By the Sword

The Modern Library / New York

By the Sword

A HISTORY OF GLADIATORS, MUSKETEERS, SAMURAI,

SWASHBUCKLERS, AND OLYMPIC CHAMPIONS

Richard Cohen

2012 Modern Library Paperback Edition

Copyright © 2002, 2008, 2012 by Narrative Tension, Inc.

Published in the United States by Modern Library, an imprint of
The Random House Publishing Group, a division of
Random House, Inc., New York.

MODERN LIBRARY and the TORCHBEARER Design are registered
trademarks of Random House, Inc.

Originally published in hardcover and in slightly
different form by Random House, an imprint of
The Random House Publishing Group,
a division of Random House, Inc., in 2002,
and subsequently in trade paperback by Modern Library,
an imprint of The Random House Publishing Group,
a division of Random House, Inc., in 2008.

LIBRARY OF CONGRESS CATALOGING-IN-PUBLICATION DATA
Cohen, Richard
By the sword: a history of gladiators, musketeers, samurai, swash-
bucklers, and Olympic champions / Richard Cohen.
p. cm.
Includes bibliographical references and index.
ISBN 978-0-8129-6966-5
EBOOK ISBN 978-0-307-43074-8
1. Fencing—History. I. Title.
U860 .C58 2002
796.86'09—dc21   2002021309

Printed in the United States of America

www.modernlibrary.com

Book design by Barbara M. Bachman

FOR *Kathy*

Preface to the Tenth Anniversary Edition

THE TEN YEARS SINCE THIS BOOK WAS FIRST PUBLISHED HAVE SEEN radical changes to the sport of swordplay. Some are technical, as revisions to this book will show. Some are administrative: a Russian billionaire has taken over as head of the international body that runs fencing, and he is determined to make it a worldwide, televisual sport. I wish him luck.

As for the United States, at the end of the first week of the 2008 Games, fully 10 percent of its entire Olympic tally was from fencing—six medals, their best haul ever. In women's saber, the remarkable Mariel Zagunis took Olympic gold in 2004 as well as in Beijing (where her compatriots were second and third), then added a world championship in 2010. There are now more than 100,000 registered fencers in America— the sport a long way from being one that well into the twentieth century was peopled by only the wealthy upper classes and the privileged, leavened by competitors from the armed services and by immigrants from the fencing countries of Europe. Fencing has become democratized.

Certainly the old order is under attack: At the last world championships, in Sicily in 2011, Italian women foilists took first, second, and third places, but mighty France was nowhere. Koreans placed third, fifth, and nineteenth, and for the first time ever at world or Olympic level a Korean won the men's individual saber. China won the same event at the Beijing Olympics—another first—while Japan took silver in the men's foil, their first-ever fencing medal. It is far from an Asian invasion, however: Estonia has the current men's épée champion; a Greek woman recently won a world cup saber event while Romania and Ukraine are new among the medalists.

For this revised edition I have corrected some errors and brought other passages up to date. For production reasons, there has been no room for stories about some of the celebrities that I have discovered fence—from Mark Zuckerberg of Facebook fame and Angelina Jolie (who early on so loved swords that she wanted her home to boast its own salle) to Nijinsky and Friedrich Engels—who, sadly, never took on his fellow fencer Karl Marx. But there is room, I think, for one recent story that epitomizes the spirit of fencing.

It concerns two Italian foilists, Andrea Baldini (born 1985) and Andrea Cassarà (born 1984). In the 2008 Olympics, the rules for participation were that each country could enter just two fencers for an individual event. Cassarà was ranked third in the world but amazingly was not in line for selection, as during the qualification period he was behind Baldini and another Italian, Salvatore Sanzo. Baldini had won silver at both the 2006 and 2007 world championships, but in the run-up to China he was on fire, and by August, just weeks before the Games, was viewed as the hot favorite for the gold. Then, on August 1, it was announced that he had tested positive for the banned diuretic furosemide, more commonly known as Lasix; it appears on the World Anti-Doping Agency's (WADA) banned drug list as an alleged masking agent. Baldini was said to have used the drug during the European championships in Kiev earlier that summer: As a result he was banned from the Games. Andrea Cassarà duly went in his place but got no further than the quarterfinals.

From the moment the drug test results were announced, Baldini strenuously maintained his innocence and protested that he was the victim of tampering—specifically, that Cassarà and the Italian team doctor had conspired to lace his drink. The prosecutors from Baldini's hometown of Livorno investigated the claim. "Sabotage? It's a hypothesis that the International Fencing Federation (FIE) has not ruled out," said the head of the Italian Fencing Federation. The next year Baldini was readmitted to competition, winning two gold medals at the European championships that July in Bulgaria. But relations between him and Cassarà were such that bodyguards were taken on to ensure that the fencers did not come to blows. In team events, where one foilist hands over his electric cord to a colleague, spectators watched as the bodyguards were kept busy. The enmity between the two champions became a talking point for the whole international fencing community.

In October, both Baldini and Cassarà were on the Italian team for the world championships in Turkey. One of them was careless in the seeding rounds, and they found themselves facing off in the quarterfinals. Other competitors stopped whatever they were doing to come and watch. As always, the fight was the first to fifteen, and the advantage swayed from one fencer to another, until the score reached 14–all. Normally, a well-timed attack scores a hit, or else a lightning riposte. Very occasionally, a phase goes to a third action—a counterriposte. The two fencers probed warily to see who would launch a final attack, forward and back, forward and back. At last, Baldini launched an attack. Cassarà parried and made a riposte. Baldini parried, and counterriposted. Still no hit. Finally, after six such actions, Baldini's weapon got through: He had won, 15–14. Indeed, he would go on to beat the Russian Artem Sedov 15–6 in the semifinals and Zhu Jun of China 15–11 in the final, to win his first world championship. But that was all anticlimax. As he took off his mask against Cassarà the audience hushed to see what would happen. The two men stepped forward and embraced each other for a long moment, both realizing that only Cassarà had the skills to allow Baldini to express his unique talent.

The crowd erupted. On the podium, Baldini displayed an Italian flag with lyrics from Bob Dylan's "The Hurricane" written on it:

> *That's the story of the Hurricane,*
> *but it won't be over till they clear his name*
> *And give him back the time he's done*
> *Put him in a prison cell but one time he could a been*
> *The champion of the world.*

As I write, in March 2012, Cassarà is the reigning world champion and the undisputed favorite going into the London Games. This time it is Baldini who is struggling for a place in the Italian team, although sentiment suggests he will be selected. As so often, fencing is about so much more than who will emerge the victor.

Contents

List of Illustrations

Prologue

*A beginning is the time for taking the most delicate care
that the balances are correct.*

—PRINCESS IRULAN, IN FRANK HERBERT'S *Dune*, 1965

THIRTY YEARS AGO I FOUGHT THE ONLY DUEL OF MY LIFE. IT
wouldn't have satisfied the dictionary definition, which requires that
deadly weapons be used—competition sabers are hardly that—but it was
certainly a "prearranged formal combat between two persons, fought to
settle a point of honor." And honor was duly satisfied, if not quite in the
way I anticipated.

Back then, Britain had one showpiece fencing event, held over two
weekends every spring in the center of London. On the second Saturday
night, the final eight competitors, dressed all in white against a black background, squared off under arc lights on a specially raised strip, or "piste."
Many in the audience of some eight hundred were in evening dress, and
radio and television covered it closely: a daunting occasion, even for a seasoned international.

The event was conducted in an elimination format, with the finalists
fencing off in pairs. Between the semifinals and the final the audience was
usually entertained with a short costume drama, but that year the organizers decided instead to offer a duel between the respective champions of the
two top-ranking clubs—the biggest in the country, the legendary Salle Paul,
and my own, Salle Boston. (Clubs are often called "salles," a holdover from
the days when French masters gave lessons in their own rooms.) The first
fencer to score ten hits would receive a purse of £100—about $1,000 today.

We had the national champion, David Acfield, so were feeling confident, but about three weeks before the fight, David told me that he had
been approached by Salle Paul to "come to an arrangement." The fight

would be rigged: Boston, the favorites, would get £60, Paul £40. As club captain, what did I think? I responded with a mixture of self-confidence, priggishness, and fondness for a gamble: first, I said, I thought David would win; second, I didn't want to be party to such a scheme; third, I liked the risk involved—all or nothing: the deal was not on. This didn't appeal to David, but he accepted my decision, if grudgingly. Not long after we talked, he injured his leg one evening at training and within a few days reported that we would have to find a replacement. The club did: me. By this time we had learned that Salle Paul was not happy with our refusal to split the purse and was determined to teach us a lesson. It was going to be a battle of honor after all.

My opponent would be Paul's top performer, David Eden. I should explain about the Eden family. David, the eldest of three brothers, had studied to be a concert pianist but had proved to be temperamentally unsuited to this. His father was a self-made businessman who specialized in wholesaling fashionable clothes to the cheaper end of the market. All three sons had gone to a state school in southwest London. In the previous decade, state schools had come under pressure to give up boxing, which almost overnight had made fencing vastly more popular, and the Edens had taken up the sport with a vengeance, all three sons going on to win international honors, David in both foil and saber.

With a foil the target is the torso, and one can score only with the point; with a saber the point may be used, but one is also free to slash and cut, and the target is anywhere above the hips—head, arms, hands are all fair game. The saber is the more dramatic weapon, more like what one sees in the cinema. And David was famously exhibitionistic. Off the strip he would dress all in black, his shirt unbuttoned to midchest, revealing thick black hair on which rested a gold medallion and chain. He sported a gold watch, gold rings, and a heavy black beard. That year he had been going out with Miss Scotland, but he later married the blond ex-girlfriend of his soccer alter ego, George Best. He was just under six feet tall, with broad shoulders, a deep chest, and a piratical smile. Altogether a bit of a lad.

He was also prodigiously talented. Between 1973 and 1974 he would win the British Open, the Commonwealth Games, and his international colors. I regularly lost to him, albeit by narrow margins. It was generally accepted that he had a short fuse: after one disputed decision I watched him hurl his mask the length of the hall, and once, in a grudge fight against a man who had seduced his coach's wife, he delivered an uppercut to his opponent's mask, hilt side on, that almost laid the man out.

By Saturday evening, it was becoming difficult to concentrate. I arrived at Baker Street's Seymour Hall, a building of faded Victorian grandeur more often used for lectures and conferences, and made my way round the back of the audience to the rooms put aside for the fencers. There was no one there, just several sets of discarded clothing, but I could hear the muffled shouts and applause as the épéeists did battle. I donned my white breeches, long white socks, and special fencing shoes, and slipped into a ragged T-shirt that I superstitiously thought brought me luck, then put on my canvas jacket. Glove, mask, and saber in hand, I walked from the changing rooms past a long line of spectators, feeling like a prizefighter about to enter the ring. As I stepped up onto the piste I saw that David was already there.

In 1972, the scoring system in saber (unlike foil and épée) had yet to be electrified, so we had two judges watching us, one on either side of the piste, who would move up and down the strip in concert with us, expected to assess every hit. Controlling the fight and posted in midpiste was the referee, whose job was to analyze the action and add his vote on hits—five judges for two combatants.

I saluted each in turn, then my opponent.

"Gentlemen, *en garde*. Are you ready?" said the referee. "Then fence."

What does one look at in a duel? The eyes of one's opponent? His face? The angle of his body, the stance he assumes? Or maybe his blade as it arcs towards its target? All of them, in a way. One is hyperaware, sensing how the audience may be reacting, while focusing on the man in front of you. One thinks at lightning speed: they say that one needs at least a twentieth of a second to decide on an appropriate action, as long again to carry it out. But often there is no time for thought at all. So fencers, whatever their level, take lessons not just to learn new moves but to hone those they already know, so that their reactions become instinctive. That is the challenge—to place what one's muscles know by heart at the disposition of what one is telling them to do.

When we changed ends at the halfway point, I found I was leading 5–1. Maybe to play up to the large crowd, David had been taking flamboyant parries, trying to predict where my blade would land, but his guesses were going wrong and each time I got through. The change of sides, however, brought a change in fortune. Suddenly David's guesses seemed telepathic, as if he knew exactly where I had chosen to aim. Three times he parried me, his ripostes whipping through. I shifted tactics, concentrating on defense; but he advanced rapidly, launching a long attack that landed across my chest. His judges' hands shot up immediately: 5–all.

Fleetingly I reflected on how such intuition comes into play far more than one thinks—that racing drivers can know exactly when to accelerate, tennis players sense just where their opponents are going to place the ball. Small comfort now. I tried to attack again, but David stretched out his arm at just the right moment, and, rushing forward too eagerly, I impaled myself on his point. As soon as the referee told us to fence again, I attacked at David's head, but he took a fast parry and, with a loud cry of triumph, riposted to my mask, using so much force that his blade whipped over the protective mesh and sliced into the back of my head. My jacket was spattered with blood. I could hear gasps from the audience.

The score was 5–8: I was down by three hits. This wasn't how it was meant to be. I was the good guy, the one who wouldn't fix the fight—the Catholic ex–public school boy, courteous and in control, up against the state school playboy villain. The hall seemed suddenly hot, and when I put my free hand to the back of my head my fingers came away red and sticky. I glanced at the audience but saw only one of David's side judges looking at me with disgust, as if to convey that no one who threw away such a commanding lead deserved to win.

I *had* to change tactics but still keep up the pressure. I tried taking smaller steps forward and hold up my attacking movement, to gain the split second that would tell me when David committed himself to a parry, so that I could alter my attack accordingly. He was so caught up in the success of his comeback that he continued to take premeditated parries; only now he was again guessing wrong. When he next attacked I caught him on the arm as he stepped forward. Soon it was 9–all.

At such a point, a bout is close to an actual duel. One hit, and it is over—not death or painful injury but defeat and, most often, elimination. A fencer becomes acutely aware that it is one on one, steel on steel.

I moved quickly down the piste, determined to be the one to launch the final attack. As I advanced, David straightened his sword arm just as he had earlier, reckoning that I wouldn't expect that move again. This time, though, I brought my saber sideways in a swift chest parry. The blades touched, and I jabbed out my riposte to the side of David's mask. As I did so I felt the tip of David's saber land hard just below my heart. Had I parried sufficiently, or would the judges rule that David's counter had gone straight through? I knew I'd been hit, but that could have been the "remise"—David hitting me only *after* my parry? I looked down at the judges on David's side of the piste. Both had their hands raised. I glanced at David. I couldn't make out his eyes, but it was obvious from the way he was standing that he too was unsure how it was going to go.

The referee turned first to David's judges. "The point counterattack—did it arrive?"

"No. I'm claiming for the move after that," said the first judge. So for him my parry was good—one vote for me.

The second judge's turn. "First parried." A second vote for me.

The referee turned to my judges, but David didn't wait. He already had his mask off and was holding out his hand. "Well done," he said.

Later that year David left Salle Paul and joined our club, gold medallion and all. He turned out to be one of the most sporting fencers I have known: no more right uppercuts. Our club used the £100 purse to help send its top five sabreurs to the annual international in New York the following March: my first visit to America. Now, thirty years on, I am sitting in my Manhattan apartment writing a history of the sport that has obsessed me for forty years.

A T THIRTEEN I WAS SENT TO DOWNSIDE, A PRIVATE BOARDING school in the heart of the Somerset countryside, whose teachers were mostly Benedictine monks from the adjoining abbey. One day, as we gathered for assembly, a monk named Dom Philip Jebb was ushered in to give us a special address. I later learned he was the grandson of Hilaire Belloc.

That morning Father Philip spoke to us about the sport he ran at the school. He told us about the three weapons, foil, épée, and saber, how each had its own character. He explained that, while you could be quicker than your opponents or technically superior, such advantages would not necessarily bring victory—you had to outthink them as well. He spoke of Downside's long unbeaten record and declared fencing the best of all sports, the most difficult at which to achieve mastery.

He invoked the traditions of honor that surround swordplay: how each fencer was expected to salute the judges and his opponent at the beginning of a bout and shake hands at its end; how, if you were hit, it was your obligation to acknowledge it. Handel had fenced, and Goethe and Michelangelo and Saint Ignatius Loyola, founder of the Jesuits.

We loved Dom Philip. He would come down to the gymnasium in off-white breeches, white socks, and tennis shoes, wearing a black leather motorcycle jacket in place of the normal white canvas jacket. The locals had dubbed him "The Fighting Monk," but he was just as keen on archaeology, and his small room in the monastery was filled with jagged pieces of stone and metal—like the silver stylus found near the Roman lead mines in the nearby Mendip Hills. Just such a one, Father Philip would say, was all that Julius Caesar had at hand to defend himself against his assassins.

It was Father Philip who taught us the rudiments of foil, the first weapon we were expected to master. He explained how the target area had been limited to the torso because that is where the vital organs lie. But that didn't mean that we could just attack each other whenever we wanted: in both foil and saber there existed a "right of way" (a priority of actions) according to which if a fencer started an offensive movement, he had either to miss or be parried before his opponent could legitimately reply. The result of such rules was that "phrases" could be built up, like a movement in music, with attack followed by riposte, itself followed by counterriposte, until there was a "conversation of the blades." There were even two kinds of "time," ordinary time and fencing time.

To begin with, much of this seemed pathologically formal, as did the weird stance we were required to adopt, feet at ninety degrees to each other, thighs agonizingly bent, nonweapon hand held up high and behind, angled over like a floppy wave. Father Philip taught us that fencing divided the torso into quadrants, each section of the chest being named for the parry that covered it. Fourth ("quarte") and sixth ("sixte") did for the top part of the torso, seventh ("septime") and eighth ("octave") for the bottom half. If it helped, we could call them respectively "upper left," "upper right," "left side down," and "right side down" until we got used to them. The position of fifth ("quint") was reserved for the saber, to parry attacks to the head. As for first ("prime"), second ("seconde"), and third ("tierce"), we would learn about them when we started saber. For now, we should try to get a feel for the blade, the all-important *sentiment du fer*.

Gradually it started to make sense. Our muscles accepted the new positions and our minds the notion that French was the language of fencing, so we had better get used to *prises de fer, coupés, doublés, corps-à-corps*, and the whole linguistic romance of steel. It really did make us feel like incipient musketeers—the more so when Father Philip told us that at university he had fought for a team called "The Cambridge Cutthroats." In due time I, too, went off to Cambridge, where I decided to concentrate on saber, which, with its cutting, slashing, and greater mobility, had captured my imagination. In 1969 I won the British Junior title and was invited to train with the Olympic squad. On my first outing the national coach, a formidable ex–Royal Marine, took me aside: "Well, son, the Junior win shows you can *fight*. Now let's see if you can actually *fence*."

Was there a difference between the two?

THERE HAVE BEEN MANY ATTEMPTS TO CAPTURE THE APPEAL OF fencing. The nineteenth-century historian of swordplay Egerton Castle saw the sport as "a superior kind of pastime, combining mental excitement and bodily exercise—the excitement of a game of skill not entirely independent of chance, together with the delight—innate in all healthy organizations—of strife and destruction—and an exercise necessitating the utmost nervous and muscular tension while it affords the refined pleasures of rhythmical action."[1]

This formidable figure was captain of the British team at the 1908 Olympics, choreographed fights for the stage, and traveled the country putting on lectures and demonstrations. He also left a remarkable monument: *Schools and Masters of Fence: From the Middle Ages to the Eighteenth Century*, a dry title for the foremost history of fencing in English, published in 1885, one so far ahead of others that many writers still shamelessly crib or paraphrase from it. Castle shows how swordplay evolved, particularly in Italy, France, Germany, Spain, and Great Britain. He deals with the watersheds of the long history of the sword: its introduction as an instrument of self-defense, its apotheosis in the age of chivalry and duel-

I execute a "horizontal flèche" against Dom Philip Jebb, wearing his trademark biker's jacket. This was in 1965, with the trees of Downside Abbey forming the backdrop.

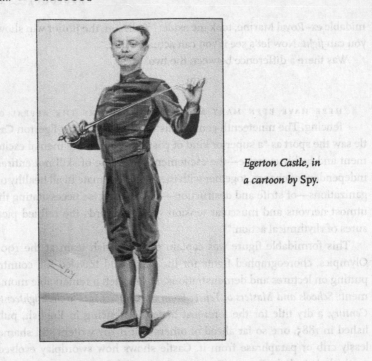

*Egerton Castle, in
a cartoon by* Spy.

ing, and finally its decline, when men of fashion determined that bearing a sword was outmoded—although that change went far deeper than a shift in taste and had to do with the fundamentals of society, both as to the means of killing and in the outlawing of private violence. Although Castle's history stops some years before the end of the nineteenth century, his work remains indispensable. I am keenly aware how much I have been treading in his shadow.

Another shade from the past has been Sir Richard Francis Burton (1821–90), possibly the most famous of all British explorers, the first European to reach Lake Tanganyika and also the first Westerner to see the Sacred Stone at Mecca and to make the pilgrimage (in full disguise) from Mecca to Medina. He was a treasure hunter, and a spy during the Crimean War. Between 1883 and 1888 he published his translations of the *Arabian Nights, The Perfumed Garden*, and the *Kama Sutra* (the "Pleasure Treatise"): he is said to have mastered thirty-five Oriental languages. Yet he would write, in middle age, "The great solace of my life was the fencing-room."

Burton started to fence almost as soon as he could walk, taught by a veteran who had lost a thumb in the Napoleonic Wars. He practiced from the start with "real, not wooden, foils and swords."[2] By the time he went up to Oxford (where he challenged a fellow student who mocked his mustache to a duel) he was taking three lessons a day, and in the summer of 1841 set off to enroll in the "famed Heidelberg fencing brigades." Some years later his wife, Isabel, urged Burton's master to teach her, so she could "defend Richard when he and I are attacked in the wilderness together." One of the coach's favorite demonstrations involved Isabel's standing motionless while he made a *moulinet*, or circular swing, at her head. "You could hear the sword swish in the air as he touched me like a fly in the act of doing it—he did it frequently to show what he *could* do, and he used to say he could not do it to any of his pupils, for fear they would flinch . . . but he knew I should stand steady: I liked that."

The Burtons finally gave up competing in 1883, when he was sixty-two, she fifty-two, after their master committed suicide. There survives a fine oil of Burton in full fencing rig, painted during his consular posting to Tri-

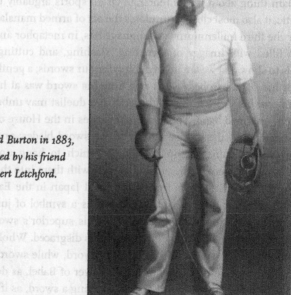

Richard Burton in 1883,
painted by his friend
Albert Letchford.

este around 1876. By then he was a fully qualified master, sufficiently pleased with his accomplishment to place his diploma after his name on the title page of *The Book of the Sword*. This was to be his great work, covering—in three volumes—the sword in all countries from the earliest times. The first volume, which takes the reader over some three hundred pages from the sword's origins to the early Roman Empire, was judged too dry by the reading public, and he never got around to volumes 2 and 3. The second volume, *The Sword Fully Grown*, was to have ranged from the decline of Rome under Constantine to "the gunpowder age"; the third volume, *Memoirs of the Sword*, to have covered "descriptions of the modern blade, notices of collections, public and private, notes on manufacturers; and, lastly, the bibliography and the literature connected with the Heroic Weapon." All that now remains of the enterprise are three green box files at the Huntington Library in California. Burton was writing *The Book of the Sword* at the same time as he translated the *Kama Sutra:* an interesting conjunction.

"SPORT IS JUST A PARADIGM OF LIFE, RIGHT?" EXCLAIMS THE NARRAtor of Richard Ford's novel *The Sportswriter*. "Otherwise who'd give a goddam thing about it?" *Is* fencing? Of all sports arguably the most romantic, it also most closely simulates the act of armed manslaughter. Ever since the third millennium B.C. language has, in metaphor and aphorism, been filled with images of thrusting, slashing, and cutting. We shake hands to show that we are not reaching for our swords; a gentleman offers a lady his right arm because at one time his sword was at his left hip; a man's coat buttons left over right, so that a duelist may unbutton it with his left, unarmed hand. The two main parties in the House of Commons are separated by the precise length of two sword blades; and each MP's locker still contains a loop of silk on which to hang up his sword. Kamikaze pilots took their samurai swords with them into their cockpits.

From the earliest days, from China and Japan in the East to Persia, Greece, and Rome, the sword has served as a symbol of justice, power, and righteous authority. With a touch of his superior's sword a man is knighted; with the breaking of his own he is disgraced. Whole armies are surrendered by the giving up of a single sword, while swords have been used as currency, even for healing. The Tower of Babel, as designed, was to have included at its summit an idol carrying a sword, as if to challenge whatever deity presumed to reign above.[3] Through the centuries, swords have been bestowed as the greatest of gifts and from generation to generation as the most emotionally and historically charged of family possessions. Some have been buried with the dead to provide protection in the afterlife, but generally swords survive their owners. As instruments that both take and preserve life, swords are often embellished with *memento mori* or religious inscriptions. In Japan, where swordsmanship is one of the classic disciplines that students of Zen must follow, blades bear invocations to the Buddhist powers. Tacitus, writing around A.D. 100, tells how a couple about to wed gave each other swords as bridal offerings. Fourteen centuries later, when Lucrezia Borgia remarried, Pope Alexander VI consecrated a sword and sent it to his daughter as his gift to her bridegroom. A leading seventeenth-century mathematician, Don Juan de la Rocha, traced fencing back to the creation of the world and the struggle between good and bad angels.

Napoleon fenced. So did George Washington, Charles Dickens, Voltaire, Karl Marx, Grace Kelly, and Alexandre Dumas, who based *The Three Musketeers* on real-life characters. Confucius liked to wear a sword. Casanova wrote a book on the duel. Anthony Chenevix-Trench, the headmaster of Eton from 1964 to 1970, who was infamous for his floggings, would sometimes, instead of beating a boy, take down two sabers from his study wall and engage him in combat. In *Moby-Dick*, an amateur midwife delivers the Indian sailor Tashtego from the sperm tank of a whale, and an onlooker suggests that both midwifery and fencing should be integral parts of a man's education. A recent Miss Venezuela was also her country's foil champion; Jim Naismith, who invented basketball, was a fencing master. When the American Academy of Motion Pictures instituted its annual awards in 1927 (nicknamed "Oscars" in 1931), the chosen trophy was a standing figure bearing, as a mark of authority, a single upright sword.

For many, modern swordplay is a source of humor. As Bill Bryson wrote during the 2000 Olympics in Sydney:

> A lot of people don't like fencing because they don't understand the rules and terminology, but in fact it's quite simple. There are basically four thrusts, known as the *cartilage*, the *chaise longue*, the *aubergine* and the *fromage anglais*, and these in turn can be parried by four defensive feints—the *pastiche*, the *penchant*, the *demi-tasse* and the *saumon en croûte*. Scoring is on the basis of one point for a

petit pois and two for a *baguette*. Points equally can be deducted for a foot fault, or *pied à terre*, and for a type of illegal lunge known as a *zut alors*.[4]

Touché. The pages that follow tell how fencing became the sport it is today. Not that the parameters of swordplay are easy to draw. People began to fence as a way of practicing for serious duels, and even now some duels—the *Mensur* contests that originated in nineteenth-century Germany—while sporting in intent, involve the participants' trying to scar each other. In war, swordfights sometimes take on a sporting quality, both in practice and on the battlefield. Conversely, so-called sporting events have often been fought bitterly and with real edge. So I have pushed back the boundaries of my subject and delved accordingly.

By the Sword is not intended as a formal or even a complete history of swordsmanship. Like any history, it must be selective, and I am aware of omissions. I say little about the phenomenal success of Soviet fencers; I cover Japan but not China, Korea, India, Indonesia, or the Philippines, all of which have traditions of swordplay; much more could be written about Cuba and Scandinavia, and the new disciplines of women's épée and saber. I touch only briefly on the history of swordplay's vocabulary—although my favorite linguistic item is the Japanese word *"tsujigiri,"* meaning "to try out a new sword on a chance passerby." The sexual symbolism of swords I have left to the reader's imagination (as far back as ancient Rome the term *"vagina"* meant a sword's sheath and *"gladius"* was slang for "penis"). Sword dreams I have avoided, although surprisingly few of Freud's books mention swords at all; as Freud, himself a heavy smoker, once observed, "Sometimes a cigar *is* just a cigar."

Swordplay has often made headlines its practitioners would have wished to avoid: blackmail, murder, and accidental death, strange love affairs and life-changing acts of dishonor all find a place in this history. I have noted the major watersheds, from the introduction of the rapier in the 1550s through the ascendancy of gunpowder (the "black arm") and the gradual elimination of the sword (the "white arm") from the world's arsenal. I have tried to describe what it was like, and is like still, to engage in one-on-one battle—to be a swordsman, as John Keegan puts it, "for whom fighting was an act of self-expression by which a man displayed not only his courage but also his individuality."[5] Above all, I have tried to portray the character of swordplay—at once graceful and brutish, fiercely competitive and technically beautiful, life-threatening and life-enhancing.

Part One

—

FROM EGYPT

TO WATERLOO

Previous page: The bookplate Archibald Corble had designed for his famous library of fencing books.

CHAPTER 1

How It All Began

*Fighting was fun—this was the thing. Fighting was
tremendous fun.*

—R. EWART OAKESHOTT, *Deadly Duels: Duels of Chivalry*, 2000

*Thrust this into another man's flesh, and they will applaud
and love you for it.*

—PROXIMUS (OLIVER REED) ADVISING MAXIMUS
(RUSSELL CROWE) IN *Gladiator*, 2000

HE GREAT AUTHORITY ON EARLY ARMS, EWART OAKESHOTT,
believes that swords first appeared between 1500 and 1100 B.C. in Minoan
Crete and Celtic Britain.¹ Remarkably quickly, they became an implement
of sport: the oldest known depiction of an actual fencing match is a relief
in the Temple of Madinat Habu, built by Ramses III around 1190 B.C.,
near Luxor in Upper Egypt. (To its right is an engraving of a pile of trophy
penises, hacked from the enemy dead—practice well, the sequence suggests, and this can be your reward.) The men are clearly not dueling—they
appear to be wearing masks, padded over the ears and tied to their wigs,
and the tips of their weapons have been covered. There are judges on either side holding feathered wands, and the score is being kept on a piece
of papyrus. An inscription records one contestant as saying, "On guard
and admire what my valiant hand shall do."

Ninus, king of Assyria, is usually given the credit for the development
of swordplay as a formalized sport. He was also the first to use professional fencing masters to instruct his troops.² The Chinese, Japanese,
Persians, Babylonians, and Romans sometimes fenced as a pastime, but
mainly they used swords to train for combat. Indian tradition has it that
Brahma taught his devotees martial exercises with the sword (priests
were warriors then), and in Hindu India's great epic, the *Mahabharata*,
we read:

Brightly gleaming their lightning rapiers as they ranged the listed field.
Brave and fierce is their action and their movements quick and light.
Skilled and true the thrust and parry of their weapons flaming bright.

This ten-thousand-verse narrative, reputedly written by one Vyasa around 500 B.C., makes frequent mention of swordfights and fencing skills and is one of the first works to examine two basic aspects of swordsmanship: ferocity and chivalry.

The Greeks believed that there was no special art to handling a sword. One reason for this was that their weapons of choice were generally short, double-edged with hilts or crossbars, and ridged from point to hilt (to stiffen the blades)—basically hacking implements. A warrior would employ it for close combat only after his spear had been thrown or broken: it was the instrument of last resort.

The Greeks placed critical importance upon drilling men to maneuver in formation, little to teaching hand-to-hand combat. It may have required special skill to throw a javelin, but with a sword it was impossible to miss at close quarters. The Greek historian and soldier Xenophon is dismissive

Egyptians fencing, seemingly with sabers, their left forearms protected
with bundles of sticks. From a wall painting circa 1200 B.C.

in his account of how the Persians trained their forces. As he saw it, skill with edged weapons came to man as naturally as breathing:

> I myself from my earliest childhood knew how to throw up a guard before the things that I thought were going to hit me. If I had nothing else, I would hold my hands before me and hinder the man who hit me as far as possible. I did this not because I was taught to do it; indeed, I was even hit just for throwing my hands before me. As for knives, from the time I was a baby I grabbed them whenever I saw them, and I never learned from anybody how to hold them either, except from nature, as I say. . . . I promise you, I cut with my knife everything that I could without being noticed. It not only came by nature, like walking and running, but seemed to me to be pleasant as well as natural. Well then, since we are left with a sort of fighting that calls for courage rather than skill, why should not we fight with enthusiasm?[3]

Despite this debatable view, it is possible to find, as early as the fifth century B.C., references in Greek historical accounts to *oplomachia* (literally, "fighting in armor"). Hoplites were the senior Greek infantry, men of substance who could afford armor, unlike the light infantrymen (*peltastai*) and shield carriers (*oplontes*), who carried slings and light javelins. The hoplites' skills eventually became a regular part of the military training program in Athens. Plato specifies how their practice sessions should be configured:

> We will institute conflicts in armor of one against one, and two against two, and so on up to ten against ten. As to what a man ought not to suffer or do, and to what extent, in order to gain the victory—as in wrestling, the masters of the art have laid down what is fair and what is not fair, so in fighting in armor—we ought to call in skilful persons, who shall judge for us and be our assessors in the work of legislation; they shall say who deserves to be victor in combats of this sort, and what he is not to do or have done to him, and in like manner what rule determines who is defeated.[4]

Combatants wore a shield, breastplate, helmet, and shin guards and carried both spear and sword. The competition was essentially a test of skill, flexibility, and physical endurance—a formal imitation of genuine warfare. While professional teachers of combat began to be highly paid and to hold prominent positions in the *gymnasia*, there were no fencing masters per se. Nor is there any account of Greek sword exercises like those of Flavius Vegetius Renatus, who wrote a whole treatise on the training of Roman legionaries. Swordsmanship in itself was not valued, it being generally believed that those who excelled in athletic games, at the Olympics, and elsewhere would naturally distinguish themselves in war. Thus the "art" of armed combat rarely found its way into public festivals, with the possible exception of funeral games.

One means of preparation came in the form of war dances, which were often performed at religious festivals and would imitate the movements and postures of soldiers—waving shields, swerving or ducking to avoid a blow, and manipulating weapons—thrusting first spears, then swords. Spartan youths practiced these dances from an early age. Socrates believed that those who honored the gods most in dances were the best in battle, while Plato, in his *Laws*, said, likewise, that dancing had combat value. The goal was to develop agility rather than strength, although Greek recruiting policy still emphasized weight and size rather than gymnastic ability: a good big one was worth more than a good little one. Only in cases of monomachy—a tradition in which the commanders of opposing armies met each other in single combat—did any individual duel openly with another.

Unlike the Greeks, the Romans admired and appreciated swordplay. Horace's friend Sybarus was a fencer, and Ovid, reflecting mournfully from his exile on the shores of the Black Sea, imagined the young men back in Rome practicing their sword skills. Gladiatorial combats—a Roman invention—date from 264 B.C. They began as a flourish occasionally added to aristocratic funeral celebrations: slaves, or sometimes prisoners of war, would fight in honor of the dead. Over the years, the contests, which could run to three hundred bouts, were extended to general celebrations. None other than Julius Caesar drew up special rules for these deadly games; he encouraged them as a means of distracting his otherwise restive people (as well as winning himself political support) and even had his own school in Campania, now recognized as "the cradle of the gladiatorial system."

Can an activity be regarded as a sport when only the *spectators* see it as such? Gladiators were of course fighting for their lives (at least, from

84 A.D. on; before that date they were often allowed to live), but ancient graffiti reveal that they were paid for each performance and could become the popular equivalent of rock stars: images of famous gladiators adorned oil lamps, flasks, and toys, and their exploits were recorded by contemporary chroniclers. Crucial to all this were the *lanistae*—the indispensable operators who functioned as trainers, slave traders, managers, and impresarios all in one. They bought, rented, or contracted gladiators for combats, set the price for seats, arranged for publicity, and hired musicians. They were generally held in disrepute—*lanista* also meant "assassin" and "bandit."

Gladiators could be formidable figures: the slave rebellion led by the famous gladiator Spartacus managed to sustain itself against powerful Roman forces for three years, and this is not an isolated example. When gladiators consistently triumphed in the arena itself, it was not uncommon for fathers to pass on the profession to their sons, and there were even families of gladiators. Occasionally, as a novelty act, women fighters appeared—the British Museum has a stone relief of two bare-breasted female performers—although such encounters were seen as exotic spectacles, on a par with dwarfs fighting, and eventually, in A.D. 200, were banned.

Combatants, as a rule, fought in pairs, and a referee (*summa rudis*), dressed in a voluminous tunic, would normally stand between them, armed with a long stick. There were various kinds of gladiators: the *myrmillones* and *samnites* were the most heavily armed, with helmet, shield, protection for their leading leg, and sword—in the beginning a short, wide weapon, later about three feet long and thinner. Thracian gladiators wore helmets and greaves (lower leg guards) and used a dagger. The *retiarii* fought with a net in one hand and a trident in the other. The juxtaposition of armed and unarmed parts of the body dictated the use of weapons and created the conditions for highly skillful swordsmanship. Left-handed gladiators were reputed to be particularly fearsome, and the style of swordsmanship was subject to precise rules for the various gladiatorial categories, which were remarkably uniform across the Roman Empire from the first through the fourth centuries.[5]

All these fighters received their instruction from the *lanistae*. Trainee gladiators learned the basic movements in groups, using wooden swords covered with leather, with leather buttons on the points. Once in the arena, as a curtain-raiser, they might put on a mass demonstration with training swords, not so different from modern TV wrestling contests.

Then the real fighting would begin. "*Gladiatorem in arena cepere consilium*," wrote Seneca—"The swordfighter reveals himself only when he gets to the arena"—an insight that would ring down the centuries.[6]

The Roman public was thoroughly familiar with the technical aspects of parrying and thrusting—many would have seen combat themselves. While Romans despised cowardice, they would reward a courageous defeated fighter, even occasionally granting a reprieve from death. There were periods when combat without reprieve was banned altogether: after all, gladiators were expensive to train. The authorities were as vigilant over the health and muscle tone of their fighters as they were over the authenticity of the fights. *Ludi* (schools) were set up all over Italy to train future performers, and several distinguished surgeons specialized in the treatment of sword and trident wounds.

Over time, free citizens, patricians, and even women frequented the *ludi* and swordplay became fashionable. No records survive as to whether visitors were limited to watching or were allowed to handle the weapons themselves, although Petronius's novel *Satyricon* has a woman of senatorial status finding gladiators so interesting that she actually trains as one. We do know that the ancient world never developed sports for their own

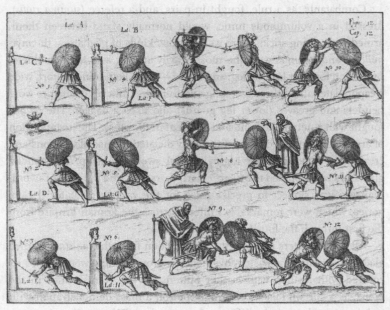

Roman infantry training at a post, as painted by Wallhausen in 1616.

sake; they played checkers—a game invented, according to legend, to overcome the tedium of the siege of Troy—and various forms of dice. Chess, however, had to wait until the Middle Ages. High society may have practiced swordplay, but that did not make fencing a sport. From an early date attempts were made to legislate against nongladiators' aping gladiators. For members of the upper class to compete in gladiatorial contests was felt to be reprehensible, so much so that when the Emperor Commodus (A.D. 161–192) announced that he would appear as a gladiator in the dress of a consul, he was murdered by his senior entourage before he could do so.

Gladiators were better coached than the average soldier, and their training methods slowly infiltrated the military, much to the disgust of die-hard purists—Pliny the Younger (c. 62–c. 114) commended one senior officer for taking on weapons training himself rather than leaving it to a professional instructor; a historian under Hadrian criticized the army for exercising with practice weapons instead of real swords.

Military training was hardly a joyride. Vegetius, writing in the fourth century A.D., describes how "a stake was planted in the ground by each recruit, in such a manner that it projected six feet in height and could not sway. Against this stake the recruit practiced with his wickerwork shield and wooden stave, just as if he were fighting a real enemy. . . . Care was taken to see that the recruit did not rush forward so rashly to inflict a wound as to lay himself open to a counterstroke from any quarter." (Vegetius makes much of training with weapons of twice normal weight, to facilitate handling the real thing.)[7] Once a recruit became proficient with substitute weapons, he would graduate to edged swords. Formal training culminated in individual combat, *armatura*, borrowed from gladiatorial schools.

In Pliny's day, Roman soldiers fighting in Spain began to adopt their enemies' superior iron weapons. From the Spanish, they also learned the advantages of using the point of a sword, and they began to practice the thrust. Tacitus would soon describe how Agricola's legions made short work of the British Celts, with their pointless and clumsy swords.[8] The Celts of Gaul, who were renowned swordsmen, were a different matter. They would whirl their weapons above their heads, slashing the air from side to side before striking downward in a chopping motion, a terrifying spectacle. The Romans eventually learned to take the first blow on the rim of their shield. The weak Celtic blade would often bend in two, allowing the legionary to counterattack. "Holding their swords straight out," Dionysius of Halicarnassus wrote of the Romans, "they would strike their opponents in the groin, pierce their sides, and drive their blows through their breasts into their vitals. And if they saw any of them keeping these parts of the body protected, they would cut the tendons of their knees or ankles and topple them to the ground roaring and biting their shields and uttering cries resembling the howling of wild beasts."[9] The evolution of swordplay, however, owed little to Rome's growing sophistication, either on the battlefield or in the Colosseum, but to a military defeat so devastating that it led to a major review of how soldiers should be armed.

IN 378 TWO THIRDS OF AN ENTIRE ROMAN ARMY WAS DESTROYED AT Adrianople (now Edirne in European Turkey). It was a stunning defeat: the emperor, all his senior officers, and some forty thousand men were killed in the space of one afternoon. "No battle in our history," declared the contemporary historian Ammianus Marcellinus, himself a Roman officer, "except Cannae [Hannibal's great victory in 216 B.C.] was such a massacre." Oakeshott argues that after Adrianople "the old days of the legions' supremacy had gone forever, and the armoured cavalryman fighting with lance and sword on a heavy horse became for the next 1100 years the arbiter of war."[10]

The imperial army of the Roman Emperor in the East, Valens, found some ten thousand Visigoths encamped in a vast enclosure of wagons and set siege. In their usual fashion, the legions massed in the center, their squadrons of auxiliary horse on the wings. The bulk of the Gothic cavalry, away foraging when the attack began, was quickly recalled. They rode down on their enemy "like a thunderbolt," and the Roman infantry was crushed together in hopeless confusion. When the Gothic footmen realized the success of their cavalry charge, they broke out from their encampment and attacked head-on, slashing and stabbing with their long swords. Dust arose in such clouds that the Romans could not see the enemy's missiles in flight or dodge them; and the ground was so drenched in blood that they slipped and fell. The Roman cavalry fled, abandoning the foot soldiers, who had to stand wedged together until they were cut down. "They were so tightly packed," Oakeshott explains, "that they could not raise their arms to strike a blow; the dead and wounded could not fall, but stayed upright in the weltering mass; many were simply crushed to death or stifled."[11] Most of the army died before the pressure eased enough for stragglers to escape. Valens himself, wounded by an arrow, made his way to a nearby farmhouse, where the Goths, discovering him there, laid up brushwood and straw and burned the emperor alive.

Some historians have argued that the simple but revolutionary invention behind this terrible rout was the stirrup, a device until that moment unknown to the Romans, which gave horsemen the power to maneuver quickly and the leverage to strike with greater force, a formidable advantage. More likely, the stirrup was an invention of far later times; but at any rate the result of the massacre was clear: for the first time in history the sword was no longer secondary to the lance or spear.

After Adrianople the thrusting sword lost ground to the slashing swords and pointed lances of Rome's enemies from the great plains. Over the succeeding centuries these weapons would be joined by an armory of others: the lance (for use on horseback), the glaive (a form of half-pike), the lance-gay (a light throwing spear), the battle-ax, the gisarme (cousin of the ax), the mace, the halberd, the bardiche, the langedebere (a spear with a large, broad blade), the hammer, the "holy-water sprinkler" (euphemism for a spiked club), the flail, the poleax (used to split the "poll," or head), the couseque (from the French, "winged spear"), the war hammer, the *Morgenstern* (a spiked club), the *Ahlspiess* (a fearful eighteen-foot-long spear), the *plancon à Picot* (a five-foot-long wooden truncheon), the *Panzerstecher* (a mail-piercing sword, with a sturdy point but no cutting edge), the rawcon or ronka (with a three-pronged head), the spontoon (a form of pike), and the voulge (a farmer's plowshare, its blade straightened to make a glaive). And there were more. That the sword would outlast nearly all these weapons was due to a combination of factors, not least its efficacy and versatility.

After the fall of the Roman Empire, the sword gained a new importance and was taken as a token of power and majesty, endowed with mystical qualities that evolved in some instances to reflect a man's true worth. This symbolism was underlined by the conduct of kings and emperors. (Charlemagne, for example, was never without a sword; he had his three sons instructed in swordplay and left them his three best weapons.*)

Initially, with copper and tin so scarce, only chieftains ("*Schwert*

---

* In the laws of the Ripuarian Franks, a scale fixed the price of different articles of a warrior's equipment in Charlemagne's time:
  A sword with sheath . . . . .7 sous
  A sword without sheath .3 sous
  A horse (entire), not blind, and sound . . . . 6 sous
  Thus a sword with sheath cost more than a good horse—a reflection, possibly, of the scarcity of swordsmiths.[12]

Adel"—"sword nobles") could carry swords. Over time, freemen and free-born women of "sword age" were also given the right to such arms. The Teutonic tribes, with their preference for using the edge, set back the advance of swordsmanship as a thrusting weapon; but they also gave birth to medieval chivalry, and in their tribal codes lay many of the notions that would make up the chivalric ideal.

Literature also had its part to play. The Old English poem *Beowulf* describes adventures closely woven into the mythic past of Germanic Europe. Composed in the eighth century, it is set in southern Scandinavia during the migrations of a quarter millennium before. Beowulf's regard for his sword, Hrunting, runs throughout the tale: "The great-hearted hero / Spoke no word in blame of the blade . . . Never in fight had it failed the hand / That drew it." Hrunting is an "ancient treasure," a "costly heirloom," "a stately sword . . . The work of giants, a warrior's joy." "No sharper steel / No lovelier treasure" can be found. Crucially, when Hrunting is wielded in hatred it will not perform for its master; it must be used with responsibility, and its powers cannot be tapped by an evil source. *Beowulf* makes a crucial distinction between a soldier (the "paid retainer of a chieftain"—one who receives *solidi*—coins) and a warrior. The latter is self-motivated and has his own agenda and a self-image of restraint; he is there not just to kill but to choose a fit form of victory. The warrior distinguishes himself from the hired killer by what he will not stoop to.

About the same time, the *Chanson de Roland*, France's great medieval epic poem, almost a blueprint for that culture's code of chivalry (from the French word *chevallerie*, "skill on horseback"), began to be sung by bards and troubadours. A dramatic account of the heroically doomed rearguard action of one of Charlemagne's captains in Spain in 778, it incorporates, like *Beowulf*, several centuries of story. In a typical moment, as Roland sees the Saracen army approaching, he says to his friend Oliver, "The Emperor gave us this host of Frenchmen, 20,000 picked men amongst whom he knows there is not one coward. . . . Strike with your lance and I will smite with Durendal, my good sword that Charlemagne gave me. If I die, he who inherits it will say, 'It was the sword of a noble vassal.' " Roland embodies all the ideals and aspirations of the age of chivalry and has become its emblem for ages to come, helping to lay the foundations for the romantic wish fulfillment on which swordplay has thrived.

The sword lay at the heart of the medieval code of honor. To it was ascribed an inner power and a true nobility; it was not to be drawn without reason. Its point could never touch the ground. Before a fight the knight kissed the cross of his sword, which often contained relics, so that the chivalrous salute passed into a religious act. Swords were associated with intelligence, unlike lances, arrows, and axes, which were the weapons of the foot soldier.

Alongside the literature of the times, there was the technological struggle. Since early armor gave only limited protection, its weaknesses led to further development of weapons and, in turn, its own improvement. Swords might still be used to crush, but to pierce through the vulnerable areas of an opponent's body armor took new skills. Armorers responded with still more efficient creations—circular discs that slid into place to guard the armpit when the arm was raised, visors with breathing vents, convex chest pieces to deflect a blade or lance, neck supports to limit tournament "whiplash"; but then they also developed the "estoc," a long, sharp, narrow-bladed sword for thrusting through an opponent's weakest areas. As in all military history, technology both responded to situations of conflict and dictated what forms future conflict would take.

After the Germanic tribes settled in the former Roman Empire, civilization fragmented. From the ninth to the eleventh centuries, tribes, city-states, and even landed magnates engaged in constant small wars. To protect themselves, they banded together in (strictly hierarchical) feudal contracts: land was divided into fiefs, and each fief had to support at least one armored mounted knight. Under the laws of chivalry, knights swore an oath of loyalty to their liege. As time went on and standards of behavior rose, knights also vowed to be honest, to defend the existing order, to protect the weak, and to show compassion to a wounded enemy. Good armor was costly* and, in light of the subsistence economy and poor communications, its use contributed to the difficulty of raising large armies, with the result that fighting became a way of life for the upper classes. The exact origins of knighthood (from the German *Knecht*, meaning "servant") are unknown, but by the twelfth century it was a phenomenon well established in France, Spain, and England.

A knight, fully armored, his leather undergarments smeared with grease, would be carrying a load of about sixty pounds, roughly the equivalent of a modern army backpack but distributed over his whole body. Everything was carefully tailored: each knight would be measured and fit-

---

* It was never called "a suit of armor," a phrase that arose only about 1600, but always "harness." The expression "he died in harness" does not mean that a man was, at death, doing his job like a horse, but that he was wearing full armor. "Armed" originally meant wearing armor—not carrying a weapon.

ted by a master armorer, and if the knight could not be there in person he would send over wax models of his limbs. The helmet would have heavy padding beneath the metal, though no armor could offer complete protection from a blow to the head or a direct strike by a mace. The well-equipped aristocratic horseman was generally regarded as the single most powerful combatant on the battlefield; yet ventilation remained a potentially deadly problem. A day's battle would leave a knight bathing in his own sweat: in *Henry IV, Part 2*, Prince Hal says of kingship that it is "Like a rich armour worn in heat of day / That scalds with safety." An armored knight was like a tank, with almost no hearing and limited vision. Hollywood films have depicted knights in armor needing the help of cranes to mount their horses, but the Metropolitan Museum in New York has conducted trials with men in armor to show how a knight could run, leap in the air, lie down on his front or back and get up again without help, and climb onto and off of his horse (always a stallion). It was exhausting but perfectly possible.[13] The total weight that a horse might carry could reach 450 pounds; in the sixteenth century bells were attached to the horse to distract its wearer from the dread sound of onrushing hooves.

The sword was used primarily to bludgeon one's opponent. (The Scots have a word for the sound a sword makes as it cuts through the air: "sough.") As late as the reign of Elizabeth I one bellicose knight, Sir John Perrot, taking part in her coronation tournament, "hit the challenger four times in the face of the helmet with the pommel of his sword," scoring more blows of this sort than any other contestant.[14] Parries with the blade were avoided, and knights either evaded blows or used their shields for defense. Swords, which could weigh well in excess of three pounds, were heavy affairs requiring strength to wield as much as skill.

Tournaments were introduced into England during the anarchic reign of King Stephen, in 1135, and continued till the end of the sixteenth century. Their heyday was 1150 to 1300, although they were still popular during the early years of Henry VIII's reign. Henry was an expert jouster who enjoyed showing off his skills, and from 1509 till 1524 he fought as chief challenger in every major English tournament. In 1524, he was nearly killed when, after he had brazenly left his visor open, the lance of his opponent splintered inside his helmet. A few months later he fought again, at the tiltyard at Greenwich and against the same opponent, his brother-in-law the Duke of Suffolk, after which he decided to call it a day.

The origin of the tournament may have been the Roman *Ludus Troiae* (Game of Troy), a warlike exercise played by two mounted teams. The game was revived in France and made its way into England and Germany, where it was dubbed "French combat." In 1056 a reference can be found to the tournament death of Sieur Godefroi de Preuilly, a Breton baron who is said to have invented the sport, although it is more likely that he simply drew up a set of rules. Such regulations came to be extremely strict, and their breach could jeopardize an offender's claim to knighthood and even cost him his life. Most of the time, however, noblemen enjoyed what they did. Their reputation rested almost entirely on their skill at arms. Initially tournaments were bloody free-for-alls, in which two miniature armies would do battle. It was considered an honor to take part, even though scores of men died or were crippled in these chaotic melees; among the notable tournaments in Italy was one in the Colosseum in Rome in 1332 that resulted in the deaths of eighteen knights.*

One of the most celebrated participants in the twelfth century was an English knight, William Marshal, who in fifteen years of competition fought successfully more than five hundred times. He had "arrangements" with other knights—partners, in effect—who would help one another, later sharing the profits. They would keep a keen eye on who was winning, who losing, and plan their fights accordingly, like somebody working a room at a cocktail party. Marshal ended up a rich man and eventually died, in his early seventies, "with his boots on"—still fighting.

During the thirteenth century tournaments showed signs of evolving from warlike exercises fought with real weapons to the comparatively harmless pageants they would become. Sometime before 1200 a concession to safety was made with the introduction of a rebated lance point—often in the shape of a crown and known as a "lance of courtesy"—sufficient to unhorse an opponent without penetrating his armor and injuring him directly. It was still a high-risk way of proving one's valor, far more dangerous than climbing Mount Everest. Over time, a system evolved by which points were awarded for each lance broken (it was easy to miss), for blows to the helmet, if the lance tips met "coronell to coronell," or for unseating a rival.

In the 1420s, a further safety device was introduced, a long wooden

---

* From 1100 to 1605 tournaments were particularly popular in France; they started to decline only in 1559, with the death of the tournament-loving Henri II, who gave a succession of them in Paris to celebrate the marriage of his daughter to Philip II, King of Spain. During the first two days Henri jousted a number of times with lords from his court and, emboldened by his success, decided to try his luck against the celebrated champion the Count de Montgomeri, who had previously wounded Francis I. Catherine de Médicis implored her husband not to fight, but he said he would break one

barrier some six feet high and covered with cloth (*toil* in French) or canvas, set up along the length of the course to divide the two knights and prevent their horses from colliding. This barrier became known as the "tilt," and soon "tilting" was the name given to the sport itself. The Germans called jousting "*über die Planken.*"

The great French writer of chivalric romances, Chrétien de Troyes, gives a vivid description of a tournament in *Erec et Enide,* written around 1170:

> A month after Pentecost the tournament assembles and opens in the plain below Tenebroc. Many a pennant flew there, vermilion, blue and white, and many a wimple and sleeve that had been given as tokens of love.... The field is completely covered with arms. The ranks shudder on both sides, and from the clash there rises a loud din, with a great cracking of lances. Lances break and shields are holed, the hauberks are torn and rent, saddles are emptied and riders tumble, while the horses sweat and lather. All draw their swords on those who clatter to the ground. Some rush up and accept their surrender, others hasten in their defence ... .[15]

These meetings became important social events, providing a necessary outlet for martial ardor and a vital means of military training. "They kept alive the spirit of international brotherhood in arms," writes Oakeshott, "which was such an essential part of the chivalric ideal."[16] A more skeptical view is that they preserved the flavor of Christian chivalry in the face of the realities of power politics. The Church tried on numerous occasions to have them banned, but in addition to their social and military value they were a significant source of revenue. A successful knight could take away rich prizes of arms and horses: among the special armor worn for jousting was a small sword for the right hand called a *gaynepain*, or "breadwinner" (but then "lord" means "loaf giver").

Tournaments throughout Europe became the most absorbing occupa-

---

more lance, in her honor. The king fought with his visor raised; whether from the outset or knocked open by a blow from Montgomeri's lance is unknown. Montgomeri's point broke off in their first interchange and the broken end of the lance then struck the king so violent a blow above the right eye, ripping across his face, that he was thrown from his horse and, deprived instantly of speech and understanding, lingered on for eleven days before he died at the age of forty.

tion of the knightly classes outside hunting and hawking—and war. No doubt the drinking and gambling that went on at these fairs were one reason for the Church's opposition, but so too was the death toll. One contest, in 1180, attracted more than three thousand armed and mounted knights. Crazed with blood lust, they galloped mercilessly over the men on foot, swinging wildly at anything that moved. Bodies littered the ground. The fighting at a tournament ended when a signal to halt was given or when a knight, near suffocation in armor so badly dented it could be removed only by a blacksmith, was unable to remain standing.

Gradually the number of participants at these meetings was pared down to small teams. Formal challenges to "joust" evolved, issued in decorous language by knights acting on their own initiative. These jousts were still condemned by the Church for their high casualty rates. In Germany a strict code of honor developed, so that one could not participate without first presenting proof of noble descent. When one knight met another he was expected to raise his visor and reveal his identity; the military salute is a legacy of this. Even today in competitive fencing one is forbidden to come on to the strip with one's mask already in place or to begin a bout without first saluting one's opponent.

Knights fought each other both à outrance ("unflaggingly"; thus "to the point of submission") or à plaisance (for fun) in three kinds of encounter: the tilt, or joust on horseback; the general melee, as already described; and the single combat on foot, with sword, poleax, ax, or dagger. In the last, the use of heavy armor and heavy weapons favored simple movements, forcing contestants to concentrate on one blow at a time, so that complicated phrases were impossible.

At the beginning of each swordfight, one combatant would strike at the other: in the case of a duel, this first blow was the privilege of the man who had been challenged; otherwise either man could strike first. As in modern martial arts, there was much preliminary maneuvering and feinting before a significant move was made. Once attacked, a knight would seek to defend himself either by taking the blow on his shield or by evasive action. Then it would be his turn to strike, while the first man was recovering from his stroke and preparing for his next; and so on. It became important to be able to change direction in midstroke as soon as you realized you were going to miss, even when this meant turning a downward blow into an upward one or a forehand into a backhand. Lighter and stronger swords were thus highly prized. Only when a shield was so cut up as to be useless were the swords themselves used for parrying, as edge-to-edge clashes were mutually damaging. Further, in fights to the death, since swords could not cut through plate metal, knights would look for weak points in their opponent's armor—pushing their sword through a man's visor or at his armpit, thus encouraging a style of fighting that used the point. This was not swordplay as we know it but was a highly skillful affair and is recognizably fencing's cousin.*

The higher-spirited contestants eventually became frustrated with just occasional jousts and introduced the *pas d'armes,* in which a knight would announce his intention to hold a designated terrain, usually a natural passage of some sort, for a certain duration against all comers. By the fifteenth century individual challenges were issued to particular knights; from the *pas d'armes* to the duel was but a short step.

DURING THE SECOND HALF OF THE FOURTEENTH CENTURY MOST OF France and much of Italy faced a new threat: rulers might requisition a fighting army, but they had no means of redeploying that army in times of peace. Thousands of soldiers were thrown out of work at the end of every war, becoming bent on rampaging and pillaging as an alternative way of life. A succession of popes first issued indulgences to those who opposed these *routiers,* as they were called; then, fearing that the well-being of the whole Christian community was at stake, organized crusades against them.** Finally they settled on a better strategy, prevailing on

---

* From 1190 to 1350 knights wore a harness of metal; then, following the French defeat at Crécy, the stronger plate metal. There was never any such thing as "chain mail." According to the *OED,* "mail" meant "little spots," as derived from the Latin *macula* (as in the Immaculate Conception), in French *mailles;* but another word, *malleus,* meaning "hammer," is a more likely derivation. It was flexible and strong, so that we read of Richard I's crusaders in 1191 fighting unharmed with Saracen arrows sticking out of their mail like feathers. It disappeared around 1650.

Up to about 1475, the fashion in armor throughout northern Europe was for slender, exaggeratedly pointed forms, with slim-fitting doublet, long-toed shoes, and a mantle, either long or short. The interplay between fashion and technology works both ways, and while this style served men for some nine hundred years, around 1495 there was a sudden and dramatic change. Within half a decade, all over Europe, the old style vanished. The silhouette of the typical knight became rotund and burly after the Italian fashion (Henry VIII's last suit of armor has a waist of fifty-eight inches—but that was not a fashion statement). Yet for another fifty years there came no corresponding change in swords.

** Papal fear was palpable. An edict of 1364 ordered the mercenaries to disband their companies, leave the areas they had taken over, and repair the damage they had

these veterans to fight in the service of a holy war—to journey to the eastern Mediterranean, to Hungary, and to Spain to fight the advancing Muslims. This strategy began as far back as the First Crusade (1095–99) and in varying degrees continued until the Eighth Crusade of 1270 to 1272 and the loss of the last Christian fortress in Syria in 1291, putting to effective use men whose whole purpose was to fight for profit. These mercenaries formed themselves into disciplined, well-organized companies with their own treasurers, secretaries, and counselors. The *routiers* were well practiced in the arts of swordplay, and from their ranks came many of the first instructors of fencing.

By the time of the Hundred Years' War (1337–1453) the missile weapon of choice was the longbow, and it was the mastery of this technology (along with suicidally brave French tactics) that gave the English victories at the decisive battles of Crécy (1346), Poitiers (1356), and Agincourt (1415). It was six feet long and three inches in circumference, made of yew, and required a force of one hundred pounds to draw it. (When the body of an archer was recovered from the dredged-up *Mary Rose*, lost in 1545, the bone of the left arm was much thicker than that of the right, and his shoulder and spinal bones were noticeably deformed.) It would be joined by its cousin, the crossbow, an Italian invention capable of piercing mail from three hundred yards away. (The Chinese would come up with an automatic crossbow that could shoot several arrows at a time.) Together the crossbow and longbow spelled the end of the supremacy of the mounted soldier.

At Agincourt, an English army five thousand strong met a French force three times its number, yet suffered casualties of just one hundred foot soldiers and thirteen men-at-arms. Some five thousand Frenchmen died: two thousand killed in action, the rest slaughtered as prisoners rather than ransomed—despite having surrendered on terms—when a last French at-

---

done—all within a month—or suffer excommunication. Clerics and laymen were forbidden to join, employ, or favor the companies; anyone supplying them with food would be anathematized to the extent that only papal absolution could release them. A further edict the following year aggravated these sentences: all towns, villages, and individuals found guilty of negotiating with *routiers* would have their privileges, liberties, and fiefs withdrawn; *routiers* and their descendants would be ineligible for public office for three generations; and their vassals would be released from their oaths of loyalty. In 1368 it was decreed that any church or cemetery where a *routier* had been buried would be placed under interdict until the corpse was exhumed and removed. As one historian sharply comments, "All that was left was the crusade."[17]

tack seemed dangerously close to success. (Ransoming prisoners was a prime means for soldiers to make money, but Henry V wanted his men to concentrate on winning the battle.) It was one of the last major engagements in which swords, rather than missile weapons or firearms, played a major role, the main support to the longbow.

However, it was on the confused battlefields of Crécy that a new power of war made its first significant appearance: gunpowder. A mixture of sulfur, carbon, and sodium or potassium nitrate, the world's oldest known explosive was invented in China, but the Franciscan friar Roger Bacon (1214–92) was its best-known proponent.* In 1911 a historian wrote typically of "Friar Bacon's villainous saltpetre," which, while it "choked Don Quixote's dream, produced the art of fence."[18] With gunpowder, "the one excuse for a complete protection of the body vanished." Even so, the revolution was a slow-turning one. Until the early seventeenth century, the longbow remained superior to any weapon using gunpowder, as it was both more accurate and more efficient. Cannon were used effectively in battering and siege work but when tried in the field met with little success; they were regarded at first as more a bad joke than a threat, at best noise makers and horse frighteners. The availability of handguns did little to alter military thinking, as their use was rare.

Armor increased in thickness, and it became common to "proof" a breastplate by firing a shot against it at point-blank range. The resulting dent was not hammered out, but retained and often embellished, as proof of the armor's quality.

It was not until the 1450s or later that guns came to be a force on the battlefield, and another fifty years would pass before they came into general use. Geoffrey Chaucer's reference in *The House of Fame* to the lightning speed of a shot—"As swifte as pellet out of gonne / When fyre is through the poudre ronne"—could refer to either guns or cannon. However, once guns came into play the effect was radical. "Would to God," wrote Blaise de Montluc in 1523, "that this unhappy weapon had never been invented."

On February 25, 1525, François I of France met the Emperor Charles V

---

* From the ninth century on, Chinese technicians developed whole new families of weapons based on gunpowder—flame-throwing "fire-lances," grenades, catapult-launched bombs, shrieking rockets, and the first true cannon. But China's ruling bureaucrats, serene in their confidence that power would always be rooted in the ancient literary classics, remained aloof, the mechanics of war beneath their interests. No one was tempted to rethink military affairs.

in the "half-light of a winter dawn" outside the gardens of a nobleman's park near Pavia. His troops were decisively beaten. "One of the turning points in political history," writes Oakeshott, "it was also a watershed in the history of armour. . . . The slaughter of France's nobility in this battle was only equalled by that of Agincourt."[19] Cavalry might retain its place in military affection till 1914, but not even overlapping armor plates could offer protection against bullets. The game was up.

Bit by bit, warriors discarded their armor and so became more vulnerable to skilled swordsmen.* Skills honed on the battlefield were already producing a body of men willing and able to teach the art of swordplay, and the codes of chivalry had defined how swordsmen should conduct themselves. The formal duel of honor had become a part of European culture, and swords were no longer the costly appurtenances they once had been. As they multiplied, there was a further need to learn the skills of self-defense.

Around the same time another invention increased the popularity of swordplay even further—what Marshall McLuhan has called "the making of typographical man." A cluster of innovations, including movable metal type, oil-based ink, and the wooden handpress, revolutionized learning. For the first time those who taught fencing could have their ideas printed and disseminated. The age of the master had arrived.

---

* Members of present-day societies for the reenactment of medieval swordplay are passionate about its high quality. The Australian historian Stephen Hand has attested that in 2001 he started researching actual medieval techniques for the use of the large shield. "The system I discovered is based around using the shield to close lines of attack, deflecting rather than blocking attacks. After about six weeks of drills with this system I was untouchable. I have been to a few reenactments since and have yet to be touched by anyone putting their twentieth-century intelligence to the problem of how to use sword and shield. The historical system is so far advanced over what modern individuals do that I was, frankly, shocked. Why should I have been shocked, though? We're modern amateurs, practicing a couple of times a week with no actual negative consequences for losing. They were trained professionals who died if they got it wrong."[20]

CHAPTER 2

Enter the Master

> Now Archery is . . . being neglected in favor of swordplay:
> for offence in every town there are not only masters to teach
> it, with his provosts, ushers, scholars and other names of art
> and school, but there has not failed also which have diligently
> and well-favorably written it, and is set out in print that
> every man shall read it.
>
> —ROGER ASCHAM, *Toxophilus*, 1545

> How people choose to defend themselves is as much part of
> national character as literature, costumes or cooking.
>
> —RICHARD F. BURTON, *The Sentiment of the Sword*, 1911

THERE IS A CLASSIC PILGRIMAGE FOR ANYONE INTERESTED IN THE history of swordplay: traveling the fifteen miles from Brussels to the small Catholic university town of Louvain. I have made the journey twice, past the Place Herbert Hoover, on to the Place Ladeuze, and up through the fresh-smelling, orderly corridors of the main library to the three rooms where I was allowed to delve into the greatest specialist collection of books on fencing in the world.

The collection was begun in 1902, when an eighteen-year-old British schoolboy bought his first book about swords. Forty-three years later, Archibald Harrison Corble had assembled his extraordinary library. "Archie" Corble had been a good sabreur in his time, winning the British championship in 1922 and competing two years later in the Paris Olympics. During his various sallies abroad he had made several good friends in Belgium and was horrified to learn, just before he went to fight in the Dardanelles campaign in 1915, that the invading German army had set fire to Louvain University, razing its renowned library. After the war Corble made a name for himself as a bibliophile and donated several books to Louvain. In 1940 the library was again set ablaze, this time by Nazi warplanes. Corble decided that when he died his collection would go to the university—and so in 1945 it did, almost two thousand books and manuscripts charting the evolution of swordplay over three and a half centuries.

This unique collection allowed me to track the arrival of the fencing master and the introduction of a new weapon, the rapier, into the alleyways and taverns of Europe, which led to a revolution in technique. Corble's legacy is in more than one sense a catholic assemblage, stretching through classic Italian works from the fifteenth to nineteenth centuries on to Josef Muls's 1929 study *Melancholia,* an examination of that affliction in twenty of Belgium's leading artists, a number of them fencers. If it touched on swordplay, Corble was interested in it.

U P UNTIL THE START OF THE SIXTEENTH CENTURY THERE WERE FEW solid principles of how best to fight with swords. Masters, mainly army veterans, passed on a hodgepodge of techniques, mixing together swordplay, dagger work, and wrestling moves—anything that would help their pupils survive. Egerton Castle's view was that "each individual master taught merely a collection of tricks that he had found, in the course of an eventful life, to be generally successful in personal encounters, and had practised until the ease and quickness acquired in their execution made them very dangerous to an unscientific opponent."[1] All that was about to change.

The oldest extant work on fencing is a late-thirteenth-century German manuscript, "I 33," now in the Royal Armouries at Leeds, which in thirty-two leaves shows a monklike figure (*sacerdos*) giving instruction to a pupil with sword and buckler, with short commentaries written in Latin. There are also wrestling moves—monks at that time were famous for their excellence as wrestlers. The next entry in Corble's library is dated 1389 and ascribed to Johannes Liechtenauer, a famous master at Nuremberg. Liechtenauer's treatise is full of hints about feints, secret thrusts, and surprise parries. Another German, Hans Talhoffer, compiled his *Fechtbuch* in 1443, recording the rules for legal duels and other single combats. Talhoffer himself served as the model for the book's sixty-five illustrations, which mix swordplay with wrestling, tripping, daggers, and cudgels; it is as much a manual for survival as a book about fencing.*

---

* Wrestling continued to have a place in swordfighting well into the seventeenth century. One of the first treatises on the sport is dated 1727, *The Inn-Play or Cornish-Hugg*

Johannes Gutenberg's invention, in 1450, of movable type ignited an explosion of books on the "science of fence"—from Perpignan (not then part of France) to Spain, Italy, and Germany. In Elizabethan England the average edition of such a book was an amazing 1,250 copies—the equivalent of a major best-seller today. By 1500 printers' workshops could be found in every important municipal center in Europe. A man born in 1453, the year of the fall of Constantinople, could look back from his fiftieth year on a lifetime in which about eight million books had been printed, more perhaps than all the scribes of Europe had produced since Constantine named the city for himself in A.D. 330. As Elizabeth Eisenstein has pointed out, it was teachers in particular who "benefited from the way their personal charisma could be augmented and amplified by the printed word."[2] Between 1516 and 1884 more than five hundred works about fencing were published. The Continent was agog.[3]

The new science was powerful enough to draw major artists to its aid: in 1512 Albrecht Dürer prepared a series of 123 etchings illustrating wrestling holds and throws and a further 58 engravings of fighting with swords, staves, and daggers. But it was the Italians who were the leading theorists, and the master most widely read abroad was Achille Marozzo. Styling himself "the Gladiator of Bologna," he published his *Opera Nova* in 1536. Marozzo was the first to establish a regular system. Parrying with the blade is ignored; he describes instead how to deflect an attack either with a dagger in the nonsword hand, with different forms of shields, or with a cloth wound around the defending arm. He advised masters to insist their students swear an oath never to fight their teacher and not to pass on what they had been taught without express permission. *Opera Nova* sold out five editions over the next hundred years, and some of its illustrations were still being plagiarized well into the eighteenth century.

Marozzo was writing for teachers of swordplay, but the demand for books on fencing was far broader than that. According to *The Book of the Courtier*, published in Venice in 1528, any man of consequence should know about all forms of weapons. The author, the great dandy and man of

---

Wrestler, by Sir Theo Parkyns of Bunny Park, Nottinghamshire. Alongside entries such as "Buttock truly Perform'd" and "Your knee in his ham To prevent his throwing his Head in your Face" are several fencing instructions, including "wrestling of use in duels" and "I illustrate how useful Wrestling is to a Gentleman in Fencing." At one point Parkyns writes, "Play-wrestling is just like French fencing, which runneth much upon falsifying, taking and spending of Time."

letters Baldassare Castiglione, observed that the ideal courtier had to possess "strength, lightnesse, and quicknesse," as well as being able to handle every kind of sword, "for beside the use that he shall have of them in war . . . there happen oftentimes variances between one gentleman and another, whereupon ensueth a combat." Castiglione's *Courtier,* along with Leon Battista Alberti's *On Painting* (1435), which rewrote the rules of painting, were the most influential and widely read of all Renaissance treatises. Fencing skills would now serve an ambitious gentry as a necessary quality for social preferment, not only as a means of self-defense.

I N 1553 CAMILLO AGRIPPA PUBLISHED *TREATISE ON THE SCIENCE OF Arms with a Philosophical Dialogue,* with engravings thought by some to have been provided by his friend and fellow fencer Michelangelo.* His book was eagerly seized on by all who could read it—or at least appreciate the illustrations. A noted architect (he built the famous obelisk in St. Peter's Square in Rome), engineer, and mathematician, Agrippa was an amateur fencer who had, Castle suggests, experienced the practical side of swordplay "during many a personal encounter in the dark winding Roman streets." Sydney Anglo, too, notes that Agrippa was "a brawler, [and] ruffian" but, free of the prejudices of a master, he was able to see the advantages of the thrust over the cut. He was so proud of the mathematical and engineering knowledge he was bringing to the problems of armed combat that he had himself depicted on the book's frontispiece demonstrating some mathematical nicety with a pair of compasses. But his insights were genuine enough. Agrippa pointed out to his readers that it was far more effective to hold the sword in front of the body, not behind it. Nor was it sensible for a right-hander to stand with his left foot forward. Agrippa identified four basic guard positions. *Prima* (the "looking at your wristwatch parry") showed his pragmatism: it was the first parry a man could make after drawing his sword. Taken with the other three, *secunda,*

---

* The great artist and Agrippa certainly fenced together, but did Michelangelo undertake the illustrations for his friend? The fencing historian Malcolm Fare recently purchased a copy of Agrippa's book, previously owned by Giuseppe Molini, librarian to the Grand Duke of Tuscany. It bears an inscription on the reverse of the title page by the sixteenth-century poet Torquato Tasso, presumably also a fencer, that runs, "*le figure intagliate da Michelangelo Buonarroti.*" Although some historians have doubted that Michelangelo was responsible for Agrippa's illustrations, citing instead Giovanni Stradanus (born Jan van der Street of Holland), the artist remains unknown; we can only speculate.

A marketplace melee, from a 1506 engraving by Lucas Cranach.
Spectators lean over a simple barrier. A tournament of this type would have
been rare by the early sixteenth century.

terza, and *quarta,* the parries effectively quartered a fencer's chest: upper and lower left, upper and lower right. Simple, but effective.

While Agrippa did not invent the lunge per se, he described a thrust delivered by fully extending the sword arm forward and moving the rear foot back. By studying the bobbing head movements of fighting cocks, he discovered the "disengage" (moving the blade from one line of attack, where it is blocked by the opposing blade, into a line that is not protected). This was possibly the first time animal movement had been used as an analogy of human movement, evidence of fencing theory being on the intellectual cutting edge of its time: Agrippa's work was significantly original. As with previous theorists, however, he did not challenge the way in which fencers fought by circling each other, like boxers, nor did he criticize their "passing" (moving to one side) in both attack and defense, requiring several steps before even getting within striking range.

Another Venetian, Giacomo di Grassi, set out "the master keys to fencing." He divided the sword blade into various parts and reduced the number of basic guard positions to three. His concern for a fencer's sense of touch in parrying is remarkable for its time, and he was equally farsighted in stressing the importance of distance, and thus footwork. The psychological insights of his treatise *The Art of Defence* transformed swordplay. No one had ever thought it possible to analyze a fight that might last only a few seconds. Di Grassi argued that, indeed, most elements of a fight could be analyzed and that the basic qualities of speed, balance, and efficient use of the body and mind could be enhanced by training.

Over the next few decades a series of Italian masters further defined the structure of swordplay. In 1610 Rodolfo Capoferro of Siena opined that in choosing a weapon a man should select a sword twice the length of his arm, a reminder that blades remained of widely differing sizes; thus, when Hamlet demands in the duel scene, "These foils have all a length?" it is not just an index of his suspicious nature but a question any good fencer might have asked. Giuseppe Morsicato Pallavicini, in *La scherma illustrata* (1670), reported how fencing was conducted day to day and describes the use of swords with protective buttons—"which, when wrapped in leather, were about the size of a musket ball." Each of these masters contributed to making swordplay an autonomous activity, separate from

Illustrations showing the four guards described by Agrippa.
It is possible the artist was Michelangelo.

the demands of the battlefield—proof that if a new art has confidence enough it can leave behind the assumptions that first gave it life.

Much of the essential procedure of fencing was now in place. The sixteenth and early seventeenth centuries saw people responding to the Renaissance idea that man could improve himself by study and avidly assimilating new ways of fighting.[4] Even Martin Luther recommended fencing (along with jousting and wrestling) to promote good health. Oakeshott is correct when he states that "the period from about 1500 to about 1620 was the greatest for the sword as a weapon for Everyman; no longer was its use a privilege confined to the knightly class."[5]

ITALY WAS THE ACCEPTED WORLD LEADER. IN BOTH ENGLAND AND France skill in swordplay had been a questionable attribute, and in the roughhouse of sixteenth-century Europe only gradually did it become apparent that swordsmanship had become a necessity. By the middle of the sixteenth century the vocabulary of fencing was Italian, and France was at best an eager pupil.

Renaissance Italy was eagerly receptive to original ideas, and its masters were quick to embrace a new weapon: the rapier. A slender, double-edged sword, rarely less than four feet long, it was developed in Spain in the early fifteenth century. Spaniards found they could go about with these swords in comparative safety and began calling them *espadas roperas* ("dress swords," from *ropera* "clothing"), as they could be worn with ordinary civil dress. When early in the sixteenth century the *espadachines* of Charles V overran Italy, they took their new sword with them. The French condensed the name to *rapière*, the English to "rapier."*

For the next fifty years, a variety of swords, even two-handed ones,

---

* The Spanish word for "sword," *espada*, is one obvious association of swords with spades. Another is to be found in playing cards. An invention of the Chinese, cards were divided into suits and symbols in the fifteenth century. Even before the invention of printing, the northern Italians produced hand-painted decks of seventy-eight Tarot cards, whose court cards included a king and queen of swords. The Germans were the first to mass-produce playing cards, changing the Italian suits of swords, batons, cups, and coins to leaves, acorns, bells, and hearts. Then the French did away with the Tarot's twenty-two trumps, reduced the deck to fifty-two cards by combining knight and page into a single jack, and introduced spades, hearts, diamonds, and clubs. These suits reflected the structure of medieval society: spades (or swords) for the warrior aristocracy, hearts (cups or chalices) for the Church, diamonds (coins or bartered treasures) for the merchant class, and clubs (batons) for agriculture, or the peasantry.

were termed "rapiers." Then the specialized rapier, a weapon ideally suited for thrusting, came into being. The blade was rarely more than three-eighths of an inch wide and sometimes as much as fifty inches long, mounted in a classic "swept" hilt—that is, curved back to protect the hand. The rapier's unwieldy length relegated the cut to a secondary action and made it prudent to combine it with a dagger or cloak, which had by this time replaced the buckler (a small shield about twelve inches across). Daggers were resilient, about a foot long, with thick blades and sharp edges, sometimes with sawlike teeth set back like barbs. Duelists took to grasping their opponents' rapiers with a heavily gloved hand, and glovemakers responded by lining the palms of their gauntlets with fine mail. For a Europe increasingly gripped by the mania for private dueling, the rapier became the ideal weapon for settling scores.

WHILE THE ITALIANS AND, FOLLOWING THEIR EXAMPLE, THE French, English, and Germans, were discovering that simplification led to progress, the Spaniards chose to make fencing an arcane and elaborate ritual. They could have dominated Europe, but instead they produced "the most elaborate, and quite the most ridiculous, treatise on fencing ever written."[7] This was the work of Don Jeronimo de Carranza, a master based just south of Seville, who in 1582 published *Libro que trata de la philosophia de las armas, y de su destreza, y de la agressión y defensión christiana.* The book, dedicated to his king, Philip II, propounds a thesis so abstruse as almost to defy understanding.

Carranza explains that he created his system by applying the entire education of a gentleman—mathematics, science, art, philosophy, and religion—to the management of arms. He called his system "*la destreza*" ("the high art") rather than "*esgrima*" ("fencing") because it expressed "art and skill at the highest level." Science, he argued, must be applied to swordsmanship, and above all the science of geometry. It is possible that he was influenced by the Muslim thinkers who formed an integral part of Spain's

---

The French were also the first to name court cards after particular historical or mythical characters. The king of spades is the biblical King David, who carries the sword belonging to his most celebrated victim, Goliath; the queen of spades, the only armed queen, is Pallas Athena, Greek goddess of wisdom and war; and the jack of spades, shown in profile carrying a beribboned pike, is Oger the Dane, a knight of Charlemagne. The jack of clubs is Lancelot, from King Arthur's Round Table.[6]

heritage—one of whom, the Tunisian-born Ibn Khaldun, wrote in 1377 that "Geometry enlightens the intellect and sets one's mind right. All its proofs are very clear and orderly. It is hardly possible for errors to enter into geometrical reasoning, because it is so well arranged and orderly."[8]

Just as Leonardo da Vinci had placed man in a circle in his examination of human proportions in 1509, Carranza organized his doctrines around a circle, whose radius bears a cryptic relation to the length of human limbs and Spanish swords. In this "mystical" circle the vertical axis bisects the body, while a horizontal chord is run through the outstretched arms. The circle is further inscribed in squares and intersected by various chords that seem to stand for certain strokes and parries. The pupil was expected to imagine a similar circle around himself and step from intersection to intersection, guided by complicated calculations. Correctly implemented, Carranza believed, this process guaranteed victory. Castle's only comment was "How the Italian and French masters must have laughed." And so they did: several Elizabethan playwrights made "the magnificent Carranza" the butt of jokes.

THE SPANISH MASTER'S TEACHING WAS ONE THING, THE SPANISH rapier another. In England, Elizabethan masters recognized that the new weapon was more lethal than any other available, and they professed as much in their work. Throughout the land men wanted to know about this new arm, "set out in Print that every man may read it."[9] It was said that there were four Spaniards to every Englishman on the streets of London, each a walking advertisement. Raphael Holinshed, the historian whose chronicles so informed Shakespeare, could write, "seldom shall you see one of my countrymen above eighteen or twenty years old go without a dagger at least at his back or side. . . . Our nobility wear commonly swords or rapiers with these daggers, as does every common serving man also."[10]*

---

* The rapier is said to have been introduced to England in 1587 by one Rowland Yorke, a desperado who in January of that year betrayed Fort Zutphen in the Netherlands to the Spanish. As Holinshed was writing the year *before* Yorke is meant to have made his introduction and other references can be found as far back as 1570—they are even listed in the armory of Henry VIII in 1540—there is reason to doubt that gentleman's place in history. More reliably, William Camden, in his *Annuals of the Queen* (1615), stated that Yorke introduced a particular way of fencing with the rapier, thrusting beneath the girdle, which had previously been considered unmanly. Yorke was evidently treacherous in matters both large and small.

Well aware that young men versed in swordsmanship would be a valuable asset in wartime, Henry VIII invited the best-known teachers in the country to join a new, royally sanctioned academy. On July 20, 1540, he granted a license to certain "Masters of the Noble Science of Defense," simultaneously outlawing independent practitioners. He forbade anyone who was not a member of his new institution from teaching and obliged all members to swear not to instruct murderers, thieves, or other undesirables. (In recent times English international teams adopted a Tudor rose as part of their costume, in recognition of Henry's patronage.) To help keep the peace, a proclamation declared that no remarks or comparisons could be made about anyone engaged in a fencing bout. Nine original masters, together with eleven provosts, were duly registered. They created four ranks, neatly appropriating the language of the universities: scholar, free scholar, provost, and master, with ascent through the ranks based on success in "prizefights."

The effect of Henry's initiative was immediate. Within five years, Roger Ascham would complain, in his classic treatise on archery, that the bow and arrow were "being neglected in favor of swordplay."[11] The new academy forged ahead. Applicants to the Masters of the Noble Science of Defense were divided into ranks by experience; and examinations and the payment of hefty fees were required at each stage. A minimum of seven years of study was required before one could apply for provost, then a further seven before contending for the Master's Prize.

"Playing the prize" (hence the modern term "prizefight") was the phrase used for the highly physical matriculations. The applicant was expected to take on all the masters within a certain jurisdiction with at least six different weapons on a scaffold erected in the marketplace. The examination was brutal, lasting two or three days, and thus requiring stamina as well as skill. The City of London's records show that when a scholar applied for guild admission the crowds were so great that nearby businesses shut down for the day. The masters would gather at theaters and taverns just outside the city limits: in Bishopsgate, Holborn, Ludgate Hill, and Newgate. Severe outbreaks of the plague, such as the epidemic that took more than seventeen thousand lives in the summer of 1593, occasionally curtailed performances, as well as limiting the number of prizes contested within the city.

Despite the popularity of these contests, the standing of masters remained on a par with that of jugglers, actors, and other vagabonds. Swordplay had been discouraged in England in the Middle Ages, especially in large towns, since it so often led to bloodshed. As far back as the reign of Edward I (1272–1307) there had been fencing schools of a sort. In 1281, and again in 1310, these establishments were banned from London "under pain of imprisonment for forty days." The instructors were commoners, never noblemen, and often little better than hired thugs, providing their services to those who preferred not to fight themselves. On the Continent, such men were called free fighters or freelances. In the instance of a duel insisted on by the courts, an appellant might hire a proxy—in England a "pugil," in France a *ferrailleur*, in Italy a *bravo*—or seek professional tuition to improve his chances. Before long, expert duelists were committing all manner of crimes, confident that they could "prove" their innocence simply by defeating their accusers—for the right to call for trial by combat was not formally repealed in England until 1819.

On the whole, though, the demand was for instruction, whether for self-protection or for self-advancement. By Henry VIII's time, commoners were able to raise the money needed to become a master of fence. Once qualified, a reasonable living was assured: Sir Philip Sidney wrote to his brother urging him to "practice the single sword, and then with the dagger, let no day pass without an hour or two such exercise." Another contemporary advised young gentlemen to put aside two crowns (120 pennies) a month for lessons—a considerable investment at a time when good beer cost a penny a quart.

Italian teachers continued to enjoy wide popularity. The French royal family employed Italian masters, and French and German aspirants continued to study in Italy. Mostly, the English followed suit, but while aristocrats might attend Italian schools, a fierce rearguard action was waged in favor of the traditional cutting sword with its heavy double-edged blade, which was seen as more manly and more English. "Sword and buckler fight," says a character in Henry Porter's play *The Two Angry Women of Abington*, "begins to grow out of use. I am sorry for it. I shall never see good manhood again. If it be once gone, this poking fight with a rapier and dagger will come up. Then the tall man—that is, a courageous man and a good sword-and-buckler man—will be spitted like a cat!"

The argument between edge and point, between aggressive Italian thrust and the more defensive English style, raged for nearly fifty years. The only surviving English fencing manual from the sixteenth century was written by the ultraconservative, formidably combative, and unashamedly xenophobic George Silver. He viewed swordplay as a practical military art and extolled English methods in his *Paradoxes of Defence*. Italian methods he dismissed as "school tricks and juggling gambols," the rapier itself as "a childish toy wherewith a man can do nothing but thrust . . . and in every moving when blows are a dealing, for lack of a hilt is in danger to have his hand or arm cut off, or his head cloven." Rapier play was not only dangerous but unmanly: a thrust could be parried "with the force of a child." True Englishmen should "cast off these Italianated, weak, fantastical, and most devilish and imperfect fights, and by exercising their own ancient weapons, be restored . . . their natural, and most manly and victorious fight again."[12] For all its invective and hyperbole, *Paradoxes of Defence* did emphasize the importance of real combat conditions and pointed out some of the limitations of the rapier.

Silver's protestations notwithstanding, the rapier attained swift ascendancy, bringing with it a new fashion in finery. In 1571, the thirteenth year of Elizabeth's reign, "began the long tucks and long rapiers," records a contemporary chronicler, "and he was held the greatest gallant that had the deepest ruff and the longest Rapier. The offence to the eye of one, and the hurt that came . . . by the other caused Her Majesty to make proclamation against them both, and to place selected grave citizens at every gate, to cut the ruffs and break the Rapier's points of all passengers that exceeded a yard in length of their rapiers, and a nail of a yard in depth of their ruffs."[13] The modern equivalent would be policemen at every street corner with a mandate to cut overlong hair and confiscate switchblades. One thing was clear: the rapier derived its popularity both from its capacity to menace and its value as a fashion accessory.

Based on the widespread enthusiasm for Italian culture in general, the upper classes succumbed to the new craze for rapiers, and several leading Italian masters came to England, including Vincentio Saviolo, Rocco Bonetti (whose pupils, according to Silver, "wear leaden soles in their shoes, the better to bring them to nimbleness of feet"), and Jeronimo Rocco ("Rocco the Younger"), said to have translated Grassi into English. Between them they taught in their adopted country for thirty years. "Teachers of offense," Silver called them, complaining that these foreign experts were receiving as much as a hundred pounds for a course of lessons—more than six times the year's pay of an army captain. Hit in pride and pocket, one disgruntled master, Austen Bagger, went armed with sword and buckler to Bonetti's house "and trampled upon him," deciding only at the last minute to spare his life.[14] On another occasion, Saviolo was invited by a master in Wells to visit his school of defense but refused in so insulting a fashion that the master boxed his ears and emptied a mug of ale over him. Both Rocco the Younger and Saviolo continued to speak slightingly of English swordsmanship, so Silver and his brother Toby challenged them to a public contest on stage. It was the first time such a challenge had been issued. The Italians, having no wish to imperil their position, declined to meet it. As for the unfortunate Jeronimo Rocco, it is said that an Englishman named Cheese, spying him in a coach with his girlfriend and, thinking it "a happy and obvious occasion for calling on him to fight" (the two men had long been at odds), went to the carriage, forced Rocco to fight him, and soon ran the Italian through, killing him outright.

Fighting had become an everyday activity—men skirmished in the streets, in theaters, in print. "Soon anyone wanting to be a good swordsman had to join a school of fence," Castle records, and aristocrats were happy to take lessons from plebeian masters. In addition to straightforward sword-work, schools taught disarms, tripping, and wrestling moves—less useful perhaps in a formal duel but vital when suddenly attacked in an alleyway or dark passage. These schools, meanwhile, became havens for assassins and cutpurses, and Castle speculates that "brutal revelry, as well as darker deeds," likely took place in comparative safety behind their walls. A contemporary is more direct: "Dead men, with holes in their breasts, were often found by the watchmen, with their pale faces resting on doorsteps or merchants' houses, or propped up and still bleeding, hid away in church porches."[15]

Between 1490 and 1550 vast numbers of swords were produced throughout Europe, at increasingly affordable cost. Sword deaths from personal quarrels rose accordingly. As London doubled in size to 200,000 inhabitants between 1580 and 1600, it saw a vast influx of restless young men. By 1586 the city had at least eight major fencing schools and many more smaller, less formal venues of instruction. In many towns the art of arms fell so low, taught by whoever considered himself capable of passing on advice, that the fencing master was also the dancing instructor—or even the local dentist. Both Henry VIII and Elizabeth passed vagrancy acts requiring fencers to have "respectable occupations to satisfy the law"—but to little avail. The playwright Christopher Marlowe was at one point charged with manslaughter after a rapier and dagger duel involving one of his closest friends; in 1593 he was killed in peculiar circumstances in a tavern brawl. Five years later, Ben Jonson was penning his play *Every Man in His Humour* (Bobadill: "You shall kill him, beyond question: if you be so generously minded." Matthew: "Indeed, it is a most excellent trick!")* when he killed a fellow actor, Gabriel Spencer, in a rapier duel. He was arraigned at the Old Bailey in October 1598, where he pleaded guilty, being released by "benefit of clergy" (a one-time plea that any literate person could employ), forfeiting his "goods and chattels" and being branded on his left thumb.

The urban calendar was littered with holidays, which became an excuse for punch-ups and attacks on brothels and bathhouses (frequently sited close to fencing establishments) or houses belonging to foreigners. Gangs roamed the streets, bearing down on anyone who stood in their way. Their swaggering manner led to their being called "swashbucklers," from the clattering sound they made bashing their dueling shields.** Fencing thugs, or "sword men," became the bullies of city life—and England was hardly alone. The French government banned all fencing schools in Paris. In Germany swashbucklers were called *"Schwertzucher," "Eisenfresser"* ("Ironeaters"), or *"Raufdegen."* A fifteenth-century German woodcut, "The Fencing Hall and the Brothel," shows fencers practicing with two-handed swords while women lure them with cries of "Come with us into the bath and enjoy yourself. You'll have such a good time you won't want to leave." A Portuguese swordfighter fell afoul of the authorities for practicing his skills on a passing breeches-maker whose hat he cut in two.[16]

Italians were more notorious still. The year 1498 saw the birth of Giovanni delle Bande Nere, the son of a Medici. Giovanni became the leading mercenary of his day and introduced the ambush into military use (so becoming, in the confined spaces of an ambush, an expert swordsman). Dubbed *"Capitano di ventura"*—"captain of fortune"—he changed sides constantly and, after the death of Leo X, a Medici relative, took up arms against the new pope. Papal favor was not unimportant: Benvenuto Cellini

---

* Act IV, Scene 7. The play is full of swordfights, and in this same scene Bobadill sets himself up as a fencing coach, well able to teach "your *Punto*, your *Reverso*, your *Stoccata*," and a host of other Italianate moves.

** Another reprobate, Roger le Skirmisour, is said to have given his name to the English language, having been called up before the Lord Mayor of London early in the fourteenth century for keeping a fencing school of dubious character. Certainly the old military name for mercenary or irregular troops, "skirmishers," is similar to the French word for fencers, *escrimeurs*, but "skirmish" has a long history, going back to its Indo-European roots (the *American Heritage Dictionary* lists more than forty words in the same family, including "scrum" and "scaramouche"). It is more likely that Roger took his name from the word than the other way around.

A fencing school and bathhouse circa 1464.

came to be admired as much for his swordplay as for his sculpture, and Pope Paul III had to explain away "Benito's" killings by declaring, "Men unique in their professions like Benvenuto are not subject to the laws." Michelangelo Caravaggio might have agreed; in 1606 he killed a man in a swordfight, probably over a squabble about a tennis-match wager, and was forced by the Vatican to flee Rome. In his case the pope was foe, not friend.

Caravaggio's weapon was the rapier, as it had been for so many before him; it was the weapon that finally brought about the triumph of the thrust over the cut. In itself, it was deadly, but after some seventy-five years of near supremacy it became outmoded. Spanish fencers continued to use it, as they continued to follow Carranza's precepts up until the opening years of the seventeenth century. Elsewhere, however, after its high season, the rapier lost its place in popular esteem. Over the mid–seventeenth century, while the Spanish clung to their great discovery, modifying it slightly into a new version, the *bilbo,* across the rest of Europe the rapier was shortened and lightened; but it was still too long for easy use, and the fencing world looked around for new inspiration.

S HAKESPEARE IS SAID TO HAVE LEARNED TO FENCE AT THE BLACK-friars Theatre, most probably under the instruction of Vincentio Saviolo, who had arrived in London when the young playwright was twenty-six. Shakespeare took his fencing seriously, on at least one occasion, in 1589, ending up on the wrong side of the law when accused of being caught in public in an affray, his sword in hand. Elizabethan audiences watched the style and execution of stage fights with keen interest: it was not unusual for unruly members of the audience to join in the action on-stage, and eventually an ordinance was passed banning the wearing of swords to the theater. In 1596 James Burbage, the leading actor of Shakespeare's company, bought the lease of the fencing school he had been attending and annexed it to Blackfriars Theatre; Shakespeare was one of his partners. Two years later the playwright, along with a theatrical group that included Burbage's two sons, decided to move the company to a less expensive site on the south bank of the Thames. Their old landlord expected (not unreasonably) that the building itself would remain where it stood. During the Christmas holiday, however, the group, armed with swords, dismantled Burbage's theater piece by piece and transported it to the new site.*

While other playwrights offered up fight scenes in profusion—John Webster would give an entire play-within-a-play to swordfighting in *Love's Graduate*—until Shakespeare no one had used the swordfight so well, or for such a variety of purposes. There are 437 references to "sword" in the Shakespearean canon (though, interestingly, only five to "duel"), and in play after play swordfights occur center stage.

Sometimes Shakespeare makes fun of the whole business, as when Slender, in *The Merry Wives of Windsor*, clumsily bruises his shin "playing at sword and dagger," or when Sir Andrew Aguecheek takes on a disguised Viola in *Twelfth Night*. In *As You Like It* Touchstone, the outlawed jester, famously ridicules the newly formed rules that applied to formal challenges, listing "the retort courteous . . . the quip modest . . . the reply churlish . . . the reproof valiant . . . the countercheck quarrelsome . . . the

---

* Shakespeare's brushes with the law have long fascinated other writers. In *Tales of the Jazz Age* F. Scott Fitzgerald has a story, "Tarquin of Cheapside," about a struggling writer toiling away when a ruffian, on the run from "two murderous pikemen . . . with short swords lurching and long plumes awry," with whom he has had a fierce passage of arms, arrives at his door and begs to hide in his loft. The ruffian, "a grey ghost of misty stuff," is of course Shakespeare, who admits he is something of a writer himself—he is at work on a long poem, *The Rape of Lucrece*. But the narrator is too preoccupied with his own efforts to take much notice, and soon "Soft Shoes," as he dubs his visitor, "flashes through a patch of moonlight" and sets off back to "the black lanes of London."[17]

lie circumstantial . . . the lie direct," while pertinently adding, "Your 'if' is the only peace-maker; much virtue in 'if.' "

There are other, more deadly encounters: Antony challenges Octavian to a duel in *Antony and Cleopatra*, Iago wounds Cassio in a brawl in *Othello*. There is a trial by combat in *Henry VI*, and in the opening scene of *Richard II* Shakespeare portrays the historic charge of treason made by Henry Bolingbroke, Duke of Hereford, against Thomas Mowbray, Duke of Norfolk, challenging him to public combat. "What my tongue speaks, my right drawn sword may prove," Henry declares.

> By that, and all the rites of knighthood else,
> Will I make good against thee, arm to arm,
> What I have spoke, or thou canst worse devise. (I, i, 80–82)

The most dramatic of Shakespeare's swordfights, however, comes in Act III, Scene 1 of *Romeo and Juliet* with Mercutio's duel with Tybalt. The verse provides a vivid description of an exchange with rapier and dagger (or perhaps cape):

> He tilts
> With piercing steel at bold Mercutio's breast;
> Who all as hot, turns deadly point to point,
> And with a martial scorn, with one hand beats
> Cold death aside, and with the other sends
> It back to Tybalt, whose dexterity
> Retorts it.   (III, i, 173–78)

The scene is also Shakespeare's chance to make fun of the Spanish school of rapier play. Mercutio derisively exclaims as he prepares to take on Tybalt that his opponent is "a villain who fights by the book of arithmetic."

Above all, there is Hamlet's duel with Laertes. Though a considerable literature exists covering this most famous of stage fights, critics disagree on what is meant to take place: how are the two swords swapped convincingly? Few eyewitness accounts of Shakespeare's plays survive, and there is not a single description of any of his fights; but we are given clues. Hamlet uses a rapier:

> HAMLET: What's his weapon?
> OSRIC: Rapier and dagger.
> HAMLET: That's two of his weapons—but well.   (V, ii, 144–46)

Hamlet is also an expert fencer and (although earlier in the play he admits to being much out of practice, a possible slip on Shakespeare's part) expects to win:

> HORATIO: *You will lose this wager, my lord.*
> HAMLET: *I do not think so. Since he [Laertes] went into France I have been in continual practice. I shall win at the odds.*   (V, ii, 210–13)

Shakespeare would have choreographed the "scuffling" called for in the text as something like close-quarter wrestling (the two men would have been far closer to each other than we are used to)—so two rapier players could easily have found themselves deadlocked and able to grasp each other's sword hand. The lunge had not yet come to England—attacks would have been by "passes," in the old style. If the swordfight were not done convincingly, the Elizabethan audience would mock or boo the actors offstage. And so the greatest play ever written climaxes in a swordfight, at once exciting, exactly described, and crucial to the outcome of the drama. It is impossible not to thrill to that moment in Act V, Scene 1, so full of foreboding and menace:

> KING: *Come, begin,*
> *And you the Judges beare a wary eye.*
> HAMLET: *Come on Sir.*
> LAERTES: *Come on Sir.*
> They play.

CHAPTER 3

A Wild Kind of Justice

> *He goes forth gallantly. That he and Caesar might*
> *Determine this great war in single fight!*
>
> —CLEOPATRA, IN SHAKESPEARE'S *Antony and Cleopatra,*
> IV, iv, 36–37

> *Men may account a* duello *an honourable kind of satisfac-*
> *tion, yet it is but a scarlet or a grained kind of murdering.*
>
> —SIR FRANCIS BACON, *Letters,* 1614

THE WORD "DUEL" COMES FROM THE LATIN *DUELLO,* MADE UP OF *bellum* ("conflict") and *duo* ("two"). A duelist was defined by Noah Webster as "one who fights in single combat." To the eighteenth-century Scots philosopher David Hume, a duelist was "one who always values himself upon his courage, his sense of honor, his fidelity and friendship"—curiously leaving out the business of fighting altogether.[1] An 1884 study of dueling, *The Field of Honor,* opts for "a professional fighter of duels; an admirer and advocate of the *code duello.*"[2] Perhaps it is best to settle on a combination of all three.

Unlike the early medieval tournaments, the scuffles between individuals in a pub-room argument, or the clan combat Sir Walter Scott describes in such convincing detail in *The Fair Maid of Perth,* the duel was fought within an imposed set of conventions. An artificially staged encounter, it was deliberately confined by formal restrictions and, as such, was the truest precursor of fencing. The two would overlap and borrow from each other over the centuries.

Dueling dominated the landscape of swordplay for more than a thousand years. A number of historians cite David and Goliath, Achilles and Hector, and Turnus and Aeneas as early duelists, but they were individual combatants engaged in a national quarrel: David and Goliath in the age-old struggle between Jews and Philistines; Achilles and Hector representing Greece and Troy; Turnus and Aeneas as rivals for Lavinia—but each with a whole army behind him. What we think of as duels were virtually unknown in the ancient world; Tacitus comes nearest, with a description in the *Germania*.[3] The Greeks and Romans had very different conceptions of what it was to be courageous: Plato for one defines courage as "the virtue of fleeing from an inevitable danger."

It is a matter of record that Antony sent a challenge to Octavius Caesar, but most historians date the origins of the duel to A.D. 501. That was when Gundebald, King of Burgundy, under pressure from a relentless bishop, drew on pre-Christian precedent to declare the wager of battle a recognized judicial proceeding. He argued that since God directed the outcome of wars, it was only right to trust in His providence to favor the just cause in private quarrels as well. (Gundebald must also have been aware that perjury was regularly being committed under the existing system of trial by oath.)* His *Lex Burgundiorum* combined Celtic, German, and Roman traditions into a single code. Victory in combat would be admissible as proof of integrity in all legal proceedings in lieu of swearing; women, invalids, men over sixty, and boys under fifteen would be exempt, and later so were priests. Why Gundebald expected God to have a freer hand in duels than elsewhere is unclear; perhaps he was guided by the belief that in a one-on-one contest God would be cornered and would have to see that justice was done. In any event, his "trial by battle" soon became the norm throughout Europe. Duels were used to decide even the most arcane and academic conflicts, so that in Toledo, in 1085, a duel determined whether Latin or Mozarabic rites should be used in the liturgy (the Mozarabic champion won).

A class of proxy fighters, known as "champions," emerged. It was a dangerous way to earn a living, as a losing duelist would have his right arm chopped off. The accused was kept just out of sight, a noose around his neck; if his champion lost, he would immediately be hanged or burned to death. As trial by battle spread, commoners were restricted by circumstance or by law to fighting on foot with wooden staves, while mounted combat and swordplay became the preserve of the nobility. Combats never started before

---

* The clergy encouraged the belief that God, whenever called upon, would work a miracle in favor of anyone unjustly accused. The power of deciding a person's guilt or innocence was then placed entirely in its hands. Thus, when red-hot plowshares were placed on the ground and an accused person, blindfolded, had to avoid them to be judged innocent, a cleric had only to place the plowshares at irregular intervals to ensure a conviction; when the accused had to handle, unhurt, a piece of red-hot iron, a presiding sympathetic priest would substitute cold iron painted red—and so on.[4]

noon, the accuser entering from one direction, the defendant from the other. The litigants would swear that they had no magic charms or potions about them (a primitive form of drug testing). Then, at the marshal's command, the challenger would fling down the "feuding glove" before his opponent, who would accept the challenge by picking it up.

If the accused could keep the fight going until the stars came out, he would win his suit. Spectators were commanded to be silent, on penalty of losing a limb. When a combatant was wounded or thrown, his opponent would usually kneel on his chest and, unless asked for mercy, drive his sword through a joint in the armor. Those last moments, waiting for the sword to slide through one's visor, must have been terrifying. The victorious knight would rarely raise his opponent's visor, as it would have meant looking into his victim's eyes. The impersonality of armor had its advantages.

Early on the Church took a stand against judicial combat: Stephen IV condemned all duels, and the Council of Valencia, in 855, threatened combatants with excommunication. But within three years Nicholas I pronounced dueling "just and legitimate" and abbots and priors began taking

*The end of a trial by combat. Outside the enclosure lies
the armor of earlier contestants.*

their share of the confiscated goods of a defeated combatant, sometimes even fighting themselves. Their weapon of choice was the mace, on the false premise that it did not shed blood (it is difficult to crush an opponent's skull cleanly). In 967 the Council of Ravenna declared judicial combat acceptable, citing David's triumph over Goliath as evidence of divine sanction. A century and a half later, there were even formulas for Church blessings of duels,[5] and a handful of saints were thought to be particularly effective if prayed to over a duel's outcome. Bishop Liutprand of Cremona was said to maintain a duelist whose function was to corroborate the truth of the bishop's statements. Certain monasteries, such as some around Paris in the fourteenth century, maintained special fields equipped with walls and viewing stalls expressly for staging judicial duels, with the monks renting out facilities as required.

However, the practice continued to worry the Church's conscience, and vacillation gradually resolved into outright condemnation. Further councils—from Limoges in 994 up to Trent in 1563—reemphasized the Church's abhorrence of dueling, and a series of early-Renaissance popes—Alexander III, Celestine III, Julius II—declared that they would excommunicate any sovereign allowing it. Similar pronouncements were made by Gregory XIII (1582), Clement VIII (1592), Alexander VII (1655), Benedict XIV (1752), Pius IX (1869), and Leo XIII (1891). None worked; as one writer put it, the warlike spirit took to the duel just as the carcasses of horses produce worms. Dueling evidently appealed to something in man that could not be reined in, even by the threat of losing his immortal soul.

Such a threat was a real one. A notable "champion for hire" was the Chevalier d'Andrieux, who by the time he was thirty had killed seventy-one men. His next opponent boasted, "Chevalier, you will be the thirteenth I have killed." D'Andrieux replied, "And you my seventy-second"—and suited his action to the word. D'Andrieux added to his reputation by regularly disarming his rivals and forcing them to forswear God, at the point of his sword and on the promise of their lives. On hearing their enforced blasphemy he would then run them through—in order, he said, to have the pleasure of dispatching body and soul in one.*

---

* There are many odd dueling stories. In 1372, a French knight, Richard Maquer, slew his friend Aubrey de Montdidier and buried him in the Forest of Bondy, near Paris. Mondidier's dog, a huge greyhound called Verbaux, said to have been present at the killing, made its way to the house of a friend of his master called Ardilliers, dragged him to the burial place, and scratched away at the ground till the body was discovered. Later, whenever the dog saw Maquer it would attack him ferociously until the suspicious Ardilliers

The judicial duel continued to be practiced, until in 1386 a duel was fought that had such an appalling outcome that even the most unquestioning began to lose faith. Jacques LeGris was accused by his old friend Jean Carrouges of raping Jean's young and beautiful wife, Marguerite, while Carrouges was away in Paris. LeGris protested his innocence, and after an inconclusive trial lasting several months the Parlement de Paris decreed that a duel be fought—in the presence of Charles VI. The two men met on December 29 a quarter of a mile north of Paris, on grounds owned by a Benedictine priory, watched by a crowd of around ten thousand. Marguerite, dressed in a long black robe, stood nearby on a scaffold, knowing that should her husband lose she would be burnt at the stake as a "false accuser." After a fierce fight, first on horseback then on foot, Carrouges thrust a dagger through a gap in LeGris's armor and mortally wounded him. The dead man's body was dragged off by the executioner, to be hanged in chains from a nearby gibbet. Not long after, a man arrested on other charges admitted to the rape, and rumors spread that Carrouges had forced his wife to accuse the wrong man to avenge an old quarrel. This was the last duel to be officially sanctioned by the Parlement de Paris, and, in France at least, such encounters lost divine authority.

One of the last judicial duels in England took place in 1571, under Queen Elizabeth I. A man named Paramour applied for trial by combat over certain disputed manorial rights, and his opponent accepted the challenge. The Court of Common Pleas had no choice but to process the application. The queen, anxious to avoid bloodshed, ruled that the suit be settled, but the duel had to proceed, as required by law. On the morning in question, officers assembled at Tothill Fields in London before a crowd of more than four thousand. Each side had a champion, the petitioner fielding a well-known fencing master named Henry Nailer. When the plaintiff failed to show up, his absence was declared an abandonment of claim, but Nailer suggested that he and the opposing champion, to "show some pastime" to the gathering, should fight each other anyway. His invitation left

---

petitioned the king, who in turn ruled that Maquer's guilt or innocence would be decided by his dueling the dog.

The exact details of the fight, held in the square of the cathedral of Notre Dame, are disputed: some chroniclers have Maquer wielding a lance, others have him buried up to his waist and armed with a stick and shield, while the dog was given a large barrel open at both sides in which he could take refuge. Whatever Maquer's defenses, they were not enough: the dog seized him by the throat until Maquer promised to confess, which he duly did.

his adversary unimpressed, and the disappointed crowd dispersed. However, the law remained on the statute book until it was cynically employed one last time, in 1817, by a man accused of murdering a girl by her younger brother. The boy was too young to fight a duel, and as no one else could be found to take his place the charges were dropped. Finally, on March 22, 1819, the judicial duel was abolished by Parliament. The accused man, shunned by the public, emigrated to America, where he soon died.

DESPITE THESE EXCEPTIONS, BY THE END OF THE THIRTEENTH century the duel of law had given way to the duel of chivalry. Initially this was a public encounter between two knights, usually on horseback, to settle a disputed possession or a point of honor. A code of chivalry was drawn up by Philip the Fair of France in 1306, and his precepts were further elaborated by Richard II and James I.

Generally, kings ignored the claims of chivalry at their peril. During the Third Crusade, Richard I (r. 1189–99) allied himself with his brother-in-law, Henry the Lion of Brunswick, and trampled on the banner of his fellow crusader Leopold of Austria. The German Emperor Henry VI commanded Richard to meet Leopold in single combat, but Richard declined, saying that Henry had no authority over him. Within months, Richard was shipwrecked off the coast of Aquileia and delivered into Leopold's hands. The emperor ruled that because Richard had failed to give satisfaction he should be kept in prison. He was released only after he had paid a heavy ransom and done public homage. This account has not yet found its way into Robin Hood mythology.

A similar violation of knightliness and judgment was made by the French king Francis I. In 1527 Francis reneged on a treaty with Charles V, the Holy Roman Emperor. Charles responded by sending back a message that he would henceforth consider Francis a base violator of public faith and a stranger to the honor and integrity befitting a knight. Francis immediately challenged Charles to a duel, which the emperor readily accepted, only to find the French king frantically backpedaling: Francis's challenge had been mere "gasconade," as windy threats were known. After that, kings and other rulers learned to leave their quarrels to diplomats and soldiers.

When people wanted to fight but had no legal case to settle, they appealed to the chivalric code, which, with its strict rules, made dueling respectable. Once the formalities of chivalric dueling grew irksome, the "duel of honor," most often private, even secret, and held at some out-of-the-way spot, without rules or umpires, became chivalry's awkward child. At first, "duels of honor" were anything but—they were free-for-alls, known as "killing affrays" or "*duelli alla macchia*." Books on fencing warned of men carrying sand in their pockets to throw into their opponents' faces and advised against shaking hands with anyone whose sword was already drawn, lest it immediately be used against them. But over time successful duelists gained something of a reputation, and the ability to vanquish numerous opponents became a mark of honor.

One such celebrated duelist was James Crichton (c. 1560–c. 1583), a noble-born Scot who was so prodigious in body and mind that by the age of twenty he could speak eleven languages (Latin, Greek, Hebrew, Chaldaic [the Babylonian tongue], Italian, Spanish, French, Flemish, German, Gaelic, and English). He could also dance, sing, and play "all sorts of instruments," according to Sir Thomas Urquhart, his first and most likely unreliable biographer.[6] Contemporary portraits depict Crichton as a handsome man, despite a red birthmark on his right cheek. He had a passionate attachment to tilting, concerts, cards, dice, and tennis, and "his memory was such that anything that he heard or read he could reproduce without an error. . . . Nor were his accomplishments as a fencer and as a horseman . . . less remarkable." In 1577 he set out on a tour of Europe.

At the University of Paris, his fellow students pinned a notice on the main gate at the College of Navarre announcing, "If you would meet with this Monster of Perfection, to make search for him either in the tavern or bawdy-house, is the readiest way to find him." Crichton parried this friendly thrust by announcing that in six weeks he would present himself to respond, in public examination, in any one of his languages, to whatever question put to him, "in any science, liberal art, discipline, or faculty, whether practical or theoretic." On the day appointed, he was examined from 9 A.M. till 6 P.M. before a large audience and performed with such brilliance that he was dubbed "the Admirable Crichton" ever after. The next day he carried all before him in a tilting competition at the Louvre.[7]

He served for two years with the French army and traveled to Genoa, where he built on his reputation as a brilliant orator; then, in 1582, he moved to Mantua. That city hosted a much-feared Italian bullyboy—in Urquhart's words, "of a mighty, able, strong, nimble and vigorous body; by nature fierce, cruel, warlike and audacious, and in the gladiatory art . . . superlatively expert and dangerous." He would travel Europe challenging all comers for a stake of 500 gold pistoles—about £400 then, a startling figure: the equivalent of about £150,000 ($250,000) today. (Some seventy years before, Henry VII had offered a prize of just £10 to any Englishman who "discovered land to the West.")

By the time Crichton arrived in Mantua, this champion had taken on three local opponents over three days, killing the first with a thrust to the throat, the second by a lunge through the heart, and the third by running him through the belly. The Duke of Mantua was "much grieved" that he had granted his protection to such a brute, and Crichton, learning of the duke's alarm, offered to fight the self-proclaimed champion in the presence of the Mantuan court. The duke gave his consent, rapiers of equal length and temper were selected, and the start of the duel was signaled by the firing of a sixty-four-pound cannonball. Both men fenced in shirts and drawers and in their bare feet.

Crichton immediately settled on defense, while his adversary—unusually, we have no record of his name—went through his entire repertoire: "he changed guard from tierce to quarte, he tried prime and seconde, he tried in high line and low line, and twisted his body into all the shapes he could to break through the Scot's defense, but to no avail."[8] Amid it all, the "sweetness of Crichton's countenance," in stark contrast to his opponent's enraged panting, charmed the court and had the ladies in a flutter (two are said to have swooned).

The watchers sensed that the Italian was tiring. Only at this point did Crichton go on to the attack, striking his opponent deliberately in the throat, heart, and belly so that, Urquhart wrote, "If lines were imagined drawn from the hand that delivered them to the places marked by them, they would represent a perfect isosceles triangle, with a perpendicular from the top angle cutting the basis in the middle." Each thrust mimicked one of the fatal thrusts against the three men who had last fought the Italian champion, and each brought him closer to death. When all was done, Crichton gave his adversary's sword to the duke and the purse to the three widows. The duke rewarded Crichton by making him tutor and companion to his dissolute son Vincenzo, "a youth of ungovernable temper."

Some weeks later, Crichton was returning from an evening visit to a lady friend when he was waylaid by masked brawlers. He fought back so effectively that he managed to disarm the ringleader, who was forced to pull off his mask and beg for his life. It was Vincenzo. Crichton fell to his knees, expressing his sorrow and explaining that he had been acting in self-defense. He handed his pupil his sword, hilt forward. Vincenzo seized it and, feeling humiliated in front of his attendants, plunged it home. So died the Admirable Crichton, not yet twenty-four, giving a phrase to the English language and a play title to J. M. Barrie.

The convergence of warriorlike behavior and civilian logic telescoped quarrels so that they were likely to become murderous with great speed; even to put one's hand on one's sword was an inflammatory act. Duels were often fought over trivial matters: in the late seventeenth century two French noblemen came to formal blows over an argument their grandfathers had had more than seventy years before. The fight extended to their seconds, then their thirds, and finally to the king's messenger, who had been sent to stop the duel but who didn't wish to miss out. In Naples, a nobleman fought some twenty duels to prove Dante a greater poet than Ariosto; at last he admitted that he had read the works of neither.

During the reigns of François II (1559–60), Charles IX (1560–74), and Henri III (1574–89), dueling in France was so popular that historians have dubbed the era "l'époque de la fureur des duels." Even though the Parlement of Paris outlawed the practice in 1559, within five years Charles IX was forced to put out an edict saying it was up to him when duels could take place. Thirty years later, Henri IV forbade dueling yet again, although in 1605 "Le Bon Henri" allowed a duel to be fought on his behalf, and on another occasion, when a subject asked permission to fight, replied, "Go, and if I were not your king, I would be your second." Contradictions between the law and actual practice reached the level of absurdity.* Between Henri's accession in 1589 and 1607, four thousand French gentlemen lost their lives dueling a rate of four or five a week, or eighteen a month while the king granted fourteen thousand pardons. Given the population of France at the time, with only about half a million people "of quality," this was a fatality rate befitting a world war.

There had to be new rules, and all over Europe, from the thirteenth century to the nineteenth, treatises outlined what such regulations should be, from the cause of a quarrel to the challenge, the choice of weapons,

---

* The enthusiasm for dueling compares poorly to the "nith-songs" of the Greenland Inuit. According to an early-nineteenth-century study, "when a Greenlander considers himself injured in any way by another person, he composes a satirical song about him, which he rehearses with the help of his intimates. He then challenges the offending one to a duel of song. One after another the two disputants sing at each other their wisdom, wit, and satire, supported by their partisans, until at last one is at his wits' end, when the audience, who are the jury, make known their decision. The matter is now settled for good, and the contestants must be friends again."[9]

and on to the fight itself. Could seconds take on a principal? Should handicapping be introduced, to make the encounter as balanced as possible? Much debated was the question of who had the advantage (presuming fighters of equal skill): the man who struck first or the one who received the first attack and launched a counterstroke.*

Some of the most vicious duels of the sixteenth century took place in Italy, where innumerable "disreputable tricks and abuses" originated. There were professors everywhere of what was called the *scienza cavalleresia* ("the gentleman's craft"); the Constable of Naples even instituted a military order, under the patronage of Saint George, to protect and maintain "this honorable pursuit." By the mid–sixteenth century a flood of treatises, emphasizing that honor was personal, led directly to the decline of the use of substitutes. In England, Queen Mary I (r. 1553–58) denounced "divers naughty and insolent persons" who had been fighting using rapiers up to five feet long and wearing armor underneath their clothing, but she could not stop the gentlemen of England from talking about duels, reading voraciously about them, and training for them.

Strangely, dueling in any formal sense did not begin in England until about a hundred years after it had taken root in France and Italy. There were full-scale private battles between grandee factions but no instance of a private duel fought in England before the sixteenth century, and very few before the reign of James I. However, in 1579 Sir Philip Sidney quarreled with the Earl of Oxford over the use of a tennis court and called him out. Queen Elizabeth intervened, reminding Sidney of "the difference between earls and gentlemen." Sidney retorted "that place was never intended to privilege to wrong"—but he still had to yield to the queen's authority. By 1650 Thomas Hobbes was writing that duels "always will be honourable, though unlawful, until such time as there should be honour ordained for

* Akira Kurosawa provides a famous scene in *Seven Samurai* in which a wise and experienced sensei scours the town with a young protégé for fitting companions to join them. They encounter two samurai preparing to duel with fresh-cut bamboo. The more mature, slighter-built combatant slowly comes on guard. His confident, rougher opponent disposes himself more quickly, shifting his weight, fidgeting, and making feints with fierce cries. The wise old observer and his student watch as the two duelists await the first blow. Suddenly the roughneck charges, seeking an advantage through speed and surprise. His opponent makes no attempt to avoid the attack but instead, a split second before the blow falls, delivers a devastating counterattack. The roughneck claims a draw, but the other disagrees, claiming, "a real sword would have killed you." The rough fencer is enraged, and real swords are soon bared. "How stupid," murmurs the old samurai. "It's so obvious." The passage of arms is replayed, this time for life and death, and the older duelist kills his man, just as he had foretold.[10]

them that refuse, and ignominy for them that make the challenge." The demands of "honor" were in effect setting up an alternative system to the rule of law, and the English nobility, like their brethren on the Continent, proved impervious to their various sovereigns' attempts to contain it. In the first two decades of the seventeenth century one in every four peers was in danger of losing his life in a duel.

But the English Crown was itself about to be brought to heel. Civil war raged between 1642 and 1646, then for a second time in 1648. Charles I had fought and lost: within months he was tried and executed, and in 1653 Oliver Cromwell declared himself lord protector, giving him supreme power in association with Parliament and the Council of State. The following year he banned dueling in all its forms, declaring that to kill somebody in such a way was still murder. He meant to have his way and on one occasion even sent troops into the Portuguese Embassy—to the horror of the diplomatic community—to remove the brother of the ambassador, Dom Tavernes de Sà, for causing the death of a bystander during an affray in Bond Street. (Dom Tavernes was taken to Tower Hill and beheaded.) For a while the number of duels dropped, only to flare up again after Cromwell's death in 1658 and the restoration of Charles II. It was said that the exiled Cavaliers brought back with them the French culture of dueling.

Soon it was back to the old routine. In 1679 Charles II proclaimed that any person responsible for killing another in a duel would be tried and punished; yet during his reign there were 172 duels involving 344 individuals, of whom 69 died and 96 were wounded. The king pardoned nearly all those who survived. Seconds, who first appeared in Italy, began to take each other on alongside their principals. Samuel Pepys alludes to the prevalence of dueling in his day as "a kind of emblem of the general complexion of the whole kingdom." Cromwell had put a stop to the whole business of public duels and theatrical entertainment, but after his death games and sports—puppet shows, circuses, cockfighting, hangings, bear baiting, tightrope walkers, wrestlers, jugglers, pugilists, conjurors—flourished again, and swordsmen were back in their element. In the 1660s Pepys recorded in his *Diary:*

> And I with Sir J. Minnes to the Strand May-pole; and there light out of his coach, and walked to the New Theatre, which, since the King's players are gone to the Royal one, is this day begun to be employed by the fencers to play prizes at. And here I came and saw the first prize I ever saw in my life: and it was between one Math-

ews, who did best at all weapons, and one Westwicke, who was soundly cut several times both in the head and legs, that he was all over blood: and other deadly blows did they give and take in very good earnest, till Westwicke was in a sad pickle. They fought at eight weapons, three boutes at each weapon. This being upon a private quarrel, they did it in good earnest; and I felt one of their swords, and found it to be very little, if at all, blunter on the edge than the common swords are. Strange to see what a deal of money is flung to them both upon the stage between every boute. So, well pleased for once with this sight, I walked home."

"Ball-rooms, masquerades, theatres, the open streets, became constant scenes of strife and bloodshed," wrote the historian Andrew Steinmetz. "Covent Garden and Lincoln's Inn Fields became the rendezvous for deciding points of honour, and at all hours of the night the clashing of swords might be heard by the peaceable citizens returning home, at the risk of being insulted and ill-treated by the pretty fellows and the beaux of the day. Duelling was in vogue, and even physicians were wont to decide their professional altercations at the point of the sword." Steinmetz then tells of two doctors, Woodward and Mead, who fought a duel under the gate of Gresham College. Woodward slipped and fell, leaving himself open to Mead's final thrust. "Take your life," exclaimed Mead. "Anything but your *physic*," Woodward replied.[12]

An entire subculture grew up in which a whole section of privileged society joined clubs with names such as "Mohocks" and "Hell-fires." These warriors went into their duels expecting to die or at the least be badly injured, with roughly the same odds on surviving unscathed as a British soldier who fought in the First World War. Other dueling clubs were slightly more sophisticated. One of these, the "Bold Bucks," accepted members only if they had fought a duel; the president was said to have dispatched as many as six opponents. Placement at banquets and dinners reflected the number of men each member had killed: those who had only drawn blood were relegated to a side table. The club did not last long; most of its members were soon enough run through or hanged.

Dueling as a partial substitute for ambushes, gang warfare, blood feuds, and assassinations was by now an accepted fact of life throughout Europe. No law had more than a transitory effect: it was like trying to ban adultery. One French wit adapted the adage "Divorce is the sacrament of adultery" into "Dueling is the sacrament of murder." Yet the distillation of sudden combat into formal duel was still evolving, and in 1720 a brawl boiled up in London with more than a hundred youths having at each other with swords and canes. A troop of Horse Guards was called out and charged into the rabble, cutting many down "ere the disturbance could be stopped, and the whole of this row had arisen because two chairmen [men carrying sedans, and proverbially very strong] were fighting."[13]

By the reign of George III public brawls were going out of style and swords were drawn less frequently in gambling halls, taverns, and chocolate houses. According to Jonathan Swift, fencing was an essential part of a "good education" in the first half of the eighteenth century, but thereafter the "noble art of self-defense" went steadily out of fashion in Oxford and Cambridge, to be replaced by country sports and team games. Men's dress had remained basically the same for almost a century; from the 1790s on swords ceased to be carried, and after 1814 trousers began to replace breeches. With the change in men's fashion, and with weapons no longer to hand, duels assumed a more regular and civilized form. The "Bold Bucks" had had their day, replaced by a more refined cadre of gentlemen—men who had no wish to be "hell-fire rakes," instead creating the "Crutch and Toothpicks." It was not long before another nickname overtook them: "The Macaronis."*

Fencing itself was a major form of popular entertainment. James Figg, a leading swordsman, established an amphitheater or academy of arms next to his house in Oxford Road, Marylebone Fields. Teaching small- and backsword, cudgeling, and boxing—"pugilism"—to gentlemen, he soon became so famous that he was praised in the journals from *The Guardian* to *The Tatler*. A show, or a prizefight, would include bouts with broadsword, cudgels, sword and dagger, sword and buckler, and quarterstaff.

Members of his troupe would advertise forthcoming events by parading the streets in fancy dress, swords drawn, colors flying, and drums beating as they handed out flyers. Figg's theater was so popular that the doors regularly opened three hours before performances began. He himself went undefeated throughout his fencing career, bar one loss to Ned Sutton, "the pipe-maker of Gravesend and champion of Kent"—but most spectators conceded that Figg had been ill at the time. In 1730 he fought

---

* "Macaroni" was simply a suitable-sounding name for anyone with Italianate pretensions. Hence the well-known ditty "Yankee Doodle went to London / Just to ride the ponies [i.e., to visit a brothel], / Stuck a feather in his cap and called it Macaroni."

his 271st public battle, cutting his opponent's wrist to the bone. A critic of the day, one Captain John Godfrey, declared that Figg was "the Atlas of the sword, and may he remain the gladiating statue. In him strength, resolution, and unparallel'd judgement conspired to form a matchless Master."[14] Horace Walpole was an admirer, as was Alexander Pope. William Hogarth engraved his calling card for him and portrayed him in his "Rake's Progress."

Before long, the boxing matches, which started as support bouts to the fencing, began to outshine the swordsmen, and Figg realized that a new popular entertainment had arisen. Changing disciplines, he became an expert pugilist and in 1720 England's first national boxing champion. One wonders why "fisticuffs" took over from swordfights in England—as they never did in France, Germany, or Italy. Maybe, *pace* George Silver, fighting your man hand to hand was a more honest activity for an Englishman.

The period is full of dueling, and journalists could not leave the subject alone. Addison, Swift, and Daniel Defoe wrote of it, and Richard

The business card designed by William Hogarth for James Figg,
showing both a typical stage and the variety of weapons used.

Steele inveighed against what he deemed its impiety and foolishness: "Death is not sufficient to deter men who make it their glory to despise it; but if everyone that fought a duel were to stand in the pillory, it would quickly lessen the number of these imaginary men of honor, and put an end to so absurd a practice."[15] Steele then to his horror found himself drawn into a duel against an officer in the Coldstream Guards, his own regiment. With honor at stake, he accepted the challenge and, to his alarm, nearly killed his opponent. The officer eventually recovered—to Steele's profound relief.

Unlike most of his literary contemporaries, Steele was actually an accomplished fencer. So was Defoe, a campaigning political journalist who was often threatened and on three occasions beat off attackers with his sword. This did not stop him from condemning dueling. He disapproved of the public fights at the Bear-Garden, where spectators came keen to see blood. Yet he could still write, "To those who understand the art, or, as the back-sword men called it, the Noble Science of Defence, the best sight is to see two bold fellows lay heartily at one another, but to be so dexterous, and such exquisite masters of their weapons, as to ward off every blow, to parry every thrust, and after many nice closes, and fine attempts, not to be able to come in with one another, or so much as to draw blood. This shows them to be good swordsmen, and perfectly skilled in their weapons."[16] Bloodless dueling, however, was a fantasy.

In 1772 Richard Brinsley Sheridan (who in later years would bring a duel into one of his comedies) moved from Ireland to Bath, where he fell in love with Elizabeth Linley, an eighteen-year-old beauty who was the principal singer at the Drury Lane Theatre—and she with him. Her father, a distinguished composer, did not immediately see Sheridan as acceptable, which left Elizabeth prey to other admirers, among them Captain Thomas Mathews of Bath, a married man who wanted only to bed her, and threatened to take her by force. She decided to flee to France, at first intending to join a convent. She confided her scheme to Sheridan, who joined her and convinced her to marry him. Meanwhile, a letter Sheridan had left for Mr. Linley explaining the situation infuriated Mathews, who arranged for a scurrilous article about Sheridan to appear in the *Bath Chronicle*, branding him "a L[iar] and a treacherous S[coundrel]." Thinking Sheridan would not return to England, he further vowed to take his life. But Sheridan *did* return, and learning of Mathews's threat decided to take him at his word. The resultant duel began at Hyde Park Corner and culminated with a fight by candlelight in the parlor of the Castle Tavern in Covent Garden. Sheridan swiftly disarmed his man, who begged for mercy. A heated argument followed, during which Sheridan took Mathews's sword, broke it, "and flung the hilt to the other end of the room." Mathews protested bitterly but begged for his life and promised he would make a full and public apology, which he did.

Mathews returned to his estate in Wales, and was universally shunned. But the captain had not given up, and a second duel was inevitable; it was fought on the crest of Kingsdown, outside Bath. This time the affair was bloody and unyielding. Although swords had been agreed on, the initial exchange was with pistols, Mathews apparently fearing another "ungentlemanly scuffle," like the first encounter. When both their first shots missed, they turned once more to swords. With his second thrust Mathews's blade broke, shivering in the middle, leaving a jagged point. He seized Sheridan by his sword arm and threw him to the ground, stabbing the playwright repeatedly with the stub of his sword. Sheridan all the while hacked away at Mathews with his own weapon. "My dear Sheridan, beg your life," implored his second. Sheridan shouted back, "No, by God I won't." Eventually, after Mathews had pierced Sheridan in more than two dozen places, he was dragged off and Sheridan was "borne from the field with a portion of his antagonist's weapon sticking through an ear, his breast-bone touched, his whole body covered with wounds and blood, and his face nearly beaten to a jelly." Eight days later he was out of danger and celebrated by returning to London and remarrying his beloved (the first ceremony had been when they were both still under age, so it was not binding), this time with her parents' approval.[17]

Elizabeth Linley was the innocent cause of Sheridan's duels, but the ladies were not always so blameless. Sounding a characteristically misogynistic note, Steinmetz lists as a regular contributing factor "the insinuations of artful, dangerous, and vicious females, and inflammatory mistresses, who prided themselves much in being the object of a duel."[18] It was certainly a public feather in many a woman's cap, and even before the time of the Sun King a woman's power of fascination could be reckoned by the number of challenges, and consequent deaths, she had inspired.

Sexual politics could be merciless. In 1668 Lord Shrewsbury accused the Duke of Buckingham of having seduced his wife. In the resultant duel Buckingham dispatched the cuckolded husband with a thrust through the body, sustaining no more than a slight wound himself. Meanwhile Lady

Shrewsbury hid in a nearby thicket, disguised as a page and holding her lover's horse ready for him to escape. That night she joined Buckingham in his bed, where he wore, as one account would have it, "the very shirt stained with the blood from the wound he had received as her champion." Charles II pardoned Buckingham, a favorite, but insisted this would be the last time he would do so. "It would be hard after this," notes Steinmetz acidly, "to say who was the most infamous, the king, the favourite, or the courtesan."[19]

Women were not always spectators. The Restoration dramatist Aphra Behn gave a distaff view of dueling in her play *The Rover* (1678). An adventuress and spy, she never herself fought a duel. In 1792, however, a Mrs. Elphinstone disparaged Almeria Lady Braddock: "You have been a very beautiful woman. You have a good autumnal face even now, but you must acknowledge that the lilies and the roses are somewhat faded. Forty years ago, I am told, a young fellow could hardly gaze upon you with impunity." Her ladyship replied that she was not yet thirty. Mrs. Elphinstone cited a well-known worthy who had let it be known that Lady Almeria was sixty-one. That was the finishing touch. Their duel, fought first with pistols, then with swords, ended with a bloody wound to Mrs. Elphinstone. At its conclusion the ladies curtsied to one other and "quitted the field with honor." This was too much for the society wits. In *The Grand Duke; or, The Statutory Duel*, Gilbert and Sullivan devote nearly fifty lines to the duel. One stanza runs:

> *When Mrs Elphinstone*
> *Did chaff the fading Braddock*
> *About her age, she had to wage*
> *A fight by Hyde Park paddock.*
> *Since nothing would atone*
> *Short of a desperate battle,*
> *The Lady B. made Mrs E.*
> *Regret her tittle-tattle.*
> *For slanders cease to be a joke*
> *Whene'er you find the women-folk*
> *Such fiery kittle cattle.*

IN HIS SHORT STORY "THE PRIVATE LIFE," HENRY JAMES REMARKS OF the writer protagonist that he "marched . . . into the flat country of anecdote, where stories are visible from afar like windmills and sign-posts." Even a selective history of dueling incurs the same risks: there are so many episodes—absurd, bloody, eccentric, or otherwise memorable. Goethe, for instance, took up fencing in the years before moving to Weimar because he believed it would make him more attractive to women. His most recent biographer remarks that "the riding and fencing lessons in the last months at Frankfurt bore little fruit . . . we hear only of one quite unserious duel."[20] When Goethe finally attained a reasonable standard of fitness, it had more to do with his sleeping regularly out of doors and giving up coffee; but he did work briefly in a swordsmiths' and wrote about fencing affectionately in *Wilhelm Meisters Lehrjahre*. Pope Clement XIV appointed the fourteen-year-old Wolfgang Amadeus Mozart a "Knight of the Order of the Golden Spur," which entitled the composer to carry a sword on certain occasions.[21] The young prodigy never fenced, however, although he sometimes signed letters "Chevalier de Mozart"—with a degree of mockery, one suspects.

Sir Walter Raleigh was such a keen swordsman that he was said to have fought more duels than any of his contemporaries. John Milton wore a sword well into his sixties and despite his encroaching blindness would boast of his skill. "When my age and mode of life so inclined me," he wrote, "I was neither unskilled in handling my sword nor unpractised in its daily use. Armed with this weapon, as I usually was, I considered my-self a match for anyone, even my superior in strength, and secure from any insult which one man could offer to another."[22] George Frideric Han-del fought a duel at Hamburg in 1704 and was lucky not to be run through; his adversary's blade broke against a button on his coat. Louis Napoléon—later Napoléon III—was a frequent duelist, on one occasion fighting Comte Léon on Wimbledon Common with swords *and* pistols. They were separated by police.

In Spain, Don Rodrigo Díaz de Vivar, "El Cid," was urged to avenge his father, who had been disgraced in a duel against the father of the Cid's lover; he took up the challenge, "and the parent of his loved one fell by his hand." In *Conquest of Mexico* William Prescott characterizes the great ex-plorer, Hernando Cortés, as someone whose "graver pursuits . . . did not prevent his indulgence of the amatory propensities, which belong to the sunny clime where he was born; and this frequently involved him in af-fairs of honor, from which, though an expert swordsman, he carried away scars that accompanied him to the grave."[23] The Spanish artists Diego

Velázquez (1599–1660) and José Ribera (1588–1652) are both said to have "handled the sword in perfection."

The same was true of Ignatius of Loyola, founder of the Jesuit order. Born into an aristocratic family from Castile, on the Spanish side of the Pyrenees, he had fiery red hair and, although just five feet one, had a "love of martial exercises and a vainglorious desire for fame." He read avidly the adventures of El Cid, the Knights of the Round Table, and *The Song of Roland* (ironic, since he was a Basque, whose countrymen had killed Roland) and at seventeen enlisted in the army. He would stride about "with his cape slinging open to reveal his tight-fitting hose and boots; a sword and dagger at his waist."[24] He challenged a Moor to a duel to the death for denying the divinity of Christ, duly running him through. Other duels followed until a musketball passed through both his legs when he was part of a Navarrese garrison besieged by the French in 1517. While convalescing, he read a life of Christ and a book on the lives of the saints, and determined on a religious career. Nor was he the only swordsman turned religious: the Abbé de Rancé, founder of the Order of the Trappist Monks, was also a regular duelist before his move to La Trappe in the 1660s.

Even more formidable was Philip Latini (1605–67) of Corleone, Sicily, an illiterate cobbler turned swordsman. He learned to fence from the Spanish mercenaries based in Palermo (Spain then ruled Sicily), and became so expert that he was known as "Corleone, the best blade of the Island." A local crime boss named Vinuiacitu (literally, "wine-turned-vinegar") sent one of his followers, Vito Canino, to see if the man could best Corleone at swordplay. The issue was soon settled: Corleone cut off the assassin's arm. Terrified that Vinuiacitu would wreak revenge, he took sanctuary in the local church until the coast was clear, staying there for a week, during which time he repented his swordfighting ways and in 1632, at age twenty-seven, became a Capuchin friar. In June 2001 he was canonized for his piety and good works as Saint Bernard of Corleone.

I N 1712, THERE WAS AN ENCOUNTER OF SUCH MALICE AND BRUTALITY that, although it did not stop dueling, it changed the way Britons perceived it. The man challenged was James Douglas, fourth Duke of Hamilton, a Jacobite grandee who had already seen prison for his part in an attempted invasion of Scotland. On his release, he had switched his allegiance to Queen Anne and the Tories and been rewarded with the embassy in Paris. However, his turncoat behavior had made him enemies, particularly among the Whigs, and commentators on the fight have argued that it was an attempt at political murder.*

The duke's opponent was Charles, fourth Baron Mohun. He was forty-seven, some years older than Hamilton, corpulent and dissipated but still a seasoned duelist, variously described by contemporaries as "the bully of the Whig faction" and "the bloody villain." Charles had been only a year old when his father was killed while seconding a duel, and by the age of seventeen he was quarreling over dice with Lord Kennedy, a fight to the death being prevented only by onlookers. Two days later he conspired with a friend, Captain Hill ("that dark-souled fellow in the pit," as Leigh Hunt called him), to abduct an actress, the delightfully named Mrs. Bracegirdle, "the belle and toast of London," as she left the theater after her evening performance.[25] The abduction went wrong, so the two cutthroats ran off to lay in wait outside her home, swords drawn. Soon there appeared another actor, William Mountfort—her lover in the play, of whom Hill was passionately jealous. Mohun embraced him in a drunken hug, allowing Hill to step forward and run his rival through. Hill then promptly made good his escape. Mohun was perfectly happy to stand trial in the House of Lords, which he did in January 1693. The case was "the sensation of the hour," with the king—that grim Calvinist William III—in constant attendance, and Mohun, still only seventeen, protesting that Mountfort had drawn first. On February 4 he was acquitted by 69 votes to 14, one peer remarking of the dead man that the fellow was only an actor and that all actors were rogues.[26] By October of the following year Mohun, "always ready for any desperate mischief," was dueling with a member of Parliament who had tried to stop him from murdering a coachman on Pall Mall.

For the next two years he took his homicidal energies abroad, serving with distinction with the British army in Flanders. By 1697 he was fighting again and was part of an affray in which his accomplice, Captain Hill, was killed. Two months on and he had notched up another murder, while seconding Lord Warwick against Captain Richard Coote in a nightime brawl in Hyde Park. All six men involved (two seconds on either side) had been blind drunk and slashed away at each other till Coote lay dead. Mohun and Warwick were charged with murder, but once again Mohun

* By 1680 members of the Green Ribbon Club—who defended Parliament and Protestantism—were called Whigs, a shortened form of "Whiggamore" (literally, "horse thief"), the name of a Scots band active around 1648 against Charles I. "Tory" was an Irish word for robber, first applied to the Conservative Party by Titus Oates in 1680.

was acquitted, this time on the grounds that Warwick had been the provoked party. Over the next decade he apparently reformed, becoming a staunch Whig and a regular speaker in the Lords. However, when the Duke of Marlborough, a colleague, was insulted by Earl Paulett during a debate, it was Mohun who visited Paulett and invited him to "take the air in the country." Queen Anne interceded and told Marlborough to call off his dogs.

Yet a dog of havoc Mohun remained. In 1701 he had inherited an estate valued at around £20,000. Hamilton also enjoyed claims on the property through his wife, and the two men had been wrangling over it for years, the bad blood thickening. Eventually, at a hearing on November 13, 1712, before a Master of Chancery in chambers, Hamilton cast aspersions on the integrity of a witness, saying that "he had neither truth nor justice in him." Mohun issued a challenge.

The encounter took place in Hyde Park between six and seven in the morning, on Saturday, November 15. "It is difficult for a Londoner at this day to imagine the loneliness of Hyde Park a century ago," wrote Steinmetz in 1886. The fringes of Mayfair were then the extreme western limit of the city. Park Lane was "a wild and desolate" region "in which dust-contractors had been permitted to carry on their business, and to accumulate mountainous cinder-heaps" stretching all the way to the Oxford Road. A few houses and one ancient roadside inn formed the village of Knightsbridge, while no one lived on the southern side of the park save an occasional cottage-dweller on the fields that rolled between Knightsbridge and Chelsea. To the north lay Tyburn, the place of execution. The ground beneath the gallows was known till the end of the eighteenth century as "no-man's land." In 1712 it was a fitting name for the entire area. The park itself was notorious as a haunt of footpads, a wilderness where affairs of honor could take place unobserved and undisturbed.

With the adjustment to a modern calendar (in 1752), November 15 then would be November 26 now. The weather would have been frosty, even snowy, following a cycle of intensely cold winters; it would have been dark then, probably smoggy, and extremely uninviting.

Mohun had spent the previous night carousing in Long Acre. The coachman who picked up him and his cronies was one John Pennington, who at the trial swore that he had stopped for them at the Bagnio (meaning "bath," so probably a brothel), a drinking parlor in Covent Garden. He had been told to take them to Kensington, but once there Mohun had insisted that they press on to Hyde Park. Pennington became uneasy.

Mohun asked if there were anywhere he could get mulled ale, and the coachman went off in search. The innkeeper he woke up refused to serve him, insisting that no one would be in the park so early other than to fight. When he returned, Pennington discovered that two other men had arrived, and it was obvious a duel was brewing. He ran back to the inn for help.

With all the parties assembled, Hamilton turned to Mohun's second, Lieutenant General George Macartney, and said, "Sir, you are the cause of this, let the event be what it will." Mohun urged that the seconds should not fight, at which Macartney demurred, while the duke, according to different sources, either looked at his own second, his cousin Colonel John Hamilton, and replied, "This is my friend, he will take a share in my dance," or else insisted, in a more "political" vein, "Macartney should have a share in the dance." However framed, those were words he would soon regret.

What happened next is terrifying and curiously hard to understand. With no regard for his own safety, Mohun rushed at Hamilton and the two cut and thrust away with no attempt to parry, obviously intent only on inflicting as much injury as possible. The most vivid account of the fight

A contemporary oil painting of the 1712 fight between the Duke of Hamilton and Lord Mohun, which led to the deaths of both men and a renewed outcry against dueling.

comes from Jonathan Swift, creator of Gulliver and an inveterate Tory publicist. His version is colored by his sympathy with Hamilton, but his narrative is clear enough:

> The dog Mohun was killed on the spot, but while the Duke was over him, Mohun shortened his sword and stabbed him in the shoulder to the heart. The Duke was helped towards the Lake-House, by the Ring, in Hyde Park, where they had fought, and died on the grass.

Did Mohun run Hamilton through, or did he die immediately? The angle of the thrust makes it far more likely that Macartney or one of Mohun's footmen, or both, stabbed Hamilton as he bent over his enemy. The ensuing trial revealed the horror of what a duel could do. Mohun had two main wounds: one, in his right side, was driven at an angle through his whole body and came out on his left side below the hips. The second made a large tear in his right groin, severing the great artery, which was the principal cause of death. The artery of Hamilton's right arm was cut through, this being the immediate cause of *his* death, but he had also suffered a diagonal wound, three inches below the left nipple and eight inches deep, and a wound in the right leg.[27] Both men's nonsword hands were deeply lacerated where each had attempted to catch hold of the other's blade—three of Mohun's fingers were almost completely severed. They had simply stabbed and hacked each other until they could take no more.

The whole story shook fashionable society. A bill was introduced into the House of Commons to suppress dueling more effectively, but after two readings it was lost. In 1852, when dueling, in England at least, was almost at an end, Thackeray retold the duel in some detail in *The History of Henry Esmond*, in elegiac tones:

> As Esmond and the Dean walked away from Kensington discoursing of this tragedy, and how fatal it was to the cause which they both had at heart; the street-criers were already out with their broadsides, shouting through the town the full, true, and horrible account of the death of Lord Mohun and Duke Hamilton in a duel. A fellow had gone to Kensington and was crying it in the Square there at very early morning, when Mr Esmond happened to pass by. He drove the man from under Beatrix's very window, whereof

the casement had been set open. The sun was shining though 'twas November; he had seen the market-carts rolling into London, the guard relieved at the Palace, the labourers trudging to their work in the Gardens between Kensington and the City, the wandering merchants and hawkers filling the air with their cries. The world was going to its business again, although dukes lay dead and ladies mourned for them; and Kings, very likely, lost their chances. So night and day pass away, and to-morrow comes, and our place knows us not. Esmond thought of the courier, now galloping on the North-Road to inform him, who was Earl of Arran yesterday, that he was Duke of Hamilton to-day, and of a thousand great schemes, hopes, ambitions, that were alive in the gallant heart, beating a few hours since, and now in a little dust quiescent.[28]

CHAPTER 4

France in the Age of the Musketeers

The whole art of fencing consists in just two things, to hit and not to be hit.

——M. JOURDAIN, IN MOLIÈRE'S
Le Bourgeois Gentilhomme, 1670

Try parrying that, Rousseau!

——REVOLUTIONARY JUDGE, SENTENCING AUGUSTIN ROUSSEAU,
FENCING MASTER TO THE ROYAL FAMILY, TO THE GUILLO-
TINE, 1793

ONE EVENING IN DECEMBER 1725, VOLTAIRE, THEN A YOUNG
bourgeois intellectual on the rise, had words at the Opera with the Chevalier de Rohan-Chabot, a well-connected nobleman and dissolute man-
about-town. Some six weeks later, as Voltaire was leaving a dinner at the
home of the Duc de Sully, one of the king's senior ministers, two by-
standers asked him to mount the steps of a carriage waiting in the street.
He did so, expecting the carriage's occupant to have something to say to
him. Instead, he was set upon by thugs and thrashed repeatedly with a
cane. "Don't hit him on the head!" shouted a voice from the carriage.
"Something good may come out of that one day!"

Voltaire recognized the voice at once: it was the Chevalier de Rohan's.
He managed to get back inside the gates and into the duke's house, but instead of sympathy or even outrage he met only laughter. Over the next few
days he bombarded the authorities with complaints, but they backed off.
"Like a herd of cows," wrote Nancy Mitford in her book on Voltaire, "one
of which has got into a shindy with a small, furious dog, the French aristocracy now drew together, staring sadly but inertly at the fray." Voltaire
decided he had no other recourse than to challenge Rohan to a duel. Although he had worn a sword for many years, he knew how to use it, to

quote another of his biographers, "about as well as a poet of the present time knows how to box." Since he was no swordsman, he threw himself into an intense regimen of fencing lessons.[1]

Suspecting that something was afoot, Rohan warned the police that Voltaire might commit some deranged act (*un coup d'étourdi*) and should be carefully watched. The police concurred and received permission from the King to arrest Voltaire should they deem it necessary. On April 16, 1726, four months after the run-in at the theater, the lieutenant in charge of the surveillance reported to his chief, "We have information that [Voltaire] is now at the house of one Leynault, a fencing-master, Rue St Martin, where he lives in very bad company. . . . It is certain he has very bad designs. . . . He is more irritated and more furious than ever in his conduct and in his conversation. All this intelligence determines the lieutenant to put the King's orders into execution, if possible, this very night."

That same evening, at last feeling confident in his dueling skills, Voltaire accosted Rohan at the Théâtre Français, and with a few well-chosen taunts elicited the challenge on which he had set his heart. A duel was arranged for nine the next morning, and Voltaire hurried back to his lodgings, unaware of the plots swirling around him. With perfect if coincidental timing, the police now acted. Shortly after arriving home Voltaire found himself borne off to the Bastille, where he was kept for fifteen days, being set free on condition that he leave the country. The chief turnkey of the Bastille was ordered "to accompany him as far as Calais, and to see him embark and set sail from that port."*

---

* Voltaire's fencing days were not entirely wasted. Seven years before, while visiting her father, he had met a fifteen-year-old girl, Emilie de Breteuil, in her Paris apartment, with seventeen rooms and thirty servants. Emilie was a tomboy and thought "difficult." According to the science writer David Bodanis, she "had long black hair and a look of perpetual startled innocence, and although most other debutante types wanted nothing more than to use their looks to get a husband, Emilie was reading Descartes' analytic geometry, and wanted potential suitors to keep their distance."[2] Her parents, worried she might grow up clumsy, paid for her to have fencing lessons, and she became good enough to take on Jacques de Brun, the head of the king's bodyguard detail, in a public contest, a performance that helped keep her many unwanted suitors at bay. At nineteen, Emilie made a marriage of convenience with a wealthy soldier named du Châtelet, then thirty, and continued her research in physics and mathematics. She also found time to translate Aristotle and Virgil, as well as to take several lovers. In 1733, eight years after Voltaire's encounter with Rohan, he met Emilie at the opera, and the two became lovers, soul mates, and fellow researchers. Emilie's work on the nature of energy was the most advanced of her time. When in 1749 she died aged forty from a late pregnancy, Voltaire wrote, "I have lost the half of myself—a soul for which mine was made."

WITHIN A YEAR OF THE INCIDENT OUTSIDE THE DUC DE SULLY'S house a new verb had been added to the language: "*voltairiser*," meaning "to voltaire, to thrash." Voltaire's humiliation epitomizes the absurdity, arrogance, and hypersensitivity of the upper classes in eighteenth-century France. Yet from the accession of Louis XIII in 1610 to the overthrow of Napoleon in 1815 it was the nobility that shaped swordsmanship into something recognizable as a modern sport—a compound of science and art.

It came about as a by-product of violence. While Louis XIII recognized that he should outlaw destructive feuding, he had a romantic fondness for the days of chivalry. During his thirty-three-year reign the country went dueling-mad—no nation, not even the German aristocracy or the Protestant rulers of Ireland, was as obsessed. Men fought at any time of the day or night, by moonlight or torchlight, openly in the streets or in secluded parks (the Bois de Boulogne was a favorite venue), on the slightest provocation. Those who wished to avoid a formal duel would resort to a collision in the street—the "*rencontre*"—which would lead to "words" and a fight on the spot without the duel's formalities: but the result was the same. Seconds were considered cowards if they did not join in, and often two or more participated. One duel, in 1652, involved four seconds a side, and there could be as many as ten, or even twenty—not melees as before, but planned encounters regulated by at least some semblance of procedure.*

It was famously said that when court acquaintances met in the morning their first inquiry was "Who fought yesterday?" and, after dinner, "Who fought this morning?" Lord Herbert, English ambassador to the court, tells in his memoirs of a young man who asked for a girl's hand only to be informed by her father that to be eligible he should fight a couple of duels first. Herbert adds, "There is scarce a Frenchman worth looking on who has not killed his man in a duel."

I like to think that, had Emilie survived, she and Voltaire might have invented fencing's electric box two centuries ahead of time.

* Employing seconds became widespread in the second half of the sixteenth century. The most notorious duel of that period was the "*duel des mignons*" of 1578, in which six of Henri III's favorites killed each other. "Once a second had killed his man," François Billacois tells us, "or put him out of action, he would go to the aid of the duelist he was seconding."[3]

Nor were duelists likely to show remorse for their actions in public. When the Marquis de la Donze was awaiting execution for killing his brother-in-law, he was asked to repent. "What!" he replied. "Do you call one of the cleverest thrusts in Gascony a crime?" Rarely were matters of honor resolved amicably: when the one-legged Marquis de Rivard was challenged, he sent a surgeon in reply and suggested that in the interests of fighting "on an equal footing" his opponent should submit to a similar amputation. The duel was called off.

This frenzy quickly spread beyond Paris, and Louis XIII, seeing how the provinces were being denuded of their most talented men, reluctantly encouraged Cardinal Richelieu to set about stemming the tide with whatever measures he saw fit. Richelieu, the austere prelate who from 1624 on was de facto ruler of France, had personal motives for taking action: years before, when he had been Bishop of Luçon, he had displeased the Marquis de Thémines. The Marquis—since he could not gain satisfaction directly from a man of the cloth—determined to challenge Richelieu's older brother. It did not take him long to fabricate an opportunity and, when the two men met, the head of the house of Richelieu, struck through the heart, died instantly.

No sooner had the younger brother become minister than he issued an edict against dueling; but he took a pragmatic view. Legislation forbidding duels had long been in place but rarely enforced. Richelieu believed that the law's severity was the reason for its nonenforcement, so in 1626 he pushed an edict through a reluctant Parlement de Paris limiting the death penalty to those whose duels actually resulted in death or whose seconds dueled with each other and ensured that these penalties were applicable even for duels fought elsewhere on the Continent and overseas. The measures failed to eradicate dueling (one duel is on record as having taken place by the light of a lantern positioned to illuminate a copy of the cardinal's edict), but they were enough to anger the *noblesse d'épée* and would soon be the mainspring of the nobility's confrontation with Richelieu.

The critical case involved the most infamous duelist of the time, François, Comte de Bouteville-Montmorency—the possessor, he claimed, "of the finest mustache in France"—who had survived twenty-one duels. At 2 P.M. on Wednesday, May 12, 1627, in broad daylight on the Place Royale, the most fashionable square in Paris, Bouteville fought his twenty-second, against the Marquis de Beuvron, for no better reason than that Beuvron wanted to avenge Bouteville's last victim. Rosmadec des

*The 1627 duel of the Count de Bouteville with the Marquis de Beuvron—
and their seconds—in broad daylight in the middle of Paris. It led to
Cardinal Richelieu's crackdown on the practice throughout France—
and Bouteville's beheading.*

Chapelles, one of Bouteville's two seconds, killed one of Beuvron's seconds. The King was livid, but it was widely assumed that he would not have a leading nobleman executed.

Richelieu had other ideas. Beuvron and his unwounded second fled to England, but Bouteville and Chapelles found themselves arrested and tried by the Parlement de Paris. The *Mercure français,* one of the main newsletters, reported that, since Bouteville had been called out by Beuvron, he had only been defending his honor, as any nobleman might. (The paper forbore from adding that Bouteville would happily have dueled whatever the situation and even ran a dueling school in his town house.) Five of the grandest ladies of the court came to the king in person to make a final appeal for clemency, but it was no use: on June 22, 1627 Bouteville and Chapelles were beheaded; effigies of Beuvron and his surviving second were hanged alongside them.

By a strange irony, the Cardinal would share his title with one of France's foremost duelists, Louis-François-Armand de Plessis, Duc de Richelieu and Maréchal de France. Born around 1690, long after the cardinal's death, the duc grew up to be "a reckless duelist, and a systematic and heartless seducer," in the words of one historian.[4] The darling of the ladies of the court (Emilie du Châtelet was one of his lovers, even though Voltaire was a close friend), he once arranged assignations with separate mistresses, leaving the arrangements to his secretary, who ineptly fixed the same hour for both. There was a scene and a duel ensued between the two women, one of them losing part of an ear. Far from tarnishing his reputation, the affair made Richelieu "the Adonis of the day."

While committed to the Bastille for the *third* time, he was moved from his dungeon to comfortable apartments at the intercession of female admirers and allowed to take a daily walk along the walls. As he paced the ramparts, a procession of elegant carriages filled with highborn admirers—all of whom either were or had been his mistresses—passed to and fro before him amid a flurry of gestures. In 1725, after having spent six years incarcerated, he was restored to favor and sent as ambassador to the Holy Roman Emperor at Vienna, then the prime diplomatic posting.

It seemed as if everyone was either writing about dueling or engaging in it—including the great philosophers. In the sixteenth century Michel de Montaigne (1533–92) had expounded at length on the iniquities of dueling, although he admitted that he was physically inept himself: "At dancing, tennis and wrestling," he wrote, "I have not been able to acquire more than a slight, vulgar skill, and at swimming, fencing, vaulting and jumping, no skill at all."[5]

René Descartes (1596–1650) was a keen fencer as a young man. In 1621, while visiting Prague, he was aboard a boat bound for East Frisia when the crew tried to assault him, and he fought them off with his sword. Later, while in Paris, he was escorting a woman friend when a drunken lout abused her. Descartes "went after the rash fool quite in the stump-stirring fashion of d'Artagnan," according to his biographer, and "having flicked the sot's sword out of his hand spared his life, not because he was a rotten swordsman, but because he was too filthy to be butchered before a beautiful lady." After completing his studies at the famous Jesuit college appropriately called "La Flèche," Descartes spent twenty years in Holland, where he continued his fencing lessons. At one point he wrote to a friend apologizing for doing so little mathematics—he had been too busy with his hobby. After his death a treatise he had written, *The Art of Fencing*, in which the "greater part of the lessons were drawn from his own experience," was found among his papers. Sadly, it does not survive.[6]

In one of his *Essays* Montesquieu (1689–1755) recorded, "When I was young the people of quality went out of their way not to be thought fine blades, and would avoid instruction therein as an activity which was too cunning by half, an enticement away from the simple path of righteousness."[7] No matter that dexterity with a sword made one more valuable to one's king on the battlefield and would help frighten off idle challenges: skill at fencing implied a shady character and would continue to do so well into the eighteenth century. However, while it was thought bad form to be known as a *"bon escrimeur,"* gentlemen still regularly traveled to Italy to improve their skills.

OUIS XIV CAME TO THE THRONE IN 1643, AT THE AGE OF FIVE. HE would reign for seventy-two years, in the opening nine of which nine hundred Frenchmen died in duels. His first edict against dueling appeared under his mother's regency in the year of his accession, followed by another in 1651, a third in 1670. . . . In all, Louis XIV published ten such edicts, but rather spoiled their effect by granting more than seven thousand pardons in nineteen years, an average of one a day. Each new edict differed little from its predecessors but was intended to show that this time the king *really* meant business. His subjects simply didn't believe him—until, in 1679, he published his "Edite [sic] des Duels," threatening the death penalty not only for the principals but for their seconds, witnesses, and attendant surgeons. Their entire property would be confiscated and the coat of arms of a gentleman offender broken by the public executioner, a terrible fate for a man of honor. At the same time, he established a Court of Honor, composed of the *maréchaux de France* (the great officers of state directing the army) to resolve disputes brought before it, as well as to penalize offenders. The court declined to interfere when the party was of insufficiently high birth, but where their peers were concerned they were vigilant. It took Louis XIV twenty-five years to enforce his edict, but by 1704 fatal encounters had almost ceased. Fifty years on, Voltaire, skulking on the Swiss border, judged the King's "abolition of duels" to be one of his greatest achievements.

Having gathered a deliberately underemployed higher aristocracy under his watchful eye at Versailles, Louis XIV elaborated endless rules of behavior and extremes of formality. Every move was prescribed by a court convention, dress was determined by social standing, and *l'étiquette* was strictly maintained. Unlike the English aristocracy, who oversaw their lands or attended Parliament, the French nobility stewed in a pressure cooker of egos and intrigue—literally thousands of courtiers all fighting for favor. (Once, walking on the terrace at Versailles, the king caught sight of an unsworded officer, the unfortunately named Marquis de Silly, and peremptorily sent for him. "You appear before your sovereign without your sword?" he demanded. "Indeed, sire," said the officer bravely. "We have been defeated at Blenheim, and I am on parole." On this occasion he was forgiven.)

A SIGNIFICANT IMPROVEMENT IN THE QUALITY OF ROADS IN THE mid–seventeenth century led to the widespread use of stagecoaches, and soon travelers learned that the long, wide-hilted rapier was not the most practical of weapons to wear in a confined space. In his diary for January 10, 1660, Pepys writes of walking to Westminster and overtaking Captain Oakeshott in his silk coat, "whose sword got hold of many people in walking." In 1663 the "suit"—the first piece of menswear to fasten in the front—made its appearance. The rapier, easy enough to carry and draw in the days of doublet and hose, did not sit well with brocaded jackets, breeches, and silk stockings. So popular in the 1640s and 1650s, it had become antisocial, "an infernal nuisance to passers-by."[8]

In the Netherlands the rapier had already begun to be replaced as early as the 1630s by swords with smaller hilts and shorter, more manageable blades. When Charles II and his followers returned to England after their long exile there, they brought these "town swords" with them. The English, who called their military blades by the medieval term of "great-swords," derided these new weapons, dubbing them "smallswords." However, it quickly became clear that the smallsword was ideal for sword-play, effective in both attack and defense. Further, it obviated the need for a dagger. When the new weapon made its way to France, the court christened it "l'épeé courte," a name that survived up to the end of the nineteenth century.*

* In 1670 Molière, the leading court dramatist, was ordered by Louis XIV to produce a "divertimento," a comedy-ballet with music and dancing. The result was Le Bourgeois Gentilhomme, in which an aspiring middle-class Frenchman struggles to ape his alleged betters. To invest himself with the appropriate affectation of nobility, he retains four teachers—of music, dancing, fencing, and philosophy. Each presents the case for the importance of his art, discoursing on the virtues of harmony, grace, verbal dexterity, and swordsmanship. To a modern ear, swordplay hardly seems to be given much of a recommendation, but Molière's fencing master was propounding radical theories: "As I proved the other day with demonstrative logic, it's impossible to be hit if you simply divert your opponent's blade from the line of your body. You do that with a simple twist of the wrist, either inward or outward."

During the fencing master's argument, Molière satirically uses the expression "mettre flamberge au vent" ("to put Flamberge to the wind") to describe the act of drawing a smallsword with a grand flourish, as if it were the great Flamberge—the other name

I T DID NOT TAKE LONG FOR FRENCH MASTERS TO REALIZE THAT THEY needed to develop a new school of fencing to suit the new weapon. Until the first half of the seventeenth century they had depended on the Italians, to such a degree that Queen Catherine de' Medici had installed several Italian masters in France to develop the sport. So successful were they that in 1567 her son Charles IX officially recognized the French Academy of Fence. Subsequent monarchs continued to patronize the academy. Louis XIV granted the association its coats of arms and conferred patents of nobility on six prominent masters. Only after studying under a recognized master for at least six years (one less than their *confrères* across the Channel) could one gain membership, and the teaching of swordplay throughout France became the monopoly of academy members.

The academy was quick to establish an "*escrime française*," a system that emphasized a more flexible way of holding one's weapon, with the thumb and forefinger on either side of the lower part of the hilt. This grip afforded a new subtlety of movement that forced hilts to become smaller and more manageable. The word "rapier" became a term of contempt, applied to a sword of disproportionate length—the weapon of a swaggerer.

It was a time for codification: the five basic steps of classical ballet were established in 1650, and treatises proliferated—on the art of war, anatomy, physiognomy, optics. The appearance of the great French Academy dictionary of the language (begun in 1638 and finally completed in 1694) ensured that French became the European tongue, the medium of diplomacy, the language of aristocracy, even of fine cooking. "For a century and more," note the historians Will and Ariel Durant, "Europe aspired to be French."[9] When a competition was held in 1783 for the best essay on why French had become *the* universal language, it was sponsored not by the court of Versailles but by that of Berlin.

In 1653 a book by Charles Besnard of Rennes, a leading master, showed conclusively that the French had finally improved on the Italians, whose masters had never allowed for purely defensive movements—every parry had also to be a thrust. Besnard (alleged to be the first to use the word "*fleuret*," the French word for "foil") saw that always trying to do two

---

of the mighty Durendal in *The Song of Roland*. Two centuries on, in his history of swordplay, Egerton Castle simply renamed this serrated weapon the "Flamberge"— and so it has been called ever since.

things at once was a mistake and separated attack from defense: Molière's fictional fencing master evidently knew what he was doing. The leading foot for the most part was kept in front, so that the fencer stepped forward or backward in one line, allowing parries and ripostes alike to become more efficient. Besnard also introduced the formal salute, a symbol of courtesy and good form.*

"The Italians had had their day," wrote a nineteenth-century commentator. "They had practiced fencing with fervour, written about it with elegance, and illustrated it with great beauty. But now they were greatly distanced by their ultramontane brethren."[11] Besnard was followed by a succession of great master theorists: Philibert de La Touche in 1670, Le Perché (who popularized the counterriposte) in 1676, Wernersson André de Liancour in 1686, and Le Sieur Labat in 1690. As the smallsword evolved, the modern one-handed technique developed, and the back arm, which had sometimes been used to parry, sometimes to grasp an adversary's sword, was now used primarily for balance.

Of all these masters, Liancour was the most influential. His quarto *Le Maistre d'armes, ou, l'exercise de l'éspée seulle* remained the standard work on defense for more than three quarters of a century. Unlike most great teachers, he published his book shortly after qualifying as a master and continued giving lessons for another forty years. *Le Maistre d'armes* has fourteen copperplate engravings of fencers executing movements in elaborate court dress, set against some of the most dramatic backgrounds in fencing literature: island castles on clifftops here, towns and harbors there; in one a troop of cavalry spurs out of a burning village; in another a besieging army is blowing up a town's defenses. In the most remarkable illustration of all, elegant gentlemen practice their sport while behind them a full-scale naval battle rages, with ships sinking and cannon smoke everywhere.

Throughout his work, Liancour omits any reference to cutting strokes, indicating that by his time the rapier had been superseded by the smallsword. He also suggests that the master have a lighter and longer weapon than his pupil, as with so many lessons to give he should not tire himself

---

* Richard Burton's archive has no fewer than thirty pages on the salute, including the handwritten note "Perhaps the most significant and certainly the most graceful part of the fencing lesson. . . . The salute proves the foilsman's method and quality. Nothing can be more unsightly than a salute stiffly or awkwardly, hurriedly or lazily executed; and it is especially unpleasant to see one of the swordsmen watching the actions of his opponent so as to follow them as best he can."[10]

unduly, and recommends removing the crossbar and shell from the pupil's weapon to ensure that the pupil hold the handle firmly. Should he parry with the wrong part of the blade, the master's blade would slip down his own and give him a painful rap on the fingers—an effective reminder of the importance of good technique.[12]

Up till Liancour's day, fencing had been in deadly earnest, as one's life could depend on one's skill. Now it became a courtly exercise in its own right, an accomplishment of a city gentleman much like music, dancing, or riding. Suppleness of wrist and careful use of one's fingers replaced the aggressive style of the Elizabethans. The notion of an artificial "right of way" transformed the sport: the fencer who started an attack must be parried (or otherwise made to miss) before his opponent could riposte, after which the *riposteur* had the right to his stroke before the first attacker could reply. Fencers learned not to attack at the same time in order not to injure one another. For further safety, ripostes were not to be made until the attacker had returned *en garde*. A "delayed riposte" (where a fencer, having parried an attack, deliberately refrains from riposting at once, so as to upset his adversary's timing) was known as *"temps perdu"*—a formulation that would have delighted Marcel Proust. Good fencers did not advance or retreat more than an inch or so but stood their ground and initiated their attacks with a light blow on their opponents' blades, almost as a conductor marks a beat with his baton.

Practice smallswords were exactly like their dueling counterparts, only

From the influential instruction manual by André de Liancour, 1686. His fencers practice their moves while a naval battle rages behind them.

with a button masking the tip of the blade. At the court of Louis XIV, however, smallswords were considered dull, and demand arose for the thrill and challenge of dueling, but without the injuries. So began a search (probably encouraged by the king's fencing master, the appropriately named Philibert de La Touche) for a new weapon, which in due course produced a blunted, lighter rectangular-section foil, the first purely sporting weapon. The French also introduced umpires (originally "nonpeers," below the social standing of the participants), whose job was to declare the winner after a bout had lasted for a set period.

The introduction of the foil marked a watershed. At first there was little difference between dueling ground and salle: foil play at both was cautious, deliberate, and technically correct. In these early days, the target lay between collar and belt, the top of which had to be at least a foot below the chin.*

Self-preservation remained a prime concern. One safeguard was the height of one's fencing hand. The greatest compliment paid to the renowned foilist Saint-Georges by his master, Texier La Boessière, was on the elevation of his hand and the consequence that his sword never touched a man in the face. Early masks were made of leather or tinplate with peepholes or a horizontal eye slit that protected only the eyes and nose. "People have had to don a mask as a precaution against attacks which could hit one's eyes even though performed in accordance with the art of fencing," said a French encyclopedia of 1755. "It is true that those who are rather less skillful at the sport can wound their opponent by fighting incorrectly, or can wound him while executing a poor parry. Certainly such a way of fencing today is quite unacceptable." So masks were regarded with some unease: donning one showed that you didn't trust your opponent not to hurt you, which bordered on the insulting. It was also seen as not quite manly to take such care of oneself.

This ambivalence about masks continued until in rapid succession three masters lost an eye. Around 1750 La Boessière introduced a new form of mask, made from wire mesh, and while the old guard continued to view it as a substitute for skill, the new mask made possible both greater speed and versatility, although it took a generation to become accepted.

---

* In 1908 the French extended the target to include the lines of the groin and the upper sword arm from shoulder to elbow. After the Antwerp Games of 1920 the upper arm was excluded. For women, the target remained at a line drawn across the top of the hips until 1964, when it was finally made the same as the men's.

Strict conventions ensured courtesy as well as formality—something of an irony, since by this time the French were gaining a reputation for being the most quarrelsome nation in Europe. But the new conventions allowed a whole repertoire of movements, known as *phrases d'armes* or sequences of play—attack, parry, riposte, counterriposte—the integral parts of what was called a "conversation" of blades.

I N A NATION OF DUELISTS HUNGRY FOR HEROES, ONE WOULD EXPECT several real-life contenders—and so there were. Cyrano de Bergerac comes down to us principally as the long-nosed lover-poet of Edmond Rostand's late-nineteenth-century play. In real life he was a well-born Parisian, Savinien de Cyrano, Sieur de Bergerac (1619–55), a moderately successful writer and playwright, far from celebrated in his own time. As a student he attended lectures with Molière, joined a group of "sacrilegious roisterers," and later killed at least ten men in duels (of which he is said to have fought more than a thousand). On one occasion, going to the aid of a friend, he dispersed a crowd of more than a hundred at his single sword's point, a legendary feat. He did have a large nose, which became even more grotesque from injuries and was the excuse for many of his challenges.

Although never a musketeer, Cyrano joined the army. He was for a time incapacitated by wounds received at the siege of Arras in 1640 and eventually retired to a life of contemplation and authorship. He tried his hand at almost every literary form; his main successes were two posthumous works, translated as *Voyages to the Moon and the Sun* (1657), a satiric form of science fiction that later suggested *Gulliver* to Swift. In 1654 a beam (the wooden kind, not from some outraged planet) fell on his head, and he eventually died from the injury several months later, at the age of thirty-six. In Rostand's play Cyrano dies more appropriately, asserting in his final breath that he will "still possess, at any rate, / Unscathed, something outlasting mortal flesh, / And that is . . . [*falls into the arms of a comrade*] My panache!" He is referring to his integrity, or individuality; there is no perfect English rendering, but Sinatra's "I Did It My Way" captures the spirit.

O THER WRITERS, FROM MADAME DE SÉVIGNÉ TO JEAN DE LA Fontaine and François de La Rochefoucauld, found themselves caught up in colorful duels, but it was four serving soldiers who captured the imagination of the public. In 1600 a special force was created by Henri

IV for his personal guard, originally armed with carbines and called "*Cara-biniers*." Louis XIII rearmed them with muskets, making them part of a company of pikemen, and renamed them "musketeers." They were disbanded in 1646, then reembodied in 1657, when they numbered 150. They were originally equipped with gray horses with long tails and known as the "Gray Musketeers" until, on a further whim, the king gave them black stallions, so that their sobriquet changed to "Black Musketeers." They were disbanded once more in 1776, reassembled again only to be dissolved in 1791, and finally faded away after Waterloo.

The King's Musketeers would be no more than a historical footnote had it not been for Alexandre Dumas—but not only Dumas was struck by their story. The inspiration for *The Three Musketeers* and its sequels, *Twenty Years After* and *The Vicomte de Bragelonne*, was a quite different work of fiction: *The Memoirs of M. d'Artagnan, Captain-Lieutenant in the First Company of the King's Musketeers*, first published between 1700 and 1701, in Cologne and Amsterdam but never in France. It ran into three editions, establishing d'Artagnan's name.

The Memoirs of M. d'Artagnan was the brainchild of a hack writer, Gatien de Courtilz de Sandras, himself a onetime musketeer, who started to write in 1678, at thirty-four, while imprisoned in the Bastille. Under the cover of being their editor, he fabricated the memoirs of about twenty people. As with his other creations, the d'Artagnan memoirs were based on fact, in this case the career of a real-life soldier, and offer a fairly accurate account of their subject's history. The real d'Artagnan found writing an onerous exercise and one rarely to be attempted, but the reading public was completely fooled. Dumas decided to continue the initial deception and presented the serialized adventures of d'Artagnan in 1848 as a true account, just in greater detail than the original autobiography. Not until 1910 did the first serious biography of d'Artagnan appear.

The flesh-and-blood d'Artagnan was born in 1615 in Gascony, which to the French of that time was a savage frontier. Its people were swarthy and "destitute to the last degree."[13] D'Artagnan's family name was Batz, which became Batz-Castelmore when his father inherited that estate. Castelmore lay on the borders of Armagnac and Fezensac, within sight of the Pyrenees. Bertrand de Batz had five sons and three daughters; his first and youngest sons were both called Charles. The elder Charles joined the Musketeers in 1633 but died soon after. A second brother, Paul, a captain in the army, governed a district in the Pyrenees for forty years and died at ninety-four, having outlived all his siblings.

The younger Charles—literature's d'Artagnan—left for Paris in 1638 or 1640; Dumas has him do so in 1625, when the real d'Artagnan was only ten. Bertrand died in 1635, at least three years before his son's departure. Nor was there any "Buttercup"—d'Artagnan's trusty steed—to carry the young Charles to Paris. The three musketeers were real enough, though. Aramis—Henri d'Aramitz—was a squire and lay priest, the nephew of Treville, in real life M. de Tresvilles, the captain of the Musketeers. Athos—Armand de Sillegue, Lord of Athos, Treville's cousin's son—fell in a duel before d'Artagnan ever joined up. Porthos—Isaac de Portau— arrived in Paris only a year before d'Artagnan and, initially turned down by the Musketeers, was forced to prove himself in action with another regiment before he was finally accepted in 1643. "Milady" was not Anne de Breuil, Duchesse de Winter, but the Countess of Carlisle, who was indeed one of Richelieu's secret agents and who *did* steal two diamond studs from the Duke of Buckingham.

D'Artagnan himself was a brave and resourceful soldier who in his first outing as a musketeer returned with a bullet through his hat and three more through his uniform. He next distinguished himself in various sieges between 1640 and 1642, getting a reputation for impetuosity, love of action for its own sake, and undertaking any adventure that could be justified as serving "the honor of France." After the Musketeers were disbanded in 1646, he was appointed confidential agent to Richelieu's successor, Cardinal Mazarin, and traveled on his behalf to Italy, England, and Germany, as well as smuggling the unpopular prelate out of Paris to Rueil, just as Dumas relates in *Twenty Years After.*

A lover of justice, a good diplomat (but never a courtier), d'Artagnan was also a skilled swordsman, probably better than Dumas makes him out to be. In the sixty-seven chapters of *The Three Musketeers* he fights just four duels. One of these he wins less through his own efforts than because his adversary, Bernajoux, impales himself. In another he does no more than disarm the baron; and against the Comte de Wardes he takes three thrusts to down his man. Only in his first fight, against de Jussac of the Cardinal's Guards, is he shown as skillful, and it is an interesting commentary on Dumas's day that d'Artagnan's swordplay is observed through the prism of accepted French style—which sometimes the young Gascon respects, sometimes not:

[D'Artagnan] fought like a furious tiger, turning ten times round his adversary, and changing his ground and guard position twenty times. Jussac was, as they expressed it in those days, a fine blade, and had been well taught; nevertheless, it required all his skill to defend himself against an opponent who, full of life and energy, had little regard for normal fencing rules, attacking him in every line at once, and yet parrying him like a man who had the greatest respect for his own skin.

This contest at length tried Jussac's patience. Frustrated at being held in check by a rival he considered a boy, he grew incensed, and started to make mistakes. D'Artagnan, who, though wanting in practice, had a good understanding of swordsmanship, redoubled his efforts. Jussac, anxious to put an end to things, sprang forward, aiming a terrible thrust at his young quarry, but the latter parried it and, while Jussac was recovering, glided like a serpent beneath his blade, passing his sword through his body. Jussac fell like a log.

In reality, d'Artagnan, far from going to the Pré aux Clercs to fight Athos, Porthos, and Aramis, had gone there with them for a prearranged duel with some of the Cardinal's guards, Athos having sent word to Jussac to bring another man to complete the party. As for Bernajoux, after wounding him d'Artagnan personally nursed him back to health, and the men became lifelong friends. The historical d'Artagnan ended up in command of the king's Grand Musketeers, "the most coveted appointment in France," but his private life was disastrous. He had married at forty, but neglected his wife for his career; after six years they separated without having had children. In 1672 he became governor of Lille, and was killed the following year, at the siege of Maastricht, a few feet away from Captain Churchill, later Duke of Marlborough, Winston Churchill's great-great-great-grandfather. His body was found two days later, a Dutch musketball lodged in its throat. In his will d'Artagnan left "two swords, one with an unpolished gold guard and a brass hilt; the other of black steel."

THREE YEARS BEFORE D'ARTAGNAN FELL, THERE WAS BORN ANOTHER champion fencer who would become a character in fiction. She was immortalized in an 1835 novel by Théophile Gautier: Julie d'Aubigny, known as "La Maupin," was the daughter of Gaston d'Aubigny, secretary to the Count of Armagnac, one of the seven great officers of the Crown. Gaston was a noted hedonist and swordsman, and his daughter's first instructor. By the time she was sixteen she could best most of the men she met at her father's salle. Slender, "with firm muscles and breasted almost like a boy,"[14] she had a beautiful face, and soon d'Armagnac claimed her as his mistress. She was found a husband, a colorless figure whom she so ignored that even before her eighteenth birthday he ruefully departed Paris for the country, leaving his young wife to her pleasures.

La Maupin felt confident enough to drop the aging d'Armagnac and set up with a certain Baron de Seranne, an accomplished fencing master, with whom she frequented the leading salles of the city, honing her skills. She was still only eighteen when Seranne, having killed a man in a duel, had to abandon Paris for the safer environs of Marseilles. La Maupin accompanied him, financing them both by exhibitions of fencing in the smoky taproom of their local tavern. She would dress as a man; one night, when revellers taunted that she was no lady, she flung down her foil and tore away her shirt "so that all could determine the question for themselves."

She was growing restless, however, and finding she possessed a beautiful if untrained contralto, gained an audition with the director of the Marseilles Academy, who engaged her at once, despite her inexperience. Her debut was a sensation: a woman contralto was a "new tone" in French opera. Seranne now passes from the picture, and La Maupin embarked on a series of celebrated affairs—with women as well as men. On one occasion, she fell violently in love with a young Marseillaise, followed her to a convent at Avignon, and promptly kidnapped her. After three months the ravished novice returned to her parents, and soon an edict condemning the "sieur" d'Aubigny to death by fire was published throughout southern France. (The erroneous title was a tactful way of denying the lesbian relationship.) La Maupin hastened to Paris, where she confirmed her reputation as a "marvelous lover and an ardent mistress." Firm-willed yet impulsive, she was also playful and warmhearted, and loyal after her fashion. She now enjoyed her first duel, calling out the actor-tenor Dumeni over a supposed insult; when he refused to fight his "male" challenger she gave him a thrashing, then stole his watch and snuffbox, parading them as trophies. Another actor who offended her and refused to fight was forced to kneel and beg forgiveness.

La Maupin entertained high social ambitions and at last found herself invited to a masked ball hosted by the king's brother, the bisexual Philippe de France, "Monsieur," the Duc d'Orléans, at the Palais-Royal. Dressed once again as a man—in a red silk suit embroidered in gold—she confidently swept her women partners around the dance floor, performing the coranto, the branle, and the pavane, all the while whispering to them lasciviously from behind her mask. Emboldened by her success, she seized a young marquise by the arm, kissed her on the mouth, and propositioned her. The alarmed young noblewoman summoned three of her admirers. As these moved in on her, La Maupin declared that she would meet all three under the first lamp bracket on the rue St.-Thomas-du-Louvre, a few minutes' walk away, and exact her satisfaction.

Off she strode to the rendezvous, only to find that the lamps had not yet been lit—but a full moon had risen, sometimes bathing the street in light, at others disappearing behind a cloud. Her opponents arrived, complaining about the darkness. "What difference does it make?" their scarlet adversary replied, and dispatched each in turn before returning to the Duc's dance floor.

Seeking out her host, she explained what had taken place and politely asked him to arrange for the wounded to be taken home. The Duc said he would petition his brother to give her a full pardon. For the next week the court was agog at the scandal and keen to see if La Maupin would fetch up in the Bastille. But the Duc was as good as his word, and the King let it be known, through the Inspector of the Opera, Destouches, that she would not be charged.[13] La Maupin wisely withdrew to Brussels, where before long she became mistress of the Elector of Bavaria, one of the four great secular princes of the Holy Roman Empire and Governor of the Spanish Netherlands (now Belgium). For more than a year she enjoyed being ex officio first lady, but tiring of her patron she decamped to Spain. Short of funds, she became personal maid to a Countess Marino, whose hauteur she rewarded by dressing her for a grand ball and secretly stuffing her hair with radishes. By the time an irate and ridiculed countess returned to rail at her maid, La Maupin had departed for Paris once more, taking a leisurely route via Poitiers and Rouen, encountering the love of her life, the Comte d'Albert, in the first city, during a swordfight, and a more than useful paramour in the second—Gabriel-Vincent Thévenard, an ambitious young singer determined to conquer Paris with his powerful bass.

Soon Gabriel had arranged for both himself and La Maupin to sing at the Opera, and she made her debut there in 1690. She continued as one of the company's principals till 1705, seeing d'Albert at regular intervals; then suddenly she turned on her hedonistic past and entered a convent, where she died shortly afterward, aged thirty-seven. "Beautiful, valiant, generous and superbly unchaste," one American biographer calls her, linking Maupin with such figures as Belle Starr and Calamity Jane, though adding, "In her skill as a fighter with a designated and particular weapon she stands in a place apart."

FRENCH FENCING HAD TWO FAMOUS AMBASSADORS IN ENGLAND, neither of whom was French. Domenico Angelo Malevolti Tremamondo (literally, "Angel Nasty Twist Shake the World") was the most renowned master of his time; William Hope, the author of an influential English-language book on French fencing style.

Born in Livorno in 1717 and first taught his craft in Pisa, Angelo, as he was known, was rich and charismatic. He traveled widely, spending some time in Venice with the painter Canaletto before settling in Paris, where he studied under Teillagory, whose style so influenced him that there was soon no trace of the Italian school in his fencing. A renowned lady-killer, he was competing in Paris when a beautiful Irish actress, Margaret Woffington, threw him a small bouquet of roses. Angelo fixed it over his heart and told the audience, "Sirs, I will defend this precious gift against all comers." The bouquet survived unscathed, and in 1755 Angelo moved to London with his conquest.

"The Angel of Fencing," as he came to be called, won the patronage of the Earl of Pembroke and introduced swordplay to George III and his children. His pupils included the actor David Garrick, the artist Joshua Reynolds, and the radical activist John Wilkes. Richard Sheridan and Thomas Gainsborough were members of his salle, as was Johann Christian Bach (son of the great composer). For more than a hundred years the club was the best in England. Through Angelo, wrote one biographer, "we gain the image of the fencing master as a man of breeding, a combination of teacher, sportsman, historian, artist, scientist and philosopher."

In 1763, at the Thatched House Tavern in St. James's Street, Angelo squared off in a famous duel against the foremost swordsman in Ireland, a certain Dr. Keys. It was a bloodless encounter, intended to exhibit each man's skill. The Irishman, a jealous rival, ferociously attacked Angelo, who put up a deft defense, not once conceding a hit. As soon as Keys tired, Angelo switched on to the offensive and landed "twelve palpable hits." From that point on his reputation was assured.

That same year he bought an impressive building, Carlisle House, in Soho, for his salle, and published his masterwork, *L'Ecole des armes*, the most lavishly illustrated fencing book since Thibault's in 1628. It boasted forty-seven full-size copperplates (for which Angelo posed himself) and was an immediate sensation, quickly reprinting four times. It was end-lessly plagiarized and imitated but was far from being just a book of pic-tures: it argued that fencing should be seen as a sport.*

Angelo was sufficiently famous to crop up in literature. As late as 1940, Rafael Sabatini's *Master-at-Arms* makes him a leading character. The tale is set in 1791, and the master, Quentin de Morlaix, enjoys "an income greater even than that earned by the famous Angelo Tremamondo, whose show pupil he had been." When Quentin receives a challenge from Redas, a rival master, Angelo is on hand to offer advice: "You will gratify him by using the *point d'arrêt*. And you will add the condition that the match will consist of a single assault for the best of six hits." The old maestro lays a finger to the side of his nose. "I know what I'm doing, child." Quentin tri-umphs, and all of Redas's pupils desert him for the Morlaix salle.[17]

THE OTHER AGENT OF FRANCE'S REVOLUTION, SIR WILLIAM HOPE, was a Scotsman (1664–c. 1730), late deputy governor of Edinburgh Castle, who in 1692 brought out his second edition of *The Compleat Fencing-master: in which is fully Described the whole Guards, Parades, and Lessons, belonging to the Smallsword*, which outlines the main features of the French school. (Hope was also the principal figure behind a parlia-mentary bill to establish a "Court of Honor" to resolve quarrels before they passed into duels. The House of Commons was preoccupied with the pro-posed union of England and Scotland, so the bill never became law.) Hope described the intricacies of fencing with a smallsword and among other things explained how the *désengagement,* changing from one line of guard to another—"caveating" is his word—began as a defense against an oppo-nent "binding the blade" rather than as a form of attack. He also claimed that the lunge—the "giving in a Thrust or making of an Elonge"—was first taught in 1676 by a French master named Jean Baptiste Le Perché de Coudray. Fencers who believe they are good but rely mainly on force he la-

---

* The full title is *L'Ecole des armes avec l'explication générale des principes attitudes et posi-tions concernant l'escrime.* The famous writer Denis Diderot contributed illustrations, but these were considered too innovative and contrary to French Academy teaching, and every printer the two men approached refused to touch them. Eventually Diderot had to go to Livorno to have them printed. There is a ghastly story attached to the book's production: Some of the plates were reportedly engraved by a man condemned to death, who was allowed a respite to finish them for the benefit of his wife and chil-dren. Once the work was done, he was hanged.[16]

bels "ignorants" and recommends that they be introduced to "sharps," practice weapons with a small part of the point exposed, so that they can learn the real level of their competence. "In the end, fencing is systematic," he wrote; "it is scientific; it is thoughtful. Fencing is control. Everything else is governed by chance."

W E COME NOW TO THE FIGURE WHO WOULD HAVE BEEN ONE OF the greatest women fencers of the late eighteenth century—had the world been altogether certain that she was in fact a woman. A contemporary cartoon shows a half woman, in wig and hoops, and half man, with breeches and sword. The mystery of the great swordsman was fomented by scandalmongers and has been variously reported (in no fewer than *sixteen* biographies). Only at the fencer's death was the matter of his/her sex finally settled. Secret agent, soldier, lawyer, diplomat, fencer, he/she had spent forty-nine years dressed as a man, the next thirty-three as a woman.

Charles-Geneviève-Louis-Auguste-André-Timothée Déon de Beaumont ("Déon" later being changed to "d'Eon") was born in the Burgundian town of Tonnerre on October 5, 1728. The young Déon was obsessed with swordplay from an early age and moved to Paris to study law, where he became proficient under the tutelage of Maître Teillagory, the master who would also coach Angelo.

The descriptions we have of d'Eon in those early years are colorful but inaccurate, as biographer after biographer has sought to add his own palette to what was already a lively story. These accounts seem to agree that d'Eon was not tall and so slender that "his friends declared that they could circle his waist with their hands."[18] He had fine light blond hair and a rose-and-white complexion, with a curved mouth, large luminous eyes, and a determined, almost arrogant thrust to his chin. He was particular and dainty in his manner but perfectly capable of being one of the boys, telling ribald stories and racing about town with friends, drinking and living it up. The one perennial absence was a girlfriend, and as late as 1771 d'Eon confided to the Comte de Broglie that he had "never wished for wife or mistress," continuing, "I am somewhat mortified to be still as Nature made me and that, since the calm of my natural temperament has never made me addicted to sensual indulgence, this has given my friends in France, as well as in Russia and England, grounds for imagining in their innocence that I was of the female sex."[19]

D'Eon flatters to deceive. A portrait by the pastellist Maurice de La Tour

"La Chevalier d'Eon," a portrait by Maurice de La Tour, sometime in the early 1750s.

shows an attractive young woman wearing earrings, a velvet ribbon around her neck, and a low-cut dress revealing a full bosom. Possibly Louis XV's cousin, the Prince de Conti, knew of this portrait, or that d'Eon liked to dress up as a woman—more likely, he was recommended to the King by an influential family friend; whatever the connection, d'Eon was enrolled in the king's secret service and sent on a mission dressed as a woman.

The notorious *Secret du Roi* was an extended bureaucracy of great complexity, a marriage of Louis's innate duplicity with his love of subterfuge. He himself would constantly issue contradictory orders, often on the same day, to his ministers on the one hand and his secret service on the other. In d'Eon's posthumously published memoirs, put together by an opportunistic journalist, Frédéric Gaillardet, such facts as they possess give a convincing description of the service as a "political and administrative distaff on which all the strands kept getting snarled and tangled into inextricable knots because no hand was strong or expert enough to guide the shaft and spin the yarn into a single thread." D'Eon was to be involved with the King's secret service until his death.

His first mission was successful. In 1755, disguised as a Mademoiselle

Lia de Beaumont, he accompanied a Scot called the Chevalier Douglas to Russia. His mandate was to gather information in the absence of any French diplomatic representation at the Court of Saint Petersburg. D'Eon later reported that he served for six months as a lady-in-waiting to the flamboyant Czarina Elizabeth, where he helped make her sympathetic toward France and did his best to thwart a possible treaty with England. The following year he went back to Russia, this time in male attire, and for his deeds there was rewarded with a commission as lieutenant of dragoons. Soon promoted to captain, he was given command of a company on the Rhine, where he fought bravely over several months in 1761.

In 1762 he was assigned to London as secretary to the French ambassador negotiating terms for ending the Seven Years' War, but continued his secret work for the King. Within weeks he had pulled off a sensational coup, having extracted secret instructions from an undersecretary's portfolio. He was rewarded with the Order of Saint-Louis, thus becoming a chevalier. At thirty-five, he was at the peak of his career and might have gone on to become an ambassador, but for a cruel piece of luck. A new ambassador was sent to London, the snobbish, mean-spirited Comte de Guerchy, whom d'Eon had antagonized during the Rhine campaign by accepting a dangerous mission that Guerchy had shirked. A bitter struggle between the two Burgundians was virtually guaranteed. D'Eon's position was a strong one. "The fascination of his ready wit," wrote an early biographer, "the lively and original character of his conversation, his taste for music . . . together with that genuine talent for the greatly prized art of fencing which had obtained for him the title of Grand Provost, soon made him appreciated and sought after in society."[20] He fenced frequently at the academy of his friend Angelo and posed for several engravings in Angelo's famous book.

About this time, rumors began to circulate concerning the chevalier's gender. Guerchy and his cronies at the embassy were happy to point out the reserved habits of the Chevalier and the absence of romantic intrigues in his life, but by now even disinterested observers mocked his effeminacy. Some said he was a hermaphrodite; ever since La Tour's portrait it had been known that he liked to dress in women's clothes and parade in them in the fashionable salles of London. D'Eon did little to set the matter straight—the only proof of his masculinity he was willing to offer was the one he imprinted "in very male fashion on the cheeks of two impertinents." Otherwise he remained silent. Then in 1769 a Russian princess arrived in London, and confidently asserted she had seen d'Eon dressed as a woman at the Russian court. The rumors gained momentum, especially after one of his breasts was removed to neutralize a mammary tumor caused by a thrust from a foil. It was presumed that only a woman would need such an operation. Nor was the gossip confined to London: d'Eon learned from the papers that the "mystery" of his sex had become the fashionable subject of conversation in the Paris salons. More bets were placed—at least one for £700 ($60,000 today)—and the odds were quoted daily on the London Stock Exchange. Soon, however, the merchants, bankers, and gentlemen of leisure who were wagering became concerned; they had money at stake, yet how was the question to be resolved? D'Eon turned down an offer of £1000 to prove his sex, and plans were made to kidnap him to settle the matter.

Barricaded in his Soho lodgings, d'Eon became involved in a series of imbroglios: extravagant debts, alleged assassination attempts (he claimed that de Guerchy had tried to poison him), and libel suits. He fired off a barrage of blackmailing letters to the French court, complaining about not being reimbursed for expenses incurred in Russia and England and backing up his requests with threats to publish highly confidential correspondence. At last he triumphed: Guerchy, finally implicated in a plot to have d'Eon killed, was recalled in disgrace, and died a broken man in 1767. But d'Eon could hardly savor his victory, for his state pension of 12,000 francs a year (equivalent to the income of fifteen working-class families) had been rescinded as a result of his blackmail. Nor did the King's actions help: at one moment he would order d'Eon's recall and arrest and at the next secretly warn him of these very orders. Eventually Louis's advisers became convinced that d'Eon had lost his reason. The King himself declared, "I do not believe that M. d'Eon is mad, but he is presumptuous and a very extraordinary person." He was terrified that his unruly subject would divulge documents in his possession, including instructions to investigate the prospects of an invasion of Britain.

D'Eon for his part was happy for the King to be alarmed but no longer was he seen at his favorite haunts; he had even deserted Angelo's famous salle, where he had previously put in regular practice. When he did venture out, he was heckled in the street—he had become the laughingstock of London. It was at this point that Louis XVI ascended the French throne: d'Eon wrote to him saying that he would relinquish the papers in his possession for 250,000 francs. The King pronounced the figure ridiculous, so d'Eon came up with another plan. The dramatist-adventurer Pierre Beaumarchais, future author of *The Barber of Seville* and *The Marriage of Figaro*, had been approached by the French government to negotiate with d'Eon on its behalf. In May 1775 they met; immediately d'Eon confessed that he was indeed a woman, and Beaumarchais believed him. This may seem incredible, but no less a judge of women than Giacomo Casanova, dining at the French Embassy in 1764, had found himself seated next to d'Eon, clad in women's clothes, and declared his companion to be "*une belle femme.*" "The voice is too clear for that of a *castrato,* and the shape too rounded for a man."[21]

Soon an agreement was reached: d'Eon promised to hand over his papers in return for the payment of his debts and the restitution of his pension. He reasoned that any charges, including the criticisms made of him in French and British society, would be quelled once it was acknowledged that he had been a woman all along. However, there was one further provision: since he was indeed a woman, he would have to declare his status officially and in future wear the clothes befitting his sex. For Louis, d'Eon's continued appearance as an officer of dragoons was an affront to public decency. After all, a transvestite was a monstrosity, a depraved creature

The caricature of d'Eon, "he/she," that appeared in the popular press when his sex was in question.

who belonged in a madhouse; but someone who admitted that she had been forced to disguise herself as a male since childhood could count on sympathetic treatment provided she agreed never to dress as a man again. Beaumarchais reported to the minister of foreign affairs, "The positive declaration of her sex, and her engagement to live henceforth in female attire, are the only means of averting scandal and misfortunes. I have been resolute in exacting this, and have succeeded."

The French authorities had another reason for enforcing this last proposal: Guerchy's son had sworn to avenge his dead father but he could scarcely challenge a woman; and the French court had no wish to see the young man pitted against a figure who was still one of the finest fencers in Europe.

Forced by law to wear clothes that all his life he had previously put on at will as an occasional pleasure, the chevalier soon learned that passing for a woman prevented him from fulfilling his obligations as a duelist, which he fervently wished to do. He wrote to the foreign minister, begging him to revoke the decree so that he might fight young Guerchy.

Unfortunately for d'Eon, the young count's mother was understandably alarmed at the prospect of such a duel and petitioned for d'Eon to be kept in female apparel. The chevalier was duly told by the foreign minister that he would not be allowed back into France unless dressed as a woman. D'Eon complied, embarking for France on August 13, 1777, having resigned himself to a lifetime in female dress: but he was not above acts of rebellion and was soon imprisoned in the Château de Dijon for wearing his dragoon's uniform.

He was now fifty, with an awkward gait and a harsh voice—and quite impoverished. He constantly declared his desire to continue his army career, while simultaneously saying he would follow his king's commands, even to "retire into a convent and cover his dragoon's head with the sacred veil." Taking pity on him, the Queen herself, Marie-Antoinette, ordered that her dressmaker and milliner attend him to see that he was properly clothed. As soon as he received the new garments, the chevalier paraded around Versailles in them, basking in the attention. Only Voltaire appears to have seen through the pretense, labeling d'Eon an "amphibian." "I cannot believe," he wrote, "that the Chevalier or the Chevalière d'Eon, whose chin is adorned with a very thick and very prickly black beard, is a woman. I am inclined to think that he has carried the eccentricity of his adventures to the point of aspiring to change his sex in order to escape the vengeance of the House of Guerchy."

In 1785 the French government was persuaded to give d'Eon 6,000 francs to cover his debts in England, and on November 17 of that year he left France, never to return. He moved once more to London, returning to his old home at 38 Brewer Street, and was accepted by London society as an eccentric old spinster with a colorful past. For years, until well after the French Revolution, this odd, muscular figure subsisted on charity. He supplemented his income by exercising another of his talents—as a chess player—taking on the first great world champion, François Philidor, and becoming in the process the first "woman" to play chess in public. A charge of 5 shillings was levied on spectators.

D'Eon also gave virtuoso displays of fencing. "He-she," as *The Gentleman's Magazine* dubbed him, provided lessons in the art and occasionally fenced in public, several times before the Prince of Wales. His most famous bout, organized by Angelo, with whom d'Eon had gone back into training, took place before the prince at Carlton House in 1787 and was recorded by the caricaturist James Gillray. D'Eon's opponent was the Chevalier de Saint-Georges, the most brilliant fencer of his generation. At fifty-nine d'Eon was nearly twenty years the elder, and was expected to fence in women's attire: triple skirts, with all their encumbrances. In the heated prose of a d'Eon biographer, we see the initial encounter through the eyes of Saint-Georges:

> Walking slowly, apparently with difficulty, there appeared in front of him a little frail old lady in a rusty black satin gown and white lace bonnet. The only touches of color about the whole amazing little person were the vivid blue of two unfaded, arrogant eyes in the white, shriveled face, and the flame color of a bit of ribbon on the black dress, over the left breast. The crowd craned their necks, tittered and whispered, as the old dame saluted the Prince with a plain, ungraved sword . . . "The Chevalier! Mademoiselle d'Eon! La Chevalière!" ran the whispers, as the quaint figure turned and saluted.[22]

What is not in doubt is the subsequent score: all the newspaper reports indicate that it was a rout, d'Eon triumphing by seven hits to one. It was a memorable victory, yet far from d'Eon's last appearance on the piste. As new debts accrued, and with his pension stopped by the Revolution, d'Eon was forced to auction off his jewels and the greater part of his library at Christie's. Now that his obligations had been swept away along with the

French crown, he was free to leave off wearing women's clothes, but he continued with them voluntarily, often finishing off his outfit with the ribbon and cross of his military decorations, though even these had eventually to be put up for sale.

Throughout these misfortunes d'Eon continued to fence, sometimes dressed in his old dragoon uniform, at others in semifemale costume; in this last garb he took part in a tournament in 1793, presided over by the Prince of Wales, and was again victorious. He decided to join forces with Jacob de Launay, his former servant, and a fencer called Mrs. Bateman, and together they toured the south of England and the Midlands giving demonstrations and inviting challenges. Newspaper reports record d'Eon's victories at Dover, Canterbury, and Oxford.

This extraordinary late flowering—d'Eon was nearly seventy—was stopped only by a serious accident. On August 26, 1796, in Southampton, he was fencing against Launay when his opponent's blade broke and entered his right armpit. The wound, exacerbated by blood poisoning, confined him to bed for four months, in the course of which he bitterly acknowledged that henceforth he would be reduced "to cutting his bread with his sword."

As soon as he was well enough, d'Eon moved back to London and set up house with a Mrs. Marie Cole, the French widow of a British naval engineer. They survived on the kindness of friends, with the help of an allowance of £50 a year from Queen Charlotte and the Prince of Wales. This was not enough to save d'Eon from being thrown into debtors' prison in 1804, at the age of seventy-six. After Mrs. Cole raised the money to secure his release, the two friends moved to 26 Milman Street, where d'Eon died on May 21, 1810, at the age of eighty-one.

The much-publicized postmortem by the celebrated medical friar Père Elysée settled the question of d'Eon's sex once and for all: anatomically, he was a man. Mrs. Cole, his companion for the past fourteen years, was, according to reports, deeply shocked. Frédéric Gaillardet, in his artificial *Memoirs*, provides a colorful chronicle of d'Eon's passing: "At the news of his death Queen Charlotte tried to ensure that the secret of his sex was buried with him. But the men she sent to guard the body could not restrain the flood of curiosity his death had aroused in high places. In spite of all the measures she had taken to try to prevent it, the corpse was minutely examined by surgeons in the presence of eminent witnesses and subjected to a post-mortem which established beyond doubt that it was that of a man." Gaillardet goes on to transform this discovery into an affair of state: "When George III, who had been in his right mind for twenty years after recovering from his first bout of insanity, heard the result of the medical examination, he *went mad again* and remained so till his death in 1820."[23]

So passed one of history's most extraordinary swordsmen. In the 1920s the sexologist Havelock Ellis made a classic study of d'Eon. Transvestism, he explained, was basic to d'Eon's nature; he linked d'Eon's love of dressing as a woman with his lack of interest in heterosexual or indeed homosexual activity. "He clearly had a constitutional predisposition," Ellis declared, "aided by an almost asexual disposition. In people with this psychic anomaly, physical sexual urge seems often subnormal."

D'Eon had a different view of his constitution. In a letter of June 18, 1800, seeking money from Charles-Maurice de Talleyrand, then minister of foreign affairs, d'Eon had written, "I have fought the good fight; I am seventy-three years of age; I have a saber cut on my head, a broken leg and two bayonet thrusts. In 1756 I contributed largely to the alliance of France and Russia. In 1762 and 1763 I laboured night and day to establish peace between France and England. I was in direct and secret correspondence with Louis XV from 1756 to the year of his death. My head belongs to the war department. My heart to France."[24]

THE ENGRAVING BY JAMES GILLRAY OF THE D'EON/SAINT-GEORGES match of 1787 shows d'Eon attacking in a full lunge. The spectators— the Prince's political friends of the time (Charles Fox, Sheridan, and Edmund Burke) and the various fencing celebrities of London and Paris—are ranged behind a barrier; George, Prince of Wales, and Mrs. Fitzherbert (his illegal wife) are easily identifiable. The prince was said to have relished the match, particularly the violent noises made by Saint-Georges during his attacks, which, as one broadsheet put it, "resembled more the roaring of a bull than sounds emanating from a human being."[25]

Who was this Saint-Georges, described at the time as a "Creole, a sort of Admirable Crichton of his day, musician, composer, athlete, horseman and swimmer . . . this worthy rival of the Chevalier d'Eon, both in swordsmanship, fashionable popularity, and wayward notoriety"?[26] He was a mulatto, the son of Georges de Boulogne, a high-ranking official under Louis XVI who owned a plantation in Guadeloupe, in the French West Indies. During one of his visits there, Boulogne fell ill and was nursed back to health by a local woman, "La Belle Nanon." The two became lovers, and

The duel at Carlton House in 1787 between Saint-Georges and the Chevalier d'Eon, as re-created by Gillray. The figure in a hat, standing, is the Prince of Wales; to his left are several other well-known figures of the time.

Nanon gave birth to a son. After Boulogne returned to France, he arranged for Nanon and their child to follow him. They traveled on board the *Saint-Georges,* and when Nanon had her son baptized she named him after the ship.*

For six years, Saint-Georges was apprenticed to the great fencing master Texier La Boessière (whose son Antoine, also a master, would write the influential *Traité de l'art des armes*). It was a Pygmalion type of arrangement: the brilliant black boy, living with a well-to-do white family, given his chance to show that he could master French culture and so rise through the system. He would see his mother only on weekends and was put through the whole rigamarole of knightly "shaping," one of the last examples before the Revolution.

Saint-Georges was a quick learner and excelled at a range of accom-

---

* According to the nineteenth-century historian Arsène Vigeant, there is another, less romantic version: mulatto births in the French colonies were generally recorded by a single name. Sometimes on the baptismal certificate the full name of the patron saint after which a child was named would be written down, hence "Saint-Georges" rather than plain "Georges."[27]

plishments, particularly as a violinist and fencer. By fifteen he was already a formidable foilist; by sixteen his speed and sense of timing were famous. Nevertheless, another master, teaching in Rouen, described the teenager as "La Boessière's nigger," at which his foster father urged him to avenge the slur: before a considerable audience Saint-Georges beat the offender by 27 hits to 3. Shortly thereafter, the tale goes, he met a fellow musician, Agatha Vessières, and the two fell in love. Their secret meetings ended, however, when another musician, besotted with a jealous passion for Saint-Georges, alerted Agatha's parents. The young man was ordered never to see Agatha again.

Whatever the truth of the matter, Saint-Georges now embarked on a succession of love affairs, as if to deaden his bitterness. Although exceptionally handsome, he never thought highly of himself, convinced that women fell for him as "an exotic bird or a curiosity from the islands."[28] He continued his fencing and would become the best swordsman in France. "Racine wrote *Phèdre*," La Boessière boasted, "but I am the one who made Saint-Georges." Angelo wrote in his *Reminiscences* that "he surpassed all his contemporaries and predecessors. No professor or amateur ever showed so much accuracy or so much strength, such length of lunge and such quickness; his attacks were a perpetual series of hits; his parade [parries] were so closed that it was in vain to attempt to touch him—in short, he was all nerve."[29] Saint-Georges was also one of the best shots of his time; one of his feats was to throw up two crown pieces into the air and hit them both before they struck the ground.

When M. de Boulogne died, he left annual pensions of 8,000 livres each to Saint-Georges and his mother (about $36,000 a year today). Meanwhile, Saint-Georges's musical career was blossoming: by now a violin virtuoso, he was also conductor and composer, with sonatas, comic operas, and string quartets to his name. Marie-Antoinette invited him to the Petit Trianon so she could play the harpsichord for him. He also continued to be "such a favorite among the ladies that his dark complexion and woolly head were forgotten."[30] However, not all was quite so idyllic—he was also the object of racist attacks and on one occasion was set upon by thugs whom a police officer, in an act of private vindictiveness, had paid to club him to death. In 1776 he was considered for the position of manager of the Paris Opera, but the leading singers and actresses begged the queen to veto him, indignant at the thought of being given orders by a mulatto.

Saint-Georges fought many duels, all successfully, although he was generally the offended party. Once, at Dunkirk, a young officer of hussars was boasting of his skill as a swordsman before several ladies. "Did you ever meet the famous Saint-Georges?" asked one. "Often," vaunted the hussar. "He could hardly land a hit on me." At this the real Saint-Georges asked if he might foil with the gentleman, to amuse the company. The officer contemptuously agreed and, of course, was quickly shamed.

During the Revolution, Saint-Georges, appointed colonel, commanded a battalion composed exclusively of colored men, which became known as "La Légion Saint-Georges"; the father of Alexandre Dumas was one of his officers. In 1793, in the manner of the time, Saint-Georges was unjustly accused of corruption and endured eighteen months of house arrest under sentence of death. He spent his last years a destitute invalid, dying in 1799 aged fifty-four.[31]

F RENCH FENCING WAS NOT ALL SMALLSWORD AND ÉPÉE. THE EIGHteenth century saw the introduction of the saber, a heavy, curved weapon descended from the Turkish scimitar. In a skirmish it was handier than the basket-hilted broadsword of the heavy cavalry and, being curved, automatically gave a slicing cut. It became the national weapon of Hungary and was immediately so effective that other armies, including the French, took it up; another variation, the cutlass, became the standard naval weapon. By the time of the War of the Spanish Succession (1701–14), the smallsword developed into a heavier instrument, as the lighter weapon was judged ineffectual for battle. With the development of the bayonet, infantry officers needed a more robust weapon and so adapted the cavalry saber. As First Consul, Napoleon habitually carried a Mameluke scimitar, brought from Egypt.

Then came 1789, the "hour of universal ferment." "The French Revolution was, after all, a great demolition," Simon Schama reminds us.[32] The Academy of Fence, so confidently created in 1567, vanished overnight, and its last president, Augustin Rousseau, private fencing master to the king, was unceremoniously guillotined not long after his sovereign, in 1793. The new revolutionaries believed that, having abolished the *ancien régime*, the duel, one of the privileges and abuses of the aristocracy, would go with it (which may explain why there is no mention of duels in the legislation of the National Assembly). When the revolutionary leader Camille Desmoulins was challenged to a duel, he shrugged and said that he would prove his courage on other fields than the Bois de Boulogne. Certainly during those dangerous times duels were to be avoided: should one challenge the wrong person, one might be denounced as a conspirator or an assassin.

Early in the Revolution one Citizen Boyer announced that he personally would confront any right-wing member of the National Assembly attempting to force a duel on a representative of the people. Concerned to meet the aristocratic challenges that might flood in, he formed a special force of revolutionary swordsmen, the Spadassinicides, to combat the threat, but their creation was an anticlimax. Although never more than fifty strong, they were enough to frighten off any of Boyer's anticipated adversaries, and never had to take the field.

The fashion of wearing swords in private life disappeared during the revolution, yet there are still numerous references to dueling, both between individual members of the Paris garrison and between civilians. Swords and sabers circulated in large numbers, which was the result, first, of the creation of the National Guard, then of its disbanding.[33] In September 1792 the Legislative Assembly decreed that all cases pending against duelists since the storming of the Bastille in July 1789 were waived. Since a number of the accused were members of the Assembly, this was hardly surprising, but it meant that the only law against dueling was submerged in the general statutes against murder and assault.

Out-of-work masters started to give lessons to the new ruling elite, who took up fencing on a regular basis. People who had never thought of having a fencing master now found them highly accessible—if only for economic reasons. Aristocrats' armories were looted, and citizens paraded with priceless smallswords. Not that they knew how to use them; when push came to thrust, they preferred to use heavily curved broad-bladed sabers. In the revolutionary armies the rule was that the more important the officer (at least, in his own estimation), the larger his sword. In Eugène Delacroix's famous "Liberty Leading the People" (1831), the figure of Liberty brandishes a musket with bayonet, and one of her three companions holds a broadsword: the intricate conversation of French foilplay had been interrupted, but when the shouting died away there remained plenty of enthusiasm for the sword.

In 1799 a coup d'état brought to power one of France's most calculating swordsmen, General Napoleon Bonaparte. He had fenced as a schoolboy, and although as a fifteen-year-old his fencing and dancing (exercises d'agrément) had been marked "very poor," once he reached military school he took to swordplay with gusto and was noted for the number of foils he broke.[34] Bonaparte spent the summer of 1788 at the University of Strasbourg, where the old fencing master would later recall fondly the lessons he had given the young Corsican. By the time Bonaparte seized power there was still no specific law banning dueling, and far from dying out the practice was once more in full flower. (Indeed, one of his foremost officers, Maréchal Ney, was addicted to dueling and once challenged every man in a theater.) Courts tended to act only when a fatality resulted from a breach of established etiquette. Napoleon, however, was firmly against the practice and knew that too many good officers were dying or being disabled by the pastime; a good duelist made a bad soldier. In 1788, when one of Louis XVI's leading admirals, Pierre-André Suffren de Saint-Tropez, was killed in a duel, the King ordered the official cause of death to be given as apoplexy; several years later, when the King of Sweden issued Napoleon personally with a direct challenge, he replied that he would send a fencing master to wait on the King; he had no intention of making an appearance himself.*

Yet Napoleon had good reason to be grateful to the sword. While still a junior officer commanding a local militia, he was visited by a teenager whose father had recently been unjustly executed. The boy had come to collect his father's sword, if M. le Capitaine would allow it. Napoleon received the boy graciously and handed over the heirloom. The next day the boy's mother paid him a visit, to thank him for his courtesy. This was Joséphine, and the spark was struck.

It is said that it was Joséphine who brought to Napoleon's attention the most notable hero in his armies. "Jean-Louis," as he was known throughout his career, had begun life a small, feeble-looking mulatto on the island of what is now Haiti, relatively close to Joséphine's birthplace, Martinique. He is heard of first in 1796, the fifth year of the first French Republic, when he arrived in France and was admitted as *"un pupille de régiment"*—a child in a regiment's care, usually a war orphan—"though at first objected to on account of his brown complexion and fragile physical appearance."[35] He was taken in hand by the regiment's fencing master, M. d'Erape, a Flemish nobleman, who was soon predicting a brilliant career for him.

Jean-Louis had a rapid, simple style, and often won bouts on parry ri-

---

* During Napoleon's time duelists took to wearing a coat of mail under their shirts, sometimes painted flesh color (known as *"supersticerie"*). To combat the practice, it soon became customary to fight naked to the waist. The Duke of Wellington, among others, sometimes wore armor under his tunic during battle. It is odd that he never learned to fence—his one duel was with pistols—despite having attended military school in France.

postes alone. He "omitted everything that was superfluous," it was said; "the affected salutes, the *contre-coups*, the capricious pauses, all shocked him, and appeared to him unworthy of such a serious art."[36] It was possibly at this time that he taught Mme. Marie-Josèphe-Rose Tascher de la Pagerie—Napoleon's Joséphine.

Two stories in particular are told of him. The first dates from 1804, when, having established a reputation as a fencer, he was insulted by a local braggart in his garrison town, who mocked him, saying "The sword wasn't invented to be used by a mulatto." Otherwise a man of even temper, Jean-Louis eventually accepted the duel his adversary had been hoping for but stipulated that whereas his opponent would have a normal sword he would fight with a buttoned foil. When friends called him mad, he replied, "I am so little crazy that tomorrow I shall administer Monsieur the punishment he deserves." Which of course he did, parrying all the bully's attacks before slashing him across the face so hard that he knocked the man over and left him bleeding.

The second adventure occurred around 1812, after Jean-Louis had seen action in Egypt, Italy, Prussia, and Russia. He was in Madrid with the 32nd Regiment of the army's Third Division. It had been a policy of Napoleon that whenever he conquered a country he would integrate men from the defeated nation into the French forces, so there were a number of Italians in his army. The campaign in Spain had been a disastrous failure, but many Italians remained stationed there, particularly in the 1st Regiment. A skirmish broke out with the 32nd Regiment, and the men started to fight each other—at bayonet point. Soon there were scores of dead and wounded. To avoid a complete slaughter, officers from both sides hurriedly convened to work out a solution. It was decided, imaginatively, that fifteen fencing masters and provosts from each of the two regiments would square off in succession until one side no longer had a man standing.

The two teams met on a plain outside Madrid, watched by the warring regiments and their entire retinue—some ten thousand men, women, and children. The first Italian master up was Giacomo Ferrari, some six feet tall, a fully qualified master and veteran of the wars. His opponent was Jean-Louis. The Italian attacked. Jean-Louis parried, held the blade to avoid a remise, then riposted through his opponent's shoulder, leaving him dying. According to the rules of the engagement, he had to remain on the field until he was defeated, so after two minutes' rest he was confronted by his second adversary. After a single action, a second victim. And so it went, man after man, until thirteen Italians had been either killed or badly wounded. Jean-Louis, his blood up if not overflowing, wanted to fight on, but representatives from both regiments managed to restrain him, and eventually it was agreed that the two remaining swordsmen, by now quaking, would not be forced to follow their unhappy comrades. "*Vive Jean-Louis! Vive le 32ième!*" rose the cry. "*Vive le 1er!*" Jean-Louis shouted back. "We are all one and the same family. *Vive l'Armée!*"

Jean-Louis was twenty-eight years old at this, his most famous encounter. His reputation spread throughout France. He refused a commission and was happy to retire to Metz, where he opened a fencing school, which in 1830 he moved to Montpellier, teaching there until his death in 1865. Earlier that year, aged eighty, he had lost his eyesight, but he continued to teach, doing everything by touch. The whole city turned out for his funeral.

Part Two

—

THE SEARCH FOR

PERFECTION

Previous page: New Japanese blades were tested on the corpses of criminals. The blindfolded figure in this seventeenth-century drawing suggests that it was not always a requirement that the perpetrator be dead before testing began.

CHAPTER 5

The Great Swordmakers

> The name of the sword sayd the lady is Excalibur, that is as
> muche to say it cuts stele.
>
> —SIR THOMAS MALORY, Le Morte D'Arthur, 1485

> Nothing is more discouraging for a soldier than to find, when
> he has dealt his adversary a mighty blow with the sword, that
> the blade twists or that the hilt comes off in his hand.
>
> —The Daily Telegraph, OCTOBER 8, 1895

MY FATHER'S FAMILY WORKED IN METAL—COPPER, ZINC, aluminum, bronze, and other alloys—for more than two hundred years. The firm that became A. Cohen and Co. was founded by my great-great-great-great-grandfather Aaron Cohen in 1799—the year George Washington died—and by the 1980s had foundries around the world, from Bulawayo to Barcelona. When my father, the fourth and youngest son of the company's chairman, was a young man, he went to work on the foundry floor, supervising the men who separated the metals. They knew about his prowess as an amateur boxer and were rather proud of him, while he appreciated their skills and the danger inherent in their work.*

---

* He was very happy there and was disappointed when promoted to more "suitable" duties. My father was a big man, six feet, two inches tall. Even at the age of fourteen, he fought as a heavyweight and went on to be named second best amateur at the weight in the country. In the early 1930s he reached the final of the Amateur Championships, where he was up against the defending champion, and by the end of the opening round he was ahead on points.

At the start of the second round, The Times reported, my father landed "a fearful blow" to his opponent's head and was alarmed to see his eyes glaze over. To the astonishment of the ringside spectators, "concerned for the man," he was heard to ask, "Are you all right?" At which point his semiconscious adversary, in a reflex action, let go "an equally violent blow," which knocked my father to the canvas and "successfully deprived him of the title."

My father was far too softhearted ever to make a champion. His sister once wrote that he "did not like hurting people but it only needed his opponent to hit him hard

A. Cohen and Co. is no longer a family business, nor, for that matter, a profitable one. A couple of years ago I went down to its single remaining foundry, in Woolwich in southeast London. The place was a sad sight. Some of the letters above the main doorway were missing, and the sign read, all too accurately, "A C HE." In its heyday the foundry produced 153 tons a week; now a weekly tonnage of 80 to 85 tons is acceptable. "The scrap industry is dying on its feet," the plant manager told me as he handed me a pair of protective goggles and led me around the pitted and blackened furnaces.

I stood by, mesmerized, as foster copper was cast into little balls of metal—"shot"—as the men, fewer than a dozen in number, injected liquid phosphorus into molten copper at a heat of 1,580 to 1,620 degrees Fahrenheit—demanding work, as phosphorus is spontaneously combustible, and dirty, too, with waste shards of metal of all shapes and sizes, dust, and grime covering the factory floor. But as the furnace roared and the orange-yellow liquid poured from one cylinder to another, I understood why metalwork has always been ascribed unearthly qualities, why alchemy has seemed a magician's talent, why even Sir Isaac Newton found "the transmuting of metals his chief design." It recalled the fascination I have always felt when watching a roaring log or coal fire. Only this was not just conjuring shapes out of flame; it was making metals, metals that in another age would have become swords.

THE WORD "SWORD" COMES FROM THE OLD ENGLISH *SWEORD*, WHICH is derived from the Indo-European root meaning "to wound." However, what follows is not even a short history of the sword in its manifold forms but rather an inquiry into what goes into producing the finest blades and the search, through millennia, for the perfect instrument of death.

One expert recently calculated that eighty-two different manipulations are required before a lump of metal is converted into a fencing blade, with

---

enough to hurt, without knocking him out, to let his temper take over, then he would box." It must have been a closely calculated affair between turning on the light and extinguishing it completely.

He fenced briefly as a teenager but stopped following an exhibition match in which he was pitted against a well-developed girl a year or two his senior. Every time he got through her defenses, his foil landed flat against her chest, her exaggerated curves giving his point no purchase. He gave up the sport in disgust.

every blade having to be fashioned by hand, the skills necessary to forge the metal alone requiring approximately fifteen years of apprenticeship.[1] The exact composition of the craft alloys and the ways they are treated have always been secrets jealously guarded by blademasters, on a par with a *botta segreta*. The discovery of a new alloy for swordmaking would have as much effect on society (pregunpowder) as the discovery of atomic power in modern times.

One thinks of a sword as a long strip of metal, of either iron or steel, with a handle; but the first swords were made of wood. Copper was forged as early as 5000 B.C., and smelting appears by the time of Christ. These first weapons of copper or bronze, and later those of iron, were of poor quality; none maintained an edge for long. The Greek historian Polybius recounts clashes with Gallic warriors who periodically had to pull out of the battleline to straighten their soft iron blades beneath their feet. Strong blades require a certain carbon content, a fact not grasped literally for ages.*

A good blade must be able to hold a keen edge, yet not break or bend out of shape under a heavy blow. Unfortunately, the more intensely steel is hardened, the more brittle it becomes. Soft iron, while hard to snap, deforms easily and loses its edge. As a way out, the earliest bladesmiths laboriously hammer-welded together thin strips of steel and iron of contrasting hardnesses to form the core of the blade, then added, separately, edges of very hard steel. The core strips were braided or twisted like rope, so that, when polished, the finished blade would display patterns of light and dark that resembled spotted snakeskin (*Würmbunt* in German), poetically envisioned as fighting or writhing dragons and serpents. To achieve this effect, it was essential that the steel's temperature under the hammer be carefully controlled, and the close monitoring of the metal's passage from dark red to white hot was best undertaken at night. This

---

* When is a sword a sword, and when a dagger? Blade lengths have varied from country to country and over time and culture, but probably any weapon that can be concealed easily about one's person counts as a dagger and a blade over fourteen inches long should count as a sword. The largest swords on record are the medieval two-handers boasting blades between 60 and 70 inches, followed by the No-Dachi blade of the Japanese at four feet long: but the longer the sword, the harder to temper accurately. The Greeks generally fought with relatively short, hacking weapons of 14 to 25 inches; the Romans used somewhat longer ones of 19 to 27 inches. A sixteenth-century rapier was between 30 and 50 inches in blade length, but by the seventeenth century the blades of most cultures stabilized at 30 to 40 inches. Current foils and épées have the same maximum length of 35$^7/_{16}$ inches, sabers 34$^{4}/_{64}$ inches.

skill of the dark hours reinforced the superstitious awe surrounding swordsmiths, who fashioned instruments made to take life and elevated their craft into the realm of magic. There evolved an entire mythology, stretching across the world's cultures, in which a master swordsmith—a Wayland Smith or Voelundr or Daedalus—achieved wondrous feats.[2]

In his memoirs Alexandre Dumas recalls his friend Alphonse Rabbe—"one of the most extraordinary men of our time"—who at the age of thirty tried to stab himself to death but whose hand was so unsteady that he missed his heart. Dumas seized upon the episode to write "The Old Dagger," an essay in praise of the instrument that had, so to speak, spared his friend's life. "Was it in the blood of a newly-killed bull that your point was buried on first coming out of the fire?" it begins. "Was it in the cold air of a narrow gorge of mountains? Was it in the syrup prepared from certain herbs, or perhaps, in holy oil?" Dumas opens one of the oddest encomiums on record: "What does this broad furrow mean which, a quarter of the length down your blade to the hilt, is pierced with a score of tiny holes like so many loopholes? Doubtless they were made so the blood could seep through."[3]

Such blade worship is not unusual. History and myth are crowded with the names of famous weapons: Ulysses' Aor in the *Iliad*, Roland's Durendal, the sword of Damocles, Tyrfing (the magic weapon that King Heidrik flings at Odin), Charlemagne's Flamberge ("The Flame Cutter") and Joyeuse, El Cid's Tizona, Oliver's Glorius, Nuada's sword in the Grail legend, and Siegfried's armory of special weapons, famously including Mimung, Gram, and Nothung. There are Hogni's sword, Dainslef, wrought by dwarves, which takes a man's life whenever drawn; the legendary sword of Samurai lore, Ama No Murakumo Tsurugi, drawn from the tail of an eight-headed dragon; and Tethra's speaking sword. Most famous of all, there is Excalibur:

> And Arthur rode across and took it, rich
> With jewels, elfin urim in the hilt,
> Bewildering heart and eye—the blade so bright,
> That men were blinded by it—on one side,
> Graven in the oldest tongue in all this world,
> "Take me," but turn the blade and ye shall see,
> And written in the language that ye speak yourself,
> "Cast me Away." And sad was Arthur. . . .[4]

In the Middle Ages, a time of intense superstitiousness, the sword-smith was believed to employ a magic compound of gold, silver, copper, and lead, a so-called *Electrum Magicum*, as part of his craft. Under the in-fluence of the stars he was held to be able to impart supernatural strength to both swords and armor. As a result, a truly crafted suit of armor became so costly that only the richest of noblemen could afford one. By 1300 steel was selling at £3 a ton, five times the cost of iron.

Throughout history culture upon culture has pursued the secret of the perfect sword, a search the more intense because swordmaking is an art with a difference: the better the craftsman, the more likely the blade's owner is to survive. Ability is not everything. A duelist with a choice of weapons could rely on the skills and cunning of his swordmaker to obtain an unfair advantage. One armorer in Milan was said to have calibrated his tempering of steel to such a pitch of perfection that in the hands of the in-experienced the weapons would actually shiver to pieces; in those familiar with them they were "as trusty as the stoutest Toledo blade." There were other legends: Otwit, King of Lombardy, received from Alberic, master craftsman of the dwarves, a blade so fine as to leave no mark after use. Among Arab smiths, a new blade's quality was tested by placing it in a river, edge pointed upstream, where it was expected to cut floating leaves in half. In the seventeenth century, the great French master Liancour made "a curious suggestion, copied by all his successors, that the point of the blade should be broken to test its quality; if it be grey, it is good, if white, it should be rejected. He does not say what arguments should be used to appease the sword-cutler's objections to this damage to his stock."[5]

T HE ART OF TEMPERING MADE SUCH CITIES AS MILAN AND AUGS-burg famous, but there were four truly preeminent centers: Damas-cus, whose blades have been legendary since the Crusades; Toledo, where the finest Spanish swords were and still are made; Solingen, home of Ger-man steel; and Japan, whose story is the most complex of all.

In 390 B.C. Celts from Gaul invaded Italy and sacked Rome. A con-temporary noted, "They would raise their swords aloft and smile after the manner of wild boars, throwing the whole weight of their bodies into the blow like hewers of wood or men digging with pickaxes, and again they would deliver crosswise blows aimed at no target, as if they intended to cut to pieces the entire bodies of their adversaries, armor and all."[6] Hacking weapons require blades that last, however, and those fashioned in Damascus came to lead the field. In Burton's research boxes at the Huntington Library I came across a late-nineteenth-century article from the *Sheffield Daily Telegraph*, "Eastern Swords and Steel," which endorses the commonly held belief that the best curved swords were made in the East:

> From the artistic point of view nothing can be better. The cimetars [*sic*] of the Persian model have a beauty of form worthy of their material, the so-called Damascus steel. The Eastern preference for a curved blade was not artistic, but arose from certain practical considerations of an apparently plausible kind. The typical Oriental warrior is always a horseman, and it is easier to slash on horseback than to thrust. Then, too, a drawing cut with a curved blade gives a singularly ugly wound.... The *yataghan*—of Byronic associations—is a very typical Oriental weapon. It is beautiful and withal terrible to look at—a sharp-pointed blade with an edge on the inside curve. But it is the sword of a nation of butchers, good for cutting throats, but comparatively useless for purposes of honest fighting.[7]

The writer does not say what "honest fighting" might be, but he never disputes the notion that Damascene swords were the best of their kind. Legends about Damascene steel abounded. It was said that before the metal was forged it was fed in small pieces to chickens, mixed up in their grain. The birds' droppings were then collected and melted, to phosphorize the steel. Another account has it that the blades, heated before their final quenching, were cooled by plunging them through the bodies of muscular, active slaves, so that the metal was infused with their strength.

How did Damascus gain such a reputation? After all, fine bronze work by Peking Man had been known thousands of years before, while Japanese curved swords, the classic samurai blades, date back to around A.D. 800. Yet for a significant period the sharpest, most sought-after weapons came from Damascus, crafted from strong, light metal whose surface was patterned like the grain in wood. The city's swordsmiths would use a mixture of iron and carbon with traces of silicon and sulfur (in so-called *wootz* ingots) from India, which would be hammered and heated into deadly weapons. The process produced the special "damask pattern," the "damascening" or "watering" that swordsmen so prized. So to two further questions: What special technology led to such a reputation? And why did Damascene craft come to so sudden an end, all those centuries ago?

In January 2000 *Discovery* magazine reported that the secret of the remarkable technology was emerging from the thousand-year-old ruins of the city of Gyaur Kala in eastern Turkmenistan, which had disclosed the remains of an ancient factory, including a high-temperature furnace fed with air from below. The innumerable steel-beaded clay shards scattered among the surrounding sands appeared to be the remains of thick-walled crucibles in which steel had been fired at temperatures of up to 2,500 degrees Celsius—far higher than any other steelmaker could then command. Under analysis, the steel revealed a mixture of low-carbon and high-carbon iron alloys, which the ancient ironmasters seem to have combined in an advanced process called "cofusion" to create a high-strength steel.[8]

Just under a year after this article, the London *Times* published an account of how, twelve years before, a professor of materials science and engineering had set out to reproduce swords similar to those of the Damascene swordsmiths. Scrutinizing pieces of a Damascene sword donated by a Swiss museum, John Verhoeven, from Iowa State University, found that the highly prized grain effect was created by clusters of iron carbide, which show up as white against the dark steel. How to create that effect? He teamed up with Alfred Pendray, a Florida blacksmith, who discovered that the clusters were induced by repeated cycles of heating and cooling. As hot liquid metal cools, impurities separate out, the ferric carbide particles congregating and growing around these impurities at each heating and cooling. It takes about six cycles to reach the damask pattern. Simple, once you know.[9]

Over the years, fewer and fewer blades came out of Damascus, and after the fifteenth century production there virtually ceased. In Verhoeven's view, this was because changes in world trade transformed the content of the ingots until they no longer offered the right blend of impurities. So Damascene steel fell victim to the international commodity market. For some years the city's reputation continued to overshadow those of other established centers of the craft—Yemen, Q'al'a in the Arabian desert, and India, so often a pacemaker and fundamental supplier—as Damascus became the point of distribution for fine weapons produced elsewhere. Much of its trade was with the West, which probably explains the reputation of "Damascene" blades.

I CONFESS THAT I AM NO SCIENTIST AND WAS MYSTIFIED BY THESE various processes. What is the difference between iron and steel? Why is carbon so important? What does the cycle of heating and cooling achieve, and why were the temperatures at which blades were "quenched" so guarded a secret?*

I fell by luck upon *The New Science of Strong Materials* by Professor James E. Gordon, a Scottish academic with a tart sense of humor (the sub-title of his book is "Why You Don't Fall Through the Floor"). "Broadly speaking," Gordon writes, "there are two problems with all metals— extraction metallurgy, the separation of the metal from its ore; and physical metallurgy, which is how to get the metal into its most useful condition of hardness, strength and toughness."[11] The latter is achieved through "the sharp instrument of fire," a power available to mankind for four hundred thousand years. As that keen fencer Michelangelo wrote in one of his sonnets, "It is with fire that blacksmiths iron subdue / Unto fair form, the image of their thought." With fire, certainly, it was possible to create a whole new class of metals, and it is no accident that the one technologist in Greek mythology to have been given the rank of a major god was Hephaestus, smith and purveyor of weapons to the Olympians. (Prometheus, who fashioned man out of clay, is only a demigod.)

Pure copper, Gordon explains, is a *soft* metal and cannot be given an effective cutting edge. It is made up of layers of minute crystals; to hold the crystals together, one needs grit. Yet if one adds a particular, yet softer metal—tin—one obtains bronze; tin's impurities combine with copper to make a far stronger alloy. Much stronger, in fact: about 5 percent tin to 95 percent copper makes bronze three times as hard as the copper alone. Bronze was discovered in the Middle East around 3800 B.C. and became, as Jacob Bronowski put it, "a material for all purposes, the plastic of its age."[12]

After bronze came iron, then the steels, a family of iron alloys. By 2500 B.C., iron, which the Sumerians called "a metal from heaven," was already in use. (The word "iron" has close English connections to the word "ire" but is also related to "holiness," "frenzy," and "defecation"—all having the common denominator "fast-moving.") Societies started to make swords

---

* In ancient Japan, one swordsmith, visiting his prospective father-in-law, another leading blademaker, dipped his fingers in the quenching trough when he thought the other smith was not looking. He was caught in the act, "and a swift stroke of the master's own sword severed his guilty hand before he had time to get it out of the tub." Thus he lost his livelihood, his hand, and the hand of his fiancée.[10]

from iron without realizing what the processes they employed did to the metals under hammer and forge—they simply judged by the results. Not until 1860, quite late in the first industrial revolution, did people start to understand carbon's role in the steelmaking process. To make cast iron, one needs about 4 percent carbon (about as much as pure iron will hold); to make steel, one needs iron and 1 percent carbon or less.

That carbon would affect the behavior of iron is easy enough to understand, but these percentages seem so small. Gordon clarifies all this by explaining that the percentage is calculated by weight, not volume—and since carbon atoms are much lighter than iron atoms, the actual volume of carbon in steel is about 20 percent.

The difficulty facing the primitive metallurgist was to get a furnace hot enough to fuse metal and carbon. Bronze melts at between 900 and 1,000 degrees Celsius, just within reach of the ordinary wood fire. Pure iron melts at 1,535 degrees—for centuries beyond the range of technology, which is what makes the achievements of the Damascene swordsmiths so astonishing. However, even small amounts (by weight) of carbon will lower the melting point of iron considerably, and carbon fuel, usually in the form of charcoal, was often used to heat iron ore. If just over 4 percent of carbon seeped into the metal, it would lower the melting point by nearly 400 degrees, a temperature just about attainable with a blown charcoal fire. The Damascenes must have discovered this technique for themselves, after which it fell out of memory for several centuries.

Hammering iron has two effects: first, it squeezes out most impurities, including what is known as "slag," a dirty brown or gray substance formed from mixing with lime or limestone; second, it reduces the carbon content of the iron, leaving only small amounts of silicon and slag, both of which protect the wrought iron from becoming too soft. When iron is heated and beaten into elongated billets, it develops a particular kind of oxide coating. A smith would then double the metal over like a piece of pastry, trapping the oxidized film between layers of hot metal. This folding process would be repeated about a dozen times, which is why top-grade swords when broken show a delicate wavy pattern, each line the sign of a beating operation. But the alloy will stand a maximum of only about fifteen such procedures; thereafter blades begin to weaken (our word "meager" is related to the French word "marcrosse," meaning "endlessly thinned out").

Next comes the crucial "quenching" phase. This hardens the steel as it progresses from its "austenite" to its "martensite" state—that is, iron once again deprived of carbon. The metal loses heat very rapidly, but a smith must still quench a blade, that is, plunge it quickly into a cool liquid, as fast as he can. If a blade is quenched too swiftly, cracks appear, especially if water rather than oil is used. So quenching hardens, tempering softens; the trick is to find the ideal balance. Preparing a steel blade entails a series of approximations, each process going too far in one direction and being offset by the next.*

Quenching calls upon a further special skill, and at this point sword-making enters into mythology. Some of the myths are true, however: it *is* better to quench a blade in urine because it cools more quickly than water. Urine also contains urea and ammonia, both nitrogen compounds, which spread into the iron, forming hard needlelike crystals of iron nitride. These again contribute to the strength of a blade, but iron has to be very hot for the nitrogen compounds to enter it—dogs do not harden lamp-posts.**

I made out the following list:

1. Cast iron—hard but brittle, with too much carbon, i.e., charcoal.
2. Blade heated—all carbon removed—metal now too soft.
3. Blade reheated—some carbon put back in again.
4. Blade quenched, to harden it—thus becoming too brittle.

---

* After learning about this I came across these lines from Ben Jonson's Introduction to Shakespeare's First Folio, "To the Memory of My Beloved, the Author Mr William Shakespeare and what he has left us":

> His Art doth give the fashion. And, that he,
> Who casts to write a living line, must sweat,
> (Such as thine are) and strike the second heat
> Upon the Muses anvile: turne the same,
> (And himselfe with it) that he thinkes to frame . . .

Swordmaking as a metaphor for wordcraft evidently has a long history.

** A simple domestic test is to heat a razor blade until it is cherry red, then plunge it into water: when it emerges, it will have become brittle. The eleventh-century alchemist Theophilus Presbyter proposed an alternative experiment: "Take a three-year-old black goat and tie him up for three days within doors without food: on the fourth day give him fern to eat and nothing else. When he shall have eaten this for two days, on the night following enclose him in a cask perforated at the bottom, under which holes place another sound vessel in which thou wilt collect his urine. Having in this manner for two or three nights sufficiently collected this, turn out the buck and temper thine instruments in this urine." He adds for good measure, "Iron instruments are also tempered in the urine of a young red-headed boy harder than in simple water." The relevance of the redheadedness is puzzling but may refer back to the time when red hair was associated with choler, one of the four elements—and so with fire.[13]

5. Blade, now tempered, reheated to 220–450°C—as it cools, becomes softer.

So much for my scientific education.

EACH OF THE VARIOUS CENTERS ASSOCIATED WITH SWORDMAKING has, unsurprisingly, been keen to assert its primacy over its rivals. Over the centuries Toledo steel has had many admirers. Andrew Steinmetz asserts that "the sword-blades of Toledo have always carried off the palm as trusty weapons; proof against all violence without breaking. One was shown at the recent French Exhibition bent into a complete circle, and yet straight as an arrow on being released."[14] Even the villainous Sheriff of Nottingham (played by Alan Rickman) in the 1990s film *Robin Hood: Prince of Thieves* muses to his cousin, as he whets his sword, "Spanish steel . . . so much stronger than our native blades."

Yet blades were fashioned in cities such as Valencia, Granada, and Zaragoza as well as Toledo. What gave to this one city such a special fame?

Toledo is situated in La Mancha, Don Quixote's stomping ground, and has always excelled in the arts. Its swordmaking reputation rests in large part on its *tornerías,* the engines that shape the blades. The Latin poet Grattius Faliscus writes of the Toledo knives that hunters carried in their belts. Even Shakespeare insists that Othello's sword came from Toledo. But the

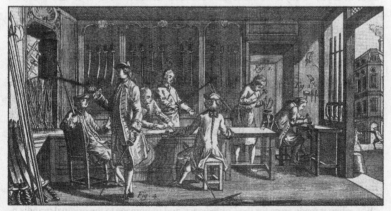

An armorer's shop in eighteenth-century Paris, designed by Diderot for his Encyclopédie méthodique, 1751–1775. *Practice—or maybe something more deadly—continues outside in the street.*

city's swordmaking dates back even earlier, to the Bronze Age. The reputation of Toledo's swordsmiths was further enhanced by local myths claiming that Hercules had added the building of Toledo to his labors and that the first hammer and anvil had been dropped on the town from the heavens, to improve the human condition. The notion even grew that Saint Joseph, the accepted father of Jesus Christ, had been not a carpenter but a smith.*

When the Romans occupied Hispania, they quickly adopted the Spanish sword, gradually abandoning their inferior flat, heavy blade. During their occupation Toledo advanced significantly, gaining ascendancy thanks to the excellence of its swordmaking and its strategic geographical situation.

The Roman order was eventually superseded by the Visigoths, under whom swordmaking declined. In 711 the Visigoths gave way to Arab rule, a bloody period during which the city's swordmaking was forced underground. Once Toledo-born Abd-er-Rahman III (r. 912–61) ascended to the caliphate, the industry revived—recognized guilds developed and there emerged *aminin*, who presided over each work community and controlled standards and productivity. Toledo further enhanced its reputation when Syrian smiths fled from the turbulent caliphate of Damascus and established their workshops in Arab-dominated Spain.

Toledo claimed that its artisans succeeded in improving on the work of Damascus by eliminating the iron veins left by their predecessors' techniques and by developing what they called their "*alma de hierro*"—literally, "soul of iron," a layer of steel that covered the intrusive vein and assured the blade a greater resilience; but this is a doubtful advertising line, since the surface rainbow effects in Damascene blades were a large part of their mystique.

The prestige of Toledo was next enhanced by the arrival around 1470 of Julián del Rey, "The Moor," a respected smith and excellent swordsman. Eight years later he was baptized, with the first king of all the Spanish kingdoms, Ferdinand II of Aragon, as his godfather. Such was Julián's prowess that Arab swords thereafter would carry his trademark, a small dog (*perrillo*), which came to be taken as a fox. Soon "fox-blade" meant any

---

* A village in Tennessee (just 1,100 souls) chose its name during the American Civil War, when it made arms for the Confederacy, and in homage to the original grandly titled itself Damascus. Toledo, Ohio, another swordmaking town, has a local newspaper called *The Toledo Blade*—a nice nod to the German word "*Blatt*," which meant both blade and a newspaper.

good sword—hence the anachronistic reference in *Henry V*, Act IV, Scene 4: "Thou diest on point of fox."

At the beginning of the thirteenth century an influx of Arab warriors known as "*zenete*," hispanized as *jinetes,* had introduced new and effective fighting techniques. This gave rise to the *jineta* sword, the weapon of choice of Moslems warring against Christians. By the fifteenth century the Christians too were using such swords—and these were largely manufactured in Toledo.[15] Even Toledo's most renowned artist, the Cretan El Greco, sported a *jineta* sword and reproduces it in at least two of his self-portraits. The swordsmiths of the city congregated into one street, "La Calle de Las Armas," where the rules of their craft could be better enforced. *Punzones* ("punches") were set as marks of workshop identity on all swords made in the city. Apprentices were expected to pass tough exams, which included tests of their ability to work with leather, thread, netting, velvet, and silk. They were also expected to make *jinetas* for use in *juegos de canas,* popular jousting tournaments that took place on feast days. Two bands of eight horsemen each got up in their finest armor would attack one another within a fixed set of rules and movements—very similar, in fact, to the old Roman version—in the first recorded example of competitive sporting swordplay in Spain.

During these years Spanish Moslem swordsmiths cooperated freely with their colleagues in Syria and so learned the craft of forging steel through the process already described—combining iron with an array of other elements such as carbon, silicon, sulfur, phosphorus, nickel, and chromium, which brought about the desired balance of hardness and flexibility. By 1561, however, the royal court moved to Madrid, and Toledo began to lose its importance. The population dropped from 125,000 to 55,000 (in 1594), exacerbated by plague at the end of the century. Apart from that, the sword was being replaced by the gun.

Toledo continued to make swords, but in 1664 a last surge of hyperinflation hit the country and a financial crisis in 1680 ruined whatever remained of the Castilian economy. Artisans abandoned their craft, and guilds everywhere were dissolved. So few native swordsmiths remained in Toledo that it suffered the indignity of having to induct foreign specialists. In 1760 the visionary King Carlos III, aware how far the rot had gone, recruited from Valencia its only remaining skilled swordmaker, seventy-year-old Luis Calixto, whom he directed to bring to Toledo the few master craftsmen he could find. In 1780 a Royal Manufactury was constructed on the outskirts of Toledo.

In the spring of 2000 I went to see Toledo for myself. A well-established stop on the tourist route, it offers swords everywhere, of all shapes and sizes—enough on show to equip an army. The city boasts two main swordmaking companies now, plus a smaller concern that specializes in bullfighting swords; but that apart, everything is made for ornamental or kitchen use. It was all vaguely depressing, as if real life had deserted the body of the town.

Throughout the nineteenth century Toledo remained a byword for excellence in swordmaking, but although the town asserts today that it has produced "the finest and most beautiful swords in the world" for centuries, from at least the early fifteenth century onward it had two principal rivals: Passau, on the Danube, at the border between Austria and Bavaria, and Solingen, a small town in the Wupper Valley in the Rhineland, near Cologne.

IT WAS WHILE CLEARING LAND FOR FARMING THAT THE INHABITANTS of the scattered villages of the Wupper Valley first discovered that veins of plentiful and easily obtainable iron ore were to be found just below the earth. Nearby beechwood forests could provide the charcoal, the numer-

A late-sixteenth-century swordsmith's, a contemporary depiction by the Italian Bernardino Poccetti. Craftsmen grind and polish blades while a variety of swords, daggers, and other arms are displayed for sale.

ous streams and rivers the necessary power. With such abundant resources, craftsmen could make high-quality, long, flexible steel swords.
That alone did not lead to high steel craftsmanship: the people of Solingen
did the rest. Even King Philip II of Spain, an Austrian Habsburg, flaunted
a sword created there, as if to keep the craftsmen of Toledo in their place.
The German town was greatly helped by the Knights of Saint John's decision to settle in the area, and during the Crusades a chosen number of the
local swordmakers would accompany these knights abroad, enabling
them to see for themselves the practices and techniques of foreign rivals.

By the fifteenth century, the reputation of the "City of Swords" shone
bright. In Solingen the term "*Kotten*" does not refer to a shed or cottage, as
it does elsewhere, but rather to a grinding workshop operated by water-
power. These *Kotten* first appeared in the river valleys and on the banks of
the Wupper. Contrary to practice elsewhere, twin workshops—*Doppelkot-
ten*—were set up, so that hammering and quenching went side by side. By
1684 there were 109 such shops. A German historian has noted that the
craftsmen would take the iron ore "and melt it in draught and smelting
ovens and fashion it into axes, spades and weapons."[16] It was these
"draught and smelting ovens" that enabled Solingen's smiths to rival the
steel refinement of Damascus.

Yet the artisans of Solingen were not the only craftsmen of their kind.
Bladesmiths elsewhere, in Prussia as well as in Württemberg, Saxony, and
the lands beyond, sought to emulate the quality and reputation of the
Solingen smiths. Some went so far as to mark their blades "Solingen,"
when the true place of manufacture was as far away as Spain or Russia.
For centuries, the most famous mark remained that of a running wolf,
still used to identify blades made in the Solingen and Passau regions.

The pirating of the Solingen name was not a one-way affair. Some German bladesmiths, recognizing the personal reputation of their best foreign competitors, applied fake markings—work attributed to Tomás de
Ayla, a prominent Spanish swordsmith, is one example. In some cases,
these forged blades were actually inferior to the German smiths' usual
product and may have been poorly made in an attempt to destroy the competitor's reputation.

High-quality blades were also forged at Augsburg, Mainz, Nuremberg,
Strasbourg, and Danzig throughout the Middle Ages and Renaissance,
their makers stamping them with the forms of eagles, lions, bears, wolves,
horses, unicorns, or serpents—and adding Latin mottos, biblical verses,
prayers, charms, curses, anagrams, and secret ciphers. Among the artists

who made designs for such emblems were Hans Holbein the Elder, Albrecht Dürer, and Rembrandt. The most famous marking of all was "Me Fecit Solingen"—"Solingen Made Me." How highly the city's work was prized may be gathered from the fact that in 1600 Pope Clement VIII presented the convert King Henri IV of France with a Solingen sword on the occasion of his wedding, while Louis XIV paid 28,000 livres to the Elector of Brandenburg and 40,000 livres to the Elector of Bavaria for their craftsmen's swords—huge sums for their day. Royal families throughout Europe ordered their swords from Solingen.

The Thirty Years' War (1618–48) sharply increased the demand for weaponry, forcing Solingen into mass production and creating intense competition among its swordmakers. The guilds enforced stringent controls over production, so a swordmaker could not make more than four broadswords daily—although he could substitute six daggers or stilettos. Trademarks were de rigueur, and bladesmiths jealously guarded their skills. "The ability to produce an artisan product in defiance of another's knowledge," writes Frederick Stephens in his history of German swords, "was the foundation stone upon which almost all the craft guilds came into existence—closed societies which taught only their own, and some other chosen few, the skills and secrets of their craft, thus ensuring for perpetuity their labour, market, and wealth from their own skilled hands."[17] Members were put under oath never to leave the jurisdiction, and by the seventeenth century three hundred specialist families in and around Solingen were producing swords.

The cartelism of the closed brotherhoods cut two ways: many who wished to become bladesmiths but were excluded left for Copenhagen, Paris, or Moscow. In 1687 a group of English merchants lured nine families of swordmakers from Solingen to settle in northern England. This came as a devastating shock to the burghers of Solingen and nearby Cologne, who threatened dire penalties. The emigrant cutlers responded by marking their blades with the famous emblem of the Solingen wolf: they were not to be intimidated. The exodus continued: a group of Solingen smiths established themselves at Tula in Russia in 1730; four decades later, groups emigrated to Eskilstuna in Sweden, Danzig in Poland, and Klingenthal in eastern France. In 1814, following Napoleon's disastrous campaign in Russia, a number of German swordsmiths set up in Zlatoust, north of Omsk. The blademaking center they founded continues today, having evolved into one of the largest weapons-manufacturing complexes of Eastern Europe.

AROUND 1875 RICHARD BURTON, WORKING ON HIS SECOND VOL-ume of the history of the sword, came to Solingen. On notepaper headed "Hotel Feder, Turin" he recalls his day "in the industrious valley of the Wupper," which is "quite enough to show the reasons why the foils and rapiers bearing that famous hand are still so popular throughout Europe." Solingen, Burton went on, "is a regular black town, one long street following the brow of a hill and splitting into a three-pronged fork to the south. It is never clear, dark with coal dust like the faces of the men." When Burton passed through, the *Gau* (district) had about 30,000 inhabitants, the town itself 14,000. "They are independent in manner," he observed. "The men drink hard and are handy with their knives."

The city had not yet been touched by the Industrial Revolution. "The hammering and forging are utterly ignorant of progress," Burton noted, with a clear contempt for this distasteful modern affectation. "The tempering is done in water as usual. . . . Solingen keeps its place in the market because [its blades are] chiefly made by hand: if more machinery were used it would soon lose rank." His statement is doubly surprising, first because water rather than oil was being used, and second because the advent of the steam engine had led to the creation of countless new engines, and by the time of Burton's visit the arduous job of forging a blade over an anvil by hand was already yielding to mechanically driven hammers. Many blade-smiths disliked and distrusted the new machines, but such innovation provided opportunities for mass production that could not be avoided.*

Business in Solingen was nevertheless brisk. The extension of trade, as well as the demands of war, meant that orders poured in from around the world, including the United States, for swords and bayonets. In 1847 a mechanism for rolling blades from long strips of steel was introduced, a painful blow to the old masters. Within the year, the swordsmiths had given up their traditional proof marks and substituted the trademarks of the newly consolidated firms. Solingen's artisans had finally been recruited to factory work.

However, after 1900 craftsmen once more came into their own, as diplomats, statesmen, and military officers requested individually made

---

* Few writers seek to evoke the *sound* of swordfights, but this is well caught by J. R. R. Tolkien in *The Lord of the Rings:* "Presently the noise of fighting broke out near at hand, just above their hiding place. He could plainly hear the ringing grate of steel on steel, the clang of sword on iron cap, the dull beat of blade on shield. . . . 'It sounds like a hundred blacksmiths all smithying together,' said Sam to Frodo."[18]

arms. Solingen flowered again, into a prosperity that lasted almost two decades. The total defeat of the Reich in 1918 brought ruin on the town. Attempts were made to convert the factories to such items as scissors and tableware, but these contributed little. Solingen would lie dormant and decaying until Adolf Hitler came to power. In April 1933 a group of city fathers went to Berlin to petition the Führer. Not only did he agree to see them, but it was at their meeting that the idea of daggers for servants of the Third Reich was proposed.

Hitler was keen to lift Germany from the economic depression gripping the developed world and to remind his countrymen of their past glories. A professor from Solingen's Industrial Trade School designed the prototype weapon for the SA and SS, and on February 6, 1934, the first orders were placed. Soon weapons fever was rampant: nearly every Nazi Party and military organization wanted its own identifying brand of dagger and sword.*

Led by Hermann Göring, who was seldom seen without an edged weapon of some fashion in his belt, the new Germany idolized the sword. One Solingen firm alone produced seventy thousand swords and daggers between 1938 and 1941, just for naval use (and the German navy was principally a submarine force)—still only a small portion of its overall output for the period.

The last three years of the war saw yet another reversal as Allied bombs shattered Solingen. The Reich's worsening position meant that even skilled craftsmen were being called up. Copper shortages forced the substitution of aluminum in pommels, crossguards, and scabbard fittings, while a diminished workforce made inferior products. With war's end, hundreds of thousands of Nazi swords were removed from Solingen's factories by Allied soldiers, who drove tanks back and forth over them.

One sunny October morning two years ago, I visited Solingen. The valleys leading into the town were bathed in a light haze, and the falling leaves imparted a melancholy beauty. It could not have been more different from Toledo, perched defiantly atop a huge hill as if challenging its en-

---

* Their purpose was ceremonial and symbolic; nevertheless, upon the outbreak of war the British War Office sent out the order "All officers will sharpen swords." The U.S. Field Manual of June 30, 1942, included directions for unarmed defense against an opponent wielding a European-style sword, based on the assumption that a GI would encounter an enemy trained in classic Western swordsmanship: "An individual trained in the use of the foil or épée will approach you in the manner illustrated in Figure A."—surely the last occasion on which a military manual gave such advice (see p. 269).

emies to besiege it. Toledo still looks like a proud medieval fortress, but Solingen bears little trace of its famous past. Now even "Old Fritz," the affectionate nickname given to its emblematic statue of a swordsmith, has been removed from the marketplace of the old town, where it stood for centuries. The one factory I visited was little more than a couple of rooms devoted to making steelware for domestic use: if I had been hoping to find glittering blades to rival those of earlier times, I was disappointed.

The author of a book I was reading on Nazi weaponry concluded sadly, "Since the demand today for edged weapons is so limited, [Solingen's] firms are turning more and more toward the production of cutlery and tableware as a full-time industry. It is extremely doubtful that the Solingen machinery for producing swords and daggers will ever again hum at the high pitch attained during the peak of the Third Reich."[19] Only an obsessive sword collector, I reflected, could regard that as a calamity.

AFTER THE WAR, A BAN ON MAKING OR POSSESSING SWORDS WAS imposed upon Japan as well as on Germany and lasted seven years—effectively until the Americans left in 1952. For the first time in its history, swordmaking in Japan came to a halt. (The practice of *kendo,* the martial

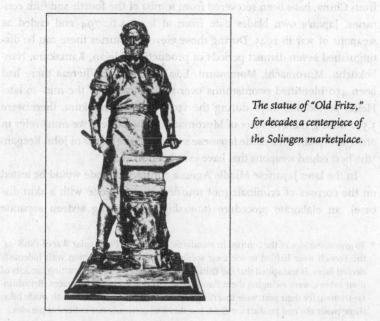

The statue of "Old Fritz," for decades a centerpiece of the Solingen marketplace.

art that imitates samurai swordplay, was also outlawed, but the Japanese soon initiated a different form of the sport, and by about 1947 were training again, in secret.)

The experience was uniquely painful. Swordmaking lay at the heart of Japan's high culture; the best swords were often ancient heirlooms, with their own names, handed down through the generations. Now they were confiscated, taken as souvenirs by the conquering troops, or destroyed. Yet these weapons had embodied something profound: blademakers had decorated their forges with religious symbols and worn ceremonial costume. A swordsmith was forbidden to engage in sexual activity for three days before beginning work on a blade or during the process, and approached his task only after elaborate rituals of purification and prayer. Swordmaking in Japan was a world apart: for all the pride in craftsmanship and the high-quality work in Toledo or Solingen, only in Japan was it a spiritual activity.

Religion was interwoven with tradition.[20] Two of the earliest authorities we have, both books from the eighth century A.D., state that Japanese iron swords and swordsmanship date back to the *shindai* (the age of the gods), which is not very helpful. Most likely, the technology that led to the development of Japan's swordmaking actually originated in China and crossed over via Korea around the fourth century. Steel swords, many from China, have been recovered from tombs of the fourth and fifth centuries. Japan's own blades date from at least A.D. 794 and ended as weapons of war in 1945. During those eleven centuries there can be distinguished seven distinct periods of production: Heian, Kamakura, Nanbokucho, Muromachi, Momoyami, Edo, and Meiji. Whereas there had been 450 identified swordsmiths over the 300 years of the mid- to late-Heian period and 1,150 during the 150 years of Kamakura, there were 3,550 during the 250 years of Muromachi. It is to these we must refer in order to explain what made Japanese swords, in the words of John Keegan, "the best edged weapons that have ever been made."[21]*

In the later Japanese Middle Ages, a completed blade would be tested on the corpses of criminals (not murderers, or anyone with a skin disease), an elaborate procedure (*tameshigiri*) involving sixteen separate

---

* To give some idea of the contrast in standards: during the Peninsular War of 1808–14, the French were baffled to see their soldiers returning from action with hideously dented faces. It transpired that the British cavalry, despairing of the cutting capacity of their sabers, were swinging them flat-on, using them as coshes or maces. British infantrymen, for their part, were inserting Japanese blades into their British-made hilts; these made the end product too rigid, but this was generally not noticed at parades.

forms of cut, ranging in difficulty, until the examiner was satisfied. A good sword might use up as many as three whole corpses before it lost its edge; the record appears to have been seven. Bruce Chatwin, in his short story "The Estate of Maximilian Tod," writes chillingly of a blade dated 1279 and signed by Toshiru Yoshimitsu, the greatest swordsmith of the time, which carried a mark that "signified that it had successfully performed, on a criminal, the movement known as *iai,* an upward thrust that severs the body clean from the right hip to the left shoulder."[22] Clan members who did the testing would generally effect three thousand practice cuts in the morning and eight hundred in the evening with blades mounted in a special grip.

This important exception apart, the process of manufacture was not intrinsically different from elsewhere, but the cultural and religious importance of swordmaking meant that greater care was taken, and it showed. The most prized Japanese blade still had to justify its aesthetic qualities by its effectiveness as a weapon. Such objects aroused, and arouse still, a mingled sense of power and beauty, awe and terror.

The "golden age" of these swords was the Kamakura period (1185–1333), when the great bladesmith Goro Nyudo Masamune of Soshiu perfected the technique of joining a hardened edge to a flexible core. He also repeatedly doubled over each steel billet, creating a multiplicity of inner surfaces, continually strengthening the blade that resulted. His disciple, Getsu, would "fold" the steel up to fifteen times—that is, creating two to the power of fifteen, or more than thirty thousand layers—infinitely thinner than tissue paper.* "It was as if he were trying to combine the flexibility of rubber with the hardness of glass," one connoisseur wrote of Getsu's work.[24] Sometimes a rose was kept nearby; only when the color of the steel was neither too red nor too orange but matched that of the rose could the folding process begin. After the folding came the tempering, until each blade "glowed to the color of the morning sun," that being the color of Japan (itself meaning "the source of the sun").

Each blade would be coated with a mixture of clay, ash, and iron filings to retard the outward flow of heat. Parts of the coating would be scraped

---

* The historian Richard Storry improves even on Getsu's record: "There exists in Japan a film showing a machine-gun being sliced in half by a sword from the forge of the great fifteenth-century maker, Kanemoto II. If this seems improbable, one must remember that smiths like Kanemoto hammered and folded and rehammered, day after day, until a sword blade contained something like four million layers [thus twenty-two folds] of finely forged steel."[23]

away, creating different patterns according to the school of blademaking and personal choice. The blade would then be heated again until it was cherry red—around 900 degrees Fahrenheit—and finally quenched. This process of "differential quenching" seems to be unique to Japan.

Samurai swords are still made, but not for military use. After 1953 smiths from what was called "the lost generation" returned to the craft, and there is now a flourishing guild of bladesmiths making *gendaito* ("modern swords"), working under strict government control. Each smith is limited to two blades a month, a figure derived from the work rate of one Akihira Miyairi, a much-revered but notably slow craftsman. New smiths must undergo not less than ten years' apprenticeship.*

The craftsman has given way to the machine, and the market today, all for sporting goods, is dominated by Britain (Leon Paul), Ukraine (Lammet), Saint Petersburg, and France (France Lames and Blaise). France Lames produced more than 150,000 new swords—almost half of them foils—in 2000 alone.

Recent improvements have been driven not by aesthetics or even cost but by safety concerns. A modern blade is functional rather than beautiful. There is no time for the Japanese passion for detail. In his book *Bushido: The Soul of Japan*, about the cult of the Japanese warrior, Inazo Nitobe describes the sword's "cold blade, collecting on its surface the moment it is drawn the vapor of the atmosphere; its immaculate texture, flashing light of bluish hue; its matchless edge . . . the curve of its back, uniting exquisite grace with utmost strength."[25] A high-flown vision; but then swordplay remains something different for Japan—no mere adjunct to religious practice but a central part of it, embodying a history of skill, philosophy, and codes of honor that provide a revealing counterpoint to swordplay in the West.

---

* And great rivalry: the most famous of early Sakoku-period swordsmiths was Kotetsu Okisato (1599–1678). He was a maker of battlefield helmets, and it was proposed that one of his products be tested by a sword forged by Kiyomitsu, a famous swordsmith. In front of a large audience, Kiyomitsu bowed to Kotetsu's helmet, which had been placed on top of a special wooden stand, drew his sword, and assumed *jodan no kamae* (an overhead combative engagement position). Kotetsu panicked and before his rival could strike cried out for him to halt. Kiyomitsu did so but was visibly unnerved—"the greater portion of his spiritual energy dissipated." Kotetsu apologized for the interruption and made a minor adjustment to the helmet.

When at last Kiyomitsu dealt his blow, it did only superficial damage, and Kotetsu was feted as a great armorer; but he was so overwhelmed by shame that he offered his apologies to his rival, abandoned the armorer's profession, and became a bladesmith.

CHAPTER 6

The Perfect Thrust

> *If any fencing expert can invent an attack which it is impossible to resist, or a parry which is impossible to deceive, I should advise him to take very good care to secure the patent rights of his invention without a moment's delay. He would certainly have no difficulty in floating a company to put it on the market in all the capitals of Europe.*
>
> —BARON DE BAZANCOURT, *Secrets of the Sword*

> *Don Jaime put the pencil down and imitated the movement of the foil with his hand, studying his shadow on the wall. . . . He always ended up with familiar, classical moves that could easily be predicted and avoided by an opponent. The perfect thrust was something else. It had to be as swift and precise as a bolt of lightning, unexpected, impossible to parry. But what was it?*
>
> —ARTURO PÉREZ-REVERTE, *The Fencing Master*

URFERS BELIEVE THAT SOMEWHERE OUT THERE ROLLS THE PERfect wave; Reichean sexologists seek the perfect orgasm; physicists long for everything to be reducible to one equation; executioners once spoke of the perfect beheading. Any skillful activity invites the notion of its distillation into an absolute ideal. For swordsmen, this has manifested itself in the quest for the perfect thrust.

At the beginning of the sixteenth century, recognized masters sought to enhance the mystique of their profession by encouraging the belief in a *botta segreta*, a special thrust that would guarantee victory. The term is Italian because the leading theorists were Italian; but throughout Europe masters cultivated a reputation for such wizardry, while also making a conscious mystery of their lessons. Pupils were made to swear never to reveal their masters' teachings, and lessons were held in the strictest privacy, with masters examining every part of a room, the furniture, and even the walls, to guard against the presence of intruders. The secret moves imparted to the fortunate initiates were called *"traccheggie"* ("acts of concealment") by the Italians and *"coups de maître"* ("masterstrokes"), *"bottes secrètes"* ("secret thrusts"), or, less politely, *"coups de malin"* ("sly cuts") by the French.

That one's adversary might use a *botta segreta* was frightening—it must have been like battling a magician—and swordsmen, declaring that it was beneath a gentleman's honor to employ them, chose to discount these secret moves by publicly scorning them. The same argument was leveled at perhaps the most famous user of a *botte secrète:* Guy de Chabot, Comte de Jarnac, who deployed his celebrated "Coup de Jarnac" against François de Vivonne, Duc de Chastaigneraie, on July 10, 1547. Their encounter, said to be the last judicial duel in Europe, contained elements of trial by combat, duel of chivalry, and duel of honor. The quarrel had begun in the reign of François I, who had refused to permit these two of his favorite knights to risk their lives. When Henri II succeeded to the throne, the two asked again, and the new king acquiesced.

Jarnac, an unwilling duelist with no great reputation for swordsmanship, was fighting only because Chastaigneraie had put it about that Jarnac had taken his own mother-in-law as his mistress, leaving Jarnac no alternative. Chastaigneraie, by contrast, was reputedly the finest swordsman and wrestler in France, a brilliant and arrogant twenty-six-year-old of exceptional strength. Jarnac took what instruction he could from one Caizo, an Italian master much favored by the court, who had his own *botte secrète,* called a *"falso manco,"* a left-handed cut at the inside of the knee.

Jarnac was well aware that the longer the bout went on the less chance he had. He used the choice of arms as a delaying tactic, proposing some thirty different weapons for combat mounted or on foot and specifying different horses with different kinds of harnesses and saddles. "This man means to fight both my honor and my wallet," sighed Chastaigneraie with bemused contempt. So sure was he of victory that he had organized a special banquet for the evening of the duel, to which the king and 150 of his courtiers were invited.

The duel was staged at Saint-Germain and attended by king, court, and a large, eager crowd. The two men exchanged courtesies, and the fight began. The opening moves were cautious as each tested for an opening. Suddenly Chastaigneraie attempted a deadly lunge. Jarnac dodged the blow, coming back at his opponent's face, and, as Chastaigneraie raised his shield, swung downward at his right knee instead, severing the right

*The Comte de Jarnac's duel against the Duc de Chastaigneraie
in 1547, re-created by a nineteenth-century engraver.*

hamstring. Too proud to reveal his pain, Chastaigneraie attempted a second, desperate thrust, at which Jarnac severed the other hamstring, forcing his adversary to the ground.

Chivalry dictated that if a defeated man asked for mercy his conquerer could grant it, but the mortified Chastaigneraie kept a furious silence. Jarnac begged him to yield in the acknowledged way. Still Chastaigneraie refused. Jarnac fell to his knees before the king and beseeched him to intervene to command the younger man's submission. When eventually surgeons came forward and dressed his wounds, Chastaigneraie was so humiliated at his overthrow that he tore off his bandages and bled to death. Henri swore never to authorize another trial by battle and issued an edict forbidding them. Jarnac found that, quite unjustly, his *coup* had passed into a proverb as a dirty trick or foul blow.

Was "the perfect thrust" by definition a *secret* move? Inevitably Burton takes up the question, and equally inevitably finds an answer. When he died in 1890, he was at work on a manuscript that appeared twenty-one years later as *The Sentiment of the Sword*. The book takes the form of a country house colloquy between himself and a group of interested friends, organized into nine evenings, on the seventh of which his interlocutor "Lord B" asks, "What is your opinion of what the French call *les bottes secrètes,* and why are they not taught in the schools?"

Burton replies that if such were taught they would no longer be secret.

> But I hasten to say that I do not believe in a *botta segreta,* any more than in the *parata universale* or in the Philosopher's Stone. *Par parenthèse,* the word *botte* has lately been pronounced too trivial for the art of arms, and we are ordered to say *coup;* the Italians are not so fastidious. . . . In France we often hear of a master who "possesses, they say, *bottes secrètes.*" A challenge has passed, and one, perhaps both, of the combatants will go to him for advice, and both probably learn the same. These passes, improperly called secrets, are mere irregularities that do not belong to everyday practice. So far I admit them, but no farther.[1]

Later in the evening, Burton yields sufficiently to list actions that fall into this category. He begins with the effective but illegal action of "pommeling one's enemy," then goes on to describe the "parries of contention," the *volta* and the *circolata* (vaulting), the *inquarto* (the sideways leap), the *sbasso* (the downward slide), the *sparita di vita* or *effacement du corps* (turning the body), the *incocciatura* (clashing of hilts), and the *balestrata* (plain tripping).

For all his proclaimed disdain, Burton had his own special attacks, perfected when he was twenty-eight and living in Boulogne. Years later his widow would write, "To this day, the Burton *une-deux,* and notably the *manchette* [an upward slash disabling the sword arm] are remembered." No doubt Burton would have characterized these as trademark moves, not actual *bottes secrètes.*

There were plenty of other actions to choose from, and examples of secret moves range across continents and over centuries. In his 1825 *Traité* *des Armes*, the French master L.-J. Lafaugère lists 1,272 different thrusts and combinations. A move known as the *"imbroccata"* (a downward thrust over an adversary's sword arm) was in vogue in Shakespeare's day, and he employs it in at least five plays. "From one truculent personage," records a nineteenth-century historian, "Tappa the Milanese, you could learn how to cut (if it so took your fancy) both eyes out of your adversary's face with a *rinverso tondo*, or circular reverse of the point."[2] Then there was *"la botte de Saint-Evremonde,"* named after another celebrated duelist, unfortunately undescribed, and the *"botte de Nouilles,"* also called the *"botte de Nevers,"* a jerky counterattack delivered between the eyes, a specialty of the Nouilles family invented by the Parisian master Le Flamand (and a recognized move in Chinese swordplay, known as "Paint a Red Dot Between the Eyebrows"). We do have details of the "Boar's Thrust," the special killing maneuver of the eighteenth-century Scottish master Donald McBane, which involves a swordsman dropping beneath the attacking blade by going down to the ground on his free hand, simultaneously bending his knee and thrusting upward.*

---

* McBane penned a remarkable book of memoirs, *The Expert Sword-man's Companion, or the True Art of Self-Defence*. Published in 1728, it remains the only fencing book written by a master who had also been a serving soldier; in all, he took part in sixteen battles and fifty-two sieges. Toward the end of his career he kept an alehouse and fencing school in London and fought thirty-seven prizes in the Bear Garden; but it is extraordinary that he survived that long.

The son of a Scottish farmer and publican, McBane enlisted in the Scots army in 1687. Five years later he won his first duel, against an army paymaster who had swindled him. Three years after that, he took part in the siege of Namur, where he was shot three times and bayonetted six. In 1697 he went home to Inverness but soon reenlisted, fought a further duel in Perth, leaving his opponent for dead, and fled to Ireland, where he set up a fencing school. Still a common soldier, he found himself consigned to Holland, where he met the man whom he thought he had killed in Perth. They became friends and set up a new academy together. On learning that four fellow practitioners ran a brothel and gaming house, he decided to take a share and fought all four until the last suddenly produced a pistol from his cocked hat and fired. The ball missed, and McBane ran him through the buttocks. The masters then agreed to cut their conqueror in, and from 1700 to 1702 he lived comfortably off the earnings.

At the battle of "Nemegen" (Nijmegen) McBane's regiment lost all its baggage, leaving him penniless. He borrowed money but lost it all in a card game, robbed the winner, was set upon by seven men, wounded five, and escaped. After sundry other vicissitudes, including being blown up by a grenade, he set up as a master a third time, simultaneously keeping a brothel with sixteen girls who doubled as his concubines. One day, exhausted after preparations for a forced march, he fell asleep and was left

McBane's signature thrust was similar to the favorite move of the Italian master Salvator Fabris, the *passata sotto*—which he would teach his pupils for a price, on condition they would not employ the action against him. (A pupil who had handed over his money for a worthless move was not likely to come back for a refund.)

behind by his regiment. "Up comes a French dragoon seeking plunder and took me prisoner, [and] drove me before him until he came to a wood where he wanted to ease nature. When his breeches were down, I mounted his horse and rode for it."

A year later he was marching with the Duke of Marlborough and in one engagement took three bayonet thrusts as well as receiving "a brace of balls that lies in my thigh to this day." None of this seemed to quench his spirit, and he was soon setting up tents for sixty "campaign ladies" as well as sixteen "professors of the sword." This was evidently insufficient, for he led a raiding party on his Dutch allies and carried off fourteen of their women. The next day two dozen Dutch swordsmen came to retrieve them. The two sides drank together, then fought until eleven Dutch and seven of McBane's band lay dead.

In 1706 he took part in a campaign that swept the French out of Flanders, in one siege hurling grenades for eight hours while receiving a ball in the head "which will mind me of it while I live." The following year he fought with a Gascon mercenary who had already killed five men. "I bound his sword and made a half thrust at his breast, he timed me and wounded me in the mouth; we took another turn, I took a little better care and gave him a thrust in the body, which made him very angry; some of the spectators cryed stand your ground, I wished them in my place, then I gave him a thrust in the belly, he then darted his sword at me, I parried it, he went and lay down on his coat and spoke none."

His next misadventure followed yet another dispute over money: he was severely beaten, thrown into a well, and left for dead, fortunately in less than a foot of water. In 1708, during one more siege of yet another town, he was knocked to the ground by the head of a comrade torn off by a cannon blast. "All his brains came round my head. I being half senseless put up my hand to my head and finding the brains cryed to my neighbour that all my brains had been knocked out; he said were they your brains out you could not speak."

In 1711, now forty-seven, McBane quarreled with two Dutch soldiers; the ensuing brawl left both men dying. Once again he was compelled to flee, only this time he was captured by the French and drafted into their ranks. It didn't take him long to kill two of his new comrades—another argument over pay—and he was arrested. The following day a drum major from Marlborough's army arrived to exchange prisoners. "Take him," the French general pleaded, "for if he stays he will kill all my men."

By 1712 the Flanders wars—in which both Cyrano de Bergerac and Guy Fawkes had fought in their day—were drifting to an end, and McBane returned to Britain, to a new marriage and a career with James Figg and his companions. He reenlisted once more, in 1715 against the Jacobite rebellion, and served until discharged because his many old wounds were troubling him. In 1726 "I fought a clean young man at Edinburgh. I gave him seven wounds and broke his arm with the fauchion. This I did at the request of several noblemen and gentlemen. But now being sixty-three years of age, resolve never to fight any more, but to repent of my former wickedness."

In Poland, cavalry officers of the eighteenth century developed the "Nyzkiem cut," a move especially effective when delivered on horseback. One of Poland's leading postwar sabreurs, Wojciech Zabłocki, showed me how the cut was made, using a replica of a hussar's saber. He turned over his wrist, palm facing down, then cut upward at an angle, as if slicing a tennis ball, so that the blade would slice from lower belly to midchest, traveling almost vertically. "It is impossible to parry with normal tierce or quarte," Wojciech explained. "You can protect yourself only by going into an exaggerated seconde"—he mimed a low-line parry, the blade pointing downward—"but made differently, with one's hand pushed out more to the left, to be strong enough against the cut." And we were not even making the cut from a horse.

The *botte de Nouilles* turns up again in the 1999 film *Le Bossu* (*En Garde* in the United States), directed by Philippe de Broca from a nineteenth-century French novel. *Le Bossu* is a well-made swashbuckler about a master sworn to avenge the death of a close friend. The "secret thrust" itself as performed is highly impractical: the move ends at the top of the bridge of the nose, where allegedly there is a small space of soft tissue. One French critic, reviewing the original book, was outraged: "The 'hit between the eyes' is of all hits the most dastardly, a total absence of dueling fair play, a mistake of chivalric honor . . . 'a tartufferie of the closed battlefield.' "[3]

Another French film, *The Revenge of the Musketeers* (1997), takes a tongue-in-cheek approach. Its leading villain, Crassac de Merindol, practices his range of secret moves in front of his henchman (later revealed to be the musketeer Athos in disguise). "I'm good in the arms room," Crassac says, then executes a *doublé doublé* and lunges while down on one knee. The Cahuzac twist? The Nemours slink? No, the Montparnasse viper, and it leaves Athos unimpressed: "It really works only with the sun behind you." At the climax Crassac tries the move on d'Artagnan's daughter, Eloïse (Sophie Marceau), to her yet greater contempt: "Everyone knows that secret thrust. *You need the sun behind you.*" As Crassac fails and realizes that his adversary is about to get the better of him, he finally asks, "Would you by any chance be using a longer blade?"—a secret recourse indeed, if not quite a fair one.

In the sixteenth and seventeenth centuries duelists were not at all worried about such notions; they wanted to learn the actions that would bring them victory. Egerton Castle observes that all these moves were "to the fencer of those times what the philosopher's stone was to the alchemist"—a phrase he coined just before Burton wrote *The Sentiment of the Sword*, with its disparaging reference to philosophers' stones. One senses a rivalry between the two men for primacy among historians of swordplay.

Castle lived by his pen, turning his hand to any topic from English bookplates to landscape gardening. He wrote plays for Sir Henry Irving, for nearly a decade was on the staff of the *Saturday Review*, and together with his wife, Agnes Sweetman, penned more than twenty historical romances, several of which became best-sellers. Some had splendid titles—his last, posthumous novel was *Pamela Pounce: A Tale of Tempestuous Petticoats*—and several drew upon his love of swordplay, one dealing explicitly with the *botte secrète*. At the climax of his short story "The Great Todescan's Secret Thrust" its hero confronts the evil Todescan: "Never, for smallest breathing-space, did the provost's terrible long blade release his own. He felt it gliding, seeking to bind, fiercely caressing; felt the deadly spring behind a tiger's crouch; felt the invincible, unknown thrust ready against his first weakening."[4] Homoeroticism may be on fine display here, but what of the secret thrust itself? All we learn of Todescan's special move is "the fierce jerky binding, the incredible turn of the wrist inwards, the infallible estocade [from the French word *"estoc,"* a longsword; thus "a blow from a longsword"] that was to have driven the point irredeemably under the armpit": hardly enough for any master to make use of in the salle.

Nearly a century on, Umberto Eco invented his own *botta segreta*, the *"coup de la mouette,"* in *The Island of the Day Before*, but again it is unclear what the actual move entails.[5] Obviously there is a difference between a surprise move and a secret thrust—although, as Burton noted, even a *botta segreta* is no longer secret after a few outings. Just as the successful general knows that his victorious strategies will first be imitated, then superseded, the fencing master gets set in his ways and does not envision the step beyond them. Like any system, fencing evolves under the steady pressure of failure.*

The search for the unbeatable action never ends. Several leading fencers have developed "signature moves," the 1963 world épée champion, Roland Losert, for instance, making two beats on the outside of his

---

* One of my earliest fencing memories was reaching the foil final of the public school–boys' championships. This was before electrical equipment, and to the surprise of those watching I made several hits by riposting with my right arm coming through behind my left—in effect riposting behind my back. I can still remember the judges collapsing in laughter as I appeared to be scratching my left buttock with the back of my right hand. Little did the judges or I know that Mihály Fullop of Hungary had won the world title in 1957 by employing the same tactic.

The "behind the back" move, as advertised in Angelo's famous treatise on fencing.
Despite the book's success, the move was still taught as a "botte secrète."

opponent's blade, feinting to make a third, then, as his adversary disengaged, blocking the blade and hitting in the low line. The great Eduardo Mangiarotti liked to make a false attack to the inside of his opponent's arm, parry by *quarte-counterquarte*, then *flèche-riposte* underneath his opponent's wrist. His publicity postcard shows him consummating such a move. The 1976 world youth foil champion, a left-handed South Londoner, delivered ripostes from behind his right ear. And the film actor Bruce Lee, who studied fencing and boxing as well as other martial arts, synthesized what he judged the best elements into a system all his own: "Jeet Kune Do" ("the intercepting fist," his translation of fencing's "stop-hit").*

* Lee produced a seven-volume work entitled *The Tao of Jeet Kune Do*. In it he reproduced long extracts from the writings of Julio M. Castello, C.-L. de Beaumont, and especially the French master Roger Crosnier. He also borrowed extensively from works on boxing, kinetics, and philosophy, throughout replacing the words "fencer" with "fighter," "blade" with "arm," and "fencing" with "JKD" (Jeet Kune Do). The rationale of this mishmash is that, as masters often refer to one's chosen weapon as an extension of one's fencing arm, why not close the distance and use one's arm as if it were a sword? In his version of this ultimate martial art, Lee's arm supplies the stop-hit, riposte, and counterattack usually offered by a sword; wrist control and circular motions become paramount. Lee never actually participated in a fencing competition—just fought practice bouts with his wife. He nicely commented on his system: "If someone comes at you with a sword, run if you can. Kung Fu doesn't always work."[6]

The nineteenth-century French philologist Emile Littré considered a *botte secrète* as no more than "an attack that one's adversary does not know how to parry." By the eighteenth century most masters knew that the philosopher's stone was also a chimera and instead concentrated on creating as complete a system as they could so that each of their pupils could select the appropriate sequence of feints and thrusts to defeat a particular opponent.

But perfect thrusts and secret moves were notions too romantic to disappear completely. In 1921 Rafael Sabatini, an Italian living in Liverpool, published *Scaramouche,* with its famous first line "He was born with the gift of laughter and the sense that the world was mad." The story tracks the adventures of a young actor, André-Louis Moreau, who vows to avenge his best friend, killed by an accomplished swordsman, and sets himself to outmatch him. He applies to one Bertrand des Amis, "Maître en fait d'Armes des Académies du Roi."

Bertrand (the real name of three generations of French masters who settled in London; Sabatini is paying a private *hommage*) is a famous teacher who agrees to take André-Louis on as pupil and part-time help. He also shows him his extensive fencing library. André-Louis duly scours it and after two months of intense immersion makes a discovery:

Swordsmanship as he learnt and taught and saw it daily practised consisted of a series of attacks and parries, a series of disengages from one line into another. But always a limited series. A half-dozen disengages on either side was, strictly speaking, usually as far as any engagement went. Then one recommenced. But even so, these disengages were fortuitous. What if from first to last they should be calculated?

He sets about testing his theory against an opponent at the salle and is delighted at its success: "In a burst of mingled generosity and intoxication, André-Louis was almost for disclosing his method—a method which a little later was to become a commonplace of the fencing-rooms. Betimes he checked himself. To reveal his secret would be to destroy the prestige that must accrue to him from exercising it." Instead, he goes back to honing his new skills, until at last he is ready to take on his teacher.

The master set himself to exert all his skill against his assistant. But today it availed him nothing before André-Louis's imperious attacks. After the third hit, M. des Amis stepped back and pulled off his mask. "What's this?" he asked. He was pale, and his dark brows were contracted in a frown. Not for years had he been so wounded in his self-love. "Have you been taught a secret botte?"

He had always boasted that he knew too much about the sword to believe any nonsense about secret bottes; but this performance of André-Louis' had shaken his convictions on that score.[7]

One can almost picture Sabatini, over several nights' enthusiastic argument at Félix Bertrand's salle, going over his ideas for how his hero would overcome the murderer. We shall see the outcome of André-Louis's secret moves in Chapter 13, but for Sabatini the perfect thrust was the ability to think well ahead of one's opponent: perfect because secret—or at least hidden from the one person who matters, the adversary.

IN 1999, JUST AS THE FILM OF LE BOSSU CAME OUT, ANOTHER FILM appeared with the same theme: The Fencing Master, adapted from the novel by the Spanish author Arturo Pérez-Reverte.[8] Once more, a master possesses a perfect thrust and must use it to conquer his enemies.

However, The Fencing Master is far more ambitious and explores the notion of whether it is possible to create a fencing system that deals with every eventuality. It is set in 1868, a time of revolution in Madrid, where Don Jaime Astarloa, aged fifty-six, maintains his salle. He is a traditionalist, a private man who avoids politics and who has lived alone ever since a failed love affair of his youth. His social life is restricted to the local coffeehouse, where he idly listens to his friends discuss whether Queen Isabella II will be overthrown.

Besides his work as a master he is trying to complete his life's ambition, a massive "Treatise on the Art of Fencing." Don Jaime reflects:

> Lately . . . he had begun to have serious doubts about his ability to set down on paper the discipline to which he had dedicated his whole life. There was another factor, too, which only added to his unease. If the work was to be the *ne plus ultra* on the subject he hoped it would be, it was essential that it deliver a master stroke, the perfect unstoppable thrust, the purest creation of human talent, a model of inspiration and efficacy.

Thus the two ideas are yoked together: the perfect system *must* include a masterstroke. Don Jaime's ruminations are disrupted by an unexpected visitor. A strikingly beautiful young woman, Adela de Otero, appeals to him to teach her; more, she will pay a large sum if he will submit to yet a further request:

> "I have made all the necessary inquiries," she said calmly, "and I was told you were the best fencing master in Madrid. The last of the old school, they say. I was also told that you are the inventor of a famous, secret thrust, which you are willing to teach to interested pupils. . . . I wish to hire your services."

At first the master refuses—he has never taught a woman—but he is smitten by her beauty, and when she picks up a foil from his salle they engage in an impromptu lesson. She is an excellent fencer; intrigued, he agrees to take her on. But her priorities are clear:

" 'They say that this secret thrust of yours is impossible to parry.' Don Jaime gave a modest smile. 'They exaggerate, madam. Once you know it, parrying it is the simplest thing in the world. I have yet to discover the unstoppable thrust.' " Nevertheless she perseveres, and he teaches her the secret move. She quickly masters it, right down to the final action—a fatal thrust to the base of the throat.

At their next lesson she asks about another of his pupils, the former government minister and well-known roué Luis de Ayala. He agrees to introduce them, then has to watch as they become first casual fencing partners, then lovers. One day Don Jaime walks to Don Luis's house for their weekly lesson, only to discover that his pupil has been murdered the previous night—by a sword thrust at the base of his throat. And Adela de Otero has disappeared.

It would be unfair to reveal more of the plot, but by the book's end Don Jaime's main adversary lies dead at his feet in his fencing room, and as the first rays of the morning sun filter through the cracks in the closed shutters, the old master is standing before the same large looking glass. Absorbed in himself, he is "trying to remember, fixing in his mind—uninterested in anything else that the universe might contain around him—all the phases which, linked with absolute precision, with mathematical certainty, would lead—he was sure of this now—to the most perfect thrust ever conceived by the human mind."

This is Pérez-Reverte's first suspense story, though the third to be published in English. Full of references to his literary heroes, Joseph Conrad and Robert Louis Stevenson, Arthur Conan Doyle and Alexandre Dumas, it is a haunting tale; and the film, which follows it closely, won several prizes, with Pérez-Reverte being hailed as "a cross between Umberto Eco and Anne Rice," the successor to Jorge Luis Borges, the successor to Stephen King.

Although *The Fencing Master* is part novel of suspense, part classic detective story, Pérez-Reverte is plainly fascinated by the idea of systems. The perfect thrust requires the ideal context in which to deliver it. Is it possible to evolve a system that deals, within its own terms, with all the problems it confronts? Readers of *The Fencing Master* may regret that the demands of the novel's powerful ending deny them the chance of learning whether Don Jaime ever writes his masterwork. But Pérez-Reverte had his own *botta segreta* in store. His next novel, *The Club Dumas*, portrayed a group of antique-book collectors in present-day Spain, its plot mirroring that of *The Three Musketeers*. One of the "classic works" the bibliophiles haggle over is the "great nineteenth-century study of swordplay by Astarloa"—so the old man *did* get to write his "great work" after all, only one has to read a totally separate novel to find this out.

Of the "perfect thrust" itself, Pérez-Reverte says that he had concealed certain elements so that it could not be followed by would-be assassins; but in truth, whatever the author's own experiences, the fencing moves in the story, though persuasive enough for fictional purposes, make little sense as actual swordplay.

As early as 1686 the great Liancour published *Le Maistre d'armes*, in which he "roundly exposed the vulgar notion (apparently not yet extinct) that there are infallible secret thrusts taught by particular masters."[9] But the perfect thrust *does* exist. In the words of the twentieth-century master Julio M. Castello, "The straight thrust and disengage with the foil, and the simple cutting attack with the sabre, *if done properly within distance*, cannot be parried. The reason is one of simple mathematics."[10]

For Pérez-Reverte, however, that was too simple, and he was yet not done with the matter. His third novel, *The Flanders Panel*, concerns a medieval puzzle painting in which two men are playing chess, while a beautiful woman, wife of one man and mistress of the other, looks on. Its legal owner, *le vieux* Belmonte, is listening to another character discuss chess, but the parallel with fencing is obvious:

"The truth is like the perfect move in chess: it exists, but you have to look for it. Given enough time, it's always demonstrable."

Hearing that, Belmonte smiled mischievously. "I would say, rather, that the perfect move you talk about, whether you call it that or whether you call it the truth, may exist. But it can't always be demonstrated. And that any system that tries to do so is limited and relative . . . there is no one system, there are no universal axioms. Systems are disparate even within themselves."[11]

This theme is followed through in the author's next work, *The Seville Communion*. Pérez-Reverte is almost playful with his fencing interest—the surname of the detective priest is "Quart," another character is named "Octavio," a third "Fr. Ferro" ("Iron"). But beyond the demands of the story, the center of interest is elsewhere: can the doctrines of the Catholic Church be regarded as a workable system by which to navigate one's way on earth?

Navigation—a matter of life or death for travelers throughout history. Pérez-Reverte's fifth novel, *The Nautical Chart*, centers on the world of maps, particularly a sixteenth-century one made by Jesuits about to be exiled from Spain for subversion. For sailors at sea, the need for reliable charts is a matter of life and death, for if their navigation fails they can lay themselves open to attack, die of thirst, or end up on the rocks. In a key passage Pérez-Reverte writes:

> Errors. At sea, as in fencing . . . everything turned on keeping your adversary at a distance and anticipating his moves. The black cloud forming flat and low in the distance, the slightly dark area of rippled water, the almost imperceptible foam breaking on the surface of the water, augured deadly thrusts that only constant vigil could parry. That made the sea the perfect simile of life.[12]

This provokes the question of whether swordplay is not also the perfect simile for life. No Western master in fiction or in fact has attempted an answer; for that we have to go to one of fencing's earliest critics.

It was Roger Ascham who, in the reign of Henry VIII, so lamented swordplay's triumphant supplanting of the longbow in the affections of the English people. A somewhat pedantic, time-serving academic at St. John's College, Cambridge, he published only two of his writings in his lifetime, a travel book about Germany and *Toxophilus*, a dialogue about the longbow, which appeared in 1545, the year pistols were first used by English horsemen.

On the strength of this one book Ascham has been praised as "one of the fathers of English prose," a writer who "has a claim on all English-reading people."[13] Samuel Johnson wrote a biography of him, and his name is still honored by archers worldwide. His book, however, is not so much a treatise on archery as one on learning any skill or body of knowledge.

Ascham imagines a conversation between Toxophilus ("lover of the bow") and his friend the rhetorician Philologus ("lover of reason"), Toxophilus declaring that the end of archery is to hit the mark—excellence is the bowman's objective. His companion disagrees, saying that there is a perfect end, unattainable perhaps, for which all aspirants must strive. Excellence is not enough—an argument in a direct line from Plato's *Phaedrus*.[14]

It is likely that archery appealed to a man of Ascham's interests partly because it provided a practical subject on which greater issues could be aligned: as Toxophilus puts it, "hytting of the marke, the ende both of shootyng and also of thys our communication." Ascham cites Aristotle's analogy between shooting and virtue, that both can be directed toward an ideal end. Once the perfect shot is set into motion, hitting the mark offers a sublime beauty. Toxophilus has it that an act may be improved by envisioning its perfect execution. The ideal archer possesses what every man must seek for: self-knowledge; thus Philologus's thirst for the perfect knowledge of his sport rather than excellence in the skill to perform it. Ascham was not writing about swordplay, but easily might have been.

CHAPTER 7

Where the Sword Is the Soul

The sword was to be far more than a simple weapon;
it had to be an answer to life's questions.

—EIJI YOSHIKAWA, *Musashi*

The Way of the Sword and the Way of Zen are identical,
for they have the same purpose—that of killing the ego.

—YAMADA JIROKICHI

W E ARE ENTERING ANOTHER WORLD, WHERE THE SWORD IS AN
instrument not just of self-protection but of intrinsic self-perfection. In
Japan, swordfighting has always been a spiritual endeavor. In the Shinto
religion, the sword is central to rituals of purification and exorcism. The
nineteenth-century master Yamaoaka Tesshu spoke of the sword of the
mind, with which, fortified by all he has learned, the fencer is spiritually
invulnerable in combat, able to rise above the concerns of life or death.
This approach is one taken by students of Zen—as an ancient Japanese
saying has it, "Nothing can set honor so right as the cut of a sword."

The basic word for sword in Japanese is *"ken,"* though a bewildering
array of terms can be found to describe this most sacred talisman.* The
earliest known Japanese swords date from the second century B.C.; anywhere from two to four feet in length, they were copies of Chinese origi-
nals, long and straight and used mainly for thrusting. At the beginning of
the eighth century A.D., a more effective model, with a pronounced curve,
appeared and quickly became the monopoly of the professional fighting
man. The refinement of the sword went hand in hand with the rise of the

---

* These include *katana, tachi, ko-bizen, kabatsuchi, no tachi, ka radachi, shinai, kyo-mono,*
kunihiro, kozuka (a side knife), *koshigatana, mamori-gatana, mino-mono, arami meizu-*
kushi, tsurugi, daisho, bokuto, soshu-mono, metezashi, tosu (a knife), *tanto* (a short sword),
wakizashi (a side sword), *tsubokiri no tsurugi, aikuchi* (a dagger), *osatune kaji, chokuto,*
agari-tachi, umabari, nodachi (a field sword), and *mikusa no kan-dakara.*

warrior class, the samurai or *bushi* (literally, "the martial elite," as distinct from conscripts, court officials, or palace guards). From 1185 on Japan was dominated by warriors, and the principal history of swordplay in Japan properly dates from that period.

In 1274 and again in 1281 the Mongol rulers of China attempted to invade the country, precipitating a revolution in Japanese military thinking. Prior to that time a battle had resembled a huge fencing match, with men fighting as individuals, not as units of a tactical formation, each soldier searching out an opponent of his social level with whom to fight, then at battle's end proceeding to his commander in chief's tent to submit for inspection the heads of those he had killed. In the fourteenth century mounted archers were replaced by foot soldiers who carried short swords, and the art of swordfighting (*iai-jutsu*) and other martial arts became essential.

It was the era of the shoguns (literally, "barbarian-subduing generalissimos" but the term later came to mean "the hereditary chancellors of state"), under whose reign society became set into five classes: the nobility, samurai, farmers, artisans, and merchants. Originally the samurai were drawn from the countryside, individual warriors who fought entirely in their own interest. By the eleventh century, they had emerged as a distinct group who pledged their allegiance to clans ruled by local feudal lords, often no more than quasi bandit chieftains. The word *"samurai"* means "retainer" and comes from the verb *"saburau,"* "to serve," and loyal servants they by necessity became. However, as their chiefs became more polished princelings, ever greedier for territory, the samurai developed into a professional military class. The private wars between warlords endured for more than four centuries, during which time the samurai evolved into fearsome warriors.

The essence of a samurai's worth lay in his mastery of swordsmanship. The sword was not just a weapon but a vehicle for *seishin tanren,* a spiritual forging that enabled the user to wipe out moral stains and to achieve *satori,* spiritual perfection. The sword, along with the symbolic mirror and jewel, played a key role in Japanese imperial life, each of the three being handed down from ruler to ruler as tokens of their supreme authority. The mirror was to catch things as they were, good or evil, and symbolized the true force of fairness and justice; the jewel represented gentleness and piety; the sword, "firm, sharp, and quickly decisive," was seen as the receptacle of "the true origins of all wisdom."[1]

IN 1573 THE WARLORD ODA NOBUNAGA BECAME SHOGUN OF ALMOST all Japan. Upon his assassination a decade later, one of his leading officers, Toyotomi Hideyoshi ("Old Monkey Face"), took his place, and, determined to consolidate his control throughout the empire, sought to eliminate all private arms. On July 8, 1588, he issued his famous "sword hunt" edict: farmers were forbidden "to keep swords, short swords, spears, firearms and other military weapons." Were they allowed to keep such "unnecessary implements," the document continued, they would be tempted to "evade their taxes" or even "plot uprisings." Political spin was then applied: "The swords thus collected will not be wasted. They will be used as nails and bolts in the construction of a Great Image of Buddha."

Within two years the entire peasantry had been disarmed (although no great statue of Buddha was raised). The measures helped support the new barrier between farmer and warrior, so that the two most important social groups of society were differentiated not only economically but also by social status, as symbolized by the wearing of swords.[2]

Hideyoshi died in 1598, and for two years Japan was torn apart by civil war. Then on October 21, 1600, on a broad plain east of Kyoto, one of the greatest clan leaders, Tokugawa Ieyasu, and his allies, some 85,000 men, took on the massed might of their enemies, the armies of the west, numbering about 130,000. By day's end Ieyasu had triumphed, and he and his descendants would rule Japan for well over two hundred years, bringing peace, prosperity, and a flourishing of the arts—especially swordplay.

In 1603 Ieyasu was appointed shogun and established his government at Edo (renamed Tokyo in 1868). He publicly venerated the divine emperor in Kyoto, the remote god-sovereign of Japan, but saw to it that within his domain law, government, and education, as well as the costume and behavior of each class, were highly controlled, almost like a nationwide eastern Versailles. What had been traditional caste consciousness hardened into a form of centralized feudalism in which the samurai—including the great nobles, senior officials, warriors, and lesser functionaries—constituted the highest class, in esteem if not in wealth. After 1600 the warrior order became a closed caste.

Ieyasu gradually disbanded the great provincial armies. Out-of-work samurai, known as "ronin" ("wave men," because they washed around like the sea) roamed the country. They found themselves in a society based on the old codes of honor yet with no place for them. Ieyasu knew that he had to contend with the threat posed by these hundreds of thousands of battle-hardened men and tacitly allowed personal duels, as well as challenge matches between the various schools of martial arts that sprouted up to cater for the demand for fencing lessons. He also encouraged the *ronin's* involvement in such arts as calligraphy and poetry. These arts soon rose to the highest form of study, inspired by the teachings of Buddhism, with its stress on self-denial and overcoming the ego, and supported by Shinto-ism, with its general anthropomorphism and Nature worship.

Buddhism had been carried into China early in the seventh century by the Indian monk Bodhidharma but was transformed under the influence of that practical civilization. The Indian word for contemplative medita-tion is *"dyana"*; this became *"ch'an"* in Chinese, and "Zen" when this form of Buddhism finally crossed into Japan around 1200, originally establish-ing itself as a separate Buddhist sect before spreading rapidly among the warrior class. Hence Zen Buddhism was the result of the spiraling inter-relationship of three great civilizations, Indian, Chinese, and Japanese. In India, Buddhism became a complex and highly intellectual system of metaphysical speculation before withering away. Chinese masters were distrustful of such intellectualism and taught that the intellect too had to be transcended for true enlightenment.

The word *"shinto"* did not come into use till well after the introduction of Buddhism and was formulated in contrast to *"butsudo"* ("the Way of the Buddha"). Shintoism, which was never more than a cult, is not a religion or system of thought but an expression of national character. The real reli-gion of Japan, however, was neither the law of the Buddha (*buppo*) nor the Path of the Gods (*shinto*), but the Way of the Warrior (*bushido*).[3]

The philosophical underpinning of samurai behavior, the "Way of the Warrior," was a direct consequence of Ieyasu's triumph of 1600. There was a need for a system to discipline displaced samurai, who at least had the leisure time to elaborate it. By contrast, as one Buddhist scholar noted, "the farmers, artisans, and merchants" ought to practice the Confucian virtues, but they had "no leisure from their occupations, and so they can-not constantly act in accordance with them and fully exemplify the Way."[4]

Kendo ("the Way of the Sword") flourished, and fencing schools, known as *ryu*, multiplied; soon there were several hundred spread throughout the country, each contributing to the cult of sacrifice and austerity as much as to the honing of skills. *Kendo* was a discipline and a continuous testing, and no Japanese would have seen it as a "sport," an alien and even frivolous concept, but the increasing emphasis on competition and the evolution of the role of masters point to how far battlefield skills were being sublimated.

One of the greatest historians of Japan, Charles Boxer, was also a keen student of *kendo*. By his account, masters were not only drawn from the warrior caste—in the early years of Ieyasu's reign, Portuguese Jesuit missionaries observed with disgust that their counterparts, the Buddhist monks, were keen swordsmen. Worse, the Franciscan friars, whose recruiting was hampered by their speaking little Japanese and who found themselves unable to hear confessions properly, were teaching "such unedifying subjects as fencing (Japanese style presumably) in order to attract potential converts to their Kyoto convent."[5]

Whereas a Westerner might say "The pen is mightier than the sword," a Japanese would reply, "*Bun bu chi*"—"pen and sword in accord." In Japanese culture, once something had been accepted as a serious activity it was developed into *michi* or *do*—a Way. This was true for such diverse undertakings as *cha-do* (the art of the tea ceremony), *kyudo* (archery), and *ikebana* (flower arrangement).

The Way of the Sword was a controlling force of life. At the age of five a samurai boy would be dressed in traditional costume, put onto a *go* board (361 squares representing a battlefield) and have a sword thrust into his belt. Thus was he initiated as a warrior. He would later be given a long sword (a *katana* or *uchigatana*), which he would wear out of doors, and a shorter one (a *wakizashi* or *shoto*), which he would carry at all times. Together they formed his essential apparel, known as "great and small" (*daisho*), to be kept next to his pillow at night. This custom of wearing two swords was peculiar to Japan. The short sword was not used in actual fighting but would be employed for cutting off an enemy's head after defeating him and also served the conquered soldier in his last resort, suicide.

The rules of conduct for a samurai varied, each feudal chief prescribing his own code, but there was a degree of uniformity. One not untypical set of regulations, formulated in the sixteenth century by the celebrated general, Kato Kiyomasa, had seven main clauses:

The following regulations are to be observed by samurai of every rank, the highest and the lowest alike:

1. The routine of service must be strictly observed. From 6 A.M. military exercises shall be practiced. Archery, gunnery and equestrianism must not be neglected. If any man shows greater

proficiency than his comrades in the way of the *bushi,* he shall receive greater pay.

2. Those who desire recreation may engage in hawking, deer-hunting or wrestling.

3. With regard to dress, garments of cotton or pongee [a soft unbleached kind of Chinese silk] shall be worn. Anyone incurring debts owing to extravagance of costume or living shall be considered a law-breaker. If, however, being zealous in the practice of military arts suitable to his rank, a man desires to hire instructors, an allowance for that purpose may be granted to him.

4. The staple of diet shall be unhulled rice. At social entertainments, one guest for one host is the proper limit. Only when men are assembled for military exercises should many dine together.

5. It is the duty of every samurai to make himself acquainted with the principles of his craft. Extravagant displays of adornment are forbidden in battle.

6. Dancing or organizing dances is unlawful and is likely to betray sword-carrying men to acts of violence. Whatever a man does should be done with his heart. Therefore for the soldier military amusements alone are suitable. The penalty for violating this provision is death by suicide.

7. Learning should be encouraged. Military books must be read. The spirit of loyalty and filial piety must be educated before all things. Poem-composing pastimes are not to be engaged in by samurai. To be addicted to such amusements is to resemble a woman. A man born a samurai should live and die sword in hand. Unless he be thus trained in time of peace, he will be useless in the hour of stress. To be brave and warlike must be his invariable condition.

Whoever finds these rules too severe shall be relieved from service. Should investigation show that anyone is so unfortunate as to lack manly qualities, he shall be singled out and dismissed forthwith. The imperative character of these instructions must not be doubted.[6]

From the earliest times the samurai code called for a peculiarly intense and self-conscious sense of personal pride and "face," often manifested in swaggering and bullying behavior. This could lead to irrational and self-defeating acts. At the end of the eleventh century, during what was called, prosaically, the Later Three Years' War, a young warrior, one Kagemasa, barely sixteen, was struck by an arrow in the left eye. With the shaft still protruding from his face, he managed to close in on and kill his adversary before falling. A colleague tried to help him by putting his foot against Kagemasa's cheek to pull out the arrow. Kagemasa indignantly cried out that while as a samurai he was willing to die from his wound he would never allow another man to put his foot on his face and jumping up tried to kill his comrade.[7]

As a rule, a sword would be grasped with both hands, the point upward and the hilt held at three quarters of an arm's length from the body. Cuts were almost entirely downward or horizontal, and a stroke's effectiveness depended mainly on a swift drawing motion given to the blade as it began to bite. There were sixteen varieties of cut, each with its own name, such as the "four-sides cut," the "clearer," the "wheel stroke," the "thunder stroke," the "peak blow," the "torso severer," the "pear splitter," the "scarf sweep," and so on.*

It was not merely the method of handling one's weapon that had to be studied. Associated with swordplay was an art variously called *shinobi*, *yawara*, and *jiu-jutsu*, whose aim was to gain the maximum effect from a minimum of effort by directing an enemy's strength against himself. Originally, expertise in swordplay was gained through experience: mastery was self-taught. However, as better swords were crafted and schools were set up, a body of fencing technique evolved. *Kenjutsu*, the art of the sword, came to be seen as a discipline of great power.

When a student had mastered one style of swordplay, he set himself to study others. An especially talented student would tour the country, fencing whenever he encountered an expert and in the event of defeat becoming the victor's pupil. Defeat was to be taken as evidence of his own inferiority, not as something to be resented or avenged; but this rule was frequently more honored in the breach than it was observed. Defeat could mean ruin: a master with a flourishing school and a healthy income might find both threatened by losing to an itinerant samurai.

Duels took place in fencing halls (*dojo*, which also meant sites devoted to religious exercises, or places of enlightenment), before shrines, in the

---

* Chinese swordplay has an even more imaginative range of names for its movements. Among them are: Tiger Crouches at the Front Door; Boatman Rows a Skull; Paint a Red Dot Between the Eyebrows; Brush Dust in the Breeze; Dragonfly Skims the Water; Turn Around and Hang a Golden Bell; Pick Up Stars with an Unerring Hand; Black Dragon Stirs Its Tail; Wasp Flies Through a Hole; Capture a Legendary Turtle in the Ocean Depths; White Snake Flicks Its Tongue; and Hold the Moon in Your Arms.

streets, and within castle walls, and were often fought to the death or at least disablement. Contrary to some reports, duels flourished almost as much as in Western Europe; they simply took different forms. They were generally one-on-one, and there was no precedent in judicial duel or trial

A nineteenth-century samurai, wearing both long and short swords.

by combat. Nor was the concept of individual honor as dominant as in the West; samurai identified instead with a clan leader and lived by a group ethic. Duels were fought not to avenge slights or slander but to prove one's supremacy as a warrior. "There were no seconds," Robert Baldick asserts, "for it was regarded as inconceivable that a knight might commit any action contrary to honor while engaging in a duel of honor."[8] That might have been the popular conception, but rules were often violated. Even after weapons, time, and place had been set, the parties might proceed as if no agreement had been reached; to do otherwise would in many instances have been to invite defeat. Duelists would employ any assortment of underhand tricks, and a swordsman might well arrive with a band of followers who would attack and cut down his opponent.

To reduce casualties and make practice duels possible, a new weapon was developed: the *shinai*, wrought from pliable bamboo slats covered with leather, which was used in conjunction with defensive armor. There was also the *bokken*, carved from solid wood, which some fencers contended was superior to steel. The stories of masters armed with nothing but *bokken* defeating opponents with the best steel swords are legion. The true *bushi* was expected to be superior to all contingencies and to be prepared for every emergency, if necessary seizing on a piece of firewood, a brazier iron, an umbrella, or a pot lid.*

The most renowned encounter involving a wooden sword is that of Miyamoto Musashi and Sasaki Kojiro, two celebrated warriors who in 1612 fought to the death on a small sandbar between the two main islands of southern Japan. This duel, more than any other, has attained mythic standing, inspiring a long succession of poems, books, and films.

Shinmen Musashi no Kami Fujiwara no Genshin was born in 1584, his mother dying in childbirth. When he was seven his father died too, and he adopted his mother's clan name, becoming known as Miyamoto Musashi. He was then put in the care of an uncle, a priest. At thirteen, he killed an experienced swordsman in single combat. Three years later, he defeated a full samurai. At that point he left home and embarked on a "warrior pilgrimage," traveling the country in search of further samurai against whom he could do battle, often meeting them in a clearing on the outskirts of a town, in the garden of a nobleman's mansion, in the precinct of a shrine, or along a wide riverbank. Musashi was by now devoting himself to the Way of the Sword, and such were his skills that he quickly became a legend. Although effectively accepted as a samurai, he was a particularly eccentric one: he ate whatever was at hand, neglected his appearance, and usually employed a *bokken* rather than a steel weapon. There were few solitary warriors traveling on foot; none had survived so many duels. Musashi was still only twenty-eight when he came to keep his appointment with Kojiro.[10]

---

* During the sixteenth century these training swords took on another role, being used by deserted wives who wished to avenge themselves on their successors. Depending on their social position, three, five, or more women would assemble on each side, headed respectively by the aggrieved lady and her successful rival, all carrying bamboo swords. No man could be admitted, except an elderly servant on each side, who transmitted the challenge and the acceptance. As one nineteenth-century traveler commented, "This contest was as interesting and harmless as it was emphatic and noisy; it relieved the pent-up hatred on the one side, and gave, perhaps, the *coup de grâce* to the honeymoon on the other."[9]

Sasaki Kojiro came from Echizen province, in the southeast. He was adopted by the head of the leading fencing school there, the Tomita, and after mastering the Tomita techniques won many duels. He soon came to create his own style of swordplay, the *Ganryu*, and was known as a merciless opponent. "His eyes shot fire," wrote one commentator. "A bloodthirsty flame burned in his pupils, like rainbows of fierce intensity, seeking to terrify and debilitate. . . . Not even Kojiro was able to grasp why the primitive urge to conquer buffeted his brain with such persistence."[11] His skill was considered almost superhuman, and he was specially celebrated for his expertise at *tsubame-gaeshi* (the "swallow counter"), an up-and-down slashing motion so swift it resembled the whirling flight of a swallow. He was the leading fighter for the local warlord, Hosokawa Tadatoshi, and was a long-standing enemy and rival of Musashi.

The duel was arranged for the "hour of the dragon"—eight o'clock—the next morning. Musashi left his lodging that night and stayed with a friend, arousing speculation that he had fled before Kojiro's mastery. The next day Kojiro was ferried out to the sandbar at the agreed time and waited in the chill. Minutes passed, then hours, and there was still no sign of Musashi. That wayward fighter, it turned out, had simply overslept; eventually he had to be woken by the innkeeper and barely had time to drink the water brought for him to wash in before he was hustled down to the shore and rowed out to the sandbar. As the boat rocked in the swells of the Kammon Strait, he dozed in the prow. At last he managed to rouse himself and fashioned two paper strings to tie back the wide sleeves of his kimono. He then took out his knife, whittled the spare oar into a crude *bokken*—and went back to sleep.

As Musashi's boat approached the sandbar, Kojiro and his waiting attendants were astounded to see that the young warrior's topknot was tied up in a towel. Brandishing his hacked-about oar, Musashi jumped out and splashed ashore. Kojiro chided him for being so late and mocked his makeshift weapon, then drew his own long blade and threw the scabbard out to sea—to prove his intent to conquer or die.

"You can't have much confidence, throwing away a good scabbard like that as if you'll never need it again," observed Musashi. He then pointed his oar at Kojiro's throat in signal that the duel had begun. The men closed on each other, each acutely aware that a single error could be fatal. There was no sound other than the lapping of the waves and the occasional caw of a bird. Suddenly Kojiro struck at Musashi, using his signature swallow stroke. At exactly the same moment Musashi leaped forward and with a great guttural cry swept his oar down with all his force. For several seconds no one could make out what had taken place. Then a gust of wind carried away the ribbon around Musashi's forehead, and the shaken onlookers saw that it had been cut sheer by Kojiro's sword. They swung toward Kojiro and only then realized that Musashi had so timed his attack to allow himself to come within a thin cloth's breadth of the opposing blade, so close that it had shorn the ribbon from his head. Yet it was the improvised *bokken* that had delivered the fatal blow. Kojiro was slowly sinking to the ground, his head crushed. Without a word, Musashi bowed to the onlookers and splashed back to his boat.

In 1971 there appeared a fictional rendering of Musashi's life, which went on to become the most popular novel ever written by a Japanese: *Musashi*, by Eiji Yoshikawa. It ends with this fight. "The sight of his own headband lying on the ground sent shivers up and down Musashi's spine," runs the last of its 970 pages.

Never in his life, he thought, would he meet another opponent like this. A wave of admiration and respect flowed over him. He was grateful to Kojiro for what the man had given him. In strength, in the will to fight, he ranked higher than Musashi, and it was because of this that Musashi had been able to excel himself.

What was it that had enabled Musashi to defeat Kojiro? Skill? The help of the gods? While knowing that it was neither of these, Musashi was never able to express a reason in words. Certainly there was something more important than either strength or godly deliverance. Kojiro had put his confidence in the sword of strength and skill. Musashi had trusted in the sword of the spirit. That was the only difference between them.[12]

In fact, Musashi's whole approach had been carefully calculated. The towering Kojiro had an especially long sword, known as "the Old Clothes Pole." Musashi realized that his own weapon would have to be as long as possible but that he would have an advantage if he could improvise such a weapon at the last possible moment, as Kojiro was a supreme judge of length where actual swords were concerned. An oar, far from being a makeshift choice, was an ideal instrument for his purpose.

Legend has it that Musashi stopped using steel swords in duels altogether after this encounter. By the time he gave up dueling, in his early thirties, he was credited with more than sixty victories, while between 1614 and 1638 he also fought six times as a soldier both in the field and in sieges.* In 1637 and 1638 he took part in the annihilation of the Christian peasantry of Shimabara in the western island of Kyushu, an event that marked the public extinction of Christianity from Japan for the next two centuries. According to his own writings, Musashi came fully to understand strategy only in his fifty-first year and by sixty had retired to a life of seclusion in a cave. It was here that he completed *Go Rin No Sho* (*The Book of Five Rings*), his book of strategy, addressed to one of his pupils, a few weeks before his death in 1645.

Musashi is the iconic swordsman-philosopher, known to his countrymen as "Kensei"—"the Holy Man of the Sword." Both in his writings and in his life he personified what a samurai should be. He became an exceptional artist, creating masterpieces of ink painting—which requires fine judgment, it being impossible to make corrections or revisions—a truly Zen form of art. Musashi was also a fine calligrapher, sculptor, and metalworker and founded a school of sword-guard-makers. He is said to have written poems and songs, though none survives. His most recent translator claims that *The Book of Five Rings* heads every *kendo* bibliography; it also flourishes as a business primer, seen as a guide not just to the principles of swordplay but to competition generally.

The great directors Kenji Mizoguchi, Akira Kurosawa, and Hiroshi Inagaki have all portrayed Musashi: Mizoguchi in *The Swordsman* (1944); Kurosawa, using the celebrated actor Toshiro Mifune, in *Yojimbo* (1961); and Inagaki in an award-winning trilogy. In the second film of that trilogy, *Duel at Ichijoji Temple* (1964), an old man watches a young, inexperienced Musashi overcome an opponent. "Of course you won the duel, but you lost as a samurai," he says. "You're really strong, but you're not mentally relaxed. That means you may win a match, but you're not yet a true samurai. You'll always remain just a tough guy." With this he wanders away.

---

* To give some context to such figures, the greatest body count credited to any one man was to George Kastrioti (1403–68), Prince of Epirus and Albania and commonly known as Iskander Bey, "the Dragon of Albania," or simply as Skanderbeg. He is said to have slain three thousand Turks with his own hand during a guerrilla campaign that lasted twenty-five years. Among the stories told about him was that he never slept for more than five hours a night and could cut two men asunder with a single stroke of his scimitar, cut through iron helmets, kill a wild boar with a single stroke, and cleave the head off a buffalo with another.

Musashi hurries after him and begs him to explain. "All I can tell you is this," says the old man at last. "Swordsmanship means chivalry. Remember, a man cannot remain forever physically strong. You're too strong. Decidedly too strong. You lack affection." Then he walks off for good, leaving Musashi still in search of the Way.

So what was this "Way"? It involved subjugating the self, enduring the pain of grueling practice, and cultivating a serenity of mind even when confronted by the knowledge of death. *Nirvana* ("blowing out," as of a candle) required that each student loose himself from earthly things and submit himself to the samurai code—a fusion of Confucian philosophy, Shintoism, and the austerities of Zen.[13] ("*Bushido*" means both "the Way of the Warrior" and "the determined will to die.")

All this passed directly into fencing strategy. It is not by chance that the word "*osho*" ("master") signifies both fencing teacher and Buddhist priest. The Itto Rye school of *kendo* taught that you should aim to strike an opponent at the very moment he strikes at you. This demonstrates a subjugation of overmastering emotions, that you are treating your enemy with appropriate respect: he must be allowed to come upon you with all his force—which is why Musashi's fight with Kojiro was so exemplary.

The Book of Five Rings divides into the five "great" essences of Buddhism: ground, water, fire, wind, and void. "By void," explains Musashi, "I mean that which has no beginning and no end. Attaining this principle means not attaining the principle. The Way of strategy is the Way of nature. When you appreciate the power of nature, knowing the rhythm of any situation, you will be able to hit the enemy naturally and strike naturally. All this is the Way of the void."[14]

Samurai scholars undertook works of history, statecraft, and political economy and produced significant volumes of theory on the martial arts and on the ideal behavior and social functions of the warrior. From this time on, the sword came to be looked on as "the mind" of the warrior.*

Much of this doctrine had an application in Chinese swordplay. The film *Crouching Tiger, Hidden Dragon* includes a fight between a masked intruder and Li Mu Bai, the renowned swordmaster. "Do you think you have a real command of the sword?" demands the figure. "Like most

---

* In his far-reaching study of fencing in Japan, G. Cameron Hurst cites what may be the primary source "for this commonly quoted Western aphorism about the sword"—that it is synonymous with a warrior's soul: an early-seventeenth-century work, *Tokugawa nariaki hyakkajo*, whose thirty-sixth article reads, "the sword is the soul of the bushi; those who lose theirs shall not be forgiven."[15]

things, I am nothing," replies Li. "It is the same for this sword. All is a simple state of mind." As they fight, he continues, "No growth without assistance. No action without reaction. No desire without restraint. Now give yourself up and find yourself again. There is a lesson for you."

Such an interchange might easily appear in a Japanese classic, but the differences between the cultures were profound. In China, the warrior was despised as a hired killer; aristocrats and commoners alike could bear swords, so there was less of a mythology about swords and their power; and obligation to family was seen as the first duty, whereas in Japan that duty was loyalty to public entities. These differences combined to produce very different histories.

To a Western mind, the teachings of Japanese swordmasters can be either deeply attractive or puzzlingly vague, but on a practical level it is easy to appreciate the samurai goal of achieving a spiritual balance to sustain oneself in battle. To fight without fearing death or defeat, being able to meet an opponent without rancor, overcoming ego, and having a profound sense of calm when under the highest conceivable pressure are remarkable assets, whatever the contest. However, even the noblest principles can become diseased. A seventeenth-century teacher, Yagyu Tajima no Kami, listed six temptations to which swordsmen are prey: (1) the conscious desire for victory, (2) the desire to resort to technical cunning, (3) the desire to display one's skills, (4) the desire to overawe the enemy, (5) the desire to play a passive role, and (6) the desire to rid oneself of any of the above.

For a samurai, mere technique was not enough to make him a master of his art; he had to immerse himself in its existential aspects, which could be attained only when he achieved a state of mind known as "*mushin*," "no mind," or "*munen*," "no thought."[16] If this were attained, the samurai was said to have *shin*, or spirit, so that his skills would flow through his body independent of his mind.

The secret documents of one of the main fencing schools of the period, the Shinkage-ryu, contain a number of *waka*, or versified epigrams based on thirty-one syllables, on the mastery of swordsmanship, part of which runs:

Some think that striking is to strike:
But striking is not to strike, nor is killing to kill.
He who strikes and he who is struck—
They are both no more than a dream that has no reality.

No thinking, no reflecting—
Perfect emptiness . . .
Victory is for the one,
Even before the combat
Who has no thought of himself,
Abiding in the no-mind-ness of Great Origin.

Here there are obvious affinities with—and significant differences from—the poetry of the Christian mystics. Roger Ascham too is not so far away.

Such precepts could be dangerous when taken to extremes. In the early years of the seventeenth century, at the height of samurai ascendancy, Japan chose to cut herself off from the rest of the world for more than two hundred years. The isolation that followed intensified the inward-looking approach of much warrior life. In the mid–seventeenth century a document known as the *Hagakure*—literally, "Hidden under the Leaves"—emphasized the samurai's readiness to give his life at any moment and declared that no great work had ever been accomplished "without going mad"—without breaking through the ordinary level of consciousness and letting loose the hidden powers lying below.[17] During the 1930s the *Hagakure* was much talked about in connection with Japanese military operations in China. "The samurai is good for nothing unless he can go beyond life and death," runs one of its sections.

One should expect death daily, so that, when the time comes, one can die in peace. Calamity, when it occurs, is not so dreadful as was feared. It is foolish to torment oneself beforehand with vain imaginings. . . . Tranquilize your mind every morning, and imagine the moment when you may be torn and mangled by arrows, guns, lances, and swords, swept away by great waves, thrown into a fire, struck down by thunderbolts, shaken by earthquakes, falling from a precipice, dying of disease, or dead from an unexpected accident: die every morning in your mind, and then you will not fear death. Once that has been achieved—when one attains a mind of "no-mind-ness"—then one can execute extraordinary deeds. . . . In *Bushido* honor comes first. Therefore, every morning and every evening, have the idea of death vividly impressed in your mind.[18]

As the great authority Daisetz Suzuki comments, "Zen's claim to handle this problem [of mastering death] without appealing either to learning or to moral training or to ritualism must have been a great attraction to the comparatively unsophisticated mind of the samurai. There was a kind of logical relationship between his psychological outlook and the direct practical teaching of Zen."[19] In this respect, Zen was the perfect religion for the samurai.

Such thinking, however, is only a short step from predatory militarism or political nihilism. This is shown in the life of one of Japan's greatest writers, Yukio Mishima, three times nominated for the Nobel Prize. Born in Tokyo in 1925, he produced some forty works of fiction as well as a stream of poetry, plays, and essays, many of which bore witness to his passion for the chivalrous traditions of imperial Japan. Throughout his life Mishima was fascinated with swords and became expert in both karate and *kendo*. In 1968 he founded the Shield Society, a group of a hundred young men dedicated to reviving *bushido*. Mishima would order his homosexual disciples to cover his body with sword cuts. In his novel *Runaway Horses* (1969), he has a student of *kendo* declare, "I lost interest in wooden swords. They have no real power." "So you think you're ready for steel?" his teacher asks. The student declares that he has to be.[20]

It was a feature of the samurai code that under certain circumstances the samurai was expected to kill himself. One especially gruesome method, practised in remote times, was submitting to be buried alive in order to join one's clan leader in death. Over the years the preferred form came to be *seppuku* ("disembowelment") or to use its more vulgar but more popular reading, *hara-kiri* ("belly slitting"). Disembowelment was performed on a number of occasions in the late twelfth century, and there are isolated examples of it during fierce provincial disorders in the northeast in the latter half of the eleventh; but the generally accepted first instance of *seppuku* proper was in 1170, when the gigantic warrior Minamoto no Tametomo (he was over seven feet tall), following defeat in battle, disemboweled himself. Thereafter this form of suicide appeared frequently in Japanese war tales. It was also used as a privileged alternative to execution (Japanese executioners were of the lowest possible caste), to atone for a misdeed or an unworthy act, and to avoid capture in battle, seen as a contemptible end for any warrior and a safeguard against likely torture. Finally, it could be a form of protest against one's lord's shortcomings. One famous act of "admonitory disembowelment" occurred in the late sixteenth century, when Oda Nobunaga, later a great general, was a wild and uncontrollable young man. A loyal retainer committed suicide in remonstrance, and Oda, greatly impressed, thereafter changed his ways.

From the early 1600s, disembowelment became the usual sentence imposed upon a samurai found guilty of a capital offense. The act was normally performed by driving a knife into the left side of the abdomen, drawing it across to the right, and giving it a final upward twist toward the chest. It was sometimes considered an appropriate gesture of bravado to draw out part of the entrails and leave them hanging. Since even a deep cut did not lead to immediate death, it became the practice to engage a "second" to administer a sword blow that would end the suffering. The suicide would sit cross-legged, rip open his stomach, then extend his neck, ready for decapitation. Ideally the second did not cut entirely through but left just enough flesh and skin to hold the head to the body and prevent it from rolling away.[21] This embrace of extreme suffering was evidently related to the deep demand for self-mortification in Zen and to the belief that the samurai should display his courage by undergoing an ordeal that mere commoners could not face. Referring to the defeated rebels of 1876, Mishima wrote, "They knew that poison was the most effective way to commit a hasty suicide, but they spurned this womanish means of putting an end to life."[22]*

There was a reason why disembowelment was the chosen form. *Hara* (the abdomen), as well as being the body's physical center, was deemed the site of man's inner being, where all his cardinal qualities were concentrated. Just as in the West one feels things first "in one's guts," for the Japanese it was his stomach where the core of a man's most precious emotions lay, even his very soul.** Mishima related *seppuku* to the concept of *makoto* (sincerity):

---

* A famous story is told of two officers belonging to the emperor's staff who met on the imperial staircase. Their swords became entangled—not a minor matter, as it suggested that one did not care what happened to the other man's sword—and words arose. "It is only an accident," said one, "and at best it is only a quarrel between our two swords." "We shall see about that," said the other, drawing his weapon and plunging it into his own breast. The other hurried away on an errand but soon returned, to find his antagonist on the point of death. He immediately drew his own sword and plunged it into his body, exclaiming, "You should not have had the start of me if you had not found me engaged in the service of the prince. I die contented, however, since I have had the glory of convincing you that my sword is as good as yours."[23]

** The Japanese word for "guts" has a far wider and more dignified sense than the English. It appears in various idioms such as *haraga okii* ("large-stomached"—hence generous or magnanimous), *hara wo tateru* ("to raise one's stomach," thus to become indignant or take offense), and *hara wo kimeru* ("to fix one's stomach," meaning to be settled in one's resolution).

I cannot believe in Western sincerity because it is invisible, but in feudal times we believed that sincerity resided in our entrails, and if we needed to show our sincerity, we had to cut our bellies and take out our *visible* sincerity. And it was also the symbol of the will of the soldier, the samurai; everybody knew that this was the most painful way to die. And the reason they preferred to die in the most excruciating manner was that it proved the courage of the samurai. This method of suicide was a Japanese invention and foreigners could not copy it.[24]

Mishima wrote these words in 1966. In November 1970 he marched into the Japanese Eastern Army headquarters and, railing to a demoralizingly indifferent crowd against both capitalism and the radical Left, committed *seppuku*. In his own mind, at least, he had proved himself the perfect follower of the *bushido*, to its ideal deadly end.

During the Second World War the same samurai spirit was invoked by *kamikaze* pilots (*kamkaz*, "the divine wind," was the typhoon that in 1281 had destroyed Kublai Khan's fleet, thus saving Japan from invasion). In 1944 a young air force lieutenant named Nagatsuka, overhearing doubts about a plan to ram Ki-27 fighters into American B-29s, evoked the ancient samurai principle of honor:

You attach too much importance to life.... If a human life has any important meaning, it is because of some relationship with other human beings. From this springs the principle of honor. Life rests on this idea, as exemplified by the conduct of our ancient samurai. That is the essence of *Bushido*.... If we cling to our own lives, we actually lose self-esteem. There are two types of existence in this world: that of animals, who simply obey their instincts, and that of men, who consciously devote their lives to serving something outside themselves.... If man merely *existed*, what a burden it would be![25]

ONE STORY FROM THE EARLY EIGHTEENTH CENTURY SURPASSES ALL OTHERS IN exemplifying the samurai honor system. It tells of the forty-seven ronin who were the retainers of Asano Nagonari, lord of Ako. In April 1701 imperial envoys from Kyoto arrived in Edo. Asano, along with two other local grandees, was appointed to receive them. One of the tactics of the imperial government was so to preoccupy the nobility with matters of court etiquette that they had little time for plotting. Unfamiliar with the proper procedure, the three nobles consulted Kira Yoshinaka, a court expert with a reputation for extorting huge sums of money from those who asked his guidance, and gave him lavish presents to ensure his cooperation. Kira judged Asano's donation insufficient and expressed his displeasure by constantly mocking his behavior. Asano eventually could contain himself no longer and in the very hall of the shogun's palace flew at his tormentor, dagger in hand. Kira escaped with minor wounds to his shoulder, but Asano's behavior so offended the shogun that he ordered the peace-breaker to disembowel himself, which Asano did that same day.

His death left his forty-seven fighting men suddenly without home or master, and they met to determine their response. Some advocated armed resistance, others swore to disembowel themselves at the castle gate; but one, Oishi Yoshio, counseled that they stay their hand, and his view prevailed. Everyone knew that the *ronin* were obliged to avenge the death of their master, and this meant that a careful watch was kept on each of them. For more than a year the forty-seven lived in seeming demoralized retreat, Oishi in the gay quarters of Kyoto, leading such a dissolute life that Kira's spies were convinced he posed no danger. But Oishi was biding his time. On January 30, 1703, flanked by his own son, Oishi and his fellow ronin stormed Kira Yoshinaka's mansion, seeking out Kira, whom they identified by the scar on his shoulder, and beheading him. That night they offered up his head at their master's grave, after which they went together to the authorities and confessed what they had done.

When the shogun heard of the *ronin*'s revenge he was extremely moved, inspired by this reawakening of ancient virtue; but to sanction a revival of feudal vendettas was dangerous: the *ronin* could not be allowed to take the law into their own hands. They were ordered to disembowel themselves, and on March 20, 1703, all did so bar the youngest, Oishi's son, who was pardoned at the last moment. The event created a great stir not only among the entire higher aristocracy but throughout the country, and samurai virtues enjoyed new respect. Innumerable works of literature described the vendetta; by 1844 no fewer than forty-seven plays had commemorated it, and the story became a great *No* play, an exemplar of righteousness and loyalty comparable to the Arthurian legend. In Japan, snow is symbolically associated with pure, heroic enterprises: it did not pass without notice that the forty-seven *ronin* had carried out their climactic attack in a snowstorm.

THE JAPANESE PREFER THE CLOSE-QUARTER BLOW TO THE BULLET; the cult of the sword and the more general cult of archaic armaments point to this. Hand-to-hand fighting has generally been more esteemed than the art of hitting from afar. Even in the twentieth century the Japanese have shown a reluctance to employ modern techniques of destruction: after demonstrating the primacy of the aircraft carrier, they still tied up untold resources building the biggest battleships in history. The Japanese tactic of ramming other planes and crashing into ships not only relates to the mystique of self-sacrifice: it also gave obvious satisfaction, as if they enjoyed the bodily contact, even at the expense of their own lives.[26]

Nevertheless, when in 1543 a Chinese cargo vessel landed at the southern island of Kyushu, and the feudal master of the island saw a Portuguese crewman shoot a duck, he immediately bought the ship's two harquebuses, primitive handguns. Within ten years, the country was manufacturing guns in quantity; by 1560, firearms were being used in battle, and by century's close guns were proportionately more common (and better constructed) in Japan than anywhere else in the world. Yet no true member of the *bushi* order wanted to use them; guns could be left to the lower classes.

Not long before, in Europe, there had been a backlash against guns, as soldiers and civilians alike realized that progress in weaponry would mean faster killing, more killing, and the diminution of human stature. One sixteenth-century Italian general was so appalled by the disgrace of having skilled swordsmen under him shot from afar by men with guns that after one successful siege he cut off the hands of every musketeer he could find. There seemed no immediate reason for the Japanese not to take to the new weapon; and yet, according to a classic book published in 1979, Noel Perrin's *Giving Up the Gun*, that is what they did for close to two hundred years.[27]

Perrin had an agenda of his own, using his book to argue that if Japan could give up advanced weaponry without ill effect, so might the Western world renounce nuclear armaments. Tokugawa Japan never in fact gave up the gun, keeping it as a "vital part" of its arsenal, and by 1876 Japan—suddenly embracing the modern world—had almost two hundred schools of firearms. In any event, ordinary Japanese had little access to weapons of any sort, including swords. However, Perrin's main case is valid: Japan largely turned its back on the "black art" and concentrated on the sword.[28]

He gives several reasons for this. For one thing, most samurai scorned guns and had no wish to be shot by a common peasant. (Don Quixote could have been speaking for any samurai when he condemned "an invention which allows a base and cowardly hand to take the life of a brave knight.") Second, the Japanese were such formidable fighters, their archepelago so hard to invade, that territorial integrity could be maintained with conventional weapons: guns were *unnecessary.* (This is questionable: the Mongols had twice sent great fleets. It is true, however, that Korea and China, the nearest potential aggressors, were preoccupied with their own problems, so for many years invasion was not likely from any source.)

Third, the sword had greater symbolic value than in Europe. The sword was a class symbol, a work of art, and a means of subjugating the lower classes. (In the early 1600s the Japanese government wanted to honor its four leading gunsmiths; it gave each of them . . . a sword.) Beyond that, the Japanese enjoyed an antipathy to foreign ideas, and the gun was an import, associated with the spread of Christianity by Spanish and Portuguese missionaries. The 1637 rebellion was raised by native Christians and fought with gunpowder. After its suppression, the country was effectively sealed off: the exclusion of authorized foreign influences became almost complete.

Perrin's final reason for Japanese resistance is perhaps most intriguing. It is purely aesthetic. This went beyond what Richard Burton called "an ugly change of dull lead for polished steel." Swords were not only beautiful; they were associated with graceful movement. "This is why," says Perrin, "an extended scene of swordplay can appear in a contemporary movie, and be a kind of danger-laden ballet, while a scene of extended gunplay comes out as raw violence."[29] A man using his sword properly is moving with beauty. A man firing an arquebus (or harquebus—lumpish and immobile) is not. Perrin quotes from a Japanese manual of 1595, whose writer apologizes for advising his students to get into positions that are distinctly ungainly: "Soldiers used to have strong wrists and arms from swordplay. Now they must get in such awkward kneeling positions to shoot guns; their elbows hurt. Hips get a strange muscle pain." Not only that, they have to contort their bodies in defiance of aesthetic principles: "*Must* separate knees to kneel and fire."

John Keegan endorses Perrin's view: " 'Style' was central to the samurai way of life, style in clothes, armor, weapons, skill-at-arms and behavior on the battlefield. . . . It seems to have partaken of the Japanese belief in the importance of unity with nature and natural forces, since muscular effort is 'natural' while the chemical energy of gunpowder is not."[30] (There are, besides, other examples of technological reversals in isolated or semi-isolated societies: the Chinese abandoned oceangoing ships after 1433, as well as mechanical clocks and water-driven spinning machines.)[31]

Firearms were never formally embargoed; rather, there was a steady series of cutbacks. The samurai-controlled government began by restricting gun production to a few cities, then introduced a requirement of a government license for producing a gun, and finally so cut down its needs that by 1610 fewer than three hundred guns a year were being ordered, and those mostly for ceremonial processions. Provincial gunsmiths were starving; several even took up swordmaking. By the end of the eighteenth century the fifteen remaining gunsmiths supported themselves with repair work and by making farm tools.

It was the arrival in Tokyo Bay of Commodore Matthew Perry and his "black ships" in 1853 that finally brought about the general reintroduction of firearms. Perry convinced his hosts that the only way to repel uninvited visitors was to deploy a moderate coastal artillery of their own. However, in 1872 a conscription law deprived the samurai of their control of the military, and four years later the new Meiji authority, finally determined to employ modern military methods and build a national army, abolished the samurai's right to bear swords. By then the last Tokugawa shogun had abdicated (in 1867), the shogunate itself had been abolished, and the three hundred feudal jurisdictions had been replaced by a central civil service.

For many of the warrior order, being stripped of their weapons was the last straw. "The sword," expostulated one grandee in a formal note of protest, "not only maintains the tranquility of the nation but also guards the safety of the individual citizen. Indeed, the one thing essential to this martial nation that reveres the gods, the one thing never to be put aside even for an instant, is the sword. How, then, could those upon whom is laid the burden of fashioning and promulgating a national policy that honors the gods and strengthens our land be so forgetful of the sword?"[32] His plea fell on deaf ears, but his people were not beaten yet.

On the night of October 24, 1876, 170 samurai, armored and swords in hand, attacked the imperial garrison stationed at Kumamoto, killing about 300 men, including the commanding general. The assault achieved little but precipitated a full-scale revolt the following year—the "Satsuma Rebellion"—in which some 25,000 samurai took up arms. The government, prepared for such a crisis, mobilized an army of 60,000 and in a climactic engagement laid siege to Kumamoto Castle, one of the three mightiest in Japan, the stronghold of 4,000 rebel troops and their leader, General Saigo. After twenty days of bitter fighting the Satsuma army was forced to withdraw, and Saigo killed himself. Thereafter the rebellion was doomed.[33] With its collapse, the history of Japanese swordplay came, in one sense, to an end. That same year the last remnants of Japan's feudal structure were abolished, and the country opened to commerce with the West.

Y ET LONG BEFORE THIS DESPERATE LAST STAND, THE COUNTRY'S attitude toward swordsmanship had undergone a transformation. Conservatives lamented this as a decline, but the samurai spirit had not disappeared. It reemerged in the determination to excel, but in a sporting form. This ultimately led to modern *kendo*, and to judo, karate, and the other martial arts. What remade Japanese swordsmanship into the competitive sport of fencing had been the widespread adoption of protective equipment during the seventeenth century. *Kendo* enthusiasts took to wearing the *men*, a head guard of heavy cotton with a metal face protector, much like a catcher's mask. They wore padded leather gloves, or *kote*, and a chest protector or cuirass made of bamboo strips covered with heavily lacquered hide, the *do*. Waist armor (*tare*), a form of apron held in place with two bands, protected the groin. Beneath all this the kendoist wore a padded blue jacket (*keiko-gi*) and a culotte or split skirt (*hakama*) that recalled the gentleman's costume of the high Tokugawa era. His two-handed sword (*shinai*) was made of four equal-sized pieces of well-seasoned, and highly polished bamboo. Bouts were for one or two hits, fenced on a "field" rather than a piste (offering considerably more space for maneuver), and specific places on the body had to be struck to score a touch: only cuts to the head, temples, wrists, and upper body and thrusts to the throat were rewarded. Fencing with these powerful swords—hitting rather than cutting—did not mean the end of purely wooden weapons, but by the end of the Tokugawa period *kendo* had become the dominant form of swordsmanship.

Even before the 1876 rebellion, the government of the Meiji epoch (1868–1912) had adopted a hostile attitude toward fencing schools, and three years after its prohibition of sword-carrying it banned dueling as well. Still, fencing did not fade away completely, due largely to the devotion of an enthusiast by the name of Sakakibara Kenkichi. Born into a poor family in a suburb of Edo in 1830, Sakakibara was a fully qualified instructor by the time he reached twenty-six. In 1872 he held a public demonstration of martial arts in a disused mansion in the suburb of Asakusa, promoting the event as if it were a sumo contest, with opposing teams, an official announcer, and much fanfare. Several leading fencers were invited to take part, including women contestants and two English-men, included to attract the curious. The event was a sellout, and soon other impresarios followed Sakakibara's lead. By September that year there were more than twenty martial arts companies in Edo; demonstrations of jujitsu, horsemanship, and other activities were added to their program. Eventually the craze wore thin, and many martial arts practitioners condemned it as degrading. However, these shows, like James Figg's sword circuses in Georgian London, greatly boosted fencing and the other martial arts just as it seemed that government displeasure might make them disappear.

The Satsuma Rebellion of 1877 also played its part, for it convinced many policemen that they should train in the martial arts, especially in fencing: too many skirmishes during the rebellion had been won by sword-wielding soldiers—on both sides. The head of the Tokyo Metropolitan Police, the former samurai Kawaji Toshiyoshi, urged that *kendo* be added to his men's basic training. "Fencing is practiced assiduously in the various Western nations," he wrote. "If Japan abolishes fencing, then some day we will have to learn it from them. Now, the saber is nowhere as

Police officers in Tokyo supervising a practice kendo session before a display for the 64th Imperial Diet during the 1930s.

sharp as the Japanese sword; so if we abolish Japanese swordsmanship and learn to use the Western saber that would be equivalent to throwing away gold and picking up broken roof-tiles. . . . Although this may be the age of the gun, the success [of police use of swords against the rebellion] is more proof of the worth of fencing than all other arguments. Moreover, fencing is of great value in training character and instilling diligence."[34] Kawaji's arguments prevailed, and several Tokugawa masters were recruited. When it became obvious that each had his own school and way of fencing, the police set about creating a unified teaching system—something never before attempted in Japan. From this emerged modern *kendo*.

Throughout the last half of the nineteenth century it was bitterly debated whether to teach the martial arts in schools. In 1884 a commission concluded that, despite their physical and spiritual values, such arts were "dangerous, violent, and detrimental to health and growth." Nevertheless, the advocates of *kendo* did not give up, and in 1911 fencing became an option in the curriculum and six years later a regular school subject. Before long, it became a means of inculcating a nationalistic spirit, and fencing suddenly found itself given an unwelcome political dimension.

It was no surprise when, after the Second World War, the Allies did their best to outlaw *kendo*, singling it out as dangerously militaristic. The very terms "*bushi*" ("warrior") and "*budo*" ("Way of the Warrior") were forbidden to be used. In November 1945 martial arts training was once again struck from the curriculum. However, *kendo* enthusiasts continued to train in secret. They devised a transitional form of fencing, using bamboo swords with Western jackets and masks—and played down the spiritual aspects.

TODAY JAPANESE FENCERS COMPETE IN WORLD AND OLYMPIC CHAMpionships, but since they first participated none had reached a final, until Yuki Ota won silver in the individual foil at the 2008 Olympics in Beijing. It may be that the search for perfection that characterized Japan's swordplay for so long cannot be twisted into sheer sporting endeavor; or perhaps modern fencers, Eastern and Western alike, have yet to rediscover that tradition.

Part Three

—

THE DUEL'S

HIGH NOON

Previous page: A sketch by Aleksandr Pushkin, one of several—
a number humorous—on his favorite obsession.
He died dueling in 1837, on his thirty-eighth birthday.

CHAPTER 8

Points of Honor

1807.   Mr Alcock killed Mr Colclough, and lost his reason,
        8 June
1808.   M. de Granpre & M. Le Pique, in balloons,
        near Paris; latter killed, 3 May
1808.   Major Campbell & Captain Boyd; latter killed,
        23 June; (former hanged, 2 October)
1809.   Lord Castlereagh wounded George Canning,
        21 September

—Haydn's Dictionary of Dates: Memorable Duels

Duels: Thunder against. No proof of courage. Great prestige
of the man who has fought one.

—GUSTAVE FLAUBERT, Dictionary of Received Ideas, 1881

ON APRIL 10, 1772, SAMUEL JOHNSON AND JAMES BOSWELL
were dining out with a small group of friends when the conversation
turned to dueling. Boswell asked the table whether they thought the practice was consistent with moral duty. Their host, a retired general, said confidently, "Undoubtedly a man has a right to defend his honor." Boswell
was asked what he would do if challenged. "I should think it necessary to
fight." Johnson weighed in: "It does not follow, that what a man would do
is therefore right." Boswell wondered aloud if dueling was contrary to the
laws of Christianity, to which Johnson replied:

Sir, as men become in a high degree refined, various causes of offence arise; which are considered to be of such importance, that life
must be staked to atone for them, though in reality they are not
so. . . . But in a state of highly polished society, an affront is held to
be a serious injury. It must, therefore, be resented, or rather, a duel
must be fought upon it; as men have agreed to banish from their
society one who puts up with an affront without fighting a duel.

Now, sir, it is never unlawful to fight in self-defense. He, then, who fights a duel, does not fight from passion against his antagonist, but out of self-defense; to avert the stigma of the world, and to prevent himself from being driven out of society. I could wish there was not that superfluity of refinement; but while such notions prevail, no doubt a man may lawfully fight a duel.

Nine days later, Boswell—still not satisfied—prompted the doctor to say more. "He this day again defended dueling," Boswell recorded,

and put his argument upon what I have ever thought as the most solid basis; that if publick war be allowed to be consistent with morality, private war must be equally so. Indeed we may observe what strained arguments are used to reconcile war with the Christian religion. But, in my opinion, it is exceedingly clear that dueling, having better reasons for its barbarous violence, is more justifiable than war in which thousands go forth without any cause of personal quarrel, and massacre each other.[1]

The great moralist may have sanctioned the "point of honor," but other men of standing condemned it. One early critic, Blaise Pascal (1623–62), labeled dueling a folly, a prejudice without rational justification.[2] Jean-Jacques Rousseau ridiculed the practice in *Julie ou la Nouvelle Héloïse*, in which the heroine, writing to her lover on the cusp of a duel to defend her good name, offers a detailed critique of dueling as a "savage prejudice" based on a false interpretation of honor. Boswell had written to Rousseau as early as 1764, but neither Rousseau's attacks nor Johnson's defense put Boswell's mind at rest, and to the end of his life he remained characteristically uncertain what to think.*

---

* Rousseau himself hated most forms of exercise, but at twenty undertook fencing lessons. As he records in his *Confessions:*

This was worse than being in the salle. After three months of instruction, I was still hitting a brick wall, incapable of putting an attack together, or being flexible enough or sufficiently strong to control my foil when my master attacked. I detested the whole business, in particular the master who was trying so hard to teach it to me. I found it incredible that anyone could take such pride in knowing how to kill a man. To bring his vast knowledge within the sphere of my understanding, my master would make comparisons with music (of which he was sin-

As the nineteenth century—known even to contemporaries as "the bourgeois century"—got under way, formalized codes appeared—in England in the 1820s, in France in the 1830s, in Germany in the late nineteenth century, and even in Russia by the century's end. Some minor points aside, the dueling codes of central Europe were much alike, being largely based on the comprehensive codification made by the Comte de Chateauvillard of the Paris Jockey Club in 1836, *Essai sur le duel,* that quickly became accepted in the Western world. By now philosophers and writers were pressing their opinions. The moralist William Paley argued that the whole rationale of the duel as a means of achieving justice made no sense: "dueling, as a punishment, is absurd, because it is an equal chance whether the punishment falls on the offender or the person offended; nor is it much better as a reparation—it being difficult to explain in what the reparation consists, or how it tends to undo the injury or afford a compensation for the injury sustained."

One would have thought that running one's enemy through might have afforded some people considerable satisfaction, but other writers agreed overall with Paley: William Hazlitt wrote against the practice, as did Leigh Hunt, who charmingly placed his essay opposite one on "Suicides of Butlers."[4] Anne Brontë condemns the duel between Lord Lowborough and Huntingdon in her *The Tenant of Wildfell Hall* as "one of the symptoms of a depraved heart";[5] while Tobias Smollett wrote of the "trade of assassinations," the idiocy of friends murdering each other, and the tragedy of a worthy man having to die because he was unlucky enough to be "insulted by a brute, a bully, a drunkard or a madman." Byron often threatened duels but never actually fought one (although while in Malta in 1809 he had to be dragged away from an officer who had insulted him). He disliked "seeing men play the fool for nothing," and thought that nine times out of ten a second could resolve a quarrel so long as he was not "a bully

gularly ignorant) and delight in finding striking analogies between, say, *tierce* and *quarte* and the same terms in music. When he wanted to make a feint attack, he would tell me to look out for a "dummy," because years ago dummies were called "feints" [*les deizes*]. When he beat my blade, and my foil jumped out of my hand, he would say with a snigger that this was a "break" [*une pause*]. To put it plainly, never in my life have I met such an insufferable pedant as this miserable creature with his *plumet* and plastron.[3]

Rousseau's antipathy to dueling may not have been fueled by moral disgust alone.

or a butcher." Elizabeth Barrett Browning hated all dueling; her husband, Robert, predictably loved the idea and has at least a hundred references to swordplay in his poetry.*

In Germany, Arthur Schopenhauer, an inveterate pessimist, devoted more than twenty-seven pages in "What a Man Represents" to tracing the origins of knightly codes and inveighing against the silliness of duels. "[This] species of honor," he wrote, "is perfectly unknown amongst Chinese, Hindus or Mohammedans ... knightly honor depends, not upon what people think, but upon what they say, as shown by the fact that insults can be withdrawn, or, if necessary, form the subject of an apology, which makes them as though they had never been uttered. ... The truth is that conduct of this kind aims, not at earning respect, but at extorting it."

Schopenhauer had spent part of his childhood in Paris and London and attended university in Berlin, where he must have come across student duelists, but he remained steadfastly unsympathetic. "The whole thing manifestly rests upon an excessive degree of arrogant pride," he went on. "This pride must not be put down to religion, but, rather, to the feudal system, which made every nobleman a petty sovereign who recognized no human judge, and learned to regard his person as sacred and inviolable. ... The theory that might is right ... has still in this nineteenth century a good deal of life left in it—more shame to us."[7]

The penalties for dueling were so draconian that they undermined their own purpose: people resisted a code that did not distinguish between willful murder and consensual combat. English juries in particular would often acquit rather than send a duelist to his death. They could see that the *code duello* was a highly ritualized affair, one main purpose of which was to eliminate random inequalities. The ceremony of the duel could mediate aggression and prevent the quarrelsome from succumbing to violent impulses. Most duels were far from barbarous acts.

Immanuel Kant was also of the opinion that a distinction should be made between duelists and murderers. He classed "killing a fellow-soldier in a duel" alongside maternal infanticide in his *Philosophy of Law,* arguing that bringing about death in such cases "must be called *Homicide,* and not *Murder,* which involves evil intent."[8] Some legal systems followed Kant's advice; others did not. For most of the century to take life in a duel was

---

* Browning's interest in fencing per se stretches from brief asides about "the sports of youth—masks, gloves and foils" to details about how he would go on walks "passing lightly in review / What seemed hits and what seemed misses in a certain fence-play." There is even a seemingly prescient reference to "the pale-electric sword."[6]

manslaughter in France, the Italian states, and Austria but murder in England and elsewhere. In the German states legislation was betwixt and between, extending tacit recognition to the duel, but then unsuccessfully seeking to secure sufficient penalties to discourage its practitioners. It was a hard line to draw—making the penalties strong enough to deter but not so harsh as to be ignored—and few European governments were willing to acknowledge that the duel had anything in its favor. Hence the difficulties in which they found themselves.

Jeremy Bentham went even further, asserting that dueling, however rudely and imperfectly, corrected a real social evil. "It entirely effaces a blot which an insult imprints upon the honor. Vulgar moralists, by condemning public opinion upon this point, only confirm the fact."[9] He proposed that offenses against honor receive the same legal protection as offenses against the person—and argued that the punishment should be commensurate with the injury.

Bentham's views notwithstanding, in 1823 an association was formed in London for the sole purpose of suppressing dueling. It included leading members of both Houses of Parliament as well as senior officers of the services. Their influence was minimal, however, and in 1829 an enterprising Irishman, Joseph Hamilton, published *The Only Approved Guide Through All the Stages of a Quarrel*, explaining in his preface how he had "held directly opposing sentiments upon the subject," first believing the duel to be a necessary evil, then viewing the practice as intolerable. However, when he appealed to leading figures—including the Duke of Wellington, who that same year would become the only British prime minister to fight a duel while in office—he got no support. When he approached Sir Walter Scott, the eminent author replied, "Doing the fullest justice to the philanthropy of your motives, I am still afraid that the practice of dueling is so deeply engrafted on the forms of society, that, for a length of time at least, until mankind may entertain much clearer views upon most moral subjects, it will hardly fall into disuse." If the duel could not be done away with, Hamilton decided, nothing daunted, it could at least be regulated. "Should any individual attempt to deviate from rules which have been so very highly sanctioned by the chief commander of the British army and others whose letters we have inserted in the Introduction," he warned, "his adversary will be justified in refusing to recognize him as a gentleman."[10] He made care to print Scott's letter in full.

Article 11 of the new code called for the duelist "to abstain from nicknames, mimicry, offensive jokes, and what is usually termed horseplay," and Article 26 stated that "an apology, with its usual accompaniment—the offer of a whip or a switch—should always be accepted for a blow." In choosing a site, one should avoid "the necessity for carrying wounded gentlemen over walls, ditches, gates, stiles or hedges"; the solemn act of tossing up for choice of weapons should be performed with "three, five or seven coins, after they have been carefully shaken in a hat"; and no duel should be fought on a Sunday, at a church festival, or near a place of public worship.

This formalizing of rules, even on a necessarily unofficial basis, helped define the duel as an affair of honor, an ethical passage of arms, as Dr. Johnson had described it. As the American historian Joanne Freeman writes, "A fair duel was a game of chance that displayed the willingness of both principals to die for their honor, not their skill at inflicting pain or death." The "polite" duelist, in certain places and times, fought "without any desire to hurt his adversary." Duels motivated by "the thirst for blood or the malignant purpose of destroying the life of another" were "ferocious, barbarous and savage."[11]

Andrew Steinmetz grants that notions of honor may sometimes have been false and that it was unlikely that opponents would be of equal skill, so there would have been many a concealed murder. But duels still served a purpose "in the absence of better laws, better police, better taste, and better manners." His advice for participants is almost comically exact:

> All practiced duelists take good care, if in an affair they puncture their adversary, to carefully wipe their sword with their handkerchief, before returning it to the scabbard. A beautiful Toledo has been known to be considerably damaged by carelessness in this respect. During the confusion that necessarily arises when a principal receives the *coup de coeur* or home thrust, such an accident to the trusty weapon is very likely to occur.[12]

By the late nineteenth century, the basic rules were clear: Seconds were expected to mark the standing spot of each combatant, leaving a distance of two feet between the points of their weapons, arms extended. Where each man should stand was drawn for by lot. Bouts were confined roughly to a 20-by-6-meter area, so that a running battle with combatants rushing about helter-skelter was impossible. The swords, rinsed with an antiseptic (carbolic acid) to avoid infection, were measured to establish that they were of equal length, and in no case was a sword with a sharp edge or a notch allowed. If, on comparing weapons, the swords were found to differ, the choice would be decided on by chance, unless the disproportion were of a material nature. The sword-bearing hand could be wrapped in a handkerchief, but no end of the handkerchief was allowed to hang down, lest the point of the opponent's sword catch in it. The combatants were requested to throw off their coats and bare their chests, to show that they were not wearing anything that could ward off a thrust. A refusal to submit was considered a refusal to fight.

At the dropping of a handkerchief, the cry *"Allez!,"* or their equivalent, the contestants would set to, the seconds standing close to each combatant, holding a sword or a cane, point downward, ready to stop the fight the moment the rules were transgressed. Unless it had been stipulated, neither combatant was allowed to ward off his opponent's blade with his unarmed hand; should either persist in doing so, the seconds of his adversary could insist that the offending hand be tied behind his back. Opponents were allowed to stoop, rise, vault to the right or left, and turn around each other, "as practiced in the fencing lessons and depicted in the various treatises on the art."[13]

When one of the parties conceded he was hurt or a wound was noticed by his second, the fight was stopped; but with the consent of the wounded man it could continue. The signal to stop was given by that man's second

A late-nineteenth-century saber duel, where one of the participants lost his head. Names and location are unknown.

raising his sword or cane while the opposing second cried out "Strike up the blades!" at which the combatants took a step back, still remaining *en garde*. All duels were to take place during the forty-eight hours succeeding the offense unless otherwise agreed; twelve hours was the earliest that a duel could be fought after a challenge. When two officers were involved, a disabling injury, if the duel had been fought with the permission of the recipient's colonel, was considered a battle wound and entitled the bearer to a pension. There were even special regulations for bishops, despite the fact that the Church had long forbidden them to fight.

The *code duello* could triumph in the most adverse circumstances. Robert Louis Stevenson may well have been drawing on fact when he depicted a challenge made in 1813 by the French hero of his novel *St. Ives* against a gnarled army veteran, an "old whiskerando . . . a brute of the first water"—with both men prisoners of war at the time. They unscrew a pair of scissors, tying each blade to a branch gathered from the prison courtyard. They fight at night, in the dark, out of view of the guards—but all strictly according to the rules of formal dueling.[14]*

One of the most articulate apologists of the practice was the German philosopher Friedrich Paulsen. "The love of honor," he wrote, "may be regarded as a peculiar modification of the impulse of self-preservation; it aims at the preservation of the self in consciousness. . . . By honor in the objective sense we mean the opinion which our surroundings have of us."[15] Paulsen believed the duel should be retained as an alternative whenever a man could not bring himself to drag an outrage to his honor before a pedantic court of law. If a man in such circumstances were not allowed to vent his anger by dueling, he would resort to some other form of revenge, thus setting off a cycle of retribution. Paulsen also defended duels as proofs of courage and assertions of worth against wealth.

For many, the duel's central purpose was not to kill but to confront death—and so to demonstrate that one was confronting one's destiny. As Cecil Woodham Smith says in *The Reason Why* (putting a twist on Francis Bacon's "Vengeance is a form of wild justice"), "though the thought of a duel provoked a shudder, dueling had a flavor of wild poetic justice."[16] To the triumphant protagonist of Joseph Conrad's *The Duellists*, "sobered by

---

* At the 2002 Antiquarian Book Fair in London, a dealer was offering a master's diploma, hand-drawn and colored by French prisoners of war in Dartmoor Prison in 1811, awarded to an infantryman who had completed the course in prison and been recognized as competent to teach fencing by twenty-six of his fellow prisoners, who had fought in the Peninsula War.

the victorious issue of a duel, life appeared robbed of its charm, simply because it was no longer menaced."[17] In another, typical case, Casanova fought a duel against Count Xavier Branicki, a friend of the Polish king, over two actresses, and was wounded in the left hand: "It became one of his favorite anecdotes," his biographer noted, "and he was proud to find that it increased his celebrity as a desperado."[18] It would be a mistake to underestimate the deep satisfaction afforded by coming through such encounters.

The formalities favored weapons that enforced physical distancing: rapiers and other forms of sword, and pistols, which did away with physical contact altogether. The pistol was the first hand weapon to rival the primacy of the sword. Which should a duelist choose? Here the argument could go both ways: for some the logic was that the greater the danger, the greater the honor; pistols were more dangerous than sabers; therefore pistols were more honorable. On the other hand, becoming an expert fencer took physical vigor, as well as much practice and technique, whereas any man could fire a pistol. A pistol fight was also considerably safer: as Lord Peter Wimsey, Dorothy Sayers's sardonic detective, puts it, as he confesses to accepting three "challenges" in his life, "A bullet, you see, may go anywhere, but steel's almost bound to go somewhere."[19]

S O DUELING WENT ITS MERRY WAY. THE FRENCH CONSIDERED IT AN essential part of a young man's education, and for the southern Irish nobility it was almost a religion. The great Hungarian mathematician János Bolyai (1802–60), cocreator of non-Euclidian geometry, was equally passionate about music and swordplay and would go to the dueling ground playing his violin. In Denmark, a Russian baron fought a Danish lieutenant over a horsewoman in the Copenhagen circus. Dueling in the Low Countries reached its high point between 1810 and 1830, and in India the British made it a regular pastime. Even ships started to duel: the *Chesapeake* and the *Shannon* squared off outside Boston Harbor in 1813 after a formal challenge had been issued.

In England, although the law against dueling was uncompromising, it was regularly flouted: the Duke of Wellington was not hanged for fighting Lord Winchilsea, nor was Lord Castlereagh transported to Australia for wounding Mr. Canning. The dukes of Norfolk and of York (George III's brother), William Pitt the Younger, Charles James Fox, George Canning, and Sir Robert Peel fought without punishment. (George III took to providing would-be duelists with a "pardon," which they would carry in their pockets to the dueling ground.) Before midcentury, however, things would change. "In England," wrote Alexis de Tocqueville in the 1850s, "all social classes dress the same way." They were coming to settle their differences in the same way too. "The intelligent artisan, the powerful and rising middle class were learning to resent aristocratic privilege," wrote Cecil Woodham Smith, "and nowhere was it more clearly manifested than in the practice of dueling. Members of the aristocracy had licence to commit a criminal offence and escape the penalty—and only, it seemed, members of the aristocracy."[20]

In September 1840 Colonel Lord Cardigan challenged Captain Harvey Tuckett (once under his command) after Tuckett had published a letter listing his faults. By this time, Tuckett had left the army, so Cardigan was not breaching the articles of war by fighting him. The duel, on Wimbledon Common, left Tuckett wounded in the ribs and bleeding profusely, and the Crown, bowing to public opinion, decided to prosecute. Cardigan became an object of public execration, with *The Times* roundly urging, "Let his head be cropped, let him be put on an oatmeal diet, let him labour on the treadmill." Perhaps the paper already sensed the inevitable: all of a year later Cardigan was finally put on trial, in the House of Lords, and acquitted. That evening he attempted to attend a performance at the Drury Lane Theatre, and as soon as he was sighted a riot took place. "Yells, hisses, shrieks, groans made it impossible for the performance to begin; it being feared that the Earl would be attacked, he was taken out of the theater by a side door."[21] The next day *The Times* thundered out a leader attacking the integrity of such a privileged judicial process and demanding that Cardigan be relieved of his command. Something had to be done, and soon Queen Victoria herself was caught up in devising legislation that might rid her country of dueling once and for all.

A new bill was launched in the House of Commons on March 15, 1844. In the debate that followed, one member of parliament reckoned that during the reign of George III there had been 172 duels, 91 of which had led to fatalities. Three days later *The Times* reported that the true figure was over 200. The prime minister, Robert Peel, revealed that the new law would deny an army pension to the widow of an officer killed in a duel the year before. His point was that an "institution predicated on the affirmation of courage and the demonstration of manliness could . . . be subverted if it brought destitution to the dependent and the weak." Thus hereafter dueling "could be rejected by individuals without the worry of taint attaching to their reputations."[22] The bill passed into law, and at last duels in England steadily declined.

ITALIANS—ESPECIALLY NEAPOLITANS—LOVED DUELING, AND ITALY clung to the *duello* more ferociously than any country besides France and Germany. In the ten years between 1879 and 1889, 2,759 duels were recorded there (this statistic is incomplete, as many were never reported); 93 percent of these were fought with swords, 6 percent with pistols, and only 1 percent with revolvers; 3,901 wounds were inflicted, 1,066 serious and 50 fatal. Thirty percent of these duels arose from political differences, 8 percent from some serious insult, 10 percent from religious disputes, and 19 percent from quarrels over cards or other games. In summer, the number of duels was five times greater than in winter, and hardly any duels occurred during Lent—an unusual argument for fasting. Out of any 100 duelists, 30 would be military men, 29 journalists, 12 barristers, 4 students, 3 professors, 3 engineers, and 3 parliamentary deputies.[23] The lower classes, it was understood, resorted to the stiletto.

A study of dueling in the Italian army, published in 1886, went through several editions and provides an interesting overview. The minimum age was determined by whether the party had been accepted into the military; the maximum was fifty-five. There were three recognized degrees of insult: simple, grave, and very grave, the last implying an insulting act—a blow or actual wound.

The author, a Signor Gelli, recommended that shortly before the combat the contestants invite their seconds to dinner, so that they may be cheered by "an atmosphere of conviviality." No one due to officiate at the duel should be invited, lest "his mere presence evoke dismal forebodings." Come the day itself, the challengers must arrive no more than fifteen minutes from the time arranged, and it was not permissible for them then to attempt to compose their differences by way of an apology. Rapiers, sabers, or pistols were the general weapons of choice, but by agreement parties might use carbines, daggers, even poison or dynamite. If so desired, they could fight on horseback. In contrast with this freedom over weaponry, clothing was strictly regulated: "It is *de rigueur* that he shall wear an English frock coat and a high hat. As for the trousers, it shall have been determined by previous agreement whether they shall be supported by a belt or suspenders." This was no laughing matter: as late as the first decade of the twentieth century, army officers fought 398 duels, probably more than any other European country.[24]

IN GERMANY AND AUSTRIA-HUNGARY, DUELING EBBED AND FLOWED, but throughout the last half of the nineteenth century the story was almost entirely one of resurgence. As late as 1900, the minister of war defended the practice in the Reichstag on the ground that there was no other way of avoiding immediate bloodshed when insults had been exchanged. Unwillingness to fight was taken as cowardice. Count Ledorowski of the Austro-Hungarian General Staff was called on to resign his commission for advising a young lieutenant not to fight a duel.[25]

By 1887, the épée, known as the *Pariser*, had become the countries' dueling weapon, though in army circles and throughout Austria the saber was still preferred, while naval officers stuck to cutlasses. When a rightist leader, Wolfgang Kapp, challenged Prussian chancellor Theobald von Bethmann Hollweg during the First World War, the chancellor declined, invoking higher duties to the Fatherland. He was supported in this by public opinion: indeed, during both the Franco-Prussian War and the First World War the German supreme command decreed a moratorium on dueling so as not to detract from the national effort.[26]

Skill in the salle could sometimes be a liability on the dueling ground. In 1893, in Vienna, a first lieutenant of the hussars demonstrated superb technique but no killer instinct as he delivered blows with the flat of his blade. His opponent noticed this tendency and stormed in, hacking off the hussar's nose, which for the duration of the combat was stuck up on the wall by an attentive second; it was stitched back on afterward.

Some duels echo down the centuries. In 1834, a Baron Trautmansdorf was paying court to the widow of a Polish general, the young Countess Lodoiska R———; he was waiting only for a diplomatic appointment before marrying her. In the meantime, a Baron von Ropp began courting her and satirized his rival in a published sonnet. Trautmansdorf called him out. Ropp first accepted, then at the dueling ground introduced a champion to fight for him, who killed Trautmansdorf with a well-practiced thrust. At this, Trautmansdorf's enraged second insisted upon satisfaction and in turn soon fell, mortally wounded in her turn: for she proved to be none other than Lodoiska herself, who had accompanied her beloved in male attire. Overcome by guilt, Ropp threw himself onto his sword and died beside the two lovers. Rather than bringing duels into further disrepute, the tragedy added to their unwholesome allure.[27] In Germany an Anti-Dueling League was established only in 1902, and as late as 1934 a history professor in Göttingen called out a colleague for dishonoring him.

For much of the nineteenth century France was the scene of passionate encounters, but far more duels were fought for form's sake and quickly stopped at the slightest sign of blood. "The duel in France," thunders Adolph Kohut in his history of dueling, published in 1888, "has deteriorated into a trivial game . . . [Its mainsprings are] in most cases enormous vanity."[28] As late as 1897 Marcel Proust, enraged by a review in *Le Journal* imputing that he was homosexual, fought a duel with its author, Jean Lorrain. One of Proust's seconds was his friend Gustave de Borda, known as "Sword-Thrust Borda"; but the chosen weapon was pistols. The combatants stood at a distance of twenty-five yards and fired into the air. "Proust behaved very pluckily, though he wasn't physically strong," a contemporary remarked kindly. Three months later Lorrain was dueling once more, against another friend of Proust, Count Robert de Montesquieu, this time with swords. Proust's biographer George Painter echoes Lord Peter Wimsey: "With pistols it was bad form not to miss your opponent, unless you had an exceptionally serious grievance; but with swords the combatants were in honor bound to go on fighting until one was hurt." The difference was still marginal: Count Robert, whose idea of dueling was to twirl his sword around like the sails of a windmill, was hit on the thumb, bled profusely, and retired from the field.[29]

Mark Twain had great fun at the expense of these heroes, many of whom, to his mind, seemed to treat dueling as a fashion accessory. "The French duel is the most health-giving of recreations because of the open-air exercise it affords," he quipped. "I would rather be the hero of a French duel than a crowned and sceptred monarch."[30] Inveterate duelists had ceased to be much respected. It was true that most citified gentlemen would fight once, *pour faire leurs preuves*—to prove themselves—but more than three encounters suggested "an odor of disrepute." During a duel at the Parc des Princes Vélodrome, on the outskirts of Paris, after a short opening clash of blades, one gallant told the *directeur du combat* that as he had now crossed swords with his opponent he would be happy to shake hands with him.

The formalities, so assiduously developed, were increasingly disregarded: salutes disappeared, seconds hardly bowed to each other, and the victorious duelist, rather than standing his ground until his wounded rival had been carried off, now left the field as quickly as he could. About the only rule that still lingered was the one that forbade duelists to speak to each other. A duel was nearly stopped in the 1850s because one of the parties shouted to the other in midlunge "*Garde à vous!*" The seconds threatened to retire until an apology was issued and silence promised—a promise scrupulously kept: at his next bout the offender was killed outright.

There is, however, one story of a duel in Napoleon's time that was never less than serious. Two officers, Fournier and Dupont, maintained a duel over nearly two decades. In 1794, at Strasbourg, Captain Fournier, a fanatical duelist, challenged and killed a young man called Blum. His commanding officer, General Moreau, who was holding a party on the evening of the funeral, suggested to one of his aides-de-camp, Captain Dupont, that Fournier's presence was surplus to requirement. When Fournier arrived and was denied admission by Dupont, he immediately challenged him. They fought with swords, and Fournier was wounded. "That's the *first* touch," he said as he sank to earth.

A month later they fought again, and this time it was Dupont who was wounded. As soon as he recovered they fought again, each receiving deep cuts. They were evidently evenly matched with swords, but Dupont had no wish to fight with pistols, as Fournier was a crack shot, reputed to amuse himself by smashing the short pipes of his fellow hussars from between their lips as they galloped by. The two men worked out an agreement that whenever afterwards they knowingly came within one hundred miles of each other, they would meet midway and renew the fight, always with swords, until one of them at last confessed himself beaten or "satisfied"— or was killed.

They wrote to each other and met and fought many times over ten or twelve years, always shaking hands, sometimes even dining together afterwards. Each eventually became a general and, during 1813, was ordered to Switzerland. Dupont arrived at his post at night, to discover Fournier billeted in the adjoining apartment. They soon set to, until Dupont ran his sword though Fournier's neck, pinning him to the wall. There he might have bled to death, but brother officers arrived in time to save him.

At this point Dupont explained that he was due to be married and wanted some conclusion to the rivalry. He proposed that the two opponents each arm themselves with pistols, go into the nearby wood together, pace off a hundred steps, counting out each step aloud, then turn and fight it out. Fournier agreed, and the next morning the men lined up for their final rendezvous.

Dupont twice tricked his rival into firing at empty clothing, first his coat, then his hat, and advanced on him with weapons primed. "General," he said, "your life is in my hands, but I do not wish to take it. I want this matter to end, however; so should you challenge me again please remember that the weapons of choice will be pistols—your favorite weapons—and that I am entitled to the first two shots—distance, three feet." And so the nineteen-year feud was dissolved.

Some time in the late nineteenth century Joseph Conrad discovered the rivalry in a ten-line paragraph in a small provincial paper published in the south of France and took it for his story "The Duel" or "The Point of Honor." "Napoleon I," it begins, "whose career had the quality of a duel against the whole of Europe, disliked dueling between the officers of his army. The great military emperor was not a swashbuckler." In Conrad's hands the two men became Ferand (a bellicose Gascon, like d'Artagnan) and d'Hubert. "What horrible perversion of madness!" reflects the old chevalier who is both uncle and confidant of d'Hubert's fiancée. "Nothing can account for such inhumanity but the sanguinary madness of the Revolution which has tainted a whole generation."[31]*

But more was yet to come. In 1977, Ridley Scott directed Keith Carradine and Harvey Keitel in a film of the story, *The Duellists*. The three accounts—the historical one and the two fictional retellings—provide a marked contrast in what we can learn from a duel and its effect on its participants. Scott's film captures the brutality and ferocity of dueling better than any other. As Conrad had summed up: "A duel, whether regarded as a ceremony in the cult of honor, or even when reduced in its moral essence to a form of manly sport, demands a perfect singleness of intention, a homicidal austerity of mood." Scott's film has that. Yet in Conrad's hands—unlike in real life and in a way quite overlooked in Scott's version—the swordfighting ("no one could deny that it was very close, very scientific") issues in a moment of redemption and, for General d'Hubert, the discovery of love through trial. Conrad's tale is the best work of fiction about nineteenth-century dueling.

* Ironically, Conrad himself fought a duel. In February 1878 he was living in Marseilles and fell in love with a fellow Pole, Paula de Somogyi. She was also subjected to the attentions of a Captain J. K. Blunt, "American, Catholic and gentleman." The two men fought with pistols, and Conrad, lightly wounded, bore the scar on his chest for the rest of his life. He used the experience—even keeping Blunt's name—in his novel *The Arrow of Gold*, published in 1920, just a few years before "The Duel" appeared in print.

A T ONE TIME THE "POINT OF HONOR" HAD BEEN OUTLAWED BY kings because it threatened their highborn retainers, but by the mid–nineteenth century butcher, baker, and candlestick maker could take to the dueling ground, just as Francis Bacon had foretold. "The practice spread to the bourgeois political classes, the literati, the journalists, the pamphleteers," wrote the British historian Gregor Dallas. The old aristocracy despaired; dueling had become democratized.[32]

French politicians knew that their country needed a new moral code to adapt to a new democratic order, and rather than turn to ancient Rome, republican France chose to reclaim the values of chivalric honor from its own past. An 1868 book by the great liberal political writer Lucien Prévost-Paradol maintained that self-interest had to be replaced by the free exercise of honor, or better still the duel, "the last powerful rampart of aging societies." France, he insisted, "is the unique example in the world of a society in which the point of honor has become the principal guarantee of good order and which enjoins the duties and the sacrifices that religion and patriotism have lost the power to inspire."[33]

He was sadly vindicated when France suffered her humiliating defeat two years later at German hands but he had already committed suicide while serving as minister in Washington, D.C., at least in part in despair at his country's declaration of war. But his cause was not forgotten. On New Year's Day 1871, a leading Paris newspaper, Le Petit Journal, expressed the conviction that though French soldiers had been badly led at the war's outset, the "honor" and "chivalric loyalty" of the ordinary fighting man had emerged unblemished. What was needed was a revival of the idea of honor along with the skills and ritual practices that sustained it. The paper felt that religion and patriotism had lost their power to inspire. What could replace them? The answer came back once more: the point of honor.

These ideas would inspire the work of the feminist playright Ernest Legouvé, who was also an avid fencer. "I would like our democracy," he wrote in 1872, "to remain aristocratic in its manners and its sentiments, and nothing can achieve that end more effectively than familiarity with the sword."[34] He advocated "the principles of today and the manners of yesteryear." Suddenly fencing and the duel experienced an enormous resurgence. Experts likened a fencing bout to a contest between nations and argued that a soldier who fenced would spill his blood in battle more readily since he believed he was defending not only his country but his "personal honor and dignity" as well. Anatole France, the critic and novelist who would receive the Nobel Prize for Literature in 1921, described the sword as "the first tool of civilization, the only means man has found to reconcile his brutal instincts and his ideal of justice."[35] "I would not want to live 24 hours in a society constituted without the duel," Jules Janin, a fellow writer, weighed in. "The duel makes of each of us a strong and independent power . . . it takes up the cause of justice the moment the law abandons it; alone it punishes what the laws are unable to punish, scorn and insult. . . . We are still a civilized people today because we have conserved the duel."[36] Other advocates argued that fencing stimulated self-regard and mutual respect.

Swordplay was central to the new republic for more than political reasons. It harkened back to a world of hierarchy and birthright, yet was the emblem of a new democracy, of modern individualism. Beyond that, Frenchmen brooded about a war of revenge that would wipe out the shame of 1870: "Think of it always," the saying went, "speak of it never." France at that time was undergoing what Robert Nye has called "a crisis of masculine identity." Hence, as he puts it, "the extraordinary revival of the idea of honor in France in the late nineteenth century and of the skills and ritual practices that sustained it."[37] Fencing, at least in theory, now recognized no social boundaries; it was "a male social universe of perfect individualism and equality." The upsurge in fencing and dueling came from a political need to restore the values of chivalry and the desire of the French male to reinterpret what kind of man he wanted to be.

Certainly the contrast is striking. By 1840 salles had dwindled to about ten nationwide. By 1890 there were more than a hundred registered masters in Paris alone, and clubs had sprouted in every provincial city. Most good-sized towns had at least two salles. Bordeaux's clubs attracted 250 fencers, and Lyons and Marseilles came close to that. Many of the new department stores and a score of Parisian newspapers maintained clubs to keep their male personnel fit.

The salle was an *école de politesse*, seen as civilizing its contestants. Fencers, it was argued, shared a freemasonry of mutual respect and a "cordiality which smoothed over the most irritating issues."[38] An experienced fencer would learn "all the ways he could avoid conflict without loss of honor or dignity."[39] The refined deportment of most masters was testimony that low-born men could be shaped by their art to a higher social calling. When a master did the season at Deauville or attended the opera, the fencing press reported the event with pride. The *Société de l'encouragement de l'escrime*, founded in 1882 for Parisian amateurs, began hosting an annual gala evening featuring the best amateurs and professionals, attracting a social elite in evening dress. At the Elysée Palace, the president of the republic's sinister son-in-law, Daniel Wilson, organized Sunday-morning sessions for the cream of the republican judicial and political establishments.

During this period *salles des armes* evolved from often unhygienic exercise rooms to tastefully outfitted clubs, with elected membership and masters engaged as salaried employees. Yet fencing was not yet a "sport." This final evolution began only in the 1890s and in many respects required the abandonment of the very qualities that fencing's early advocates had hoped would build men of integrity. Once innovations such as scoring and formal competition arrived, fair play came under attack; winning at all costs had come to stay. In this new world France would for a long time remain supreme.

ONE OF THE MOST ARDENT SWORDSMEN OF THE PERIOD WAS Georges Clemenceau, who served as prime minister of France from 1906 to 1909 and again from 1917 to 1920. "The Tiger" was always a fierce political radical, even if by the end of his career a somewhat overtaken one. He fought twelve duels: seven with the pistol, five with the sword, at both of which he was expert, a first-class marksman and an even more gifted fencer. He preferred the sword, but in most of his encounters he was the challenger and rarely had choice of weapons. His rivals generally chose pistols, possibly because they believed he would never aim to kill and might opt to miss altogether; whereas with an épée he might satisfy himself only with significant bloodletting. It was said in the Chamber of Deputies that there were three things about Clemenceau to dread: his sword, his pistol, and his tongue; but in all his duels only one of his opponents was ever seriously hurt.*

---

* In one of G. K. Chesterton's Father Brown stories, "The Duel of Dr. Hirsch," a character tellingly comments, "I cannot speak like Clemenceau and Deroulède, for their words are like echoes of their pistols. The French ask for a duelist as the English ask for a sportsman." Chesterton evidently had a fondness for dueling, and he brought it into at least three of his stories. In "The Chief Mourner of Marne" he inserted a speech that probably reflects his own views on the morality of the practice: "It seems to me that you only pardon the sins that you don't really think sinful. You only forgive criminals when they commit what you don't regard as crimes, but rather as conventions. So you tolerate a conventional duel, just as you tolerate a conventional divorce. You forgive because there isn't anything to be forgiven."[40]

There survives an engaging book, dated now, by the American journalist Wythe Williams that includes a detailed discussion with Clemenceau about fencing. "The adversaries who dared face the point of his sword had no chance," writes Williams with evident admiration. "He delighted in first disarming them with a flashing but terrific *coup en seconde*, the most powerful blow in swordplay, almost paralyzing the arm. The Tiger would laugh,

A duel in Paris around 1900. First blood was usually enough to finish the affair.

mockingly, and bow while waiting for the weapon to be retrieved. Then he would flick his opponent in a part of the anatomy of his own choosing. He would perform the operation delicately, with just enough damage for the satisfaction of honor, and the termination of the affair."[41]

This kind of heroic archaism, fostering a belief that willpower alone could triumph over mere material opposition, helped inspire a wartime doctrine that sent hundreds of thousands of young men to their deaths: a terrible consequence that finally snuffed out dueling, along with much else of the old order. The grand phrases that might be appropriate to the salle did not apply to wooded countryside packed with enemy machine guns; yet Clemenceau was unapologetic about his conduct. Whenever a political rival provoked his ire, he would demand satisfaction. "You see, we had been taught as children that one could not honorably escape a challenge," he told Williams. "I was never one to believe that a wrong could be righted by a bullet or a swordthrust, but, following my upbringing, I made up my mind to give a proper account of myself if provoked to a point where a duel was unavoidable. As a result, I left my mark several times with pistol and épée, and in turn I carry scars."

Dueling regularly meant practicing regularly, so Clemenceau attended a salle in the rue Monsieur le Prince. It was run by one of the most famous masters in Paris, a robust character named Emile Mérignac, a handsome man with twirled moustache and pointed beard who would talk constantly during a bout and particularly loved to quote from the famous duel scene in *Cyrano de Bergerac*, rounding off attacks with "At the end of the thrust I arrive!"

He admired Clemenceau as a fencer even more than as a statesman and believed that had he ever really competed he would have rated as highly as Lucien Gaudin, France's leading swordsman. "Monsieur Clemenceau had a powerful arm and his fingers were of steel," Mérignac explained. "He was stocky but could glide with the speed of a jungle beast. Frequently he terrified his opponents at the very beginning of a fight. On a number of occasions we argued about our respective methods. I always favored the lighter foil over the épée, but this, according to *Le Tigre*, was a fancy, defensive weapon. 'Going on to the attack is always my way,' he told me. 'It gives me authority. It opens up the target, confuses my opponent, and sets up my decisive thrust.'" For Mérignac, Clemenceau's fencing strategy, his character, and his political style were as one.

R USSIA SCRAMBLED TO IMITATE ALL THINGS FRENCH—BUT WHEREAS the French were by now content with sporting and ceremonial bouts, Russia experienced a burst of enthusiasm for a practice previously held in contempt, one that brought about the deaths of such great writers as Pushkin and Lermontov. Both men wrote of their dueling days, and the subject also captivated Chekhov, Tolstoy, Turgenev, and Dostoevsky (appearing in *all but two* of his works, a unique preoccupation).

For a long time dueling was both socially discouraged and formally outlawed, and regulations were stringent. Under Czar Peter I (r. 1682–1725), even those contemplating a duel could be hanged, along with their seconds. On one occasion the czar, seeing his favorite courtier dance with his sword at his side, slapped him hard across the face. All this was before the duel arrived in Russia; but several wars would take its army abroad, where it would come into contact with the dueling tradition. "We would fight with sabers over nothing," recalled one veteran, "then would make up, and would not remember the quarrel."[42] The court soon succumbed to its seductive appeal.

In 1787 Catherine the Great issued a *Manifesto on Duels* that distinguished between the offender and the offended. She commanded her nobles to regulate themselves, tacitly admitting duels by the back door. Her son, Paul I, thrust the door wide open, even laying it down that European monarchs should challenge each other, their prime ministers serving as seconds, rather than fight wars. True to his word, he duly challenged Napoleon Bonaparte to fight him in Hamburg. He received no answer.

As usual, pro-dueling sentiments did not hold sway for long. Three years into his reign, Nicholas I (r. 1825–55) published an entire corpus of laws against the practice. Even mention of dueling in the press was banned: papers did not report Pushkin's fatal duel until almost six weeks after his death. The Russian aristocracy considered the practice barbaric, disliking it for its foreign origin and believing it epitomized irrational submission to alien ideas. One essayist ridiculed those of his countrymen who "borrowed from the French their *point d'honneur* for the sake of fashion."[43] In theatrical comedies, dueling was featured as something to be laughed at.

Yet the monarchy's efforts to ban dueling were as ineffective as those of its European neighbors, and the practice began, slowly and begrudgingly, to be accepted. As elsewhere, early examples resembled common brawls, breaking out uninvigilated at the moment of offense. Turgenev came to lament that Russia's weaknesses could be accounted for by the absence of a culture of chivalry. By the end of the nineteenth century, with Moscow and Saint Petersburg in love with all things French, no self-respecting officer or gentleman could ignore the new sensation. The first codes appeared after 1894, when Czar Alexander III effectively legalized dueling, but the practice was enthusiastically pursued long before that.

Dueling finally came to Russia for almost the opposite reason it had been reborn in France: as a refuge from the suffocating tyranny of the czars. It acquired distinct political overtones, serving as a statement of opposition to the existing order. "The independence and initiative it accorded to an individual," Irina Reyfman writes, "made it Russians' favorite regulator of personal conflicts."[44] A Frenchman would send his seconds to a rival; but Russians delivered their challenges violently, with a face slap (at least) inescapable.

Chest, the Russian word for "honor," ranges in meaning from proven valor and virtue to recognition for social eminence, respect, honesty, and, in later usage, human dignity. It denotes both externally recognized social standing or merit and internal appreciation of one's own worth. Montesquieu had written of honor being the foundation of monarchies and the defining possession of the noble class.[45] He was speaking ironically, but the Russian nobility was keen to distinguish itself as a class. They took to dueling as a means of doing so.

Aleksandr Pushkin (1799–1837), a Byronic figure celebrated as much for the figure he cut and for his antics as for his emotive romantic poetry, was one of Russia's most legendary *bretteurs* (Russians used the French word for anyone who dueled frequently). Short and slight of build but hardy, Pushkin had a furious temper, inherited from his father. At school he excelled in two subjects: poetry and swordplay.[46]* Early on he acquired a taste for the joint pleasures of taking offense and taking satisfaction. Although dueling was still illegal, no one with pretensions to being a gentleman could ignore a challenge if personal honor was at stake.

Shortly after graduating, Pushkin—so lively a swordsman that he was nicknamed "the Cricket"—challenged his uncle to a duel for stealing his dancing partner at a country festival. Family intervened, and the fight was stopped. He once challenged a Greek merely for expressing surprise that he had not read a particular book. One winter he challenged Baron Korf, a former schoolmate, for taking a cane to Pushkin's drunken servant, whom he accused of impudence. Korf chose sabers but would not fight his old friend over such a trifle, proposing instead that they drown their differences in champagne. This time the matter ended there. On another occasion, Pushkin was placed in protective custody for slapping the face of a Moldavian merchant whose pretty young wife had repulsed his advances at a party. He spent the fortnight in jail lying on his bed, shooting wax bullets from a dueling pistol at flies on the ceiling. Within weeks he was dueling again, reportedly waiting for his opponent to take the first shot while he nonchalantly ate cherries. The wife of a friend wrote in a letter that "Pushkin figures in a duel almost every day."

Pushkin's last opponent was his brother-in-law Georges Charles d'An-

---

* A few masters taught during the reign of the czars. The most prominent was Adolphe Grisier, who spent ten years teaching various princes and noblemen of the imperial court. His book *Les Armes et le Duel* is dedicated to His Imperial Majesty, Nicholas I. From the time of the Russian Revolution until 1945, fencing was considered a bourgeois sport and effectively ceased to exist. The Soviet Union first participated in international competition in 1946 and went on to dominate the field.[47]

thès, and the two met at 5 P.M. at an isolated spot on the Black River on the outskirts of Saint Petersburg—each twenty paces away from a barrier, pistols in hand. The river was frozen solid, the snow knee-deep. D'Anthès, who knew that to kill the famous poet would be disastrous for his military career, planned to give Pushkin no more than a flesh wound in the leg, but Pushkin wanted d'Anthès dead and rushed the barrier. To save himself, d'Anthès fired first, but his aim was off and the bullet took Pushkin in the lower abdomen.

D'Anthès positioned himself sideways on, his pistol raised to protect his head, his other arm held against his chest, and waited to see what his stricken rival would do. "Bravo!" cried Pushkin, who fired, then tossed his pistol aside. The bullet went through d'Anthès's right arm, was deflected by a button, and left him with no more than a few bruised ribs. But Pushkin was dying. In pain and bleeding badly, he was wrapped in a fur coat and borne home, still able to joke and tell dueling stories along the way. Back in his house, he looked around his study and addressed his books: "Farewell, friends." He died the following morning, on his thirty-eighth birthday. His death was met with widespread grief and taken as evidence of the high tragic dignity of the duel. (Boris Pasternak arranged a duel against a fellow writer as late as 1914 on the anniversary of Pushkin's encounter.) A Russian historian judged that Pushkin's life "and even his death, now a national legend, have become in posterity's eyes the paragon of high moral virtue, the measure of honor and dignity."[48]

Dueling had developed from a rare literary affectation at the beginning of the eighteenth century into a ubiquitous national pastime. Its semi-legalization in 1894, just as so many European nations were giving up the practice, provoked widespread discussion, from many points of view—social, legal, religious, and philosophical. Yet the debate, and the degree of empathy and disgust, were fiercest of all in Russian literature. Leo Tolstoy, for one, was keenly aware of dueling's flaws: its cruelty and its capacity to overwhelm judgment and good sense. He accepts as much in his 1855 short story, "A Billiard Marker's Notes." Yet twice in those early years he issued challenges: first in 1856, when he was twenty-eight, to a journalist, Longinov. "God knows what will become of it," he wrote two days after calling for the duel. "But I shall be firm and bold." In the end friends pleaded with him, and Tolstoy reconsidered. Five years later, incensed over some perceived insult, he challenged Ivan Turgenev, who wrote back a groveling apology—which he sent to the wrong address. This farcical disagreement lasted for nearly eight months before subsiding. By the time

Tolstoy came to write *War and Peace* his views had changed: now he was most concerned about the duel's dangerous ineluctability, the fact that, once set in motion, it was almost impossible to prevent a bloody conclusion. In the novel an almost inexorable force seems to drive the duel between Pierre Bezukhov and Dolokhov: "A feeling of dread was in the air. It was evident that the affair so lightly begun could no longer be averted but was taking its course independently of men's will and had to unfold."[49] In *Anna Karenina* he uses Karenin's reluctance to challenge his wife's lover as an index of weak character: Karenin's fear of dueling undermines any criticism he has to make of the practice.

Dueling plays a role in several of Anton Chekhov's plays but takes center stage in a novella, *The Duel*, written in 1891. Ivan Layevsky, twenty-eight, the typical Chekhovian "superfluous man," a lazy failure, works in the Ministry of Finance. His mistress is Nadezhda, "the prettiest young woman in the town," whom he neglects; while the town's zoologist, Kolya von Koren, a German with "a resolute, strong, despotic nature," openly despises him. Early on Layevsky acknowledges that "the duel is a survival of medieval barbarism," yet, almost without intending to, filled with frustrated self-loathing, he ends up challenging his tormentor. Koren, speaking to the deacon Dr. Sheshkovsky, gives the story's central speech:

> Here tomorrow we have a duel. You and I will say it's stupid and absurd, that the duel is out of date, that there is no real difference between the aristocratic duel and the drunken brawl in the pit-house, and yet we shall not stop, we shall go there and fight. So there is some force stronger than our reasoning. We shout that war is plunder, robbery, atrocity, fratricide; we cannot look upon blood without fainting; but the French or the Germans have only to insult us to feel at once an exhalation of spirit; in the most genuine way we shout "Hurrah!" and rush to attack the foe. You will invoke the blessing of God on our weapons, and our valor will arouse universal and general enthusiasm. Again it follows there is a force, if not higher, at any rate stronger, than us and our philosophy. We can no more stop it than that cloud which is moving upwards towards the sea.[50]

Dostoevsky was more sympathetic, and throughout his writing career harped on the duel's ambiguous moral standing. He was the grandson of a priest and a merchant; and his father had been a doctor in a hospital for the poor, so the aristocratic ideals of the dueling code were alien to him. He never fought himself, had no personal experience with affairs of honor, and tried to work out in both his fiction and his essays how one could avoid fighting a duel without dishonor. He insisted that a man had the right and the obligation to defend himself—and that included the duel, which he felt was governed by character rather than by impersonal forces. His notes for *A Writer's Diary* read in part:

> *The duel.* In a human being there is a personality as well as a citizen. A judge judges the citizen and sometimes does not see the personality at all. Therefore there is always the possibility that this invisible personality has some feeling that stays with him exclusively, and a judge will see nothing of it. Even the law cannot foresee all the subtleties. But to take away the personality and leave only the citizen is impossible.[51]

In his novels, characters who choose to disregard the code of honor reveal themselves either as unprincipled or, worse, as spiritual monsters. Dostoevsky continued to ponder how one might avoid fighting a duel without losing one's standing. Later in life he would come to see dueling, as Chekhov would, as a silly Western custom that Russians had imported to their detriment. In *The Brothers Karamazov*, written in his sixtieth year, he made this clear:

> "I think duels are so nice," Maria Kondratievna remarked. "How so, miss?" "It's so scary and brave, especially when fine young officers with pistols in their hands are shooting at each other because of some lady friend. Just like a picture. Oh, if only they let girls watch, I'd like terribly to see one." "It's fine when he's doing the aiming, but when it's his mug that's being aimed at, there's the stupidest feeling, miss. You'd run away from the place."

In nearly everything Dostoevsky published there is some mention of dueling ("The Landlady" and *White Nights* are the two exceptions), but at last he concluded, "European moral things should not be copied: vindictiveness, retaliation, cruelty, chivalric honor—all this is very bad. Their faith is worse than ours."[52]

The debate, however, was being taken out of his hands. No institution can survive prolonged ridicule, and duelists were being mocked rather than admired. "To the age of railways, steamers and gaslight, of popular education and popular science, dueling appeared criminal and absurd," wrote Woodham Smith. Legislation remained mostly unchanged, only now it was effective as duelists knew they would be apprehended. The activity had lost cultural legitimacy. New pastimes had emerged: organized football, cycling, competitive yachting for the well-off, and the pleasurable risks of mountaineering, barely known in 1800, yet by 1900 one of the glamorous new outdoor activities. Increasingly popular team games such as cricket and football promoted the tendency to regard the individual as primarily part of a larger group, and individual interests and needs were subordinated to those of the collective. For those who wanted to put their lives on the line, there were better ways of doing it than a duel at dawn: in southern Europe bullfighting was made more dangerous, while Franklin D. Roosevelt went "ice yachting" at 100 m.p.h., faster than any contemporary airplane. Duels continued; but as Oscar Wilde had said, to abolish war, show it not as wicked but as vulgar. Dueling had become vulgar. When in the 1890s Lord Queensberry publicly insulted Wilde at a London club, the latter started legal proceedings rather than issue a challenge. Although the language in which Wilde's biographer reported the incident in 1918 was that of the duel—"challenge," "mortal combat," "fight," "death duel"—single combat between two such contestants was no longer an option.[53]

Richard Burton, writing as the century drew to its close, makes the same point: "The duel is one of those provisional arrangements which, like cannibalism, slavery, polygamy, and many others, belong to certain stages of society, and which drop off as decayed and dead matter when, no longer necessary, they become injurious excrescences upon the body social." But, he adds, "Those who look only at the surface of things consider these temporary institutions as unmixed evils, forgetting the immense amount of good which they did in their own day."[54]

Dueling had been intertwined with the art of swordplay. Fencing in turn had borrowed much of its allure, as well as its skills and its code of honor. As dueling vanished, fencers suddenly felt a cold wind, as they found themselves practitioners of a sport with a compelling past but an uncertain future.

CHAPTER 9

A Pursuit for Gentlemen

> Court dress is not likely to be required. Top hats and frock
> coats are almost certain to be wanted.
>
> —ADVICE FROM THE FOREIGN OFFICE TO THE BRITISH TEAM
> IN THE 1906 OLYMPICS

> The marksman's special skill was drifting towards sport, as
> archery had, as swordplay had, as throwing the javelin and
> the hammer had; the commonplace weapon of one age be-
> coming the Olympic medal of the next.
>
> —DICK FRANCIS, *Twice Shy*, 1982

KARL MARX LEARNED TO FENCE AT THE UNIVERSITY OF BONN. He was copresident of a private society called the Trier Tavern Club, about thirty students whose main purpose was to get drunk as frequently and riotously as possible. The Trier crowd regularly came to blows with members of the Borussia (meaning "where Prussians gather") Korps, and eventually Marx received a challenge to a saber duel.[1] The future revolutionary—a "short-sighted swot," his biographer Francis Wheen calls him—found himself up against a trained soldier and was lucky to get away with a slight cut above his left eye. "Is dueling so closely interwoven with philosophy?" his father wrote to him in despair. "Do not let this inclination . . . this craze, take root." In 1837 Marx left for Berlin and more sober studies, but was still keen to show his fencing mettle when he arrived in London in 1851, virtually an exile. It did not take him long to make contact with a certain Emmanuel Barthélemy, a fencing master with something of a reputation who had arrived in the capital the previous year.

Barthélemy was a French revolutionary who had been active in secret societies during the reign of Louis-Philippe. At seventeen he had been imprisoned for killing a police agent, but had been released in a general amnesty in 1847, after serving ten years. Not content to follow his calling as a fencing coach, he took part in the June uprising of 1848, was sentenced to life in prison, and managed to escape to London in the summer of 1850. Within weeks of his arrival he had opened a salle in Rathbone Place, off Oxford Street, "where fencing with sabers, épées and foils and pistol-shooting could be practiced." It was there that Marx met him.

What we know of Barthélemy and of the author of *Das Kapital* as a sabreur comes from the memoirs of Wilhelm Liebknecht, Marx's companion in many a pub crawl, a lifelong member of his university dueling corps, and a fellow socialist. Liebknecht relates how Barthélemy, "a fierce-eyed muscular ruffian" who still bore on his shoulder the indelible brand of a galley convict, became a frequent visitor to Marx's house: "Mrs Marx did not like him. There was something uncanny about him, and she found his piercing eyes repulsive."[2] But Barthélemy was useful to Marx both on and off the piste—furnishing him, for instance, with firsthand accounts of revolutionary activity that Marx used to good effect when he turned his series of articles *The Class Struggles in France* into a book.

Marx attended Barthélemy's salle regularly, giving "lusty battle" to his coach. "What he [Marx] lacked in science he tried to make up in aggressiveness," Liebknecht recorded, "and unless you were cool-headed he could really startle you." There is no evidence as to how good Marx was, but one can imagine how the great advocate of proletarian revolution might have fought—with controlled fury. Liebknecht noted that he rarely took notice of the opinion of others and that his usual reaction to opposition was anger.

Barthélemy was a good teacher, but his heart was still with the Revolution. He befriended one of Marx's enemies, the revolutionary August Willich, and announced that he would no longer give Marx lessons: he was insufficiently radical and "would not conspire and disturb the peace." Within a few weeks Barthélemy agreed to second Willich, who had called Marx out. Marx refused the challenge, which was taken up by a friend, who was critically wounded by a bullet in the head. Barthélemy and Marx never spoke again.

Two years later Barthélemy fought his own duel over a political difference and killed his opponent outright. Once more he found himself in prison but somehow managed to get out in two months. Thereafter he was shunned by the London émigré community. Undaunted, he hit upon a new plan: he would assassinate Napoleon III. "To make quite sure," Liebknecht explains, "he planned to shoot him not with a bullet but with deer shot steeped in sulphur; and if that did not work he would stab him." In December 1854 Barthélemy obtained an invitation for the next grand ball at the Tuileries, but on his way to the ship that was to take him to

France he suddenly remembered that he was owed money by an ex-employer. As he was near the man's home, he decided to stop by, words turned to blows, and Barthélemy killed two men.

At the "sensational trial that excited all England," he claimed to have acted in self-defense. He was convicted, and this time he would not escape. Some months later, Liebknecht visited Newgate Prison, where Barthélemy had been put to death. "Among the plaster casts of the faces of men who had been hanged was that of Barthélemy, with the impression of the hangman's noose still visible. His expression was changed very little—his face still showed an iron determination."

Marx fought only one more duel—this time with pistols; he had apparently lost interest in the sword, and there is no mention of fencing in his letters to Engels. However, ten years before he ever met Barthélemy he did commit this view to paper, that the "principal thesis [of political economy] is the renunciation of life and of human needs. The less you eat, drink, buy books, go to the theater or to balls, or to the public house, and the less you think, love, theorise, sing, paint, fence etc the more you will be able to save and the greater will become your treasure which neither moth nor rust will corrupt—your capital."[3]

B Y THE TIME OF BARTHÉLEMY'S DEATH, A NEW KIND OF MASTER WAS coming into being. Instruction in the noble art had come a long way from the days when it was a school of quick tricks for anxious duelists and public entertainers. Beginning in the early 1870s, evening galas featuring international fencers could bring in thousands of spectators, but this did not mean that there were many active fencers generally. While fencing was popular in Italy and France, as dueling declined, so the sport too fell off throughout the rest of Europe. Masters might become cultivated and socially adept, but they were catering to a diminishing clientele. Fencing stood at a crossroads.

In Britain, the first club (as distinct from a salle belonging to a master) was the London Fencing Club, founded on July 13, 1848, by an ex-student of Angelo *fils*, one George Chapman. The membership came to embrace the Earl of Cardigan, Lord Desborough (possibly the finest athlete Britain has produced),* and Prince Louis-Napoleon, who was briefly a member

---

* Born in 1855 as William Grenfell, Desborough was a cricket and soccer star at Harrow, where he set a school mile record that stood for sixty-one years. At Oxford he was pres-

while in exile. (He was described at the time as "a wild, harum-scarum youth riding at full gallop down the streets to the peril of the public, fencing and pistol-shooting, and apparently without serious thoughts of any kind.")[4] The Queen's consort, Prince Albert, had taken up fencing while at the University of Bonn (winning prizes for his skill with the broadsword), and he passed on his interest to his children, the Prince of Wales (later Edward VII) and Prince Alfred, Duke of Edinburgh. Both princes were members of L.F.C. from 1865 till the end of the century. The stage was represented by Edmund Kean and Henry Irving, music by Sir Arthur Sullivan, and literature (ancestrally) by Byron, who was known to pass out from excitement while watching theatrical performances and who had a sword made for Kean, in homage to his performance as Othello.*

Byron is always reported as having a clubfoot, but this did not stop him from becoming a keen fencer. He learned the sport from Henry Angelo at Harrow and tried to get Angelo to teach him at Cambridge too, but the city's mayor refused the master permission to rent premises.[5] Through Angelo, Byron met the ex–champion boxer "Gentleman" Jackson, who shared rooms with Angelo in London. He took lessons in both fencing and boxing (wearing especially heavy clothing for the former, to make him sweat more freely) and became friends with his two teachers and "their strange assortment of high-class demi-monde associates in theatrical and sporting circles," as his biographer Leslie Marquand put it.

Whatever the character of Angelo's friends, at the London Fencing Club a strict decorum prevailed. To make a remise (in which one fencer

---

ident of athletics and the boat club and rowed number four in the famous 1877 boat race, the only one to end in a dead heat. He was punting champion of Great Britain three years in succession, sculled from Oxford to Putney, 105 miles, in a day; stroked an eight across the English Channel; and fenced for Britain in the 1906 Olympics at the age of fifty, winning a silver medal. He climbed extensively in the Alps, including three successful assaults on the Matterhorn, by three different routes; went big-game hunting in India and shooting in the Rocky Mountains. In one season's stalking in Scotland, he bagged a hundred stags, and during three weeks' fishing in Florida caught a hundred tarpon. He twice swam Niagara Falls, the second time in heavy hail and snow. As the *Daily Telegraph*'s war correspondent in the Sudan in 1888, he once confronted the dervishes alone, armed only with an umbrella.

* After Kean's death the weapon was auctioned off. Around 1935 John Gielgud was playing Hamlet when a dealer came backstage and presented it to him. Gielgud kept the sword for fifteen years, looking for a suitable successor, then one day was so overcome by seeing Laurence Olivier as Richard III that he passed it on. Who next? Richard Burton? Paul Scofield? Alec McCowen? In the end Olivier kept it; maybe he thought no one else was good enough.

La Leçon d'Escrime—a French postcard from the turn of the century: "Lunge well, be both bold and graceful."

pushes on with his attack rather than waiting to parry the riposte) was frowned upon and required an apology. Counterattacking was likewise considered bad form; a consistent offender might not have his membership renewed. As one early-twentieth-century historian put it, "Pedantry was, as it had been before, the bane of fencing."[6] Some masters had their pupils take lessons standing in tea trays, to teach them to limit their foot movement. One master described a typical bout in which two fellow *maîtres d'armes* would place themselves *en garde* and the first would then make an *appel*—a stamp with the front foot—with a violent "*Voilà, monsieur!*" followed by another beat of the foot and an elaborate lunge, perfect stylistically but "not erring on the side of quickness." His opponent would form, with exquisite precision, perhaps half a dozen parries while the original attacker would attempt to deceive them, but almost in slow motion: "no unseemly scrambling."

The L.F.C. set its face against publicity and shunned contact with other clubs: "Any member who took part in competitions outside the Club was regarded with considerable disfavor," records the official history. "Members fenced for exercise and for the love of *belles armes* . . . and regarded their Club as an exclusive establishment where they could enjoy physical development and the pleasure of (strictly male) company."[7] Good manners required that outside of competitions both fencers should leave the strip with the illusion of being equally matched: even to count touches was un-heard-of.

Similar attitudes prevailed on the continent. In Paris there were the Salle du Cercle de l'Union Artistique, the Salle du Cercle des Eclaireurs, and a handful named after their founding masters: Boyer, Jacob, Manniez, Mérignac Fils, Mimiague, Pellenq, Pons, Neven, Robert, Ruze, Staat. The tone of relations between the clubs can be gleaned from *Les Salles d'Armes de Paris* (1875), which describes the doyen of the Paris professionals, the seventy-seven-year-old Alphonse Pons: "He speaks pompously, he fences pompously and he has pompously called his salle 'Academy of Arms.'"[8] Nevertheless, the club had more than a hundred members.

Despite all attempts to outlaw dueling, masters were happy to give lessons to would-be duelists, but the days when instruction was based on life-or-death situations had long since gone. The artificial conventions of foil fencing, establishing rights-of-way, limited targets, and extended phrases now dictated how even duels should be fought. The influence of the military meant that the bayonet and the singlestick lingered on, but generally the weapons of choice had been whittled down to foil and saber. The épée was hardly used in the salle, while "even duels," noted Burton, "are mostly fought with French foils, which I have called mere bent wires."[9]

To prepare their pupils for more deadly encounters, masters would simply adapt their normal lessons at foil. While the foil and the épée were in reality very different, their guards being differently shaped and their blades differing markedly in both shape and weight, after the invention of the mask the style of foil became more mobile and vigorous, thus blurring any distinction even further, and foil technique came to be held by many as sufficient preparation for dueling.* But that was about to change.

By the 1850s a group of Parisian fencers were beginning to rebel against the stranglehold of foil technique. In 1862 the Baron de Bazancourt published *Les Secrets de l'Epée*, in which he argued that fencing in the salle should imitate real fighting. His message was reinforced when a well-known army captain, considered an expert salle foilist, nevertheless met

---

* Sydney Anglo points out that even Castle—"whose primary interest lay in the evolution of swordsmanship towards the sport of his own day"—recognized that "things are done with the foil which would never be attempted in earnest with a sword" (Castle's words), and accepted that modern play is artificial and that "foil practice may in fact be looked upon as 'diagrammatic' fencing."[10] As Anglo points out, "What is at issue here is the psychology of combat."

his death in a formal duel against a far less experienced opponent. Bazancourt launched a revolution. During the last quarter of the century, Parisian masters increasingly prepared men for duels with standard dueling épées, differing from the real thing only in that their tips were capped. Purists immediately dubbed the new fashion a prostitution, and referees, still using the naked eye to award hits, would favor the épéeist whose style most paralleled foil wherever possible. Once introduced, however, the fighting épée was seen to have merits well beyond its uses in formal dueling; its practitioners had to develop the duelist's mentality: hit without being hit.

It took time to develop an independent body of technique for the new weapon, but between 1884 and 1893 four leading masters, Claude La Marche, Jules Jacob, Ambroise Baudry, and Anthime Spinnewyn, all produced major studies in which they discussed the differences between fencing in the salle and conditions of an actual duel and reached parallel conclusions: new techniques had to be taught. Pupils began to be instructed to use the guard of their épées to divert attacks, to parry and riposte in one movement, not two (as in foil), and to keep their feet closer together.[11] Once épées were given blunted tips and épéeists taught to aim for the hand and wrist, the guard was enlarged the better to protect the hand.

This debate over dueling technique coincided with an extraordinary national scandal. From October 1894, when a French army captain, Alfred Dreyfus, was first accused of high treason for betraying military secrets to Germany, until 1906, when he was formally reinstated, the "Dreyfus Affair" aroused exceptional passions in the French. Journalists, editors, and politicians found themselves obliged to defend their views and their honor on dewy mornings in the Bois de Boulogne. The Affair was probably the last political issue to provoke duels.

Challenged novices frequently approached Baudry for a quick lesson before a duel. He is said to have stipulated that if his new pupil lost he need not pay anything, but if the pupil won he would be required to take fencing lessons for a year. His clients accumulated more than three hundred victories and Baudry had to take on five assistant masters. Fencers soon formed special clubs devoted exclusively to épée. "Foil play is dead," declared Jean Joseph-Renaud, one of the most noted of the new enthusiasts. "Fencing is the art of fighting a duel, and it is nothing else."* Epée

* In 1896, Joseph-Renaud won the amateur foil championship of France, but by 1900 had decided that it was foolish to practice both foil and épée (mixing disciplines to the

theorists repudiated the idea that they had evolved a new kind of sword-play, insisting instead that all they had done was return to first principles, stripping away accretions that were often dangerous "in the field."

Two seemingly disparate forces—the romantic movement (and, flowing from it, a newfound cult of chivalry) and the invention of cheap paper (allowing the rise of the popular adventure story) now combined to give swordplay a special place in popular culture across the face of Europe.

John Ruskin coined the word "medievalism" to describe an epoch in architecture, but it soon came to inspire a movement that would permeate almost every aspect of modern life. Private individuals began to collect armor (the first recorded sale being held at Christie's in 1789), and Sir Thomas Malory's *Le Morte D'Arthur* was republished for the first time since 1634. There followed the Oxford Movement in religion, the Arthurian revival in art, the Gothic Revival in architecture, and the Young England movement in politics. The first of Tennyson's Arthurian poems, "The Lady of Shalott," based on a medieval Italian novella, came out in 1832. Tennyson had been inspired as a boy by *Le Morte D'Arthur* and spent forty years (from 1830 to 1870) completing his epic cycle *Idylls of the King*. Arthur and his Round Table were reinstated as national symbols. Equally celebrated was Arthur's sword, Excalibur, with its "blade so bright that men were blinded with it." Blinded indeed: as one historian records, "myth was restored and the quasi-historical Arthur now troubled only historians. Tennyson spoke for his age."[12]

The second revolution, in publishing, took place in 1806, when two

---

detriment of both), so devoted himself entirely to the "new" weapon—a considerable act of principle, as by this time he was one of the foremost foilists in Europe. Four years later, in London for a major épée competition, he rose from his sickbed to help the French team to victory and the next day won the individual épée championship, much to his own astonishment. In 1908 he was a member of the French team that came fourth in the Olympic Games—at saber. Over the years he refereed several hundred private duels, justifying his role by saying that "generally both parties are so nervous that nobody gets hurt, the offended hero soothes his honor and everyone goes away happy." He lived until 1953. In addition to his career as a championship fencer, he was a journalist, playwright, and novelist, with more than sixty books to his credit, ranging from a meditation on the institution of marriage to a study of French and English boxing.

Huguenot brothers, Henry and Sealy Fourdrinier, patented a design for a papermaking machine that would produce a continuous sheet of paper. Cheap printing was suddenly a reality, and Europe was awash in a literature that sought to satisfy the new longing for the adventures of chivalrous knights of old. No matter that European knights of the eleventh century, the "perfect gentlemen" of Tennyson's poem, were actually an inglorious bunch, loutish, cruel, and rampaging. (The Germans still have a proverb, "*Er will Ritter an mir werden,*" "He wants to play the knight with me," where "knight" means "bully.") The enthusiasm embraced musketeers, crusaders, highwaymen, explorers, outlaws (from Robin Hood to New World frontiersmen), pirates, secret agents, court intriguers, and dashing army officers. And heroes and villains alike would resort, in a tight corner, to cold steel.

This new genre of stories redefined how swordplay was perceived. Sir Walter Scott (1771–1832), an early but crucial figure, effectively invented the historical novel, and his popularity soon swept the Continent; it was said that everyone in Berlin went to bed with *Waverley* under his pillow and read *Rob Roy* while sipping his morning chocolate. Scott himself may never have fenced (a leg withered before he was two years old prevented that), but his Waverley sequence alone includes some thirty scenes involving duels or challenges.[13] He fomented a burgeoning school of British historical novelists—W. Harrison Ainsworth, Edward Bulwer-Lytton, R. D. Blackmore—as fiction evolved from the novel of manners to tales full of heroism and derring-do. By the 1830s imitations of *Ivanhoe* and *Kenilworth* proliferated. Scott and his immediate successors had little interest in exploring nuances of motivation; his writing—at least of action scenes—was like a modern adventure film, crammed with drama and special effects.

Not even Dickens was immune, regularly attending Salle Bertrand, the rival of Angelo's as the leading London club, where he practiced for stage fights. His forays into amateur dramatics included his oft-played role as Captain Bobadill in Ben Jonson's *Every Man in His Humour,* where C. R. Leslie painted him in the part, lounging nonchalantly, a foil by his side, as if waiting for a fellow member to invite him onto the piste. In *Nicholas Nickleby,* Dickens disposes of one of his less admirable characters, Lord Frederick Verisopht, in a duel, and when Nicholas enters Mr. Crummles's establishment looking for work there is a fight scene between two theatrical sailors of such range and detail that one feels Dickens must have encountered such a bout at first hand.* (The comic duel thus enters literature very late—only when the sword truly diminishes as a battle weapon can it be considered funny.)

Between 1880 and 1914 more than five hundred adventure novels were published, and nearly all featured swordfights. Captain Marryat, R. D. Blackmore, H. Rider Haggard (much admired by Freud), P. C. Wren (*Beau Sabreur,* and also onetime fencing champion of West India), and Anthony Hope (whose *Prisoner of Zenda* sold 500,000 copies over four decades in its British edition) were stalwarts in the first team. Robert Louis Stevenson (constantly complaining about his lack of invention) would patrol the midfield, with Joseph Conrad, a foreign signing, leading the line. Baroness Emmuska Orczy, author of *The Scarlet Pimpernel* (1902) and its successors, was (at the least) an energetic cheerleader.

Across the Channel, German pre-Romantics such as Goethe, Friedrich von Schiller, and Friedrich von Schlegel were laying the groundwork. "Chivalry is itself the poetry of life," wrote Schlegel in his *Philosophy of History.* Richard Wagner did his bit for Arthurian romance in *Lohengrin, Tristan und Isolde,* and *Parsifal.* Popular literature found its champion in Karl May, whose adventures of Kara Ben Nemsi, a sword-wielding traveler through northern Africa and the Middle East in the 1870s, are said to have been among the favorite light reading of Hitler, De Gaulle, and Albert Ein-

---

* Several novelists fenced but never made use of their experience in books—for instance, Richard Adams, Peter Cheyney, Paul Gallico, John Dickson-Carr, and Anthony Burgess (despite a cameo appearance of a swordstick, "a fine starry horrorshow cut-throat britva," in *A Clockwork Orange*). Among those who did are Mervyn Peake (in *Gormenghast*), Georgette Heyer (in *The Quiet Gentleman*), Robert A. Heinlein (in *Glory Road*), J. P. Donleavy (in *A Singular Man*), Edgar Rice Burroughs (but not in his Tarzan books), W. G. Sebald in *Vertigo,* and Desmond Bagley in several thrillers. Rex Stout has Nero Wolfe investigate a murder committed with a tampered weapon ("the épée that was sticking through him had no button on it . . .") in *Over My Dead Body,* but the details are slapdash. Friedrich Dürrenmatt has a play, *Der Besuch der alten Dame,* featuring a woman duelist defending her honor, and William Boyd a hilarious account of a lesson with an irascible master in *Stars and Bars.* Most famous of all, Holden Caulfield is manager of his school fencing team in *The Catcher in the Rye* and manages to forget all their kit; but that is all we learn of his enthusiasm.

Dueling was another matter: in *The Tragic Comedians* (1880) George Meredith depicts under the most transparent disguise the fate of the great socialist intellectual and friend of Bismarck, Ferdinand Lassalle, killed in 1864 defending the honor of a countess; Anthony Trollope includes an unlikely duel involving an MP in a Palliser novel (and Arthur Fletcher, the decent politician of *The Prime Minister,* regrets that he cannot shoot Ferdinand Lopez, the mysterious man whom the woman he loves seems to prefer); and Thackeray, another member of Salle Bertrand, wrote at length of the Mohun-Hamilton duel in *Henry Esmond.*

stein. The Viennese writer Arthur Schnitzler may have abominated the duel, but it appears in work after work, almost an obsession. The brothers Grimm included a memorable fairy tale in their great collection. "The Three Brothers" follows the well-worn theme of a man with three sons who tells them to go out into the world to learn a trade; on their return, "he who makes the best masterpiece shall have the house." The eldest son becomes a blacksmith, the second a barber, the youngest a fencing master. During his apprenticeship the youngest son suffers many a blow, but he is never discouraged—"for," he says to himself, "if you are afraid of a blow, you'll never win the house." The three return home, where the elder two duly display their skills. Just as the youngest son's turn comes, the sky opens up into a torrential downpour. Drawing his sword, he flourishes it so fast that not a drop falls on him. His father is amazed. The story illustrates the new respect and revived sense of magic that now attended skilled swordsmen.

In France, nineteenth-century novelists sought inspiration in their own more recent history. *The Adventures of François, Foundling, Thief, Juggler and Fencing Master During the French Revolution* chronicles the progress of the eponymous François, who apprentices himself to Gamel the Fencing Master and "is given a rapier for wear in the streets, which was not yet forbidden." While his master teaches "middle-aged gents in the morning; the Jacobins about two," François fights several duels and unsurprisingly takes all before him:

> Twice he touched the man's chest, and by degrees drove him back, panting, until he was against the door. Suddenly, seeming to recover strength, the Jacobin lunged in *quarte*, and would have caught the marquis fair in the breastbone had he not thrown himself backward as he felt the prick. Instantly he struck the blade aside with his open left hand, and, as it went by his left side, drew his rapier savagely through Amar's right lung and into the panel of the door. It was over. Not ten minutes had passed.[14]

The father of all such writing is of course Alexandre Dumas (1802–70). Dumas's own father was a general—a mulatto, the son of a French nobleman and a Haitian slave—who served under Napoleon, as did the father of his friend Victor Hugo. Dumas also founded newspapers and a theater, indulged in political adventures with Garibaldi, fought in the streets during the revolutions of 1830 and 1848, supplied arms (paid for out of his own pocket) to radical movements abroad, and stood for the National Assembly.

Mainly, however, he wrote—by most estimates some three hundred volumes of plays, memoirs, travel, and fiction. In his early thirties he turned to historical romances; profiting from the vogue for serialization in popular newspapers, he set his stories anywhere from the Middle Ages to the nineteenth century. The facts were always secondary to a good story: "True, I have raped history," he boasted, "but it has produced some beautiful offspring." It was Dumas, sometimes said to be the most widely read author of his age, who did more to popularize swordfighting than anyone in history—because so many people read him and because he created the archetypes who would reign again in cinema. He was himself taught fencing three times a week by the renowned foilist, Adolphe Grisier, the model for his 1859 novel *The Fencing Master*. He also wrote the preface to Grisier's treatise *Les Armes et le Duel*—and may have contributed more than that, as there are touches in the main text that are pure Dumas.* "I possessed all the physical advantages which a rustic life gives," he once explained. "I could ride any horse ... and was pretty smart with the foil." Dumas describes a duel he fought and won, to his great surprise, almost by mistake—his opening thrust caught his opponent off guard. "I attacked him *en quarte*, and without making a pass with my sword in order to feel my way with my man, I thrust out freely *en tierce*. He leapt backwards, stumbled over a vine-root and fell head over heels." Dumas's sword had pierced his shoulder—and "the sensation it had given my opponent was

---

* Grisier wrote that during the wars with England the French prisoners in the English hulks found themselves "abandoned to measureless and dangerous idleness." Accordingly, they organized various pastimes, including fencing; but most knew little about the sport and, cut off as they were, even those with some experience fell into bad habits. When peace came and the prisoners were released, France was "flooded" with a crowd of swashbuckling irregulars, *"une masse de ferrailleurs,"* who, having little else to turn their hands to, set up as masters. Thus was founded a new school: *"la méthode venue des pontons d'Angleterre."*

Grisier goes on to give a dramatic description of the various wickednesses of the school, which include *glisser la monture* (to let the grip slide in the fingers to increase the available length of the sword), "a trick of the worst kind," and standing square on, ignoring the *"effacement"* of the body inculcated by the old school. The new villains would also jump about wildly, rush in with their heads down, thrust without taking aim, advance without covering themselves, parry in the wrong line, refuse to give the blade, even counterattack without the right of way. Grisier—or Dumas—had great fun, and came near to describing the foil techniques of today.

so startling that, lightly though he was wounded, the shock had over-turned him. . . . It turned out that the poor lad had never handled a sword before!"[15]

One of Dumas's biographers insists categorically that all the duels he claimed to have fought were fakes and cites one where the only "real" fighting broke out by accident. To impress the unwitting seconds, Dumas drove himself into a frenzy, swishing his sword dramatically with shouts of "Come, defend yourself! Ha! A victory over you would be but a paltry thing!" This was too much; his opponent seized his sword and landed a hit on the arm. Dumas looked at the blood staining his sleeve, and cried out, "What's that for?" The "duel" had run its course.[16]

It is a pity that Dumas rarely took time in his books to re-create the swordfights with the authority he must have gained; maybe only d'Arta-gnan and his companions taking on the Cardinal's men at the start of *The Three Musketeers* and d'Artagnan's later duel with Jussac are truly convinc-ing. He wrote the original novel in installments between March and July 1844, the same year that he penned *The Count of Monte Cristo*, collaborat-ing with one Auguste Maquet on both books, as well as on the first sequel to *The Three Musketeers*, *Twenty Years After*, and the next work in the se-quence, *The Vicomte de Bragelonne*. Dumas described all these books as "easy literature," and certainly action dictates everything. If there is an im-portant theme in his writings, it is the wronged outsider who comes to the fore—the embodiment of the Romantic myth.

Other French popular writers put swordplay front and center, not merely as a chance for action. Edmond Rostand's famous play about Cyrano de Bergerac premiered in Paris in December 1897, making Cyrano one of the classic figures of popular sentiment. Théophile Gautier pub-lished *Mlle de Maupin*, his romance of the real-life singer, actress, and swordswoman, in 1835, and a swashbuckling romp, *Le Capitaine Fracassé*, in 1863. Guy de Maupassant's *Bel-Ami, or, The History of a Scoundrel*, the tale of a young provincial seeking to make good in Paris, is in many ways autobiographical. Its hero displays a compulsive interest in dueling, and the account of an evening *en gala* is the funniest sketch of a fencing exhibi-tion we have. The passage is too long to quote in full, but what follows gives its flavor. The evening opens with a bout between a couple of professionals,

two good masters, if not of the first rank. They appeared, both spare, with a soldierly bearing and somewhat stiff in their move-ments. After making the appropriate salute like two robots, they began to fight, looking in their canvas and white leather uniforms like two soldier clowns fighting for a joke.

Every so often, you heard, "*Touché!*" And the six judges nodded their heads in a knowing way. All that the public could see were two live puppets who were jumping about sticking out their arms; they did not understand at all what was happening; but they were pleased.[17]

No matter that fencing on the Continent was of a higher standard than anything Britain could produce. A number of British authors—Alfred Hutton, Frederick Pollock, Cyril Matthey, and Carl Thimm among them— played a dominant role in charting both the history and technical advances of swordplay. Perhaps this was because they saw it not as a timeless mystique but rather as an evolving discipline. Coming up behind them was Egerton Castle and, dominating all, Richard Francis Burton. Yet even though nineteenth-century literature was exploding with scenes of derring-do, people wanted their swordplay in fantasy and romance, not in reality, and by the end of the century fencing was in danger of going the way of real tennis or Eton fives.

The fact that it did not can be credited, indirectly, to our final author. He was six feet four, weighed 235 pounds, and he was keen on golf, ballooning, bicycling, billiards, bowls, boxing, cricket (especially), fishing, football, foxhunting, motoring, tricycling, even baseball. The one sport he had no interest in would seem to be fencing, but his friends did, in particular a group involved with the magazine *The Idler:* Anthony Hope, of *The Prisoner of Zenda;* James M. Barrie*; E. W. Hornung, creator of Raffles, the amateur cracksman; and Jerome K. Jerome, the magazine's editor. The author who never picked up a sword was Sir Arthur Conan Doyle. And Sherlock Holmes *did* fence.

The first Sherlock Holmes story is "A Study in Scarlet," which appeared in *Beeton's Christmas Annual* for 1887. (Conan Doyle received £25

---

* There is much swordplay in *Peter Pan*, which climaxes in a duel between Peter and Captain Hook: "Without more words they fell to and for a space there was no advantage to either blade. Peter was a superb swordsman, and parried with dazzling rapidity: ever and anon he followed up a feint with a lunge that got past his foe's defense, but his shorter reach stood him ill and he could not drive the steel home. Hook, scarcely his inferior in brilliancy, but not so nimble in wrist play, forced him back by the weight of his onset, hoping suddenly to end all with a favorite thrust, taught him long ago by Barbecue at Rio."

I would have liked to have had a lesson from Professor Barbecue.

for this "shilling shocker"—not bad, given that his earnings as a doctor were £300 a year.) Watson draws up a list of Holmes's "limits" (or characteristics of his new friend). Number 11 reads: "Is an expert single-stick player, boxer and swordsman." Several cases on, Holmes himself tells us that, during his two years at "Camford" (Doyle's amalgam of Oxford and Cambridge), "bar fencing and boxing I had few athletic tastes." In "The Five Orange Pips," the Great Detective's skills are listed as "violin-player, boxer, swordsman, lawyer and self-poisoner by cocaine and tobacco." Yet there is not a single story where Holmes matches blades with an enemy.[18] The only partial exception occurs in "The Illustrious Client," in which Holmes uses his skill with the singlestick to beat off ruffians in Regent Street.*

But Holmes was not the end of the story. Not for nothing did Conan

---

* The singlestick has a long history. Originally a round stick of ash of about 34 inches, thicker at one end than the other, in its original form it was known as the "waster"—in the sixteenth century merely a wooden sword used in practice. By the 1720s the sticks had become cudgels with sword guards, and under the first and second Georges were immensely popular under the names of "cudgelplay" and "singlesticking." The rules had players close together, their feet not moving and each stroke being delivered with a whiplike action of the wrist from a high guard, the hand being held above the head. Anywhere above the waist was a valid target, but all blows except those aimed at the head were employed solely to gain openings, as each bout could be decided only by a "broken head," i.e., a cut on the head that drew blood. At first the nonsword hand and arm were used to ward off blows not parried with the stick, but near the close of the eighteenth century the unarmed hand grasped a scarf tied loosely around the back thigh, the elbow being raised to protect the face: there is a lively description of cudgel play in *Tom Brown's School Days*. With the introduction of the light saber the singlestick's days were numbered, although French cane fencing is similar; the French version, however, is designed more for defense with a walking stick—which is how Holmes uses it.

Conan Doyle may have been influenced by a report that appeared in *The Herald* of September 13, 1891, headed "The Italian Sword-cane Fencing Fad," which, the paper recorded, "is being introduced in London, although it is hard to see what use it will be in a country where the possession of a sword-cane is a crime. The fencer uses the blade to attack, and the sheath to assist in defence. The sheath is held in the left hand, and the blade in the right. When standing on guard the sword-arm is farthest from the enemy—an exact reversal of the rule in ordinary fencing." Holmes would have had no truck with such an ungentlemanly weapon.

Several years later, in 1927, the great master Léon Bertrand wrote scornfully in *Cut and Thrust:* "I declare the singlestick to be of little if any value to the cause of fencing. Rigid as a poker, the singlestick could not possibly be employed as a thrusting medium. Its lack of pliability precludes any development of legerdemain . . . sense of touch, and its very grip affords little scope for skillful manipulation." No one dared argue with him.[19]

Doyle's gravestone carry the inscription (from Robert Louis Stevenson) "Steel true / blade straight." In 1891 he published the first of his historical novels, *The White Company*, about "men who loved honor more than life," set during the Hundred Years' War. He also began planning a series of stories based on a real-life soldier, the Baron de Marbot, one of Napoleon's lieutenant generals. Marbot's own picaresque memoirs, published in Paris some fifty years earlier, had just been translated into English, and Conan Doyle was captivated by the recollections of this vain, yet innocent and chivalrous man, with "a head as thick as his heart is strong." The outcome was a character named Brigadier Etienne Gérard, the best horseman in the French army, an inveterate ladies' man, an innocent braggart, and an expert swordsman.

The Brigadier made his appearance in 1896—the year of the first modern Olympics. In the very first story, the Brigadier is given a message to carry to Napoleon. His superiors, believing him to be so obtuse that he will inevitably fall into enemy hands, deliberately write the message to lead the British astray; but Gérard wins through—to the fury of the emperor and his marshals. Having set off on horseback, he encounters an enemy force, fires his pistol, cuts his way through enemy lines, fords a river, and runs cross-country to his destination. Sixteen years later, these five disciplines were to be incorporated into a new sporting event—the Modern Pentathlon, at the 1912 Olympics.

WHAT WOULD BECOME KNOWN AS THE OLYMPIC GAMES EMERGED in 776 B.C. as part of a festival held at the summer solstice on the plain of Olympia, in the district of Elis. Aethlios, first King of Elis, is said, erroneously, to have given his name to the word "athlete," though the word translates as "one who competes for a prize." There were several other "games," varying in size and importance, a number of them taking place in or around Athens, the first of which dates from 1370 B.C. At Olympia, entries were confined to Greek male citizens, who had to agree to train under strict supervision for ten months. There was only one event, a sprint the length of the arena. The distance (170 m) was said to have been measured out by Hercules himself: it was as far as he could walk while holding his breath.

The prize for the victor was a crown of wild olives, part of the cow that had been sacrificed at the festival, and the right to leave a miniature likeness of himself in the temple. Competitors initially wore clothes; then, after 720 B.C., they ran naked. Explanations for this change vary: for some, it was to demonstrate the beauty, strength, and grace of the human figure; for others, the change occured after one of the contestants, Koroubios, threw aside his loincloth so as to run faster—one of the first instances of streamlining gear in order to win.

There is a third reason: married women were not allowed to watch the race, a rule dating back to the time when fertility rites played a major part in the celebrations. Women caught spectating were dealt with in a clear and direct way: they were thrown down a steep mountainside. One woman, Callipatira of Rhodes, who had coached her son Pisidorus after his father's death, crept in disguised as a man. When her son won, she jumped over the barrier dividing spectators and judges and her clothing came loose, giving her away. Since she came from a great family of athletes (her brothers had all been champions, and her father was one of Greece's most famous boxers), she was forgiven. However, to avoid any recurrence, it was decreed that all contestants and coaches should henceforth appear naked.

Later, in the years of Spartan ascendancy, women were not only allowed to attend but encouraged to compete. The Spartans added wrestling (often highly bloody encounters); a three-part event made up of running, jumping, and spear-throwing; and the discus—but still no swordfighting. With the Roman conquest came boxing—more vicious than wrestling, as competitors wrapped their fists in leather thongs, sometimes embedded with nails. Mutilation was a mark of honor.

For about twelve hundred years the Games continued to be held at the base of Mount Olympus. Rows over professional status, doping, bribery, politics, and boycotts were commonplace. The first publicly disgraced cheat was Eupholus of Thessaly, who bribed three boxers to lose intentionally (it is not clear quite why) in 388 B.C. He was fined, and the money used to erect a statue of Zeus outside the stadium, to appease the god and warn others who might be similarly tempted. Before long there was a line of these statues, called "zanes," each bearing on its base a description of the offense and a note of praise to the actual victor.

A truce on all political disputes was declared for the duration of the Games. Even during the protracted Peloponnesian War hostilities were suspended and the belligerents competed in the festival. Eventually, in A.D. 393, the Christian emperor Theodosius banned the games as pagan—

despite which they continued for another thirty years, until the site was destroyed. In the sixth century an earthquake buried the ancient Olympic arena completely, "cheat" statues and all.

Yet the idea of an athletic festival persisted. The Greeks revived gatherings for which they used the word "Olympic" in 1859, 1870, 1875, and 1889, but these festivals, like most others, were strictly local. The Much Wenlock Games in Shropshire date back as far as 1636 and were held regularly thereafter; among the later events were such abstruse contests as tilting at a ring and tent pegging, as well as cricket and lawn tennis. In the summer of 1866, London held an Olympics that drew ten thousand spectators, with twenty-four events, including fencing with bayonets and a saber competition won by one G. Henderson of Liverpool. The great English cricketer W. G. Grace, then eighteen, entered a twenty-flight hurdle race and won by twenty yards. Other games had been held in France, Sweden, and Germany, and as early as 1788 the president of Harvard was petitioned to restart the Olympics in America. The first true prototype, however, emerged in Sweden, host to a festival "in commemoration of the Ancient Olympic Games" in 1834 and again in 1836.

Enter Pierre de Frédy, Baron de Coubertin, scion of a family whose title went back to 1477. After brief military training and a few months at law school, the young baron felt a vocation as a social reformer. As a boy he had experienced the "humiliating defeat" of the French in 1870, which he attributed (questionably) to the physical inferiority of his country's youth. French schools concentrated on high academic standards and generally ignored physical education. Coubertin decided that English education, with its emphasis on sport, was far superior. When he came across *Tom Brown's School Days,* Tom Hughes's novel of life at Rugby School sixty years before, he felt he had discovered a paradigm of how education should work, with Dr. Thomas Arnold, Rugby's headmaster, "his lifelong hero, prophet, and father-substitute."[20] As much tract as novel, the book is hardly enough to shape a philosophy, but Coubertin thought *"l'éducation anglaise"* offered the right pathway to French manhood. A visit to Rugby consolidated his view, and as he plodded toward his vision of a new Olympic Games he carried a copy, in English, of what became his bible of the strenuous life.

Financially Coubertin had no need to work, so he could afford to dabble in quasi-political good causes. He became one of the 2,731 members of the Unions de la Paix Sociale, a member of the Société d'Economie Sociale and of numerous educational committees, in which capacity he helped bring sports to French schools and initiated interschool competition. In

1889 he organized an international conference on physical education and went to the Paris Exposition, joined to which was a medieval-style sporting meet that he dubbed "great competitive pageants for school youth."[21] During his speech at the conference, almost as an afterthought and inspired in passing by a campaign in the newspaper *Le Temps*, he brought up the idea of a modern Olympics, which he repeated during a lecture tour of the United States and again on a visit to London. Three years after the initial conference, in November 1892, at a meeting at the Sorbonne, he appealed for a "splendid and beneficent" sports festival.

Events moved quickly after that. In the fall of 1893 Coubertin made a second tour of America. The timing was right: numerous rowing clubs had sprung up throughout the United States from the 1830s on, and by 1869 the first international contest had taken place. Yacht racing also dates from the 1830s, with the America's Cup first contested in 1857. Track and field athletics took shape in the 1870s; both football and rugby were well established, while baseball was being referred to as "the national sport" as early as 1856. Parallel with these upper-class sports, a host of other recreations had grown up in the 1870s and 1880s, ice skating, bicycling, and long-distance walking among them. These were but the prime channels of an extraordinary outpouring of participatory and spectator sport in the United States in the latter decades of the nineteenth century. Coubertin was impressed and heartened, convinced that his ideas were timely.

In June 1894 the London *Spectator* dismissed his brainchild as "a harmless whim," but by the fall, at yet another conference in Paris, the little Frenchman was pressing for the capital to host the first revived Olympic Games, alongside a "Universal Exposition," by the turn of the century. By conference's end (the British delegates having failed to have "amateur" formally defined by social class) the thirteen nations present voted overwhelmingly to undertake the Games. Twenty-one other nations sent written support.

It is unclear what process led to the choice of participants and events for the first modern Olympics (for romantic reasons, the committee decided to hold them in Athens; the original starting date of 1900 was brought forward to 1896 at the suggestion of the Greek delegate), but Coubertin himself ensured that both foil and saber were among the original events. Although he was little over five feet tall, the baron had been a fencer, and his memoirs display a photograph of him fencing outdoors, his slightly squat figure making an appropriate *beau escrimeur*. In 1906 he even drew up the rules for saber on horseback.[22] Richard Mandell evokes the Coubertin of those years:

> His mustache was splendid. It was carefully pruned, with sumptuous tendrils that swooped out to wisps at the end, beyond the width of his canted ears and broad, asymmetrical forehead. He looked like a whiskered cat destined for a long life. . . . His heavy eyebrows and piercing eyes were always dark. In fact, his eyes were so dark as to appear to be without pupils. They were a bit popped, with Italian verve. . . . Dazzling and aggressive, they were the eyes of a man continually gauging the possibilities for action . . . this man with a peppy organgrinder's good looks.[23]

The revived Olympics were a great success: 245 athletes from twelve nations competed in forty-three different disciplines. But they almost did not take place: no invitations were sent out till December 1895, just eight months before the event, and more than 60 percent of the eventual entries came from Greece, with Germany, France, and the United States sending 21, 19, and 14 contestants respectively. Britain sent 8, and both the British and French teams were unofficial. Such was the informality of the Games that a British lawn tennis player entered the Olympic tournament simply to secure a court to play on. Nevertheless, on March 25, 1896, a dreary, rainy Wednesday, cannon were fired, doves were released, and after 1,471 years the Olympics were reborn.*

Throughout the history of the modern Games only fourteen events have been held at every Olympics: the 100-, 400-, 800-, and 1,500-meter races, the marathon, the 110-meter hurdles, the high jump, pole vault, long jump, triple jump, shot put, and discus, the 1,500-meter freestyle swimming—and the individual saber. Individual foil was excluded only in

---

* The Greeks were determined that one of their countrymen should win what was almost their national event, the marathon, held over twenty-six miles between Marathon and Athens. George Averoff, the wealthy local architect who had largely funded the Games, was so caught up in the general fervor that he offered the Greek runners his daughter in marriage, along with a dowry of a million drachmas—exactly the cost of reconstructing the main stadium. Of the twenty-five runners, twenty-one were Greek, so the odds were favorable, and sure enough a local postman, Spiridon Loues, crossed the finishing line first. Fortunately for Averoff, Loues was already married, but he was happy to accept a voucher for 365 free meals, free shoe-polishing for life, and a plot of land known thereafter as "the field of Marathon."

1908, when the London organizers decided it was unsuitable for competition. In 1896 the fencing was mainly memorable, in so amateur an enterprise, for the inclusion of a foil event for professional masters; but then Coubertin was ever the pragmatist, and in 1931 admitted:

> Amateurism. That! Always that. It had been 16 years since we had naively feigned to be done with it. . . . Today I can risk the confession; I was never much concerned about the question of amateurism. It had served me as a screen to convene the Congress to Re-establish the Olympic Games. Seeing the importance that others lent it in the sporting world, I would show the expected zeal in that direction, but it was zeal without real conviction.[24]

At any rate, fencing was the first sport in the Olympics with an event for professionals (won by Leon Pyrgos of Greece); in 1900 it was extended to saber and épée. In 1904 there was a singlesticks event and two years later "three-cornered saber." The Olympics of 1906 have always troubled the statisticians and figure in hardly any record books, yet after the St. Louis Games in 1904 it had been decided that, wherever else the Olympics might be staged, there should be another Olympics, also on a four-year cycle, sited permanently in Athens. A fencing team was sent by Britain, captained by Theodore Andrea Cook, president of the British Olympic Council. Cook was required to write an official report, which he did in *The Cruise of the* Branwen, "being a short history of the modern revival of the Olympic Games, together with an account of the adventures of the English fencing team in Athens in 1906."

It is a bizarre production. For a start, the *Branwen* was a 135-foot-long yacht owned by one of the team, Lord Howard de Walden, aboard which four members of the fencing squad traveled to Athens. Cook admitted in his preface that "This modest volume has no pretensions to be a very serious contribution to the history either of sport or travel."[25] While a detailed account can be found of the performances of the twenty-four-man British team, one also encounters quotations from Greek, Latin, and French literature, an extended discussion of the techniques, ancient and modern, of javelin and discus throwing; descriptions of Vesuvius, the Parthenon, and *Oedipus Rex* (as performed in the main stadium of the Games); two full articles, in French, reprinted from a magazine to which Cook had contributed; and a long report on what the fencers saw on their journey home.

The Games themselves drew 901 competitors. In overall results Britain came second to France, Greece third, and the United States fourth. "The gospel of good sport has spread," wrote Cook, "until it has reached nations that were previously untouched by any single spark of athletic emulation. . . . England no longer stands alone, as once she did, as the apostle of 'hard exercise.' "

Most of the crowned heads of Europe attended the opening ceremony, and once the Games were under way up to thirty thousand people crowded into the stadium, sited just below the Acropolis. The customary gymnastic displays culminated in the performance of Colonel Black's Swedish team, who gave "an almost excessive testimony to the practical results of that gentleman's persistent energy in the cause of national calisthenics." The six-man British fencing squad included two peers and one knight, yet it was representative enough and on its return home roundly beat a Rest of Britain team. Howard de Walden fought at foil, saber, and épée; since the previous week he had won the Craven Stakes at Newmarket, it was "a record which will be difficult to beat." Cook points out that "the average age of the British team (43) greatly exceeded that of any other team, as I have no doubt its average height and weight did also." Britain's first match, against Germany, was watched by Edward VII, who was so impressed that on his return to London he agreed to be patron of British fencing.*

Even though the Athens experiment was not repeated—by 1908 the Games were already a costly affair—*The Cruise of the Branwen* remains a beguilingly offbeat account of an international sporting event. Lord Howard and his passengers must have sensed that too, because they composed a fourteen-verse poem, the "Song of the *Branwen*," whose final stanza runs:

---

* One member of Britain's épée team, Sir Cosmo Duff Gordon, would travel on the *Titanic* on its fateful voyage in 1912. The night she went down, April 14, Duff Gordon offered the sailors on the lifeboat that had him and his wife on board £5 each (roughly three weeks' pay) to make up for the wages they would lose by the ship's sinking; but he also argued that they should not go back to pick up those struggling in the water. There were 2,340 souls on the liner, lifeboats for only 1,100, and in the chaos just 651 escaped. But the sailors, feeling they had been undercompensated, blew the gaff. One of the actual checks Duff Gordon made out was displayed at the official inquiry, and Duff Gordon spent the rest of his life in disgrace, since many felt he had in effect bribed the men to let others die. He underwent the ultimate social indignity of that time: his entry in *Who's Who* was expunged.

The fencing venue at the "unofficial" Athens Games of 1906. Edward VII came to watch and was so impressed he became the patron of Britain's fencing association.

The young Bulgarian dreams it
As the stars pale in the sky;
Dalmatians, Turks and Magyars
Have heard its battle-cry;
And a nameless terror seizes
The wives of Paris town
When they read the name of Branwen
And her swordsmen of renown.

The privileged atmosphere in which fencing was conducted, and the small number who practiced it, meant that several celebrities had time to take up the sport and could excel at it without encountering too much competition. In France, Gustave Eiffel, who raised the great tower, fenced until his seventy-fourth year. Paul Gauguin was keener still. André Maginot, responsible as minister of defense for the ill-fated Maginot Line, took particular pleasure in fencing, even teaching his sister at foil.[26]

In Britain, another young fencer to make his mark was Winston

Churchill, who took up the sport at Harrow. At the age of seventeen he wrote to his mother, "I have won the fencing. A very fine cup. I was far and away first. Absolutely untouched in the finals." Churchill was chosen to represent Harrow at the Public Schools championships, the toughest event open to schoolboys in those days. He wrote home excitedly, "My fencing is now my great employment out of school as now that I represent the school it behooves me to 'sweat it up.'" Come the day, according to *The Field*, "although only a boy in appearance, he quickly showed the spectators that in the use of the foil he had been well tutored." He beat boys from Eton, Winchester, Bradfield, and Tonbridge before facing the intimidating "Deanley [actually Dearnley] (Late First Life Guards) of the Gymnasium, Oxford, and winner of the Army fencing championships on three different occasions."

The bout was for the best of seven hits. "Master Churchill at once went for his man and cleverly won the first point, following this by adding two more hits. The guardsman, however, secured the next two; but with astonishing rapidity the next was added to Churchill's score. The final bout produced some 'smart fencing' and, amid great applause, the son of the illustrious statesman [Lord Randolph Churchill] was hailed the victor. . . . Churchill is undoubtedly one of the smartest competitors with the foil ever seen at these annual contests." "His success," added *The Harrovian*, was "chiefly due to his quick and dashing attack, which quite took his opponents by surprise. Churchill must be congratulated on his success" as his opponents "must have been much taller and more formidable than himself." It is odd that a guardsman should have been allowed to fence in a school competition; possibly the fight-off was arranged immediately after the championships, or else Dearnley was allowed to take part as the event was held at the army barracks in Aldershot.

After Harrow, Churchill may have dabbled at his chosen sport during his army days in India, but there is no evidence of it. It was in India that in 1897, commanding a small detachment in open country during a rearguard action against Pathan tribesmen, he decisively rejected the sword. As the Pathans closed in on the small hillock he and his men were defending, the adjutant of Churchill's battalion scrambled up and panted, "Come on back now. There's no time to lose. We can cover you from the knoll." At this Churchill pocketed his ammunition (it was a standing order to let no bullets fall into enemy hands) and was on the point of retreating when a fusillade killed the man next to him and struck five others, one of whom, Churchill later recorded, "was spinning around just behind me, his face a mass of blood, his right eye cut out." Recovering the wounded was a point of honor, as torture was inevitable if they fell into Pathan hands. Churchill and his command were halfway down the slope, carrying their casualties, when some thirty tribesmen charged them. In the resulting chaos the adjutant was hit. Churchill ran to rescue him, but a Pathan swordsman got there first, butchering him with a stroke. At this point, Churchill recalled his championship and promptly drew his saber. "I resolved on personal combat à l'arme blanche." But he was on his own by now, and more Pathans were hastening toward him. It occurred to him that these clansmen were not public schoolboys. "I changed my mind about cold steel." Instead, "I fired nine shots from my revolver"—and leapt to safety, an Indiana Jones before his time.[27]

I T WAS MILITARY PRESSURE THAT LED TO THE INTRODUCTION OF THE modern pentathlon at the Stockholm Games of 1912, although the hand of Coubertin is evident. Conan Doyle's Brigadier Etienne Gérard had been translated into French in 1898, and who could resist such bravura passages as this:

"You are, as I understand, a good swordsman?" said he.

"Tolerable, sire," I answered.

"You were chosen by your regiment to fight the champion of the Hussars of Chambarant?" said he.

I was not sorry to find that he knew so much of my exploits.

"My comrades, sire, did me that honor," said I.

"And for the sake of practice you insulted six fencing masters in the week before your duel?"

"I had the privilege of being out seven times in as many days, sire," said I.

"And escaped without a scratch?"

"The fencing master of the 23rd Light Infantry touched me on the left elbow, sire."[28]

The London Times recently wrote of the modern pentathlon in an editorial that "this event is said, implausibly, to replicate the five skills . . . needed by an Ancient Greek officer to escape from enemy lines."[29] Very implausibly. The original pentathlon (from the Greek penta, "five," and athlon, "contest") was featured for the first time in 708 B.C., after Spartans had complained that too many Olympic events favored civilians and did nothing to reward the skills of warriors. It consisted of running (the length of one ancient Greek stadium, now deemed to be 192.27 meters), jumping, discus, javelin, and wrestling—the first four events held on a knockout basis until there remained only two competitors, who would then wrestle for the crown. The pentathlon was immediately positioned as a major event of the games, and the winner was named "Athlete of the Festival."

The modern version consists of a freestyle swim of 300 meters, a twelve-object show-jumping course on a horse previously unknown to the competitor, twenty shots from 25 meters at a target 155 millimeters in diameter, a 5,000-meter race across country, and a fencing *"poule unique"* in which every contestant is matched successively against everyone else, for a single hit. The notion behind the event was that a gentleman officer might, in battle, be compelled to gallop across broken country, cut his way through enemy lines with sword and pistol, swim a river, and run many miles to deliver an important message—a remarkable vision, but exactly what Gérard underwent in that very first adventure, "The Medal of Brigadier Gérard."*

A junior officer, even in 1912, would have carried a cavalry saber; Coubertin, in deference to the Olympic hosts, substituted épée, at which Sweden had long excelled. Having initiated the event, he then immodestly declared that it would be the one contest that would "test a man's moral qualities as much as his physical resources and skills, producing thereby the ideal complete athlete."

---

* Over the years, attempts have been made to change the basic disciplines, for example replacing horses with motorbikes and fencing with judo. So far they seem unlikely to succeed. An article in *L'Escrime Française* in 1954 reported the findings of the International Council of Military Sports (CSM) concerning the value of sports to military training, and in particular for the requirements of modern air combat. Medical opinion in Europe placed fencing at the top of the list of recommended sports for air force pilots. An Italian expert stated, "There is a profound analogy between aviation and fencing. . . . Fencing is a particularly good sport because it accustoms [the pilot] to an evaluation of the strength of the opponent, to the use of reasoning and the exercise of courage." The secretary of the committee summed up: "Fencing develops serenity under fire, because the fencer does not have to deal with an object but with a thinking person—his opponent—in a struggle fought at terribly close quarters and with movements of lightning rapidity."[30] Years later, when Polish fighter pilots arrived in Britain during the Second World War, one of their first inquiries was for a fencing master and a place to train.

ONE BENEFICIARY OF THIS ADDITION TO THE OLYMPICS WAS A young American soldier who made his international debut at Stockholm: George S. Patton, the flamboyant American combat commander of the Second World War, who would conquer Sicily in thirty-eight days. Patton graduated from West Point in 1909. Fencing was part of his coursework, and although he had never encountered the sport he threw himself avidly into learning all he could. The official West Point team fought at foil, but Patton organized a special broadsword group and even, despite his marked dyslexia, wrote a poem about his new enthusiasm—as well as other pieces about his recollections of his conduct as a swordsman in previous incarnations, much to the amusement of his brother cadets. He would practice on his own for hours, giving free expression to his teenage belief that to be a fine swordsman was an essential trait of any great general. In 1905 he wrote home, "If I never amount to anything else I can turn instructor with the broadsword, for I am the best of the best in the class." In fact, he was an all-around athlete, setting a record in the 220-yard low hurdles and being an effective football player until he broke both arms at the end of his first year. He was an excellent swimmer and also became adept with rifle and pistol—a range of skills that, taken together, made him a natural candidate for the new Olympic discipline.

In 1896 twelve nations had sent about 100 sportsmen to Athens to compete with 150 Greeks. By 1912 there were twenty-eight nations and a total of 2,547 athletes. The pentathlon was limited to military contestants. Each competitor carried out his own training program, and Patton fed himself a diet of raw steak and salads. On May 10 he was chosen to represent the United States, the only American to take part. The competition was in early July, and forty-two athletes were entered. Patton fancied his chances.

The day before the opening event, he practiced his shooting, scoring 197 points out of a possible 200, good enough for a medal. The competition proper began with the swimming event, in which he did well, finishing seventh. Then came the fencing, in which Patton beat twenty-one of his twenty-four opponents, placing him third. He later recorded, "I was fortunate enough to give the French victor the only defeat he had." Fencing the first to make three hits, the Frenchman, Lieutenant de Mas Latrie, took a 2–0 lead, but Patton fought back to win convincingly: it was a good victory.[31]

At this point Patton was in line for a medal, but then came the calamity

*Second Lieutenant George S. Patton, Jr. (left), takes on fellow pentathlete
de Mas Latrie of France during the 1912 Stockholm Olympics.
Patton won the bout 3–2, the Frenchman's only defeat.*

of the shooting event. He scored a miserable 169, coming in twenty-first.
He complained that he had been penalized for missing the target completely on one of his shots, when in fact the bullet had gone through a previously made hole. Much argument ensued, but a miss was recorded: had
Patton's view been upheld, he would have won the gold medal, but there
was no evidence to support him. Despite good performances at riding,
where he came in sixth, registering a perfect score, and running, where he
came in tenth, he ended up fifth overall. Of the top seven finishers, six
were Swedes.

Naturally enough, the local papers gave several columns to the event
and picked out Patton's fencing for special mention: his calm had been
"unusual and calculated. He was skillful in exploiting his opponent's
every weakness." Other commentators were more critical: "Patton's pu-
gnacious, slashing, give-no-quarter attacking style easily made him a
crowd favorite but tactically often left him vulnerable to the finesse of his
competitors, most of whom were far more experienced. . . . To attack was
to succeed, to defend was to invite defeat." Another commented, "[The
American's defense] was the despair of his teachers, for the aggressive Patton was interested only in offense. His method of parrying was to counterattack."

He must have made an impression, however, as the U.S. fencing team now enlisted him for the saber competition, despite his having trained mainly at épée. His own view of the Games was starry-eyed. The Olympics were the closest approximation to the heroic ideal of his fantasies. As for the modern pentathlon, he recorded, "the high spirit of sportsmanship speaks volumes for the character of the officers of the present day. There was not a single . . . protest or any unsportsmanlike quibbling or fighting for points. . . . Each man did his best and took what fortune sent like a true soldier, and at the end we all felt more like good friends and comrades than rivals . . . yet this spirit of friendship in no manner detracted from the zeal with which all strove for success."[32]

Patton asked some of his fellow contestants who was the best fencer in Europe, and was told it was Brigade Sergeant-Major Charles Cléry, professional champion of Europe, who taught at the Saumur Cavalry School. Patton at once made his way to Saumur and for the next two weeks took lessons from Cléry at épée and saber. On returning to the United States, Patton set about redesigning the 1840 U.S. cavalry saber (referred to colloquially as "old wrist-breaker") and wrote a new army manual for its use, with a foreword by Major General Leonard Wood, a family friend and expert fencer—he frequently practiced with President Roosevelt in the White House. Patton was subsequently assigned to the Mounted Service School in Fort Riley, Kansas, where he was given the official title "Master of the Sword." The first to hold the position, he was thus acknowledged as the foremost expert in the army. For a young second lieutenant, this was prominence indeed.

On his twenty-eighth birthday, the following year, Patton wrote to his wife, Beatrice, "When I get less hair than I now have I will look like a German duelist." A decade later he would spend five more months at Fort Riley, taking an advanced cavalry course. One day he approached a young instructor, Lieutenant (later to be Brigadier General) Paul Robinett, to swap extra tuition in machine-gun technique for Sunday-afternoon fencing lessons in the attic at their quarters.

Robinett later recalled, "It was a grim business. With every thrust he would shout some such remark as 'I've knocked his eye out! See the blood spew! I've bored him through the heart! I've ripped his guts out!' One by one we stepped up to be dismembered. On and on Patton would go, until almost exhausted."

Patton competed only in the Stockholm Games, as the First World War put paid to the next Olympics. When the Games returned in 1920, fencing was established as a key sport in its own right as well as being one of the mainstays of the pentathlon. However, for most people the "festival" was still small beer: amateurs were not expected to be of the same standard as professionals, there was no sponsorship and little publicity, and the whole notion of international sports meetings had not yet broken through into the world's consciousness. Instead, there was a different discovery that was making people sit up and take notice, one that in its way did even more than international sports meetings to help keep fencing alive: and that was the cinema.

CHAPTER 10

Swashbuckling

> SWASHBUCKLER. 1560. One who makes a noise by striking his
> own or his opponent's shield with a sword. A swaggering
> bravo or ruffian. A noisy braggadocio. The swashbuckling
> manners of a youth of fashion in the reign of Elizabeth I.
>
> —The Shorter Oxford English Dictionary

> Make the viewer feel the blow.
>
> —YUEN WO PING, FIGHT CHOREOGRAPHER FOR *Crouching
> Tiger, Hidden Dragon* AND *The Matrix*

IT IS SAID THAT CINEMA BEGAN IN PARIS ON DECEMBER 28, 1895,
when thirty-three people crowded into the basement of a café in the Boulevard des Capucines to watch twenty minutes of primitive flickering images.[1] The new medium developed with astonishing speed, even if many
of the earliest examples of the filmmaker's art were ornate fantasy sequences or trick shots, such as *The Execution of Mary, Queen of Scots*
(1895), which shows the doomed queen's headless body—a trick achieved
by putting a dummy in place while the camera was stopped.

The first full-length film featuring swordplay was probably Italian, *The
Crusades* (1911), followed by the epic *Quo Vadis?* (1912), "the most ambitious photodrama that has yet been seen here," but there was little in either of adept swordsmanship.[2] Fencing in general, however, pervaded
early cinema and became a staple with both American and European filmmakers. In particular, 1916 saw *D'Artagnan*, which cost $15,000 to make
and brought in seven times that in profit. In the years that followed there
were versions of *The Three Musketeers, The Prisoner of Zenda,* and *Ivanhoe,*
as well as a 1920 *Mark of Zorro*—films crowded with flashing swords and
extravagant postures but with no thought given to anything resembling
technical accuracy. They were, as one film historian put it, "little more
than knife sharpenings."[3]

In this the cinema took its lead from theater. For most of the nineteenth century, a prime qualification for matinee stardom had been sword-fighting ability. Many a poor play was staged as an occasion for an exciting fight scene, and no melodrama was considered complete without a climactic set-to between hero and villain. Most actors took their stage fights seriously, one American actor launching into Richard III's final combat with such fury that on one occasion he refused to yield at all and pursued his terrified antagonist off the stage and out into the street. Most performers just hacked away, waiting for the appropriate amount of time before one of them could fall dead, for no apparent reason. Lionel Barrymore, toward the end of his career and playing a villain, once stopped in mid-performance during a climactic duel after the play's young hero had managed to lose his sword during their skirmish. "*What* am I meant to do *now*?" he asked rhetorically, "*Starve* to death?"

Generally, swordfights were a compound of saber and épée. A number of well-known routines were used, selected according to the needs of the play but not created for a particular production. These routines, referred to in the profession as "the Square Eights," "the Round Eights," "the Glasgow Tens," and even one called "the Drunk Combat," were made up of a series of cuts, or whacks of blade on blade, repeated as often as necessary.*

In London in the late nineteenth century, the majority of the leading actors of the day became pupils of the "Master of Fence," Félix Bertrand, who helped stage the most celebrated duels—between Herbert Beerbohm Tree and Fred Terry in *Hamlet*, for instance, in Charles Wyndham's *Cyrano*, and Johnston Forbes-Robertson's *Macbeth*. Not all stage fights were planned, however. During the climactic scene between Henry Irving and Squire Bancroft in *The Dead Heart*, only the final thrust was rehearsed. The rest, night after night, was improvised. "This fight," says William Hobbs, who is seen by many as Bertrand's successor, "set all Lon-

---

* Mark Twain, typically, picked up on the problems some actors could have with fencing terms. In *The Adventures of Tom Sawyer* (1876) Tom is in a forest when he encounters his friend Joe Harper and, waving his wooden sword, declares that he is Robin Hood. Joe soon gets into the act: "Then thou are indeed that famous outlaw? Right gladly will I dispute with thee the passes of the merry wood. Have at thee!" They at once strike "a fencing attitude, foot to foot, and began a grave, careful combat, 'two up and two down.' Presently Tom said: 'Now if you've got the hang. Go it lively!' So they 'went it lively,' panting and perspiring with the work. By and by Tom shouted: 'Fall! Fall! Why don't you fall?' 'I shan't! Why don't you fall yourself? You're getting the worst of it.' 'Why that ain't anything. *I* can't fall; that ain't the way it is in the book. The book says "Then with one back-handed stroke he slew poor Guy of Guisborne." You're to turn round and let me hit you in the back.' There was no getting around the authorities, so Joe turned, received the whack and fell."[4]

don talking, and no wonder!"[5] Both men put great energy into their duel—yet Irving was nearsighted. They must have been good fencers to have survived without injury. Bram Stoker (of *Dracula* fame, and Irving's manager and biographer) observed with a certain admiration of a production of *Romeo and Juliet* that the swordplay was so spirited that on most evenings at least one member of the cast required medical attention. Once, in the fight between Romeo and Paris in the tomb, when Paris failed to die on cue, Romeo (Henry Irving) seized his adversary's sword, hit him over the knuckles with his own, prodded him in the stomach with his knee, and cried, "Die, my boy, die. Down, down, down"—then elbowed and pushed his wretched victim into his grave.

Another important feature was flying sparks. Irving so loved the effect that that he would attach flints to his blade. Later, with the advent of electricity, he would go even further and had his weapons wired, so that they would discharge sparks throughout the fight. He soon added rubber insulation.

The net result was that filmmakers knew that swordfights made for great box office; but at first they paid little attention to how such fights should be orchestrated.* This was still true when Douglas Fairbanks produced *The Three Musketeers* in 1921. Demonstrations outside and inside the theater and throughout its first screening—when Fairbanks was called upon to make a speech before the film started, during the intermission, and a third time at the conclusion—confirmed that he had a success on his hands. Two-dollar tickets went for five.

Although Fairbanks was later considered the embodiment of d'Artagnan, the idea of making a film inspired by Dumas's hero crept up on him slowly. In 1918 he made *A Modern Musketeer*, a strange hybrid based on the now-forgotten novel *D'Artagnan of Kansas*. It opens with a scene showing Fairbanks as d'Artagnan, then switches to a modern accident-prone hero, "always chivalrous, always misunderstood," and his attempts to woo a flapper, Elsie Dodge, away from her suitor, Forrest Vandeteer, "the richest man in Yonkers." The opening credits ask, hopefully, "Do you remember

---

* Years later, Alan Sillitoe was to satirize this approach in a children's book, *The Incredible Fencing Fleas* (1978):

Frederick was breathless. "Now what do we do?"
    "You jump over my sword," said Ferdinand, "and I'll jump over yours."
    "What good will that do?"
    "It will give us something to do."

d'Artagnan of France? Can you recall the thrills you got from the adventures of that famous swash-buckling gallant of three centuries ago?" (It was long believed that only the first reel had survived, but recently the missing reels have resurfaced, and the whole of this brilliant film should shortly be available.)

Capitalizing on the success of Fairbanks's *The Three Musketeers,* the Alexander Film Corporation quickly rereleased its 1916 *D'Artagnan* under Fairbanks's title, while the French comedian Max Linder rushed out a knockabout takeoff, *The Three Must-Get-Theirs.* With Linder as "Dart-in-again," it contained several marvelous spoof dueling sequences, all based on classical foil play, carefully arranged by the Belgian master Fred Cavens.

Linder's comedy was seen by Fairbanks, who, far from being affronted, asked Cavens to work with him on his next batch of films. Of all the actors who have fought with swords the best actual athlete remains the five-foot, five-inch Douglas Elton Ulman—Douglas Fairbanks, Sr. Yet he made all his swashbuckling movies after the age of thirty-five. As Jeffrey Richards says in his authoritative *Swordsmen of the Screen,* "After Doug the swashbuckler took off as a cinematic genre, in which physical movement and vi-

Douglas Fairbanks, Sr., in practice for his role of d'Artagnan in his 1921 version of The Three Musketeers. *Note the expression on the stuntman's face, and also Fairbanks's casual attire. To the right stands their swordmaster, Henri J. Uyttenhove.*

sual style predominated. But for sheer verve and vitality there was never anyone to equal Doug."[6]

The appeal of the athletic Fairbanks may seem obvious today, but in 1920, when he launched *The Mark of Zorro*, he did so with trepidation, having been advised not to abandon his previous comedy-adventures; after all, four years earlier D. W. Griffith's historical epic *Intolerance* had failed at the box office. But *The Mark of Zorro* ("*zorro*" is Spanish for "fox") was an enormous success, and suddenly swashbucklers were all the rage. Seeing Fairbanks's films over a three-day period, in the Museum of Modern Art's new viewing rooms in Queens, I could understand why: they have an infectious exuberance, a disarming confidence, and rich humor to go with their impressive gymnastics. "Why do you wear a mask?" Zorro is asked. "Perhaps to hide the features of a Bergerac," he replies with a boyish grin. As d'Artagnan, he is twice brought up before Richelieu, his life in the Cardinal's hands. "If you were about to die, what would you do?" Richelieu asks him each time, and each time he replies, "Your Eminence, I should write the history of France." On the second occasion, having just

The scene as it appears on film. Fairbanks did all his own fencing stunts, even though his swashbuckling films started only after he was thirty-five.

been bested by d'Artagnan over the queen's jewels, the prelate "whose genius had re-created France" says, "Then set down in your book, M. d'Artagnan, that Richelieu was a generous foe"—handing him back to his fellow musketeers and into the arms of Constance.

Following the First World War, disillusionment and a widespread thirst for escapism led to a longing for romance, heroism, and adventure. Fairbanks caught these aspirations brilliantly. He created "the Fairbanks picture," showing that people could be effective as individuals. In his wake, other stars from the silent film era donned cape and sword: among them Ramon Novarro (*Scaramouche*, 1923; *The Prisoner of Zenda*, 1922); Rudolph Valentino (*Monsieur Beaucaire*, 1924), fencing left-handed; and John Barrymore (*Don Juan*, 1926, with one of the screen's great duels—although he had the experience of a hundred and one Broadway *Hamlets* to help him, he got overexcited before the camera, swinging about wildly and dangerously, and Fred Cavens had to double for him).

Cavens, a graduate of the Belgian Military Institute, worked with Fairbanks on three of his films: *Don Q, Son of Zorro* (1925), *The Black Pirate* (1926), and *The Iron Mask* (1929). He had long considered how screen fights should be staged and became a great innovator. "All movements—instead of being as small as possible, as in competitive fencing—must be large," he declared, "but nevertheless correct. Magnified is the word. The routine should contain the most spectacular attacks and parries it is possible to execute while remaining logical to the situation. In other words, the duel should be a fight and not a fencing exhibition, and should disregard at times classically correct guards and lunges. The attitudes arising naturally out of fighting instinct should predominate. When this occurs the whole performance will leave an impression of strength, skill and manly grace."[7]

Cavens was not only an inspired fight arranger, he was lucky in his timing. Over the next twenty years he worked with all the great swashbuckling stars of the period, in some of the best films featuring swordfights: Douglas Fairbanks, Sr. and Jr. (the latter in *The Corsican Brothers* and *The Exile*), Errol Flynn (*Captain Blood*, *The Adventures of Robin Hood*, *The Sea Hawk*, *The Adventures of Don Juan*), Louis Hayward (*The Man in the Iron Mask*, *The Fortunes of Captain Blood*), Cornel Wilde (*Sons of the Musketeers*), and Tyrone Power (*The Mark of Zorro*). Of these only Power never looked the part. Errol Flynn was a natural sportsman who had narrowly failed to make the Australian Olympic team in 1932 as a boxer; Douglas Fairbanks, Jr., learned to fence when he was twelve, and usually did his own fights; and Wilde, the 1934 American intercollegiate foil champion, trained with the 1936 Olympic squad. Born in Budapest, in several of his films he would change hands midfight, to show his dexterity.

Throughout his career at Paramount, Cavens received only a single screen credit—for *The Vagabond King*, in 1956. He not only taught the films' heroes how to fight, he also taught the villains. The most memorably dastardly of these was Basil Rathbone, otherwise known as Levasseur in *Captain Blood*, Guy of Guisborne in *The Adventures of Robin Hood*, and Captain Esteban Pasquale in *The Mark of Zorro*. Rathbone was a good club fencer who prided himself on his expertise—"a skilled swordsman," as he described himself—and in *The Adventures of Robin Hood* (1938) he and Flynn crossed swords with a minimum of doubling. Nick Evangelista, in his *Encyclopedia of the Sword*, rates Rathbone's duel with Tyrone Power in *The Mark of Zorro* as "the finest example of movie swordplay Hollywood has ever produced." Rathbone himself considered Power "the most agile man with a sword I've ever faced before a camera"; but the truth is that Power had to be doubled by Fred Cavens's son, yet was *still* so unathletic he managed to undermine the fight scenes. By contrast, Rathbone did all his own swordplay, wearing high, stiff boots to accentuate the dramatic line of his lunge. The powers that be at Twentieth Century Fox expressed alarm that the forty-eight-year-old Rathbone, at that time the highest-paid character actor in Hollywood, should be performing his own fights, but Cavens declared, "I doubt that he would do well in competition, but for picture purposes he is better than the best fencer in the world."*

---

* During his years in London Rathbone had been a pupil of both Félix Grave and Léon Bertrand. He could be generous to fellow actors. Discussing *The Court Jester* (1956), in which he played opposite Danny Kaye in a deliberate spoof of medieval melodramas, he wrote in his autobiography, "We had to fight a duel together with sabre. I don't care much for sabre but had had instruction in this weapon during my long association with all manner of swords. . . . After a couple of weeks of instruction Danny Kaye could completely outfight me! Even granted the difference in our ages, Danny's reflexes were incredibly fast, and nothing had to be shown or explained to him a second time."[8] Rathbone put Kaye's aptitude down to his being a brilliant mimic (about the same period, the French mime Marcel Marceau was also an excellent fencer), but his memory played him false: at the insistence of the production heads Kaye's fencing was doubled—partly because Rathbone was then sixty-four, partly for the timing of the comedy effects, and partly for Kaye's own safety, as he had to parry a number of cuts to head and legs with his eyes closed.

Later, after his success in *The Court Jester*, Rathbone was at his Hollywood club taking a foil lesson watched by two old fencing hands. Each time he neared them they

Basil Rathbone (Guy of Guisborne) battling Errol Flynn in The Adventures
of Robin Hood *(1937). Rathbone had taken up fencing at school; Flynn never
really learned swordplay, but he looked the part.*

The first cycle of swashbucklers ended with the coming of sound. As
the studios concentrated on talk-laden scripts, action films were momentarily forgotten: in his last silent film, *The Iron Mask* (1929), Fairbanks
symbolically dies. The swashbuckler owed its resurgence to unlikely advocates. During the early 1930s pressure groups such as the Catholic Legion
of Decency remonstrated against the content of new releases—their eroti-
cism, their glorification of crime, the general immoralities halfway glori-
fied. Hollywood's response was an increase in "safe" subjects, such as
adaptations of classic novels and historical dramas. The swashbuckler,
with its enthusiasm for the chivalric code, was an obvious candidate. In
1934 MGM produced *Treasure Island* and United Artists *The Count of
Monte Cristo;* the following year Warner Bros. made *Captain Blood,* and a
full revival was under way. The success of *Captain Blood* was helped by the
defection of the original choice for the main part, Robert Donat, who was

would intone, recalling the famous exchange that runs through the film, "Get it? Got
it. Good." Finally Rathbone could stand it no longer. Flinging off his mask he turned
and seethed, "Please *stop it*."

replaced by a twenty-six-year-old Tasmanian, the son of a professor of marine biology: Errol Flynn.

Flynn made eight swashbuckling films in his heyday, a further three by 1959, and it doesn't matter that he did few of his fight scenes himself (in *The Warriors*—released in the United Kingdom as *The Dark Avenger*, 1955—his double was R. R. V. [Raymond Rudolph Valentino] Paul, the British foilist who would reach the Olympic finals the following year). Flynn was athletic, looked the part, and remains the most convincing swordsman ever to have appeared on film. His sincerity and impudent charm do the rest. In *The New Adventures of Don Juan* (1948) he even gets the job of running the Royal Fencing Academy of the court of Spain, and with it some choice dialogue. When told by the king, "We consider Don Lorca the greatest living duelist in Spain," he shoots back, "That's certainly the mark of a good duelist, your Majesty: to be living." But as ever with Flynn, one forgives him a good deal. And who would not envy his reply to Olivia de Havilland in *The Adventures of Robin Hood*? "Why, you speak treason!" "Fluently."

Amid the many terrible lines to which the genre gave birth, there is

Rathbone during practice. On the left is the Belgian swordmaster Fred Cavens. Hollywood took on a succession of Belgian masters, considering them more amenable than their French counterparts.

one glorious exception. It comes during one of the finest of all film duels, between Ronald Colman as Rudolf Rassendyll and Douglas Fairbanks, Jr., as Rupert of Hentzau in the 1937 version of *The Prisoner of Zenda*. As the two men fight in one continuous take, around murky dungeons, up and down winding staircases, and through the shadowy main hall of the castle, they spar verbally with equal expertise:

RUPERT: *Touché*, Rassendyll. I cannot get used to fighting with furniture; where did you learn it?

RUDOLF: That all goes with the old school tie.

RUPERT: Well, then, here's your last fencing lesson. Look out for your head. Why don't you stand your ground and fight?

RUDOLF: "He who fights and runs away"—remember?

RUPERT: I see. You want to let the drawbridge down. I've just killed a man for trying that.

RUDOLF: An unarmed man, of course.

RUPERT: Of course. . . . You English are a stubborn lot.

RUDOLF: Well, "England expects that every man . . ."—you know.

RUPERT: Your golden-haired goddess will look well in black, Rassendyll. I'll console her for you . . . kiss away her tears. What, no quotation?

RUDOLF: Yes, a barking dog never bites.

RUPERT: Aargh! You'd be a sensation in a circus. I can't understand it. Where did you learn such roller skating?

RUDOLF: Coldstream Guards, my boy. Come on, now, when does the fencing lesson begin?

RUPERT: Stand still and fight, you coward.

RUDOLF: Bad-tempered fellow, aren't you, underneath the charm?

RUPERT: Why don't you let me kill you quietly?

RUDOLF: Oh, a little noise adds a touch of cheer. You notice I'm getting you closer to the drawbridge rope?

RUPERT: You're so fond of rope, it's a pity to have to finish you off with steel. What did they teach you on the playing fields of Eton? Puss in the corner?

RUDOLF: Oh, chiefly not throwing knives at other people's backs.

This was the third in a run of five Zendas—to date. There have been four film versions of Zorro and as many of *Captain Blood*, with a *Son of Captain Blood* thrown in. *The Count of Monte Cristo* has had twenty-one incarnations, plus two Countesses of Monte Cristo and a TV serial; Robin Hood has had ten films, as well as a long-running TV series; and there have been so many *Three Musketeers* (by my count, more than thirty) that it is almost easier to tot up the years when a new version has *not* appeared. In 1931 St. Louis even hosted an open-air opera of the tale, starring, of all people, Cary Grant as d'Artagnan.

THE SECOND CYCLE OF SWASHBUCKLERS ENDED DRAMATICALLY WITH America's entry into the Second World War in 1941. Cinemagoers wanted to see films that reaffirmed the fundamental values of American life, and this led to a major revival of Westerns. Douglas Fairbanks, Jr., joined the U.S. Navy, Power and Hayward the Marines. Flynn, to his dismay rejected on health grounds, made war movies such as *Desperate Journey* and *Objective Burma*. When hostilities ended, swashbucklers returned, with the old senior players joined by a new group—Cornel Wilde, John Derek, and Richard Greene—all challenging for stardom.

By 1949 Hollywood had been hit by strikes and other labor problems, and the bitter days of the Red Scare had arrived. Most threatening of all, television was burgeoning. There were cutbacks in production, together with a flood of "bread-and-butter" swashbucklers, produced at speed with standardized fight scenes and with Western directors in charge.

By the mid-1950s television had overtaken the cinema. In Britain, the small screen was filled with swashbuckling series, rapidly exported to America. There were some notable successes—*Robin Hood* with Richard Greene; *Ivanhoe* with Roger Moore, a nascent Bond in armor—enough to turn Hollywood away from the swashbuckler and toward the epic. As Jeffrey Richards concluded, "So d'Artagnan, Scaramouche and Captain Blood gave way to Alexander the Great, Cleopatra and Ben-Hur."[9] He notes that since the 1950s there have been sporadic revivals of swashbucklers—a wave of Italian-made imitations during the early 1960s, for instance—and in the 1970s Richard Lester's contributions, *The Three Musketeers* (1973), *Royal Flash* (1975), and *Robin and Marian* (1976). But he saw this revival as illusory; swashbucklers were more likely to be parodies than truly felt adventures: "The keynote is requiem rather than renaissance. The swashbuckler in fact shows little sign of real revival because while the style may be imitated, the underlying ethic has been irreparably undermined."

This pessimism has been disproved by events. In the twenty-five years since Richards made these observations there has been a steady stream of swashbucklers, and of films in which swordplay has played a key part. From the fights in *Star Wars* to those in *Gladiator*, from *First Knight* to *The Mask of Zorro*, from *Rob Roy* to *The Mists of Avalon*, from *The Princess Bride* to *Crouching Tiger, Hidden Dragon*, from *Lord of the Rings* to *The Count of Monte Cristo*, filmmakers have found that for the sheer excitement of pitting hero against villain in one-to-one combat there is still a place for the swordfight, whatever new costumes the combatants may be wearing.

THE ROLL OF ACTORS WHO HAVE FENCED IN FILMS IS EXTENSIVE, and on occasion surprising. It includes George Sanders (who hated every minute and even lost the part of villain in *The Mark of Zorro* because he shirked the duel scene), Bob Hope, Tony Curtis, John Wayne, Kirk and Michael Douglas, Robin Williams fencing Dustin Hoffman in *Hook*, Michael Caine, Gérard Depardieu as Cyrano, and Anthony Hopkins as Zorro.

Then there are Stewart Granger (leaden in *The Prisoner of Zenda*, acrobatic in *Scaramouche*, where he became so involved in the fencing scenes he needed twelve stitches in his leg and sustained a shoulder injury that plagued him the rest of his life), Kevin Costner, Charlton Heston, Arnold Schwarzenegger, Gregory Peck as Horatio Hornblower ("That was wonderful swordsmanship, sir." "Mr. Langley, when I was a midshipman I was bottom of the class in swordsmanship"—a becoming modesty given his wooden swordplay, although both he and his opponent, Christopher Lee, were both well over six feet tall and the restrictions of the fo'c'sle left little room for footwork), Orson Welles (who fenced at school, and always wanted to play Cyrano), Peter Ustinov, Peter O'Toole, even Robert De Niro.

One should not forget that over the years several actresses have also wielded swords: Maureen O'Hara, most notably in *Lady in the Iron Mask* and *At Sword's Point*, with "a helter-skelter climax that resembles a fencers' convention" (*The New York Times*); Jean Peters—most convincing of all— in *Anne of the Indies*; Lana Turner coaching Roger Moore in *Diane*; Lucille Ball of *I Love Lucy* fame; Grace Kelly in *The Swan*; Natalie Wood in *The Great Race*; Catherine Zeta-Jones in *The Mask of Zorro*; and Sophie Marceau in *The Revenge of the Musketeers*. Not always happily: *The New York Times* described Jean Peters, unfairly, as having "the swashbuckling airs of a lass in Miss Twitt's Finishing School," and when Marion Davies, William Randolph Hearst's longtime companion, was forced to play Mary

Tudor in the costume drama *When Knighthood Was in Flower* (1922), she complained, "I had to learn fencing for that picture. Every day for four hours, for four months. I had a mask for the first month and buttons on the ends of the swords. Then they took the mask away and then they took the buttons off. I was frightened stiff. And my legs were stiff, too, from lunging. . . . I couldn't walk, but the director thought I walked just like a princess."[10]

Throughout the history of the cinema, however, staging swordfights has been the responsibility of very few individuals. Before the 1950s there were just four fight arrangers of note: Cavens, maybe the best of them all; Henri J. Uyttenhove, another graduate of the Belgian Military Institute; Ralph Faulkner, the one native-born American; and Jean L. Heremans. Uyttenhove was the first to bring expert staging to screen duels, coaching Fairbanks Senior in *The Three Musketeers* and *Robin Hood* and choreographing the early versions of *Scaramouche* and *The Prisoner of Zenda;* but he worked exclusively during the silent era and with the advent of talkies moved into formal instruction. Even so, his contribution should not be overlooked: *Variety* commented on *The Three Musketeers,* his first film with Fairbanks, "Fairbanks . . . must have toned up his fencing considerably for he displays work with the sword that has not been approached."[11]

Of the four, Ralph Faulkner was the best fencer. Born in Abilene,

Grace Kelly in The Swan *(1956). Her tutor is Louis Jourdan,*
who tells her: "A fencer is always in danger of revealing his
intentions to his adversary—and that he must never do."

Kansas, in 1891, he moved to Hollywood in 1922. Good-looking, athletic, and debonair, he entered silent films, appearing opposite Mary Astor, Marion Davies, and Ronald Colman. During the making of *The Man from Glengarry* he tripped over a log and injured his left leg. After a cartilage operation he took up fencing to strengthen his knee and was soon practicing three hours a day. In 1928 he won the Pacific Coast saber title and that same year became the first Californian fencer ever selected for the Olympics. Although he made no impression at the Games in Amsterdam (where, the modest but unmistakably attractive Faulkner later told friends, he became involved with the German gold-medal winner, Helene Mayer), he came in second that summer at an international épée competition in Belgium and took first place at a saber event in Dieppe.

Faulkner competed again at the Olympics in 1932 and was a member of the six-man squad that took fourth place in the saber; but by now he was heavily engaged in film work. He played various roles in the 1935 remake of *The Three Musketeers* ("I was killed five times") and portrayed fencing masters in at least two other films: prophetic roles, because he later became a full-fledged master and coached several national champions at his Hollywood salle, Falcon Studios. He learned to stage fight scenes under Fred Cavens, whom he met during the shooting of *The Three Musketeers*, but the friendship foundered once they became competitors. Faulkner applied to work on the 1937 *Prisoner of Zenda* and was sitting in an anteroom at the Selznick Studios following his interview when Cavens walked in. "What are you doing here?" asked his surprised mentor. Faulkner had nothing to say. Cavens mused aloud, "*Bien*, I guess we're rivals now."

Faulkner got the job and proceeded to do his best work, doubling for the two principals and playing the role of a henchman. The climactic saber duel required four weeks of rehearsal. Three years later he would work with Cavens and Errol Flynn on *The Sea Hawk*, a propagandistic piece that equated sixteenth-century Spain with Nazi Germany. Somewhat humiliatingly for Faulkner, Cavens was in charge, while he played a palace guardsman. Faulkner received no official credit either for doubling the main villain in the set-piece palace duel or for coaching Flynn, presumably because after only two days' work on the climactic duel he was replaced, as director Michael Curtiz considered his footwork not "in period": he looked too much like a modern fencer.

For the next four decades Faulkner coached and doubled Hollywood's leading players (*The Court Jester* was his personal favorite). During his varied career he was a real-estate agent, shipyard worker, and dancer, even appearing in a couple of New York ballets in 1931–32. He retained his good looks and lithe figure well into his seventies, doing crowd scenes when no longer doubling. "Those big melees aboard pirate ships were the worst," he recalled. "There were so many fellows in those battles who knew nothing about fencing or swords. They'd wave their blades around like there was no one within a mile of them, and all the time everyone would be so packed together you couldn't step a foot in any direction."

Faulkner's fencing sequences are criticized now, as are Cavens's, as "tit for tat"—too repetitive to be convincing; but in his best work, as in *Prisoner of Zenda*, Faulkner produced some of the most exciting swordfights on screen. He in turn hated what he saw of the early 1980s—what he called the "kick 'em in the crotch" school of fighting. He died at the grand age of ninety-five, in 1986. One pupil called him "a swashbuckling Mr. Chips."[12]

In the 1940s and '50s the leading fight arranger was Jean Heremans, another Belgian fencing champion, first hired in 1948 for the MGM remake of *The Three Musketeers*. For this he created one of the longest screen duels ever recorded, lasting five minutes. The job was to have gone to Fred Cavens and his son, but they were working on *The New Adventures of Don Juan*, which because of industrial unrest (the Mafia was said to be trying to muscle in on Hollywood) took more than eighteen months to complete. It cost them their footing at MGM, where Heremans would reign for the next fifteen years.

The Three Musketeers was given a budget of nearly $3 million, almost a record for a nonmusical. It starred Gene Kelly, who threw himself into the role of d'Artagnan so completely that when Lana Turner, playing Milady de Winter, broke a rib after an overvigorous bedroom tussle, he happily used the period of her recovery to take extra lessons with Heremans.

Kelly at one point argued that *The Three Musketeers* should be made as a musical so he could use his singing and dancing skills. His ballet training, he reflected later, had special value when it came to the swordfights. "In both," he said, "the feet are always placed outward, making it possible to move quickly from side to side and use your body to the full. Unless your toes are turned outward, period costumes made it very difficult to move easily in a duel. So when I first started fencing I had no problem in moving around but the difficulty was to train my reflexes to deflect with speed and then come back at my opponent."[13] (He failed to mention that he was extensively doubled in the film in both the fencing and riding sequences.) Of all his nonmusical films, *The Three Musketeers* was Kelly's favorite. His enthusiasm for swordfighting made him keen to play the hero in *Cyrano de Bergerac*, which had never been filmed in English. Louis B. Mayer, the studio head whom he approached, told him outright that just one false nose would ruin his career. It was left to José Ferrer, another able fencer, to make the picture two years later.

In just one year, 1952, Heremans was involved in remakes of both *The Prisoner of Zenda* and *Scaramouche*—for many regarded as the classic film of swordplay, which climaxes with absolutely the longest swordfight in screen history, six and a half minutes. At the beginning of the story, its villain, Gervais, Marquis de La Tour d'Azyr, kills Philippe de Vilmorin in a duel he forces on the younger man. Philippe's friend André-Louis Moreau—the part played by Stewart Granger—vows revenge. At the book's climax, with hero and villain in love with the same lady, Thérèse de Plougastel, they duel; André-Louis's bloodlust is frustrated when he badly wounds the marquis and the fight is stopped before he can finish his enemy off. At the book's end, however, André-Louis realizes that the countess loves La Tour d'Azyr. "My God!" he cries aloud. "What she must have suffered, then, if I had killed him as I intended!" He lets out a sigh and turns to his companion. "It is perhaps as well that my lunge went wide."[14]

This was too subtle for Hollywood tastes, and in the film version the final duel receives the works. The marquis still survives, but this time because André cannot bring himself to deliver the final blow—which he later realizes is because La Tour d'Azyr is his long-lost brother. (A bowdlerization of the original Ramon Novarro version, where the marquis turns out to be André-Louis's *father*.)

The Granger-Ferrer fight in *Scaramouche* is far from being the best ever, as has been claimed, but it caught the public interest. It also caught the attention of the great Italian champion Aldo Nadi, who was by this time living in America, where he hoped to make a career in films. In his memoirs he sets out to make an example of *Scaramouche*, employing all the self-righteous scorn he could muster. Of the main duel, he says, "not twenty seconds, when coldly viewed, could be called, even by the wildest stretch of any Hollywood press agent's imagination, genuine swordsmanship. . . . The time has come to try—merely try, of course—to call a halt to such utterly ridiculous spectacles which crudely offend one of the noblest arts and sciences of the world. . . . *Scaramouche* had everything that typifies Hollywood swordsmanship—with a vengeance."*

---

* To give Nadi's invective some support, a list, "Things You Need to Know About the Movies," is currently circulating on the Internet. Entries include:

Reviewing the main locale of the fight—theater stalls, the grand stairway, the foyer, the stage itself—Nadi declares:

> No duelist in his right mind would ever even consider fighting on such a terrain. . . . Not only did we see the fighters more than precariously balanced in the air, leaning out of the theater boxes or dangling from ropes also suspended from said boxes, *and* fighting *all* the time; we also saw, after the foolish interlude of the staircase, the duelists walk, that is, balance themselves, on the tops of the orchestra seats from the back of the theater straight on down to the stage, *and* fighting *all* the time—or at least whenever they could, poor fellows.[15]

This is using a sledgehammer to kill a fly and in many ways wrongheaded; but it reminds us how far swordplay had been taken by Hollywood in the search for entertainment. *Scaramouche* was a popular success, and, although Ferrer is a mediocre fencer and Granger handicapped by a heavy frame and general lack of deftness, they go at it enthusiastically enough. Granger—who had a double for *The Prisoner of Zenda* but did the fencing himself in *Scaramouche*—took lessons from a top British coach whenever he was in London. "Mel Ferrer did some of his own fencing, but he wouldn't concentrate," Granger revealed in a 1980s interview. "If a pretty girl came on to the set, his eyes would wander." Ferrer's "fencing acting," however, is excellent: as the climactic fight wears on he convincingly tires, visibly running out of moves.

Granger's double was meant to be Paul Stakker, who also doubled for Johnny Weissmuller (a.k.a. Tarzan). "He was a wonderful fighter and swimmer," Granger recalled, "but he fenced as if he were boxing. He didn't have the style. The first time I saw him being photographed for me as a double, I said, 'Wait a minute, Paul, you must watch me and see the

---

Should you wish to pass yourself off as a German officer, it will not be necessary to speak the language, a German accent will do;

Police departments give their officers personality tests to make sure they are deliberately assigned a partner who is their total opposite;

The Eiffel Tower can be seen from any window in Paris;

You can always find a chain saw when you need one;

—and so on. The one on swordplay reads: "It does not matter if you are heavily outnumbered in a fight . . . your enemies will wait patiently to attack you one by one by dancing around in a threatening manner until you have knocked out their predecessors."

Stewart Granger (right) takes on Mel Ferrer in the 1952 version of
Scaramouche. *The acerbic Aldo Nadi wrote—as an intended insult—that the film
"had everything that typifies Hollywood swordsmanship—with a vengeance."*

way I fence. I have a certain style. You've got to copy the style, because if
the style's no good it won't look right.' He looked at me puzzled, and I
said, 'What the hell, sit down, I'll do it.' And ended up doing the whole
darned film."

At one point during the duel, Granger fell, actually knocking himself
out. As he came to, he became aware of voices. "One said, 'Darn, George,
he's bad.' George was the director, and the man talking was the assistant
director. . . . I could see his face peering down at me, so I kept my eyes
closed, pretending to be out, and he said, 'George, my God, I think he's
dead.' Then George says in this loud voice, 'Oh no, what are we going to
do? We haven't finished the film.'" At that point Granger opened his eyes
and grinned.

Scaramouche has some interesting technical innovations. The director
cut the music for the fight scenes, so all we hear is the clash of steel, the
grunts of the swordsmen, and the vocal reactions of the audience in the
Ambigu Théâtre. Kinetic scenery was used for the first time, that is, special microphones hidden in the scenery picked up the sound of the blades
as they landed on curtain or balustrade. The audience also sees part of the
fight through the eyes of the fencing master who has taught both men.

Despite Nadi's strictures, Stewart Granger was praised for his fencing.

A typical review described him as "a high-handed Bourbon who is 120 proof with the sword." Granger and Errol Flynn kept up a friendly rivalry over who was the better swordsman: "Basil was a tremendous fencer, but Errol was not very good," recalled Granger. "You watch him. He's got a wonderful figure, and he's so beautifully coordinated he gives the impression that he's a good fencer, but he rather slaps the swords together up in the air. I knew him well, and we used to kid each other. I would say, 'I'm a better fencer than you, for crying out loud; have you seen me at it?' And he'd say, 'Yeah, I know. You're pretty good; but I have slimmer hips.'"[16]

W HAT IS THE RELATION OF COMPETITIVE FENCING TO THE WORLD of film dueling? Often swashbucklers offer a nod to fencing technique—but not more than that. In *The Swan* (1956), Louis Jourdan plays fencing instructor to Grace Kelly, in her last film role. During a couple of lessons, naturally conducted without masks, we see Kelly performing very proficiently—a long lunge, a beat attack, then parries in prime, seconde, quarte, and octave, finishing with a doublé. "We must practice the art of making a feint," Jourdan tells her, "it's a sham attack followed by a genuine one in another quarter. A fencer is always in danger of revealing his intentions to his adversary—and that he must never do. His opponent must never know from one moment to the next what he is thinking. Like everything else, it's a question of practice." Then there is the master in *Scaramouche:* "Fight with the head. Forget the heart. . . . You have a demon in you this fine day. Lose it, or you'll not live to see another."

Scriptwriters were generally willing to turn a blind eye to anachronisms (most versions of Robin Hood use techniques—the lunge, various parries—not developed till centuries later), but they seemed to have caught on to the way in which thrusting weapons overtook the broadsword. In *The Mark of Zorro* (1940) Tyrone Power declares, "Dashing about with a cutlass is quite out of fashion. . . . It hasn't been done since the Middle Ages," while Errol Flynn in *The Master of Ballantrae* (1953) is exhorted by the French pirate captain, in mid-duel, "Keep the arm supple at all times—it's one of the elementary rules." But then verisimilitude was rarely the point: Fred Cavens had Flynn performing counterparries and lightning feints that would have been impossible with the long, heavy weapons of the time; and Dumas himself described duels in *The Three Musketeers* in terms of nineteenth-century fencing. On the other hand, in *The Mississippi Gambler* (1953), when Tyrone Power triumphs in a takeoff of a nineteenth-century French duel, his victim sneers admiringly, "That same low-line hit again." His next opponent adds, "My compliments. . . . You have courage to let the point come so close before parrying." Both moves were typical of the fencer who claims to have choreographed the fights—none other than Aldo Nadi.

WHEN STEWART GRANGER TOOK LESSONS FOR *SCARAMOUCHE* IT was from the British national coach, Bob Anderson—and in Anderson we meet Cavens's true successor. Born in 1923, Anderson began fencing while a Royal Marine, breaking into the English team in 1950 in both foil and saber—although he was a fine épéeist, too, and later British professional champion in all three weapons. At the 1950 world championships he retired with a damaged thumb just before the final eight and never again had such a good opportunity to enter the top flight. He reached the quarterfinals at the Helsinki Olympics but had already begun coaching, and on his return from the Games he resumed his work as assistant to the then national coach, Roger Crosnier.

The following year, Crosnier returned to France and Anderson was his obvious replacement. He proceeded to rack up another six Olympics as a coach, won a top European saber competition in 1962, and oversaw Britain's rise to third place in the fencing pantheon after France and Italy. But the public-school ethos remained dominant, and Anderson, who never had his own salle, was treated largely as a packhorse, traveling around the country running courses, often for beginners. He kept going for fifteen years before emigrating to Canada.

There were no such problems with his Hollywood career. A friend introduced him to Errol Flynn, who liked his athletic, ultraromantic style of fencing. The two worked together on *Ballantrae*, with Anderson as stunt double, but during filming in Sicily he pierced Flynn in the thigh. Flynn said immediately that it was his own fault—he had been distracted by a boat passing by—and soon the two men were off drinking together. For years afterward, film crews would tell new cast members, "Watch out for Anderson—he's the one who skewered Flynn!"

The Master of Ballantrae was followed by two further films together, *Crossed Swords* and *The Dark Avenger*, and thereafter Anderson was rarely out of film work, coaching Roger Moore in *Moonraker*, Ryan O'Neal in *Barry Lyndon*, Michael Caine in *Kidnapped*, Sean Connery in *Highlander*, Eric Roberts in *By the Sword*, and Richard Gere in *First Knight*, among others. He even appeared in front of the camera as Darth Vader for the fight scenes with Mark Hamill in *The Empire Strikes Back* and *Return of the Jedi.* "Since Mark played Luke Skywalker without any protection at all, it was realized that due to the restrictions on Darth Vader's costume, especially when it came to the field of vision from behind the mask, Mark could easily be injured. So they needed an expert swordsman." During the fight in the Freezing Chamber Han Solo is carbonized. "They had to keep the stage at a very high temperature so that the steam did not disperse. This meant that I was swordfighting with Luke Skywalker all day in this temperature for about five days. I lost fourteen pounds." The swords had a carbon-fiber blade, painted with reflective paint, so that they could simulate laser light.

Anderson was swordmaster for the Royal Shakespeare Company in Stratford for several years and held the same position with Walt Disney Films from 1972 to 1980. I first met him in 1966, when I signed up for a course he was teaching in west London, and ended up taking lessons from him as part of the British team from 1970 on. In the summer of 2000 I drove down to his house on the south coast of England, near Bognor Regis, and we talked about his career over seaside fish and chips. "What I

Darth Vader, as played by Bob Anderson, crosses beams with Luke Skywalker in The Empire Strikes Back. *If anything, as the Star Wars series goes on, swordplay has become an even more important element.*

usually do," he says, "is put together a basic routine as it comes into my head, with a high amount of concentration on getting the rhythm right. The most important thing concerning the final choreographed fight is the changing of the rhythm of the blades. If it all goes along at the same tempo it gets boring, so you have to do moves that are broad and slow, then change to fast and fluid." One thinks back to the vision of Fred Cavens eighty years before.

During the 1970s styles changed. In Aldo Nadi's opinion, "the difference between competitive fencing and stage or screen dueling is as vast as the difference between life itself and the tenuous illusion of it offered on the screen," a view that, however tendentiously put, has haunted directors for decades: they want duels to *look* as if they were being fought by experts. Then, some time in the 1970s, there was a spate of swashbuckler parodies, and when the "straight" version returned it did so in earnest—swordfights didn't have to look authentic from a purist's point of view, they had to look as if the combatants' lives were truly at stake. Ridley Scott's *The Duellists* (1977) had its principals, David Carradine and Harvey Keitel, flailing about exhausted, stopping to care for even minor wounds, getting covered in blood, needing time for recovery. For the first time in a film a duelist desperately clutches his opponent's blade with his nonfencing hand, with predictable results. Suddenly, wounds *hurt*.

In 1988 Anderson was invited to organize the fight scenes for *The Princess Bride*, adapted from William Goldman's tongue-in-cheek novel, alongside the stunt coordinator Peter Diamond: "It was a turning point in my career. I was beginning to think that my style, built on the Flynn model, was out of date. 'Reality' was what everybody wanted. But the film showed that the romantic kind of swordplay hadn't been displaced."[17] The male leads in *The Princess Bride*, Mandy Patinkin and Cary Elwes, besides discussing the finer points of swordplay, got so involved that they would wander off fighting hammer and tongs just for the hell of it and had to be brought to order by Anderson so filming could continue. One sound recordist typified the film's cult status by memorizing its entire dialogue, and one can see why it was so popular: "What in the world have you been learning?" "The sword." "Madness. You have spent ten entire years just learning to fence?" "No, not *just* learning to fence . . . I squeezed rocks." This was parody and romance at the same time.

Anderson's work on this film led directly to his being asked to arrange the fights for the 1993 remake of *The Three Musketeers*, this time with Chris O'Donnell as d'Artagnan. "The odd thing about all this is that a lot of modern swordmasters think that the old fights of the Errol Flynn and Douglas Fairbanks era are passé. Fortunately, Rob Reiner, who directed *The Princess Bride,* wanted exactly that type of fight. I remember thinking that maybe it wouldn't go down well, but everyone raved about it. It's nice to know that people still like the romantic sort of swordfight, where there's no hacking, with blood all over the place and gimmick stunts."

The blades used were once steel, but more recently have been made of wood, Duralumin, aluminum, plastic, or carbon fiber. Since these replicas sound dull, the actual clash of steel against steel has to be added later. Under Anderson's instruction, actors begin with slow-motion choreography, then build up to movements in real time. For the 1993 *Three Musketeers* this process took a month. But the care is necessary. Errol Flynn, recalls Anderson, nearly cut off Christopher Lee's thumb during the filming of *The Warriors* (1955), while Fred Graham, the stuntman who fenced Flynn in Basil Rathbone's place in *The Adventures of Robin Hood,* first injured his foot during the duel on the staircase at Nottingham Castle, then later plunged several feet from the balcony to the studio floor while filming Guisborne's death fall and ended up in hospital. In a duel during *The Sword of the Avenger* (1948), Ralph Faulkner caught his foot on a wire and pitched forward directly onto his opponent's sword, whose point just missed his eye. David Niven (with whom Bob also worked) tells of the time when he tripped during a fight sequence while playing Bonnie Prince Charlie, his blade going straight into the leg of a nearby extra. To his relief, the limb proved to be made of wood. Or so Niven would have us believe.*

---

* In another Flynn movie, *They Died with Their Boots On,* a 1941 film of the years leading up to Custer's Last Stand, the actor Bill Mead was thrown by his horse, and although he had the presence of mind to cast his sword forward to avoid falling on it, it stuck in the ground hilt down and he impaled himself fatally. More recently, Laurence Olivier listed the injuries he suffered as an actor. They include:

3 ruptured Achilles tendons
Untold slashes including a full thrust razor-edged sword wound in the *breast*
Landing from considerable height, scrotum first, upon acrobat's knee
Hurled to the stage from 30 feet due to faultily moored rope ladder
Impalement upon jagged ply cut-outs
Broken foot by standing preoccupied in camera track
Broken face by horse galloping into camera while looking through finder
One arrow shot between shinbones
Near electrocution through scimitar entering studio dimmer while backing away from unwelcome interview.[18]

OFFICIALLY ANDERSON RETIRED IN 1991, BUT IN 1993 CAME THE Dumas remake, then in 1996 he was lured back with another *Mask of Zorro*, in which all three principals, Anthony Hopkins, Catherine Zeta-Jones, and Antonio Banderas, were keen to do their own fencing. "Catherine was an ex-dancer, which helped. Hopkins thought he was Flynn. He'd say, 'That's pretty good; I like that,' and when I told him that was enough, he'd counter with 'Just five more times.'" Anderson rates Banderas as the best natural talent with whom he has ever worked. "You need four elements to make a champion: anticipation; a superb sense of rhythm; timing; and physical ability, particularly leg strength. Banderas had them all." Despite a recent brush with cancer, Anderson had just returned from four months in New Zealand for *The Lord of the Rings*, a $360 million project encompassing three separate films, and was busy plotting his next assignments, the new James Bond adventure at Pinewood Studios (in which Pierce Brosnan is doubled in the swordfighting sequences by the British international épéeist Steven Paul—whose father Raymond doubled for Flynn back in the 1950s), *Pirates of the Caribbean*, with Johnny Depp, and a sequel to *Zorro*. He was laughing at the fate of Liv Tyler in *The Lord of the Rings*. Cast as the young heroine, Arwen, she had bridled at the notion of rehearsing for a fencing scene. An angry Anderson told her he was going away for a while, leaving her with his assistant. He told her he'd give her one chance to shoot the scene on his return before giving it to the director for his approval. "When I came back I could see a gleam in my assistant's eye: she did the best fight sequence I've seen a girl do."

ANDERSON, WHO DIED ON NEW YEAR'S DAY, 2012, HAD ONE FORmidable rival as the world's leading fight director: a British Australian now in his seventies, William Hobbs. Born in North London in 1939, Hobbs was brought up by his actress mother after his father, a Royal Air Force pilot, was killed in the last months of the Second World War. It was a bohemian upbringing: his aunt was a dancer with the renowned Windmill Theatre and once won a prize for "the second best legs in England"; his elder half brother went into the circus. The family lived in Australia for several years, and it was there that "Bill," as he had become, began fencing in 1954. He narrowly failed to make the Australian team for the Melbourne Olympics in 1956 and in 1957 moved back to London to enroll at the Central School for Speech and Drama; Judi Dench was a contemporary, as was Vanessa Redgrave.* "Most actors say that they are good fencers," Hobbs says. "That's a lie: they're not." While a student, he asked the Central's registrar why fencing had always been taught there. "For grace and deportment," she replied. Hobbs recalls being shown four fight positions in all his time as a student—that was it. In his book on stage fighting he quotes with obvious scorn Simon Callow's comment in *Being an Actor.* "There were no classes at the Drama Centre in fencing, dialects, or clog-dancing. They reckoned that if you needed them, you could pick them up in ten minutes. They were right." Hobbs spent hours training actors for their roles.

He spent 1959–60 doing weekly repertory and describes both his experience and his acting as "awful." "Give it up, baby," was Olivier's advice. Instead—inspired, he says, by the scenes in *Scaramouche*—he began to direct fights: Peter O'Toole's *Hamlet* at the Bristol Old Vic, then to London's Old Vic with Franco Zeffirelli and *Romeo and Juliet,* with Dench as Juliet. His duels won rave reviews, almost unheard-of for theater notices. Hobbs spent nine years as fight director at Laurence Olivier's National Theatre Company, then was fencing master at the Central for fifteen years.

By the time he was invited to move into film, Hobbs was well prepared. In 1972 Ridley Scott approached him to orchestrate the fights for *The Duellists*—where the duels take up at least half the movie. "I don't want any of that old tosh—I want it real," Scott told him. Hobbs was in complete agreement: "From the beginning I wanted to break away from all the Hollywood stuff I'd seen. What interested me was the story, the drama. I was excited by the *people.* The pauses we put into the fights in that film were phenomenal, but we wanted to get across the awful feeling that you believe you'll be dead on the floor. In the end, the realism is in the fear." A fencing

---

* During my time in publishing I commissioned both the memoirs of Vanessa Redgrave—a fencer of great potential, let down by poor eyesight—and a book about their father, Michael, by her younger brother, Corin, who won the public schools saber in 1956, and later, in 1960, came close to Olympic selection.

In 1995, performing the title role in *Julius Caesar* at Houston's Alley Theater, Corin jumped onto a table and, seeing that someone had inadvertently left a dagger there, decided to exploit the opportunity. With his next speech he kicked the dagger away forcefully, only to watch in horror as it made a gentle arc into a crowd of attendants, lodging itself in the forehead of an elderly actress. The assistant director, watching the performance from the stalls, rushed backstage. The wound was only superficial, but the assistant director, overcome by the sight of blood, fainted away, crushing his glasses as he fell. It is now mandatory on the London stage that any play with swordfights have a "fight rehearsal" before *every* performance.

phrase, he says, should have the same feeling as two serpents recovering their balance before resuming their attacks on each other. "The best such scenes—Orson Welles's *Chimes at Midnight*, or *Seven Samurai*—are good precisely because they don't show you everything. Men running through fields, a body falling in mud, a momentary clash of blades: the audience supplies the rest."

Since *The Duellists*, Hobbs has worked on *Cyrano de Bergerac* with Gérard Depardieu, *Hamlet* with Mel Gibson, *Dangerous Liaisons*, Richard Lester's *Musketeer* films (in the first of which he plays an assassin, intent on murdering Porthos), Polanski's *Macbeth*, *Rob Roy*,* *Shakespeare in Love*, and many others—most recently the highly enjoyable remake of *The Count of Monte Cristo*. He will turn down projects that do not interest him—even such high-profile films as *The Mark of Zorro* and *Gladiator* he let go. Over the years, he has worked on twenty-one *Hamlets* (one prince, Laurence Payne, who was *not* coached by Hobbs, actually lost an eye in the duel scene). He was fight arranger on Richard Lester's *The Three Musketeers* around the same time as Bob Anderson's version but sees his work as very different. "Despite the humor in it, ours was a much grittier, muckier world—we wanted to get the physicality of the period." Such scenes can be expensive to stage—in Mel Gibson's *Braveheart* an entire swordfighting scene was cut in postproduction, at a cost of £500,000.

Hobbs reckons that Gene Wilder was his most promising actor-pupil, having worked with him in *The Adventure of Sherlock Holmes' Smarter Brother*. "He could actually fence." He also rates highly Ralph Fiennes, with whom he has worked in both film and theater. Fiennes started fencing in *The Avengers* and enjoyed it so much that he took extra coaching, even joining Hobbs's London club, Swash and Buckle.

Bill Hobbs describes the swordfights in pre-1960 movies as "two cuts high, two cuts low." Their actual nickname in Britain was "Meat and Two Veg"—a variant on the French *"batterie de cuisine"* and *"concert de casseroles."* He quotes his old friend and stunt coordinator Richard Graydon as saying to a new group of stuntmen, "In the old days, every stuntman was happy as they had in their repertoire three very effective sword

---

* Rob Roy was the perfect historical figure on whom to pin feats of swordsmanship. A contemporary of Donald McBane, Roy was a dedicated cattle rustler but with Robin Hood–like leanings. On one occasion, he encountered an officer of James II and a party of soldiers, who were hanging four peasants from a tree on the bigoted grounds that they were Noncomformists. Roy set about them with his broadsword to such effect that he killed both the officer and eleven of his men, the remainder taking to their heels.[19]

moves. Then Bill Hobbs came along, added a fourth, and made it *complicated*." Of course he did far more than that; he stressed that sword-fights should not seek to emulate classical fencing; parries had to be wider (or even newly created) and attacks specially conceived, so that they would *look* convincing. As Errol Flynn confessed in *My Wicked, Wicked Ways*, "I'm not a fencer. I'm a thespian. But I know how to make it look good."

The latest form of cinema swordfight can be found in the high-tech world of *The Matrix* and *Crouching Tiger, Hidden Dragon*—both of which had the same fight arranger, Yuen Wo Ping.* He is now styled the "Action Choreographer," and we have progressed far beyond the world of doubles or even of stuntmen. The new technology makes actors almost redundant, now that limbs can be excised in the editing room and figures made to bounce off the branches of trees and run up the side of walls. (Even though the cameraman for *Pirates of the Caribbean: The Curse of the Black Pearl* had to wade into duels encased in plastic armor.) While trick photography goes back to those earliest days of 1895, the swordfights in *Crouching Tiger* are exhilarating but exist in a make-believe world: at least with Fairbanks and Flynn we knew that someone was wielding the sword and were happy to believe it was the star himself, as often it was. Now it all seems like conjuring, a distant cousin to the fencer's art. Yet *Crouching Tiger*'s director, Ang Lee, has declared, "Fight sequences are not about beating someone up or a kind of health exercise. It's really all about an energetic cinematic language." Perhaps the powers of high technology, allied with Eastern martial arts, are teaching Western audiences a new language for swordplay; if so, that language, in its turn, may have something to teach fencers—that it is not enough to find the balance between classic swordplay and realism. Keeping faith with the imaginations of the audience matters too.

---

* The theater, by contrast, finds it hard to compete with films for stupendous action sequences, and most stage swordplay comes now from the classic repertory. The last time I saw modern fencing on stage was in the Broadway revival of Arthur Miller's *The Price*. Was America's greatest playwright a closet fencer? I asked Miller about the role of Vinnie, the policeman on the edge of retirement who twice rehearses the fencing moves he recalls from college.

Miller said that he had based it all on a boyhood friend who'd been on the university fencing team at Columbia. "I used to fool around with him at foil—when I wasn't working on a job: I didn't have the money to go to school yet. I was the target."

CHAPTER 11

On Mount Rushmore

JOHN WAYNE: *We'll be sorry to see you hanged.*
STUART WHITMAN [INCREDULOUS, HAVING JUST WON A DUEL]:
They've never enforced the laws against dueling before!

—*The Comancheros*, DIRECTED BY MICHAEL CURTIZ, 1962

Among those who control the world
and protect the State
There's no one who doesn't employ
swordsmanship in his mind.

—YAGYU MUNEYOSHI (1529–1606)

HEY LOOM SOME 3,064 FEET HIGH, CARVED FROM THE MOUN-
tain granite of the Black Hills of South Dakota—the heads of George
Washington, Thomas Jefferson, Abraham Lincoln, and Theodore Roosevelt, four of the greatest presidents of the United States. The Mount
Rushmore National Memorial was begun in August 1927 and finished
only in 1941, two years before the death of its creator, Gutzon Borglum.
The original idea is said to have come from the superintendent of the local
historical society, but was soon taken up nationally and made a reality by
President Coolidge. The memorial was conceived as a "shrine of democracy," with the four presidents representing the founding, expansion, and
preservation of the United States. Washington was an inescapable choice,
although his carving bears a nose a full foot longer than initially calculated. Jefferson joined him less for his intrinsic greatness, Borglum explained, than for "taking the first steps towards continental expansion"
with the Louisiana Purchase. Lincoln was added for his "preservation of
the Union." Roosevelt was a trickier decision. He finally got the nod for the
Panama Canal—as Borglum described it in a letter to Roosevelt's niece
Eleanor Roosevelt, thus "breaking the political lobby that had blocked for
half a century every effort to cut the Isthmus."[1]

Borglum was a rare bird. The son of a Danish Mormon immigrant, he came to specialize in monumental edifices. He had completed another, of Woodrow Wilson, for a huge memorial in Warsaw: it was under Wilson's presidency and due to his support that Poland had won its independence. Borglum became a voluble critic of Hitler only after 1939, when the Führer had the sculpture torn down. It was an antagonism he might not otherwise have felt so keenly, being himself a racist bigot and an active supporter of the Ku Klux Klan. Borglum was an outdoor type who loved boxing, fishing, riding, and hunting and had one other great enthusiasm: fencing. I like to think that as he chiseled away, he knew that each of the formidable statesmen he was sculpting had shared that passion.

At least three other presidents took up the sword: Andrew Jackson, Harry S Truman, and Ulysses S. Grant, who fenced at West Point, though he does not mention it in his memoirs. (Second Lieutenant Ronald Reagan, U.S. Cavalry Reserve, was celebrated between 1937 and 1942 as his regiment's "greatest swordsman," but alas the accolade was metaphorical.) Of all the American presidents, Washington was by far the most committed fencer. At ten years old, he was already whittling sticks into makeshift swords and battling away in imitation of his elders. "In those days," writes one biographer, "when battles still were decided by hand-to-hand fighting with the 'cold steel,' when gentlemen were expected to settle their quarrels sword in hand, and when all men of fashion, except clergymen, still wore light swords when in full dress, dexterity in swordplay was expected of all Virginia cavaliers."[2] Washington's paternal great-grandfather had wielded a sword in battle; his father had carried a cutlass as captain of his own ship; his stepbrother, while at school in England, had been taught to fence by a fashionable master. Young George was trained by his father, his brothers, and their friends, first to use a cutlass and later at foil, the French smallsword, the claymore, and the cavalry saber.

In his expense ledger for 1756 there is an entry for £1, 1s, 6d paid to one Sergeant Wood, a fencing master. Later coaches included a Dutchman, Jacob Van Braam, and George Muse of Fredericksburg, under whose tutelage Washington blossomed, until he was reputedly "the best swordsman in Virginia." He even founded a club, called the "Virginian Fencibles," with Van Braam as resident master. Van Braam was as much friend as coach, accompanying Washington on three long marches through the wilderness against French forts in the French and Indian War, where Washington made his reputation; the two are said to have relieved the tedium of these journeys with bouts of swordplay.

Washington's other teacher, Muse, became an adjutant in the army.

When he was discharged for cowardice he petulantly wrote to his old pupil, attempting to blame him for his behavior. He received the marmoreal reply:

> Sir,
> Your impertinent letter was delivered to me yesterday. As I am not accustomed to receive such from any man, nor would have taken the same language from you personally, without letting you feel some marks of my resentment, I would advise you to be cautious.

Such a letter generally presaged a challenge; but Muse, evidently knowing his man, backed down.

A S FAR AS THOMAS JEFFERSON IS CONCERNED, WE KNOW VERY little—only that as a young man in Virginia in the 1760s he was "acquainted with dancing, boxing, playing the fiddle, and small sword." Jefferson was an excellent violinist and kept it up in later life. It is possible that he did so with his fencing as well, but we have no record of it.[3] An old children's book shows him in friendly swordplay with the Marquis de Lafayette, and the third president of the United States may have done some fencing while minister to the court of Louis XVI in the 1780s—he records buying a sword and belt in August 1784, most probably to be properly turned out for levees—but he is unlikely to have fenced with Lafayette in America. The Frenchman *did* challenge the Earl of Carlisle, one of England's commissioners to the United States during the Revolution.

A NDREW JACKSON HAD FOUGHT AT LEAST FOURTEEN DUELS, MAINLY with pistols, by the time he was elected president in 1828. Ambitious and quick-tempered, he was known as the most famous duelist in the old South. He too met Lafayette, sometime between 1824 and 1826, placing a saber and pair of pistols on a table between them; but the Frenchmen was interested only in examining the two guns. Later Jackson came to be involved in one of the more ludicrous quarrels ever decided by a sword. In his time there was a vogue for minimally orchestrated violence, resorted to when a duel proper could not be arranged—or perhaps was not wanted. A man might scorn the effete, rule-bound "satisfaction" of a duel and prefer to have it out with his antagonist, rough and tumble. Jackson, habitually truculent, got into an argument with Governor John Sevier, founding father of Tennessee, and the two agreed to meet just beyond the state's borders.

Unlike the governor, Jackson arrived in good time, waiting for two whole days before giving up and starting back for Knoxville. He had not gone a mile when he saw Sevier in front of him. Indignant at this further impertinence, Jackson sent off a letter of justification, which the governor refused to accept. Jackson spurred furiously to within a hundred yards of his man and, leveling the cane he was carrying like a medieval jouster, charged. The astounded governor dismounted, and in so doing stepped on his own scabbard and fell prostrate under his horse. That was that. The whole affair seemed so ridiculous that the argument was soon patched up and the two parties rode off together.

I N THE FIRST EIGHTY YEARS OF THE REPUBLIC IT WAS HARD FOR ANY prominent public figure, especially in the South and especially one with a militia commission, to avoid a duel of some kind. Abraham Lincoln was caught up in at least two challenges (as well as a third, but that involved flinging cow dung at twenty paces). The first took place in 1832, when a fellow militia officer in the Black Hawk War, James Zachary, called Lincoln a coward. Captain Lincoln of the Illinois militia, as he then was, answered, "If any man thinks me a coward, let him test it." Captain Zachary replied, "You think you can get away with it, just because you are larger and heavier than me." Lincoln told him, "You can guard against that. Choose your own weapons." But Zachary, like Washington's opponent, backed off.

Lincoln's second challenge effectively won him both honor and a wife. It touches on his romantic history and deserves a brief digression. The problem was that once any woman was attracted to him Lincoln tended to lose interest, unable to believe that any person of judgment could find him worth loving. In 1835 he thought he had found the woman he wanted to marry, a cheerful twenty-two-year-old from New Salem, but she suddenly died of a fever, leaving Lincoln heartbroken. Within a year he met and proposed to another girl, Mary Owens, and was decisively rejected.

Around Christmas 1840, two months shy of his thirty-second birthday, Lincoln found himself romantically involved once more. This time the girl was a pretty twenty-one-year-old, Mary Todd, with a quick, sarcastic tongue. Lincoln proposed to her, was accepted, then within a few days wrote saying that it was all a mistake. Mary wrote back, saying she was dev-astated but understood. Her letter must have been artfully worded, because its effect on Lincoln was immediate and persuasive. He reversed himself once again, announced that he should never have given her up, and fell into such a deep depression that friends began to fear for him. To his law partner, John Todd Stuart, he confessed, "I am now the most miserable man living." Eventually, Mrs. Simeon Francis, "the matchmaker of Spring-field" and wife of the editor of the local newspaper, the *Sangamo Journal*, decided to take the matter into her own hands. The following summer she invited Lincoln and Mary to her house, without warning either. "Be friends again," she urged. They were "shyly delighted" and agreed to try.[4]

Lincoln had for some time been penning satirical squibs for the *Journal* under the pseudonym "Aunt Rebecca," a couple of which had been aimed at a prominent local Democrat (Lincoln was then a Whig), James Shields, later a general and a senator of three different states. Shields, a "gallant, hot-headed bachelor" of County Tyrone, Ireland, then occupied the influ-ential post of state auditor of public accounts. In his thirty-six years he had been a sailor (and indeed shipwrecked) and had been wounded fighting the Indians in Florida. A genial, rather dressy ladies' man, he was quick to take offense, especially at criticism of a personal kind. That autumn, the Dem-ocratic state officers had been forced by the sudden collapse of the state bank to repudiate their own currency, forcing on Shields the "unhappy fate" of informing the people of Illinois that their banknotes could not be used to pay their taxes; only gold and silver would be accepted.[5]

This was a heaven-sent gift to the Whigs. Lincoln's first article about the auditor appeared in August 1842. It was uncharacteristically personal: "Shields is a fool as well as a liar. With him truth is out of the question." At the outset, Shields kept silent. Mary Todd and a friend, Julia Jayne, wrote a further gibe, also as "Aunt Rebecca." Baiting Shields had become a summer sport. Lincoln wrote the next piece, in which he referred to the unfortunate auditor as "floating about on the air, without heft or earthly substance, just like a lock of cat fur where cats have been fightin'." A fourth article followed, again by Mary and Julia Jayne, then a fifth, this time in rhyme, asserting that Shields had "won" Aunt Rebecca and that the two were to be married. It was lame stuff, but Shields's patience broke. He sent an envoy, General Whiteside, to Francis's office to de-mand his attacker's true name, under threat of exacting satisfaction from Francis himself.

Shields, though not tall—about five feet nine—was active and alert. As a boy, he had imbibed a good deal of military science from veterans of the Napoleonic Wars, and had actually taught fencing while stationed in Quebec. The large, portly Francis was most unwilling to fight. Nevertheless, he refused to disclose Whiteside's identity to his correspondent.

The next day, Francis encountered Lincoln in the street and poured out his alarm. Lincoln said airily, "Just tell Shields that it was me" and left for Tremont, where he had legal business. As soon as Shields and Whiteside heard that Lincoln had declared himself the culprit, they set off in pursuit. Meanwhile, two of his friends, Dr. Elias Merryman and Mr. Butler, fearing he might be attacked unawares, also took to horse, passing Shields and Whiteside in the night.

The two men were hardly emissaries of peace. Both believed Lincoln to be "unpracticed" in swordplay and the "diplomacy" of dueling, but they were anxious to have him fight. Merryman, a fine swordsman, was combative by nature; his first piece of advice was not on how to avoid a confrontation but for his friend to choose the strong cavalry broadsword as his weapon. (This was not surprising; since the middle of the eighteenth century sabers, in one form or another, had become predominant, making up more than 80 percent of all European and American swords; by 1800 the gentleman's dress smallsword had virtually disappeared.)

As it turned out, their man was not the greenhorn they supposed. Although pacific by nature and physically lanky, he was very tall—just under six feet five—and strong: in his younger days in the militia, he had "had, it is said, only one superior in the whole army" in the art of wrestling. According to the later testimony of Major J. M. Lucas, who knew him well, Lincoln had been thoroughly drilled by another officer in broadsword use and had gained experience with cavalry swords during the Black Hawk War—around the time of his confrontation with Captain Zachary. Lucas "had no doubt Lincoln meant to fight. He was no coward, and he would unquestionably have held his own against his antagonist, for he was a powerful man in those days, and was quite well skilled."

Shields and Whiteside arrived in Tremont on Saturday, September 17. Shields immediately sent Lincoln a note: "I have become the object of slander, vituperation and personal abuse." Merryman, who had already started giving Lincoln dueling lessons, wrote Lincoln's reply for him. It was highly aggressive in tone and called on Shields either to back down or be prepared to fight, since Lincoln had no intention of apologizing.

On the old northwest frontier, men often settled their differences by force, but that usually meant a fistfight. In the self-consciously patrician circles with which Lincoln was increasingly associated, however, disagree-ments were expected to take a more formal turn. For someone like Shields, an ambitious and self-made immigrant, to appeal to the *code du-ello* was a way to assert his pretensions. Thus a duel was inevitable—but could not be held where they were. The practice was outlawed in Illinois, under penalty, at least in theory, of up to five years in prison. Even to send a challenge or make an oral agreement to fight could entail heavy fines. Quickly—for the news had spread—the parties made their way outside the state, choosing a neck of land near the confluence of the Mississippi and Missouri, just outside the towns of Springfield and Alton, Lincoln quipping that the site was most conveniently close to the penitentiary. The two men reached Springfield late on Monday night—to find, as Merryman later recorded, that "the affair had got great publicity . . . and that an arrest was probable."

Lincoln, as the man challenged, now set out his "instructions," under four headings. First, the weapons were to be "cavalry broadswords of the largest size, precisely equal in all respects." Second, he specified the terms of engagement: "A plank ten feet long, and from nine to twelve inches broad, to be firmly fixed on edge, on the ground, as the line between us which neither is to pass his foot over upon forfeit of his life. [It is not clear here, or in other dueling literature, who would implement this threat.] Next, a line drawn on the ground on either side of the said plank and par-allel with it, each at the distance of the whole length of the sword and three feet additional from the plank; and the passing of his own such line by ei-ther party during the fight shall be deemed a surrender of the contest." Third, the time was set as "On Thursday evening at five o'clock if you can get it so." Finally, the place was fixed for three miles outside of Alton, "on the opposite side of the river, the particular spot to be agreed on by you."

The conditions were accepted, and on the day chosen the two parties made their way to the dueling ground, known as Bloody Island. Before the bout could begin, however, two horsemen rode up: an associate of Shields, Revill W. English, and John J. Hardin, a political colleague of Lincoln and a kinsman of Mary Todd. Hurried words passed, Lincoln and Shields agreeing to exchange apologies, and a reconciliation took place. Lincoln even proposed to Shields that they play a game of "Old Sledge" to deter-mine who should pay for the expenses of their trip. Shields "pungled"—chipped in his share.

Lincoln's later attitude to the fight was by turns bellicose and prag-matic. "I did not intend to hurt Shields unless I did so clearly in self-defense," he explained. But "if it had been necessary I could have split him from the crown of his head to the end of his backbone." He repeated this claim to Major Lucas: "I could have split him in two." Another witness, General Linder, had a different impression:

After this affair . . . in a walk we took together, seeing him make passes with a stick, such as are made in broadsword exercises, I was induced to ask him why he had selected that weapon with which to fight Shields. He promptly answered, in that sharp, ear-splitting voice of his, "To tell you the truth, Linder, I did not want to kill Shields, and felt sure I could disarm him, having had about a month to learn the broadsword exercise; and furthermore, I didn't want the damned fellow to kill me, which I rather think he would have done had we selected pistols."

Never again would Lincoln write a pseudonymous article, and for the rest of his life he would be ashamed of the episode. Once during the Civil War, when an officer asked him at a White House reception if he had ever fought a duel, the president reddened and snapped, "I do not deny it, but if you desire my friendship never mention it again." Even so, at least in one respect his actions had done the trick. Mary Todd was deeply struck that he should have protected her part in rousing Shields in such a way, while in the whirl of their reconciliation he was able to put aside his own misgivings. Ten days after the duel was called off, on November 4, 1842, they were married.

Had anyone bothered to take a closer look at Lincoln's carefully worded instructions, they might have dismissed his later braggadocio, even while admiring his cunning. The cavalry broadsword was large and heavy; it was designed not for artful swordplay but for slashing. To wield it effectively required considerable strength and technique. More important, the two men were separated by a plank nearly a foot high, then by a sword's length, and a further three feet on each side. Lincoln had eight inches on Shields and disproportionately long arms to boot. Thus he had specified rules that allowed him to reach his opponent, leaving the latter unlikely to land a single blow.[6]

U. S. GRANT'S ACTIVE FENCING WAS CONFINED TO HIS DAYS AT West Point, where exercise at smallsword and bayonet was compulsory. In Grant's day there was no physical training and no organized sport—indeed, there was no gymnasium for the 112 cadets—but from the academy's founding in 1802 swordplay was "for a long time the only regular athletic activity other than horseback riding" that was considered an essential part of a cadet's training.[7]*

Grant graduated in 1843, aged twenty-one, and was posted as a lieutenant to the Fourth Infantry. He was drilling his company one day when his company commander, a captain, walked by accompanied by other officers and asked, "Where are the rest of your men, Lieutenant?" "Absent, by your leave, Sir," replied Grant. "That is not true," snapped the captain. At this Grant turned to his sergeant, telling him to take over command, and dismissed the company. He then took out his sword and placed its tip against the breast of his senior officer. "Unless you apologize for this insult," he said in level tones, "I will run you through." The captain apologized, and Grant, fortunately, was not court-martialed for his insolence.[8]

Ulysses was not done with the sword. On Palm Sunday, April 9, 1865, he famously made his way to Appomattox Courthouse, Virginia, where as general in chief of the armies of the United States he accepted the surrender of General Robert E. Lee, commander of the army of Northern Virginia and, in effect, all the Confederate forces.

Lee was wearing his full dress uniform, replete with his ceremonial saber, his "Maryland sword." Grant, in the careful words of Lee's chief biographer, "a man of middle height, slightly stooped and heavily bearded, came in alone. He was dressed for the field, with boots and breeches mudbespattered."[9] He was not wearing any form of sword—a symbolic gesture, as generations of historians have agreed, to show that as the victorious commander he had no need of one.

The truth is more prosaic. Not only did Lee not offer Grant his sword, as has also been alleged, but the only talk of sword came when Grant apologized to Lee for not wearing his saber, "saying," Lee later recorded, that

---

* In 1814 Pierre Thomas was appointed "swordmaster," becoming the first full-time physical education instructor in any institution in America. His successor, Herman Koehler, was called "master of the sword," a position dryly renamed "director of physical education" in 1947. In 1953 both fencing and horsemanship were discontinued, applied psychology and electronics being introduced in their stead. Fencing returned to the academy as a club sport in 1957. The U.S. Naval Academy at Annapolis taught fencing from its founding in 1846, one of only three sports in which cadets could engage. Naval boarding parties still used cutlasses, so every sailor was drilled in fencing; but in recent years Annapolis has dropped it too. Only the U.S. Air Force Academy still teaches swordplay.

"it had gone off in his baggage, and he had not been able to get it in time."[10]

Maybe it was a symbolic meeting all the same—just accidentally so.

I N THE WINTER OF 1873, WHEN THEODORE ROOSEVELT WAS FOURTEEN, he visited Europe for the second time. He stayed with the family of Herr Minckwitz, a German politician. "The two sons were fascinating students from the University of Leipsic [sic]," he later wrote in his *Autobiography,* "both of them belonging to duelling corps, and much scarred in consequence. One, a famous swordsman, was called *Der Roth Herzog* (The Red Duke), and the other was nicknamed *Herr Nasehorn* (Sir Rhinoceros) because the tip of his nose had been cut off in a duel and sewn on again."[11] Before long Roosevelt was himself a student and while at Harvard was challenged to "a real French duel by a real Frenchman." He took such a vehement delight in furthering arrangements for the fight that his opponent, worn down, apologized and invited him to dinner.[12]

Roosevelt's interest in swordplay is possibly the least surprising in any of the fencing presidents. One of 821 students at Harvard, he boxed daily, wrestled, and competed in several track events, despite being a wiry 135 pounds. He was keen on a variety of outdoor pursuits, including hiking, mountaineering, and fishing, while also enjoying jujitsu, tennis, and big-game shooting. And he loved fencing, not as a passing interest but as a recreation he carried into the White House. Roosevelt was six weeks shy of his forty-third birthday when he succeeded McKinley, thus making him the youngest man ever to occupy the presidency. A story in *The New York Times* from April 26, 1903, when he was forty-four, records that he had arranged to take fencing lessons from a teacher in Baltimore, a Professor Giovanni Pavese. "I find Mr. Roosevelt one of the keenest sportsmen I have ever met," Pavese is quoted as saying. "He has the quick eye and aggressive movement that will make him a good fencer. His physical development will adapt him to the exercise, which he will find strenuous enough to please him. I believe I will find him a pupil as apt as he is distinguished." President Roosevelt was usually given lessons once a week, a room in the White House having been specially fitted up as a salle d'armes for the purpose. "During the interim between lessons," wrote a contemporary reporter, "the President devotes as much time as he can spare from his official and social duties to the arduous practice which is necessary if one would become a skillful swordsman."[13]

Professor Pavese's commission was not unique: in the 1890s the president of France, Félix Faure, regularly took lessons from a master at the Elysée Palace.* But Roosevelt's interest in swordplay ranged widely. In *Theodore Rex* Edmund Morris describes how every evening in the residence the president would compel his friend Brigadier General Leonard Wood (onetime military governor of Cuba) to don padded helmet and chest protector, and armed with singlesticks the two men would "beat each other like carpets" in the upper rooms of the executive mansion.[14] Roosevelt joked, "We look like Tweedledum and Tweedledee." In one session his right arm was so severely whacked about that he had to greet his evening guests left-handed.

THIS LEAVES ONE AMERICAN FENCING PRESIDENT UNACCOUNTED for, and he perhaps the least likely: Harry Truman. With his squeaky voice and delicate frame, Truman was the antithesis of a sportsman. His schoolmates called him "Four-eyes" on account of his spectacles, and he recorded disarmingly, "Without my glasses I was as blind as a bat, and to tell the truth, I was kind of a sissy. If there was any danger of getting into a fight, I always ran." Fencing proved the exception.

At high school Truman found himself drawn to the girl who was the class's foremost athlete, Elizabeth Virginia Wallace, a fine tennis player, the best third-base player in the school, a tireless ice-skater and all-round track star—and, of course, the girl he would later marry: Bess. According to their daughter's biography, Bess "was the best female fencer in town, and she was probably better than most of the boys . . . and she was pretty besides."[15] St. Louis, a bustling, cosmopolitan city known as "The Gateway to the West," had a long tradition of French influence, so it was not surprising to find fencing a respected sport. Anyway, the two teenagers used to meet after school at Truman's cousins', the Nolands', and go over their homework together. That, at least, was the pretext for meeting; in fact, they spent their time fencing.

In 1965, Mary Ethel Noland, Truman's first cousin, recorded:

* In February 1899 Faure died in the Elysée Palace from a heart attack while in the arms of his mistress, whose hair was gripped so tightly by the stricken president that she could not struggle free. Luckily, a sword-armed garde Republican was on hand, and the mistress, slightly shorn, was soon able to make her way home. She later became a character in an Agatha Christie novel and ended her life as Lady Abinger, dying in Brighton in 1954.

[Harry] had two foils, or rapiers, or whatever you call them; and so we would sometimes practice fencing, which we knew absolutely nothing about, but it was fun to try, and we had the porch and we had room here to play and have fun, generally, which we did, with a little Latin intermingled, maybe. Though I'm afraid Caesar had a very slim chance with all that was going on.[16]

One can picture the bespectacled boy and his Miss Wonderful, laughing and playing around with their foils and textbooks.

FOR ANY RECENT PRESIDENT, FENCING MIGHT SEEM A THROWBACK to a much earlier age, but swordplay has actually had a long, if sometimes disreputable, tradition in the New World. The first recorded duel fought in North America took place at the newly settled Plimoth Plantation on June 18, 1621, between two servants of a landowner, using swords and daggers. They were literally bound to keep the peace: their punishment was to have their hands and feet tied together for twenty-four hours, without food or drink. Their suffering was such that they were freed after an hour—an act of mercy when one considers that another New England miscreant, in 1644, was beheaded with a sword, the last such execution recorded in North America. In 1719 Massachusetts passed a law depriving duelists of political rights and rendering them ineligible for any public office for twenty years; should a duelist fall or otherwise be killed, his body was to be "appropriated to anatomical demonstration." America was outdoing Europe.

The first reference to fencing as such in North America that I have been able to find is in a manuscript in the British Museum, dated 1675. In a short account of life in New England, a note reads, "One Dancing schoole was set up, but put down. A Fenceing schoole is allowed."[17] Thereafter a reference can be found to one John Rievers, a Dutchman, teaching fencing and dancing to colonists in 1754 in New York, on the corner of Whitehall and Stone Streets, on the encouragement of British officers garrisoned there.

The sport took root in several colonies, most notably in Virginia, where plantation owners carried on the traditions of their (usually rather notional) English forebears. This also meant dueling—a practice introduced by the French and Germans immigrants as much as by the British—which functioned as a means of gaining social status and demonstrating bravery. The *code duello* also reinforced the honor system and, in a society dependent on slavery, emphasized ritualized authority. Slaves and the lower orders should show deference; one's peers should show courtesy—a gentleman would not duel with someone outside his class but would take up a cane or horsewhip, to show his contempt for his victim.

Writing in 1831 on the American duel, de Tocqueville noted the differences between the European and the New World models. "In Europe," he observed, "one hardly ever fights except in order to be able to say that one has done so; the offence is generally a sort of moral stain which one wants to wash away, and which most often is washed away at little expense. In America one only fights to kill; one fights because one sees no hope of getting one's adversary condemned to death. There are very few duels, but they almost always end fatally."[18] Tocqueville could be credulous: even in America, both duelists usually survived.

Americans used pistols for choice, but also shotguns, rifles, carbines, and bowie knives, with deadly results. Outside the aristocracy, most Americans had neither time for nor access to fencing instruction, whereas using a pistol was easy; all one needed was iron nerve. Wherever the French had settled marked an exception. The Francophone population of Louisiana certainly honored its heritage, with sword duels still being fought in New Orleans up through the early twentieth century. The practice first invaded New Orleans at the end of the eighteenth century, after the arrival there of immigrants from San Domingo and, later, officers and soldiers from Bonaparte's army. As late as 1883, when dueling of all kinds had almost been eradicated elsewhere, a rapier duel between a soda-water seller and a catfish dealer lasted eighty-three minutes before either combatant drew blood.

That same year, the editor of the Charleston *News and Courier* was created Knight of the Order of Saint George by the pope in recognition of his persistent opposition to dueling. Journalists (and politicians) were by then the main duelists throughout the United States, as they were in Europe. About this time a mode of fighting became known as "the American duel," part suicide pact, part Russian roulette. An intermediary would offer the two principals the ends of a handkerchief, one of which would be tied in a knot: the person who drew the knot would be expected to shoot himself voluntarily. Some Americans protested against the name—rightly so, as the hybrid was practiced mainly in Germany. The appellation was the result of xenophobic Germans voicing their abhorrence of "Americanization."

New Orleans had a number of masters at the time of the Louisiana Purchase in 1803—generally foreigners—and a special site where people went to learn to fence. "The whole stretch of Exchange Alley," wrote Lyle Saxon, "was filled with fencing masters, and in the afternoon or evening those passing by in the street could hear the rasping of the swords, and the cries of the spectators who watched these contests with approving and critical eyes."[19] The city boasted several rich families, whose young men were sent abroad to be educated—usually to Paris, where they did as they pleased, gambled, fought, and made love. There had been swordplay in New Orleans since its founding, but by the 1830s the rich young Creoles of the city, back from their travels, had adopted a high style of studied dandyism, and "the word 'honor' hung in the air like the refrain of a popular song."[20]

Dueling quickly became a lifestyle. From 1834 on there was even a regular venue, known as "The Dueling Oaks," which saw ten to twelve such encounters a week. A cafe nearby specialized in serving coffee to contestants before a duel. Many fencing masters plied their trade in New Orleans, forming a cadre of their own. They would be pointed out as they walked by, often even more elaborately attired than their pupils. One master, a lawyer from Bordeaux, having made a fortune teaching fencing to young officers during the Mexican War, gained notoriety early in his career in Louisiana by fighting seven duels in a week. Another, the splendidly named Bastile (Basile?) Croquère, a mulatto, is described as parading the city in a suit of green broadcloth, with spotless linen and a wide black ruff. He was famous for his collection of cameos and would wear breast pin, bracelet, and cameo rings. His skills were so phenomenal that the highest Creole gentry flocked to him for lessons, despite the prevailing prejudice against "men of color." Another well-known duelist was José (or Pepe) Lulla, a wealthy Spaniard, who was famed with both sword and pistol. With the latter he was said to be able to shoot coin from between a man's fingers or an egg from a man's head. (He once shot an egg off the head of his own son.) He fought twenty duels, but died from natural causes in 1888, at the age of seventy-three.

At first, fatalities and even serious wounds were rare, and "a scratch usually sufficed to bring the combat to an end."[21] Then encounters became more deadly, and as dueling spread to neighboring states, the South became known as "a seedbed of national violence," producing a stream of young men with "obsessions about reputation and vengeance and deadly weapons with them."[22] Public opinion was united against the practice,

The Famous New Orleans Duelling Ground.

A café adjoining "The Dueling Oaks," as the ground was known,
served coffee to anxious participants. One unstoppable bretteur fought
seven duels in a single week—making his reputation.

condemning it as a foreign importation, "a remnant of Gothic barbarism."[23] Yet the code of honor actually grew in the South and the south-
ern-influenced frontier states after 1810. Mark Twain blamed this on the
disastrous effect of Walter Scott and the rise of romantic literature, citing
such novels as *The Antiquary* and *Ivanhoe* and such romantic notions—
this from a duelist in *The Bride of Lammermoor*—as "If one of us falls, all
accounts are settled; if not, men are never so ready for peace as after war."*

Surprisingly, attempts to control dueling in America, and the population's response, were the inverse of those in Europe. While European
rulers made every effort to suppress the custom—even dragging the mortally wounded from the dueling ground to a place of execution—only to

---

* Twain himself describes a particularly grisly duel in an almost two-page footnote on
such encounters in *Life on the Mississippi*: "Two 'highly connected' young Virginians,
clerks in a hardware store at Charlottesville, while 'skylarking,' came to blows. Peter
Dick threw pepper in Charles Roads's eyes; Roads demanded an apology; Dick refused
to give it, and it was agreed that a duel was inevitable, but a difficulty arose; the parties
had no pistols, and it was too late at night to procure them. One of them suggested that
butcher knives would answer the purpose, and the other accepted the suggestion: the
result was that Roads fell to the floor with a gash in his abdomen that may or may not
prove fatal."[24]

find that dueling flourished, in America the practice was generally regarded with disapproval but the laws up to 1850 made it neither criminal nor contemptible. Not until 1838 did Congress outlaw challenges in the District of Columbia, and even then a senator from Delaware maintained that, though he thought dueling immoral, "it was not of that class of crimes which should subject offenders to the cells of a penitentiary and make them the associates of felons." Similarly, a senator from Missouri declared that "from what I have seen, fighting is like marrying: the more barriers that are erected against it, the surer are the interested parties to come together."[25]

The first recorded fatal duel took place in Massachusetts on July 3, 1728, when after a quarrel over cards two young Bostonians, Woodbridge and Phillips, took their differences, and their swords, out onto King Street—State Street today—and Woodbridge was found dead on the Common the following morning. Phillips was not charged, but the practice nonetheless remained rare. Views hardened almost exactly a century later, after the legendary encounter of August 1827, when Colonel James Bowie used his infamous knife in what was reported as "the bloodiest affair of the kind on American record."

Bowie's attack was the culmination of a running feud between two groups in the Red River parish of Rapides, in Louisiana. The principals were Dr. Maddox, Major Wright, Colonel Robert Alexander Crain, and the Blanchards on the one side, and the Wellses, Curreys, and Bowies on the other. When a challenge passed between Dr. Maddox and Samuel Wells, a duel was arranged to take place opposite Natchez, Mississippi. The site was a large sandbar, a favorite place for men to settle their differences by dueling, and on the appointed day about forty spectators, divided equally among friends of the two sides, gathered at opposite ends of the sandbar to watch. Bowie was carrying a large knife made from a blacksmith's rasp, a file used for horses' hooves. Bowie's brother had advised him it was "strong, and of admirable temper. It is more trustworthy in the hands of a strong man than a pistol, for it will not snap." And so it proved.

What ensued was terrifying. After an initial exchange of shots, Crain and Bowie closed in. Crain neatly avoided Bowie's knife and clubbed him over the head with his pistol. Bowie fell, momentarily stunned. Crain then stepped back, allowing his friend Major Wright, a noted duelist, to advance and thrust his swordstick into the stricken man. The blade struck Bowie's breastbone and went around the rib, but did not kill him. At the same moment Bowie seized Wright, pulling the slighter man on top of him. "Now, Major, you die," said Bowie coolly, plunging his knife into Wright's heart. Meanwhile the savagery had spread to the forty onlookers and ended only when at least six had been killed and fifteen wounded. This, recorded a contemporary historian, was "the grand fight which gave origin to the bowie-knife, the fearful fame of which is spread over all countries."[26]

Bowie's weapon, with a blade typically eight to twelve inches long, was not a sword, but it had its effect on swordplay. The bowie knife (and its first cousin, the "Arkansas toothpick") became a favored weapon of the Southern aristocracy, one especially suited to killing.[27] When, in 1849, Kentucky attempted to outlaw dueling, one opponent of the bill observed, "I ask gentlemen which has produced most misery and mourning in Kentucky, the duel or the bowie knife? Which, I ask, has shed most blood, the fair and open combat or the knife of the assassin?"[28] People's fear of the bowie knife made them more tolerant of formal duels.

"The bowie-knife," ruled the Texas Supreme Court in 1859,

is an exceedingly destructive weapon. It is difficult to defend against it, by any degree of bravery, or any amount of skill. The gun or pistol may miss its aim, and when discharged, its dangerous character is lost, or diminished at least. The sword may be parried. With these weapons men fight for the sake of the combat, to satisfy the laws of honor, not necessarily with the intention to kill, or with a certainty of killing, when the intention exists. The Bowie-knife differs from these in its device and design; it is an instrument of almost certain death.[29]

All this helped the duel's cause. In the 1920s in Georgia, another state with a culture of violence, no white male ever went about unarmed. "It is no wonder that thoughtful men, not only in Georgia but also over the rest of the South and the Western frontier, argued for the duel as a check on general murder," wrote the historian William Stevens. "In a duel conditions could be made reasonably equal, and seconds often had an opportunity to effect a reconciliation."[30]

Other states took a similar view. Dueling was unlawful but far from a capital offense. In Vermont and Connecticut, the punishment was a fine and disqualification from office; Illinois passed a law against dueling at some point before 1815, but the law, never published, was finally repealed. In Rhode Island, a convicted duelist would be carted to the gallows with a rope about his neck and made to sit for an hour "exposed to the peltings of the mob" but not actually hanged.[31] In 1836 Nathaniel Hawthorne reported how in old Massachusetts duelists had been severely punished. "In the U.S. now," he wrote, "non-fatal duels cause public hissing. We should imitate the British and encourage the custom to fade away."[32] Despite this declaration, the following year Hawthorne learned from his lover, Mary Silsbee, that an acquaintance of his, John Louis O'Sullivan, "had been guilty of an attempt to practice the basest treachery upon her," and he immediately called him out. O'Sullivan apologized profusely, and eventually the novelist withdrew his challenge.[33] In general there were far fewer examples of duels in the North. A single dueling society is known to have existed in the United States—in Charleston, South Carolina, in the early nineteenth century—and that was quickly disbanded after the death, in a duel, of its president.

With the discovery of gold in the Sacramento Valley in 1848, dueling moved westward, along with tens of thousands of Americans, many of them southerners, infected with "California fever." Tournaments, modeled on their medieval forerunners, remained popular in Maryland, Virginia, and South Carolina as late as 1865 but were never the reckless or chivalric displays they had been in Europe.[34] In the West, nearly all duels were fought with firearms. By the 1860s, even in California, the practice was on the decline. It was not just because of public disapproval and sterner legislation: as with the First World War in Europe, the appalling toll of the Civil War made dueling seem foolish and more obviously criminal. On the battlefield itself the Civil War cavalries charged saber in hand, but a trooper's revolver and carbine carried more weight than his sword. U.S. troops made their last traditional cavalry charge in 1906 against Moro rebels in the Philippines, but this was already an anachronism; by then swordplay had moved safely indoors, into the confines of the movie theater and the fencing hall.

MODERN FENCING WAS BROUGHT TO AMERICA BY THE GERMAN *Turnvereiner* in the late 1840s. These highly organized gymnastic societies were part of the movement for national renewal in Germany and would eventually give focus to the dueling fraternities there. They emphasized physical training through gymnastics and included fencing in their regimen. After the Civil War, many colleges and sports clubs adopted fencing along with the rest of the *Turnverein* program. The constitution and by-laws of the Boston Fencing Club, published in 1858, recorded that each member was expected to "provide his own foils"; "no females . . . under any pretext whatever. . . . No dogs shall be kept in the clubrooms," under pain of a 50-cent fine. No fine is recorded for harboring a female.

A striking proponent of fencing was James Naismith, the inventor of basketball. In 1891 Naismith was working at the Young Men's Christian Association training school at Springfield, Massachusetts, teaching psychology, Bible studies, and boxing and other sports when his senior teacher asked him to think of an indoor game to break the monotony of constant gym during the winter months. He tried lacrosse, football, soccer, and even indoor cricket before coming up with the rudiments of basketball, using nine players on each side and with just thirteen rules. When his students showed they enjoyed the game, he wrote up his idea in the school paper, *The Triangle*, and from then on basketball took off. In 1897 the number of players per side was reduced to five, but by then Naismith had moved on to the University of Kansas, where he taught a range of sports.

"Fencing equipment at the University of Kansas was acquired by chance," his biographer records, "in 1896, two years before a fencing instructor, namely Naismith, was available. The university had purchased for its athletic department all the fixtures and equipment . . . of a defunct gymnasium in Atchison, Kansas. Included in the equipment happened to be the masks, foils, plastrons, and other accoutrements of a fencing class. The gear looked impressive enough, but no one knew, or cared, much about it. When Naismith came along, though, action began."

Although the university had remained uninterested in so frivolous a sport, fencing was becoming popular in the United States (in 1893, over twenty thousand people flocked to an international tournament fought on horseback with sabers in New York's Madison Square Garden), and in 1894 the Intercollegiate Fencing Association was founded. Naismith had become adept at fencing before he came to the Midwest, and he liked the sport. Therefore, when he found equipment in the storeroom of the gymnasium, he dusted it off, organized classes in fencing and broadsword, and became responsible for raising student interest in fencing, with few lapses, throughout the rest of his career at the university. Naismith continued to teach fencing until he was past seventy-five, sparring regularly with his students. A skillful performer as well as a good instructor, he liked to show off the finer points of the sport by using a yardstick against a student with a broadsword—and winning.[35]

By the end of the nineteenth century a number of U.S. universities considered it a mark of standing to have fencing facilities, and a majority of cities had clubs. The sword was regarded as either a deadly weapon or a slightly effete instrument of exercise for a gentleman, and clubs existed as little islands of aristocratic diversion, not greatly different from their European counterparts; but fencing made slower progress than in Europe. It was not until 1874 that the first salle was opened in New York. Its master, Karl Senac, and his son, Peter, also published one of the first—and most reprinted—American books on the sport, *The Art of Fencing*. When that same year masks were reworked to be more effective, they were adopted by baseball coaches as the first catchers' masks. (As a grim postscript, Senac Senior would stuff a rag soaked in chloroform into one of the new masks when, some years later, he committed suicide.)

In 1888 the Amateur Athletic Union had initiated national championships. Fencers were unhappy with the arrangement and on May 6, 1891, formed the Amateur Fencers League of America, with 108 original members. The following year national championships were held under the auspices of the new body. The first AFLA Rules for Competition provided that "The English language only shall be spoken by the judges (3) during the competition." This was not the only oddity: the winner was de-

The U.S. War Department assumed in 1942 that its GIs would encounter an enemy trained in classic Western swordsmanship, and responded accordingly with a field manual on how to deal with swordsmen.

termined not by counting victories but by tabulating the aggregate number of hits in a round robin. The three judges awarded hits for defense, attack, and "general good form." Each competitor wore "a dark fencing suit so that white chalk marks [from the weapons' tips] can easily be seen."

These rules remained in force till 1897, when white jackets were introduced for foil and chalk was discontinued. Dark jackets remained the norm for épée until 1911. Five-touch bouts were also discontinued. Foilists were to fence for a full four minutes; the winner was whoever was ahead when time was called. The foil target was also a movable feast: originally it ran up and down one side of the torso, from collar to hip; in 1906 it was extended to the entire torso, front and back; then in 1923 the groin was added. In both foil and saber contestants were required to acknowledge touches; failure to do so cost two points.

On April Fools' Day 1905 a new and unconventional set of regulations was recommended for all foil competitions. "Judges are requested to give points for the general bearing," exhorted the lawmakers,

> for form shown in defense and attack, and for the value of the touch itself. A good parry, even if not followed by a touch, should be credited with some value. Touches made in poor style should not receive the consideration of a well-executed touch, which should be worth at least two points in comparison. Rushing, pounding, failing to cross foils, or to make the parry, dragging the feet, throwing forward the body, dodging, coming on guard poorly, failing to use the left hand correctly, or offending against form in any way, should be counted against such offenders; and should the opponent have better form or fewer faults, it should be counted in his favor and so expressed in points in the judge's score.[36]

It was a noble if doomed attempt to govern fencing on aesthetic principles, a decade at least after Europe had given up the battle. These criteria set America apart for nearly twenty years. At the poorly supported and badly organized 1904 Olympics in St. Louis, only the United States and Cuba fielded teams, and the isolation of American fencers was not felt. At the London Games of 1908, the organizers decided that since foil was an art the result should not be recorded by the mere scoring of touches, so an exhibition event was held. The British captain, Theodore Cook, declared, "Foil fencing is the instrument of perhaps the most graceful and most courteous form of athletic exercise in the world and its whole spirit is de-

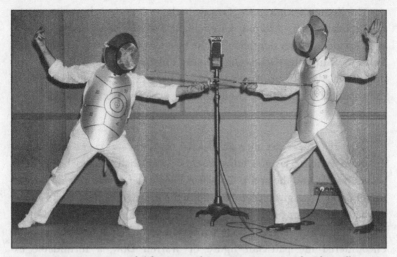

A 1937 attempt to improve foil fencing: each weapon was equipped with small suction cups, which stuck to the spot where a hit was made. The heart and other vital organs are diagrammed and points awarded accordingly. The system's inventor, Ray Gross (left), awarded 100 points for a hit at the heart, 20 points for the right breast.

stroyed by mere combativeness." Following the Games of 1912 and 1920, however, the Americans returned home keen for their sport to be integrated with the European model: in 1923 it finally was, with the same target area and scoring systems.

Foil was the leading weapon throughout this period, with saber and épée some way behind. Between 1920 and 1956 America won two individual medals at the Olympics—silver for foil in 1932 and bronze for épée in 1928—along with four team bronzes. Then came the Hungarian Uprising and the diaspora of 1956: suddenly the country was flooded with top-class Magyar fencers. It made a difference—the saber team came fourth in 1960—but not a significant one. There were already leading masters in place—Aldo Nadi on the West Coast, Giorgio Santelli at the New York Athletic Club, among others—but somehow the sport remained resolutely a minority interest, appealing only to a moneyed white upper middle class.*

---

* Several of America's keenest fencers of this period found fame in other worlds. Admiral Forrest Sherman—who in 1943 was Admiral Chester Nimitz's "right arm, if not

The Rome Olympics of 1960 saw perhaps America's best chance of a gold medal. Albert Axelrod, an ebullient, volatile New Yorker, came in third in the foil after demolishing the best talent of Western Europe, but failed to disturb the two excellent young Russians who took first and second places. After 1960 American teams became the worthy also-rans of international competition. Then arose the explosive issue of race.

SOME YEARS BEFORE THE ROME GAMES, "INTER-SETTLEMENT RECREation Fencing League tournaments" were instituted to bring more young people into the sport. One year, the winner of the girls' foil event, Violet Barker, was given membership in the prestigious New York Fencers Club as part of her prize. Some days later, clutching her new card of admission, she went to the club to participate in an AFLA competition and encountered the patrician figure of Warren Dow, a formidable ex-Olympian who had been association secretary during three different presidencies between 1942 and 1948, and who effectively ran U.S. fencing. "What are you doing here?" he asked. Barker was black. She explained. Dow asked for her card and, standing in front of the club's heavy oak doors, tore it in two. "We don't let niggers fence here," he told her.

Both Barker and her coach were too poor and felt too powerless to lodge an official complaint, but soon after that two black members of Columbia University's fencing team were denied access to the even more prestigious New York Athletic Club, and *their* coach, the newly appointed Joseph Velarde, insisted that his whole squad enter the NYAC by the front door like everyone else. When his request was refused, the team set off back home. Two stories appeared in *The New York Times*, representations were made, and eventually a committee of the AFLA was convened to discuss the matter. Dow was present and made his feelings clear: "If we let *them* into this club that will be the end of fencing at the NYAC, and that will mean the end of fencing in the United States." He looked around the table, facing each member in turn, then added, "Look, we know how we're going to vote, let's get it over with and go back to fencing." "No, Warren,"

---

a major part of his brain," and became chief of naval operations after the war—was reckoned one of the finest swordsmen of his time. Richard C. Steere, a member of the bronze medal–winning team at the 1932 Olympics who fenced on into his eighties, was General Patton's leading weather expert, determining Patton's strategies in the North African landings, defying Washington and London's forecasts, and earning from Patton the nickname "Commander Houdini."

someone said quietly, "you don't know how I am going to vote." To everyone's surprise, it was the association's president, Miguel de Capriles. Turning to the others, he said, "Gentlemen, it's time we addressed the fact that fencing has changed from the aristocratic thing that it was to the democratic thing it now is." His speech carried the day.[37]

Black children from all walks of life began to fence. One was to transform the sport in America. Peter Westbrook was born in 1952 to a mixed-race couple living in the Hayes Homes housing project in Newark, New Jersey—one of the poorest and most violent areas in the state. Westbrook's father, Ulysses, had been a GI during the Korean War; his Japanese mother was a war bride. The young Westbrook's memories are of his father beating his mother; his father putting out cigarettes on his mother's face; his mother on the floor, her leg bleeding. Ulysses left for good when Peter was six, but by then the boy had already used a knife to carve a "Z" for "Zorro"—a television favorite—on his mother's coffee table.

A life in the projects was not what Mariko Westbrook wanted for her son, and she was soon mapping out his escape. Peter would travel to school with cardboard masking the holes in his shoes and grew up a thief and a fighter—a good fighter, he says; taunted for his ancestry, he had to be. He not only scrapped in the streets but boxed in the Police Athletic League. In his autobiography, published in 1997, he described this early world. "I often think about the kids from my neighborhood," he writes, "how they never had a chance. I would say that 90% are dead, 8% are in jail, and I have no idea what happened to the remaining 2%. Stinky, Buddy, Carter and Horse are the nicknames of some of my buddies that didn't make it. Drugs or homicide took their lives: one was shot in the back for robbing a store, another murdered by a rival."[38]

Not the normal background for a champion. By the time he was fourteen Peter had started to fence: "My mother could trace her lineage back through many samurai. This was a source of great honor, great pride. For her, fencing was a sport of nobles. She thought, If I get Peter into fencing, he'll meet noble people. But it wasn't all that stuff about her family that got me interested. She offered me five dollars if I took a lesson."

The inducement worked. He won an athletic scholarship to New York University, gained a place on the 1976 Olympic team, and in 1984 took a bronze medal at the Los Angeles Games. In answer to those who saw the L.A. Games as "soft" because so many Eastern Europeans were absent, he made the world championship finals in 1989. For more than twenty years he dominated saber fencing in America, qualifying for six Olympics and winning the national title an unprecedented thirteen times. His lithe, cat-like movements made him look like a boxer, which he had once been: his right shoulder leaning slightly down and forward, his back arm held out wide.

Sometimes he met with racial slurs, but used them to spur him on. If he had a white opponent, he conjured up a white face and recalled an insult from a white man. He never saw his father's face when he attacked—his father had hurt him only indirectly, he explained. He was always a picture of calm and courtesy on the strip, impassive, but judges standing close by could hear him muttering obscenities under his breath, too low for the referee to pick up.

"I could have killed somebody every day," he told a *New York Times* reporter.[39] "It's a great fuel for the sport, but it started to seep out in life. Somebody might step on my toes in the subway, I'd start a fight with my fists." He went into therapy. When he eventually came around to writing a memoir, he chose the title *Harnessing Anger*. In the passages where he touches on his early experiences his words have an edge that few other writings on the sport can match:

> I had one objective only: to win. If I am fencing with you my whole heart and soul are concerned. How can I do this gracefully and effortlessly? I absorb your body language the way a dry sponge absorbs water. My objective is to get to know how you think, to anticipate your next move. I try to become aware of your slightest weaknesses, the ones you don't even know you have. Then I capitalize on them. That's how I can defeat you.

Having grown up on the rough side of the tracks, he had no qualms about preying upon his enemies' weaknesses.

> To do this in life is a crime, but to do it in the sport of fencing is to create beauty and art. It's all about negative manipulation and emotional intimidation. With each opponent I immediately try to gauge, *How weak is this man? How many times will I have to beat him down in order to shatter him?* I try to think beyond a single match. I ask, *Can I scare him so bad that he'll bow down to me forever? How can I keep him as my prisoner for life?* I don't think that people who have grown up in mainstream society know how to do this.

But mainstream society was impressed. Peter carried the American flag at the Barcelona Games in 1992 and again at the Pan-American Games in 1995. His last Olympics were those of 1996, but by then his life had taken another turn. In 1991 he had established the Peter Westbrook Foundation, largely from his own savings, an organization to help disadvantaged inner-city youth not only to learn fencing but to improve their overall performance in school. At the first meeting six children turned up; now there are more than a hundred people enrolled, ranging in age from nine to twenty-one. The foundation has become one of the most successful inner-city sports programs in the country, producing four of the country's current top five saber fencers and several strong women contenders too. Keeth Smart and his sister Erinn were among the half dozen who appeared at that first class in 1991; both went to the Sydney Olympics in 2000.

Westbrook worked for IBM in the 1970s and is an adept marketing man, ensuring that newspaper articles on his club appear regularly and making TV appearances. In an interview in 1999, *Sports Illustrated* recorded, "Westbrook has a simple rule: Do well in school or don't fence. He hires tutors and holds bi-monthly essay-writing contests, awarding $50 prizes to the top three entrants. He charges kids for private lessons so they'll feel obligated to get the most from their investment. The fee is a rock-bottom $20 a year, and he often reduces even that."[40]

The foundation pays instructors' salaries, equips the fencers, and rents the current premises on Twenty-fifth Street. In effect, it has folded itself into the old Fencers Club, a nice irony. It provides money for travel to competitions—all on a shoestring annual budget of around $175,000, which Westbrook raises on his own. As a "black-almost-white guy" and a member of the U.S. Olympic Committee, he knows he is ideally placed to speak to both sides, but he is also not beyond motivating his charges by reminding them of their blackness in what is still predominantly a white man's sport. "Why do inner-city kids make the best fencers?" he says. "They've got more rage, more anger, great fighting spirit. That anger and rage is what it takes to be an Olympic champion."

One of Westbrook's most promising pupils is Ivan Lee, a slim, 160-pound left-hander now on a full athlete's scholarship at St. John's University, where several of the foundation's members have found harbor. "Where I'm from, the sport of fencing is about as far removed from the people as square dancing and classical music," he wrote in one of the es-

Peter Westbrook (center) flanked by his pupils Akhi Spencer-El and Keeth Smart. Both Spencer-El and Smart made the 2000 Olympics, and by March 2003 Smart was ranked the number one sabreur in the world.

says he prepared for Westbrook. "Honestly, how many skinny, black, 16-year-old boys with glasses do you know that fence?"

I first met Westbrook when we fenced against each other in a team match at the World Championships in Grenoble in 1974, and we have kept up our friendship over the years. In April 2000 we were sharing a coffee together near his club when Ivan Lee came by. He had narrowly failed to win the world youth title, ending up in third place, and was reporting in to discuss why he had fallen short. Lee admitted that in the semifinal he had felt afraid, not only of what his opponent might do but even more of the prospect of victory. He had refused to acknowledge it, and that had made him seize up. "You didn't *use* the fear," Westbrook told him, grasping the boy's upper arm. "We all feel that fear; you've got to learn to bring it out into the open."

They agreed to work on the problem together. A year later Lee came second in the same tournament, ending up number two in the world youth rankings—and, even more impressively, came third in a top senior event, beating most of the world's leading fencers. Small wonder that in March 2002 Disney paid to develop a film based on Westbrook's life, and have "fast-tracked" the project, or that *The New York Times* dubbed Westbrook "the most influential fencer in New York today."

The paper might have gone further but for another great change in American fencing. Following the collapse of Soviet hegemony in 1989, scores of top-class fencers and masters have emigrated to the United States—not only from Hungary, as in 1956, but from Poland, Russia, and Bulgaria. A onetime U.S. team captain told me, "We currently have the greatest concentration of coaching strength ever—and I'm including Italy." In the world championships in 2000 the United States won its first-ever team gold medal—at women's saber. The women's coach was a Pole based in Oregon. Luck, said some; and women's saber was a new event and therefore less competitive. But a year later, at the world championships in Nîmes, the Americans took bronze in the women's foil, besting a strong German team 45–43.

While still outside the top ten fencing nations, the United States has started to dominate the youth international circuit, as the French, Germans, Italians, and Russians have done for years. There are currently a hundred thousand fencers in the country and about eight hundred clubs. The many Eastern Europeans jockeying for coaching jobs throughout the United States have yet to prove they can manage a club, not just give excellent individual lessons, but the future looks bright. From comic strips such as "Peanuts" and "Tank McNamara" to cartoons in *The New Yorker*, a teenage Lex Luthor fencing in *Smallville*, and doctors on *ER* staging impromptu fencing bouts, consciousness of the sport is growing nationwide. All that is necessary, one might cynically add, is to relocate the country in the middle of Europe.

Part Four

WOUNDED WARRIORS

Previous page: A German student, restricted by his injuries
following a Mensur duel, drinks as best he can.

CHAPTER 12

Spilled Blood

*Haven't you ever wondered what it would be like? What
would be that feeling of a real blade entering another man's
body? That initial resistance . . . and that sudden giving?
The surprise on another man's face!*

—THE VILLAINOUS MASTER (ERIC ROBERTS) IN
By the Sword, 1991

*Wounds of the flesh a surgeon's skill may heal,
But wounded honor is only cured with steel.*

—FROM A NINETEENTH-CENTURY
CHALLENGE TO A DUEL

IN THE SUMMER OF 1995 A "SWORD-SWALLOWING GUIDE" APPEARED
in *The Sword,* the official magazine of the British Fencing Association. It
opens:

> Bored with practice sessions with foil, épée or sabre? Try swallow-
> ing the weapon instead! According to a recent newspaper report, a
> surgeon who has studied the technique of swordswallowing claims
> that "once you have learned to do it properly, it is harmless." A
> novice starts by swallowing a ball attached to a strong cotton
> thread, which he repeatedly pulls up until the gag-reflex is sup-
> pressed. He then graduates to swords of increasing length to a
> maximum of two feet. A big meal prior to performance weighs
> down the stomach so the sword dramatically disappears up to the
> hilt.
>
> But don't hiccup. Last century an Indian swordswallower hic-
> cuped during a performance in London. His beautifully dissected
> esophagus and the sword are on display at University College
> Hospital.[1]

When this article appeared I was a member of Britain's Board of Fencing, with particular responsibility for safety. A colleague phoned me shortly after the magazine had been distributed to say that there was a real danger of a young fencer experimenting: we should circulate every subscriber with a warning. I opted for inaction, and fortunately no pioneer hiccupped that summer. But the practice exerts an odd fascination. Shakespeare wrote about it (in *Henry VI, Part II:* "I'll make thee eat iron like an ostrich, and swallow my sword like a great pin, ere thou an I part"), and the practice is recorded long before—Lucius Apuleius (c. A.D. 123–170) and the Spanish humanist Ludovicus Vives (1492–1540) both mention it.*

By the mid–eighth century sword-swallowing was popular in Japan, having first traveled from Greece to India and on into southern China. In the Middle Ages sword-swallowers, like other "magicians," were condemned and persecuted by the Church, and it was not until the mid–seventeenth century that they could wander Europe more or less freely. They became popular in America from 1893, when their acts were one of the features of the Chicago World's Fair, but still their veracity was doubted, with *Webster's Dictionary* defining a sword-swallower as "a performer who pretends to swallow a sword." Some performers use a guiding tube of thin metal that they have already ingested, but for most the act is genuine, with all its attendant risks.

In 1895 the editor of a London magazine described one Signor Benedetti, who had just performed at the Westminster Aquarium and Canterbury Hall. The blade used by Benedetti, we learn, was thirty and a quarter inches long. "The point of this sword," the writer added,

when passed up to its hilt down Benedetti's gullet, can be felt in the left groin, so close to the top of the leg that another inch would carry it into the limb. For a man of Mr Benedetti's height (5ft 8ins,

---

* "I saw with these eyes a Juggler that swallowed a two-hand sword, with a very keene edge, and by and by for a little money that we that looked on gave him, hee devoured a chasing speare with the point downeward. And after that hee had conveyed the whole speare within the closure of his body, and brought it out againe behind, there appeared on the top thereof (which caused us all to marvell) a faire boy pleasant and nimble, winding and turning himself in such sort, that you would suppose he had neither bone nor gristle, and verily thinke that he were the naturall Serpent, creeping and sliding on the knotted staffe, which the god of Medicine is feigned to beare."¹ Vives for his part recorded, "to the great fear and horror of spectators, [he would] swallow swords and vomit forth a power of needles, girdles, and coins."

without his boots) the ordinary distance an instrument could be passed would be from 24 to 25 inches. Benedetti tells me that sometimes, though very rarely, his long sword stops when passed at a distance of about 25 inches, and at a spot which would be in the proper line of the bottom of the stomach.

Without a trace of humor, the article continued, "Being a wise man, he does not attempt on these occasions to push the sword further, but immediately withdraws it." The rationale for this feat exercises a certain fascination:

In seeking for an explanation for this remarkable accomplishing [*sic*], it seems more probable that the sword passes out of the stomach rather than that the stomach is of such an extraordinary size that it extends as far as the groin, especially when we remember the difficulty there is sometimes experienced in passing anything beyond the natural distance, and on the supposition that the sword passes out of the stomach, it must pass either into an elongated pouch, or into a natural elongation of that organ. But the outlet into this natural continuation is normally placed at right angles to the opening of the gullet into the stomach, and about 5 inches from it, and therefore is in such relation to the gullet orifice that a straight rod, passed through the latter, would not go anywhere near the former.

The writer argued that the passage into the Italian's stomach was, unusually, in a direct line with his gullet:

If the sword entered into a pouch of the stomach it is difficult to understand how it is that no trouble is ever experienced with the food. With such a blind sac of five inches in length, there must of necessity be at some time or another some disturbance to the system from the detained accumulation of food, but no inconvenience ever seems to occur to M. Benedetti.

Signor Benedetti had first attempted this act in 1863, at the age of fourteen, when he discovered he could pass down a blade of almost the same length as the one he came to employ in his prime. So his act was not the fruit of any gradual process of stomach distension through constant practice. However, honing his art over the next thirty years, he so accustomed his stomach to steel that it could take a sword for some minutes without disturbance.

There remained the danger of hiccups—or, at the least, of coughing. Here any would-be swallower is given a tip: in passing a blade down the gullet, unless the head is thrown back,

> it is necessary to keep the instrument pressed against the back of the throat—that is, against the vertebral column which forms the posterior wall of the gullet. If this is done, no fit of coughing need occur in using a moderate-sized and flexible instrument, although it can be borne but for a very few seconds.[3]

This fascination with swallowing a potentially lethal weapon must have been keener in the times when swords were the preferred instruments of death. From this description one can almost feel what it was like as Benedetti's sword traveled down his body. The ways a sword could do damage varied sharply: the hacking of a Roman soldier in gladiatorial times differed from the cutting of the broadsword, which differed again from the thrust of a Renaissance rapier; and the consequences of each also differed. Then there are the injuries incurred in fencing and the mishaps of stage and screen.

Toward the end of *The Courts of the Morning* John Buchan makes the point that the basic human instinct is to *grapple* with one's enemies, to engage them body to body. The use of a distancing weapon—one that confers space—requires a quite separate temperament; the encounter becomes multidimensional: one's feet are set free, and sheer strength is no longer so vital an element. No animal regularly uses a weapon in conflict situations.* Swordplay is thus not an alien activity, but it is an unnatural one.

---

* There are some exceptions. The eighteenth-century French traveler M. L. Jacolliot was at the court of the Rajah of Mysore when he witnessed a squad of elephants trained in fencing by a master who had taught them foil, which would fence between themselves and the local soldiery. Each elephant would attack by extending its trunk and parry by retracting it. According to Jacolliot, it was almost impossible for even the most skillful man to hit them anywhere other than on the trunk, and that only rarely. As soon as foils were crossed, the elephant would shoot out his trunk at great speed and its opponent would be hit on the chest. At times they would toy with their adversary and, without bothering to make a hit, would envelop the other foil with such rapid circular movements that no attack was possible.

During the latter part of the nineteenth century, about a fifth of the duels in Germany ended in death. The medical adviser to British fencing, Dr. Raymond Crawfurd, hazards an even higher rate for European duels overall: "I have seen a figure of 60 percent quoted. Presumably that means that in a minimum of 10 percent of duels *both* parties died! On reflection, I think that figure must be too high, when you allow for duels that only went to the first blood. Nevertheless, the penetrating blade injury is a highly lethal one." Even if a victim's internal organs were not hit, the raggedness of the opening and the almost certain likelihood of infection made rapier wounds fearsome. Duelists typically would ensure that they cleared their bladder and would not eat before an engagement, partly to make a slimmer target but also, should they be pierced in gut or stomach, to limit the danger of infection. Most died long after the actual fight; in 1578 one Jacques de Quelrus, a favorite of Henri III, took thirty-three days to expire. In England, it has for centuries not been considered murder if one's victim took more than a year and a day to die.

What happens when a human being is struck by a sword? How deep does a wound have to be to take life, and where does it have to hit? In G. K. Chesterton's story "The Sins of Prince Saradine," two duelists set to with "two long Italian rapiers":

the ringing of the rapiers quickened to a rattle, the prince's arms flew up, and the point shot out behind his shoulderblades. He went over with a great whirling movement, almost like one throwing the half of a boy's cartwheel. The sword flew from his hand like a shooting star, and dived into the distant river. And he himself sank with so earth-shaking a subsidence that he broke a big rose-tree with his body and shook up into the sky a cloud of red earth—like the smoke of some heathen sacrifice.[5]

A vivid image, but one suspects that a simple collapse was not what Chesterton was looking for. Adventure fiction can paint a convincing picture of painful sword combat when it wants to, however. Bernard Cornwell sets a grisly scene on horseback in one of his novels:

"One day," Jacolliot recorded, "the Rajah armed two elephants with real swords. Immediately they attacked one another furiously and it was extremely difficult to separate them. When this was finally achieved, they were already severely wounded. It appeared . . . that despite their fury these elephants continued to observe the rules taught by their master.[4]

Sharpe stood his ground, his right arm facing the attack. The Lieutenant, like all good French skirmishing officers, carried a light curved saber; a good slashing weapon, but not the most accurate blade for the lunge. This man, eager to draw first blood, swerved as he neared Sharpe, then leaned out of his saddle to give a gut-slicing sweep with the glittering blade.

Sharpe simply parried the blow by holding his own heavy sword vertically. The clash of steel jarred up his arm, then he kicked his heels back to force the stallion towards the road. . . . Sharpe was deliberately . . . letting the eager Frenchman overtake him, but just a heartbeat before the sun-bright saber whipped hard down Sharpe jerked the long sword back and upwards. The heavy blade smashed brutally hard into the mouth of the Lieutenant's horse. The beast reared up on its hind legs, screaming, with blood showing at its lips and teeth. Sharpe was already turning the stallion across its front. The Lieutenant was desperately trying to stay in the saddle. He flailed for balance with his saber arm, then screamed because he saw the heavy sword coming at his throat. He tried to twist away, but instead his horse plunged back onto its forefeet and threw the Lieutenant's weight fast forward.

Sharpe held his straight-bladed sword pointed at the Lieutenant's throat and locked his elbow as the Frenchman fell onto the blade. There was an instant's resistance, then the sword's point punctured skin and muscle to tear into the great blood vessels of the Frenchman's neck. . . . Then the Frenchman was falling away, and his dying weight ripped his body clear of the long steel blade.[6]

Loss of blood has always been the most common danger. While a duelist's surgeon would be able to stanch the peripheral bleeding caused by limb injuries, he would be able to do little for deep cuts to the head or trunk. The victim's only hope would be that the bleeding could be sufficiently contained to allow time for transfusion or emergency surgery. After massive bleeding (exsanguination) and infection, most deaths are caused by air in the bloodstream (embolism), suffocation (asphyxia), or collapsed lung (pneumothorax). Even if major arteries are cut and severe loss of blood ensues, an adult can remain fully conscious from two to thirty seconds, with death occurring from between three seconds and two minutes later. Even mortally wounded duelists were sometimes able to continue fighting effectively long enough to take the lives of those who had taken theirs. A stricken man frequently does not feel the full effects of his wound and, blinded with rage, may simply throw himself on his opponent with renewed fury.

The many deadly encounters in France in the late 1800s are listed in Christoph Amberger's *Secret History of the Sword*. In each case only one duelist survived. "This is not surprising," writes Amberger. "After all, the weapon itself is designed for antagonistic combat. Its point can indeed be described only with the cliché of 'needle-sharp.' It will snag veins, arteries, and muscles on its path through the body, tearing them as the blade progresses. (A blunted tip, such as that of the modern sports saber, will push them aside rather than tearing them.) The resulting damage is a function of organs hit and depth of penetration."[7]

Yet outright kills depended as much on sheer luck as on skill. A thrust would kill for sure only if it penetrated the internal organs, not when it jammed against a bone. Amberger continues, "Given the anatomical variants of the opponent's body, a deliberate attempt at an instant kill with a thrust into a 'vital point' could be compared with trying to impale an airborne fly hovering behind a curtain." Some years ago my own doctor was stabbed in the back with six inches of steel by a New York serial stalker, whom the policed dubbed "the Spiderman," but Spiderman missed his fly. Dr. Kinkhabwala was back at work within two days.

One Marseillais turned himself into a deadly duelist to avenge the deaths of his bride, parents, and family at the hands of Jacobins and Bonapartists. He picked his victims by their choice of reading: the *Figaro* or the *National*. His strategy was clear, if chilling: "If I thrust *en quarte*, I pull out with a barely perceptible shift of hand position into *tierce*, or vice versa. That kills. He'll stay down for ever . . . because the lung then is damaged, and sepsis will follow."[8]

Sword wounds caused particular problems for the doctors called in to mend them. Dr. Richard Wiseman, surgeon to Charles II, gives a detailed account of dealing with such injuries, as when a blade remains embedded in its victim's body. A doctor may have to "consider whether you may with safety pluck out the Weapon or no. Some will live a day with the Weapon in their Body, who would expire upon the moment of Extraction. But if your judgment suggest to you that the Patient is recoverable, make haste, out with it before the Part be inflamed."[9]

One problem with puncture wounds is that they are prone to prolonged suppuration, which antiseptic dressings normally assuage. Some treatments are distinctly unorthodox. Oscar Kolombatovitch has had a long and varied career as weapon maker and fencing master (he taught at both West Point and the Metropolitan Opera, his pupils including an ungainly Pavarotti). He also found time to work for the OSS. In Italy during the 1930s, he fought several duels and on one occasion was badly wounded in the groin. "Bleeding like a stuck pig," he was rushed to the very rudimentary local hospital. "My main worry was the hospitals there—they had already killed Puccini and Caruso." Here he was attended by a pretty young nurse, who to his surprise kept offering him the local cigarettes, "Nazionale," which tasted like "horse dung with toilet paper." "Why are you doing this to me?" he growled. The nurse looked up from his injury. "I want to see whether the smoke comes out down there."

FENCERS WERE OFTEN DUELISTS, ESPECIALLY IN ITALY, THE MOST notable being Aldo Nadi, who before he left Italy for America was continually getting into arguments with his fellow countrymen, with predictable results. Despite many challenges, he fought only a single duel, but being a surprisingly gifted writer he recorded the experience in one of the best accounts we have of what it is like to duel (particularly if one is a fencer) and how it feels to be hit by a sharpened blade.[10]

His opponent was Adolfo Cotronei, fencing editor of the Milan newspaper *Corriere della Sera*. The quarrel began in 1924 when the great French champion Lucien Gaudin was to fight *en gala* against the Italian champion, Candido Sassone. The site for the match was the Hotel Augusteo in Rome. "Mussolini was present," Nadi writes. "Somebody took me to his box, and I was introduced to the dictator." It being an exhibition bout, no strict score was kept, but Nadi reckoned that Gaudin ran out the clear winner. At a dinner following the match, Nadi announced his views to the assembled company. Cotronei, who was present, said nothing but a few days later published an article asserting that Sassone had won 9–7. "Apart from the fact that in exhibition fencing the reporting of a definite score simply is not done," Nadi states dryly, "this was the biggest lie of the century." He goes on, "It must be remembered that this was Fascist Italy; and no champion belonging to Fascist Italy could possibly be defeated by any foreign and non-Fascist champion, let alone in the presence of the Number One."

Nadi did nothing at first, but it was reported to him that Cotronei had publicly called him a "*mascalzone*." "The word," Nadi wrote, "belonging to Tuscan slang, cannot possibly be translated into English. But you may rest assured that such an appellation is very insulting indeed." He issued his challenge.

Cotronei was in his early forties, the survivor of five previous duels; Nadi was twenty-five and had never dueled before. The rendezvous was the paddock of the famous Milan racetrack of San Siro. Nadi arrived there shortly after dawn and recalled having been at this same track a few weeks before, and losing heavily. A few yards away he noticed Cotronei talking idly with his seconds and remembered that he was a racing *aficionado*; the editor seemed as relaxed as if awaiting a training gallop.

Nadi underscores that being a champion fencer was no guarantee of going home alive: "The layman . . . may have certain romantic notions about dueling, and even see some sort of glamour in it, while the [modern fencer] knows it is, at best, a thoroughly unpleasant, grim business. . . . One is a world of hate, courage and blood; the other of courtesy, courage and skill."*

He could see a couple of doctors in white shirts silently laying out a "hideous assortment of surgical instruments" on a little table. Before putting on his glove, as dueling regulations required, his seconds fastened a white silk handkerchief to his wrist. "What's that for?" he asked. "To protect the main arteries." It was not the most comforting of explanations. Nadi looked around. There was a small crowd of celebrated artists, writers, and journalists and several equally well-known sportsmen, including a number of well-known masters and amateurs. He quickly picked out the master who trained Cotronei. He could beat *him*, all right, but felt less sure about the pupil. The only member of his own family there was his brother Nedo—"a great fencer, but he seems absolutely terrified." Aldo had told his brother that, as the injured party, he had chosen épées rather than sabers. "While saber duels may be bloodier than épée ones, they are less deadly . . . if a few inches of an épée hit a vital organ you've had it." Nedo had winced.

The doctors had meticulously sterilized the épées, and only then did both men pick up their weapons. "Despite its narrow width, you know

---

* This was a widely accepted view, not just Nadi's special pleading. Burton reflects, "Many men attend the schools for years and never take the trouble of trying the experiment how they would react if opposed to a vigorous and resolute man who has never had a sword in hand. The attack—I would call it the wild-beast style . . . may sometimes succeed by chance. I have heard of an English naval officer who, utterly ignorant of the foil, when placed before his opponent began to use it like horsewhip, and succeeded."[11]

only too well that it is practically unbreakable. It certainly won't break when it meets your flesh! You cannot help being mesmerized by its point, its needle sharpness reminding you that it can penetrate your body as easily as butter."

As if on cue, the referee said in a strong voice: "Gentlemen, *en garde!*" Nadi continues:

You have got *en garde* thousands of times before, but never like this. In competition the good fencer takes his time weighing up his opponent before starting in. But in a duel this isn't possible, because your adversary immediately executes a plan which he has obviously thought out in advance: *surprise the youngster at the very beginning; take advantage of his lack of dueling experience, possibly neutralize his ingrained technical superiority; work on his nerves and morale. Get to him at once.* Disregarding the risk, old Cotronei attacks with all the viciousness he can muster, letting out guttural sounds as he does so. . . .

You counterattack, and your sword-point lands precisely where you wanted it to—at the wrist, piercing both the glove and the white silk. But during your opponent's flurry of action his blade has clashed with yours, and its point whips into your forearm. . . . "Halt!" shouts the referee. Oblivious to your own wound, you look at once at your opponent's wrist, then up at his face. Why on earth does he look so pleased? Wasn't he the one to be hit first? Yes, but this is not like a competition bout. He has every reason to be pleased at having wounded you. . . .

The doctors take care of both wounds. What? They are bandaging up your wound but not his! Preposterous! You feel furious with everything and everyone—but above all with yourself. You curse, but silently, under your breath, as if in a competition. . . . You are on guard again. Fine. The duel continues, with more touches, more wounds. While these are being disinfected and the blades elaborately sterilized, my seconds repeatedly suggest that I accept the proposals from my adversary's seconds to call a halt. I do not even bother to reply.

After the sixth set-to they again ask us to stop. I could hardly say that at this point I lost my temper—that had long since gone. . . . Quietly but firmly I said: "Stop annoying me. I am going to fight till daybreak if I have to." Remember, I was still young. Much later I

The Adolfo Cotronei–Aldo Nadi encounter. "If I'd known there was going to be such a turnout I would have sold tickets," boasted Aldo Nadi (left) in his memoirs, but at the time he was anything but confident.

was told that it was at this point that one of the spectators muttered: "I think he's going to kill him." My own doctor, a young scientist, was as white as a sheet and looked ready to collapse. . . .

Up to that point the slippery pebbles of the paddock, on which my street shoes (dueling regulations again) could not gain purchase, had prevented any truly aggressive movement. . . . Now it was a different story. . . . I wanted to lunge, and lunge I would. My left foot went to work at once. Pawing and pushing away like a dog after a rabbit, it cleared the little stones beneath it and settled in the sticky ground underneath. I was ready—but first a vicious curiosity made me look up at my opponent's face.

It was distorted physically and morally. It displayed none of the defiance and self-control it had shown just before the fight. His eyes seemed hypnotized by the point of my blade. It dominated his whole world. He seemed so drained of energy that he could hardly keep on guard: all his reserves were exhausted. He was in my hands, unable to escape. . . . *Now was the time to press that attack.*

The outcome of Nadi's duel can be discovered in his memoirs; but suffice it to say that both he and Cotronei survived, honor dented but vital organs intact. Almost immediately Nadi set off for Cannes, where he won an épée tournament and spent the night making love to a woman he met at his hotel.

A S FOR COMPETITIVE FENCING, ONLY IN THE GERMAN *MENSUR* ARE wounds actively encouraged, and these are never inflicted with dire intent. But the sport has its dangers. One is still simulating an attempt to kill, and even within a protected environment swordfights can go wrong.* Up until the nineteenth century it was generally accepted that if you fenced for any length of time you would finish bruised, minus an eye or tooth, or even dead. Eye injuries remained a constant hazard. In the seventeenth century a Scots gentleman, who had procured the assassination of a master in revenge for having had an eye destroyed during a lesson, pleaded at his trial that it was the custom to "spare the face." In the early 1600s John Turner, a leading English master, had a reputation for hitting his opponents in the eye and had killed one John Dun in this way. John Maningham recorded the bout in his *Diary:* "Turner and Dun, two famous fencers, played their prizes this day at the bankside, but Turner at last ran Dun so far in the brain at the eye that he fell down presently stone dead; a goodly sport in a Christian state, to see one man kill another." Later, Turner was to put out the eye of the Scottish laird Robert Crichton during a practice bout, and it was for this Crichton had him assassinated.**

---

* It would be wrong to present fencing as other than a very safe sport; but as recently as 1983 Britain suffered its only fatal accident, when a modern pentathlete died after his opponent's épée blade broke on his chest, the broken end lifting the bottom edge of the bib of his mask, transfixing the trachea and left common carotid artery. Commenting on his death, Raymond Crawfurd noted that fencing ranks fifth in the league table of incidence of sports injuries (*not* fatalities) after soccer, Rugby Union football, and women's and men's hockey.[12]

** Eye injuries are particularly gruesome. In his account of the death of Christopher Marlowe his biographer Charles Nicholl records the evidence given at the inquest: "The dagger aforesaid of the value of twelve pence, gave the said Christopher a mortal wound above his right eye, of the depth of two inches and of the width of one inch." From this wound Marlowe "then and instantly died." "Judging from this description," comments Nicholl, "the point of the dagger went in just above the right eyeball, penetrated the superior orbital fissure at the back of the eye socket, and entered Marlowe's brain. On its way the blade would have sliced through the major blood vessels: the cavernous sinus, the internal cartorid artery. The actual cause of death was probably a massive haemorrhage into the brain, or possibly an embolism from the inrush of air along the track of the wound."[13]

As far on as 1840 John Tenniel, later the famous illustrator of *Alice's Adventures in Wonderland,* was taking his daily fencing lesson, without benefit of masks. The master concerned, a pupil of Angelo, was Tenniel's father. The button fell off the senior Tenniel's foil, and the blade, flicking across his son's right eye, blinded it. Tenniel Junior—only twenty at the time—made no sign that he had been seriously wounded, and his father, amazingly, never learned what he had done. It was later said that the blinded eye may have caused the loss of dimension in Tenniel's drawings.

Such accidents were all too common. Angelo's son Henry tells in his memoirs how he once, "in fencing without a mask, swallowed some inches, button and all," of his adversary's foil. When researching among

"A Fatal Fencing Accident," as captured in the nineteenth-century magazine Bystander.

Richard Burton's papers, I came across a four-part article on the history of fencing dated spring 1881. The author's name is not given, but I suspect it was Burton himself, notably from one paragraph:

"One would think that the fencing of the last century would have been deliberate, even to tameness in comparison with ours if such accidents were not constantly happening. . . . At this day we should think fencing without a mask the merest foolhardiness; and it is now usual to protect not only the whole of the body but the leg down to the knee; though as late as 1847 Grisier, one of the last lights of the formal academic school, condemned thigh-pads and leather jackets as an extravagant new-fangledness, tending only to encourage wild fencing."[14]

One of the most dramatic of accidents overtook the French master Alphonse Pons during a bout in London with the hot-tempered Lord Geffrin. Incensed at being continually parried, Geffrin launched a furious attack. Again Pons parried, and the force of the blow broke Geffrin's blade some eight inches from the tip, but the foil went on to penetrate the master's chest. Pons was carried to a sofa, where he called for pen and ink. He then dictated a brief letter to his daughter: "My daughter, I am dying. It was my fault, I should have parried twice." Happily, he recovered.

The Geffrin-Pons fight raises the question of the differences between injuries caused by an intact weapon and those caused by a broken blade. The specific threat posed by the latter is a recent discovery. It is much easier to make body armor effective against a bullet than against a dagger, the cross-sectional force behind which is colossal by comparison (at its tip, roughly 3.75 tons per square inch, vibrating at 3,600 mph). A British épéeist, Ron Parfitt, has conducted several experiments with broken blades. They can function like a dum-dum bullet. "The essential point," he says, "is that the blade bends increasingly until it snaps, when it flicks out straight and hits the jacket with a shearing action which cuts across the fibres rather than just pushing a hole through them. Again the forces are very considerable but different from the thrusting action of a dueling sword. An intact épée, by comparison, has a relatively large surface area at the tip and so penetration is less likely and will also go less deep."

It took until the middle of the nineteenth century for attention to turn to safety. Leather jackets, a variation on the jerkins worn under coats of mail, were introduced, later giving way to stiff canvas jackets and breeches. Special shoes with long projecting leathers at the toe, which gave the leading foot "a resonant sound," began to be worn (Burton objected, saying that "practice does this with the common cricketing shoe easily and loudly enough"). Gloves varied widely, but most had special patches of stiff leather. Eventually—as late as 1970—thick canvas was discarded in favor of light, figure-hugging cotton costumes. Electric fencing provoked a new rush of problems. Despite the constant bending and straightening blades underwent, there was little regulation over how they were made or how they performed. (Administrators were more intent on scrutinizing how the tips of any new electric device were attached to the blades: they could not be glued or soldered on and had to have a thread of a certain diameter.)

After a Finnish épéeist was killed at the Stockholm championships of 1951, canvas plastrons came in, specifically to guard beneath the arm.

Eleven years later the existing épée point (which could pierce a mask's mesh) was replaced with one with a flat top. The French master Michel Alaux, writing in *American Fencing*, sounded a warning:

> Now we face the problem of a new point whose edged cutting actions resemble those of the punch press used in steel production to test the resistance of metal. . . . While giving lessons I personally have felt the penetrating power of this new point. This is of some concern, and raises other questions. Has the point been tested against the mesh of the mask? Is the change a real improvement? Might it not be better to require a stronger mesh for the mask and forbid the use of rusty masks? Does this point's shape reduce the force of penetration through the material of the jacket?[15]

In the next issue another distinguished master, the film fight–arranger Ralph Faulkner, articulated what he saw as the "real" cause of accidents: that the point wasn't the point, but rather the nature of the activity itself:

> If two 180-pound chunks of bone, flesh and muscle come together head-on, with sword arms outstretched and lethal steel aimed at the chest (or elsewhere), something is going to give and it doesn't matter if the point is round, flat, conical, laminated, pulsated or animated. If the point doesn't pierce whatever it comes in contact with then the blade will break and the danger will be even greater.[16]

Meanwhile, people kept on getting killed or mutilated. In 1971 Vincent Bonfil, a friend of mine and a foilist about to break into the British team, was fencing without a plastron when his opponent's blade broke, entering under his armpit. No doctor was on hand, and within five minutes he had bled to death. In 1977 the top American sabreur was Peter Westbrook, who in his autobiography describes the time he and his Hungarian coach, Csaba Elthes, were practicing a routine drill at the New York Fencers Club:

> As I ran at him to perform a new move, Csaba thrust his blade out in front of me. I was supposed to deflect it and hit him on the head, but he did it so fast that I actually impaled myself on the tip of his saber. The blade of a saber is about two-and-a-half feet long and is very flexible. But as I kept advancing like a battering ram, I heard it snap about a third of the way from the tip. Realizing that Csaba

now had in his hand not a flexible blade with a blunt tip but a rigid knife with a jagged, razor-sharp tip, I threw my head back to avoid his deadly weapon. That move allowed the tip to project below my mask bib and pierce my throat. It went through my larynx and my oesophagus, an inch-and-a-half of it. . . .

I felt like there was a big chicken bone stuck in my throat. The next thing I knew I heard a hissing sound, *pssst pssst,* like when somebody calls to you on the street. I looked around the room. Who was hissing? What was going on? I suddenly realized that the sound was coming from my own throat. That scared me. When I put my hand over the hole in my throat, the hissing sound stopped. As soon as I removed my hand, the hissing continued.[17]

His master had performed a perfect tracheotomy. Doctors later told Peter that he had been extraordinarily lucky: the neck holds so many blood vessels—not to mention the spinal cord—that if the tip had penetrated a centimeter elsewhere, Peter would have died. Others were equally lucky. During the Olympics of 1980, a Russian foilist was run through the chest with a blade that severed a blood vessel but missed his heart, and a broken blade entered under the bib of a Ukrainian sabreur, again without causing major injury. World or Olympic championships are now obliged to have ambulances standing by, but these are still a second line of care. At the 1985 world championships in Barcelona, a French foilist was impaled by a broken blade entering his thigh, and the official medic on duty, a Romanian, had no idea what to do; the fencer's life was saved only when a Spanish doctor in the audience leapt from the stands and came to his rescue.*

The watershed proved to be the Rome world championships of 1982. The program had reached its halfway point, with the men's team foil event. During the match between what was then West Germany and the USSR, Matthias Behr, a team gold medalist for Germany, faced Vladimir Smirnov, the twenty-eight-year-old reigning world and Olympic champion. As Smirnov advanced, Behr—indeed a great bear of a man, six feet, three inches tall and heavily built—went on the attack. The German's

---

* Until 1966, in Michigan, it was a misdemeanor punishable by up to a year in jail or a $500 fine to "be present at the fighting of a duel with deadly weapons as an aide, or second or surgeon." The statute made no distinction between dueling and fencing, so for a fencer to wear a mask, glove, and jacket would be an admission that he was using a "deadly weapon" under the law. An alert law student spotted the ambiguity, and the statute was changed.

blade broke against the Russian's guard as he tried to parry and traveled on through his mask. The converging lunges of these two powerful men drove the blade—now in effect a stilletto—through Smirnov's eye and seven centimeters into his brain.

In the audience was an American team official, Marius Valsamis, a professor of neuropathology from Brooklyn. He was immediately summoned and gave the Russian mouth-to-mouth resuscitation, to no avail. Smirnov was rushed to the nearest hospital, the Gemelli clinic, and the blade removed. Both Valsamis and the Russian doctor pronounced Smirnov brain-dead, but Smirnov was a superb athlete whose off-training hobby was karate: his body was still functioning. The authorities kept him on a life-support machine for four days, until the championships were over. The USSR team, fighting without its strongest member, honored his memory by storming to the gold medal.

Three elements came together to cause the Smirnov catastrophe: Behr's blade being under enormous stress when it broke, the stump still in his hand discharged stored energy like a spring suddenly released. That it struck Smirnov's jacket at the same time as the Russian drove himself forward initiated a compound process of cutting and thrusting. The tip would have been snapping back toward repose with maximum potential from the whole stump's deformation. Behr would not even have been aware that he had hurt his opponent; indeed, those watching recall him turning round and walking toward his end of the strip, quite unaware of Smirnov stretched out behind him. Little force is needed to stick a knife into soft tissue: in this case it was as if the Russian had dropped from a second-story window onto a smashed metal fencepole.

There had been dreadful fatalities before* but none so horrible or to such a famous athlete. The Italian examining magistrates determined that there was no proper regulation of the sport and threatened to charge the organizers of the championships—the FIE and the Italian Fencing Federation—with manslaughter. The danger of the international fencing body being prosecuted en bloc was avoided, but only after promises to make significant changes.

---

* In July 1892, in Fall River, Massachusetts, Professor Castaldi was giving one of his pupils, Dr. Terry, a well-known surgeon, his weekly lesson when the master's blade broke and drove through Terry's mask, inflicting a flesh wound near the nose. Terry got a new mask and Castaldi a new weapon; the lesson continued. Within a few moves Castaldi's second blade broke, the jagged end going through Terry's mask and right eye into his brain. He died three hours later without recovering consciousness.

A full two years later, a special meeting in Paris to examine safety measures led to changes in the standards for masks: minimum and maximum thicknesses for the wire and a maximum hole size for the mesh were stipulated. The problem of clothing safety seemed to defy solution, and for a while it looked as if there was no material both suitable and able to meet the safety requirements. The answer was Kevlar, a trade name like Hoover or Kleenex, a lightweight, high-strength material used in everything from ropes and car tires to composite plastics such as fishing rods, sailing masts, bulletproof vests, and the shells of U.S. Army battle helmets. Kevlar has almost miraculous qualities: with five times the tensile strength of steel, it has half the density of fiberglass. It was discovered in 1966 by Stephanie Kwolek, a scientist who had joined the U.S. chemical giant DuPont to fund her way through medical school. After six years in development, it was launched onto the market in 1971—eleven years before Smirnov was killed.

New clothing made from Kevlar and ballistic nylon was approved for international fencing competition. Then on French television a reporter held up a sample jacket and thrust a fountain pen straight through it. The designers went back to the drawing board. Subsequently, cloths of (heavy-duty) woven Kevlar yarn and composite woven and knitted materials were used to make clothing pen-proof; then, some years later, it was discovered that Kevlar could be weakened by sunlight and by certain detergents and bleaches. It has now all but been replaced by the newer polyethylene fibers such as Dyneema™ and Spectra™, which are even stronger and do not degrade under washing or drying in the sun. Fencing kit is now also made from high-density composite woven cloths originally developed for stab-resistant police wear.

As for the blades, the federation looked for a material that could withstand repeated bending without breaking. Barry Paul—marking the third generation of his family to head up Leon Paul, as well as being on the British team for many years and having been a close friend of Vincent Bonfil—is heavily involved in the FIE's quest. Visiting him at his works headquarters in north London, I asked whether such a metal or alloy yet existed. "No," he told me, "and when a prototype composite fail-safe blade with a relatively soft inner core was developed, it proved so expensive it was never put into production." Maraging steels developed for military use, specifically in jet engines, were found to have the necessary attributes and lasted a long time before failing, but "in the end they too would break, and people would still be killed." Since maraging steel contains no carbon, he explained, it is questionable even to classify it as steel—the "clash of steel" may be a sound of the past. As Barry took me around his factory, he elaborated on what the alternatives might be. Fiberglass blades have their advantages, he conceded, but they neither sound nor feel right, and when they break tiny glass splinters inflict particularly nasty injuries. He and other manufacturers are now experimenting with certain superalloys again derived mainly from the aircraft industry.

Since 1984, further improvements have been introduced, but new problems have kept them company. To make fencing more TV-friendly, the FIE has promoted see-through masks, but competitions revealed that poor production (by one of Paul's rivals) caused the visors to crack around their fixing holes, precipitating a fencers' revolt. More stringent testing is under way. Across five seasons of U.S. fencing (2003–2008), for instance, involving almost 80,000 male and female participants of all ages and skill levels, the rate of time-loss injury (i.e., one severe enough to cause withdrawal from competition) was 0.3 per 1,000 athlete exposures. Fencing-unique injuries, specifically puncture wounds, accounted for less than 3 percent of reported events, and none resulted in permanent damage. There has not been a single reported fatality in the history of U.S. fencing.

Compared to their predecessors 150 years ago, fencers are bigger and fitter and weigh more; they deploy more force in their swordplay, and action time has been reduced: all thus imparting a greater potential for deadliness. "Yet there are so few injuries," Barry told me, "that most insurance companies don't even offer coverage—the research figures are too small for them to reach any conclusion." He picked up a brand-new blade and bent it on the floor till it formed a deep bow. "We're pretty close to the time where safety precautions won't get any better," he concluded, letting the blade spring back in his hand. "At a certain point, either you destroy the sport or you accept a degree of risk. Fencing *is* a combat sport. People *will* get injured."

CHAPTER 13

Scars of Glory

> For what's more honorable than scarrs
> Or skin to tatters rent in Warrs?
>
> —SAMUEL BUTLER, *Hudibras*, 1658

> I rejoice at every dangerous sport which I see pursued.
> The students at Heidelberg, with their sword-slashed faces,
> inspire me with sincere respect.
>
> —OLIVER WENDELL HOLMES, JR. *The Soldier's Faith*, 1895

THE SCENE: A SOCIETY CAFÉ IN BERLIN, EARLY IN *THE LIFE AND Death of Colonel Blimp*.

BRITISH VISITOR: Dueling's very popular here, I believe?

YOUNG WOMAN [DEBORAH KERR]: Oh yes. It's a proud father that has a scarred son, and vice versa. German girls find scars very attractive. A book was recently published on the German colonies in which it was specifically stated that one of the advantages of possessing dueling scars was that the natives of Africa look with more respect on a white man who bears them than on those who do not.

In Michael Powell and Emeric Pressburger's famous 1943 film, Roger Livesey plays a young British diplomat visiting Berlin in 1902, who finds himself challenged to a duel by a Prussian officer. Livesey stands by bemused as the opposing seconds produce a rule book for the bout. His equanimity is somewhat shaken when he hears his second offhandedly remark, "I heard of one chap whose nerve broke. . . . I say, I hope our chap doesn't get killed. Create an awful stink if he does." The chosen weapon is a cavalry saber, and both men end up in the hospital—where they become firm friends.

Unlike most films featuring swordfights, the details here are well researched, but above all the encounter captures the extraordinary enthusiasm Prussians displayed for dueling, setting to with gusto as the practice was winding down elsewhere. They even adapted a form of fighting that had originated in late-medieval France to develop their own weapon, the *Mensur* (a word derived from the "measure" or space between fencers), by the sixteenth century almost unknown outside the student fraternities of Germany and Austria-Hungary, where it has persisted for more than three hundred years. It is either gruesome and barbaric or fascinating and a true test of courage, depending on one's point of view.

Up till the early 1700s student fights were rough affairs, involving cudgels, daggers, and whips. Those who fought duels were known contemptuously as "*Knoten*," lumps, not yet licked into shape, possibly after "*Knotenstock*," a gnarled cudgel. At some point in the early eighteenth century codes of behavior were developed, the sword replaced the cudgel, and a special vocabulary was introduced: students were "frogs," "mules," "camels," "fat foxes," "burnt foxes," "mossy heads." Challenges required little more than a simple insult. By the 1730s two methods were commonly employed. One could place a light in one's window or carry a lantern, either of which would constitute a challenge. If the light were not put out on request, it would be pelted with stones, which would usually provoke a duel. Alternatively, the challenging student would approach his adversary and cry out "*Pereat*," to which the correct reply was "*Pereat contra*," which established that both men were ready to fight. These "*Rencontres*" died out around 1780, and a new and broader code, the "*Komment*," took their place. This decreed that no formal duel or *Mensur* could be fought without just cause. A maximum and minimum number of rounds were set out, as was how to fix a venue and time. However, the formalities were frequently ignored, and simply calling one's opponent "*dummer Junge*" ("young fool") was generally sufficient to start a fight.

The weapon of choice was the *Stossdegen*, similar to a modern epée, only with a larger guard and a three-sided blade. The edges were not sharpened, so the main object was to skewer one's opponent. Following a particularly gruesome death at Göttingen in 1767, a sword was developed that produced less gory injuries, and this led to the *Schläger* ("striker"), derived from the rapier. Universities east of the Elbe River adopted a bell-shaped guard like an inverted saucer (referred to humorously as "the soup plate of honor") and an obliquely pointed blade, while elsewhere students used the *Korbschlager*, with a basket guard and a squared-off (i.e., nonpiercing) tip, whose edges were as sharp as a razor for about eighteen inches along each side. These new swords changed the *Mensur*: the style of the bouts adapted to the need to parry the swinging blade, while distances contracted with time until combatants kept their back feet entirely stationary. The most vulnerable parts of the body were shielded, while the ubiquitous student cap, originally worn to protect the eyes (with pieces of plaster of Paris secured by tape just under the eyes), was replaced by specially constructed goggles.

In most universities the venue was always an inn on the outskirts of town. At Heidelberg, *Mensuren* were fought in Hirschgasse ("Stag Lane") in the room of a hostelry paid for from fraternity funds. A junior fraternity member would be sent to inform the "*Paukarzt*," the attending surgeon. Two seconds, two witnesses, and a referee were required, and the room was often thronged with spectators.

Most detailed accounts of *Mensuren* have been left by foreign guests. One of the best is Mark Twain's, who devotes two chapters to them in *A Tramp Abroad*. Twain describes the venue as a two-story public house set in a narrow valley: "We went upstairs and passed into a large whitewashed apartment which was perhaps fifty feet long, by thirty feet wide and twenty or twenty-five high. It was a well-lighted place. There was no carpet. Across one end and down both sides of the room extended a row of tables, and at these tables some 50 or 75 students were sitting."[1] Twain stayed from 9:30 in the morning until 2 P.M., witnessing four *Mensuren* and one formal duel.

Between 1848 and 1870 the duel and the *Mensur* assumed contrasting characters. While the duel kept most of its original features, the rapier blade of the *Schläger* gave way in the *Mensur* to a curved saber blade, about three feet in length, and the distance between opponents contracted to a single blade's distance from chest to chest. The target shrank too, simply to the head, partially protected by goggles. Thus the *Mensur* exposed a small, vulnerable, but generally not fatal area, while in the duel both head and torso were fair game.

Each fighter was brought into the room by his second and his witness, after which he would don his cap, whose size varied from ordinary student headgear to a much larger contraption with a broad peak. Divinity students always fought in these peaked caps, as a scar would terminate their careers. Eventually the caps were replaced with massive glassless iron goggles. Next came a wide scarf, usually reaching up to the chin and pulled in tightly. For the sword arm, whose binding had to give protection while not restricting the action of the wrist and elbow, a fine leather glove was used, bound and secured to the wrist with a silken ribbon. The *Stulp*, a thick, well-quilted silk arm cover, was pulled down over the glove and fastened with more ribbons.

Finally the duelist climbed into his *Paukhosen*, thick leather trousers laced together behind by leather thongs, which rose over the stomach and ribs to form a cuirass. Even so, it left a good part of the chest uncovered. A second thick glove was fastened to the back of the *Paukhosen* to keep the nonsword hand firmly out of the way throughout the fight. Combatants removed their coats, waistcoats, ties, and suspenders and slit their shirt-sleeves from wrist to shoulder to leave the arm free, regular challengers keeping special shirts for the purpose.

Once fully kitted, the opponents would be conducted into the dueling room, where they would strut up and down, each supporting his sword arm on his witness. The seconds would mark out the boundaries of the fight with chalk: if either man retreated behind his line three times, he was dismissed "with shame and insult." The rules recognized at least six different forms of engagement, from "twelve rounds with the great cap, until a conclusive wound" to a single round lasting fifteen minutes. A round would continue until one combatant had landed a clear blow, this being defined as one of at least two inches, deep enough, to use the student phrase, "to cut through the two skins." When such a wound was made, the wounded man's second ended the fight by crying out "Remove him!" or (to the umpire) "Please declare a bloody one" [a *"Blutigen"*].

One foreign observer described these encounters as "not very dangerous" and records students who "have fought from 30 to 40, and even 60 times, and yet have come out of them all with a few slight wounds in the face."[2] All such fights were quite against the law—the last legal sword-fighting in the German lands had taken place back in 1793—so the students had to employ an elaborate warning system, stationing "foxes" (first-year students) on each side of the road every hundred feet to signal the approach of the "poodles" (*Pedellen*), the university beadles. Once the alarm sounded, the combatants would strip off their gear and rush into the woods. Sword handle, guard, and blade could all be unscrewed and hidden, the hilt and guard under a cloak, the blade inside a hollow walking stick. If a student was too slow to get away, there was always a neighboring cornfield or the garret. At one time, two undergraduates regularly hired the garden shed next to the inn so that escaping duelists could be presented to the authorities as visiting friends. Eventually the police forbade anyone to rent the building.

A British traveler in the 1930s, Robert Southcombe, was allowed to attend both a *Duell* with heavy saber and a *Mensur* contest. The morning Southcombe went to watch, there were one young doctor and two or three medical students present. On a table near a window he could see basins of water, sponges, and a number of crooked needles threaded with coored silk. Cuts were washed in cold water. "As I understood it," Southcombe commented dryly, "a salt preparation was rubbed in to preserve the scar. To flinch unduly, or even at all, when cut in *Schlager* fighting was to court social ostracism."[3]

Twain's account of fifty years before suggests that nothing much had changed. "The student is glad to get wounds in the face," Twain explained, "because the scars they leave will show so well there; and it is also said that these face-wounds are so prized that youths have even been known to pull them apart from time to time and pour red wine in them to make them heal badly and leave as ugly a scar as possible. . . . I had seen the heads and faces of ten youths gashed in every direction by the keen two-edged blades, and yet had not seen a victim wince, nor heard a moan, or detected any fleeting expression which confessed the sharp pains the hurts were inflicting."[4]

James Morgan Hart, another American visitor, was less impressed. "Bloodshed aside," he recorded, "the general appearance of the duelists is very comical. The pad and cravat and spectacles made them look somewhat like a pair of submarine divers in their armor. Then, it is interesting to watch the left hand pulling on the tag in convulsive sympathy with the movements of the right hand. . . . I doubt whether the civilized world can afford an odder sight."[5] Hart later asked a friend, a corps student and first-class *Schläger* fencer, what he really thought of the *Mensur*. "Oh, it's a horrible piece of nonsense (*ein grässlicher Unsinn*)," he said, "but at any rate it's better than street-fighting."[6]

Each of these accounts is accurate so far as it goes, but relatively sanitized, and avoids mention of the copious drinking that was so vital a part of fraternity life and does not describe what *Mensur* fights could be like at their worst. Around 1900 the English actor, playwright, and author Jerome K. Jerome biked through Germany and wrote up his travels in *Three Men on the Bummel*,[7] a sequel to his earlier great success, *Three Men in a Boat*, his voyage with two friends up the Thames. Most of the book offers a sympathetic portrait—but not his report on dueling.[8] The Germans, he wrote, believed that the *Mensur* built character. (Ten years before, the Emperor Franz Josef of Austria had suggested that dueling clubs provided "the best education which a young man can get for his future life.") "Their argument is that it schools the German youth to coolness and courage," wrote Jerome derisively. The student "fights not to please himself, but to satisfy a public opinion that is two hundred years behind the times." Far from being a virtuous exercise, "all the *Mensur* does is brutalize him."

The fight might be brutish and short, he continued, while "the whole interest is centered in watching the wounds. They come always in one or

The dueling students measure the distance. On their left are
their seconds, on the right the official attendants.

two places—on the top of the head or the left side of the face." Sometimes a portion of hairy scalp or section of cheek flies up into the air, "to be carefully preserved in an envelope by its proud possessor, or, strictly speaking, its proud former possessor, and shown round on convivial evenings." Each bout produces "a plentiful stream of blood. It splashes doctors, seconds, and spectators; it sprinkles ceilings and walls; it saturates the fighters, and makes pools for itself in the sawdust. At the end of each round the doctors rush up, and with hands already dripping with blood press together the gaping wounds, dabbing them with little balls of wet cotton wool." The point, of course, is to "go away from the University bearing as many scars as possible" and so merit the admiration of one's peers, the attention of the fairer sex, and, eventually, "a wife with a dowry of five figures at the least."

The second act of the spectacle took place in the dressing room. The "doctors" in evidence there were generally medical students, "coarse-looking men" who seemed "rather to relish their work" and who carried out their repairs without much regard to the pain or physiognomy of their charges. This is all part of the ritual, since "how the student bears the dressing of his wounds is as important as how he receives them. Every operation has to be performed as brutally as may be, and his companions watch him during the process to see that he goes through it with an appearance of peace and enjoyment. A clean-cut wound that gapes wide is most desired by all parties. On purpose it is sewn up clumsily, with the hope that by this means the scar will last a lifetime."

One student from Göttingen recalled a duelist's nose being hacked off. Another attested, "These seem to be no light matters; the wounds were sometimes formidable, and I have seen blood spurting an inch high from a vein."[9] Visitors to German universities would see students walking around town with their faces and noses swathed in bandages. Richard Burton, on a journey to Heidelberg, wrote of a particularly grisly encounter:

> Sometimes too heavy a cut went into the lungs, and at other times took an effect upon either eye. But the grand thing was to walk off with the tip of the adversary's nose, by a dexterous upward snick from the hanging guard. A terrible story was told of a duel between a handsome man and an ugly man. Beauty had a lovely nose, and Beast so managed that presently it was found on the ground. Beauty made a rush for it, but Beast stamped it out of shape.[10]

WHEN ONE LOOKS AT PORTRAITS OF HIM IN LATER LIFE, THE STERN, unforgiving stare above the huge walrus mustache, it is hard to imagine the future Prince Otto Eduard Leopold von Bismarck as he must have been as a student in the early 1830s. Göttingen University, in the kingdom of Hanover, had fifteen hundred students, and by the time Bismarck matriculated, ostensibly to read law, it was recognized as one of the best in Germany.

Bismarck was a Prussian Junker—"from Pomerania," as he styled himself—the son of a rural, clodhopping father and a neurotic urban intellectual mother, and by all accounts he quickly became one of the sights of the university. He dressed wildly, in top boots with iron spurs, his long untamed hair swinging beneath a cap of flaming crimson and gold, with enormous wide trousers, a chaotic dressing gown, and a big brass ring on the first finger of his left hand. Strapped about his waist was a leather girdle into which were thrust two large horse pistols along with a long basket-hilted dueling sword. Shrieking children would follow him down the street.

Although "as thin as a knitting-needle," Bismarck was unusually tall and regularly drank his fellow students under the table. He invented his own special draught, "black velvet," a particularly deadly concoction of champagne and porter, but was equally at home consuming enormous quantities of wine or beer in student *Kneipen* (drinking bouts). He spoke of "my friend, the flask" and attended lectures only on the rare occasions when he had nothing better to do. He was forever at odds with the authorities, whether for setting a fox loose in the middle of a university ballroom, going on drunken midnight swims, or randomly discharging his pistols. He committed so many offenses that he spent considerable time in the college jail; the student prison door still bears his name, carved while serving ten days for acting as a second. Contemporaries dubbed him "Mad Bismarck." He owned two dogs, one a dachshund named Ariel. On one occasion he threatened to duel with a passing student who admitted to having laughed at his dog unless the student apologized directly to the dachshund. Ariel got his apology.

Bismarck loved dueling. He joined the Landsmannschaft Hanovara, a dueling fraternity whose members came mainly from officer and civil service families in Hannovera, and was soon a legendary figure, given further nicknames, including "Achilles the Invulnerable" and "Baby-Head." In all he fought twenty-five *Mensuren* between the summer of 1831 and his departure in 1834, receiving seven bloody hits and two illegal (*incommentmässig*) ones. He was both lucky and skillful, for the biggest cut he received was made by a fellow student named Biedenweg, whose sword, the press recorded, "flew from its socket," and cut Bismarck, depending on which authority one believes, from the left side of his jaw to the corner of his mouth or from the tip of his nose to the edge of his right ear. Such was his skill that other students were careful not to challenge him—though obviously, from his tally of victories, not careful enough.

Bismarck struck up a friendship with John Lothrop Motley, a reserved New Englander from Boston who later became a noted historian and diplomat, serving in Vienna and London. The two became inseparable. A few years after leaving Göttingen, Motley wrote a novel, *Morton's Hope, or the Memoirs of a Provincial*. In it Bismarck is fictionalized as Otto von Rabenmark, otherwise known as "the fox." Motley evidently attended many of Bismarck's duels, two of which he describes in detail. Here Rabenmark fights a student called Kopp:

> For an instant they remained motionless, and eyed each other warily, but undauntedly. Suddenly Rabenmark raised his weapons, and making a feint at the heel of his antagonist, directed a violent blow at his breast. It was skillfully parried by the opposite party, who retorted with a savage "quart," which, if successful, would have severed him nearly in two. The fox caught it on his sword, with a skill which I hardly believed him capable of, and then becoming animated, aimed a succession of violent and rapid blows, now "quart" and now "tierce," upon his adversary. They were all parried with wonderful precision and coolness.

Motley writes with an almost brotherly concern, but with admiration too; he follows the convention of the time by referring to attacks to tierce and quart rather than flank (beneath the sword arm) and chest, as we would now. He goes on:

> I perceived that the dexterity of my friend was nearly exhausted, and expected every instant to see him stretched upon the floor. At last, Kopp aimed a prodigious blow at Rabenmark's head. It came within a quarter of an inch of the frontlet of the cap before Rabenmark succeeded in beating it off with a desperate and successful backhand stroke. The fox, now throwing himself entirely off his guard, rushed wildly upon his adversary. He beat down his sword before he had time to recover his posture of defense, and with one

last violent and tremendous effort he struck at his adversary's head. It was unexpected, and too late to parry; the blow alighted full upon the cheek of the enemy. Its force was prodigious; the Westphalian, stunned and blinded, staggered a few paces forward, and then his feet slipped, and he fell upon the floor.

"Alighted" is an oddly decorous choice of word in the circumstances; Motley was presumably trying to keep the reader's sympathy for his friend even as he vaunted his ferocious fighting powers.

I went up and took a look at him. The Pauk-Doktor was busy sponging away the blood, and an assistant was applying restoratives to awaken him from his swoon. The side of the cap had been cut through by the violence of the blow, and a deep and ghastly wound extended from the top of the head across the temple and the cheek. The whole side of the face was laid open. "He has enough for the next six weeks," said Rabenmark, coolly turning towards the dressing room.

"*Verfluchter Fuchs*" ("Cursed fox"), murmured the wounded man, reviving at the sound of his adversary's voice for an instant, and then relapsing into his swoon.... From that day Fox Rabenmark was the most renowned *Schläger* in Göttingen."[*]

Bismarck left Göttingen in August 1833. As his political career gathered momentum, he openly recommended violence as an instrument of policy—hence his famous slogan "Blood and iron." "When I have an enemy in my power, I must destroy him," he declared. "Passivity is taken for weakness and is weakness." In September 1848, when Berlin was shaken by revolutionary movements, he told his wife regretfully that "unfortunately" blood was not likely to flow. In 1866, after seven weeks of war,

---

[*] Thirty years later, in 1869, Motley became his country's minister to London. On his arrival there, an enterprising publisher decided to reissue the book. Motley was horrified and searched in vain for a copy. He discovered that the only one that remained in Europe was in the British Museum. He could not lay his hands on it, as it had been withdrawn by a member of the publishing firm, who was engaged in copying it in the reading room. Motley finally got permission to read his own work one Sunday afternoon, when the reading room was closed to the general public. A few days later the publisher was surprised by a visit from Motley, who offered to pay a considerable sum for the book's withdrawal. To this day, the only public copy of *Morton's Hope* in Europe lies buried in the British Museum.

he threatened to throw himself out of the nearest window if the king didn't agree with him. In March 1886, at a cabinet meeting, he insisted that the government had to make "war to the knife." He must have been saddened when, in one of the many duels he fought as an adult, his opponent—the leader of the moderate Liberal Party in the Prussian Chamber—chose pistols, not swords. Although Bismarck's second suggested sabers, the two adversaries ended up firing one shot each, and both missed. Bismarck mused in a letter to his mother, "I should have been glad to have gone on with the combat, but dueling etiquette forbade it."

WHAT KIND OF APPEAL COULD A SPORT HAVE THAT MADE A CULT of such injuries? Nicholas Mosley, son of Oswald Mosley, the British Fascist leader, has Max Ackerman, the hero of his novel *Hopeful Monsters*, move with his father to Heidelberg, after which he is sent to Freiburg University. The year is 1928. It is not long before Max encounters the dueling halls, and he is simultaneously attracted and revolted. "If this sort of thing is a ritual," he asks his father, "is it more sophisticated or more silly than just to be decorated by tribal witch-doctors with knives?" The senior Ackerman replies, "What would be sophisticated, I suppose, would be to be able to look at why one wanted to be cut by knives."[12] A fair point, but for an answer we need to return to Germany's past.

When in 1348 the first Central European university was opened in Prague, the student population was divided, as was customary, along geographical lines, and the many foreign students were housed according to their "nations," home countries or provinces. The same principle was followed when an exodus of scholars from Prague founded Leipzig University in 1409. This practice spread to other universities, and soon any new student, or "bean," had to undergo initiation before being accepted by his comrades. The ceremony was usually concluded with the "bean" having his mouth filled and salt and wine being poured over his head, symbolically absolving him of his callowness, his *Beanismus*. These rites were never subtle affairs. As early as 1385 students at the University of Heidelberg were forbidden to attend fencing schools.

By the 1780s students were quartered in small groups called "*Kränzchen*." In 1798 the *Kränzchen* at Onoldia in Erlangen became the first fraternity to put "corps" as a prefix to its name. With defeat at the hands of Napoleon at the Battle of Jena in 1806, nationalism came into student life and a new association for all German students grew up, known as the "*Deutschen Burschenschaften*"—one of which branches was forced by the authorities to disband in 1817 partly because of dueling.

The following year fourteen of these *Burschenschaften* adopted a constitution pledging their members to the ideals of a Christian-German physical and intellectual education for the service of the Fatherland. Foreigners and Jews were excluded. There was considerable rivalry between various wings of the association, and at certain universities violent dueling was common. These transformations may seem interminably convoluted, but they marked attempts by student bodies to organize themselves, and with each development came a renewed emphasis on the importance of loyalty to the new order. "The student's most valued asset was his word of honor," wrote the historian R. G. S. Weber, "for it was that which allowed him access to the university when taking his oath at matriculation. It was his word of honor which allowed him to have credit authorized by the university. The student was honor bound to keep his word, for it was his only negotiable possession and his word of honor was seen as the outward indication of his true character and worth."[13]

By the late nineteenth century each federation of fraternities—the exclusive Corps, the slightly more "democratic" *Burschenschaften*, the *Turnerschaften*, and the rest—had established their own criteria of what constituted honor. This ideal was multifaceted and less a measure of social status than a reflection of the inner man. How did a student become an educated gentleman? The corps decided that there were three elements: self-observation, self-answerability, and self-control.

It was here that dueling played its part, as an activity that required and embodied all three. The corps expected their members to exercise self-control and to fence well regardless of where or how badly they were hit. Thus the student fraternities, to echo Coriolanus, "by rare example turned terror into sport." Jerome put it succinctly: "That he may fight the better for the Fatherland, the German lad must be made indifferent to wounds and suffering: so the *Mensur* with all its bloody paraphernalia was conceived."[14]

Only some of the student bodies were fencing fraternities, but these tended to produce particularly successful alumni. Fraternity members fought both *Mensuren* and duels, but the two were very different. The *Mensur*, with its antecedents in medieval chivalry, was a challenge that fostered character and camaraderie. To use the words of the old Catholic Catechism, it became a means of showing "an outward sign of inward grace"—demonstrating inner qualities through outward indications of honor. Thus the scars of a *Mensur* were a badge that told the informed observer that the bearer was a man of worth. A duel, conducted with the intent to maim or kill, was a sinister and less honorable affair.

Given such an intellectual underpinning, it is not surprising that the *Mensur* was so popular. About one student out of ten in Prussia in the nineteenth century dueled at some stage during his undergraduate days. Heinrich Heine, the poet, fought a number of duels. Theodor Herzl, the intellectual father of modern Israel, trained for four hours a day, fighting his obligatory *Mensur* on May 11, 1881. Every member of Herzl's fraternity had a *nom de combat;* his was Tancred, the hero of Benjamin Disraeli's novel who goes to Palestine.[15]*

German students traditionally divided into three groups: scholars, careerists, and cavaliers. It was the last, the swaggering cavaliers, who would join a fraternity that took pride in fighting for their honor. And those fraternities, besides their bloody encounters with swords, went in for showy uniforms and endless carousing.

In the spring of 1882 Max Weber enrolled at Heidelberg, heading off to the fencing room every morning to work out. By his third term he had fought his first *Mensur* and received his fraternity ribbon. Although he was considered skinny when he first entered the university, fraternity drinking soon had its effect. His widow and biographer, Marianne, records that "the lanky youth became broad and strong, and he inclined towards corpulence."[17] By the time he was nineteen, Weber was so stout that none of the uniforms in his army barracks fitted him: he had to be squeezed into a mess sergeant's. When his mother saw him for the first time following his *Mensur,* corpulent and scarred across the cheek, "the vigorous woman could think of no other way to express her astonishment and fright than to give him a resounding slap in the face."

For all the emphasis on camaraderie, the members of a dueling fraternity were not particularly friendly toward one another. Although firm friendships did form, this was against the prevailing zeitgeist. "The brothers did not associate with friendly warmth, but were cold as ice towards one another," Weber's widow records with rancor. "Friendships were regarded as unmanly. Everyone kept his distance but paid close attention

---

* When Herzl came to draft a constitution for the State of Israel, his old enthusiasm resurfaced and he legislated that dueling was to be virtually without restriction, "in order to have real officers and to impart a tone of French refinement to good society. Dueling is permitted and will not be punished, no matter what the outcome, provided that the seconds have done their share towards an honorable settlement. Every saber duel will be investigated by the dueling tribunal only afterwards."[16]

to what the others were doing. There was mutual criticism as well as friction—all decreed by an ideal of manliness that attached the greatest importance to formal bearing. . . . Anyone who managed to hold his own within this community felt extremely secure, superior and blasé towards the rest of the world." Weber himself admitted, "There were no problems for us; we were convinced that we could somehow solve everything that arose by means of a duel." "Say what you like against the practice," wrote another contemporary, "but to feel oneself man to man, with cold steel in one's hand, does one good." In later years, Weber publicly supported dueling, especially *Satisfaktionsfähigkeit*, the right to vindicate one's personal honor by such means, and when in 1910 Marianne Weber, an activist in the bourgeois women's movement, was insulted in a newspaper, he at once declared that he was ready to defend "the honor of his wife" in a duel. Only the refusal of his adversary prevented an actual fight.

As it happened, Germany had an unusually keen follower of duels in its future kaiser, Wilhelm II. Born in 1859 with a withered left arm, the young Wilhelm ensured that his good arm would be doubly strong and for some years took fencing lessons every day. "It is not for mere love of the sport, but for medical reasons," one British source confided. "He suffers sometimes from difficult breathing—a difficulty which riding on horseback rather increases than diminishes. His medical advisers have therefore suggested daily exercises at fencing."[18]

The prince attended Bonn University, where he was not allowed to duel at his club. A recent biographer records that though he joined one of the fraternities, the Borussia corps, "its members' behaviour repelled him with their love of duelling, gambling and heavy drinking."[19] Maybe. A little over a decade later he was at a summer symposium of the university, which was always attended by the dueling clubs. Replying to a toast in his honor, he declared:

It is my firm conviction that every youth who enters a corps or beer-drinking and dueling club will receive the true direction of his life from the spirit which prevails in them. . . . He who scoffs at the German students' corps does not penetrate their real meaning. I hope that as long as there are German corps-students the spirit which is fostered in their corps, and which is steeled by strength and courage, will be preserved, and that you will always take delight in handling the duelling-blade. There are many people who do not understand what our duels really mean, but that must not lead us astray. You and I, who have been corps-students, know better than that. As in the Middle Ages manly strength and courage were steeled by the practice of jousting or tournaments, so the spirit and habits which are acquired from membership of a corps furnish us with that degree of fortitude which is necessary to us when we go out into the world.[20]

The less attractive aspects of corps life—arrogance, drunkenness, and aggressive swagger—would suggest that the fraternities might have been natural homes for *Hitlerjungen* once the Nazis took power. In fact, although some fraternity members did become Nazis, the opposite was the case. From the Fascist perspective, just as Mussolini saw the Mafia as a highly integrated organization that represented a threat and sought to destroy it, so the National Socialists saw the fraternities as rivals that had to be broken down.

Hitler became chancellor at the end of January 1933. By July one of his senior officials declared that any fraternity member who had time to be quarrelsome was obviously not fulfilling National Socialist goals. This "suggestion" was received differently by individual fraternities. In Kiel, the local student leader issued a decree suspending all fencing fraternities for a period of at least two terms. Elsewhere the pronouncement was ignored. The Nazis, or rather their main mass movement, the National Socialist German Workers Party (NSDAP), tried to set up rival fraternity houses. In August it was proclaimed that all incidents involving questions of honor—in other words, that might lead to a duel—should be reported to the authorities. The students would not back down, and an uneasy standoff began.

That summer, wearing fraternity colors was forbidden. In Freiburg, during the winter term of 1935–36, members of the Hitler Youth adopted the habit of tearing off fraternity members' tricolor bands whenever they saw them. Corps members responded by lining their bands with razor blades. Eventually, however, the uncompromising stance of the fraternities brought about their overthrow: each was so intent on preserving its individual independence that bit by bit the student arm of the Nazi Party gained more power, and by mid-September 1935 the majority of fencing fraternities had been disbanded.

The Nazis' own student fencing corps, the *Kameradschaften,* were not a popular alternative, and by July 1936 it looked as if they might founder completely. In November a new head of the organization was appointed, Dr. Gustav Adolf Scheel, who had been a member of a dueling fraternity at Tübingen. In order to induce the old fraternities to fold themselves into the Nazi student organizations, Scheel announced a new code of honor requiring all NSDStB members to fence a *Mensur* if challenged. The NSDStB forbade dueling, so for a while nothing happened. Then, in April 1937, another leading Nazi wrote an article saying that any serious German student should adopt the laws and customs of his university community—in other words, that he should duel when required to do so.

That spring, Hitler let it be known that any self-respecting German should be willing to fight for his honor. Before long, instruction in fencing was made mandatory for NSDStB members. At the same time the Wehrmacht, the SA, and the SS all accepted that their members should "give satisfaction at arms," and soon enough all had thriving fencing clubs. "For all members of the NSDStB and its *Kameradschaften*, offended honor can only be redressed by force of arms," proclaimed Scheel. "Any other concept of arms will no longer have any currency among German students." Suddenly, all German students were required to fence. It was quite a turnaround, even though only light sabers were to be used, not foils or épées and certainly not *Schläger*.

Confusion abounded, because the NSDStB itself still forbade the *Mensur*. Further, all students were required to belong to a Party-affiliated organization, none of which allowed dueling. So in theory *Mensur* fencing was mandatory, only no one was permitted to do it. In several centers dueling continued, in strict secrecy; but secrecy had always been part of the *Mensur*'s history—and of its appeal.

When war broke out, many universities closed down. By the time they reopened, the composition of the student bodies had changed; only the German zest for swordplay, despite its illegality, did not die away. In 1941 a group of officers at the University of Bonn clubbed together and approached the head of their local *Kameradschaft* for permission to conduct *Mensuren*. In Münster, the Ambulance Medics fenced in elaborate secrecy—under the protection of several local officials, including the chief of police. The University of Freiburg, home to a particularly enthusiastic group of duelists, hosted some five hundred *Mensuren* up until 1944, when investigations by the NSDStB forced it to close down. Even then, the duelists were so well organized that a hunting cabin in the Black Forest was provided for recuperation: anyone caught with fresh wounds would ipso facto have been in contravention of NSDStB regulations. Fighting a *Mensur* became an explicit act of defiance. Sensing that the governing powers could not stamp out dueling, students revived other traditional practices, including local fencing organizations—all illicit and carried out under the noses of the Nazis. As R. G. S. Weber wrote, "Although not in the proportions of the plot against Hitler on 20 July 1944, the actions of the corps were none the less actions of resistance against the totalitarian regime with which they fundamentally disagreed."[21]

A number of corps alumni were prominent in the German Resistance. Of those executed in the July plot, seven, including its nominal leader, Adam von Trott zu Solz, were ex-*Mensur* fencers. One of the conspirators, who managed to survive the war, noted that meetings of corps alumni in Berlin during the war served as a means of exchanging antiregime information. The alumni network was also used to enlist support for the Resistance. Fraternity brothers, even if they could not help directly, could be trusted to keep secrets.

With the collapse of the Third Reich, the Allied military governments temporarily banned most German organizations, including student fraternities. Various Nazi laws were rescinded, and the *Mensur* was reduced to the status of assault with a deadly weapon, punishable by imprisonment. Until June 10, 1950, the *Schläger* was deemed by the occupying forces to be an offensive weapon, whose mere possession was a punishable offense. Slowly, however, the fraternities crept back, so that by 1951 there were sixty-three corps in Germany, fifty-nine practicing the *Mensur*.

At a special conference on May 19, 1951, it was ruled that any *Korpsier* not already qualified would be required to fence at least one *Mensur* or be released from membership. *Mensur* fencing was still officially forbidden in Germany, but in January 1953 the Federal High Court of Justice acquitted several students charged with lethal assault on the grounds that the protective equipment worn and strict procedural regulations involved meant that the *Mensur* could not be judged an assault with a deadly weapon under the law. Similar judgments in 1960 and 1962 placed the *Mensur* beyond further legal action. A correspondent for *Encounter*, writing in the mid-1950s, reported that several corps had been re-formed: until 1954 the rectors of Bonn University had opposed their reintroduction, but there was now no law against them, "only one under which one party may denounce another for inflicting bodily harm, and this of course no corps dueller would do."[22] So it has remained up to the present day.

A BOUT FIFTEEN HUNDRED TO TWO THOUSAND *MENSUREN* ARE STILL fought every year in Germany, Austria, and some of the Swiss cantons. In the summer of 2000 a friend of mine, a Polish sabreur, visited Berlin and dined one night with the city's mayor, who told him that he was delighted that he had effectively outlawed so barbaric a practice. The next evening my friend attended the local fencing club, of which a fellow Pole is now the resident master, and photographed several *Mensuren*. The pictures he later showed me are full of beaming young Teuton faces, streaming with blood.*

Later that year I made a special journey to Solingen to visit a local swordsmith named Wolf Peter Unshelm, who makes *Mensur* swords by hand in a small house in a beautiful valley on the outskirts of the town. There are four small workrooms, with a lathe made in 1888 and a mask-making machine, part of which has Mr. Unshelm's ancient car jack holding the masks in position. One of the restrictions imposed on Germany after the war was a ban on the manufacture of weapons. When in 1956 the ban was lifted, Wolf Peter began a three-year apprenticeship. For the last twenty-five years he has run his own business, making about two hundred *Schläger* a year and about sixty *Mensur* swords, as well as weapons for ceremonial and ornamental use. Then there are the masks and the special gauntlets, stacked in a corner in one of the tiny workrooms.

Now in his early sixties, Wolf Peter has never fought a *Mensur* himself, but as he proudly took me around his workplace he picked up one of his

---

* J. Christoph Amberger, a German based in Baltimore, fought seven *Mensuren* between 1985 and 1987. His account of one of these bouts, held in Göttingen in 1987, is the best description of what a *Mensur* is like at the sharp end. After a prodigous to-and-fro, Amberger, already badly cut, at last gets in what turns out to be a winning hit:

> I can still see my opponent's sweat-drenched face. A hair-fine line appears across his forehead, five, six inches long. Then a red curtain falls, turning his face into a mask of oily scarlet, from which the inch-high rims of the goggles stick out black and ghoulishly.
>
> Commotion. My opponent disappears behind the tattered leather back of his second. The doctor approaches, looks and shakes his head. A moment later the second will turn around, request silence while unhooking his gauntlets, and courteously thank [me] for a fair fight.
>
> Suddenly all the tension that has drained me for an hour has evaporated, my lungs expand, and a breeze seems to cool my face. And not even the prospect of having needles shoved through the gaping fringes of my cuts can dim the elation. I know I won't feel a thing: the combination of wound shock and adrenaline will take care of anaesthesia.[23]

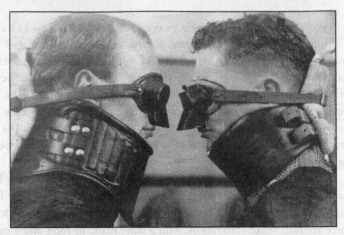

Modern-day corps brothers swear loyalty in a ritual ceremony.
The upper reaches of certain leading German companies are still said
to require a dueling background.

weapons and immediately got on guard in the perfect *Mensur* posture, moving his fencing arm deftly through the various positions. He is a slight, friendly man, about five feet seven inches in height, and the big sword looked strange in his hand.

Duels with the heavy saber are still forbidden in Germany, although Wolf Peter was not sure of the current law. I asked how many clients he had, and he showed me a well-thumbed order book containing a hundred names and addresses—each a fraternity club, the names of the club secretaries evoking Germany's nationalist past. There was one customer in America, another in Scandinavia, a couple in Switzerland, but the rest were all in Austria or Germany. He was, Wolf Peter said, kept extremely busy. For the last fifteen years he has been the only maker of *Mensur* and *Schläger* swords in Germany and, so far as he knows, in the world. He has no assistant, no apprentice; his daughter, he told me, now grown up, takes no interest in his calling. So there will be no one to continue his skills when he retires, maybe in three years' time.

I drove off leaving Wolf Peter standing outside his workshop, gently waving good-bye. Somehow, I felt, a successor would be found. The *Mensur* may be an anachronism, but there is a call for it still. And since the 1920s its practitioners have not suffered a single fatality—making it, ironically, one of the safest sports in the world.

Part Five

GREAT POWERS

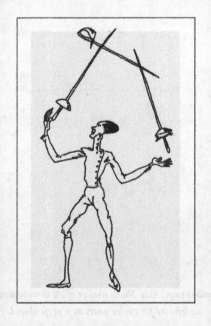

Previous page: Aldo Nadi, master of all three weapons,
undefeated for twelve years as a professional.

CHAPTER 14

The Fascist Sport

> *The only instrument with which one can conduct foreign*
> *policy is alone and exclusively—the sword.*
>
> —DR. JOSEPH GOEBBELS, *Der Angriff,* May 28, 1931

> *The contentious concept of sport summarized in the phrase*
> *"Sport for sport's sake" is a fiction. Fascism has exploded this*
> *fiction once and for all.*
>
> —LANDO FERRETTI, PRESIDENT OF THE 1928 ITALIAN
> OLYMPIC COMMITTEE

WHEN MY FATHER DIED IN 1994, I HAD THE RESPONSIBILITY OF going through his possessions to decide what to throw away. After clearing out an old clothes chest, I glanced at the newspaper lining the bottom of a drawer. It was from the *Daily Mirror* of Saturday, March 11, 1933, and I still have it, yellowed and almost crumbling. "HITLER BECOMES SUPREME IN GERMANY" runs the headline, alongside an article on Franklin Roosevelt's inauguration. The subheading reads, "Reign of Terror by Nazi Troops—Three More States Taken Over." "Britain Asked to Help 'In Averting Another European War,'" the subheadings continue, "American Couple's Home Raided . . . Consul Protests Against 'Brutal Nazi Attack' . . . A sensation has been caused by a three-day suspension of the *Berliner Tageblatt,* the most celebrated newspaper in Germany. No reason is given."

What struck me then is how clearly a popular paper saw the menace of Nazism, only weeks after Hitler assumed power. If the *Mirror* could recognize the brutal nature of Nazi rule, why did it take others so long? I was reminded of the old saw about a frog in boiling water: drop it straight into a boiling pan, and it will jump out at once; heat the water gradually, and it will swim around happily until it is too late.

The fencing community did its share of swimming. The right-wing drift of the sport was a gradual process, and when the fascists took over fencing in several countries there was no one to stop them. Right-wing politicians in particular seem to have had a fondness for fencing. Heinrich Himmler had something sim'lar. At the end of the First World War he was at university in Munich, where he longed to be part of the dueling fraternities but was held back by his strong religious beliefs, as dueling was against Church doctrine. His desire to duel won out, and he joined a war veterans' league, the Reichskriegsteilnehmerverband, where he went into training for his first duel.

In the summer of 1922, aged twenty-one, he at last secured the duel he had longed for. Despite his small stature and spindly frame, he felt he performed well, and noted in his diary: "I certainly did not get agitated. Stood very well and fought technically beautifully. My opponent was Herr Renner, Alemannians [fraternity], he struck honest blows."[1]

The fight, the thirteenth of fifty scheduled that day, was stopped when Himmler had taken five cuts, for which he received five stitches and a ligature. "I did not flinch once," he recorded. Afterward his head was buzzing, and he slept badly—a small price to pay: he had proved himself. By the time he became leader of the SS, like many Nazis, he patterned his cult of honor on the chivalric medieval archetypes that fencers so identified with. His headquarters at Wewelsburg boasted a vast dining hall with an oaken Round Table around which Himmler's twelve most prominent *Obergruppenführer* clustered. As he once reminded a similar assembly, "Never forget—we are a knightly order." Then there was Hermann Göring, who at grand state occasions would wear a crusader's sword; while Hitler's desk had on it a motif of a sword being drawn from its sheath. But Goebbels had no duels at all.

Enthusiasm for fencing among military leaders was not confined to the Third Reich. It was the favorite pastime of the sports-obsessed dictator Juan Perón (husband of Evita), who was his country's army champion; while General Franco fenced as a cadet in Toledo and won a decoration for gallantry after a desperate fight with sword and dagger with a Moroccan tribesman, from which, he would recall with pleasure, he "still had the glorious scars on his head."[2]*

---

* General De Gaulle was a notable exception—at military school he had to practice every day from 7 to 9 A.M. at swordplay (as well as gymnastics and horsemanship), but despite being nicknamed "Cyrano," knowing Rostand's play by heart, and being six feet, five inches tall, he came close to the bottom of his class in fencing. His only other connection with the sport came when he was courting his future wife, Yvonne Vendroux; they went to watch her brother compete in a fencing tournament in Paris, and later that same day De Gaulle proposed.

Apart from military figures, Ezra Pound was at the same fencing club at university as his fellow poet William Carlos Williams. Williams had no fascist leanings, but Pound's sympathies led him to broadcast from Italy during the war, and after he had been imprisoned he gave lessons to his fellow internees—using a broomstick. He also wrote a poem in memory of his fencing master, which is unusual in seeing Death as a keen fencer:

> Gone while your tastes were keen to you,
> Gone where the grey winds call to you,
> By that high fencer, even Death,
> Struck of the blade that no man parrieth.

Pound's political hero, Benito Mussolini, was once asked by a journalist which was the greater, the pen or the sword.* He replied immediately, "The sword—because it cuts. Cuts. Ends things. *Finish.*" In Italy, fencing came to be known as "the Fascist sport." The country's record in competition was formidable: in the sixteen years of European and Olympic championships leading up to 1935, Italians won twenty-four gold, twenty-seven silver, and fourteen bronze medals, and finished fourth seventeen times. Such success, nearly all achieved under Mussolini, had political implications: the government looked fondly on fencing and helped promote it. Mussolini himself had always been attracted to swordplay, a passion that could be traced back loosely to his schooldays, when he had been expelled for stabbing another boy with a penknife; he continued into adulthood to carry a knife wherever he went (though, incredibly, he never learned to use a razor properly, and "shaved himself as though in a fury with hasty and careless strokes."[3]).

Throughout his life Mussolini craved various forms of release. He would cycle eighteen miles for flying lessons, sandwiching in driving instruction and the occasional duel; but despite his determination to excel he was as clumsy with a sword as he was behind the wheel of a car—even on mountain roads, with the engine boiling, he never saw the need to

---

* The original adage dates back to 1839, when Edward Bulwer-Lytton wrote *Richelieu*. In Act II, Scene 2, we hear:

> Beneath the rule of men entirely great,
> The pen is mightier than the sword.

It was also Bulwer-Lytton who begins his 1840 novel *Paul Clifford* with the memorable opening "It was a dark and stormy night."

change gear. "All through his life to acknowledge defeat was to risk exposing himself to ridicule—the one thing he feared above all," wrote Richard Collier, one of his biographers. "Though he wielded his rapier like a bludgeon, grunting and grimacing, he threw out challenges with the aplomb of a d'Artagnan—fighting under bridges, on the banks of streams, once in a rented room after the seconds had piled all the furniture on to the landing."[4]

On a typical day, he would be up at seven, take a cold bath, swig back a glass of milk, then go off riding for an hour, leaping onto his horse cowboy-fashion. After that he would fence. According to a sympathetic biography published in Italy in 1928, he generally preferred the saber, and with his teeth set in grim determination would fight "with a style that was totally personal, full of clever ruses, sudden counterattacks, blows unexpected according to the logic of his adversary, which the *Duce* launches like the punishment of God."[5]

In his early days, Mussolini would use a special code with his wife, Rachele, whenever he went off to duel, to avoid frightening their children. "Have spaghetti today," he would say. Rachele would take out the blood-stained shirt in which he fought all his duels, while the family handyman, Cirillo Tambara, set off for the local store to buy pitch, with which Mussolini would coat his fencing glove so that no adversary could inflict shame by disarming him. Hemingway once said that really brave men do not have to fight duels. Nor do they have to pose for photographers with a tame lioness or drive at breakneck speeds along bad roads and boast about it. Mussolini was not a physical coward, but he was scared of being thought one.

Five of his duels took place while he was still a journalist, mainly between 1915 and 1922, the most memorable in October 1921, against the socialist Francesco Ciccotti-Scozzese, an old friend become a sworn enemy. The Ministry of the Interior learned of this duel and was determined to stop it, not least because Ciccotti-Scozzese had a heart condition, but the two men left their homes in Milan and traveled to Emilia to fight—closely followed by the police. They went on through the Cisa Pass, then Livorno, with the duel finally getting under way at a house in Antignano. At this point a local official, Marcello Vaccari, discovered them, and they fled once more. The fight ended in Livorno on October 27, after fourteen separate starts, and then only because of fears for Ciccotti's health.

In his autobiography, Mussolini describes this last encounter with pride: "I had a duel of some consequence with Ciccotti-Scozzese, a mean figure of a journalist. . . . Among other various imperfections, one might say he had that of physical cowardice. Our duel was proof of it. After several assaults the physicians were obliged to stop the encounter because of the claim that my opponent had a heart attack. In other words, fear had set him all aflutter." He continues in typical vein, "I think I have some good qualities as a swordsman—at least I possess some qualities of courage, and thanks to both, I have always come out of combats rather well. In those combats having a chivalrous character, I endeavor to acquit myself in a worthy manner."[6]

As he grew older, he devoted more time to cultivating physical fitness. His most intimate retainer besides his housekeeper and cook was Camillo Rodolfi, his riding and fencing instructor, who enjoyed a well-paid sinecure as a noncommissioned colonel in the Fascist militia. By 1923 Mussolini had given up alcohol and tobacco almost entirely. To demonstrate his youthful vigor, he would run down a line of soldiers when inspecting a parade. Foreign newspapers were not allowed to refer to his age, and he successfully concealed the fact that he needed to wear spectacles; occasionally he even invited foreign journalists to watch him fence.

Shortly after he seized power in October 1922, *Il Duce* had created the Colosseum of Mussolini, a sports center whose aim was to turn out winning international teams over a whole range of sports, much like the academies that now exist in many advanced nations. The best amateurs and

Mussolini practices under the watchful eye of his coach.

*Nedo Nadi in 1931, shortly after his return from Argentina. By 1932 he would
be Italy's team captain at the Los Angeles Olympics.*

professionals in various disciplines were selected with few other requirements than to prepare for competition, then win. Fencing was one of the
chosen sports. Even so, Mussolini's interest might well have cooled, had
circumstances not provided him with an unusual opportunity.

At the 1912 Olympics an eighteen-year-old from Livorno, Nedo Nadi,
won the gold medal at foil. Eight years later he broke all records at
Antwerp, winning individual gold at foil and saber and gold medals in all
three team events, where Italy made a clean sweep. Following these
Games, Nadi returned to a country in political ferment. Within two years
Mussolini was in power, and demanded that all Italians show their support by joining the Fascist Party. Nadi made no attempt to do so: by nature,
he was apolitical, so much so that in the 1914–18 war, after having been

decorated for bravery, he was sharply reprimanded for being openly friendly to one of his Austrian prisoners whom he discovered had been a fencer. "I just treated him as a human being," Nadi insisted, but he was stripped of his medal all the same.

Back in his home town of Ardenza, just outside Livorno, the local *Fascisti* tried various means to make the country's new hero into a party member. He was not interested. He was happy, he said, teaching alongside his fencing-master father at their local club. The Fascist militia refused to let matters rest there. Mussolini had recently survived an attempt on his life, and to celebrate his deliverance special processions were organized throughout Italy. It was decreed that all Italians should hang Fascist flags out of their windows for the duration of the proceedings. Nadi refused. Blackshirts went by his house yelling abuse, and when this had no effect they decided that more positive action was required. A group of them held a secret meeting and planned to ambush Nadi on his way home from work. The plotters selected a pinewood grove about a hundred meters from Nadi's club, electing to do more than just give the recalcitrant sportsman a good beating: they would break his sword arm.

One of their group, a well-built boy called Piero Polese, happened to be a pupil of Nadi. As soon as he heard about the new plan, he drew his gun and dared anyone to try to harm his teacher. Polese then went to see Nadi's formidable wife, Roma Ferralasco, to tell her that her husband's life was in danger. For some reason, Roma chose not to tell her husband. Instead, she arranged for Polese to accompany Nadi from the club every afternoon; he told his master that he had a girlfriend who lived along the same route. Then, from 4 P.M. on, Roma, who would by then have finished her work as a physical-education teacher, would take over. Soon she was shadowing her husband around town, a revolver in her handbag. Support for the ambush melted away. Throughout, Nadi appears to have had no idea what was going on.

When the next Fascist parade day came round—there were one or two a month—Roma again refused to put out the required flag. As the Fascists stomped past, shouting, throwing stones and trying to see inside the house, she shouted back, "If you have something to say, say it to my face." Her husband, meanwhile, continued to devote himself to books, classical music, and fencing. It was as if everyone knew he was walking a tightrope except Nadi himself.

The Fascists decided that their next move would be to burn down the Nadis' house, but again Roma was tipped off, and the attack averted. Still the threats continued. The local chief of police, one of the leading Fascists in town, took to walking up and down the street outside their home, whip in hand, his glistening boots clicking on the cobblestones. He would stop and gaze up at the Nadis' windows. At other times he would spur round on a large white horse he used for official occasions and repeat the exercise—an unnerving exhibition of power and intimidation.[7]

Roma determined to act. She wrote to Mussolini's right-hand man, the secretary of the party, Augusto Turati—an ex-fencer who knew and admired Nadi. Turati in turn spoke to Mussolini, and within twenty-four hours the chief of police was "transferred." Some weeks later the policeman's corpse was found in a ditch, the victim of a Blackshirt hit squad. When Il Duce decided to act, there were no half measures.

By now, Mussolini's interest in Italy's great champion had been roused. He must have imagined Nadi as some Italian Gary Cooper—tall, unassuming but wonderfully accomplished, with great natural dignity—the perfect representative of the new Italy, if only the obstinate fencer could be made to play his part. Mussolini had recently coined the line "The plow makes the furrow, but the sword defends it." Nadi was the incarnation of such a slogan.

Acting on Mussolini's instructions, Turati invited Nadi to Rome: "He [Mussolini] often asks me about you, he reads the exceptional reports from ambassadors and other Ministers about your fencing in the capitals of the world. . . . Let me know when you might be able to visit him, and I will set up a meeting." Nadi ignored the letter. Turati wrote again; once more there was no response. When a third letter came, Roma told her husband he would have to make the journey. "You're selling me out," Nadi said angrily; but this time he went.

Taking Roma with him, Nadi set off in a three-gear car. When he finally met Il Duce, on October 28, 1929, he greeted him not with the Fascist address expected of visitors but with a sharp military salute. He was playing with fire; but Mussolini took a liking to the independent sportsman, and the moment passed. The two men were like a comedy act, Mussolini, barrel-chested and squat, Nadi towering over him, sleek and slim. The meeting, scheduled to last fifteen minutes, went on for forty-five. Mussolini was quite clear as to what he wanted from his guest. He told Nadi he hoped he would come to Rome. He could bring his father down with him, and they would be provided with anything they wanted: their own fencing club, money, the freedom to come and go as they pleased. Mussolini would promote Nadi's entire program. And Mussolini's two sons—would Nadi teach them to fence too?

Throughout the interview, Nadi remained studiously polite, but also adamant: he had no wish to move. Mussolini did not fly into one of his rages—perhaps intrigued that Nadi, unlike other visitors, had not asked for any favors. But he was not yet finished. Over the years, Nadi had received many awards from other governments—a major decoration from Hungary, the Légion d'Honneur from France—and Mussolini was keen to show he could be just as appreciative. As Nadi prepared to leave, Mussolini asked him to accept a photograph of a celebrated Italian actress, Ghitta Garrel. It showed her in a pretty white dress, not at some formal Fascist event. "You're not going to turn this down as well, are you?" he joked. Slightly abashed, Nadi took the photo. Mussolini hugged and kissed him, and the interview was over. Only later did Nadi turn the photo over. Mussolini had written, "To Nedo Nadi with sympathy and admiration." It was as if a virus had found a point of entry.

Waiting in one of the anterooms were Cardinal Ascalesi of Naples and Italo Balbo, one of Mussolini's main henchmen. Aware of the length of time Nadi had spent with Il Duce, Balbo, who knew Nadi through a family connection, exclaimed, "Hey, Livorno boy! You must have won him over!" Nadi said nothing and walked straight past the two men. He picked up Roma and, still silent, took the elevator down to the palace gardens and walked to the car. They drove through the Corso Umberto until they reached the Campidoglio Gardens; it was only then that Nadi started to talk. "He's a fascinating man," he told his wife. "Not like a dictator at all. A friendly eccentric. I felt sorry for him—he's really passionate in what he believes in: he's going to have a hard time of things."

News of Nadi's meeting with Mussolini spread quickly, with reports in the newspapers and on the radio. The Fascists in his hometown were dumbfounded. What were they meant to do now? They decided to cross Nadi off their list, and all intimidation stopped. But Mussolini knew that he was on the way to getting what he wanted. Nadi went off to Argentina to become master at the Jockey Club of Buenos Aires—then not only a city with many fine fencers but, with the new wealth of the Argentine aristocracy, one of the world's capitals of high-quality sports—but Mussolini kept up the courtship, raining a succession of official honors upon Nadi. By 1931 Nadi returned to Italy, to move to Rome to take up a five-year contract under Mussolini's patronage as coach to the Italian national team—at a reported salary of $3,000 a month, quickly making him a lira millionaire. He would captain the team at the 1932 Games in Los Angeles and again in Berlin. Photos of the 1936 Olympics show him dressed in the infamous black shirt—and giving the Fascist salute.

Nadi proved to be an inspiring captain, and at the Berlin Games the Italian fencers won four gold medals, three silver, and two bronze. The Germans, who had put high hopes on the fencing, ended with two bronze medals, a silver, and no gold. The other three gold medals (there were seven in all then) were all won by Hungary, so that the final fencing points table read Italy 68, Hungary 37, Germany 19. The triumph of the three fascist nations was complete.

Despite Germany's relatively poor showing in the fencing events, the 1936 Games were a huge propaganda coup for the Nazis. In the overall tally, it came first, well ahead of the United States, having swelled its victories by adding several events such as women's gymnastics and yachting, in which it was strong, as well as irrelevant "sports" such as arts competitions. Hitler himself came to watch the fencing (where épée was fought electrically for the first time), which, with three hundred contestants from thirty-one nations, was the most cosmopolitan of any sport at the Olympics.

THERE WAS ONE UNEXPECTED ABSENCE FROM THE FASCIST RANKS AT these games—that of the British épée team's most infamous fencer: Oswald Mosley. He had been successively a Conservative, Independent, and Labour member of Parliament and a member of the 1929 Labour government, serving as Chancellor of the Duchy of Lancaster, with particular responsibility for unemployment. A brilliant speaker, he was often mentioned as a future prime minister—of either of the main parties—but his career came off the rails dramatically in 1931, when, dissatisfied with traditional alignments, he founded the New Party. Following a visit to Italy, he folded his organization into the British Union of Fascists, of which he soon became leader. Violently anti-Semitic, the party foundered at the polls, and Mosley ended in disgrace. He vacillated wildly in his political affiliations, but throughout everything he was consistent in one respect: he was a dedicated fencer.

He had taken up the sport at fifteen at Winchester College, having reluctantly surrendered his first love, boxing, on medical advice. Nine

Oswald Mosley, the British fascist leader, at an open-air épée practice in the mid-1930s. His injured right foot, the result of the accident he suffered at Sandhurst, is clearly visible.

months later he won the foil and saber public school titles (both the double victory and the early age set records). Later, training as an officer cadet at Sandhurst, he injured his right foot when he fell from an upstairs window, an injury exacerbated by a plane crash. Unable to lunge or flèche, he was forced to give up fencing.

When, in February 1931, Mosley started the New Party, many illustrious names followed him, drawn by his personal magnetism. The economist Maynard Keynes assured him of his vote, as did Harold Nicolson, the writer and diplomat; Winston Churchill's twelve-year-old nephew Esmond Romilly campaigned for him at his preparatory school, and the Sitwell family, lions of the London literary world, were keen supporters. In another sphere Peter Howard, captain of the Oxford Rugby XV and soon to captain England, joined the pack. Leading Labour intellectuals such as John Strachey and Alan Young added weight to the group.

Early on, Mosley said he was keen that his followers should be "fit" and "in training," and for that reason he resumed fencing. He joined the London Fencing Club, where he was not popular with older members, most of them Tories who felt he had been a traitor to their party. Disregarding them, Mosley was so quick to regain his previous skills that within a year he was joint runner-up in the national épée championships. "To have returned with a gammy leg from a twenty-year lay-off to become runner-up in the British Epée Championship in 1932 was a formidable achievement," his biographer Robert Skidelsky comments. "It also took up a formidable amount of time. Throughout 1932 he was fencing all over England."[8] His obsessiveness continued to bear fruit: in 1933 Mosley came third in the same championships: he was thus one of the leading épéeists of the time and for at least two years was a regular member of the British team.

At the time of the general election of October 1931, the New Party was still attracting major figures: the novelist Peter Cheyney, himself a keen club fencer, Brendan Bracken and Randolph Churchill all joined, while Christopher Isherwood wrote for the Party's magazine, *Action*. Although Mosley had not yet adopted the fascist name, his friend Malcolm Campbell carried the fascist colors on his car "Bluebird" when it broke the land speed record. But the election itself was a disaster for the New Party, which could muster only 36,377 votes from twenty-four constituencies. Even the Communists garnered 70,844. Mosley decided that dramatic action was necessary. That April, he adopted the fasces as his party's symbol, the bundle of rods symbolizing unity, the ax the power of the state as carried by the lictors of ancient Rome. On October 1, 1932, the British Union of Fascists was formed; in 1936 Mosley introduced a new emblem, a flash of lightning within a circle. He also brought in the famous black shirts—black, "not only because it was the opposite to red but because at that time," he explains in his autobiography, "it was worn by no one else in this country." As a gesture toward their leader the fascists modeled the new uniform directly on the fencing jacket.[9] Mosley, using the language of the catechism, described the dress as "the outward and visible sign of an inward and spiritual grace."

In 1935 Mosley was a member of the British épée team that came fifth at the European Championships at Lausanne and could reasonably have expected Olympic selection in 1936. He gives the background to his exclusion in his memoirs: "It was decided that the British team in the traditional march past should not give the Olympic salute," which had been invented by the Greeks more than two thousand years before Hitler or Mussolini were born, and consequently long before anyone thought of calling it the fascist salute. "As the French and nearly every other team decided to give the salute, it seemed on the one hand invidious that I should refrain, and on the other that it would show a lack of the team spirit appropriate to the occasion if I had been the only member of the British team to give it. So discretion became the better part of sportsmanship."[10] An unlikely and self-serving story, but not impossible. The following year, he was a team member (at forty-one) for the world championships, after which he drifted away from the sport. One of his last acts connected to fencing, shortly before the war, was to ask the British swordmaker Leon Paul to supply his party with knuckle-dusters (brass knuckles); Paul declined.

H OWEVER HATEFUL, EVEN MALEVOLENT, MOSLEY'S CAREER WAS, IT pales besides that of the man whom one historian has called "almost certainly the most evil figure in modern history." Reinhard Heydrich, head of the Sicherheitsdienst (SD), the internal security section of the SS, was one of the grandees of the Third Reich, the most powerful man in the country after Hitler and Heinrich Himmler. By 1936 he was deputy head of the Gestapo, as well as the Reich Criminal Police, the Frontier Police, and the Counterespionage Police. As Himmler's deputy, he was directly responsible for implementing the "Final Solution"; Adolf Eichmann, among others, reported to him. Yet Heydrich was an enigmatic and complicated man. The son of an opera singer and composer (he was christened "Reinhard Tristan," in homage to Wagner), he was a violinist of concert standard, a good chamber musician, and a passable pianist and singer.

Heydrich had light blond hair, striking blue eyes set close together, and a beak of a nose dominating a long, equine face. His voice was high, and he had an unfortunate bleating laugh, which gained him the nickname "Ziege"—"nannygoat." At the naval school in Flensburg-Murwick he was a brilliant pupil, one of its best tennis players, a good swimmer and keen sailor. He took up riding and trained for cross-country events, becoming a member of the naval pentathlon team in the mid-1920s. His outstanding skill, however, was as a saber fencer, an aptitude he displayed from the age of eleven. His widow recorded that he trained at least an hour every morning, before the day's work began. Then on weekends there were competitions. "He became one of the most formidable swordsmen in Germany," records a French biographer; "at one moment he thought of participating in the Olympic Games in Berlin in 1936."[11]

Reinhard Heydrich at the time of the Berlin Olympics, the end of his aspirations as an international fencer.

Heydrich was not, however, of true Olympic caliber, and his attempts to inveigle his way into the German team were never likely to succeed. He would appear at competitions swathed in a freshly laundered white toweling robe emblazoned with Nazi insignia, with junior Gestapo members at hand to attend to his needs—and also, no doubt, to help intimidate opponents. It didn't work: his fellow fencers would surreptitiously throw fights to each other to ensure that Heydrich never progressed to a stage from which he could seriously lobby for team selection. (When in 1930 Oswald Mosley had visited Italy he had been invited to take part in an épée match and won all his bouts but was aware that his hosts had made sure he would.) Undaunted, Heydrich set about creating the best club in Germany by enticing promising fencers into the SS, and in 1940 the SS club in Berlin won all three weapons in the German championships. Heydrich also recruited Joseph "Pepi" Losert, a 1936 Olympic saber finalist, to give him lessons—an extraordinary commitment for a man known for working all hours and whose range of sinister responsibilities was enormous.*

Heydrich displayed a rare benevolence in helping a former fencing champion, Paul Sommer, a Jew, to emigrate to the United States. Other kindnesses have been reported, notably to the Polish 1936 épée champion, Roman Kantor, whom Heydrich is said to have taken to Berlin (where he pumped him for information on Polish training techniques); but the official records show that Kantor was removed to Majdanek concentration camp in 1942 and died there the following year.

It would be a mistake to underestimate Heydrich as a fencer. The expert coaching he received bore fruit. In November 1936 he came in fifth in épée and third in saber in the first SS Fencing Masters Tournament. In December 1941 a match was scheduled between Germany and Hungary, and at the last minute one of the German team dropped out. Heydrich took his place and performed second best of the German sabreurs. A sports journalist covering the match commented that this was "an almost unimaginable result when one considers the amount of other work he still managed."

Testimonies about Heydrich's swordplay are of slight relevance set against his enormous crimes, but one senior officer in the SS, Walter Schellenberg, has provided an intimidating portrait in which the qualities he picks out could, in a different context, describe a fencing champion: "[He] had an incredibly acute perception of the moral, professional, human and political weaknesses of others," Schellenberg records. "His unusual intellect was matched by the ever-watchful instincts of a predatory animal always alert to danger and ready to act swiftly and ruthlessly. Whatever his instincts pinpointed as useful he adopted, exploited and then if necessary dropped with equal swiftness. Whatever seemed redundant or to offer the slightest threat or inconvenience was thrown out." The emphasis on simplicity and effectiveness would have certainly appealed to the great masters of the nineteenth century. Less so Schellenberg's conclusion: "He was inordinately ambitious. He had to be the best in everything, regardless of the means."[12]

Imbued with his services' dogma of Aryan superiority and utterly convinced of his own invincibility, Heydrich hated to lose. Civilians in particular tried to avoid fencing him. One evening in the late 1930s, a

---

* Losert (1908–93) also represented Austria in foil and épée, winning all three national titles in 1951. He taught both his children to fence. His son, Roland, won the world senior épée title in 1963. His daughter, Ingrid, elected to fence for Germany and was ranked in the top six in the world.

more-than-capable Austrian sabreur, Dr. Arthur Ferrarres-Waldstein, on a visit to Berlin, came to the SS club for practice. "There's a new face—come here," Heydrich said. The two men took to the strip, where the Austrian, unaware of Heydrich's reputation, hit his opponent almost at will. Later he told another club member that he couldn't understand the cold anger of his adversary. "You are expected to lose against him," his horrified friend said.

Heydrich was a notoriously bad sport. "He can never lose, only complain," a fellow fencer noted. In 1927, when the armed services failed to invite him to take part in their championships, he seethed for months. When, a year later, he finally did enter the naval pentathlon, he came only third out of five and took it characteristically badly, blaming the referee.[13] Around this time he, his instructor, and two other naval officers took part in the second German officers' tournament, held in Dresden. Heydrich was eliminated in the preliminary rounds and, in public view, flung his sword angrily to the floor after his final defeat and stomped away, swearing. His teammates looked on aghast.[14]

His longtime master eventually had to take him aside and remind him that he was supposed to be a role model for SS fencers. Heydrich got the point and asked his master to let him know at once if at any future competition he acted in an unsporting way. Not long after, during the elimination rounds of a saber event, he again started to grumble at a judge's decision. The referee reprimanded him publicly, saying, "On the fencing strip the laws of sporting fairness apply and nothing else." Heydrich bit his tongue.

When the occasion arose, he could swallow his beliefs. At the 1936 Olympics, in the negotiations over the jury just before a saber team match involving Germany, Heydrich made it clear that he wanted to have four Americans as side judges. "But they're Jews!" he was told. "Yes, I know," he replied, "but they're still the fairest." He favored a hierarchy of criteria, in which what was best for Germany took pride of place. Not only as a competitor did he feel he had to win. In 1937, he traveled as nonplaying captain to a tournament at Brussels. In a key team match the Belgian referee became aware that the German judges were cheating. He changed the entire jury, and the Germans lost. That evening the competition ended with a dinner dance, and one of the young British fencers, Mary Glen Haig, who would be an Olympic finalist in 1948, found herself waltzing with the German captain. "I said to him, 'Bad luck on losing this afternoon.' He said, 'What do you mean, losing? We won.'"

His plans for competitive glory frustrated, Heydrich turned to the sport's administration. He announced that it was his aim "to raise [saber fencing] to that high level to which, on account of the stature and power of the Reich, it was entitled even in the international arena." His ambition focused on the post of president of the International Fencing Federation (FIE). In pursuit of this new sinecure he would combine intimidation and intrigue to a remarkable degree.

At the outbreak of war the FIE was based in Brussels because its president, the Belgian fencer Paul Anspach, lived there. Anspach had been elected in September 1939; his presidency was set to run until December 31, 1940. His successor would in due course have been chosen at a congress in the spring—but it never took place because of the German invasion. In the days before Brussels fell, a number of Germans and suspected Nazi sympathizers had been deported, and some murdered en route. At a hearing organized by the Occupation authorities it was established that Anspach, although under suspicion, had played no part in the murders; but the interrogation revealed his place in the fencing hierarchy. This was duly reported to Heydrich, who at once sent a detachment to seize the FIE archives and take them to the Nazi Party headquarters in Prinz-Albrecht-Strasse in Berlin. Heydrich, meanwhile, was busy consolidating his power over fencing in the Reich, a goal he duly achieved in December 1940, when he was elected head of the German Fencing Association. This gave him quite a different authority for dealing with Anspach, whom he now summoned to Berlin. As part of the new order in Europe, he explained, the German federation, together with those of Italy and Hungary, would found a new European alliance to replace the FIE. The archives would thus remain in Berlin. Heydrich reminded Anspach that his term of office had already expired and that he was entitled to carry on FIE business only because a new election was impossible. Anspach was "invited" to transfer his powers to Heydrich until a new congress could be convened. Refusal to comply could mean years in jail.

Anspach replied that he was the elected president of world fencing, and so he would remain. Despite this defiance, he was allowed to return to Brussels unharmed, but a letter from Heydrich soon followed, demanding his resignation. Again Anspach refused. He did not write back directly to Heydrich but instead sent a furious letter to the president of the International Olympic Committee. For Heydrich, however, as one historian puts it, "watching suspiciously and parrying an opponent's intentions, reacting with lightning speed to unforeseen situations" were second nature. He simply tried another move, enlisting the help of the chairman of the Italian Fencing Federation, Dr. Basletta, who was a friend of Anspach. This time Anspach yielded. Heydrich thus added yet another office to his burgeoning portfolio; but for several weeks Anspach had resisted with almost suicidal courage. Maybe Heydrich respected a brave man when he met one.

The fencing world did not have its new leader for long. On May 27, 1942, while serving as an all-too-active deputy "protector" of Bohemia and Moravia, Heydrich was wounded when three Czech parachutists, acting in concert with the British Special Operations Executive, ambushed his official car. That morning "his dark-green, open Mercedes was unescorted and still unarmored as his driver slowed and changed down for the sharp bend where Benes' agents waited," reported the British historian Peter Padfield (Edvard Benes had been president of Czechoslovakia until shortly before Hitler's invasion). "One gave the signal of his approach. Another at the bend stepped forward, raised a sub-machine gun from beneath his raincoat, aimed and squeezed the trigger. The gun jammed. The third man, waiting in reserve with a specially designed bomb, lobbed it at the car. It exploded under the rear wheel, driving fragments of metal, leather seat-cover, stuffing and pieces of Heydrich's own uniform into his internal organs. Despite this he leaped from the car with pistol raised, giving chase and firing at one of his attackers before collapsing."[15] Afterward he was rushed to hospital and operated on by Czech doctors, but the damage was too great, and on June 4 he died. In retaliation, Hitler razed the entire Czech village of Lidice, massacring its adult male population and enslaving the women and children.

Anspach survived the war, but the FIE records were accidentally burned by American troops after the fall of Berlin, when disinfecting the sports stadium to which they had been moved. After the war, another kind of disinfection, a "commission for purging," was set up by the FIE, and by 1947 eighteen fencers were expelled by their federations for "acts against the FIE": three Czechs, four Austrians, five Norwegians, a Pole, two Dutchmen, and three Belgians. Not one German.

I T IS TEMPTING TO CONFINE THE STORY OF FASCISM AND FENCING TO the major "villains"—to Mussolini, Mosley, and Heydrich. But other stories from the period paint a more complex picture of honor and betrayal in the world of fascist fencing.

In 1936, four days before the saber event at the Berlin Olympics, the Polish team's coach, Leon Koza-Kozarski, was giving a lesson to his country's number one sabreur, Antoni Sobik, when his blade broke and pierced Sobik's right hand. The two men went at once to the first-aid post, where the German doctor on duty examined Sobik carefully, took him for X rays, and over the next two days dressed the wound twice daily. The blade had gone deep but had missed vital muscle and tendons, and Sobik was able to fence after all, reaching the final and coming seventh.

At the outbreak of war in 1939, Koza-Kozarski was commanding a regiment on the southwestern border in Silesia. "We fought in a forest, and I had so few soldiers that I had to place them every 50 meters," he later recalled. When the German infantry got too close, he would shout, "Fix bayonets!" The Germans learned to recognize the characteristic sound of the rings being slapped into place and held back, not wanting to risk hand-to-hand combat. By September 20, after holding out for several days, the Polish troops were finally encircled and cut down by German machine guns. Koza-Kozarski feigned death among the corpses of his men, but when a young soldier kicked his back hard he cried out. He was taken prisoner and sent to a camp in Hohenstein Fort in the Owly Mountains, where "unwanted" Polish officers were confined to be physically and mentally broken. "The living conditions were quite unbearable. Because of my knowledge of German I was appointed an interpreter." Despite this slightly privileged position, his health deteriorated and he was convinced that he had not long to live.

One day the officers were mustered in the main courtyard. The camp was being visited by an important military commission. Because of his duties as an interpreter, Koza-Kozarski was in the front rank during the inspection. One of the colonels brought himself up short and asked tersely, "What are you doing here?" Koza-Kozarski shivered in fear: if he were recognized as coming from Poznán, where he had participated in the 1918 Polish Uprising, he would be shot.

"Don't you recognize me?" the German officer went on. It was the doctor who had treated Antoni Sobik in 1936. "I can't speak to you now. I will do my best to see if I can get you transferred." That was the last time the two men met, but a few weeks later Koza-Kozarski was removed to a camp in Murnau, where living conditions were much better. "I owe my life to that German doctor," he said.

After the war he had returned to his home town of Katowice, where he met Antoni Sobik. "Do you remember how you cut my fencing hand in

Berlin?" Sobik asked him. "We were both lucky it was nothing serious." "Yes," said Koza-Kozarski, "it was a lucky wound all right."[16]

THE POLISH COACH WAS NOT THE ONLY FORTUNATE ONE. NICOLO Perno was born in Naples in 1910, graduated from the famous masters' school in Rome, and was regularly his country's saber and épée professional champion. By 1936 he was one of Italy's top épée coaches. After their successes at the Berlin Games the Italians were approached by the German federation, who asked if a senior coach could help rebuild German fencing. Nedo Nadi, a great admirer of Perno's, asked if he would accept the post. Perno was soon coaching the German épée team.

In 1943, when the Italians changed sides, Perno became overnight an enemy alien in his adopted country. He was stationed at the Italian consulate in Frankfurt, and it was there that two Gestapo agents arrested him. He was allowed one last visit to his eight-months-pregnant wife. As he was saying good-bye, the telephone rang. One of the agents answered and made terse replies to the caller, whose name Perno never learned; but he came to believe that a pupil had ensured that he was not taken to a camp but placed under house arrest instead.

A few days later, as the city suffered a massive air raid, Perno and his wife were spirited away by his young fencers to a castle in the south of Germany, a thousand meters above sea level. This was the home of Siegfried Lerdon, one-time épée champion of Germany and a member of its team at the 1936 Games, whose wife had studied in Milan and spoke perfect Italian. Perno and his family stayed there for several months, in which time Perno built a special hideaway in the estate's forest, where, when the Gestapo returned, he hid for a year, surviving on what he could catch or eat. Then in 1945 the Americans came.

By 1948 he was back training the German épéeists, but in 1954 he returned to Italy where he became accepted as one of the leading masters of his time. Over the years he trained the Italian Pentathlon team, the Mexicans, the Puerto Ricans, and the Taiwan Chinese. For twenty years he taught fencing at the National Academy of Dramatic Art, and was president of the Italian Masters' Academy. The Germans gave him their most prestigious medal. In his ninety-second year, he wrote to me: "The fencing strip has always seemed to me a metaphor for life itself: he who knows how to move on it, how to overcome a rival by honest means, has really discovered how life itself must be."

CHAPTER 15

The Woman Who Saluted Hitler

> Athletes, by and large, are people who are happy to let their
> actions speak for them, happy to be what they do. As a result,
> when you talk to an athlete . . . he's never likely to feel the
> least bit divided, or alienated, or one ounce of existential
> dread. . . . His is a rare selfishness.
>
> —RICHARD FORD, The Sportswriter

> I had an old acquaintance, Otto Kahn, who walked down
> Fifth Avenue with a deformed friend. "You know," said
> Kahn, "I used to be a Jew." His friend responded, "Really?
> I used to be a hunchback."
>
> —STORY TOLD BY GROUCHO MARX

IN 1928 A YOUNG FENCER, NOT YET EIGHTEEN, REPRESENTED GER-
many at the ninth modern Olympics, in Amsterdam. Forty-six teams took
part, the largest number ever, for a festival that stretched from May 17 to
August 12. She was already a phenomenon, having won her country's national title at the age of fourteen. She sensed how hungry her defeated nation was for success, since in the first Games after the war, in 1920, the
Belgians had pointedly not invited their invaders of 1914; and four years
later the French, while allowing the other former Central Powers, Hungary, Turkey, Bulgaria, and Austria, back into the Games, again excluded
Germany. Now at last German sportsmen had a chance to reassert their
country's athletic reputation. The girl was Helene Mayer, and she won the
gold medal—Germany's first Olympic fencing title.

Mayer was born on December 10, 1910, the second of three children of
Ludwig and Ida, a happily married middle-class couple. Her brother
Eugen had been born the previous year, and Ludwig Junior followed in
1915. Helene had taken up fencing as a child, encouraged by her father

and taught by a coach of the old school, Cavaliere Arturo Gazzera, one of several Italian masters then in Germany. But she was more than a prodigiously talented fencer. She was strikingly beautiful, with fine open features, the body of a model, blue eyes, and long corn-blond hair. When fencing she would wind her tresses around her ears and keep them in place with a wide white headband; sometimes, in the heat of competition, they would escape in an unruly cascade. Back in Germany she quickly became a national celebrity and was given the nickname "Blond Hee," a shortening of her name that caught the public's imagination.

Helene was a celebrity, a *Höherer Tochter,* Germany's privileged daughter. President Paul von Hindenburg invited her to tea. In Offenbach, her hometown, a torchlight parade was held in her honor. Plaster of paris statuettes showing her in white figure-hugging fencing kit sold by the thousands. "Helene," which means "shining" in Greek, seemed the perfect name for the country's first postwar heroine, uniting national success with the favored influence of Greek culture and sports.

There was, however, one detail in Golden Hee's history of which the public was ignorant: her father was Jewish. At that moment, it seemed a good time to be a Jew. In 1871, Jews had been conclusively granted civil rights when the German states united to form the empire. Over the next half century, German Jews assimilated into society, so that by 1910 they had a profound sense of belonging to the Fatherland. It was no secret that Helene was the daughter of Dr. Ludwig Karl Mayer, a prominent Jewish physician, chief of sanitation in Offenbach, where his father had been honorary mayor. Ludwig Mayer was not a practicing Jew, and Helene was not brought up as such, but he was president of the local chapter of the influential Central Organization of German Citizens of Jewish Faith, founded in 1893 to combat anti-Semitism. Helene's mother Ida was Christian, in a time when intermarriage between Christians and Jews was increasing: by 1910, 13 percent of Jewish men and 10 percent of Jewish women had married a Gentile. Not that Jews were ever more than a small minority: 0.83 percent of the population, 500,000 out of well over 60 million people. There were about 2,000 Jews in Offenbach.

By 1928 *Mein Kampf* had been published and Hitler was already using the slogan "The Jews are our misfortune," but his party was still a minor force: in the elections held that year the National Socialists won 810,000 of 31 million votes cast and only 12 of 491 seats in the Reichstag. Helene felt untouched by it all. In the district where she was brought up, she was called "the Jewish Mayer," to distinguish her from "the Christian

Mayer"—a girl of the same name who lived next door. Why was she not called "the sporting Mayer" or something less loaded, especially as she looked the perfect specimen of Aryan girlhood? Anti-Semitism was there, lurking, but Helene had little connection to or interest in her Jewish background: forced expulsions, murderous prejudice, pogroms seemed to belong to another world.

In her childhood and teens, Helene excelled at riding, swimming, skiing, and dancing. She was good enough at ballet to have appeared at the age of seven as a soloist, and she continued her ballet training until 1923, when, at thirteen, she performed an evening of dance in her hometown. But her father had been a fencer, and her elder brother, Eugen, had also enthusiastically taken up the sport. Now above all she wanted to fence. She would practice in the family backyard each morning at 6 A.M. before going off to school, using Eugen almost literally as her foil. She first entered the German senior championships in 1924, coming second to an Offenbach teammate; in 1925 she won the title and proceeded to win it again an unprecedented six years in a row.

Helene was still a schoolgirl and every day would take the *Strassenbahn* (street railway) from Offenbach to Frankfurt, where from 1921 to 1930 she attended the Schillerschule, named after the celebrated poet. On her first entering the school her father wrote to its principal, asking "to excuse my daughter, Helene Mayer, from participation in *Israelitischen* religious instruction." His wish, based on his own liberal atheism, was granted, so his daughter grew up without ever exploring her Jewish inheritance. She was a good student, though, bright and lively and intent on going to university.

When Helene captured the gold medal in 1928, her classmates were delighted. The school noticeboard boasted, "Our *Unsere Unterprimanerin* [twelfth-grade student] Helene Mayer has won first prize at the Olympic Games in Amsterdam. Heil Hee!" The school commissioned a life-size portrait of its new heroine, which was hung in pride of place in the entrance hall.

Helene was soon traveling all over Europe, and in 1929 won the European title—effectively the world championship—repeating this victory in Vienna two years later, comprehensively defeating the local champion, Ellen Preis, 5–2 in the final. She also fell in love for the first time, with a naval cadet, Alexander Gaihardt. In April that same year her father died, severing her last tenuous connection with Judaism. By then she was enrolled at Frankfurt University, where she chose to study law and modern languages, planning to join the diplomatic service. But by 1930, spurred by an economic depression that left a million Germans out of work, the Nazis had become the second largest political party in the country, and in April 1932 a failing and unconvincing Hindenburg only narrowly managed to keep Hitler out of the presidency. While Helene fenced, her fatherland was in turmoil.

The 1932 Games were to be held in August in Los Angeles—one of the earliest signs of Hollywood power. The German Olympic Association allotted two places to fencing—the only combat sport open to women as well as men for more than one hundred years and in 1932 one of just three in which women competed—and Helene was chosen, alongside Erwin

The gamine Helene continued as a ballet dancer up to her teens. It gave her invaluable flexibility and balance for her fencing.

Casmir, who had won the silver medal for foil at Amsterdam. As a consequence of the recession, each athlete was required to contribute 3,000 DM to cover their costs, a large sum that Helene nevertheless raised with ease after a visit to sponsors in Berlin. She was the reigning Olympic champion, only twenty-one yet widely seen as the foremost fencing stylist in the world.

Helene was superbly athletic, with exceptional balance, grace, and stamina. Her training as a dancer gave her an acute sense of her own body and what it could do—and also exceptional speed of reaction. Her coach had grounded her technique in the best Italo-German tradition. At just over five feet, ten inches—very tall for her time—and weighing 150 pounds, she would dominate her opponents, often beating men at practice—even at saber, which she sometimes did for fun. "On the strip she was a tigress: you felt her domination as soon as she put her mask on," I was told. An American contemporary, who had tied for second place in the 1948 Games, told me, "I fenced her only twice, and each time she beat me badly. It wasn't that she had any favorite move. Her fencing was so rounded, *everything* was marvelous."

Would she be the first woman to retain an Olympic title? The press certainly thought so: on her arrival in Los Angeles reporters surrounded her. A *Los Angeles Recorder* article, "Queen of the Fencers," reported, "Her arrival at the Chapman Park Hotel created quite a furore among the other girl athletes, most of whom have short bobbed hair and envied this pretty miss her novel coiffure." She was "a physical counterpart of a Superwoman. . . . Her arm is like iron, her grip like steel and her wrists are as dainty as a ballet-dancer's."[1]

Two days before the women's competition started, Helene learned that the German training ship *Niobe* had gone down with all her company, including her boyfriend, Alex Gaihardt. Still she fenced on, and managed to win through to the final, topping her semifinal, but in the final she came in only fifth. Some reports recorded that she had seemed "ill."

The gold went to her young former opponent, Ellen Preis (later Müller-Preis). According to two American observers, Curtis Ettinger and Leo Nunes, Preis sat with her Austrian colleagues and with German supporters, most wearing the black armband of the Nazi Party.* Their odious jeering was demoralizing; when they learned of the death of Mayer's beau, they used it to fuel their taunts. Preis may not have been an active part of

---

* Curtis Ettinger (1901–81) was Austrian foil and saber champion a dozen times and an Olympic semifinalist. He escaped Austria at the time of the Anschluss and practiced law, first in Paris and then, from 1941 on, in the United States. He knew Mayer well.

this claque, however. In her memoirs, published in 1936, she writes sympathetically of her great rival, "What happened to Helene, who had fought so well, and without a single defeat, throughout the earlier rounds? She seemed nervous and tense, and teammates would gather round her, all talking at her, some criticizing her for not doing better. They don't know how easy it is to lose—just a small thing going wrong, not noticeable to others, can take the edge off one's performance."[2] Without family to comfort her, alone and in a foreign country, it is amazing that Helene performed as well as she did. Had she won the three bouts that she lost 5–4—including a vital bout to Preis, whom she led 4–1, only to be hit with four ripostes in a row—she would have tied for the gold. But defeat hurt her deeply. She knew she was the best—only she had lost.

Before the Games, Helene had accepted a two-year fellowship to study foreign languages at an exclusive women's college, Scripps, in Claremont, some forty miles east of Los Angeles. Established in 1926, with about two hundred students at the time Helene enrolled, Scripps was one of the few institutions on the West Coast dedicated to educating women for a career. She threw herself into campus life that fall, continuing to fence but also becoming president of the Franco-German Society, the most popular club in college, with a hundred members.

Her figure started to change. She had always had a healthy appetite, a reaction, she would explain later, to the hunger she had experienced during the severe food shortages of the First World War. Throughout her life she would suck the marrow out of bones, and she also displayed the characteristic German love of beer. "Helene Mayer's magnificently willowy figure," an American obituarist would write years later, "and blonde braided tresses, tightly rolled over each ear, became the symbol of Europe's athletic womanhood." But even at the Games the slim, model-like contours of the eighteen-year-old were being replaced by what another historian unkindly described as the look "of an Aryan brood mare" with "a rather beefy face and a strong jaw." In a remarkable series of nude studies she made with the photographer Imogen Cunningham in 1938, she appears like a buxom *Hausfrau*, physically powerful, sensual, but Junoesque, the one-time dancer who had come to enjoy the good life.

Yet Helene remained striking, even beautiful, with unabated self-confidence. She would sport brightly colored capes and scarves, American Indian jewelry, and close-fitting evening gowns. She loved grand entrances and would burst through the doors to a fencing meet and cry to the assembled company in a deep, powerful voice, "I AM HERE!" Maxine Mitchell,

Helene, in trademark headband and pigtails,
dwarfing the Italian foilist Oreste Puliti.

the American who tied for sixth place in the 1952 Games, recalled how Helene "livened up every party": she "always made her final touch with a flourish, an explosive attack, then off with the mask, a shake of the hand, and a walk off the strip. 'But, Helene, sometimes your attack doesn't arrive!'—'I know. It's my reputation. You go and make reputation too, and you see!'"[3]

Her fellow students described her as "exuberant," "jolly," "more fun than a barrel of monkeys," "unforgettable." In the words of one biographer, "she was vivacious, flippant, and flirtatious . . . there was an informal quality in her nature that Americans found unexpected and likeable." She was invited to ranch barbecues, camping trips in the desert, a formal ball, even to meet Hollywood filmmakers, and found herself giving technical advice on swordfighting scenes. The official Scripps catalogue included a photograph of her in fencing kit, with the text "Miss Mayer's presence on the campus is a feature of the life at Scripps. . . . She has persuaded the whole college to follow her own love of this sport."

Events back home presented a stark contrast to life in America. Within six months of Helene's matriculation at Scripps, the Weimar Republic had drifted to its end. Unemployment had ballooned to 6 million, fighting had broken out in the streets, and the parliamentary regime had lost control. On January 30, 1933, Hitler was named chancellor. Almost immediately a flurry of anti-Semitic legislation was pushed through; outbursts of violence against Jews escalated.

How much of this reached Helene in California is unclear. Fellow students recall her once calling Hitler "mad," but otherwise, "she spoke rarely of politics. . . . She was always very fond of Germany." Then, in April, she learned that the new "racial laws" in Germany had prompted her fencing club in Offenbach to cancel her membership; her name had been removed from its notice boards and scrolls of honor. When her family protested, a club spokesman explained, "They were not suspended, but they were no longer registered as members"—a piece of doublespeak that was a harbinger of things to come. The German Fencing Association declared that the actions of the Offenbach club did not affect Helene's membership in the national federation: she could still fence for Germany.

Helene's story, of course, was part of a much wider picture. On May 31, 1931, the IOC had selected Berlin as the site of the 1936 Games. Initially, the leading Nazis had not thought well of the Olympics—its ideals of international goodwill and partnership were far from Hitler's notions of racial purity and military strength. At the time of the 1932 Games, one Nazi writer described them as an "infamous festival organized by Jews." Hitler went even further, deriding the Olympics as "an invention of Jews and Freemasons—a ploy inspired by Judaism which cannot possibly be put on by a Reich ruled by National Socialists." Goebbels, however, convinced his leader that the Games offered an ideal opportunity to show the world the "new Germany"; the Nazi view quickly changed.

As soon as the Nazis came to power, they pursued their racist policies while the government tried to protect the Games in Berlin. In April 1933 Jewish boxers and referees were forbidden to take part in German championship matches. In June, Helene traveled to Chicago, where she won the U.S. national championship. In August, Jewish athletes were banned from competing with Aryans in Germany and sporting clubs were ordered to expel Jewish members. By October, Jews could train and compete only with other Jews. Back at Scripps, Helene discovered that her exchange fellowship had been rescinded on "racial grounds." The college generously said it would absorb the costs of her completing her course. Her thesis subject was hardly that of a professional sportswoman: "The Influence of French Symbolism on German Lyricism."

Helene graduated in the spring of 1934 and that same month traveled to New York to win the national foil title for the second year running: she would be U.S. champion eight times (there was no bar on non-Americans entering until many years later). Now, stranded and uncertain, she accepted an offer from Mills College, a prosperous liberal arts institution in Oakland, California, one of the oldest women's colleges in the United States. She would teach German and fencing.

On September 25, as Helene was settling into her new life, an article appeared in the college newspaper, headed "Hitler Threat Detains Fencing Champion in U.S.": "Fraulein Helene Mayer, arresting, statuesque blonde, arrived at Mills College a few days ago, enthusiastic about the physical education department and anxious to begin teaching her class of twenty girls in fencing. The thing she likes about Mills, she says, is its tradition." There followed a short encomium on the virtues of Mills, then: "The German girl fears return to Germany because censors opened a letter to her mother allegedly criticizing Hitler. She cannot return to Germany in safety and, as she is here on a student's passport, she can stay in the U.S. only so long as she remains a student. A teaching fellowship awarded her by Mills College solves her immediate problem."

Nowhere does Helene link her plight with German anti-Semitism, yet that November Hitler's sports minister issued a decree forbidding "any German athletic organization to affiliate with a non-Aryan. . . . Every personal contact with Jews is to be avoided." Helene issued a statement saying that she would be pleased to represent Germany in international competition. Six months later, interviewed again for the student newspaper, she declared that "should Germany invite her to participate in the 1936 Olympics, she would consider it an honor."

Matters were far from that simple. As early as May 1933, Jews in New York mobilized and called for a boycott of the Games. The following month, the International Olympic Committee met in Vienna, and American members pushed to remove the Games from Germany if discrimination against Jewish athletes continued. The next day a government spokesman in Berlin announced that "as a principle" Jews would not be excluded from German teams. One of the Americans, Brigadier General Charles E. Sherrill, the head of his country's athletics association, in order to have concrete proof that the Germans would keep their word, asked that Miss Mayer specifically should receive an invitation to join the German Olympic team. Helene had become a test case.

On November 21, at a meeting of the American Amateur Athletic

Union, the delegates voted to boycott the Games unless Germany's position was "changed in fact as well as in theory." According to Richard Mandell's *The Nazi Olympics,* the American protests "frightened the Nazis."[4] But they were too clever to succumb. In January 1935 seven German-Jewish athletes received a letter from their local sports authorities saying that their results were inadequate, so they had not qualified for selection. Surely Germany should not be forced to put Jews on its team on the grounds of their race alone?

On a reconnaissance mission in Germany in the summer of 1935, Sherrill continued to harry Nazi officials, pointing out that despite their promises two years earlier they still had not sent an invitation to their leading gold-medal prospect. That August, another senior American athletics official, Judge Jeremiah T. Mahoney, urged that the United States withdraw, pointing out that the Nazis had made it impossible for Jews to qualify for German teams: they were eligible only if they belonged to a Nazi athletic organization, which by law they were not permitted to join. The boycott movement spread to other countries—Britain, France, Belgium, Canada, and the Netherlands—but while it was vociferous it remained small, and there were powerful voices on the other side, saying that politics must be kept out of sport; it was not for other countries to dictate to Germany whom it should select.

That August, Helene received a cable from the influential Jewish-interest magazine *American Hebrew.* It posed four questions: "Did you receive and accept reported invitation to participate in the Olympics for Germany? Do you think in light of continued discrimination, America and other countries should withdraw? Do you regard yourself a refugee from Germany? Did you know Nazi papers repeatedly and tendentiously reported your suicide?"

She cabled back, "I cannot understand newspaper write-ups because have not received invitation from Germany to participate in Olympic Games. Unable to answer your second question. Am absent from Germany since 1932 and therefore do not consider myself a refugee. Amused at suicide rumors." She might have added that she did not feel close to the Jewish community; did not practice its religion; and did not want to be seen as a Jew.

Meanwhile, the German government was preparing another bombshell. On September 15 were enacted the draconian Nuremberg Laws. Jews were returned to an almost medieval standing. A person defined as a Jew could not be a German; and a Jew was someone "of any religious preference who had at least one Jewish grandparent." Helene was no longer a German citizen. She could not fence for Germany.

Ten days later, the head of the German Olympic Committee arrived in the United States on a goodwill tour. "The Olympics without America simply would not be the Olympics," he told *The New York Times*. He added that he was mailing a personal invitation to Helene to attend the German trials in February. "We do not know or have any way of knowing if she has retained her skill after four years, but we hope she will come over. Believe me, we wish more than anybody in America that we had some Jewish athletes of Olympic caliber. But we have none."

No letter ever reached Helene, nor was any explanation forthcoming as to how this new approach squared with the new laws. On September 27, the *Times* had a new story. Under the headline "Reich Recalls 2 Jews to Olympic Team—Invites Helene Mayer, Fencer and Gretel Bergmann, Highjumper to Be Members," the paper reported that the German sports minister had given these assurances by letter to General Sherrill, "evidence that Germany is acting entirely within the spirit of the Olympic statutes and that these members of the German team will receive the same treatment as other candidates, although they are Jewesses" (a term used quite unselfconsciously by a paper with a Jewish proprietor).

Texts of the letters sent to Helene and her high-jumping compatriot were provided. That to Helene read in part, "I beg you to consider yourself as a member of the pre-selected German team which will definitely be composed in the spring of 1936 after test matches. If you are prevented from taking part in these text matches, I am prepared to accept American sports tests as sufficient qualification."

General Sherrill told the *Times* that on the strength of these assurances he would now support the Games. The following day the paper reported that it had heard directly from Helene Mayer that no invitation had reached her. She did not believe that "any had been extended or would be forthcoming." Over the next few weeks there were further exchanges between Sherrill, the Nazi sports authorities, and interested American parties without anything being decided. Then, on November 5, a Mills College spokesman boldly declared that Helene "would represent Germany only if granted full German citizenship rights. She has not received a reply to that offer. If the German committee and government refuse to grant such citizen rights, Miss Mayer will decline."

This was electrifying. Even if no one else would do so, Helene was recognizing the reality of the Nuremberg Laws and going over the heads of the sports authorities direct to the Reich government. Three days later, the government announced that it understood that Miss Mayer had already accepted her place without any conditions. Helene repeated her stance, and so the war of words continued. Privately, Helene consulted the German consul general in San Francisco, and on November 18 he sent a lengthy but revealing report to his embassy:

According to the implementation regulations of the Nuremberg Laws, which are as of now only known through the American press, a number of non-Aryans are granted the possibility to obtain Reichs-citizenship. Helene Mayer has two Jewish grandparents (on her father's side). She declares that she is free of any religion and that she has never been in touch with the synagogue community with the exception of her school years during which she had to participate in both Jewish and Christian instruction. She further explained to me that she feels all the more bitter about her present situation because she does not want to have anything to do with Jewish circles and that she regards herself in no way as Jewish nor does she want to be regarded as Jewish by others.

Regardless of the previously mentioned fact that Miss Mayer under no circumstances wants her petition with the Reichs sports leader to be considered as a condition, she is now of the opinion that she can compete with conviction for Germany in the Olympics, only if she has certainty that she will be regarded as an equal member of the national community. She specifically pointed out that she has to live in an environment which would not understand, if she were to compete for a country which regarded her as a political underling.

From my last conversation with her I have gotten the distinct impression that she expects to be granted the Reich's citizenship and that—in the event that it will not be granted to her—she will have to take back her confirmation under the pressure of her current environment which she cannot leave right now. The pressure exerted on her by the press is particularly strong and she does not know how she will be able to escape this daily badgering any more.

Under these circumstances I would consider it suitable and advisable that the question about granting citizenship to Miss Mayer should be settled immediately and with a positive outcome. Otherwise it is to be expected that Miss Mayer who has an impulsive temperament and does not always weigh her words carefully will let herself be carried away into making remarks which will do us unnecessary harm considering the typical, prominent big spread of the American press.[5]

The German response to the letter was ambiguous. According to a *New York Times* report of November 26, the authorities had received Helene's acceptance of an invitation to compete. At the same time they could assure her that she would indeed be considered a full German citizen despite her "Jewish blood." How could that be? Jews were adjudged to be persons of 75 percent or more "Jewish blood." She did not fall into this category.

It appeared that back in Germany a groundless and insulting story was circulating that Ludwig Mayer might not have been Helene's true father; so if she accepted that she was not legitimate, any trace of Jewish ancestry would be eradicated. But where did the 25 percent figure come from?

Back at Mills College Helene ignored both the slur/compliment and the lack of logic. She let it be known that she had still received no direct word from German Olympic officials and so could say nothing; but she did call once more on the consul general. On December 3 he wrote to his embassy, "After Helene Mayer received a telegram from her mother yesterday, according to which her brothers are Reich citizens, and from which she concludes that Helene also has Reich citizenship, [she] has definitely decided to participate in the Olympic Games."

So that was the solution Helene had come up with: her mother had declared her a citizen! Her brothers had been recognized as citizens, *ergo* she was one too. There was no official documentation of this wonderful way out—for all parties—but no German official confirmed or denied Helene's assertion. There remained the Nuremberg Laws, however. Helene had not disclaimed her official parentage: she still had a Jewish father and two Jewish grandparents. She was Jewish, whatever her citizenship; but so long as everyone turned a blind eye she was also on the Olympic team.

Why was no one pointing out this obvious contradiction? Besides, if Helene was no longer Jewish, the claim of American and other sports leaders that they had been successful in getting a Jew accepted was no longer valid. Evidently both the American and the International Olympic committees had decided that they had to insist that Germany select at least one qualified Jewish athlete; this achieved, the Games could proceed. So, bizarrely, the German and American Olympic authorities became allies.

The American press did not surrender quite so easily, several papers arguing that Helene had been forced to appear for Germany out of consideration for her family; had she refused to fence, her mother and brothers could have ended up in a concentration camp.

Helene did not emerge unscathed. The journalist Georg Bernhard called her "Goebbels's little heifer."[6] Much later, after the Games were over, in a radio talk broadcast all over the United States, Germany's leading novelist, Thomas Mann—who had narrowly eluded arrest in 1933, fleeing first to Switzerland and finally to the sanctuary of Southern California—publicly upbraided Helene for throwing her mask in with the Nazis. Instead, he declared, she should have used her position to warn the world of the dangers of Hitler's Germany. But in truth, as 1935 drew to a close, the heat went out of the Olympic debate—it had gone on too long, with too many equivocations on all sides. On February 13 Helene sailed to her homeland on the German liner *Bremen*. Upon landing, after an absence of four years, she told a reporter, "I've always intended going back. Once you've been in the Games you will understand. It's a tremendous experience. And besides, I want a chance to win back that championship I lost in Los Angeles."

Helene was the only Jewish athlete to represent Germany at the summer Games. In the winter Olympics, held in the Bavarian Alps that February, there had been another contestant with one Jewish parent, Rudi Ball, on the German ice hockey team; but this was hardly noticed by the world's press, or even in Germany, where only one family in five took a newspaper. What, however, of Gretel Bergmann, the high jumper, who also had publicly been told by the authorities that she would be part of the German team? Her story makes an interesting contrast to Helene's.

Born of Jewish parents, Bergmann had been accepted into the University of Berlin when, in 1934, her admission was withdrawn. She left for England to further her education and within the year won the British women's high-jump championship. She was then told that the Nazis wanted her to return home to try out for the national team. She duly did, only to find "it was a charade. The handful of Jewish track and field athletes were not allowed to be in the German Athletic Association because we were Jews, and that's where the best training and competition existed. We were forced to train in potato fields."[7] Even so, on June 30, 1936, just one month before the Olympics, she was permitted to jump at the last major Olympic trial and won easily.

"I remember all the Nazi flags and official saluting and I jumped like a fiend," she said. "I always did my best when I was angry. I never jumped better." Her winning jump of five feet, three inches (1.6 meters) equaled the German record.*

On July 16 Bergmann received a letter from the German Olympic Committee informing her that she was not after all to be included in the team: "obviously your performance did not qualify . . . looking back on your recent performances, you could not possibly have expected to be chosen." When the high jump event was finally held at the Games, the winning leap was five feet, three inches, the same as Bergmann's at the trials. But the Nazis knew what they were doing: the letter had been timed to arrive the day after the American team had set sail from New York—positive proof that they would not now pull out.

Bergmann never met Helene Mayer and feels that the Nazis allowed her to compete because she was not "100 percent Jewish" and could be presented, however inaccurately, as an Aryan sportswoman—and because fencing was hidden away in a side stadium, not, like the track and field events, performed in the main arena in front of huge crowds. "I believe that the Nazis knew as early as 1934 just what they were going to do in 1936."

In 1937 Bergmann settled in New York. Within two years she was American high-jump champion. In 2002, aged eighty-seven, she was living in Queens. I went to visit her and was introduced to her ninety-year-old husband, also a Jewish athlete (a middle-distance runner). She showed me her many trophies and recaptured the years of anger and yearning. "The thought that I might have to represent Nazi Germany sickened me, yet I desperately wanted the chance to compete. But my motivation was different from any other athlete and not at all compatible with the Olympic ideals. I wanted to show what a Jew could do—to use my talent as a weapon against Nazi ideology."

Helene had no such agenda. Although to outside eyes she was an ideal selection, a reigning world champion, she had no wish to be tagged a "Jewish athlete." She didn't have anything against Jews; she just didn't *feel* Jewish—she felt "like a German." As she later told an American friend, "I

---

* Something of the Nazi ambition to come out on top at the Berlin Games can be seen in Bergmann's story of her roommate at several athletic meets: "She never used to undress in front of me and I'm sure she never got in the shower at all. I remember thinking she was weird." The girl, Dora Ratjen, was a fellow high jumper in more than one sense. After the war she reemerged as Hermann Ratjen, a waiter in Bremen; the athlete had been told to masquerade as a woman in order to win medals for Germany.

never knew I was a Jew until the NSVD said I was, and now I don't give a shit."[8]

During her months back in Germany, she lived among a protective coterie of friends and family and spent all the time she could training—not in Offenbach, whose club had expelled her, but at a salle in Königstein, near Frankfurt. There were training camps too, one in the north, then another in the south of Germany, with Hungarian and French coaches on supply, but Helene dubbed them "ghastly" and commissioned extra lessons from an Italian coach, Francesco Tagliabo. Her longtime teammate Erwin Casmir was now responsible for organizing the German fencing effort. "Helene Mayer's ability was not even a question," he recorded. "Nevertheless I had to inform myself about her present strength in fencing because we knew little about that." Come the trials, "she qualified as top of all those who entered and nothing stood in her way after that."

A reception was held for the team in Berlin, where Helene shook hands with Hitler: as with other athletes who were introduced to him, no

At the Olympic Village, 1936. Helene kept this intimate portrait in her scrapbook of the Games.

words were exchanged. Then came the march at the opening—4,000 athletes from fifty nations, with 100,000 people crowded into a stadium intended for 80,000, where Helene stood out as the tallest woman on her team. Then, at last the competition.

On August 5 *The New York Times* reviewed the film *Road to Glory*, scripted by William Faulkner. That same day the women's foil was contested in Berlin—a nice coincidence. Helene outshone her fellow team members, Hedwig Hass and Olga Oelkers, fighting her way without difficulty through the other forty-four competitors to the eight-woman final. The amphitheater where the competition was held was packed—unusual for a fencing event: the controversy surrounding Helene's inclusion had led to an expectant and partisan audience.

It soon became clear that the gold medal lay between three fencers: Ellen Preis, the reigning Olympic champion, who would go on to capture the world title in 1947 and 1949; a young Jewish Hungarian, Ilona Schacherer-Elek, delicate and stylish (off the piste she would promenade with a long cigarette holder at her lips) who had won the European title in 1934 and 1935 (when Helene had not competed) and who would win again in 1948 and 1951; and Helene herself, already a three-time champion. The 1936 final, even without its attendant dramas, brought together three of the finest women fencers of all time.*

The system then for deciding the gold medal was confounding. As was customary, the eight finalists were to fence the others in the pool, in three fights each for the best of nine hits (unless time ran out, as it would prove to do). Individual touches were then added up to decide the winner. Sure

---

* It is worth putting these three into the context of other champions, past and future. No woman before them achieved what they did; but since then there have been some fine champions. The Soviet Union produced a crop of notable foilists in the 1960s and 1970s, including Valentina Sidorova and Elena Belova; Germany has two three-time champions in Cornelia Hanisch and Anna Fechtel. Perhaps most remarkable of all is the Hungarian Ildiko Rejto, world champion in 1963 and Olympic champion in 1964, who was born both paralyzed and profoundly deaf. (Her early years were spent in a wheelchair until, aged fourteen, one day she stood and could soon walk.) None, though, so dominated their opponents as Elek or Mayer did, while Preiss's eighteen-year span at world-champion level speaks for itself.

When Rejto finally married, it was too late to bear children. Her husband's brother, however, had a family of five, and his wife was expecting a sixth. Rejto suggested to her husband that he ask his brother if they could adopt the new child. His brother agreed, and the newborn son was handed over. Shortly after, Rejto complained to her husband that it was not good for a child to be brought up on its own, without siblings. Again her brother- and sister-in-law were approached, and again they complied. Rejto and her husband are now part of a happy family of four.

enough, it emerged that the gold medal would go to one of the three favorites; but which one? As Adrianne Blue recounts in her book *Faster, Higher, Further:*

> Tension was high. The crowd was warned to be silent. There was no sound as Mayer, who towered over Elek, lunged at her in the first of their encounters. Ilona Elek was small but quick, a left-hander. She had none of Mayer's classic style, and she had a shorter reach but she was an excellent strategist.[9]*

The crowd was willing her to lose, but Elek fought on, winning their three bouts, 3–2, 4–4, and 5–4. But only time would tell who would eventually be Olympic champion. Mayer went on to beat all her other opponents including every Aryan she faced. She must, it seemed, be ahead on points.

Now came the crucial encounter of the finals: Mayer versus Preis, her tormentor in Los Angeles. To pick up Mandell's account, here was "perhaps the most dramatic fencing match of the age. . . . In an atmosphere so tense that the crowded spectators were almost too choked to express empathetic satisfaction or dismay, the two great athletes lunged stormily or dodged with uncanny agility." Incredibly, the match ended in a draw: 2–2, 3–3, 4–4. The judges hurriedly added up all the finalists' hits: a Jew had indeed taken the gold medal, but it was the Hungarian, Elek, by a single hit over Mayer; Preis had the bronze. One of Helene's friends on the German team, Doris Runzheimer, a track athlete, was watching and later wrote, "There were four international judges at the last crucial match. Dubious decisions were made." Others present, more objective, thought the judging fair.

Hours later the three medalists stood on the winners' rostrum in the main Olympic stadium, medallions around their necks, laurel wreaths in their hair. In the photograph cabled around the world, Elek and Preis are at attention, Elek holding in her left arm one of the oak saplings given to every victor at the Games. Helene is standing at attention too, but her right arm is extended in a stiff Nazi salute.

The gesture seemed a clear affirmation of Hitler's power, a pledge of

---

* In *The Nazi Olympics* Richard Mandell makes an intriguing comment: "In their match early in the finals the young Hungarian perceived her opponent's weakness. By means of irritating affectations, she succeeded in making Mayer nervous."[10]

A crowd of 100,000 stands to attention for the Hungarian National Anthem,
while each of the three medalists wears an olive-branch coronet.
And Helene Mayor salutes the Führer.

allegiance to the Third Reich and all it stood for. All Germans who
mounted the podium were required to make it. According to Susan D.
Bachrach of the U.S. Holocaust Memorial Museum, "the film footage of
this moment shows Mayer hesitating awkwardly as she gave the salute."[11]
Perhaps. Would there have been any real danger to her or her family had
she kept her arm by her side? Would, say, Gretel Bergmann have given the
Nazi salute? "I ask myself that question every day of my life," Bergmann
herself says. "I don't know the answer. I might be dead now. There was a
terrible climate of unimaginable fear in Germany, and very few heroes."

After the ceremony, Reinhold Heydrich, who had closely followed all
the fencing events and who knew the Mayer family through university fraternity meetings with Eugen, came up to Helene and said in a voice loud
enough to carry to one of her coaches, who passed on the story, "You Jewish c***. You've lost us the gold medal." Helene replied, "I am really very
sorry, but you're a fencer yourself and know that some days you win, some
days you lose. Today I lost. *Auf Wiedersehen.*" A few days later she left for
America on the *Heidelberg.*

Helene had been in Germany for six months. Back in the haven of
Mills, she picked up the threads of her American life. By September 22 the
Mills College Weekly was featuring a long interview with the college's "am-

bassador" to the Olympics. Everything Helene told the paper was painfully superficial and bland, almost a Nazi propaganda sheet: "Helene returned with several good-looking suits, sports outfits, and fencing costumes which the German government generously gave to its athletes. In addition she brought back beautiful scarves and pins given her by the German government and several fine leather bags. To quote Helene, she 'collected more stuff this year than ever before.'"

The following month, Helene gave a talk to the student body, during which she referred casually to Hitler as "a cute little man." There was no irony in her words: one of her audience recalls even today the shock of hearing her talk in such terms. Why did she deliberately block the full range of what she had experienced? Did she still believe that her German citizenship would be returned to her? (It never was.) In the principal account of Helene's life—by a fellow Californian, Milly Mogulof—the author invokes "victimology theory," according to which, as situations worsen, victims have diminished capacity to acknowledge their enemy. Mogulof also quotes Primo Levi on how victims are "tempted or teased into becoming accomplices in the atrocities committed against them . . . a corrosive process against moral values and moral choices."

It is possible to view Helene Mayer in this way, but it may be too kind. Above all, she wanted to be accepted as a good German and to triumph as the great fencer she knew she was. In 1937 she competed again for Germany in the world championships in Paris, found herself in the last eight along with seven of the Berlin finalists, and triumphantly took first place, Elek landing the silver medal and Preis once again the bronze. It was Helene's last appearance at a world or Olympic championship, but perhaps she felt she had proved her point.

In 1938 the Gestapo went to Helene's mother's house and threatened her, but Helene made representations and the threats were not repeated. During the 1936 Games Helene had also made some attempts to get Eugen to Peru, but nothing came of it and he ended up, with his brother Ludwig, doing national service—not in the Wehrmacht but in the Organization TODT, involved in sending drafted workers to the mines. Eugen's widow Erica told me that Königstein seemed like "a forgotten village" for much of the war, but in 1945 both brothers fled their posts and hid out in the Black Forest until Germany surrendered. "We should have listened to Helene," Eugen concluded.[12] Their uncle Georg August Mayer had died in Theresienstadt camp in 1942.

When she realized there was no future for her in Germany, Helene set about making California her permanent home, settling into a three-room cottage near the Mills campus with her trophies, books, mementos, and photographs, including the photo of Hitler shaking her hand at the 1936 Games. She continued to speak German, to eat German food, to sing German songs; but in 1940 she became an American citizen. On top of her teaching responsibilities she was made a professor of political science at the City College of San Francisco. She cofounded a fencing club in San Francisco, then, during the war, helped teach German to American servicemen: one of the tasks she set them was to learn a map of Berlin by heart. In 1946, after winning the U.S. title for the eighth time, she considered training for the 1948 Games, but in the 1947 U.S. championships she lost a bout marked by doubtful decisions to an inspired local fencer, Helena Dow (wife of Warren Dow), and had to accept second place. This seems to have had a far greater effect on her than a minor setback should have, for thereafter she gave up serious competition. It is difficult to see how she could have envisaged herself at the Olympics again; not until 1964 were athletes who had represented one country allowed to compete for another, and Helene could hardly have fenced for Germany as an American citizen. But she must have looked on enviously the following year in London as Elek took her second gold medal; Preiss, yet again, was third.

It was in 1948 that Helene first began experiencing sudden pain, weakness, and fatigue—the initial symptoms of the breast cancer that would kill her. In February 1952 she took leave of absence without pay from her work to return to Germany for a "recuperative period." Three months later, in May, she married a "quintessentially Bavarian" aristocrat, Baron Erwin von Sonnenburg, an old family friend, and settled down to live with him in Germany. She had had several lovers in America and a number of proposals of marriage, but this dignified engineer was the first, she said, who came up to her standards.

The 1952 Olympics were held in Helsinki. Germany was allowed to reenter, having been banned from the London Games. Ilona Elek, now forty-five—three years older than Helene—seemed on her way to a third gold when she was defeated 3-4 by the eventual winner, an Italian. Helene followed the Games keenly and wrote to her old fencing friends for gossip and details of the championships. Following a series of operations, she thought that she had beaten her breast cancer, but the disease had metastasized into her spine and the end came quickly. She died on October 10, 1953, two months short of her forty-third birthday and less than a year and a half after her marriage. Throughout these years she never spoke publicly about the 1936 Games, and even close friends have only insubstantial memories of occasional expressions of regret.*

What would have happened had Helene Mayer refused to allow herself to be the "token Jew" and not negotiated with the Nazis? Might she, one individual, actually have been able to change the course of events? As Milly Mogulof formulates the issue, "Had she demurred . . . the entire Olympic enterprise might have been threatened, leaving the planners in an awkward situation. Would they have scurried about in an unseemly, time-consuming search to find another 'suitable' German-Jewish athlete? Faced with a mounting dilemma, the United States as a major player and other Western democracies might have bowed out of the Games." That is pitching it high; but it is just possible.

What of Helene's own decision? How much were her actions motivated by fear of reprisals against her family? The evidence suggests very little, although it was undoubtedly a factor. Her dogged adherence to Germanness and her ambitions as a fencer seem greater elements. She was probably the greatest woman foilist ever; but she was the wrong person for the times and for the exceptional choices she was forced to make.

In 1968, in the run-up to West Germany hosting the Olympic Games, its post office issued a series of special Olympic stamps. These portrayed, among others, Pierre de Coubertin and also Carl Diem, the sports educator who had planned much of the 1936 Games. Only one woman athlete was honored with a stamp: Helene Mayer, "Blond Hee."

---

* I was part of the British team at the Munich Games in 1972 when the Arab terrorist assault on the Olympic Village ended in a shoot-out in which eleven Israeli athletes, a West German policeman, and five terrorists were killed. There was much talk in the world's press about calling off the Games as a mark of respect for the murdered Israelis. I remember writing to the London *Times*, arguing that sportsmen were neither stupid nor coldhearted but that it was right for the Games to continue. I still believe it. Eighteen years later, the Soviet Union invaded Afghanistan and Jimmy Carter and Margaret Thatcher decided to boycott the Moscow Olympics. Again (letter-writing to newspapers being an occupational disease for certain kinds of Englishmen) *The Times* printed a letter I sent them arguing that such a boycott was inappropriate: if selected, I intended to go. As the year went on, however, I met friends from Eastern Europe, and without exception they said they hoped Western athletes would stand up to the Soviets and not take part. In the end the weight of the moral argument was too much: weeks before we were due to fly out, I elected not to go. But I well remember the agonized to-ing and fro-ing I went through trying to make up my mind, over issues far less onerous than Mayer's.

CHAPTER 16

The Champions

> To become a champion is not so very difficult. What is
> extremely difficult is to remain one.
>
> —ALDO NADI, *On Fencing*

> In swordmanship, always train and discipline yourself,
> But don't show it—hide it, be modest about it. . . .
>
> —YAGYU MUNEYOSHI (1529–1606)

*A*T THE SYDNEY GAMES IN 2000 THE OFFICIAL FENCING PRO-
gram asked, "Which nation will be first in history to win 100 Olympic
medals—France or Italy?" These two started the Olympics with 99 and 95
medals respectively, tallies far outstripping their nearest competitors.
France reached its century first, when Hugues Obry won the individual silver in the épée, and by the end of the Games had gathered another 5, for a
total of 105 (36 gold, 37 silver, 32 bronze), and Italy had just reached three
figures (40–35–25); but the rivalry had begun long before the advent of the
modern Olympics and showed itself most intensely at foil.

With Paris setting the agenda, fencing in France has always managed
to remain remarkably homogeneous. In 1877, the Ministry of War published *Manuel d'escrime,* a handbook that provided the foundation for its
successor, the *Règlement d'escrime* of 1908, which became the bible of
French fencing. In Italy there was no such unity: competing schools—in
Naples, Milan, Livorno, Bologna, and Florence—bitterly disputed rules
and techniques.*

---

* It would take—and has taken—separate treatises to describe the main differences between the French and Italian schools, but a few pointers may be useful.

　Italian foils and épées had as their principal characteristic the crossbar, a direct de-
scendant of the Spanish sword, but with the ends cut down so that they did not pass
beyond the edges of the guard. In the old days the extended crossbar was used to snag
an opponent's sword against one's bar and blade, allowing the fencer to close the distance and attack with his "free" hand—which often held another weapon. The purpose

Sometime in the early 1870s, the new Italian government, having recently unified the country and keen to reestablish its place among the great nations of the world, decided as part of this policy to codify its fencing practices. In 1882, the Neapolitan-Sicilian masters persuaded the Ministry of War to hold a competition for the best fencing treatise. The winning entry would then be adopted, as had been its counterpart in France, for use throughout the army—an oblique tactic for breaking northern control over military fencing. The southern faction believed their northern and more cosmopolitan rivals to be contaminated by foreign influence and saw themselves as custodians of a "pure" system of Italian swordplay. The northern master they singled out for particular criticism was Giuseppe Radaelli, whose influential manual struck at fencing's historically defensive character by encouraging counterattacks rather than parries.

Ten works were shortlisted, including Radaelli's. The judges began their deliberations on November 15, 1883, the final choice falling between Radaelli and a Neapolitan, Masaniello Parise, whose grandfather and father were fencing masters (his grandfather Raffaele had insisted that his bride-to-be learn to fence before their wedding could take place and made sure their five sons learned too). While the commission deliberated, Parise's supporters vigorously attacked Radaelli, claiming that he advocated cuts from the elbow, that his pupils hit too heavily, and that his system encouraged counterattacks rather than parries—influenced by Radaelli's notorious saying "The parry does not exist."

In the end, Parise won, his victory prompting the government to

---

of reducing the crossbar was to give greater strength both to parries and to attacks on the opponent's blade.

The French eliminated the crossbar completely when they discovered that skillful use of the fingers could compensate for and surpass the use of the wrist. The Italians would bind the pommel of their foil to the wrist, making finger-play almost impossible. In an Italian *en garde* the arm would be extended, as in the old Spanish style, bending only in order to parry. At the outset, the French called for the arm to be held no more than three inches from the body, the elbow bent, the weapon pointed at the opponent's eyes. The legs were also positioned slightly differently, and the two countries developed different systems of parries. The Italians seldom made attacks with a simple lunge, but always began by advancing and "taking" (that is, hitting or otherwise controlling) the blade, the movement being initiated from outside lunging distance and often completed by a coupé (passing *over* the opposing blade). The stiffness of the arm, another legacy of the Spanish school, made force an essential component.

The French advocated deep, long lunges, and advancing only to get close enough for an attack. Actions on the blade were unusual. Against Italians, the stop-thrust was often used, but rarely against fellow Frenchmen.

establish the Scuola Magistrale, an academy of the sword for masters in Rome, with the thirty-four-year-old Neapolitan as its dean. Parise quickly dispatched cadres of masters to all parts of Europe and the Levant to study every type of fencing, and incorporated the best of their reports into his blueprint for how the discipline should be taught. He would remain dean until his death at the age of sixty-one, and in that time oversaw the training of some of Italy's greatest masters: Italo Santelli (graduated 1889), Arturo Gazzera (1893), and Francesco Tagliabo (1897)—the last two of whom would later coach Helene Mayer. But it was the earliest graduate of them all, Agesilao Greco (1887), who with his brother and nephew would have the most profound effect on Italian swordplay.

Agesilao's father was a Sicilian nobleman who had fought for Garibaldi—and indeed every romantic cause that he could find. He was badly wounded in one of the battles for independence against Austria and tossed into a mass grave. Left for dead, he remained there for an entire night before fighting his way out. This will to survival he passed down to his two sons, Agesilao and Aurelio, and to their cousin Enzo.

Aurelio had wanted to be a painter, but his father dictated otherwise, and the chastened fifteen-year-old entered an international foil tournament at Bergamo: in a field of 180, he took first prize for fencing style as well as winning the competition itself. In 1902, in a competition for professionals in Turin attracting 300 contestants, he won the foil without receiving a single hit—one of the exceptional achievements in fencing history. His successes grew until in 1922 he capped his career in a public contest in all three weapons against the champion of Rome, winning 20–8 at saber, 20–2 at foil, and 20–0 at épée. Thereafter he devoted himself to teaching, becoming a leading manager, administrator, and master, and ultimately creating the Italian Federation of Fencing. He and Agesilao between them wrote seven books, covering all three weapons.

Enzo was less strong than his uncles as a competitive fencer, but became one of the great fight arrangers, working on such films as *Cleopatra*, *Ben Hur*, *El Cid*, *William Tell*, and Visconti's *The Innocent* and with actors such as Charlton Heston, Errol Flynn, Richard Burton, and Claudia Cardinale. He would quote a famous fencing epigram, "Every sword is like a small bird. Hold it too tightly and it will suffocate. Too lightly, and it will fly away." The line would eventually be given to the fencing master in *Scaramouche*. Even Visconti gave Enzo a free hand over fight scenes, except when he suggested that a duel scene between two women in a Gina Lollobrigida vehicle be fought with the actresses stripped to the waist.

*In 1922 Aurelio Greco took on the Italian champion Candido Sassone in what
journalists dubbed "the duel of the century," and which was even filmed.
It lasted six months, over seven different venues, and ended with Sassone's defeat.
The whole argument arose from a difference of opinion about fencing theory.*

In the 1880s, matches and competitions—nearly all fought in the open
air—were formal, academic affairs, where the scoring of hits was based on
the classicism of the performance and whether the touch in question
would have delivered a mortal wound, not simply on whether a hit had
arrived.* This of course left wide room for interpretation, depending on
the particular school of the fencer and jury. A French jury would favor a

---

* An Italian rulebook on etiquette in the salle runs: "Article 2: On entering, as on leaving, it is necessary to shake hands with everybody in the room; Article 5: It is absolutely obligatory every time when one is hit to announce the touch, saying "*Toccato*";
Article 6: if a fencer is by chance disarmed, the other, regardless of his social rank,
must pick up the weapon and hand it to his adversary by the guard, in order to avoid
even the idea of haughtiness."[1]

Frenchman, an Italian jury one of its own; after one team event in 1895 an Italian judge claimed that the Italian fencers had won by 540 hits to 36. As a result, matches frequently degenerated, with challenges being issued whenever a fencer felt that his reputation had been impugned. Regular duelists despised sporting matches.

Nonetheless, Agesilao Greco was regularly called on for more legitimate tests of his mettle. On June 17, 1889, he led a four-man team in one of the first encounters between the Scuola Magistrale and leading French masters. The contest was held in the banquet hall of the Grand Hotel in Paris, but even so the French found themselves at a disadvantage, confronted with a system based chiefly on dueling technique, and lost heavily. *Le Figaro* observed, "*Above all,* the purpose of fencing to Italian fencers is combat; and they seek to attain their goal with all the resources they have available; their aim is to hit and not be hit. . . . We, instead, admire, *above all,* aesthetic bouts."[2]

Greco's fencing may not have been aesthetic, but it was effective. In the same paper the noted teacher Arsène Vigeant acclaimed him as "a young master with a great future, gifted with marvelous power and originality in tactical approach," while *Il Secolo* of Milan described Greco as "the hero of the evening." *Evénement,* however, took a different view, declaring that "The Roman masters have not yet abandoned theatrical postures." The "useless movement and contortions, and the continuous beating of the adversary's blade, which they search for systematically in monotonous fashion. . . . After Saturday's competition opinions were mixed: some amateur foilsmen admired the Italian fencers, but the majority, while recognizing great qualities in the Italians, nevertheless saw their fencing as trickery." This became the standard criticism of the Greco school: it was theatrical and relied on deception rather than technique—Neapolitans were always trying to trick you.*

In 1903 Agesilao fenced the great French champion Lucien Mérignac in Buenos Aires before an audience of over four thousand. The following year, again in Buenos Aires, he fought a draw against another powerful Parisian, Alphonse Kirchoffer. The Frenchman was short and awkward, and his unclassical style so upset Greco that he twice protested to the jury about his

---

* Agesilao had his rivals even in Italy, chief among them Eugenio Pini from Livorno, who could be just as short-tempered. When he fought Rue "The Invincible," the French master who, hit twice in succession, failed to acknowledge being hit as etiquette dictated, Pini pulled the button from his foil and with his next attack ripped open Rue's jacket. He then tore off his mask and shouted, "I suppose *that one* didn't arrive either?"[3]

Agesilao Greco was always looking for an excuse to duel. He was in a café in Naples when another customer started throwing snail shells at two girls seated nearby. By the third shell Agesilao had issued a challenge in defense of the girls' honor: the resultant duel lasted nearly four hours.

opponent's roughhouse tactics; by the bout's end opinion was divided on who had landed the most hits. Following the match a report appeared in *La Nación* lauding Kirchoffer. Greco was incensed and accused his opponent of deliberately attacking low. Kirchoffer denied the charge and departed for Montevideo. Greco claimed that the Frenchman had fled the country to avoid a rematch. When Kirchoffer refused to fight again, the Sicilian challenged him to a duel; but on this occasion nothing materialized. Seven years later, learning that Kirchoffer's entire right foot and part of his left had had to be amputated, he immediately volunteered for the benefit gala. The event drew an audience of eight thousand, including the prime minister of France, Aristide Briand, and was a showpiece for the best fencers of Italy and France. The Italian side included a seventeen-year-old Livornese: Nedo Nadi.

THUS WE COME TO THE THIRD GREAT ITALIAN FENCING FAMILY: Nedo, his father, Beppe, and his younger brother, Aldo. Their story encompasses the reflowering of fencing in the north of Italy; the transition from professional fencing as the highest form of swordplay to international championships, where amateurs reigned supreme; and the extraordinary Nadi family itself, with Nedo and Aldo ranking among the half-dozen greatest fencers the sport has seen.

It is hard to say why the northern school flourished after the Scuola Magistrale had been created in Rome, or why Livorno should have become so important. The city had been built by the Medici as a free port for international trade and consequently became a staging post for immigrants, where fencing masters could prosper. By the end of the nineteenth century few noble families remained, and a thriving mercantile class had taken their place. Luigi Barbasetti says in his classic book on foil fencing, *La Scherma di Spada*, that for all the enthusiasm for the sport in

Nedo, Beppe, and Aldo Nadi in Livorno, 1933. "Nedo will defeat everybody," predicted Beppe, "and when he tires of being number one he will pass the title on to Aldo." He was not far wrong.

Naples, Sicily, and Rome the standard was higher in Livorno because northerners had, as he puts it, a more calculating disposition.[4]

Whatever accounted for Livorno's success, Beppe Nadi was its most famous master. His father was chief of the fire department, and Beppe drifted into the same line of work. His father was also a coach at the Academy of Via Ernesto Rossi, where Beppe himself was soon fencing. In 1892 he started his own club, Circolo Fides Livorno—"Circolo" because it suggested a more friendly environment than the more usual "salle," and "Fides" from the city motto, which proclaimed its citizens' loyalty to the Medicis. The fencing room was minuscule, and students were called upon to pay just one lira a month. Although the city had maintained a central generator since 1888, there was no electricity: members had to practice by candlelight. The neighborhood was filled with such establishments as "The House of Appointments" or, as it was officially known, "The House of Tolerance." Four years later Nadi moved to a more salubrious area with electric light—though still only a single room to fence in plus a couple of showerless locker rooms. At first he did not allow women to join the club; when various young actresses came to fence, he gave them lessons in secret. They would change in his small master's closet, which was separated from the main changing room by a single door. Students used to peek at them through holes in the door as they undressed—"It had more holes in it than a Gruyère cheese," one recalled.

Beppe had been a good fencer. In 1893 he so dominated a competition in Hungary that he was invited to stay on and coach there. "I am from Livorno," he replied, "and in Livorno I stay." Nedo was born in June of that year, Aldo six years later. Beppe's two sons would become both his victims and his obsession. Nedo was the first to be subjugated. "I will make him the strongest fencer in the world," his father told his friends. "Nedo will defeat everybody, and when he tires of being number one he will pass the title on to Aldo." Nedo had his first lesson at the age of six and took two lessons a day thereafter, morning and evening, and finally three. For his first few months he was permitted to make a set number of moves, then for two years he was forbidden to free-fence with the other boys; he could only practice, and if he made a mistake or did not complete an action to his parent's satisfaction, he would be struck hard on the legs with his father's blade.[5]

Nedo remained under strict supervision even outside his lessons. He was not allowed to fence anyone at the club other than the three or four top members, so that he would fight only those of a standard he might meet in international competition. He spent his whole childhood fencing—few friends, no games, no forms of escape. At the age of twelve he won the Italian foil championship. Two years later he was desperate to fence in the 1908 Olympics, but his father told him he was too young. In 1909 he traveled to a prestigious international tournament in Vienna, where he won in all three weapons with ease. "We have just seen fencing's Mozart," reported a Viennese newspaper. But Beppe wanted his son to concentrate on foil and saber, telling Nedo that épée was "the prostitution of fencing." The champion-in-waiting was beginning to rebel, however, and would sneak off to fence the forbidden weapon with a friend. Otherwise his progress continued, and within two years he was selected for the Stockholm Olympics.

He traveled there by train, second class—the Italian government was too preoccupied with its war in Libya to find money for sportsmen—and arrived suffering from bronchitis, with his foil event the very next day. Nedo's look of youthful innocence contrasted with his aggressive style on the piste, and the crowd took to him, applauding every hit he made and anointing him its favorite. Never seriously challenged, he swept to the gold medal. By the time of the saber event he was exhausted and came in only fifth. He did not compete at épée because of an ear infection. Beppe was delighted with his son's performance and threw a huge party for his return. The menu read: Olympic soup; boiled fish with Swedish salsa; vegetables "on the strip"; veal roasted in foil; fencers' salad; cookies "gold medal"; tricolor fruit; and "July 8" coffee—the day of Nedo's victory.

The following year Nedo went to Bucharest. The Romanian capital, eager to ape Paris, gloried in receiving the Olympic champion of "France's sport." Prince Carol, himself a fencer, introduced Nedo to his parents, Queen Marie and King Ferdinand, who inducted the nineteen-year-old into court society, then effectively kidnapped him, urging him to stay in Bucharest to give their son lessons. After twelve days, Nedo begged his father to find some urgent excuse to recall him to Livorno. The Romanian king kept up his interest in Nedo, sending the young lieutenant food parcels and "military advice" throughout the First World War. Nedo was suitably embarrassed, and every time he moved to a different unit had to explain his "Bucharest connection." The war made a great impression on him. In one engagement, near Venice, Nedo left a village unprotected while he and his troops went to blow up a nearby bridge. The village was attacked, and many of its inhabitants killed. This tragedy, and the death of several friends, left him melancholic and reflective. When he and his wife would stay at home listening to classical music, Aldo would scoff at them as "those two poor *fessi* [fools]."

FOR MOST OF THE NINETEENTH CENTURY NATIONAL CHAMPIONSHIPS at any sport, let alone international competitions, were simply inconceivable. When young men competed with each other it was on the battlefield. Outside the British Isles (the English were known to be a sports-crazed people, better left alone), there was minimal literature on sport; what little could be found was about riding, boxing, maybe single-stick fighting. But by the final quarter of the century a new atmosphere was detectable, and sports of all kinds came to be seen as instruments of national pride and personal development. Partly this was a consequence of the age of steam and the telegraph; international consituencies of specialized activities could keep in touch with one another, and with communication came uniform standards of excellence. A new world of sporting contacts had come into being.

Fencing was slow to respond to these changes. In November 1913 the Fédération Internationale d'Escrime was founded at the Automobile Club in Paris. Eventually the first European individual tournament—at épée—was held, also in Paris, in 1921. The following year a saber championship was added, and eight years later individual championships, with a complete program of team and individual events for men in each of the three weapons but offering women only an individual foil championship. A European women's team event was held from 1932 on but did not become part of the Olympics until 1960.

One reason for this slow development was the acrimony between France and Italy. In 1912 the French stormed out of the Olympic foil event when their proposal that the upper arm be included as part of the target was rejected, leaving the way open for Nedo's victory. Within hours an Italian proposal, that the length of the épée blade be extended, was likewise rejected, and it was the Italians' turn to walk out.

Fencers in other countries began to wonder if all nations could ever agree to a tournament in which everyone could participate. The 1916 Olympics, which were, ironically, to have been held in Berlin, were a casualty of the Great War, and until 1919 there was no official Franco-Italian encounter. That year the French and the Italians participated in the Inter-Allied Military Games. Nedo and Aldo, as officers in the Italian armed forces, both competed, Nedo coming first in foil and Aldo third in foil, second in saber, and fifth in épée. The following year saw the Antwerp Olympics and Nedo's five gold medals. Nedo's main rival was Lucien Gaudin, who the year before war broke out had defeated him at a key encounter in Spain. Gaudin was in his prime and considered unbeatable at foil; but first came the team event. "After Italy and France had defeated all other nations easily," Aldo explains in his autobiography, "they were to meet for the championship. As a rule, the captains of the teams meet in the opening bout, but Nedo, partly because he feared Gaudin like the plague, partly because he knew that I didn't care one way or the other when I fenced him, put me down first on the team order so that the match started with Gaudin and me. Further, Nedo realized that if I succeeded in defeating the French captain, the victory would give our team a tremendous shot in the arm. It worked perfectly. Officially I defeated the so far invincible (or so he claimed) Gaudin three to one."[6]

Gaudin, possibly demoralized, scratched from the individual events, saying he had hurt his foot in a match against the United States. The Nadis had the field to themselves, and Nedo failed to take all six gold medals on offer only because he decided not to fence in the individual épée, citing exhaustion: he had been competing sometimes eighteen hours a day for seven days in a row.

Following the Games, Nedo turned professional. After the months of intimidation by Blackshirts back home in Livorno and his meeting with Mussolini, he left for Argentina. His departure should have prompted his brother to step into his shoes. Aldo had certainly been groomed well enough. He had started to fence even younger than Nedo, at the age of four, in the blouse and short skirt worn by young children of both sexes at that time. By eleven he had won his first championships, open to all Italian fencers under eighteen, at both foil and saber. Nedo was his exemplar, but he also had to live in his shadow, and when Nedo had won saber gold in Antwerp and Aldo the silver it was generally understood that the younger Nadi had been under instructions to lose. Unsurprisingly, Aldo developed an all-consuming urge to outdo his brother. The two became estranged—although, whenever anybody criticized Nedo, Aldo was the first to defend him.

After Aldo's defeat of Gaudin in 1920, the stage was set for a return match. It eventually took place in Paris on January 30, 1922, before a crowd of seven thousand, some three thousand more having to be turned away. The best seats went for 100 francs and were resold on the black market for as much as 1,000—the equivalent of two weeks' income for an

American family then. Cabinet ministers in evening dress were out in force, and the press had come from all over Europe. But Aldo made a fatal mistake: keen to prove his superiority, he accepted the French request to count hits on the upper swordarm as valid. He lost 20–11, with more than half the Frenchman's touches, he later claimed, arriving in the conceded area. (Léon Bertrand later wrote that he had counted only five hits so awarded.) Other attacks by Nadi were ignored by the judges, some spectators recorded, even when he had to straighten his foil blade after the hit. Aldo was twenty-two, Gaudin thirty-five. Aldo tried repeatedly to entice his adversary into a third encounter, but Gaudin systematically refused. Eventually, in 1924, they fought an exhibition match in Florence, in a huge arena filled with fellow fencers, personalities from other sports, members of the European press, and other fans. No official score was kept, and each side claimed its champion the winner.

"Hundreds of experts had their paper and pencil out to count the touches," recalled an American fencer in the audience that night.

> The two great adversaries fenced superbly for about twenty minutes. . . . I can still feel the excitement, the enthusiasm of that evening. Toward the end, every Frenchman present was convinced that Gaudin had an edge of a touch or two; every Italian was ready to swear that Aldo was slightly ahead. They were superb and very evenly matched. Then the director [referee] asked for the last three touches . . . and Aldo had one of those superhuman moments. In quick succession, he scored all three touches against Gaudin, who called them in a loud voice as a tribute to the greatness of his opponent. After Florence, Gaudin stated: "No one will defeat Aldo Nadi in the next twenty years," and the prediction came true.[7]

Both fencers were amply paid for their appearance—although Aldo typically squandered his entire fee on the Monte Carlo gaming tables the following day and had to wire his father for the train fare back to Italy. Worse was to follow. The FIE, French-controlled, told Aldo that the fee he had taken made him a professional: he was no longer eligible for the Olympics. Gaudin suffered no such fate, as he gave his fee of 40,000 francs to his federation (which may or may not have repaid it in goods and services) and went on to win two gold medals in 1928. Neither Aldo nor Nedo ever fenced the French champion again. Gaudin died suddenly in

1934, at forty-eight—but for ten years he kept his distance, and much of his reputation.*

When Aldo was made a professional, he was just twenty-two. In the mid-1920s individual matches between top fencers were regarded as a step higher than international tournaments, Olympics included. These matches ranked among the foremost sporting events of Europe, with a system similar to world championship boxing: the two best men were set against each other, and the event was built up in the press. Public interest translated into huge crowds and considerable financial rewards for the promoters (and occasionally for the contestants). It was in such matches that Aldo excelled, and he was soon commanding extraordinary fees—as much as $50,000 for an evening's fencing—which enabled him to live in the most expensive hotels in Europe, enjoying the life of a playboy. A compulsive gambler, he thought nothing of making $15,000 from one event (for fifteen minutes of fencing), then blowing it all on a night at the gaming tables. After a succession of romantic conquests, in 1925 he married Ruby Malville, a Scotswoman descended, she claimed, from George III of England. Ruby was a society beauty who shared Aldo's love of good living. They flitted between Cannes, Nice, Deauville, and Biarritz, dined with the Aga Khan and Noël Coward, played chemin de fer with Winston Churchill, befriended Maurice Rostand (son of the author of *Cyrano de Bergerac*, with whom Aldo rather identified), and stayed up into the small hours drinking with Douglas Fairbanks, Sr. In Vienna in 1928 he was given the leading role in a Jean Renoir silent film, *The Tournament* or *Le Tornai dans la cité* ("*Allez-y, Aldo, faîtes votre scène!*" the great director would cry), and won admiring reviews in the French press.

During the next seven years Aldo won fifty-six international contests, defeating every opponent set before him. The French champion René Haussy later wrote, "Aldo Nadi is unquestionably the most difficult adver-

---

* While from 1921 on the world's fencers came together each non-Olympic year, no world title was at stake: no one thought of calling these championships anything other than "European," since the main fencing nations were all to be found in Europe. Then, in 1937, the competitions were rechristened "World Championships," and for a curious reason. At that time Italy, under Mussolini, was energetically pursuing sporting success for national prestige. Anyone who carried off an Olympic or world title received decorations and considerable privileges, such as free travel and free seats at state theaters. Italian fencers found that the European titles they won were not considered for such rewards, and mainly to oblige them the FIE—of which Italy was one of the most powerful members—accorded the European championships "world" status.

Paris, January 1922: Aldo (right) takes on the great French foilist Lucien Gaudin before a crowd of over seven thousand, with three thousand more being turned away. Aldo's accommodation of allowing upper arm hits as valid proved his undoing.

sary I have ever encountered," while Roger Ducret, an Olympic champion also among Aldo's victims, called him "the living sword, the phenomenon of fencing, the best man with all three weapons." Other eminent fencers spoke equally highly of him.

Then, between 1929 and 1931, Aldo, plagued by marital troubles, gave up fencing completely (a fact he omits in his autobiography) and settled in Florence. Shortly afterwards his marriage failed, and by November 1932 he was back on the exhibition circuit, beating the French épée champion in Paris 12–4. In 1934, after a convincing win over yet another French champion, the authoritative Italian *Sport d'Italia* wrote prophetically, "Will this latest victory of Aldo Nadi's mean . . . that our champion must stop fighting because there will be no one willing to take him on? Who would want to meet him again when his power and class literally expose to ridicule whoever faces him?" Another paper declared, "Not everyone is longing to face Aldo Nadi. For this great champion is anything but a diplomat. In front of an opponent he knows only this law: to beat, exceed, laminate, destroy, reduce to dust." By 1935 the French federation forbade its members to compete with him, believing that such bouts would hurt their careers. The supply of opponents had dried up, and the Great Depression had sounded the death knell of professional fencing competition. Aldo decided to call it a day.

WHAT HAD MADE ALDO SO SPECIAL? HE NEVER HAD HIS BROTHER'S strength and all-round technique. After losing to Gaudin in Paris, he decided that the aggressive attacks taught him by his father were not the answer and set out to create a style of his own. He practiced parrying at the very last moment, allowing the tip of his opponent's blade within an inch of his body—thus bringing his adversary all the closer for a counterattack. He aimed constantly to surprise. When an opponent started to advance, Nadi would not retreat, to preserve distance as others might, but went on the attack, to take advantage of the advancing fencer's slight loss of balance.

Throughout his life Aldo was always catching colds and fighting off pneumonia, and though six feet, two inches tall weighed only 130 pounds. Nedo could make strong, repeated attacks, each with equal force; Aldo could not. Given his limited stamina, he could not preserve a constant intensity throughout an entire bout, and so would relax, then suddenly summon his energy into an all-out attack. He would put particular pressure on his opponent toward the end of a bout, when both men were tiring and when his adversary might be losing concentration.

Further to fluster his opponents, he would attack not into their weak spots but into their best protected lines, forcing them to counterattack when they did not wish to. In a 1941 article, he wrote, "Napoleon said: 'The whole art of war consists in a well-thought-out defensive, together with a swift and bold offensive. . . . One must lead one's opponent to give battle under the most unfavorable conditions, then, when his last reserves are engaged, destroy him by a decisive attack . . . the dominating features of any successful campaign are energy and rapidity. . . . Energy, speed in analysis, decision and execution of a plan, boldness, these are the qualities of a good soldier.'" He did not need to add, of a good fencer too.[8]

Who was better, Aldo or Nedo? "They were both great champions, two perfect machines, both thoroughbreds," recalled the memorably named Bino Bini, one of their contemporaries. "It was Aldo's luck to have had Nedo, who taught him even more than their father." That is to sit on the fence; but it is difficult to compare them. For a start, the brothers were so different in character. Where Nedo had a faultless style, a superb competitive temperament, and great charm off the piste, Aldo was unpredictable, a daredevil fantast, vain, and contrary. In his early days in Livorno, fellow club members called him "Saber" because of his cutting tongue. He would shrug this off: "Life would be very dull without enemies." At the 1920 Olympics, he got into a fight with an Italian weight lifter, who advanced on him with a large stone in his hand. Aldo was carrying a small whip, which he flicked at his opponent, lacerating the man's arm so badly that he was unable to compete. He then went around boasting of his feat.

In 1935 Aldo left Italy for France but, finding no work, emigrated to the United States, teaching first in New York, then in Los Angeles. In 1943 he wrote his treatise on foil, a copy of which, with characteristic hubris, he sent to Bernard Shaw, who replied with a three-hundred-word letter and two photos, one with the caption "This is the only portrait of me in which I could pass as a fencer, which I never was." Twelve years later Aldo completed his autobiography, a well-written and vainglorious absurdity. Not published until 1995, long after his death, it evokes a lifestyle radically different from that of any other fencing champion.

From 1935 to 1943 Aldo taught in New York, in two large rooms on the third floor of the Savoy Plaza Hotel. Then his friend the beautician Elizabeth Arden opened a salle for him in her premises in the heart of Manhattan. He was still able to live, as he put it, "in a princely manner," going dancing with Dorothy Paley, the wife of William S. Paley, the head of CBS, and in due course remarried—to Rosemary, another Scot with an illustrious forebear (this time the warrior chieftain William Wallace). But the American fencing scene was totally different from that of Europe, and an older Aldo was no longer welcomed everywhere as a sporting phenomenon. "In their abysmal ignorance about fencing," he hissed, "my compatriots and Hollywood seem nearly always to prefer fourth-raters to me. . . . This, of course, while not remotely affecting my vanity, shows the obvious truth that here whatever ability I possess is completely wasted."[9]

Some months before the outbreak of war he sailed for Europe, hobnobbing with Tyrone Power and "my old friend" Charles Boyer. In Venice he met up again with Fairbanks, "who happened to be talking with Goebbels, Hitler's vitriolic minister of propaganda." Aldo may have been an elitist, but he was no Nazi. After Pearl Harbor he tried to enlist in the American army but failed the physical.

It was time to pursue a film career in earnest. According to his own account, Aldo had been offered an MGM contract by Louis B. Mayer at $300 a week, but his memoirs are full of proffered roles that never came to anything. He worked on *Frenchman's Creek* with Basil Rathbone, training the leading man, Arturo de Cordova—his "co-ordination, thank God, was good"—then, having taught foil to Walter Huston's wife when Huston came to Broadway to play Othello, he was put in charge of the swordfights in the opening act. And so it went on. Lillian Gish "fell in love with fencing at first sight. She took several lessons and I must say she was quite proficient at it." He tried to sell a top nightclub act with "a (very) struggling actor named Cornel Wilde," who was "anything but dependable"; Rosemary had to stand in for him.

He was offered a part by Errol Flynn in *The Adventures of Don Juan*, doubling for him in the dueling scenes, but when Flynn said he would have to demonstrate his skills to the film's director Aldo made it clear that "I did not care in the least to be examined by anybody, since my record as a fencer positively required approval from no one—least of all from movie fencing ignoramuses." He never got the job and settled instead for putting on a display at Flynn's home in front of a Hollywood audience, in which he and one of his pupils fought at foil and saber; afterward Gary Cooper complained that they hadn't fenced épée too.

The final ignominy came when Aldo was promised a leading role in Howard Hawks's classic *To Have and Have Not*. He gave a copy of his book *On Fencing* to the film's scriptwriter, William Faulkner, whose daughter, Faulkner told him, wanted to learn the sport. He then waited to see what role he had been given. It turned out to be that of a minor gangster, and he had just four words to speak: "Come with me, please." In the final reel he is shot by the film's hero, played by Humphrey Bogart. By the end of his first decade in America his arrogance had so alienated the fencing community that when the scene was played in cinemas fencers in the audience regularly cheered.

All this time Aldo had been teaching, at his own salle on La Cienega Boulevard in Los Angeles, reached by a narrow staircase next to the dance studio on the ground floor. He proceeded to turn out champions at all levels within the small world of American fencing, but knew that all chance of performing on a world stage had disappeared. Aldo's last years were spent alternatively teaching and firing off furious tirades against current fencing atrocities, Hollywood desecrations of real swordplay, and any attempt to raise other fencers above the record of himself or his brother. On the evening of November 10, 1965, students at the Aldo Nadi Fencing

Academy were disturbed when their maestro failed to appear. A visit to his home disclosed that, quite out of character, the great champion had died peacefully in his sleep.

THE ITALIAN TRADITION OF REMARKABLE FENCING FAMILIES WAS far from ended by the deaths of the Nadis. At the turn of the century Giuseppe Mangiarotti, the prosperous son of a celebrated soprano, was sent by his mother on a six-year European tour to acquire commercial experience. Upon his return home to Milan he opened a garage specializing in De Dion–Boutons, the superb French automobiles. Dining out one evening with his friend Alberto Costamagna, who edited the French sports magazine *La Ciclette*, he was introduced to Olderico Rizzotti, the magazine's fencing correspondent. Mangiarotti, unimpressed by Rizzotti's spindly appearance, maintained that he could destroy him with his little finger if ever they had to fight. As the two started to argue, a diner at the next table leaned forward to introduce himself as Baron Lancia Di Brolo, assistant master to Eugenio Pini in Buenos Aires. He was on holiday in Milan for the next four weeks. If Mangiarotti were willing, he would instruct him in the noble art. Giuseppe accepted and after a crash course defeated Rizzotti 20–17.

Enjoying this new hobby, Giuseppe went on to study in Turin, Paris, and Budapest (under Italo Santelli) before returning home when Hungary went to war in 1914. In 1919 he founded his own salle. He also produced three sons, Dario (born 1915), Eduardo (1919), and Mario (1920), who took up from where the Nadis had left off. Mario fenced with three weapons, Eduardo with foil and épée, and Dario as an épéeist.

It was épée that Giuseppe Mangiarotti loved the most, and the school he founded dominated international competition for nearly four decades. His middle son, Eduardo, was the strongest and by 1936 was on the Italian team. He was still at high school in Milan and had to be given special leave as "an excellent young Fascist" to take a month off to train for the Berlin Games. Although as a seventeen-year-old he was judged too young for the individual event, where the three fencers selected came first, second, and third, he was put in against the French in an attempt to upset the reigning champions. He proceeded to win his first three bouts 3–0 (every single hit made by a perfectly executed taking of his opponent's blade and flèche) and tie his last 3–3—an exemplary performance for a fencer of any age. Two years later he took the épée silver in the world championships in Slovakia.

Then came the war. In September the Italian government transferred its young champion to Malnate, on the Swiss border. With Italy's change of side, Eduardo, rather than be taken prisoner by the SS, voluntarily led several hundred infantrymen to internment in Switzerland. Soon he was appointed camp lieutenant and was spending weekends training with the leading Swiss fencers in such cities as Berne, Zurich, Lausanne, and Geneva while during the week attending to his duties as an internment officer.[10]

As soon as the international situation allowed, he was back into his stride, coming third in foil at the 1947 Lisbon world championships and, the following year, third in épée at the London Olympics. How the French must have hated these Italian dynasties, one rising up even before its predecessor disappeared. Not to be outdone, Mario fenced on the 1951 épée team that took the silver in Stockholm, while Dario won individual épée gold at Cairo in 1949 and the silver in both 1950 and 1952, plus a 1952 team gold. During his Cairo victory the heat was so intense that Dario twice collapsed with cramp, and his thighs had to be bound with string to prevent his muscles from seizing up.

It was Eduardo, however, who lays highest claim to a special place in fencing history. Over an international career lasting twenty years he won six Olympic and thirteen world-championship golds. Then there were his thirteen silvers and seven bronzes. His thirty-nine-medal tally makes him the most successful fencer in world history—despite six of his prime years lost to the war. He has been criticized as an automaton, a Pavlovian specimen put together by his father,* but a young American fencer, Maria Tishman, who would reach the Olympic final in 1948 and knew good fencing when she saw it, vividly recalls her first trip to a European championship: "I had always thought of men's épée fencing as two long-legged figures standing around for a long time poking and jabbing at each other. Then all of a sudden this guy—Mangiarotti—comes along, sleek and good-looking

---

* Even the Italians are hard on their great champion. An international sabreur from Padua explains, "You must understand that Mangiarotti was an épéeist—the dead weapon of the dueling tradition. As the saying goes, Italy has always liked épée, but she is fascinated by saber and loves foil as her son." Claude Lévi-Strauss has also noted, it doesn't matter how much an activity claims to be a brotherhood against the rest of the world: there is always a hierarchy—and an enormous amount of concealed hostility.

*Eduardo Mangiarotti executes a flèche attack against his father,
Giuseppe. In 1925 Giuseppe had shared the Italian professional épée title
with Aldo Nadi, and in 1926 with Nedo Nadi.*

and—magnificent. He made it all look like a different game. He made it
so *exciting.*"

No one piles up a record like Mangiarotti's on technique alone. It requires character too. For instance, he had originally been right-handed,
but from the age of ten his father made him fence with his left, modeling
him on Gaudin. In Stockholm in 1951, in the foil semifinals, a German opponent struck Eduardo on his left index finger, with two bouts to go.
Changing to his right, he went on to win both matches and take the silver
medal in the finals. A couple of days later, reverting to his left hand, still
heavily bandaged, he won the épée title.

And yet, and yet . . . if one steps back from the long list of medals won
and honors gained, there is one obvious lacuna. Despite placing second
four times, he never won an individual foil gold. Someone would always
come to take that great trophy away from Italy. And that someone was
French.

F RANCE HAD BEEN LONGING FOR A SUPERSTAR OF ITS OWN EVER
since Gaudin's retirement, and when the new prodigy arrived he
turned out to be everything his country could have desired. Christian
d'Oriola was graceful and technically masterful, with an extraordinary
sense of time and distance. And in individual competition not once did he

have to bow the knee to any Italian, as had Gaudin. Once asked the secret of his success—he garnered more world championship and Olympic medals than any other foilist in history—he replied, "I don't know. I was certainly extremely quick and I always had a fighting spirit." He might have added that being a left-hander helped; and he provided his country-men with something more than medals—he exemplified the quintessen-tial French style, which many other fencing cultures have tried to copy but never achieved.

D'Oriola's early years were markedly different from those of his Italian rivals. He began to fence when his father told his three children that they were all to take up the sport for a year; after twelve months Christian was the only one who wished to continue (a cousin, Pierre Jonquères d'Oriola, would become an Olympic show jumper, winning gold in 1952 and 1964). He was then eight years old. His father, a farmer in the southern city of Perpignan, was a club-level fencer and soon handed over coaching duties to two local professionals.

D'Oriola won his first competition in 1942, a local under-fifteen event. "The night before, I lay awake thinking only that I would go all out on at-tack, but during the competition I got most of my hits with defensive movements." After a second competition his father's presence made him so nervous that he asked him not to watch, which he wouldn't do again until after his son had won his first Olympic title.

Christian was training just three times a week and only for two hours, a regimen that hardly changed throughout his career (now, a top fencer would expect to train six to eight hours a day). In 1947, at eighteen, he was runner-up in the national championship. "When I phoned my father to tell him, almost his only comment was 'Why didn't you win?'" Later that year d'Oriola went to Lisbon for the world championships—his first ap-pearance in international competition. He won the foil outright. "I was surprised how hard the Italians hit. They all tried to beat me by closing dis-tance and using their superior weight." The next year, in his first Olympics, he was runner-up to his fellow Frenchman Jehan Buhan but won the world title again in April 1949. The following month he collapsed with severe kidney pains and withdrew from competition for two years. During his time in hospital his then master, Michel Alaux (later U.S. na-tional coach) would smuggle foils into d'Oriola's ward to give him lessons simply on hand actions.

Having missed gold in London, d'Oriola traveled to Helsinki in 1952 determined to make amends. The foil's *nine* finalists numbered three

Frenchmen—d'Oriola, Buhan, and Jacques Lataste—three Italians, two Egyptians, and a Hungarian. According to one of the losing semifinalists (who was also one of the judges in the final), the Egyptians had already arranged to give their fights to Eduardo Mangiarotti, whose compatriots were also under orders to donate their fights to him. So the Italian champion had four of his eight bouts already in his pocket. At this point the French captain, René Lévy, elected that d'Oriola should be given victories by his two teammates. Buhan objected, saying that it was the usual practice in international finals for such fights to be ceded to whoever was that year's French champion, and that was he. Lévy ruled that he would examine his judgment halfway: whoever in their encounter reached three hits first, Buhan or d'Oriola, would be given the bout, plus Lataste's. (If one was a good fencer, losing a bout was an art in itself.) D'Oriola got there first. In the crucial bout against Mangiarotti he won easily, 5–2, and ended the final undefeated. Witnesses said that as finely as Mangiarotti fought, it was like watching a master class. D'Oriola merely commented, "I didn't make any special hit against him—I could guess easily what he was going to do."[11] It was a simple statement of fact.

D'Oriola's performance in the team final against the Italians was even more impressive: he won 5–0, 5–0, 5–1, 5–2, giving the French the match, and the title, 8–6. The last two bouts didn't even have to be fought. The young Frenchman was in his pomp. Contemporaries speak of him as having so fast a hand that one could not always follow his actions; "He moved like a giant cat ever ready to pounce or spring away"; "It was like fencing a telescope—suddenly a long arm would come out and hit you." I have a picture of him from a world final, extended in a full lunge. His rear leg seems to go on forever, almost touching the ground for its entire length: like Spiderman in the cartoon strip.

After his Olympic victory in 1952 he won the world title again in 1953 and 1954. From the decade beginning in 1947 he dominated foil fencing as surely as the Nadis had in the 1920s. Unlike Aldo but like Nedo, he was modest and unassuming—though perfectly able to fight his corner: in the first round of the Helsinki Games he was badly off form and seemed likely to be eliminated. His referee was an Italian, Terlizzi, and it was obvious that any doubtful hits were going against the French champion. Finally d'Oriola put down his mask, went up to Terlizzi, and took him by the lapel, saying in his harsh Gascon accent (as one of the side judges heard it), "I'm fencing quite badly enough on my own account without your help!" (D'Oriola's version is that he was simply explaining that the Ital-

The three foil medalists at Helsinki: Eduardo Mangiarotti, Christian d'Oriola, and Manlio Di Rosa. Di Rosa's brother Livio was to become Italy's leading foil coach, helping to transform the sport and producing a stream of world and Olympic champions.

ian's refereeing was increasing his motivation.) He went on to gain promotion by the narrowest of margins, eventually winning the competition. By 1955 he had come first six times and second once in his seven world championships—still a record. Then something happened that precipitated a revolution in the way foil was fenced: the world championships went electric.

To appreciate the effect requires a little history. Electric foil had been around in various forms for more than seventy years (as opposed to "steam" foil, so called from the language of the railways when a "steam" engine was outmoded compared to the more modern electric locomotive). In 1885 a Belgian inventor appears to have constructed such an apparatus for scoring hits. Eleven years later a British surgeon developed "an automatic electric recorder," involving a special jacket with wires attached to the collars of each fencer. "To accomplish his responsible work satisfactorily," reported the *Daily Courier* of June 25, 1896, "it is necessary for the judge to possess the eye of a hawk and the agility of a tiger." Although an exhibition at Salle Bertrand in London was judged "an unalloyed success," nothing came of the experiment, and for the next forty years other inventors tried their hands, none with success.

In May 1939 Béla de Tuscan, a former Hungarian army saber champion by then based in Detroit, who was in London to perform with his wife—"the only professional woman sabreur in the world"—demonstrated an electric foil with a deep bell-shaped guard made of red transparent plastic. There was no central apparatus, no reels or outside wires, and each fencer carried on his hip his own control unit, battery, and relay in a compact the size of a cigarette case, plus, mounted on top of his mask, a "signalization unit." It may have worked, but it offended the purists, still smarting from the effects electric épée had caused on its introduction at the Berlin Games three years before.

By 1954 the FIE decided that the chief technical difficulties had been overcome and was further encouraged by a demonstration held in Milan between French and Italian fencers. It showed that 75 percent of hits were decided at once by the electric box alone; 22 percent where lights went on for both fencers were decided clearly by the referee without difficulty; and only 3 percent gave rise to differing interpretations.

Even after the introduction of the new equipment, including the special lamé metallic jackets that had to be worn over the usual clothing and the new foils themselves, there were severe teething problems. The foil, slightly shorter than the nonelectric version, was point-heavy and whippy, its lack of balance impairing the quality of its use. Worse, unlike electric épée, with its simpler wiring system, the new equipment inflicted shocks whenever a fencer perspired heavily. "The men sweated so much that they caused short circuits through the mask," recalls Gillian Sheen, the Olympic gold medalist of 1956. "They had to wear our shower caps to protect themselves."[12] Even if the shocks were "almost always" confined to those who used all-metal handles, fencers were advised to change their clothes in midcompetition.

They were as likely to do that as change their way of looking for hits. Competitors took to atavistically whipping off their masks in an effort to intimidate the machines. No less a fencer than Eduardo Mangiarotti had, in the early days of electric épée, once got down on his knees and invoked God to witness that the box had lied. For the more powerful nations, the objectivity of the machines seemed no improvement over "sympathetic" juries.

Then there was the effect on foil fencing itself. One early critic worried that the new weapon would "always be clumsier than the normal foil, and . . . will favor the more robust play of the Italian school to the detriment of the finger play of the French."[13] Others saw épée "time" replacing the foil principle of right-of-way. Remises would multiply, given the tendency of fencers to look at the box, even in the middle of a phrase, then to jab away furiously until a light came on.

What no one doubted was that a revolution had indeed come about. What kind of revolution? "The electric scoring system demands simplicity," explained one Hungarian master. "Because of this simplicity the fencer must increase his speed, which makes his fighting more athletic. The high-speed lunge, the surprise flèche, the hurried retreat—all require athletic ability. These movements can be mastered and properly executed only by the practice of supplementary training in short sprinting, high-jumping, broad jumping, etc."[14]*

The French team at the 1955 championships was aghast. For the first time in the history of the event, they not only failed to win either the individual or team foil but left without a single gold medal, as if the failure of their foilists had infected the other weapons as well. As d'Oriola rationalized the loss, "France was the only country using foil blades to FIE regulations, but these frequently did not register hits"—the flat French points slipping off the smooth metallic lamé surface of the new jackets, while the "shaped" Italian points could register over approximately twice the area. For the individual event, some of the team changed to Italian points, others to Hungarian, and in the final, thus reequiped, they placed second, third, fourth, and fifth. It was a fine fight-back, and d'Oriola failed to win only by losing twice to a twenty-one-year-old Hungarian, József Gyuricza, in the final and in the fight-off for first place. A silver was no disgrace, but he had seen his title taken away from him.

He was inconsolable. "The electric foil completely changed the technique of foil fencing," he reflected many years later.[15] "No longer did the hit have to be seen, and the possibility of hits on the back and so on [was] introduced. Technique in itself was no longer necessary, and some of the great fencers of the steam foil era . . . were unable to adapt to the new style. Speaking personally, fencing with an electric foil was not nearly as enjoyable." He announced his retirement immediately after the championships. Then tongues began wagging: D'Oriola was not a great champion because he could not adapt to the new weapon. He had retired because he

---

* The following conversation, supposedly overheard at the first "electric foil" championships, was widely quoted: First bystander: "What a beautiful counterriposte!" Second bystander: "Yes, old habits die hard."

had neither the courage nor the skill to win where the electric box reigned impartially and individual referees could do little. That same year Aldo Nadi's autobiography, initially entitled *Mask Off*, was published. Its fifty-ninth chapter, "Comparisons,"[16] begins with typical directness:

> To judge by the results in recent years in the most important international contests such as the Olympics, world championships and others almost as significant, one man seems to emerge above all fencers. His name: Christian d'Oriola, a Frenchman obviously of Italian blood, and Olympic foil champion. True, I have noticed that he is not always the winner—anything but. Once, for example, in the Coppa Gaudini fought every year between the six best Italians and the six best Frenchmen, M. d'Oriola had no less than four defeats in six bouts—something that simply cannot happen to a great fencer. Also, in 1954, he was defeated many times by Manlio Di Rosa, who was world champion back in 1951, and positively past his prime.

Nadi then glides in the stiletto: "I shall merely add that a great fencer wins with any kind of weapon and with any jury."

If anything could have been calculated to goad d'Oriola, this must have been it, although he insists he never read the book. He announced his comeback; he wished to fence at the Games in 1956 and was soon traveling with the French team to Melbourne. He could not stop the Italians from winning the foil team event, although in the final he won all his bouts with just seven hits against him. Two days later came the individual. Gyuricza could manage only fifth; Giancarlo Bergamini and Antonio Spallino, both of Italy, took the silver and bronze; the gold went to d'Oriola. He retired again, petitioning to the FIE that electric foil be discontinued—"it is decadent fencing." He had won in Melbourne, he said, only to prove that an able fencer could master that "inartistic game," adding, "I naturally had to alter my game to be more efficient."

Recently I spent almost four hours in Eduardo Mangiarotti's neat offices in central Milan. At one point he reached for a substantial volume published in 1904. "Nearly a hundred years ago. Yet it lists all the Italian masters who left Italy to teach in other countries. And *it takes a whole book*."[17] He regards his own record as "probably now unbeatable." What of d'Oriola; how would he judge between them? Well, he, Mangiarotti, had superb technique; "but d'Oriola had technique too, and he was always

*Christian d'Oriola's extraordinary lunge, seen here in 1947 during a
ten-hit match against the French professional champion, André Gardère.
For once d'Oriola came off second best, Gardère triumphing 10-7.
The referee is Roger Crosnier, later British national coach.*

better than I." A strikingly generous admission. How so? "He had something I never had—*fantasy.*"

Was this d'Oriola's view too? I met him in 2001, when he was seventy-
three and living in Montpellier, in the grip of Parkinson's disease. Thinking that it would please him, I opened with Mangiarotti's comment. "*Non,
non, non,*" he interrupted sharply. There was no sign of weakness in his
voice, just the forceful tones of the skilled insurance specialist he had
become. It wasn't fantasy that had led to his victories, "*c'était flexibilité.*"

Flexibility: the quality Aldo Nadi had invoked to describe his own fencing. Later, in correspondence, d'Oriola corrected himself: "It is not 'flexibility' that should be quoted but the word 'anticipation.' My main weapon
against all my opponents, including Mangiarotti, was anticipation." Best
to leave it there.

D'Oriola died in 2007, leaving no son or daughter to continue his
name, and while Mangiarotti's daughter Carola fenced for her country, it
was without her father's success. With the coming of electric foil the hold
of the French and the Italians was broken. In 1960 the foil gold and silver
medalists came from the Soviet Union; over the next twenty-four years the

Soviets would win twelve world and Olympic titles. A new tradition was taking form, led by the Belorussian Alexandr Romankov (five times world champion between 1974 and 1983) and the Ukrainian Sergei Golubitsky, winner of three consecutive world titles, 1997 to 1999. A recent issue of the French magazine *Escrime* grandly describes Golubitsky as "today considered the best foilist ever."[18]

S HORTLY BEFORE HIS DEATH, ALDO NADI LEARNED THAT THE ITALIAN authorities were to honor Mangiarotti as the country's all-time outstanding fencer and immediately challenged Mangiarotti to a duel; not with swords, as the sixty-two-year-old had recently injured his neck, but with pistols. Mangiarotti replied that he used guns only to shoot pigeons, and nothing further came of it; but Aldo's outburst was not entirely unjustified. All Mangiarotti's silver and bronze medals, he asserted, were tokens of defeat. Conveniently ignoring Nedo's fifth place in saber in 1912, he recited his brother's unblemished roster of Olympic victories—six medals, all gold: what could be better than that? So to the end Aldo attacked, fashioning his argument to get the result he wanted. Fantasy? *Flexibilité?* Or anticipation?

Is there in fact some common denominator for champions? Barbara Tuchman, in a revealing essay on "Generalship," quotes the Maréchal de Saxe (himself drawing on Aristotle): "Courage is the first of all qualities." Without it other qualities are of little value since they cannot be used. She goes on: "I think 'courage' is too simple a word. The concept must include both physical and moral courage, for there are people who have the former without the latter . . . physical courage must also be joined by intelligence, for, as the Chinese proverb puts it, 'a general who is stupid and courageous is a calamity.' Physical, combined with moral, courage makes the possessor resolute, and I would say . . . that the primary quality is resolution. That is what enables a man to prevail."[19]

CHAPTER 17

Exodus

> Az okos gazda a kárt is jóra fordítja. (A clever master turns
> even a loss into a gain.)
>
> —HUNGARIAN PROVERB

> If you want to find out about fencers, go up behind one as he
> faces a practice target. Burst a balloon behind his back. The
> foilist will immediately lunge at the pad. The épéeist will
> stand his ground, immobile but alert. The sabreur will swing
> round and assault you.
>
> —HUNGARIAN AXIOM

IN THE EARLY 1950S THE SCIENTIFIC ADVISORY BOARD OF THE U.S. Atomic Energy Commission convened in Washington, D.C. A first count of the members showed a minority absent, but still a quorum; another count enabled the chairman to ask his colleagues, in his faultless native Hungarian, "Shall we conduct this meeting in the mother tongue?" Agreed and done.[1]

Hungary doesn't just produce—and export—nuclear physicists. Hungarians have consistently proved good at odd things: water polo, a branch of mathematics involving game theory, boxing—and fencing. As Giorgio Santelli, the Italian master brought up in Budapest, said, "The Hungarians are a very warlike people with martial traditions. After all, they have been fighting the Turks for centuries." Hungary remains the only country with a sabreur—a resplendent nineteenth-century hussar on horseback—on one of its banknotes. (Though Denmark has a centaur brandishing a short sword.) Yet the country failed to win independence from the Hapsburgs in 1848 and was defeated again in 1956; maybe as a nation accustomed to defeat the Hungarians are more adaptable, and able to get their own back.* Anyway, and above all, Hungary is a nation of

---

* Their language is also a factor. Quite unlike any European stock, it is at best cousin to Finnish and Estonian, probably closest to Korean. Polysynthetic and glottal, it effec-

sabreurs. This chapter tells the story of Hungarian saber, and of an extraordinary exodus.

In Hungary saber is accepted as the national weapon, the chosen arm of the country's wars against the Tartars, Ottoman Turks, and other invaders, ever since the conquering Turks introduced them to the curved weapons of the East in the sixteenth century. The scimitar, with its keen arc-shaped edge, is the child of the Persian *shamsheer,* and by the late eighteenth century both Hungarian and Polish cavalry were armed with versions of it. Hungarian duels were consequently fought with cavalry sabers, and the first sporting sabers were derived from this heavy and powerful instrument.

The first modern school of fencing opened its doors in 1851, when "the father of Hungarian saber," Joseph Keresztessy (1810–72) began to teach his students simple, short swings and parries that emanated from circular wrist motions, pioneering a new Hungarian style. Not long after, an Italian master, Carlo Pessina, went to Russia to study Cossack swordsmanship. He returned home convinced that the Steppe horsemen were so accurate with their sabers because they were cutting not from the wrist, as was being taught elsewhere, but from the elbow, holding the wrist "in one piece" with the forearm, this enabling them to perform astonishing feats with absolute sureness and precision. This style was taken up throughout Italy and documented in a widely disseminated book by the northern Italian master Giuseppe Radaelli.[2] It was Radaelli who invented the light sporting saber, giving Italians a priceless advantage against opponents armed with the heavy conventional military weapon. The target in saber fencing is restricted to everything above the hips, a fact that is generally attributed to the mistaken notion that mounted cavalry would not strike the enemy's legs or horses. The truth is that the leg remained a valid target in both combat and competitive saber well into the second decade of the twentieth century.*

_____

tively gives Hungarians a secret tongue, so that they operate like some public closed society.

* From the eighteenth century until the 1870s, the curved-blade saber was reckoned a subcategory of the broadsword, and the leg and thigh were thus both valid targets. Most manuals of the time discuss leg cuts. Only around 1870 did views change, the Austrian master Gustav Hergsell, for example, referring to hits below the waist not being used out of politeness (*der Anstand*). The influential master Luigi Barbasetti echoed this, saying that such cuts should be excluded in all "chivalrous and honorable combat"; but then Barbasetti used the same justification for outlawing cuts to the sword arm. Away from competitive fencing, cavalrymen were explicitly instructed to hit at both an adversary's sword arm and bridle hand.[3]

Part of the attraction of this new style was that it followed the actions of actual duels. Cuts were made with "draw"—in other words, they were made to penetrate an adversary's skin. Any attack had to be firmly parried or completely avoided, just as in a real fight. The cuts, when they arrived, were so powerful that fencers had to wear padded clothing and line their masks with iron and leather to avoid being knocked out. Sabreurs looked more like deep-sea divers than lithe athletes.[4] The sabers were correspondingly heavier than anything used today: the blades at this stage being 10 millimeters wide, contracting successively to 6 millimeters, then 4 millimeters, until finally the ultrathin, V-section blade evolved. The weapons of the 1880s literally required strong-arm tactics.

Hungarian fencers, increasingly frustrated at the lack of opportunity to test their skills against foreign competitors, constantly debated which style was better, their own or that of the Italians. Until the 1930s Hungarians trained only at saber: parents sent their children to clubs specifically to learn the weapon, to prepare them to win duels.

In 1896, the year of the first modern Olympics, Hungary elected not to take part. Instead, the Hungarian Athletic Club (MAC) organized a Millennium Exposition tournament (to mark the Hungarian Conquest of Central Europe) in foil, épée, and saber; it would transform Hungary's standing in the sport. All the leading European fencers were invited, amateurs and professionals alike—and they came. The Italians and French carried off the laurels, with Hungarian amateurs picking up the occasional victory. A Hungarian actually came second-best amateur among the forty-four contestants in the saber event, but Hungary's outmoded techniques meant its fencers otherwise languished well behind those from the leading nations.

Seven of the saber finalists were Italian, and the event was won by a young army officer, Italo Santelli. Using a lighter saber and fast footwork, he appeared, in the words of one Hungarian, to be "the Edison of fencing. . . . Even for the layman, it was an obvious pleasure to watch his brilliant technique, his perfect movements, his lightning-quick hands. He fenced with the stunning self-assurance of a juggler."[5]

Santelli was invited to stay on in Hungary and teach at the leading club in the capital. The Italians were not worried—they had masters enough—and Santelli was pleased to go. In September 1896 the twenty-five-year-old moved to Budapest with his wife and young family. Not only did he have to change the way Hungarian sabreurs made their cuts; they had little or no footwork. Santelli did not discard everything from their style but combined it with what he had learned in Rome. He taught that it was not shameful to foil an attack simply by moving out of distance, and with lighter blades he could teach feint actions and faster handwork. He explained that he was joining Italian cunning to Hungarian passion— by which he meant "temper." But he also discovered that many Hungarians had an uncanny sense of timing, a skill he set out to exploit to the full.*

Santelli soon became a popular figure in the city; even his inability to master the Hungarian language, though he would live in the country more than forty years, became endearing. He would use verbs only in their infinitive form, saying, "Well, young man, you to be very clever must to work much more" or "How you to be?" Before long his students had picked up his mannerisms and had started speaking like him whenever they came to the salle. Yet despite his reputation as the friendliest of men, Santelli was a man of strict discipline, and his lessons stretched his pupils to the limit. They might laugh at his difficulties with their tongue, but they respected him as a teacher—and as a fencer.

Even so, accounts of their master's eccentricities circulated through the city. There was the story, for instance, of the student who avoided paying for his lessons. Once, at the end of a session, he looked out of the window of the salle and to his horror saw his tailor below. He ran to Santelli and asked for help. Santelli told him not to worry and instructed him to get a newspaper and hold it up before his face, as if reading it. The tailor duly made his way up to the salle and asked Santelli where his young charge had gone: he owed money on a suit. Santelli—aware that the young man could hear their conversation clearly—replied, "My dear sir, I to be afraid we are not to deal with a gentleman. He a villain who cheat everybody. He not to pay for lessons for a year." The young man rustled his

---

* In several countries, fencers exercising with heavy practice sabers worked out side by side with the new breed of sabreur using the lighter weapon. The contrast between the two was highlighted at the turn of the century, when the Italian maestro Giuseppe Magrini introduced the sporting saber to England. He appeared for his first exhibition bout resplendent in black satin breeches and silk stockings, holding a fragile-seeming silverplated saber. His opponent, an army officer, wore heavy canvas shin guards and a cagelike mask, and clutched a blunted cavalry sword. At the command "Play" Magrini executed several lightning feints, ending with a delicate cut across his opponent's chest. After one wild attempt to follow the blade, the officer abandoned defense and slashed at the Italian's head. His blade curled over Magrini's mask to hit him solidly on the back of his scalp. After this experience was repeated Magrini took off his mask and with deliberate calm said, "Thank you, sir. You are a very much better man than I."

paper but couldn't say anything. After the tailor had left, he not only paid for his back lessons but thereafter settled his accounts without delay.

Santelli gave private lessons to anyone who would pay for his services. He was a handsome man with winning ways, popular wherever he went. Two of his private pupils were beautiful young ballet dancers, to whom he gave morning lessons. Both girls worked with him in leotards or the then-equivalent. One day his wife appeared at the club, kicked them out, and set about her husband with an umbrella. Far from being ashamed, Santelli regularly told the story, saying that it marked his first and only defeat on Hungarian soil.

With the advent of the First World War, Hungary and Italy found themselves on opposite sides. Most Italians in Budapest were immediately regarded as aliens, but Santelli was never ostracized. The Hungarians didn't think of him as "really" Italian, while his home government respected him for all he had done for fencing and gave him the title "Cavaliere"—the equivalent of a British knighthood. Santelli just went on teaching.

The habit of dueling was still alive, and various *salles d'armes* specialized in offering quick instruction to men facing duels who had previously never fenced.[6] Santelli's club in Pest was one such; his salle took over the whole of one floor and was the city's main venue for illegal duels: the changing rooms at either end had peepholes in their doors, through which spectators would illicitly watch. But not all duels were held there. One evening Santelli was approached by an overweight middle-aged man who asked for a lesson. What happened next is the fencing equivalent of an urban myth, but I am assured that it actually took place.

The new recruit explained that he had to fight a duel. "When?" asked Santelli. "Tomorrow morning." The master threw up his hands. "What can I to do in an evening? What do you expect?" He looked at the man evenly. "What is the name of your opponent?" When he was told, he became even more exasperated. "He is a well-known duelist. And to my knowledge, he has never lost." Santelli thought for a moment. "Well, I have an hour to give you. Maybe I can to teach you a move or two. But I must tell you that your opponent will not be satisfied with first blood; he likes to disarm his rivals, then to kill them. There is chance to hit him as he attempts to disarm you—if he thinks you are novice he to be overconfident. Let us see what we can do." They were soon at work, although after about forty minutes the older man was exhausted. It did not bode well.

The following day Santelli went to his salle as usual and was surprised to find his new pupil there, his face wreathed in smiles. "I did just as you told me," he bubbled. "As he went for my blade I did the move under his arm, aiming at his wrist. Only I was so wound up I did it too fiercely and cut off his entire hand." Santelli accepted the profuse thanks offered but was further surprised when the man continued, "I have one more favor to ask: will you now teach my son?" The boy was a teenager, so there was no duel in sight. His godfather had given him fencing kit for his birthday, and after being teased by his friends he had joined a fencing club, just to spite them. Santelli was pleased to take the boy on. What was his name? Endre Kabos, he was told.

In 1933, in Budapest, Endre Kabos, watched by his master, won the European championship in saber, beating Gustavo Marzi in the final. He won again the following year, in Warsaw, and in 1936 became the Olympic champion, once more pushing Marzi into second place. Kabos had been taught by Santelli to fence left-handed. He was one of six Jews on the Hungarian team. Another, Attila Petschauer, also a sabreur, and a very good one, came second three times and third three times in world championships between 1925 and 1931. He failed to win a medal at the 1932 Games, but a fellow Hungarian told me that he would have won the gold had anti-Semitic judging not robbed him. "He was emphatically the best there—the most natural fencer I ever saw in my life." Both Petschauer and Kabos had to withstand considerable prejudice in Hungary, where the anti-Semitism of the reactionary government pervaded many sports. Fencing officials openly disdained Jews, even their Olympic champions—including Kabos, despite the several medals he had won in the First World War. Both men died in the Second World War, Kabos the day before his thirty-eighth birthday, when a tram crossing the Margaret Bridge in Budapest was blown up by the Germans, who had put mines under all the main bridges across the Danube, and, without warning, exploded them all. Petschauer was tortured to death in a Hungarian concentration camp.

Recently the lives of both men were formed into one composite figure in the film *Sunshine* (2000), the story of three generations of Austro-Hungarian Jews, the Sonnenscheins. In the second of its three sections, young Adam Sonnenschein (Ralph Fiennes) becomes a promising fencer. The film's Oscar-winning director, István Szabó, had himself been a fencer, but he put the swordfighting scenes into the hands of László Szepesi, who had just completed a coaching assignment with the French saber squad.*

* Each actor was given a real-life sabreur with whom to train. Ralph Fiennes took lessons from Szepesi himself (who was given the part of the presiding referee for the gold-medal bout) and was taught to fence both right- and left-handed, as he does in the

Surrounded by anti-Semitism, Adam changes his surname to "Sors," "something more Hungarian"—although, in Latin, it also means "prophecy" or "fate"—and converts to Christianity. He also moves to Budapest, where the Italian master of the Officers Fencing Club (Santelli, but given a different name here) changes him from a right-handed sabreur to a left-handed one—with immediate results. Sors is chosen for the 1936 Olympic Games and amid mounting excitement beats his Italian rival to take the individual gold. With the outbreak of war, he is imprisoned and eventually tortured to death in front of his teenage son.

SANTELLI TRANSFORMED HUNGARIAN SABER, PRODUCING A STREAM of world and Olympic champions and first-class masters. Yet he was not alone. Two home-bred masters formed with him a famous triptych of Hungarian coaches: "The Officer," László Borsodi (who looked down on Santelli, only a sergeant), and "The Professor," László Gerencsér.

Following Santelli's lead, a special school for training masters was created, the Toldi Miklos Royal Hungarian Sports Institution. During the 1930s and 1940s its director was Borsodi, a strict disciplinarian whose countenance was partly hidden behind an immense Prussian moustache. The club that emerged from the school was the MAC, probably the strongest in the country, which, because all its members were military men, was a place of strict order and discipline. Everybody knew his place.

Borsodi was a martinet, unfriendly and with a painfully sharp tongue. As soon as his lessons were over he wanted no further conversation with his pupils. Nobody liked him, but he was revered because he was such a fine teacher. He worked exclusively with fencers who had already completed their basic training, and although he would correct his pupils' technical errors, he was more interested in tactics and strategy, teaching his students how to observe their opponents on the piste and how to exploit their weaknesses. Before major competitions he would reveal to his favored pupils some secret or little-known move, tricks he guarded jealously and demonstrated only out of sight of other club fencers. Once a year he pitted trainee masters against one another, stripped to the waist, with only

---

film, but once swapped hands in midlesson. "That was a very bad idea," says Szepesi; as a result that day the actor was unable to fence effectively at all. Fiennes took to the sport, however, and Szepesi later asked me to arrange for him to have further instruction in London. He was to fence in both *The Avengers* and, onstage, in *Coriolanus*.[7]

The three great masters
of Hungarian fencing:
Italo Santelli (top left),
László Borsodi
(bottom), and
László Gerencsér.

gloves and masks for protection; in this way, he argued, his charges could experience the physical and psychological sensations of the duelist.

Eventually a group left the MAC and established their own club, the HTVK. This too was open to officers only and soon had a dictator every bit as dominating as Borsodi. His name was Colonel Endre Somogyi, and, although not a coach, he played a vital role both before and immediately after the Second World War. Somogyi recruited the army's best fencers into the HTVK, so that the club became the principal conduit into the national team. Anyone who did not fit in, for reason of character or ability, was likely to find himself posted far away from the capital. Somogyi would position himself opposite referees during national competitions, indicating by a look or gesture which way a hit should be given. This is one reason why Petschauer never won a national title and was so often runner-up. Somogyi was as much hated as respected but he was credited with masterminding the successful selection of Hungarian teams. During the Second World War, he went to the highest official body and gained exemption for team members from being sent to the front. One top coach—

Béla Bay—was actually on a truck ready to leave when the order came to recall him. Petschauer was not so lucky.

Borsodi's principal rival, Dr. Gerencsér, a professor and former lawyer, was of an altogether different cast from either Borsodi or Somogy. He taught at the main university club, the BEAC, where he was a stickler for good technique. If Santelli's lessons were marked by speed of execution and Borsodi's by their emphasis on strategy, Gerencsér was an astute planner of training programs. He had been an excellent track athlete in his day, some of his records going unbroken for years. Given a sympathetic audience, he could theorize endlessly; but his actual lessons were inspiring—and could last for an hour and a half or more. What interested him was the *science* of fencing, how its movements could be broken down into different components. What might appear to be second nature, an instinctive reaction, could to his mind be honed into a conscious and scientific procedure. Unlike the MAC or HTVK, the atmosphere in the BEAC was friendly and relaxed, and to avoid conflict with the two army clubs the students there tended to concentrate on foil and épée. They still produced several champion sabreurs, even if they knew that doubtful calls in national competitions would generally go against them. Like Santelli, Gerencsér was a much-loved figure. His club became a haven for Jewish fencers during the war.

All three masters emphasized fluid footwork and insisted on the need to separate hand and foot movements, so that during one foot action the hand could complete as many as three different moves—an innovation that prompted yet another overhaul of fencing tactics. Borsodi and Santelli combined in the late 1920s to introduce the flèche (French for "arrow"), a fast-running attack that has the fencer throw himself at his opponent in what is half leap, half run, similar to a sprinter propelling himself from his starting block. They also pioneered anatomical, motion-mechanical, and motion-dynamic studies and invited input from masters of complementary sports.

The Second World War took its toll: Borsodi, whose real name was Bloum but who had changed it on joining the army and converted to Catholicism soon after, shot himself in 1941, the day after it was announced that Jews had to wear stars on their clothing. Santelli died during the siege of Budapest, and his story is even sadder: as the Allies pressed for victory, Santelli liked to stand in his yard with his daughter, Fiorenza, and count the American planes flying in to attack. Early in 1944 his daughter was killed by one of their bombs, and in his grief the heartbroken master simply gave up eating and wasted away.

The combined effect of these remarkable teachers would endure to produce an unparalleled run of champions. Only the United States, with its records in men's diving and in pole vaulting, surpasses it. From 1908 on, when Hungary took first, second, and fourth places (third uniquely going to a Bohemian) and won the team gold, this nation of some 10 million people dominated the saber. In the 1912 Games, seven of the eight finalists were Hungarian, with a lone Italian—Nedo Nadi—in fifth place; thereafter, countries were restricted to entering three fencers per event. Competition stopped during the First World War, and Hungary was barred from taking part in 1920; but from 1924 to 1964 its sabreurs won the individual gold at every Olympics. They won every European or world tournament from 1925 until 1957, with the exception of 1938, 1947, 1949, and 1950, when they did not compete (due to a compound of political pressures and lack of funds). In the team event, after coming second to Italy in 1924, they won each year they competed until 1959, the first year of the Polish renaissance. They took gold medals in the Olympics and world championships for fifty-one straight years: an extraordinary record.

During this entire half century, only thirty individuals represented Hungary at saber. Team members soldiered on until well into their thirties, even their forties. One, Aladár Gerevich (1910–96) can claim to be the most successful fencer in history. (Originally his name would have been "Gurevich"—literally, "Ben Hur.") He won seven gold medals during a career that stretched from 1932 to 1960, the only athlete in any sport ever to win gold over six Games—he was fifty when he won his last medal, a team gold in Rome. And he should have won even more: in the 1952 final he was at match point with his countryman, Pál "Foxy" Kovács, in the fight that decided the gold, when Kovács acknowledged a hit. The referee, however—Paul Anspach of Belgium—mistakenly awarded the touch to Kovács. Gerevich, said a fellow team member, György Jekelfalussy-Piller, was so far ahead of the field "he would have won wielding a pencil." He was also six times Hungarian foil champion, and fourth and fifth in the épée.

The prevailing philosophy behind such feats informs a story told me by seventy-year-old Csaba Pallaghy, now an American citizen, who as a young man was an ambitious and talented Hungarian sabreur. In 1956, just before the Melbourne Games, the national championships were held in Budapest. Pallaghy, then in his mid-twenties, reached the semifinals and saw his chance of making the Olympic team. He had only to beat the seasoned international László Rajcsányi (who had won a world bronze as far back as 1934) to make his first final. The score stood at 3–3, and the referee was György Piller, three-time world champion in the 1930s and thus an old colleague of Rajcsányi. Pallaghy made a fast attack to his opponent's head, which arrived just before Rajcsányi could parry. Piller called "Halt!" and asked the judge on Pallaghy's side if the attack had landed. "Yes," replied the judge. "The *attack*?" Piller asked again, menacingly. The judge stood his ground; but the cowed second official, effectively threatened, abstained.

Then as now a referee has a vote of $1\frac{1}{2}$. Thus he can be outvoted by two judges voting together, but if one judge abstains he can outvote the other. Piller now said "Parried" in a strong voice, and Rajcsányi was given the hit: 3–4. Eager to make his point, Pallaghy decided he would try the same action, but this time even more quickly. Exactly the same thing happened: his hit arrived, only to be overturned by Piller, giving victory to the older man. Pallaghy was eliminated and lost his chance to go to Melbourne.

Furious, he went to his coach, a product of Borsodi's academy and indeed his eventual successor, Béla Bay. "Master," he said, "both those last two hits were mine!" "Yes," replied his coach. Bay then turned to look at the stream of spectators taking their seats for the final. "But look at those people. Do you really think they have come to watch you? No, they have come to watch Rajcsányi."

Pallaghy was not so easily to be pacified. "But I won—surely that's the point. I deserve to be in the final." His master took his arm. "No," he said firmly, "that's not the point. When you can score five hits that no referee can deny you, when you are so far ahead of your opponent that your supremacy is undeniable, then you will deserve your place." The Hungarian way was hard, but it produced results.

THAT AUTUMN SAW THE INVASION OF SOVIET TANKS TO QUELL THE Hungarian national uprising. That some 200,000 men, women, and children fled the country might imply there was a period of relatively easy access to the West. The opposite is true. One Hungarian master, only ten at the time and now teaching in Britain, recalls the few days of "freedom" as "very simply, a riot. . . . It was impossible to tell what was going on. It began with a well-intentioned demonstration by university students, then everything got out of hand. Prisons were opened up and criminals set free who from revenge went about killing people at random. Many innocent young people lost their lives." Those who left the country did so in great haste and often great danger. "Along the border," wrote Noel Barber, author of *Seven Days of Freedom*, the best firsthand account of the uprising, "the Russians stalked the fleeing refugees, particularly on the deathly still, frost-bitten zone by the Neusiedlersee, a reed-filled lake separating Hungary from Austria. Hungarians hid in the reeds, waist deep in the icy water, while marauding patrols hunted them."[8] Many who wanted to leave were arrested and thrown into prison. The diaspora was a desperate affair.

For its fencing community, it was a heartbreaking time. The previous year had been Hungary's most successful ever, with five gold medals at the Rome world championships, and sufficient silver and bronze to win it the coveted "Grand Prix"—marking it as the best fencing nation in the world. It was similarly dominant at under-twenty-one level.

When news of the Uprising reached the Olympic team it was at training camp in Tata, some forty miles from Budapest. "It was unbelievable to hear about shouting, people dying, buildings on fire," one fencer recalls. "Everyone was in a state of shock." Would they be allowed to travel to Melbourne? What about uniforms, visas, bills? What about afterward?

Béla Bay, the overall captain, assembled his team and told them, "My friends, neither I nor anyone else can tell you what is going on in Budapest or in the rest of the country. I have no idea how or when these events will end. I know only one thing: we are here to do our best at the Games. I will not allow anyone to upset that aim. Now—back to training." A week later they received permission to travel from the Ministry of Sport.

Once in Melbourne, it was hard to concentrate. Not only was news filtering through from the thousands who had fled Hungary, but both fencers and coaches were approached with offers to desert their team and continue their careers elsewhere. Many were tempted, and more than half the Hungarian delegation at the Games took time to travel in the "free world" before returning home. Others never returned, while many fencers who were not even at the Games seized their chance to leave for a new country.

By 1956, the "great old saber team" of the 1920s and 1930s—Sándor Posta and Ödön Tersztyanszky, then Piller, Kabos, and Petschauer—had been followed by the "big team" of Kovács, Gerevich, Tibor Berczelly, Rudolf Kárpáti, Rajcsányi, and Imre Rajczy, then by the young hopefuls Mendelényi, Delneky, and Zoltán Horváth. Now Attila Keresztes, Orley, Dániel Magay, and Jeno Hamori all left (the last two to join the Nobel Prize nominee Éde Teller at his atomic energy research institute in the United States). More important, the best coaches from the Toldi Miklos Institute departed for other countries: Csizmadia and Béla Somos to Germany, Béla Balogh to Italy, Resolovics to Austria, Béla Imregi to Britain, Adam to Holland, Imre Hennyey to Canada, Rajczy to Argentina. János Kevey was already in Poland. Csaba Elthes, who for many years would coach the U.S. saber team, emigrated to New York, as did Csajághy and Niederkirchner, while Dánosi went to Detroit, Nicholas G. Tóth to Colorado Springs, Pokay to Buffalo, Marki and Julius Palffy-Alpar to San Francisco. György Piller, head of the Hungarian Fencing League from 1931 to 1947, settled in San Francisco.[9] This exodus was unpredented in sporting history. And others would follow.

Not all the coaches who left Hungary had been saber masters. Béla Rerrich, for example, had early given up the idea of being a sabreur—"It was more difficult to get into the Hungarian team than to win an Olympic medal," he wrote to me. Instead, after starting the sport in 1929 under Gerencsér, he adapted to become a foilist, twice winning the Hungarian junior championship. One day, returning from a senior competition, he told Gerencsér that he had been eliminated by dishonest refereeing. "Right," said his coach, "we'll make you an épéeist." The strategy worked. Rerrich would become national champion four times and by 1937 was in the team for the world championships.

By 1956 he had retired from competition and was a respected épée coach; with the Soviet invasion he seized his chance to leave but deliberately did not make for America—"too big a place to make champions"—and settled instead in Sweden. In the whole of that country, with its population of about 7 million, there were about one hundred fencing clubs and at most two thousand fencers. The center of the sport was Stockholm, where fencing had taken root about 1880 and whose two main clubs had some two hundred regular members. When Rerrich arrived, the city had just two masters. By the mid-1960s, his pupils were winning medals at junior championships; in 1968, one of his fencers, Ferm, won the modern pentathlon world title; and by the 1970s, Sweden had become the finest épée nation in the world.

In 1973, in the Göteborg world championships, one of Rerrich's épéeists, Hans Jacobsson, took second place. In 1974 and again in 1975 the Swedish épéeists took the team gold while another of their squad, Rolf Edling, was champion in 1973 and 1974. In 1977 the team came first again. In 1980 it was the turn of Johan Harmenberg to become Olympic champion; in 1984 Björne Vaggo took the silver. Rerrich went on teaching until well into his eighties, dying at eighty-seven in June 2005.

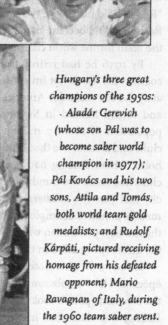

Hungary's three great champions of the 1950s: Aladár Gerevich (whose son Pál was to become saber world champion in 1977); Pál Kovács and his two sons, Attila and Tomás, both world team gold medalists; and Rudolf Kárpáti, pictured receiving homage from his defeated opponent, Mario Ravagnan of Italy, during the 1960 team saber event.

Such dedication is unworldly, an attribute that was also true of my own master, Béla Imregi, a remarkable athlete ranked in the top ten in Hungary in the decathlon, who became a senior coach in skiing and tennis as well as in fencing. At the time of the Russian invasion Imregi was a member of the revolutionary committee for sport. He was also a major in the Hungarian army, and, condemned to death by the Russians as a class enemy, fled to London. He had coached épée and women's foil with the Olympic team in 1948, but Hungary's reputation for saber entailed his being asked to teach what was his third weapon, and for the next thirty-five years he did so with great brilliance, producing even so champions in all three weapons.

To Imregi, fencing was the highest way of life. Like Italo Santelli, he had trouble learning the language of his adopted country. In "Bélarese," as his fractured English came to be known, he would say, "Necessary you sleep with saber under pillow." As long as you loved fencing, he would do anything for you. In 1972, in the run-up to the Munich Games, he took his most promising pupil (now a professor of cardiology) on holiday with his family, teaching him free of charge throughout the summer. The pupil duly defeated the eventual silver medalist—a Hungarian.

I joined Béla's salle in 1977. I was already over thirty, but under his tutelage enjoyed my best results. One evening, having won the British title the previous weekend and feeling pleased with myself, I went to the club for my usual lesson. Imregi sat me down and for twenty minutes demonstrated that I had yet to learn the correct way to hold a saber.

He had little interest in personal advancement, almost none in financial compensation, and was not primarily concerned that his charges won: they had to *fence*. Pupils would be invited back to his home in the southeast of London for lessons in his tiny garden or in the house itself, his living room ceiling scarred by ill-directed cuts. Passersby would stop to marvel at the Peckham Park bandstand he regularly used as an impromptu fencing strip, the clash of steel replacing more familiar melodies.

He was stubborn, quick to anger, passionate in his beliefs. You crossed him at your peril, and once crossed he was slow to forgive. He had a formidable list of enemies, even if many of them were ignorant of their elevation. Beneath his famous beetle eyebrows, his eyes were full of mischief. On one occasion, when a fencer playfully slapped him on the back, Béla—then seventy-eight—fell prone, seeming to die on the spot. A few anxious seconds later he jumped to his feet, delighted with his trickery. Again, in hospital with various tubes and wires plunged into his chest, he pointed to them: "What this? One BBC, one ITV?" A week of training missed, and the errant pupil would be met with "Hello, my name Imregi. Who you?" He gave up teaching only in 1991, when he was eighty-three.

A host of such stories are told of other coaches of the diaspora—not always fondly: when the American sabreur Peter Westbrook suffered his near-fatal neck injury, his Hungarian coach, Csaba Elthes, simply sat down, lit a cigarette, and muttered, "Typical: I create champion; then I kill him." Another time Elthes stopped teaching a teenage pupil to say, "Go phone your mother. Tell her to come collect you now. There's no point teaching you. You never make fencer."

Elthes was the most successful master ever to teach in the United States. Born "de Elthes," a Hungarian nobleman, in 1912, he became a doctor of law in 1936 and was assigned an important post in the Ministry of the Interior. He had been made to take up fencing on his thirteenth birthday by his father, who explained that a man of his class would in all likelihood be challenged to a duel and must learn to defend himself. The best way to avoid a challenge was to have the reputation of being an expert duelist. "I had no love for dueling," Elthes later explained, but conceded that "It made people think twice before they spoke ill of another." In 1933 he enrolled at Budapest University and became a pupil of László Gerencsér. By 1938 he was competing internationally.

During the war Elthes served as a cavalry lieutenant on the Russian front. Provisions were so inadequate that he spent three months scavenging for food. At one time he was ordered to attack the Red Army positions armed only with his Sunday dress sword. The sole enemy he admitted fearing was the Russian cavalry: they had better horses. It was during the war that he learned to recognize an important sound—that of Russian airplanes approaching. Later, back in Budapest, he would hear the sound again and saved his wife's life and his own by going early to one of the few bomb shelters in the city. During those times, he said, he once drank tank petrol neat when he could find no alcoholic alternative.

After the war, by now in his mid-thirties, Elthes started to fence again. In 1951 he came fifth in the national championships, but his career was cut short when, the following year, the Committee on Athletics refused to allow him to travel outside Hungary because of his "political instability." Finally denounced in January 1957 after he had taken part in the October uprising, he abandoned his wife and daughters and fled to Yugoslavia, where he spent eight months in an internment camp before making his way to the United States. By 1960 he was a U.S. Olympic coach. His influence on his adopted country's fencing was extraordinary. Between 1970 and 1986, no fewer than 106 of the 116 finalists in the national championships were his pupils. His teams won the championships twenty-four times in twenty-five years.

Csaba Elthes had the appearance of an American Indian chief. He walked with a pronounced limp, the result, according to unkind observers, of a drunken accident back in Budapest—though others insisted he had taken a bullet in his knee during his escape. It was actually the result of a riding accident. He died, still teaching, in 1997. Up to the end, he never lost his acerbic tongue. On one occasion, teaching at the Fencers Club on Seventy-first Street and aware that a crowd of experienced sabreurs was watching him instruct a particularly unresponsive pupil, he stopped the lesson to pronounce, "I not only have to put technique into his body, I have to put a *brain* into his *head!*" "Sorry," said the student. "Too late!" replied Elthes. On another occasion a cockroach scuttled across the salle floor. Elthes squashed it under his shoe. "Aach!" he exclaimed theatrically, "*Pleasure* fencers!" Those who didn't train seriously were beneath contempt.

WHEN A COUNTRY LOSES SO MANY TEACHERS OF HIGH QUALITY within a few months, what happens to those who remain? For years one used to see at world championships a slight, withdrawn figure who, with his black mustache, balding head, and reserved manner, reminded me of a bank clerk or maybe some younger, shyer brother of Groucho Marx. One couldn't tell if he were a coach or held some managerial position within the Hungarian team, but I at least imagined, observing the respect he was given, that he might be some political commissar, responsible for reporting on the team's behavior. I could not have been more wrong.

His name was Béla Bay, or, more affectionately, "Béla Bacsi" ("Uncle Béla"), and he had saved Hungarian fencing. His father was a nobleman from the far east of Hungary, now Romanian Transylvania, and Bay grew up in his father's sprawling forests, where he learned to hunt. When his parents divorced, he moved to Budapest with his mother, training as a lawyer. Taught to fence by László Gerencsér, before long he was accomplished at all three weapons, winning the national title twice at both foil and épée and reaching the Olympic épée final in 1936, the year before he graduated. By the time the war came he was captain of his club. As such, he was ordered to expel all Jews. He duly summoned every fencer whom he knew to be Jewish and made each write out a letter of resignation—but without dating it. Thereafter, whenever a visiting official asked after a particular fencer, he would date the letter and present it; meanwhile the Jewish members fenced on. Other Jews he hid in his flat in Budapest or in the homes of friends. He also made sure that his father's forests were put to good use, so that by war's end scores of Jews had Béla Bay to thank for their lives.

After the war came the Soviets. Bay realized that to be an aristocrat in the new Hungary was at best to court unemployment, possibly a labor camp. Fencing offered a lifeline, so he gave up law and turned to coaching. At first he feared that the Communists would view the sport as decadent and upper class, and do away with it entirely. He helped his new rulers see that sport could be of propaganda use. It was a simple equation. Fencing events involved four weapons, offering the possibility of one gold medal for each individual event, plus another five for team events—a total of twenty-four golds. His logic prevailed, and fencing was reprieved.

In 1948 the Communists appointed István Kutas as unofficial sports commissar. Kutas was not a minister but rather a Richelieu-like figure who exercised the real power while officials made the day-to-day decisions. He kept his position for more than twenty years. Kutas soon took a liking to the cultured and obliging coach who would take him wild boar–hunting on his old estate, and Bay was appointed overall captain of all international fencing. Kutas was no fool; he had a good eye for talent, and in 1952 Hungary returned from the Olympics with sixteen golds. At first he told Bay that he wanted the old military schools like the Toldi Miklos Sports Institute kept closed. (The Soviets regarded the Hungarian military as suspect, as they had fought against them during the war.) But Bay turned even the schools' closure to advantage.[10]

In 1951 two leading fencers told him in desperation that under the Communists they had no hope of getting jobs suitable to their qualifications. "Do the one thing you can do better than anyone else," he told them, "teach your sport." One of these men was György Piller; the other was József Hatz, a onetime army colonel who went on to train Ildikó Rejtö, Olympic foil champion in 1964.

Bay argued with Kutas that to replicate Hungary's achievements with new, Communist-trained athletes could take twenty years. Why not restore the old system, he cajoled, putting top athletes into a special military sports academy? Soon a "sports military unit" was created, with top coaches from every discipline as well as amateurs of talent. Thus Rudolf Kárpáti, saber gold medalist in 1956 and 1960, by profession a musicologist, was commissioned into the army. Years later he died a general without ever having seen active service.*

Hungary was thus able to continue as the top saber power regularly winning in foil and épée as well. There was hardly a blip on the graph of success. A new generation of masters, such as Hatz at foil, Imre Vass at épée, and János Szucs at saber, grew up and prospered in the new Hungary. Bay was always the technician, insisting that his pupils learn a wide repertoire of movements. The advent of electric foil suited the Hungarians, who produced a young, fit, and fast team. Then came the October invasion and the mass exodus. Bay could have emigrated—traveling out of the country was relatively easy for him—but he chose to stay. Why?**

When I was last in Budapest, I talked to Jenö Kamuti, twice world and twice Olympic silver medalist and arguably Hungary's most successful

---

* Kárpáti owned a substantial collection of classical and semiclassical records and for several years hosted one of Hungary's most popular radio shows. He also wrote a lecture series on the relationship between music and fencing footwork. He once withdrew from an army tank exercise in order to take part in a saber competition. He later ran into his commanding officer, who began, "Do you realize I am COLONEL KOVACS?" Hungary's fencing hero replied, "Yes, and I am MAJOR KARPATI." No further action was taken.[11]

** In 1958 at the world championships in Philadelphia the Soviet team reached the saber final to face Hungary. The Hungarians crushed them, not only winning easily but talking and joking among themselves even on the piste, as if their opponents were of no concern. When the Soviet manager asked Bay to give up a few bouts to his team, he was turned away with contempt.

In those days the team event was held before the individual—the order being reversed only in 1963. Five fencers of Hungarian origin who had moved to the United States and renounced their citizenship had entered the championships. At the FIE congress, held the day before fencing began, the Hungarian delegation objected, arguing that the fencers were not stateless, as they claimed, since Hungarian citizenship could be voided only with the consent of the Hungarian government. The U.S. delegation pointed out that an individual's right to renounce allegiance to a government was fundamental in most legal systems, and particularly in the United States. The U.S. had accepted the statelessness of the fencers concerned, and as the championships were being held on American soil the FIE would have to accept that ruling. A vote was taken, and the applicants were declared stateless. In an effort at compromise, the FIE now ruled that only three stateless fencers would be allowed to compete per weapon, based on an ad hoc selection principle. The Hungarians accepted this decision. Three days later, however, after a telephone call from Budapest, the Hungarians withdrew from the two events still to be fought, saber and épée, which included stateless fencers.

male foilist. A surgeon by profession and currently director of one of the largest hospitals in Budapest, he had been one of Bay's favorite pupils. I asked him what had governed his old master's decision to stay when so many others had left.

We were stretched out on the grass outside a sports hall about three miles from Budapest; both of us had been taking part in the veterans' world championships. Kamuti, dressed again, had loosened his tie and grinned in recollection. There were three reasons, he said, why Bay had never left. First, by 1956 his mother was old and unwilling to move. He could not leave her behind. And he was obsessed with hunting, which he was still able to do in forests he knew well. Most of all, he had told his protégé, "Fencing saved my life. I have a duty to give something back. If I leave Hungary now, fencing here could die."

He also feared that in the midst of the upheaval of 1956 there might be civil war, that the Soviets would come in, and that his country would end up as a Soviet state. Was he sympathetic to the Communist government, then? Kamuti shook his head. "No, no: he made a *pact* with communism—he didn't agree with it." The politicians tried to get their top sportsmen to accept the system, but Bay had a different agenda. He told his pupils not to ram their heads into the wall—not to take the system on headfirst. They should work around it, as had he.

"He was more than a master to me—like a second father," reminisced Kamuti. "He would give me advice about everything. When I was about twenty—the year before the uprising—he started giving me books I should read. There were many of them, but one I remember was Lawrence's *Seven Pillars of Wisdom*, to help me understand the Arab world. Another was *Country of the Czar*, by Maurice Paleologue. It explained why communism could take hold in Russia, but only there. This book was forbidden reading in Hungary. Béla Bacsi didn't agree with communism—he *made use* of it."

Bay died in 1999, still hunting into his nineties, having married his girlfriend of thirty years at the age of seventy-five. According to Kamuti, the only time he had seriously thought about leaving Hungary was when he was invited to be the number-one huntsman in New Zealand. But he had turned that down too.

There was a further piece of accommodation, however. In December 1951 Bay was asked to send twenty-four top fencers and coaches to Moscow to train with the young Russian team. They stayed there for several weeks, while the Soviet coaches watched, made notes, took pho-

*Béla Bay, "Uncle Béla," whose obsession with hunting
helped keep him from fleeing to the West.*

tographs, and recorded endless reels of film. They made literally hundreds
of pictures of Gerevich, including a complete film of his movements.
"With infinite patience and industry," a Hungarian épéeist recalled in
1960, "they worked out a complete choreography of fencing movements
and they conducted systematic research—with the help of doctors, psy-
chotherapists, medical sports institutes, etc.—into the motor reflexes, ca-
pabilities, reactions and even mental concentration of fencers."[12] The
Soviets liked gold medals too.

The Soviet Union entered its first Olympics in 1952. Overall, it ran a
close second to the United States in total points, but Soviet fencers were
still learning and were content to play the sidelines. By 1955 the Soviet
saber team came third at the world championships, and the following year
Lev Kuznetsov took the bronze for individual saber, his country's first
Olympic success in fencing. Two years later, at the top-rated Martini Foil

competition in Paris, the leading Soviet foilist, Mark Midler, beat the renowned French number two, Claude Netter, 10–0—a result one top coach judged "without parallel in the history of fencing."[13] Then, at the 1960 Rome Games, the fledgling Russian team took eight medals: three gold, three silver, and two bronze. Hungary won four: a gold (Kárpáti) and silver in the individual saber, a team saber gold, and a silver in the women's team foil. By then there were eighteen principal fencing centers in the Soviet Union and more than 30,000 federation members.

Béla Bay may have helped save Hungarian fencing, but he also handed over the secrets of its fifty-year supremacy to the Soviets. Between 1960 and 1980, Hungary won thirty-one Olympic medals in fencing, ten of them gold; the USSR won forty-one, seventeen gold. In saber alone, in the four Olympics from 1972 to 1988, Hungary won a silver and three bronzes; the Russian team four golds, four silvers, and two bronzes. Since 1964, the Russian sabreurs have reached every Olympic final—bar 1984, which the Soviets boycotted. The pupil had become the master.

Part Six

—

FAUSTIAN PACTS

Illustration: John Dyatta's drawing of two Stone Age figures showing contrasts. In every age it is possible to honor fair play.

Previous page: John Updike's drawing of two Stone Age figures observing the
courtesies. In every age, it is possible to honor fair play.

CHAPTER 18

The Burden of Gold

> Sow an action and reap a habit; sow a habit and
> reap a character; sow a character and reap a destiny.
>
> —RALPH WALDO EMERSON

> Better a fallen star than never a burst of light.
>
> —OSCAR WILDE

ONE BLUSTERY DAY IN BUDAPEST IN THE AUTUMN OF 1991, A predominantly male gathering was making its way to the main crematorium in the city. The mourners were well dressed for a cross section of the citizenry, for they belonged to an unusual elite. Most were Hungarian fencers or ex-fencers, though a delegation from the Polish Fencing Federation had made the journey from Warsaw, and there were Italians too, some Germans, even a Romanian. The dead man's widow was there, of course, as was his daughter. Conspicuous by their absence were any representatives of the Hungarian Federation. Someone else was absent, perhaps the person closest of all to the man being buried. But we will come to him later, and the role he had played in sending his patron into exile.

They had come to pay their respects to one of the greatest Hungarian masters, János Kevey. Two years after the end of World War II, Kevey had left his country to teach in Poland, where he initiated a saber revolution that finally put an end to Hungary's hegemony. But that is only part of the reason why no Hungarian officials came to honor him.

KEVEY'S STORY IS A COMPLICATED ONE. GERMAN BY BIRTH— "Richter" was his family name when he came into the world on February 28, 1907—his parents soon took up Hungarian citizenship and adopted the name "Kevey," from Kevevara, the village in southern Hungary where they lived. In the early 1930s János studied law and fenced. He was universities champion at foil and saber and went on to represent his country at the Student Games in Darmstadt, where he won a saber team gold. Thereafter he trained as a coach in the Budapest Military Academy and early in his career survived a vicious duel. In 1938 he spent a year teaching in Poland, training its national saber team.

By 1939 Kevey found himself in the army, where he became aide-de-camp to Miklós Horthy, a determined anti-Semite, whose fascist views he shared. He continued to fence and in 1940 won the Hungarian épée championship. When the country was overrun by German troops he fought on the side of his new masters. In 1945 the Soviet forces took Budapest and Kevey changed allegiance again, being appointed a major in the New Democratic Army. However, in the months after the capitulation the Russians instigated a series of political trials, and Horthy was prosecuted for war crimes, in particular for his actions against Jews during Hungary's alliance with the Nazis. As soon as the archives were examined, Kevey was indicted as well and summoned to court as a witness for the prosecution. Alone of those who testified, he declared his commanding officer innocent. It did little good: Horthy was executed soon afterward. Kevey was charged with collaboration and sentenced to several months in prison.

He spent this ample opportunity for reflection in reviewing the way saber had been taught, and decided that a new method was possible, based on a limited repertoire of fast, simple movements and above all on mobility. He would organize all attacks around the flèche. No one knows whether he persuaded his fellow prisoners to be his guinea pigs, but once his sentence was over he walked out of prison eager to put his theories into practice. However, there was no work for him in Budapest, where he was viewed as a traitor. Luckily for him, others felt differently. Following the invasion of their country in 1939, many Polish officers had escaped to Hungary, keen to continue fighting the Germans. When Hungary came into the war on the German side, Kevey had been one of those who helped hide these officers; after 1945 a number of these men won high office in Poland and proclaimed him a hero.

Poland was desperate to reconstruct itself. Thousands of young men and women saw sport as the key to a new life, and the Polish government, initially less under Moscow's sway than other Eastern European countries, was open to new ideas. Within the world of fencing, foil was generally considered a weapon for girls and beginners; épée, in Poland as in Hungary, was introduced comparatively late, whereas saber had a long history as a traditional weapon of the Polish cavalry. Young Poles eager to take up fencing were encouraged to turn to saber, and Kevey was invited to take over the national team.

He was not content to bring together a new cadre of athletes; over time, he inveigled the best of the younger fencers throughout the country to leave their current masters to come to his special training camps in Warsaw. Once he had drawn together a group of the quality he wanted, he told them what he had in mind. To emulate the Hungarians would take at least twenty years: there was no shortcut to perfect technique. But he did have a shortcut to success. The Hungarians were vulnerable to speed, and by working on a limited range of quick strokes he would give his squad the edge to win.

One of his pupils, Wojciech Zabłocki, an architect in training from Kraków, remembers Kevey teaching them to make direct attacks from relatively close in, flèching so quickly that it was impossible to parry. Kevey progressively extended the distance while keeping the tactics. "I used to practice thousands of flèches against the wooden door of my room. The door ended up partly destroyed, and I hurt myself too," recalls Zabłocki. "As I was light and had strong legs I developed a flèche that was horizontal, and Kevey adopted this for his school. We took photos that amazed everyone—but this was partly because the camera was down low so the flèche seemed exaggeratedly high."[1]

The training program upon which Kevey insisted was exacting, but at first there was little to show for it. From 1948 to 1956 the medals went the way they always had—to Hungary, then Italy, with the occasional French intervention. Poland was improving, but slowly, and to complicate matters a new rival appeared: the Soviet Union. To win, the Poles were going to have to beat the Russians too—only the Russians were their overlords and expected them to share their new techniques.

In February 1952 Kevey took a squad to Moscow to demonstrate his training methods. On arrival he was enthusiastically feted—flowers, banners, cheering. As the team negotiated the welcoming throngs, Kevey suddenly paled; several of the team thought he was going to faint. That evening he explained that he had recognized a man in the crowd as the officer who had interrogated and beaten him in prison. Throughout the rest of the visit the normally assured coach was terrified that he might be arrested again. Nothing happened that time, but several years later, the day after Warsaw honored him with a state award for his services to Polish sport, Kevey learned that the Hungarian government had demanded his extradition for complicity in German war crimes. Again he was fortunate: the president of the Polish Committee for State Sport was a friend, and the request was ignored.

It is hard to underplay Kevey's impact upon his contemporaries. He had the build of a stocky boxer, surmounted in middle age by a shock of perfectly white hair over a broad, heavily lined face. He was a dominating figure, full of life, who liked to control those around him, an insatiable womanizer who always seemed to be married to a different rich wife. Paradoxically, he would not allow his fencers any sexual activity in the week preceding competition, although he advised it the night before, "to help quicken them." He would monitor his protégés' food and drink. They could take salt but not sugar, while alcohol, coffee, and other stimulants were forbidden. In training camps he would wake his pupils at five or six in the morning and order them to go swimming, even in winter, in the ice-cold water of a nearby lake. In a short memoir of his teacher, Wojciech Zabłocki describes him discounting other coaches, claiming any success as his own, and becoming "father, mother, creator—God."

By 1953 results started to roll in. At the Under-21 world championships in Paris, Zabłocki took first place. The silver went to Jerzy Pawłowski, a legal student tied to the army. At the senior world championships in Brussels, Poland took a bronze team medal, its first success since 1934. At the next championships, in Luxembourg, Pawłowski came fourth behind three Hungarians. The following year, in Rome, it was Zabłocki's turn—fourth again. In Melbourne in 1956, Pawłowski was runner-up to the great Hungarian Rudolf Kárpáti. The Poles also took the team silver, ousting Italy. Kevey immediately asked for a pay raise but was told that, though his work was greatly appreciated, he was asking for a higher salary than the new first secretary, Władysław Gomułka.

However playful this repulse, Kevey knew that for his Polish masters the goal was gold, a dream as elusive as ever. The idea began to circulate that maybe Kevey, so long seen as the solution, was in fact becoming the problem. One team official was told by a discerning German coach, "I'm surprised such intelligent youngsters put up with such stupefying training." The message was passed on.

Kevey's young charges were becoming restless, but what could they do? "The only way to get rid of him was to lose," admitted one. "But we wanted above all to *win*." Kevey realized that his fencers no longer trusted him and began to exercise his authority more heavily. At the 1957 world championships came the victory for which he had been longing. In the eight-man saber final were two great Hungarians of the old guard, Kárpáti and Kovács, and two newcomers, Horváth and Mendelényi. Overconfident and focused on securing all four top places, the senior Hungarians gave their bouts to their younger colleagues, and although Kárpáti easily beat Pawłowski he was saddled with two "losses" and had to watch as the young Pole beat his three countrymen to take the title outright—Hungary's first loss since 1920 and Poland's first victory ever—so unexpected that the organizers had not laid in a recording of the Polish national anthem.[2]

The following year Kevey was convinced that his team would take the gold—but it lost to the Russians in the semifinals, and managed only a bronze (Twardokens) in the individual. Kevey called a press conference, at which he roundly berated his team. Accusing them of "immoral behavior," he declared, "They didn't want to use my methods." Spearheaded by Pawłowski, the saber squad wrote a letter to its association saying they no longer wanted Kevey as their coach. So public a declaration of disillusionment could not be ignored. By 1958 Kevey's contract was terminated, and he was on the move again, this time to Italy.

With its teacher gone, the Polish team found the impetus it needed

János Kevey playacts with his young charges during an outdoor training session. Soon the rebellion would be all too real.

and in the 1959 world championships finally upended the Hungarians. For the next five years it dominated world saber. It narrowly lost the team gold to Hungary at the Rome Olympics, but retained its world title in 1961, 1962, and 1963. Pawłowski failed in Tokyo in 1964 but took a second world title in 1965 and a third in 1966. In 1967 he came second to a Russian, Mark Rakita. In Mexico in 1968, the whole fencing community waited to see if he could at last triumph at an Olympics. He was thirty-six; time was running out.

There was a six-man final: two Russians, Rakita and Vladimir Nazlimov; the defending Olympic champion, Tibor Pésza of Hungary; one Italian, Rigoli; and two Poles, Pawłowski and the rising star Josef Nowara. Pawłowski lost 5–2 to Pesza, an old nemesis, but won his other bouts, leaving him to fight a barrage with Rakita for the gold. Rakita was one of the great stylists of Russian saber; the son of a prizewinning nuclear scientist, he was notably intelligent and, although not as fast as some rivals, would destroy them on tactics and technique. But that day he could not stop Pawłowski from taking a 3–1 lead. Slightly against character, Rakita then attacked twice, each time Pawłowski counterattacking too late. Next the Russian executed a sharp parry-riposte to take the lead 4–3—a single hit from the gold. Probably expecting a third badly timed counter, he made a third direct attack, but this time Pawłowski took a parry and made a fast riposte: 4–4.

It was a given in the saber community that one did not try to hit Rakita at his head: his quint parry was rock-solid, and he always seemed to know when an attack or riposte was coming there. Now Pawłowski feinted, as if to attack again. Rakita launched into his own attack, but the Pole was ready for him, parried—and hit Rakita in the center of his mask. Poland had its first individual gold, in one of the most popular victories of all time.

THE TEAM KEVEY HAD CREATED WAS REMARKABLE IN A NUMBER OF ways. It was not a cadre of professional athletes, sportsmen with little in mind except the precepts of the fencing hall. Pawłowski, who had taken up the sport late (at sixteen, in 1948), was a qualified lawyer (whose dissertation subject had been "A Critique of Hayek's Neo-Liberal Conception of Liberty and Law") and a major in the army, and a protégé of General Wojciech Jaruzelski, later the Polish head of state. Zabłocki would become one of the world's leading designers of sports stadiums as well as an exhibited watercolorist and an authority on the history of fencing. Zbigniew

Jerzy Pawłowski lands his second world saber title in 1965. This newspaper cutting was stuck inside the scrapbook of his team colleague and fellow Olympic champion Witek Woyda; years later Woyda learned that throughout this period Pawłowski was sending reports back about him to the Polish authorities.

Czajkowski, another key member of the group, would qualify as a doctor and write over twenty books on fencing and sports psychology. He became manager, then head coach, of Polish fencing (as he is still, in his eighties), helping to take Polish foil and épée to the same level as saber.*

Then there was Ryszard Parulski, world youth saber champion in

---

* Early in the Second World War, Czajkowski was fighting the Red Army and Belorussian partisans in eastern Poland when he and four other teenagers were captured by partisans. "They wanted to hang me; they'd even prepared a rope," he recalls.[3] Instead, two Soviet officers ordered him to Kobrýn, to be interrogated by a military commissar. After a short interview, he was sent home. In April 1940 he was captured once more, this time by Soviet troops, and spent more than a year in prison. Still only eighteen, he was sent to the infamous labor camp at Vorkuta in the Arctic north, where more than 2 million Poles would perish. In September 1941 he escaped, making his way by foot,

1959, world foil champion in 1961, and in 1963 a member of the gold-medal-winning épée team: he became a leading lawyer, representing Solidarity in the 1980s, and president of Polish fencing from 1979 to 1982. Two others on the team were Emil Ochyra, world individual silver medalist in 1961, a depressive who would commit suicide at the age of thirty-five by throwing himself from a window; and Ryszard Zub, who would leave Poland in 1969 for Padua, to become, within three years, saber coach to the Italian team—a remarkable reversal in the normal traffic in top coaches.

But Pawłowski was the group's prince and seemingly never aged. In all, he was a world finalist eighteen times. In 1973, at the Göteborg championships, he reached the final for the last time at forty-two, only narrowly missing a medal, nearly twenty years after his first. That same year he published his autobiography, *Trud olimpijskiego złota* (*The Burden of Olympic Gold*).[4]

Pawłowski was a hero not only among fencers. His book on the Olympics, his regular appearances on television, and his talks to sports clubs and army units made him a known figure throughout Poland. He received the highest decorations the state could bestow, and under his auspices fencing grew into one of the country's most popular sports. Appointed president of Polish fencing while still an active team member, he was also central to dealings between the government and Legia, Warsaw's leading club, which was subsidized by the army. "So great was the country's pride in Pawłowski's prowess," *Time* magazine was to report, "that Polish Party chief Edward Gierek is said to have brought the fencer with him to an informal meeting with Soviet Party Chief Leonid Brezhnev."[5] In the mid-1960s, while studying law at Warsaw University, Pawłowski drove around in a Mercedes 300—the same model as used by his country's prime minister. By this time he was living in the center of Warsaw, on Warecki Street, in a five-room apartment full of antiques, expensive books, and good paintings. But people didn't begrudge their hero his way of life: he had earned it. He was popular outside Poland too; he spoke several languages with ease, and his mischievous charm won him

---

donkey, camel, and barge to Uzbekistan in Central Asia. By February 1942 he had reached the newly formed Polish forces within the USSR and begged to be allowed to join the Polish navy. Rejected, he made a second extraordinary journey by way of India, Persia, and South Africa to Britain and enlisted at the Polish naval base in Plymouth, where he was assigned to the *Oelazak*, Destroyer L26. By the end of 1942 his ship held the record for the number of German planes shot down. Czajkowski served in the Dieppe raid and the landings on Sicily and at Salerno.

friends worldwide, especially in Britain and America. The ladies loved him and the gentlemen envied him, for the most part without rancor.

Then there was his fencing. At a dinner in Budapest in the 1960s, the U.S. saber captain jokingly said to Pál Kovács that Pawłowski was "the last Hungarian Olympic champion." Kovács, so great a champion himself, paused only for a moment before agreeing. By then the lightning-fast tear-away of the 1950s had been replaced by a supreme technician with the footwork of a dancer. Not only could he win; he displayed an extraordinary grace, combined with an acute strategic sense. A rival team manager reckoned that Pawłowski had eight different ways of moving forward—eight styles of footwork, each calculated to induce a different reaction.[6] One teammate recalls Pawłowski's lessons with Kevey, their blades moving so fast that even an experienced onlooker could not follow the action.[7] In his final years in Poland, Kevey took to giving Pawłowski lessons with a saber in each hand, so that the old coach could parry and riposte almost simultaneously: "Why waste time?" he would say. Pawłowski just got faster.

Pawłowski stories are the stuff of legend. In the early days, before the Hungarians had been toppled, Kevey was still unsure that his young team could win on talent alone. In the late 1950s, during a competition in Budapest before a partisan home crowd, he told Pawłowski—set to fight Zoltán Horváth, who regularly beat him—that if he used his usual tactics he was sure to lose yet again: Horváth's technical repertoire was too great. Instead, he should use his speed to get an early hit by counterattacking to the head as the Hungarian came forward. Horváth would take note and expect a second flèche; instead Pawłowski should sit back and wait—play with distance, make an occasional false attack, but not commit himself. The crowd would get restless and taunt their champion for not polishing off this diminutive Pole. Horváth, a vain man much given to brooding when his plans went awry, would become frustrated, get too close in his anxiety to score—and Pawłowski could trust himself to flèche again.

The match went ahead as foreseen. Pawłowski scored the first hit, then seemed to do nothing. The crowd started to chant—"*Hughue, hughue, hajra!*"—exhorting its man on in the words of an ancient battle cry dating back to Attila the Hun. After a few moments of chanting, Pawłowski suddenly stopped, took off his mask, and started to conduct the audience with his saber. Eventually realization dawned—among those looking on, and for Horváth. In Russian the word, pronounced phonetically "Hughie," coincidentally means "penis," or, more accurately, "prick"; in Polish, the word is spelled "*Huj*" but pronounced similarly. The crowd was unintentionally insulting its champion. The fight resumed, Horváth pressed angrily forward, and Pawłowski hit him again and again, to win with ease.[8]

Pawłowski became adept at playing not only audiences but juries and referees too. In the Buenos Aires world championships of 1962 he confronted Horváth once again, in the culminating match for the team gold. Horváth was set on revenge, especially as there were many Hungarian emigrants in the audience who had come to see their old country triumph; but time and again the judges seemed to miss his hits and give their votes to Pawłowski. Not once but twice Horváth became so furious that he laid mask, glove, and saber on the strip and glared successively at his opponent and each of the five judges. On both occasions Pawłowski—beaming, cracking jokes, winking at the audience—collected Horváth's equipment and with extravagantly demoralizing courtesy handed it back to him. Poland soon had its second team gold.

The following year, at the world championships in Gdańsk, a similar drama unfolded. In the individual final Pawłowski was forced to accept second best, losing to the Russian Jacob Rylski. Three days later came the saber team final, pitting the Poles against a fast-improving Russian side. The match ended in eight victories apiece, which meant that each team would have to nominate one member to a winner-take-all fight-off. Zabłocki had won three of his four bouts, while Pawłowski had lost two, including a 2–5 defeat by Rylski. The Poles told Zabłocki to warm up, which he did energetically, while Pawłowski took a lesson in secret behind the stands. The Russians, deceived, did not put forward Rylski, their new champion, but Ouimar Mavlikanov, as their only fencer to have beaten Zabłocki; and were astounded when Pawłowski took the strip. Minutes before, Pawłowski had been given a shot of neat vodka, which seems to have done the trick: he trounced Mavlikanov 5–0, staggering theatrically off the piste into his teammates' arms.

This showmanship extended beyond the fencing hall. In 1973 the world championships were held in Göteborg, a city renowned for its nightlife, particularly its sex shows. One distinguished French referee recalls that, taken to the most celebrated of these, he found himself in an audience crowded with fencers from all nations. The show was a pageant of celebrated women from the past, each girl coming on stage "dressed" as a famous figure from history. At its climax, a particularly pretty actress sashayed onstage in an approximation of Marie-Antoinette and slowly, layer by layer, took off the top half of her clothes until she was naked from

*Pawłowski on the attack against Viktor
Sidiak of the USSR, gold medalist of 1972.*

the waist up. Below, she still wore the enormous bustle of eighteenth-century court fashion. As she moved center stage the bustle, which was hinged, suddenly parted—to reveal Pawłowski, milking the moment for all it was worth. The two performers, straight-faced throughout, took a bow to rapturous applause. How he had inveigled himself into the show, he never revealed.

Pawłowski was still part of the Polish team the following year, at the world championships in Grenoble. He had been ill in the weeks leading up to the event and was not sufficiently prepared: even so, it was a surprise when he was eliminated in the quarterfinals. What none of us knew then was that we would not see him again for more than a decade. It was later alleged that he had planned to stay on in France after the championships. However, his poor showing meant that he was still 2.5 points (the equivalent of a silver medal) away from overtaking Eduardo Mangiarotti as the most successful fencer of all time—an accolade calculated from world and Olympic top-three placings. His plan, he later revealed, had been to get to the Montreal Games, achieve his goal, then apply for asylum in America. Instead, he simply disappeared "as if he had fallen through the earth," as a Polish reporter put it.

News leaked out over that summer that he had been arrested "for crimes against the interests of the state." Then other rumors started to make the rounds—that he had committed suicide in Modlin Prison outside Warsaw; that he had been engaged in illegal currency trading (which would not have been unusual: most East European sportsmen dabbled in foreign exchange) or was involved in a smuggling ring; then that he was working for the French, that he was working for NATO, for the KGB, for the British—nobody in the fencing community seemed to know anything for sure. Only one fact was clear: Pawłowski was an army officer; if tried and found guilty of spying, he would face the death penalty.

A rumor began to circulate that a disaffected ex-CIA agent, Philip Agee, had just completed a book, *Inside the Company, a CIA Diary,* which, while it did not specifically name Pawłowski, nevertheless incriminated him.[9] According to the *Los Angeles Times,* the two had met in Mexico City in 1968, where Agee was working under the cover of special Olympic attaché at the American embassy. When the book appeared in late 1975, it was hard to tell whether it implicated Pawłowski or not. Soon after, in a follow-up volume, *On the Run,* Agee strenuously denied that he and Pawłowski had ever met and said that the suggestion that he had "fingered" the Pole was an Agency attempt to discredit him because of his criticisms.[10]

Some time later I heard another version of events, this time from Zbigniew Czajkowski, by now Poland's head coach. In 1974 a spy working for a NATO power defected to the Bulgarian Embassy in Havana and revealed that he had five coagents. One of them was "Pawel"—Pawłowski's principal nickname (although he had several others: Polish counterintelligence knew him both as "Szczery," "The Sincere One," and "Gracz," "The Card Player," because of his fondness for poker; he was also sometimes called "Papuga," "Parrot"). That same year Pawłowski had been in Moscow and had spent a night with a woman in his hotel room. While she slept he looked inside her handbag and discovered that she had taken his secret notebook, with all his Western addresses and contacts. He recovered it, but sometime later it was stolen from his car. He went once more to Moscow, to sign a publishing deal, but instead was met by security officials at the airport. His friend General Jaruzelski, at that time Minister of Defense, came to his aid, insisting that it was impossible for Pawłowski to be a spy. He was an honest and courageous Pole, against whom there was no conclusive evidence. As with Kevey twenty years before, the case was seemingly dropped, under hazy circumstances.

But a number of Pawłowski's friends and colleagues knew that something was in the wind. A foil team member had been told that the police were closing in and in January 1975 passed on a warning when they met at training camp. Pawłowski applied for a visa to go abroad and for the first time was refused. One night after practice, when showering with another friend and rising saber star, Jacek Bierkowski, he confided that he was having problems with his passport and admitted that he was desperate.

Even then, he was desperate with style. Just days before his arrest, he and Zabłocki drove to a film set in the countryside outside Warsaw, where they had been invited to take part in a production of Sheridan's *The Rivals*. They got chatting with two girls in the makeup department, and Pawłowski suggested to Zabłocki that they stay overnight to see what might come of it. Zabłocki made his excuses and left his friend in sole possession. Whatever else one makes of this episode, it shows remarkable sangfroid. Two weeks later, at the beginning of May, Pawłowski was arrested. Radio Free Europe broadcast the news on June 11.

Just before he was taken into custody, Pawłowski had been pronounced the most outstanding sportsman Poland had produced in more than a decade. *Time* would call him "the undisputed sports hero of Poland."[11] Thus, as the influential *Neue Züricher Zeitung* put it, "the news of his arrest shocked the Polish public, especially the army and young people, for whom he was almost a national idol." The Polish government had "added to this dismay by removing his name from its prominent position in its 'Program of Patriotic Education.'"[12]

Almost immediately, continued the *Zeitung*, influential figures in the government and the army had tried to cover up the affair, convinced there would be "unpleasant consequences" if Pawłowski were brought to trial. At the same time, the Russian representative on the Warsaw Pact High Command demanded "an exemplary sentence"—in other words, the death penalty. Pawłowski was interrogated for two and a half months—which explains why his appearance in court was so long delayed—and eventually put on trial before a Polish military tribunal meeting in secret. It found him guilty and gave him a sentence that had no standing under Polish law—twenty-five years' imprisonment—for espionage "on behalf of an undesignated NATO country." There was talk that he had been spared the death sentence because he had used to go out hunting (he was a fine marksman) with Jaruzelski; but the court itself declared that it had not invoked the ultimate penalty because he had admitted his crimes, revealed his contacts, and provided a detailed account of all his spying activ-

Pawłowski entered the army while a student and rose to the rank of major; in Polish law his treachery carried the death penalty.

ities. There had been a tense struggle between the military and civilian authorities as to who would try the case. Had it gone to the civilian courts—more under Moscow's thumb than the military—Pawłowski would have been unlikely to have survived.

One of Pawłowski's friends, Jerzy Kosinski, for many Poland's leading literary figure, wrote of the affair in *Blind Date*, a roman à clef published in several languages, which in the absence of an official version became accepted as the most nearly accurate account. The novel revolves around the adventures of its mysterious central character, Levanter. One of his old friends is "J.P.," a legendary figure: "three times world fencing champion, Olympic gold medalist, winner of scores of other international meets, J.P. ranked as the greatest fencer of all time."[13] After various adventures, Levanter is warned by an Arab diplomat that the Polish government is poised to act against J.P., who sure enough is arrested as he steps off the plane after a trip to New York and taken to a fortress. Kosinski continues:

> For a while there was silence about his fate. Then the first ominous sign appeared. In one of the country's official publications, a well-known Party hack published a cartoon showing J.P. as a hooded, trench-coated, saber-rattling spy, superimposed on a graph of military secrets, his weapon broken, his leg chained to a ball. The word

was soon out that J.P. had refused to co-operate and play into the hands of his accusers. . . .

From various leaks and rumors, the following picture of J.P.'s interrogation had reached Western intelligence. J.P. had been seated in a chair in a large, stark room, the diplomat told Levanter, and had been grilled under glaring lights. After a long session of loaded questions clearly designed to wear him down, the fencer had pointed to his arm and shouted, "You can't destroy what this arm stands for. It belongs to the people!"

The officer in charge got up from behind his desk and entered the circle of light to stand behind the fencer. "Is this the arm you speak of?" he asked calmly, tapping J.P.'s right shoulder.

J.P. swung around in his chair to face him. "Yes, Colonel, this is the arm," he said, extending it with pride.

The officer looked at the outstretched arm. Swiftly he grabbed it with both hands and, putting all his weight on one leg, pushed the chair away with the other. Like a peasant breaking a twig in two, the colonel bent the fencer's arm over the back of the chair, then pressed down. The elbow snapped with a loud crack, and the arm went limp. J.P. howled and tried to pull free, but the colonel twisted the broken arm sideways and brought the wrist down over the back of the chair. Now the wrist cracked, and the hand went as limp as the arm. Moaning, J.P. slid from the chair onto the floor. "So much for the arm of the people," said the colonel, returning to his desk.

This horrific description, by an author who had won numerous international prizes, buttressed with inside information about Pawłowski's career and arrest, was taken as authoritative: both the *Los Angeles Times* and *Time* magazine, among others, reported it as fact. It was totally fictitious; but the word circulating among the fencing community was that Pawłowski's fencing arm had been broken.

The rumor mill had not finished grinding. Within weeks *Der Spiegel* reported that another Polish fencer, Witek Woyda, who had taken both the foil individual and team gold at the Munich Olympics, had fled to the West and that a third sportsman, a field athlete, Marek Bodynski, had been shot dead trying to escape.[14] Neither story was true, although Woyda did leave Poland for Italy, finally settling in America. A final rumor had Pawłowski committing suicide: according to the officer who first interviewed him after his arrest, following the verdict, "he asked me when he'd be taken off to start his prison sentence, because, he said, he wanted to finish his life 'honorably.' Everyone understood he meant to take his own life, but then he turned up bang on time for his sentence."[15]

The authorities were not content to throw their former hero into prison. Shortly after his arrival, two inmates, apparently put up to it by their guards, jumped Pawłowski; he had to fight them off. But over time his treatment improved. When Jacek Bierkowski took the individual silver at the Budapest world championships that summer, Pawłowski was allowed to send his protégé a congratulatory telegram.

Pawłowski's arrest had immediate repercussions. A number of other officers were convicted with him and sentenced on similar charges. Some 120 Polish fencers were interrogated. Several senior officers were replaced, and even the head of the Polish navy was relieved of his post. A few weeks later the fifty-three-year-old admiral died suddenly, "in mysterious circumstances."

Many unanswered questions remained. For example, to what secrets could a sportsman have access? Pawłowski knew several senior officers as friends and moved in exalted circles. One close associate told me that he had passed on radar codes for military aircraft. Pawłowski said he had simply compiled intelligence reports on various people he met, "character assessments," but if that had been the full story it is unlikely his arrest would have caused such an upheaval.

On June 11, 1985, after serving a little over ten years of his sentence, Pawłowski was exchanged for three East European spies arrested in Belgium. He was taken to the Glienicker Bridge between East and West Berlin and given back his passport; extraordinarily, he was not stripped of his citizenship. At this he turned around and asked to be driven back to Warsaw: "I am a Polish patriot." According to Roman Zajkowski of Polish counterintelligence, "To the last minute we didn't know what he was going to do. Throughout the plane journey there I sat next to his wife Iwonka, but he didn't say a word." Later Pawłowski did somewhat let down his mask: "It was a strange feeling, being in my mid fifties, watching those who went across while I stayed. I knew I was disappointing the Americans, but I have never regretted not going to the West. If I'd gone I'd have given the Communists ammunition for showing me in a negative light. By staying I shut them up."[16]

Soon after, Pawłowski went to one of the main Warsaw clubs, Marymont, where his old teammate Ryszard Parulski, now president of Polish fencing, was happy to let him practice. He took on most of the young bloods there and won nearly every fight. A few weeks later he entered a classification tournament, just missing the final. Janek Koniusz, who would win silver at the 1989 world championships, recalls that "his legs had gone, and he couldn't concentrate on any subject for any length of time, but his hand was as fast as ever." There was much talk as to how he would fare in the Polish national championships, but this time Parulski did not allow him to take part; parents of young fencers had told him that they did not want their sons shaking hands with a traitor. It was the last time Pawłowski attempted to fence in competition.

So what had made him a spy? Pawłowski had fame, unlimited travel privileges, and a pampered life in Poland. He was a zloty billionaire, owning a sheep farm just outside Warsaw and a share of a restaurant (both farm and restaurant were confiscated on his conviction), and all agreed he was a patriot. So why?

"My heart is Polish, my mind American," Pawłowski has said; but East European friends at the New York Athletic Club, where I now fence, laugh at the notion that his motive was ideological. "With Jerzy it was always money," they say. At the end of August 2000 I spent several days in Warsaw, including a day and a half with Pawłowski. We talked both afternoons at his favorite ice-cream parlor, where he was warmly welcomed, at his home, and in the house of his longtime friend and rival, Wojciech Zabłocki. My first meeting was with Zabłocki, who had his own view of matters: "Jurek [as he calls him] always liked to take risks. Gambling made life more interesting—made the adrenaline flow—and if that could be combined with getting more money and hurting the Russians, so much the better. But taking risks was at the heart of it: it's what made him such a good fencer." It also gave him a secret life, I reflected, making him different from those around him. I recalled the British spies of the 1930s and 1940s, Guy Burgess, Donald Maclean, and Anthony Blunt, homosexuals when homosexuality was illegal, living two secret lives at once; and thought about how fencing depends on deception, on suggesting the opposite of one's real intentions . . .

Zabłocki described how Pawłowski loved to negotiate deals during trips abroad, selling equipment he had been given and using the currency to buy foreign goods, which he would then resell, often openly cheating his teammates, even telling them what he had done afterwards. Once, in the late 1950s, he told Zabłocki, after selling him a watch, that he had paid considerably less for it, expecting his friend to be affronted. Zabłocki had been through this too often to take the bait. Pawłowski pressed on: "So, you know, I cheated you on that exchange." Zabłocki did eventually reply, "Yes, I know," but without displaying any anger or resentment. Pawłowski never cheated him again.

At least, not on currency matters. But there was one fencing encounter that Zabłocki has never forgotten. Unlike the Hungarians and the Italians, the Poles did not fix bouts among themselves—Pawłowski and Zabłocki were so competitive that they always fenced for victory—and in 1959 they tied for first place in a big international tournament in Italy, having to fight off to determine who would be champion.

The great Eduardo Mangiarotti was asked to referee the fight. Though primarily an épéeist and foilist, he fancied himself a saber referee, yet again and again he gave doubtful hits in Pawłowski's favor, until Zabłocki was defeated. Afterwards an exultant Pawłowski explained to his teammate that before the bout he had sought out Mangiarotti to urge that he put himself forward as referee. "You are easily the best person here. You never make mistakes; it would be quite wrong for them to ask anyone but you." Mangiarotti needed no second bidding and richly repaid Pawłowski's initiative.

I can still remember fencing Pawłowski at the Vienna world championships in 1971. It soon became clear that the final place among those who would be promoted in an early round rested between myself and an American, Al Morales, who then beat me 5–2. My last fight in the pool was against Pawłowski, who had not lost any of his other bouts, and I knew I could win promotion only by beating him. There were several classes of ability between us, but I knew that Pawłowski rarely tried his hardest against weaker opponents, and that although he loved to win he would fall back on certain set moves. I reckoned that I knew what these moves would be and managed to take the bout 5–1.

As we walked off the strip I mumbled something apologetic to Pawłowski, who said, with a wave of his hand, "My present to you." At the time I thought this gracious, but afterward I reflected that I had *earned* that victory; it wasn't my fault if he didn't want to put himself out against me. I had chosen the *right* moves—why couldn't he admit as much? Or maybe he hadn't been trying at all. . . . Years later I learned that Morales, a graduate of the U.S. Naval Academy, was rumored to have been working for the CIA. Rivalry among spies? And there was the simple fencing explanation: two years before, in Poland, Morales had beaten Pawłowski in

The desperate last-hit flèche by Walter Köestner to defeat Pawłowski during their match for the final at the 1964 Olympics. Pawłowski later claimed he had stopped fencing and was trying to help the German up.

a competition the Pole had expected to win. So what had really been going on that morning in Vienna?

Pawłowski made fencing look so easy that it was hard to know when he was totally engaged and when he was coasting. At the Tokyo Games in 1964, he had been the firm favorite, the reigning world champion and in top form.* In the last sixteen he was drawn against the German Walter Köestner: the first to land ten hits. He rapidly drew ahead 7–2, then started to toy with his opponent. The score went 7–3, 7–4, and on, until the two men found themselves at 9–all. At this moment Köestner launched himself in a desperate horizontal flèche, throwing his whole body forward, both feet off the floor. The attack landed on Pawłowski's arm: the world champion had been eliminated. I spoke to Köestner about the fight, and he remembered the last hit in detail. Pawłowski had a different version:

---

* Shortly before the Games, the Polish fencers had challenged their Olympic soccer team to a match, with the goals slightly reduced in size. Zabłocki was keeper, Pawłowski the leading forward. The fencers won 5–3, creating a storm in the home press.

he had seen the German stumble and stopped, holding out an arm to help him. As he did so Köestner's cut had landed. The last hit was an accident.

But I too remembered the hit—an extraordinarily dramatic picture had appeared in *The Times* the next day, making the German's all-out attack clear. Pawłowski could not admit the truth. But to his credit he did say that some time after his prison sentence was announced Walter Köestner had been among a group of German fencers who approached the Polish government offering half a million DM for Pawłowski's release. The deal was turned down flat.[17]

Zabłocki arranged for me to visit Ryszard Parulski, Pawłowski's teammate back in early 1960s, now in charge of the campaign to get the Olympics to Poland in 2012. I was invited to his office, reached through two sets of locked iron gates and furnished with plush black leather sofas and chairs. Parulski was dressed in similar style: black leather pants, a black open-necked shirt, and white silk scarf. He has drifted far to the right since his Solidarity days and is seen as Pawłowski's fiercest critic among Polish fencers. I told him Zabłocki's view of their famous contemporary. "Liberal nonsense," he snapped. "Pawłowski joined the army, then signed up as a Party member. He didn't have to do either—I didn't. He's trying to remake himself as a hero against communism, but he was always interested in money." He looked at me hard. "He took advantage of everyone; you *never* betray your country for money."

Afterward, Zabłocki picked me up and took me back to his house for lunch. I told him what Parulski had said, and he thought for a bit. When Pawłowski first got out of prison, he said, he had tried to clear his name—or at least win back his reputation—and planned to confront General Kiszczak, the minister who had been in charge of investigating him, to show that the accusations were unjustified. For a while the government did nothing, but after Pawłowski started proclaiming his innocence in public his trial transcripts were released, and in 1991, with a post-communist government, a leading magazine, *Prawo i Zycia* (*Truth and Life*), revealed that it had come out during the trial that Pawłowski had been spying for the Polish State Security services since August 1955—on his own teammates.[18] In the early 1960s he had even sent in three reports about his friend Witek Woyda, saying the foilist was selling his furniture in anticipation of fleeing the country. Soon other papers were commenting on the trial transcripts. They revealed that Pawłowski's job had been to tell the security services which athletes were planning to defect, who supported Israel, and who might be open to approaches. His spying ceased abruptly in March 1962, when it was judged that he was using his position "for personal gain."

The trial papers also revealed the results of a personality profile that the security services had run on Pawłowski, judging him to be egocentric, independent, able to predict an opponent's intentions, blessed with amazing reflexes, arrogant, lacking in self-criticism, presumptuous, respectful of those stronger than himself, suffering from an inferiority complex, and given to flattery. At Pawłowski's trial, a judge went further, describing him as "a traitor to his country, a careerist, and quite devoid of any noble feelings."

These reports were even more damaging to Pawłowski's reputation than the original charges. Typically, however, he has recently proclaimed that he was wrongfully, indeed fraudulently, indicted. He was enraged with two Polish journalists in particular, and was considering legal action. Zabłocki has urged him to lie low, as he knows the government has yet further accusations to make—that he had agreed while in jail to spy against Solidarity prisoners.

As Zabłocki and I were finishing lunch, Pawłowski arrived to pick me up. I spent the rest of the day with him and all the next day, until he and his wife of thirty-seven years, Iwonka ("Yvonne"), drove me to the airport. Pawłowski is tubby now and almost bald, but, though close to seventy and having recently survived a bout with cancer, still moves with deft assurance. "I am as strong as an ox." His house, a large, open-plan building he designed himself, is about twenty minutes from the city center. He was gracious and friendly throughout—except for one moment of startling anger, when he shouted at one of his three wolfhounds to behave. He seemed willing to talk about everything, showing me his large cellar with a sophisticated do-it-yourself kit, his paintings and mementos, but on almost every topic where he might be open to criticism he gave only vague replies.

Had he spied on his teammates, as the trial transcripts asserted? Pawłowski's face took on a crafty look, and he said simply that no one knew just when he had started to spy for the CIA—it was certainly before 1968. How much long before? 1952? He couldn't say more—it would incriminate people still alive. Furthermore, I shouldn't believe anything Parulski told me—"it was he who took on the task of getting rid of me from fencing." He then handed me a copy of his second book, *Najdluzszy pojedynek* (*My Longest Duel*) (1994),[19] an account, plain and simple, of his days as a spy. Unlike the first book, it is written in a sparse, dynamic style, colloquial and opinionated: a Polish friend of mine called it a "turn-pager." Throughout the Russians are the villains and Pawłowski the hero: "I will show those sons of bitches. We will see who will win in the end."

The book relates how he was approached during a trip to Padua—date unspecified—by an American named Joe Baker. From the first, Pawłowski writes, he insisted there be no payment; he was acting out of patriotism and a determination to exact revenge for what had been done to his country—the Katyn massacre of 1940, the torture and murder of members of the Polish Underground Army up to 1956, the Russians' betrayal of the Warsaw Uprising of August–October 1944, when they had deliberately stopped their advance, leaving the Germans to crush the rebellion. As a twelve-year-old he had been part of the uprising, and that desire for freedom motivated him still. Throughout his days with the Agency he had accepted only one gift: a holiday in Nice.

On the espionage itself he was extremely reticent: he had been involved with the army general staff, and one of his contacts had been "Jan Kowalski"—the Polish equivalent of John Smith. He insisted he had been doctrinally anti-Communist since the Games in Helsinki, when he had seen what life was like in the West. When I asked again about his ostensible collaboration with the Polish secret police, he went off on a tangent, replying that his longevity as a CIA agent could be evidenced by the KGB's many attempts to kill him. His book details two of their more extreme "countermeasures," when his car was sabotaged, once in Poland and once in Belgium—"I was a well-known figure; it was easier than charging me as a spy"—but each time he had escaped. His eventual trial was, he claimed, a victory for Communist propaganda: "See, we try our heroes."

In 1990 a German lawyer and ex-fencer, Wolfgang Lange, was empowered by Pawłowski to write to *Der Spiegel* to see if the magazine would commission an article about his life. Lange's letter reads in part:

> We represent the interests of a Polish client . . . against the U.S. government. We have attempted to contact the U.S. government re this matter but unfortunately have had no response. Therefore we are going public.

It details his imprisonment and release, then adds:

The embarrassing part of this arrangement for the U.S. was that our client's camouflage was revealed through betrayal in the headquarters of the CIA. David B., a CIA official, was paid $90,000 by the Soviet Union in exchange for the names of spies who worked against the Soviets—among them was our client.

Our client was recruited by the USA because he was a famous athlete and he could travel without suspicion between the East and West. Point of contact at that time was Colonel Lunkuist, head of the military service in Frankfurt. The first meeting of our client and Colonel Lunkuist took place during a fencing competition in Padua. Colonel Lunkuist was also a famous Formula One driver.

At the time our client was assured that, due to his work for the American secret services, he would never face financial problems of any kind and that after ten years of espionage he could emigrate to America. Money would not be a problem.[20]

So Pawłowski wanted a CIA pension, had got nowhere, and was trying to publicize his case. Lange's enquiry never came to anything, and although the German fencers put together a new life for him, with an undemanding role in their saber program, they never heard from him again. Understandably, those who offered help feel let down—but not surprised.

I had heard that when Pawłowski was first taken off to prison, to a decaying structure built in 1902, he was given a room on his own—cell 7—as no one would share with him. According to Pawłowski, there were *seven* men in his cell, pedophiles, psychopaths, and mentally deranged prisoners: "the worst types—people on the edge of society." Early on, he had to make it clear he was no "*swel*"—the lowest of the low among the prisoner population, who would rent his body out to others. He was allowed 112 zlotys—little more than a dollar—a week, one letter a month, two parcels a year. When life got easier, his son was even able to smuggle in chocolates and cigarettes during visits.

After his release Pawłowski cooperated on a film of his life for Austrian television. It has some interesting information not found elsewhere, such as the assertion that Pawłowski's formal accusation named two non-Poles as co-spies: a West German, Dieter Fenger, a national épée team member in the early 1960s, and an Israeli, "Checki" Zinnober. But mainly it gives its subject a very sympathetic ride, beginning with shots of him in straw hat and tartan shirt painting swans on a nearby lake. "I had a moral problem," he says. "To spy against my own country was the most effective way I had of fighting the enemy." The narrator asks at the film's end, "Was he a hero or only one who played too high?" Pawłowski gets the final say: "The real hero was my wife . . . in every day of my hard life."

All over their house, which he and Iwonka share with Iwonka's mother, are Pawłowski's paintings. Unlike Zabłocki, with whom he has exhibited, he paints only in oils. It is a hobby he took up in prison, using a toothbrush. He gave his first painting to another inmate, who asked him for it. He also became a jailhouse lawyer, helping inmates with their complaints. One prisoner, Fidel the Filipino, serving a life sentence for murder, became his chess partner. Fidel suffered from terrible head pains, and one day, in consternation, Pawłowski laid his hands on his friend's head. The man felt a strong heat and after a while said with intense relief, "Thank God—the bitch has left." His migraines never returned. Since then Pawłowski has taken this apparent gift seriously and turns up three times a week at one of the hospitals in Warsaw to help patients. Once, he says, he even helped cure his wife.

Later that day Iwonka, plump and pretty in a pink suit, joined us and confirmed his story: on holiday in the Canadian mountains, she fell and was convinced she had broken her leg. Pawłowski put his hands on her, and by the time she was brought down to the hotel and X-rayed there was no sign of any damage. "I myself didn't feel anything," Pawłowski says. "I was too angry—she was wearing such stupid shoes for climbing."

After her husband was taken into custody, Iwonka was told that her work as an obstetrician at the military hospital near their home would be imperiled if she did not file for divorce. She says, "I smiled and told them if that was their condition then I would give up being a doctor." Soon after, she lost her job. Only after her husband's release did she start working again. She and Pawłowski seemed very happy together. Was she in fact his third wife, or fourth? "Third!" he replied. "No—first—you know Arab saying? Third wife is first!"

Soon it was time for me to leave, and Pawłowski offered to drive me to the airport. In the car I was reminded of the only other visit Western fencers had made to the Pawłowski house. Roland Boitelle, former president of the FIE, and an American official, Ralph Zimmerman, had gone there for dinner during a top saber competition in Warsaw in the spring of 1986, within months of Pawłowski's release. Pawłowski doesn't ordinarily drink alcohol (bar that special medal-winning shot of vodka), but he raised his glass toward the central light, which he obviously thought was bugged, toasting "Poland and Freedom." At the end of the evening he gave Zimmerman an engraving he had done—of a suffering Christ. Then he drove his guests back to their hotel, setting off into the night like a demon. At one stage he drove through a red light, just as a police car came by, as if daring the car to give chase. He was still gambling.

On my own ride to the airport Pawłowski became mournful. He had been out of prison by the time Kevey died, he said, but no one told him, so he had never even tried to go to Budapest for his old teacher's cremation. "We may have argued at the end, but we were very close. We spent so much time together—we even shared girlfriends. When I left prison, he came to Poland just to see me. I hold it against them all that they never told me. I should have been there."

Kevey, who after his time in Poland had taught for several years in Turin, finally returned to coach in Hungary but never had the success in either country that he had enjoyed in Poland. The truth is that there he had had his pick of the country's most promising young fencers; although his teaching style had the veneer of a new system, he was basically propounding the classic Hungarian method. His horizontal flèche was eventually banned, and later flèching itself was outlawed. Nevertheless, he was a great teacher, the only saber coach worldwide to have worked at international level with three leading fencing nations, just not the original he declared himself to be. When Zabłocki, one of the two Poles at the memorial service, saw the urn carrying Kevey's ashes, he thought to himself: what a small urn for such a big man.

In *My Longest Duel* Pawłowski returns again and again to a famous figure from Polish mythology, Konrad Wallonrod. In the greatest of the romantic poems in which he appears, the young Wallonrod swears revenge against the German Knights of the Sword who have ravaged his country. He later joins them and leads them into a ruinous ambush. So he is both seeming traitor and hero-patriot—displaying what is called "double patriotism." It is a compelling image but for Pawłowski a self-justifying and unconvincing one. There is a Polish word for it—"*bajka*," a fairy tale.

Pawłowski was the great champion of my competitive days. "It is strange," wrote the journalist Simon Barnes, "how some athletes have this additional quality of watchability; something that makes them not only a great athlete but also a star. They draw every eye to themselves in triumph and disaster or when they are just having an ordinary day. Talent is something you take for granted at the high level of sport; watchability is something different."[21] Despite all the issues his life raises, I prefer to think of

Pawłowski as I saw him first: balletic, effortless, his compact body advancing and retreating under such control that his torso seemed not to move even as his legs carried him onward. He would launch into outlandish actions that had no right to succeed, even against his main rivals, just so he could set up a final hit with a flick to the wrist or the latest of parries, to leave audiences gasping at his audacity. Then the courteous smile, the slight nod, and that knowing look, as if he and the onlookers were sharing some secret.

Perhaps we were.

CHAPTER 19

Honor Betrayed

Escrimeur: (sport) fencer
[Immediate next entry] Escroc: crook, swindler, shark, con-man
—Collins French Dictionary, 1995

Honour! Tut, a breath,
There's no such thing in nature; a mere term
Invented to awe fools.

—BEN JONSON, Volpone, 1606

CHEATING HAS INFECTED FENCING, A SPORT ROOTED IN NOTIONS of honor and chivalry, since competitions began just as dueling, a procedure of honor, was always haunted by foul play. In the early years of international meets, France, Italy, and Hungary were so dominant that it was axiomatic that fencers from those nations would be given preferential treatment by juries, who were either too scared or too prejudiced to award hits fairly. (Most smaller European countries understandably concentrated on épée, the first weapon to be run electrically.) Dishonesty is rife and has been since the first modern Olympics, if not before.

That a sporting contest had to be continually scrutinized for false play was a late-nineteenth-century admission; and even then the idea that participants might systematically find a way round the rules was slow to take root. Cheating, particularly in Olympic sports, became a cause for concern about the time of the 1956 Games, by which time governments as well as individuals could see the advantages to be gained from sporting success, and fencers, particularly from Communist countries, could make a significantly better life for themselves with victories on the piste. Dr. Manfred Hoppner, East Germany's last chief of sports medicine, found guilty of feeding body-changing drugs to his charges, declared in his defense, "Competitive sport and sport for health are different things. Competitive sport begins where healthy sport ends."[1] Such a view is not limited to competitors from the old East Bloc: as standards of training, nutrition, and recruitment have risen, championship fencing has demanded more time and dedication, and most contestants have become professional in all but name. Any fencer who hopes to compete successfully on the international scene is expected to be able to "look after himself."

Until the advent of electrical épée in the late 1920s, hits were judged by eye. Up till 1932, one had to acknowledge touches—hence Laertes' "A hit, a palpable hit." And the target itself was strictly limited, a matter as much of good form as good fencing. "Imagine what it was [like] when every man wore, upon the breast leathers of his fencing jacket, a fine, big heart of red cloth, which told the world where the thrusts were to be and not to be," mused Richard Burton. "A point denting any other part of the garment was considered not only a failure but a blunder; it was not merely condemned by the rule of arms, it was overwhelmed with contempt. Circles, equally limited, were traced out for everything in the shape of attacks, parries, and ripostes."[2]

Burton was writing about foil in the late eighteenth century; by his day new measures had been introduced, particularly for épée, where the critical issue was who arrived first. The practice épée was given a blunt point, similar to the flat head of a nail, "made still more incapable of penetration by winding round it a small ball of waxed thread, such as cobblers use."[3] For competitions there were various forms of "boutons marqués," all unsatisfactory. For a while points were tipped with a red dye, so that a good hit would leave a woundlike daub on an opponent, and the intervals between fights would be spent rubbing the incriminating areas with removing fluids. One veteran Olympian recalls the distinctive smell of fencers' changing rooms—"a mix of perspiration and vinegar." In the 1950s the Russians invented an improved dye, which was soaked into cotton-wool pads on the tips of foils, to stain clothing for about thirty seconds before disappearing; but it proved totally impractical, since it could not record good hits and off-target hits in sequence.

At the same time that dyes were being used, the so-called point d'arrêt—literally, the stopping point—became popular. Introduced in 1883, it was a single sharp tip protruding 2 millimeters from the cord binding wrapped around the top of the épée. It was pronounced "most useful," for by catching in the clothes it showed where a hit had been made. Eventually it was condemned as dangerous, as well as too costly on clothing, and in 1906 a triple point was introduced, named after its inventor, Léon Sazie. It is difficult to imagine that his épée was once considered state-of-the-art, a real advance over previous weapons, considering that at day's end fencers would find their jackets honeycombed with tiny nicks, especially along the sleeve. Gauntlets that covered the sleeve were soon introduced, and the stiff corded cotton from which jackets were made replaced by sailcloth.

Although primitive electrical scoring systems had been developed early in the history of épée (a French catalog of 1914 shows one such apparatus), the first practical one, invented by a Swiss engineer, Laurent Pagan, was introduced in November 1931 at a tournament in Geneva. The first European championships with electric épée were held in 1935; the first world championships with electric foil in 1955, saber in 1988. Each innovation was acclaimed, yet the criticism persisted that hits were still not being awarded with sufficient accuracy. Of course, even within the parameters of modern sport, fencers have been expected to acknowledge touches; but, as the intensity of competition has grown, this has become a tradition honored more in fine words than in substance.*

It is no secret that all games are played in continuous tension between their formal rules (or laws) and a shifting convention of what players find acceptable. The great British all-rounder C. B. Fry took this a stage further: if both sides decide to cheat, cheating is fair.[5] (He conveniently overlooked that spectators are part of the relationship too.) Fencers have quietly adopted the same axiom, partly because at international level most are manipulative masters of the rules, partly because they are genuinely creative. It was accepted that cheating was wrong; there were myriad rules to penalize it; but there were inevitable gray areas, and soon a double standard evolved, which distinguished "tolerated" cheating, which most fencers might try as long as they could get away with it, from cheating that was beyond the pale in any situation.

A fencer can cheat in scores of ways, ranging from the simple act of knocking off the clip that makes one's electric jacket function to subtler manipulations: in the days before electric saber a German international

---

* Epée was always intended to reflect the conditions of a duel, so bouts were initially fought for one hit, as they still are in the pentathlon. The number of hits increased over the years, until in the 1950s it was set at five, as with foil and saber. This offended the purists, especially when a fencer finished a bout with a double hit—that is, when both épéeists land at the same moment, each thus scoring on the other. Such hits, in the words of one critic, "twisted the game into the opposite it was intended for."[4] When, at the 1948 Olympics, one third of the hits in the final (of six) were doubles, one master grieved, "Epée fencing might just as well never have been thought of." By 1960 the time interval between hits, which the first boxes had been able to judge to one fifteenth of a second, had been reduced to one twenty-fifth.

sabreur (now a senior judge) would loosen the pommel of his weapon so that it gave a *click* similar to that of a blade's striking its target. Here are some of the more dramatic cheating methods and how they have been applied.

1. *Parrying with the back arm.* Fighter pilots say that a particular kind of offensive fire "lies in the grass"—that is, so low to the ground that radar cannot detect it. Fencing is now so fast it can be difficult even for seasoned referees to follow. It is illegal to parry with one's unarmed hand, yet some fencers are adept at doing so. Opponents are allowed to ask for special judges to watch out for the offense; but by and large if a fencer can get away with the odd illicit parry he wins a certain amount of grudging admiration.

2. *Favoritism.* In 1979 the Hungarian world saber champion of 1977, Pál Gerevich, son of the famous father, told an interviewer, "Saber fencers have a saying, 'For the first half of your life you work to gain authority; for the second half your authority works for you.'" Even though electric equipment has helped unknown fencers gain hits on those with a reputation, referees still favor the known fencer. Back in the days of "steam" foil, the hot favorite in the women's event in the 1952 Olympics was the great Ilona Elek. At the three-quarters stage, leading a final pool of eight with five wins and no losses, she fenced a little-known American, Maxine Mitchell. The audience looked on as Mitchell landed ten hits in a row, but got credit for only four. Elek herself wasn't cheating—the jury, consciously or unconsciously, was doing it for her. By a rough justice, by the time the Hungarian notched up enough hits to win, both women were exhausted, and Elek lost her next two bouts and with them her chance at gold.

3. *Drugs.* There are a few well-known cases, but fencing is relatively clear of this particular problem.* One of the world's top ten sabreurs during the mid-1980s was convicted of drug taking by the FIE and never again fenced in international competition: he now coaches in South America.

---

* Drink is another matter. The 1965 épée world champion, Zoltán Nemere of Hungary, was so fond of the bottle that he lost his driving license, then a year later was involved in a car accident, for which he was jailed. The year after that, he received a special parole to attend the world championship. Two years later, in the very first bout of the épée team final at the Mexico Games, the Russian Gregori Kriss took advantage of the freshly introduced doping controls to complain that Nemere stank of alcohol. The Hungarian manager, Béla Bay, was asked if he would accept official testing of his fencer. Bay said he would, on condition that all the fencers be so tested. The protest was withdrawn.

The 1984 Olympic saber champion Jean-François Lamour tested positive for excess caffeine after winning the world championships in 1987. A second urine sample was clear, so Lamour was not suspended. He told me that if he had had the alleged amount of caffeine in his system—36 milliliters—he wouldn't have been able to get on guard, let alone win a title. Yet he still worried that somehow he might have been guilty as charged. "It was as if the sky had fallen in. I kept asking myself if perhaps I had made a mistake. I tried to remember how much coffee I had drunk, how many times I'd been to the toilet, how much water I had taken. Even now I have not received any official letter saying I am cleared—yet the laboratory responsible for the tests made a lot of mistakes, not just with me, and six months after my positive test the lab was closed down."*

The one other celebrated drug case involved the Italian Dorina Vaccaroni, world foil champion in 1983. At a top competition in Germany the previous year Vaccaroni, just eighteen, reached the final, where "she fenced like a maniac—I'd never seen her fence like that before," her opponent, Cornelia Hanisch, told me. Vaccaroni then tested positive for a banned substance that in small doses acts as a stimulant but in substantial doses can induce epilepsy. Although Vaccaroni denied knowingly using a prohibited substance, the German girl was awarded the championship.

4. *Illicit equipment.* In the 1936 Olympics the defending épée champion, Giancarlo Cornaggia-Medici, said to possess the most precise stopthrust ever developed, was fighting in the quarterfinals when he became perplexed by three successive double hits. He stopped and asked for the length of his adversary's weapon to be measured. It was found to be just half an inch over the limit.

More recently, a German fencer took to varnishing the top half of the

---

The sad postscript came early in 2001, when Nemere was killed in a car crash, driving home late one night from a friend's wedding. He had not been drinking.

* At the championships, the FIE doctor was the Hungarian Jenö Kamuti; had Lamour been suspended, the saber title would have gone to the silver medalist—a Hungarian. At the time some of his fellow countrymen murmured that Kamuti had bent the findings so that Lamour was cleared, since Kamuti, a contender in the FIE presidential election, due a few months later, needed French votes to win. But Kamuti has a reputation as an honest man, and his version is convincing: "It was the first year that caffeine had been on the list of forbidden drugs, and laboratories were not sufficiently prepared. As it was, there were four different samples. The first showed up so positive it was impossible for anyone to have taken in that amount; the second showed up negative; the third didn't work; and the fourth was on the limit. So my decision was an easy one."

point of his épée. When he tested his weapon on his opponent's guard at the beginning of a fight to ensure that no hit would register on the coquille (the steel guard), he carefully made contact with the *lower* half of his point, so that nothing seemed untoward; then, once the fight started, the varnish, effectively becoming the "target" that the German's épée was hitting, caused the electric box to register as soon as he struck anything hard—a free hit to the German. In the meantime, the hit rubbed off the incriminating varnish.

In a similar move, an American Olympic épéeist would come *en garde* with a thin circle of tape on his finger, which, after the weapons had been tested, he would slip onto his épée tip, causing the electric box to register as soon as the épée struck any target, valid or not, then peel away the tape before a referee could check his weapon. In each case, the cheating gained only one hit; but at international level one hit per fight is a huge advantage.

5. *Fights are bought and sold.* In the run-up to the 2000 Olympics, a Spanish fencer in an "A" grade saber tournament in Athens needed to beat a leading Russian, thrice world champion. The Spaniard won, thus gaining his berth to Sydney. The price of victory was said to have been $3,000. When I asked the tournament's leading administrator about it, he said, "I am sure it was only $2,000." Everyone at the competition knew what had happened, but versions of this story are commonplace. After the Polish saber squad had qualified for the Sydney Games, they went off to one of the season's remaining competitions, in the words of their team manager, "knowing that it wouldn't hurt them to lose, and it was their chance to make some good money."

6. *"Arranged" fights.* For years each of the stronger nations would decide, usually at the final stage, who on its team had the best chance of ultimate victory, and the weaker members would be ordered to throw their bouts to the designated standard-bearer. In the individual foil final of the 1924 Olympics, unusually of *twelve* fencers, four Italians, Puliti, Marcello Bertinetti, Bini, and Giulio Sarocchi, qualified. To make "arranged" fights harder (purely in the sense that the nation cheating had to put its money on the right man—and there have been many cases when it got it wrong), members of the same national team are required to fight off against one another first: Oreste Puliti beat his three compatriots with ease. The judges were not happy and, led by Imre Kovács of Hungary, maintained that the three losers had thrown their bouts. Outraged, Puliti threatened

to cane Kovács and was summarily disqualified. The other three Italians walked out in protest.

Two days later Puliti and Kovács ran into each other at a music hall. Words were exchanged. Kovács told Puliti he couldn't understand a word of Italian, whereupon the furious fencer struck him in the face, saying that Kovács surely couldn't fail to understand *that*. The two were pulled apart, but further words passed and a formal duel called for. Four months later Puliti and Kovács faced each other just over the Hungarian frontier. Puliti attacked at once, wounding Kovács in the arm, and the president stopped the fight; Kovács's wound was dressed and the two embraced, parting the best of friends. "*Vive le sport!*" What may in part have fueled Puliti's wrath was that for years he had not been allowed the chance to fight for the gold medal cleanly. As his obituary recorded in 1958, "the politics of fencing, officially denied and declared mere fiction by all team captains throughout the centuries, kept him in second or third place at the height of his athletic powers."[6]

In the 1958 épée world championships, the final pool of eight contained five Italians (led by the redoubtable Eduardo Mangiarotti, already three times champion); two Russians; and a lone Englishman, W. H. F. "Bill" Hoskyns. One by one the Italians dutifully lost to Mangiarotti; Hoskyns beat the two Russians. In consequence, however, Mangiarotti was hardly warmed up when he came to fence the Russians and lost to both. He then beat Hoskyns easily, but having suffered two defeats had to watch as Hoskyns triumphed over each of his compatriots, to end with six victories and the world title. Mangiarotti beat his head against the wall. Had he fenced "cleanly," he would likely have won.

7. *Intimidation and seduction.* Nearly all fencers try to influence referees and juries by body language or open appeals for favor, and nearly all fencers play to the gallery. A seasoned American international described the sport as "90 percent marketing, 10 percent skill." That is deliberately putting it high, but undoubtedly there is a charm to deception that is paramount in some people's makeup. Is this cheating? Most fencers would see the question as a matter of degree. The operatic Italian sabreur Mario Aldo Montano, fighting a top Russian in a world semifinal in 1971, at the end of one phrase, strutted round the entire stadium, clucking a victory chant like an inebriated cockerel. He returned to the strip only to discover that the referee had awarded the touch to his opponent. He simply grinned. The next year Italy was up against the Soviet Union in the team final, and

Montano had the deciding bout. He had already been warned by the referee for taking off his mask to protest decisions he didn't like;[7] another such display would cost him a hit and as the score was at 4–all would thus lose him and his country the match. When he scored (as he thought) the winning touch, he made to tear off his mask in victory before the referee had made any decision. As one man, his teammates fell upon him to ensure he kept his mask on—and won the gold.

Italians are past masters of working round the rules. After a long run of triumphs up through the 1950s, their fencing slumped and a new manager, Attillo Fini, was appointed. He decided that for Italy to regain its position he would not only have to act as a virtual dictator over his fencers but also work his way to ascendancy over juries and referees. By the early 1970s Italy was back at the top. Rival nations watched in horror but generally did nothing. One Bulgarian referee was so knavishly pro-Italian that on retirement he was given a top coaching post in Turin and his wife a job with Fiat. Some time later, he moved back to Sofia.*

8. *Combines.* During the 1960s and 1970s Hungary had an outstanding épée squad in which nearly everyone was qualified as a doctor, engineer, lawyer, or diplomat. It was also renowned for being difficult.[8] Among them they helped promote this "acceptable" form of cheating, which was to bedevil fencing for more than twenty years. The combine is the trading of a bout, usually between fencers from different countries, for a future favor. It is difficult to say precisely when the practice began, but by the late 1960s it was rife. The FIE hurried to change the rules for major championships—five times between 1960 and 1970—but this gesture only confused officials and fencers alike, while failing in its objective: for the combine continued and wore itself out only in the 1990s, when direct elimination was introduced.[9]

---

* Other nations register their feelings differently. During the 1971 world championships Hungary met Sweden in the épée team final. The match was close and hard fought, with the Swedish manager, the Hungarian-born Béla Rerrich, constantly leaping up to protest. On one of these occasions his complaint required an official inquiry (*jury d'appel*), leaving audience as well as competitors waiting. The Hungarian épéeist involved, Csaba Fenyvesi, eventually got down from the raised piste, picked up a table, and told his three colleagues to bring chairs. Soon the four were busily playing cards. The audience burst out laughing at a sight unprecedented in fencing, let alone at a world final. Time passed, and still the officials were debating in some upstairs room. Eventually the leading Swedish épéeist, Rolf Edling, went up to the Hungarian foursome, looked over each player's hand, and asked if he could join in. The official complaint became irrelevant, and the match soon resumed.

Combines took various forms, but in the main there were three variations: in rounds before the final, a weak fencer might have a fight thrown to him to ensure that his victory would eliminate a feared rival; a fencer who already knew midway through a pool that he was going to be eliminated could throw a fight advantageously to another; or—the dominant form—in exchange for a victory in the immediate round a fencer would repay the debt in the following round, or when the fencers next met. Combines featured frequently in semifinals, where seeding was no longer relevant and the "losing" fencer thus lost nothing by ceding a fight. It is said that the 1964 Olympic épée champion, Gregori Kriss, won a Russian championship in which all seven cofinalists owed him their fight.

The Hungarian épéeists put a refinement on this procedure—almost a purification. They saw themselves as professional sportsmen who, in a Communist society, needed to maintain a high rate of success to ensure their standard of living. They had no time for "lucky" amateurs on a hot streak or second-tier fencers sneaking an unwarranted victory and used the combine to weed out weaker épéeists, so that that the final pool of six would contain the "right" fencers. Once these six had successfully won through, they could fence among themselves to decide the winner. It was cheating, but with its own subversive logic.

Everything depended on trust, and a peculiar code of honor grew up to regulate the combine and other forms of cheating. As combine deals could often be struck only in snatched interchanges, there was ample room for misunderstanding. On one occasion Jerzy Pawłowski was approached by the Hungarians in midcompetition with word that Rudolf Kárpáti would give him a fight but expected to be repaid in the final. No deal, said Pawłowski; he intended to win the bout anyway, as he duly did, against Kárpáti's lackluster opposition. Come the final, Kárpáti, expecting repayment, was incensed not to receive it. "I want it back," he snarled in Russian. Pawłowski replied, "I never took it"—and went on to win their second bout as well.

General acceptance of the combine reached the point that, after the individual saber of the 1987 world championships, the silver medalist, Geörgy Nebald of Hungary, raged to a leading newspaper that he had lost in the final because one judge, a Canadian sabreur who had been knocked out earlier in the day, had skewed his decisions out of spite at having been the victim of Nebald's earlier combine. How could the man harbor such a grudge when the gold was at stake?

Maybe combines weren't really cheating. Each fencer, after all, was doing what was in his best interests.* The FIE was in a quandary. It knew that such an argument was specious, but every one of its senior members represented a country whose fencers were regularly taking part in combines. C. B. Fry again: if all parties agree to cheat, it is no longer cheating (but then neither may it be sport). Anyway, as harassed FIE officials explained, it was almost impossible to prove a case. (John F. Kennedy would regularly quote a Spanish quatrain, in translation: "Bullfight critics, ranked in rows / Crowd the enormous plaza full / But there's only one who *knows* / And he's the man who fights the bull.")

The turning point would come in 1971, at the world championships in Vienna. In the women's foil semifinals, a Romanian, Ana Pascu, who was certain of promotion, gave her bout to the reigning world champion, Galina Gorokhova of the Soviet Union. Pascu's surrender did not go unobserved ("Thievery!" muttered the Italian camp, whose fencer had been eliminated by the loss), and we were all keen to see whether the Russian would repay the obligation.

But who was going to accuse the world champion of cheating? The referee in a fencing bout has possibly the widest range of powers, both explicit and discretionary, of any official in sport. He or she is responsible for the flow, interpretation, and scoring of a fight, and also for maintaining proper technique and punishing errors. However, there is a large gap between the provisions of the rulebook and their interpretation and enforcement. Who was to referee the crucial bout?

The choice fell on Guido Malacarne, an amiable middle-aged bachelor

---

* What are the limits of what is honorable and dishonorable? As one seasoned foil international said to me, "If everyone else is doing it, you're putting yourself at a disadvantage if you *don't*." Competitors become hardened and determined not to give anything away. In a key team match in 1978, against a Cuban fondly known as "The Truck," I was denied a hit I had undoubtedly made but my opponent acknowledged it, reversing the decision so that the touch was recorded. Later in the bout, on the deciding hit, he made a valid riposte and looked to me to acknowledge it. I said nothing. "Ah well," he said, "so much for honor." I felt ashamed.

However, four years later, in the European championship, I was fencing a Spaniard. When he made an attack at my head that I thought got through my parry, I was surprised when both judges—this being in the days before electric saber—said that I had parried. I raised my hand, and the hit was recorded against me. I felt that "The Truck" might have nodded in approval. Later in the bout, almost the same hit was made in reverse; this time the Spaniard stood his ground. At the end of the fight one of the side judges, a coach with the Polish team, said to me in his all-too-clear English, "This is an international tournament: you don't acknowledge hits, and you don't expect others to, because they won't. And by the way, you were wrong—you *did* parry his attack; it was his renewed attack that hit you."

Galina Gorokhova of the Soviet Union, world champion of 1970, awaits to hear
whether the organizers of the 1971 championships will disqualify her for cheating.

who had never been a top fencer himself but was a regular official with the
Italian team. Behind his back the Italians called him "Mr. Coupon-Cutter,"
a reference to the monthly dividend he received from a family timber business. For all his intelligence and integrity, he was considered a bit of a
joke. So when the Directoire Technique, the officiating body, asked him to
take the Gorokhova-Pascu bout it was done condescendingly, the offering
of a poisoned chalice: "Now, Guido, you're the best—the obvious man to
take this one."

If the FIE thought Malacarne would buck the challenge, they would
soon learn how wrong they were. No one had reckoned with a crucial factor: here was a world final, all of it televised, and the Russian, an intimidating, bulky figure with a hard, morose stare,* was too vain to want to

* Gorokhova was also well known for her backhand parry. Even her teammates looked
askance at this—"she fences with two hands," they'd joke sourly—but her coach was

make her "defeat" seem honestly arrived at—she wanted the world to know that she could beat Pascu any time she chose and made no attempt to score until 1–3 down. At this point Malacarne warned her, in his precise French, to fence properly and not to favor her opponent. After a lecture from her coach, she did score two hits to reach 3–all—with one last touch to come.

The Russian now reverted to her former passivity, with Pascu making desperate attacks, most of which missed and frequently ended with her toppling onto her opponent, who carefully avoided making the decisive hit accidentally. The Directoire Technique hurriedly convened beside the piste and agreed with Malacarne that he should be allowed to disqualify Gorokhova, which he did. The Russians at once appealed, asserting that their fencer had not been feeling well—a liver complaint—and besides, she had scored two hits after the warning. It did no good; at the appeal Gorokhova was expelled by an overwhelming majority.

At this time I was editing *The Sword* and invited the American official Marius Valsamis to write about the affair. He entitled his article "The Sheriff of Dodge City," likening international fencing to a lawless town in which crime, both organized and disorganized, runs rampant. Finally the law-abiding citizens hire a lawman to clean up the town: Wyatt Earp or, in fencing's case, Malacarne.[10] Had the 1971 disqualification been Malacarne's only intervention, this might have been overstating his contribution, but at the 1975 Pan-American Games he once again took a brave line—during the fight-off for first place between Argentinian and American épéeists. A year later he would play a crucial part in exposing the most dramatic scandal in fencing's history.

On July 20, 1976, for the only time ever, a story about fencing appeared on the front page of *The New York Times*. It was hardly an advertisement for the sport. Filed from the Montreal Olympics under the headline "Soviet Fencer Disqualified for Cheating," it laid out how an illegal device that had been detected in the épée of a Soviet athlete, Boris Onishenko, fencing in the modern pentathlon, had enabled him to set off the electronic recording machine at will. The disgracing of Onishenko, who

---

a high-ranking KGB officer with wide-ranging influence within fencing, so she was inviolate. A couple of months before the championships, she was quoted in a leading Russian sports magazine as saying, "Sport teaches us to be alert and brave." Her many rivals must have laughed. At the beginning of one world final an Italian, the beautiful if tempestuous Vannetta Masciotta, got up on the piste and hissed, "Drop dead!" Gorokhova replied, "You first!"

was quickly dubbed "Dis-Onishenko," became a major story of those Games, second only to the orchestrated walkout of more than a dozen African teams to protest South Africa's apartheid policies.

At the time of the Montreal Games Onishenko was thirty-eight, nominally a major in the Red Army, with a part-time job teaching at the Dynamo Sports Institute in Kiev and leisure interests in cars, music—and electronics. He had first excelled as a swimmer, but after making the Soviet pentathlon team in 1967 he had established himself as one of the world's best pentathletes. In the 1972 Olympics he came in second to the Hungarian András "Bandi" Balczo, although Balczo was second to Onishenko in the fencing section.

No one knows how long Onishenko's épées had been doctored. His performances had shown remarkable improvement since 1970; without question he was a very fine épéeist and a favorite to win the discipline. Fencing in the pentathlon is sudden death—the first hit in each bout wins—and the individual and team competitions are combined into one and so offer the best return: unlike in the other disciplines, success means another's failure—every time Onishenko hit an opponent he gained points and they lost them.

The modern pentathlon began on the first day of the Games with each three-man team fencing off among themselves. Then, at 8:45 A.M., the Soviet Union trio was up against Great Britain's Adrian Parker, Jim Fox, and Danny Nightingale. "After a while Adrian Parker and Boris Onishenko faced each other on the piste, had their weapons tested and began fencing," Malacarne recalled. "An attack from Onishenko made his light go on, and I ruled that Parker had been hit. However, Parker took off his mask and assured me that the hit had not arrived. I pointed out that I had distinctly seen Onishenko's point go very close to his forearm and that perhaps he had not felt the hit arrive because it landed on a fold of his glove or of his sleeve. Parker again assured me that no hit had arrived, and I therefore proceeded to make a rapid inspection of Onishenko's épée. The point was marked with the pass sign [i.e., the Games' armorers had officially approved it, as they were required to do with all swords presented for competition use] as were the blade and coquille, while inside the guard the two wires were separated by a sheet of plastic. I again told Parker that I had no reason to annul the hit, and I signaled to the score table that Parker had been defeated. However, the incident had left its impression on me and I asked for the name of the Soviet fencer to be repeated to me: Onishenko. I would be on my guard."[11]

The other two Soviet fencers, Lednev and Mosolov, fought their bouts; then it was Onishenko's turn, this time against Jim Fox, a top-class fencer, good enough to have been placed sixth in the British épée rankings and who had been watching Parker's fight closely. "Adrian swore that Boris had not hit him," Fox told me. "When I fenced him I jumped in, deliberately opening myself for a stop-hit. I was still outside hitting distance when I picked up Onishenko's blade—really high, before his point was anywhere near me. His blade was above my head and I smacked it [my épée] into his chest—but the light was already on." As soon as Fox challenged the touch, Onishenko said, "No, no, Jimmy, there was no hit. I will change the weapon." Fox was adamant that he should not do so. Malacarne again: "As they fenced, I had a distinct feeling that Onishenko's light came on at the mere contact of blades . . . and I immediately signaled that the hit was annulled. At that point I asked Onishenko to surrender his weapon to me.

"Since I had already made a summary check on the piste of his épée before he fenced Parker, it was clear, as he must have realized, that I was going to proceed to examine his sword more rigorously. Anyway, he pretended not to understand what I was saying and hurried to the end of the

Moment of truth: Boris Onishenko (left) attacks Jim Fox of Great Britain during their 1976 pentathlon match, but Fox jumps back, out of range. Yet the light for a valid hit comes on.

piste, where his companions had already brought out another épée to exchange with his own. I ran up to him and stopped this happening and ordered them to give me the correct weapon—which I made sure I had not
lost sight of at any time. The Russians protested that the weapon which
Onishenko had been using was not the one I indicated, but the other
which they had produced. I replied that I was sure it was the first weapon
and that that was the one I intended to confiscate. There was a slight argument, after which I took possession of the épée and sent for one of the
FIE controllers."

A French FIE official arrived and agreed that the weapon in question
should be taken to Control. Onishenko was later to argue that the rigged
épée was not his, despite the fact that it was made for a left-hander and the
rest of the Soviet team, reserve included, were right-handed. Even now
there is confusion over the exact nature of his épée. The organizers describe it in their report as a pistol grip; Fox is convinced it was a French
handle. "Anyway," he says, "it was bent round slightly, with a protrusion
placed behind the forefinger which his finger could touch as it slid back."
But even that was not immediately clear. After the French official had had
his say, a senior Hungarian, Tibor Szekely, himself a onetime international épéeist, arrived on the piste carrying Onishenko's épée and a testing
kit. Together he and Malacarne ran over the weapon's various parts.

"The point was correct," says Malacarne. "So were the blade and coquille, while inside the coquille the two wires were in place and perfectly
legal. But the wires, covered by the insulating plastic, showed two distinct
breaks in the insulation, and these seemed to connect if one pressed one's
fingers against the coquille. Certainly the wires touched, if not every time
then a number of times for both of us. The question I asked Tibor Szekely
was 'Could this break in the plastic insulation have been deliberate—with
a knife or razor?' (For I was certain that the hit which had come up on the
lights had never arrived on the target.) Szekely's answer was no, it was not
possible to prove that the break had been made maliciously. At that point
I had no alternative but to confirm that the hit had been annulled and to
give Onishenko an official warning—which, should a faulty hit be repeated, would become a ten-point penalty."

Watching all this from high in the stands was the then head of British
fencing, Mary Glen Haig. With her was Nicholas Bacon, the twelve-year-
old son of friends who was suffering from a brain tumor (of which he
would die four years later). He had been brought to the Olympics before
his next bout of surgery. Nicholas been observing Onishenko keenly and,

jumping up and down with indignation, insisted that the Ukrainian was cheating. Glen Haig, who was also a member of the IOC committee and always a formidable presence, made her way down to the fencing area and told a *third* official, Carl Schwende, the chief of discipline for the fencing event, that a warning and confiscation were not enough.

Schwende replied that it could not be proven that Onishenko's épée had been deliberately tampered with. Spurred on by Glen Haig, the British team put in an official protest, claiming that the evidence pointed overwhelmingly to dishonest alterations, for which the penalty was disqualification. All this took place within fifteen minutes of the first challenge.

After long discussion, the FIE decided that Onishenko's épée should be taken apart. Only then did they discover the full extent of the "engineering"—that the handle had a hole bored through it, and that it had been fitted with two extra wires, leading to a small metal disc, which, when pressed, produced a contact, and thus a hit, at will. The whole was encased in a tight-fitting chamois leather cover. "[It] was camouflaged to perfection," says Malacarne. "But for the reluctance of the Soviet team to hand over the weapon, the incident might have had a completely different outcome. The apparently small defect of the two wires would have earned only an official warning—as at first it did—and might have prevented any more thorough examination."

"There was no joy in it for me," says Jim Fox. "Boris was fencing brilliantly—there's no doubt about it, he was a great fencer. After the incident he came up to me and said, 'Jim, I'm so sorry about all this,' and I said, 'That's all right, Boris.' We then both went off to our respective pistes to fence new countries." Back in 1972, when Onishenko had finished second, Fox had come in fourth, losing to him in the fencing. 'I ended just twenty-four points behind him, which a fencing victory over him would have reversed. If he was already cheating, then he did me out of a medal."

Could Onishenko have fooled the international fencing community for that long? The then president of the World Pentathlon Association reckoned that he had been cheating for two years, but others are doubtful. "It is very hard to believe Onishenko had been using the weapon before," says Michael Proudfoot, the British manager, "simply because he was so easily found out. . . . The Russians—including Onishenko—came to London for a pentathlon international in April that year, and we videotaped nearly all their fights. I have studied the film in great detail since and cannot find any evidence of doubtful hits. But then again it is difficult, because you really need the box or light and the épées simultaneously on video."

There remain two mysteries. One of the other officials at the match was Patrick Vajda, among the best referees in the world and a relaxed observer of the fencing scene. We have spoken at length about what happened in Montreal, but I was not expecting what he told me one day in his Paris insurance offices in early 2000: that he was convinced that Onishenko himself had been innocent and that the Russian coach and manager had engineered the scam. I find that too much to swallow. How could Onishenko *not* have known that he was using a rigged épée? It may seem implausible, but Carl Schwende agrees with Vajda. "After we disqualified him, I walked out of the committee room with Onishenko," he explained. "He said to me, in German, 'It's not me. You know me.' I really think it's most difficult to establish what procedure was followed and who the guilty party was and who the victim. The incredible part of all this is that Onishenko did not need this kind of trick to win. He could easily have done very well without it."

This seems almost determinedly unjudgmental. After Montreal, Onishenko had been due to become coach of the Soviet pentathlon team and to be promoted to lieutenant colonel. He must have been keen to go out with a bang—which could only mean winning the individual gold. To quote the generous opinion of Jim Fox, "The pressure to be top . . . was so great you can almost forgive anyone for doing anything."[12]

Mark Rakita, the Russian world saber champion of 1967, was a close friend of Onishenko. "Psychologically I can understand it," he told me. "He wanted to finish at number one, end things cleanly. His dream was to win the Olympics. He had also undergone being persecuted for being too old. The policy then was to get rid of the old-timers, and after 1972 people wanted him out. But he was a good guy as well as being a friend of mine, and I still don't know why he did it. How could he live with himself, even had he got away with it?"*

---

* Rakita also told me that, so far as the sabreurs were concerned, the Russians did not cheat because they had no need to—they were confident that they were better than anybody else. This certainly had seemed to be true, but then he told me about how he had taken part in a combine. I also recall Zbigniew Czajkowski's memories of his days in Moscow in the early 1950s, when the Russians were cheating "like mad!" After a while the cheating was so blatant that he took off his mask and smiled. One of the Russian officials asked him why. He explained that it was his reaction to the constant dishonesty. The official disregarded this and simply snapped, "Smiling is not allowed."

Sandy Kerekes, a Hungarian-born sabreur and pentathlete who has lived in Canada since 1950, was the overall competition director for the pentathlon back in 1972. He believes that the Soviet team coach may have forced their key fencer to act as he did. The manager, Oleg Chuvilin, was a popular character, unlikely to have been part of so gross a plot, but the coach, Fleischman, was a shadowy figure who had suddenly appeared as a fencing master in 1972 and disappeared as quickly after the Games were over. "Onishenko may have been the hand that pulled the trigger, but did he have a wife or children? Might he have been open to blackmail on other counts? Who knows what pressures he was under or what he was told to do?" Kerekes adds that Chuvilin had enemies in Moscow and had survived an assassination attempt. "But Chuvilin would deny everything about Onishenko. They just wanted to take care of it themselves."

In any event, only one man was punished. Onishenko was unceremoniously ushered back to the Soviet team ship anchored in the Saint Lawrence River. No other Russian épées were found to have been tampered with, and the organizers' fear that the Russians might walk out en bloc, followed by other Eastern European countries, was not realized. The offense was presented as the crime of a single individual: Onishenko returned home to be stripped of his medals and discharged from the army, and his salary as a top-class athlete was cut off. But his uncle was the secretary of the Ukrainian branch of the CPSU. Within a year he was managing a large swimming complex in Kiev, then was made director of the Central Republican Sports Stadium—with a capacity of 100,000, the largest in the Ukraine.

Bizarrely, I was told by several leading fencers that around 1991 Onishenko was found drowned in the swimming pool he had once administered. The rumor spread that he had been killed by the KGB, though from what motive nobody knew. Yet Ukrainians based in New York say they have spoken to him within the last three years, one of them face-to-face. A BBC team making a radio program at the end of 2000 believed that it dealt with him on the phone. Or was it someone impersonating him? "Onishenko" told them that his life was fine; he was sixty-three, and had a twelve-year-old granddaughter; only she wasn't interested in fencing, she preferred mathematics. Game theory, perhaps.

At the time, Soviet officials insisted that Onishenko was a one-off case; no one should think that some great cheating strategy was afoot. It is true that since 1976 the combine has almost died out, but other ways of skirt-

Boris Onishenko
during the
Montreal
fencing event.

ing the rules have replaced it. Highly competitive people will always push regulations to the limits in any sport. The FIE has enacted endless new rules to ensure the sport's good name: tantrums are now penalized heavily, talking to referees is strictly regulated, and referees themselves are heavily scrutinized. At the 2000 Sydney Games the organizers invited a roster of thirty referees, drawn from officials worldwide; fifteen were never used. However, special interests still proliferate.

Just before the 1992 Barcelona Olympics the head of world fencing, the Frenchman René Roch, was asked by an IOC official to confirm that the current rulebook was the one to be used at the Games. "Yes," he affirmed. His questioner went on, "There are six hundred or so rules in your book, M. Roch—75 to 80 percent of them measures against cheating. Does your sport have a problem?"

At the first classical Olympics, competitors were flogged for cheating and wrestlers were called "lions" for their addiction to (illegal) biting. The origins of boxing, racing, and athletics are, to quote a London *Times* editorial, "sunk in a mire of gaming and cheating."[13] But dishonesty is particularly shocking in fencing, because of its history. "Perhaps sporting heroes are especially vulnerable," one commentator mused, "because a champion's will to win is an impulse close to greed. Supreme athleticism does not always leave room for moderation or common sense."

CHAPTER 20

The Demon Barber

*Folly never thinks it has enough, even when
it obtains what it desires.*

—CICERO, *Tusculanae Disputationes*
(ON THE EMOTIONS), 44 B.C.

*I'll have them wall all Germany with brass,
And make swift Rhine circle fair Wertenberg
I'll have them fill the public schools with silk,
Wherewith the students shall be bravely clad.*

—CHRISTOPHER MARLOWE,
The Tragical History of Dr. Faustus, 1592

TAUBERBISCHOFSHEIM IS A TOWN OF JUST 12,000 INHABITANTS,
set between the Main and Tauber Rivers in the northeast of Baden-
Württemberg. The area is known as "Badisch Sibirien," a nod to its
anonymity and isolation. Surrounded by hills, forests, vineyards, and
farmland, before the 1970s the town had little economic or political sig-
nificance, and few, even in Germany, knew of its existence. It was there
that in 1936 the wife of a local barber, Herr Beck, gave birth to their thirteenth child. He was christened Emil, and grew up ungainly, short, and
overweight. By 1953 he was apprenticed to his father.

Of Emil's twelve brothers and sisters, six died in childhood. Emil himself displayed boundless energy and surprising strength but looked the
antithesis of an athlete. Yet that is what he longed to be. One day in his
teens he saw a government training film extolling fencing. The following
day he went back to see it again: he had been bitten. After the Second
World War Germans had been banned from fencing internationally because of the sport's connection to Nazism. Germany was readmitted in
1949 and had been competing for only four years when to general astonishment Emil decided that he wanted to become a fencing coach. The
nearest club was eleven miles away, a hilly trip through rolling vineyards

to the town of Bad Mergentheim. The only way he could make the journey was by bike, an arduous trip even for a fit athlete. But Emil was determined. Every spare evening, he bolted from his father's shop, grabbed his ragged fencing suit (made from flour sacks stitched together by his sister), and cycled off. He started practicing foil but soon changed to épée, coaching himself along the way; he never received an épée lesson in his life.

Time magazine would later write that Emil had "always been the wildest Beck, so uncontrollable in kindergarten he had been thrown out after five days, so wild at home his older brothers would leash him to a tree with the goats." The same independence of spirit informed his assessment of the new world he had entered. "Why does a man need to hold a foil with his fingers?" *Time* has Beck asking. "Because the French did? *Pah.* Your fingers get tired that way; why not use the palm of the hand? And why thrust the blade only from here? Because the Hungarians and the Italians did? My God, if it will bring you a hit, why not jab the thing at them from behind your back?" Or, one could add, over your shoulder or crouching down close to the ground. The electric box, Beck pointed out, gives no points for style, does not react to soulful looks or angry tirades, but *does* light up for hits that land on the back, under the arm, or in crevices in the groin; or that are flicked over like fiberglass fishing rods with a whip-cracking wrist action. Two particular classic doctrines he discarded: no longer was it necessary, he declared, to lead with the arm—one could lead with the feet instead. And feints need not be targeted on an opponent; they could be directed anywhere, so long as they had the desired effect. The point was to seize the initiative, then ensure that one landed on target. To put across his new vision Beck knew he had to start a club of his own. He continued to work in his father's shop from 8 A.M. to 6 P.M., but then it was off to train in the boiler room behind the town grammar school—the only venue he could find.

Soon he was scouring libraries, pestering coaches in other cities, a maverick unbound by any law. He used foil technique to teach épée, telling his charges that they must look for the "dead point"—the *"tote Punkt"*—in their opponent. Find his weakness, then exploit it—by whatever means. Beck's students began to enter local competitions; on one early occasion the celebrated club at Heidelberg thrashed his team 15–1, "holding up their noses so high they gathered rain," as he would growl years later. But within two years his team was back, to emerge victorious.

Beck needed pupils. So far he had been content to recruit customers in his father's shop. Now he persuaded children in the village to drop by his club, where he would flip five balls into the air to see which child caught what. Those who snared at least two he kept. He became their substitute father, fretting over their schooling, arranging jobs, doing favors. "You must train. *You have no choice*," he would bark at eleven-year-old Matthias Behr. Then he would give the boy an admonitory smack across the cheek and trundle away with what became his trademark rolling gait. "I'm not a winner at heart," Behr told me. "You have to be a special man to get a gold medal. At vital moments I don't feel it's that important to win." Yet Beck took Behr to Olympic gold in 1976 and three silvers, as well as steering him back to fencing after the nightmare bout in Rome in 1982 that ended in the death of Vladimir Smirnov. Beck knew, to the point of obsession, that to be very good at something is not natural. Certain formal disciplines—mathematics, say, or music—may produce naturals, but training for a sport is like training for war. "Fencing is fighting," he would say, "if you don't fight, you're not fencing." His pupils had to be disciplined so that they could discover in themselves qualities they never dreamed that they possessed.

But training was only one part of this brave new world. Beck would be not just teacher and manager but also fund-raiser and organizer, and he crisscrossed West Germany in pursuit of equipment, transport, and money to take his club beyond that tiny boiler room. Daimler-Benz, DuPont, Sony, and Adidas all helped out, as did banks and bakery chains, brewers of beer and distillers of schnapps—fifty-two sponsors in all, splashing their names and jingles across the town.

By 1971 Beck's own center had arisen among the apple trees on the outskirts of Tauberbischofsheim. This did not guarantee success. Beck was put in charge of the Olympic team at Munich, but it collapsed, failing to win a single medal before its home crowd. There was an outcry, and Beck nearly quit; but he decided to press on, only with renewed energy. The amateurism of the young barber had long since gone. In its place was the Beck ideology. "To complete his lessons you have to be a machine," sighed Matthias Gey, who would take the world foil championship in 1987, having been taught by Beck from the age of two and a half. "We do everything so fast and hard, there is barely time to breathe. He works so many hours, he doesn't understand we have lives outside of fencing." "I give my lessons *unmöglich schnell*," boasted Beck; "Impossibly fast."

Beck had little interest in turning out standard models. "I don't force fencers to perform the same way, I adapt what each person can do. That's why Tauber fencers tend to look different. Most coaches try to push *their*

technique onto athletes; I investigate what will be good for each person."
True to this philosophy, Beck's one technical book on fencing, *Tauberbischofsheimer Fechtlektionem*, shows him teaching two of his most famous
pupils, Matthias Behr and Alex Pusch, to hit around the back of the head,
while running forward, or in *en garde* positions very different from the accepted classic stance.[1]

"Who else but Beck, after sending his athletes through weightlifting
and gymnastic sessions, three-mile jogs and fast-paced lessons, would
hold a tournament each night, breaking down the fencers into pools of
twelve or fifteen and assigning to each one a number of victories he must
achieve?" asked *Time*. "Who else but Beck would tell the fencer who fails
to reach that number that he is an invisible man: sorry, you never came
that night, you must redo the session. Too many invisible nights and Herr
Beck withholds the monthly stipend the government pays West German
athletes—hey, boys, nobody rides a Mercedes for free." It was Darwinism
in fencing form: only the fittest would survive. Fencers gave the Tauber
Center a special nickname: "TBC" (tuberculosis). Among the non-

*Emil Beck—nicknamed "Piggy" by his pupils—was by 1972 Germany's
head coach, director of the center he had created at Tauberbischofsheim,
and Olympic team manager. For the son of the local barber,
it was a meteoric success story.*

Germans it was believed that Beck created codes for his fencers, seemingly innocent words he would shout from the side of the piste, illegally instructing them to change tactics in midfight.

The magnetism and willpower of the man they privately called "*Schweinchen*" ("Piggy") were formidable. "He'd lay down his life for one of his fencers," reflected Volker Fischer, a four-time gold medalist, fondly. Elmar Bormann, épée world champion in 1983, asserted, "When Emil Beck says, 'Sit down,' we don't look behind us to see whether there is a chair." Work, work, work, train, train, train. "Man was born to work," says Beck. "Without work, he could not exist. I work fourteen to eighteen hours a day, seven days a week. Vacations? They are an invention of modern times. Man doesn't need a holiday."

Soon the ignominy of 1972 was replaced by glory. At the 1976 Olympics, nine fencers from Beck's academy won eleven individual or team medals, including five golds. In 1984, eleven of his fencers won twelve medals, seven of them gold. There were nearly thirty other first-class fencing clubs in West Germany, yet in 1988 thirteen of the country's team of twenty were Beck's pupils.

Such success brought further opportunities. Beck began to harbor political ambitions. He got to know Chancellor Helmut Kohl sufficiently well to slap him on the back and call him by the informal *du*. Anything seemed possible. Then in 1985 Beck suffered a stroke and was hospitalized. Even then, he would slip out of his ward to work secretly all night. He was soon back full-time.

The center at Tauber continued to expand. Even at the beginning it had a cafeteria, weight room, physiotherapy department, and photographers' lab. Today it boasts a soccer field, basketball and tennis courts, a sauna, a massage room, a weapon repair shop, a computerized Cybex, and a pulsimeter to monitor the condition of each fencer; full facilities for disabled fencers, an isokinetic center, a twenty-meter "warm pool" for stretching and underwater massage, a "fango" room for mud treatment, and fourteen bedrooms, purpose-built with extra space to accommodate fencing bags. The medical department is twelve strong, with facilities for operations and doctors who base their practice within the club, with patients from the town happy to have such state-of-the-art treatment. The center, with its staff of 100, is attended by more than 600 fencers who travel in, 150 to 300 each day, from the two dozen clubs around Tauber. There are forty-five full-length pistes and now a gym equipped for "wireless fencing," in anticipation of the time when electric cables are phased out. There is a boarding school, a fleet of twelve cars and four Mercedes buses, and thirty more Mercedes cars either loaned for free or leased cheaply to fencers, according to achievement. What twenty years ago was a grassy field has become an apartment block with flats for twenty-two, again custom-built to accommodate disabled residents—a 12 million DM project paid for half by the club, half by federal and local governments. In the last ten years, nearly $20 million has been sunk into the site. Even a golf course is planned.

In October 2000 I made the two-hour journey from Frankfurt to Tauber, to keep an appointment to see Beck. In the parking lot stood his personal Mercedes, number plate TBB E1. It was like visiting a space-age village. Every facility was in use or in preparation for use. Onetime champions did duty as coaches and general tutors. Beck was demonstrably proud of his center. "Our aim is to cater for everyone, from children of three through to Olympic champions, and to do all the educational things, not just the sports stuff. And one of the successes here is that it's not all for the wealthy—we can look after the poor and underprivileged." He cited three of his champions, all products of one-parent families. Later he handed me a book extolling his achievements.[2] Beck's fencers have won 147 gold medals in world, European, and Olympic championships, senior and junior.

"It's like a carousel ride," said Beck. "Once you get on, you must ride it to the end. My life is one long storm. My enemies are waiting for me to fail. They try to pull me down, but they only push me higher." When he judged that there was insufficient talent among home-born Germans to meet his ambitions, he effectively moved into the transfer market. Foreign nationals—Romanians, Russians, Cubans—were brought to Tauberbischofsheim: thus the triumphant German team in 1992 included a onetime East German, Uwe Prosske; Robert Felsiak, a Polish immigrant of just three years' standing; and Vladimir Reznitchenko, who had won a bronze for the Soviets in 1988. A Russian from Estonia, he had gained his German citizenship just in time to be eligible for the world championships. It was all still legal—just.

Other German clubs resented Tauber's power. When a Tauber member fought anyone from the main club in Bonn, the clash was more ferocious than those against foreign competition. Fencers from other countries dreaded taking on the Beck machine; referees felt intimidated. In the Hamburg world championships in 1978, the great French épéeist Philippe Riboud was fencing the last bout of the six-man final against Jabłowski of

Poland. The score stood at 4–4 as they entered the last minute. If Riboud won here he would be champion, edging out Alex Pusch, the 1976 Olympic champion, who stood tied in second place with two others. As the seconds ticked away Riboud, panting stentoriously (he has only one functioning lung) launched a last desperate attack. The box lit up—the referee gave him the hit—the Frenchman was champion! His teammates threw him delightedly into the air . . . but Emil Beck, stationed at the side of the piste, noticed that the official clock showed several seconds past closure. No official had called "Time!" as the rules demanded. He made an official protest; for three hours the *jury d'appel* deliberated, then decided that Riboud had not won after all; a "double defeat" was registered against the two fencers, which meant that four épéeists were tied for first place, with three victories apiece. Most of the audience left in disgust.

In the fight-off that followed, after a five-hour marathon that ended at midnight, a new champion emerged: Beck's student, Alex Pusch. It was rumored that the clock had been left running after the final bout to check its accuracy and that the buzzer had certainly sounded a few seconds before the end of time. (This so enraged the senior French official that he grabbed the German timekeeper by the throat.) No one suggested that Beck had instructed the officials to act as they did or had in any way cheated; but of all the coaches I can think of, only one—the Italian Attilo Fini—might have done what Beck did. And he and Beck had an understanding: wherever possible, in a key bout, an Italian would get a German referee, a German an Italian; things worked out so much better that way.

NEMESIS WAS AT HAND, IN THE FORM OF A TALL YOUNG MAN called Arnd Schmitt. Schmitt was born in Heidenheim in 1965, the second of three sons of a comfortable upper-middle-class family, the father working for Zeiss lenses and the mother as a translator. Schmitt's father had competed as a show jumper and knew the demands of international sports; he would be a crucial support for his son in the events that followed.

At first Arnd concentrated on track and field, becoming regional schoolboy champion in the high jump and high hurdles; but Heidenheim, despite its population of some 50,000, had for years been the venue for a huge international épée competition. It was impossible not to be caught up in the excitement each spring as the best fencers in the world converged on his hometown; Arnd and his brother, Ulrich, three years his junior, decided to try their hand. Arnd became national junior foil champion, and also qualified for the world youth team at épée: he was a natural at the sport. However, the reserve in the German foil squad came from Tauber: Beck was soon protesting to the Federation that no fencer should be allowed to compete at more than one weapon. The Federation, under such pressure from their national coach, caved in, and informed Schmitt he would have to make a choice. So he did—épée; the vacant foil place went to Beck's pupil.

Schmitt might have turned his back on Beck after such brinkmanship, but he knew Beck admired his talent, and there was a powerful reason for moving to the Tauber Club. German national service was looming, but the government allowed selected athletes to opt for a two-year training period at a suitable sports center in place of the normal fifteen months of compulsory service. Tauber was such a center; Arnd made his decision, and jumped. The Federation, alarmed at Beck's ability to hoover up the country's young talent, responded by banning Schmitt from competition for three months. It made little difference to the young Heidenheimer: in his first outing following the ban, an épée event in Ulm, he won with ease.

He joined Tauber in 1984, aged nineteen. A little over a year later, Ulrich, now seventeen, and a bronze medalist at foil in the World Under-20 Championships, joined him. At first, the brothers prospered in the hothouse atmosphere, but not for long.

Two years ago, I learned the full story of what had happened, visiting both Beck and Schmitt, the latter at the club in Bonn where he now fences, TSV Bayer Leverkusen. A dentist now, when we spoke he was still the reigning world épée champion, having won the title in 1999 in his thirty-fifth year. It was early in the morning, and we sat in the club's spacious bar, with only cleaners and the occasional club official looking in. Schmitt was at first uneasy, continually fingering the shiny brown briefcase that he had laid on the table between us. Slowly, however, he began to talk about his time under Beck's rule. He had quickly become disenchanted. "Beck's not really a coach. People think he's the most successful master in history, and he has this list of all his champions. But only about ten percent of them has he trained personally. For the rest he was more their manager. And I soon learned what he was like. He's not an honest man at all, and I hate what he does to people."

I felt this harsh and thought back to the times I had watched Beck giving his pupils warm-up lessons in world championships or Olympics—of his having Alex Pusch lunge at him again and again and again, hitting him in a veritable *Blitzkrieg,* so fast and unremitting a barrage that it seemed irresistible.

Schmitt soon drew attention to himself because, on his father's advice, he had turned down a club Mercedes and the chance to borrow money free of interest. "So I didn't owe him anything. It was then that I started to fight with Beck—not because I wanted to, but because I had to." One day in 1985 he was called into Beck's office. "Why don't you want my help?" the coach asked, listing everything that Schmitt had turned down. Soon tears were running down Beck's face as he plaintively urged the teenager to join his system, "to be a part of us." By his account, Schmitt responded politely that he did not need more than he already had. Beck's whole demeanor changed. "He got really angry. He pushed his head into mine and yelled, 'I'm going to destroy you—you're never going to become a champion. Never.'"

The next thing Schmitt knew, all the fencers at the club—bar himself and his brother—were summoned by Beck and told that they should not talk to Schmitt: he was to be ostracized. Beck tried to make the other squad members believe that Schmitt had wanted more money from Beck (national junior team members were already at that time getting from non-

Arnd Schmitt in March 2000. He was a fittingly heroic figure amid the morass of German—and international—squabbling during the 1980s and early 1990s.

Tauber sources 100 to 1,300 DM a month, depending on results) and that he had decided to kick him out as soon as his alternate training was over.

The next few months were like something out of *The Trial*. Schmitt had many friends at Tauber, and these continued to talk to him; only as soon as they saw Beck or one of the other coaches approach they would abruptly turn their backs. Ulrich was too young to help much, and besides, his knee collapsed under the heavy training program, and after two operations he was forced to give up the sport. Arnd, not yet twenty-one, was on his own. He discovered that other fencers were being paid as much as 500 DM to beat him in important competitions. He had been granted a travel allowance of 300 DM a month but saw none of that money for two years. "Beck put all the money he received into one big pot and played God with it, distributing it as he saw fit." If Beck thought he could break the young épéeist, he had chosen the wrong man: after leaving Tauber Schmitt would become the spokesman for the German union of fencers and would be appointed the representative for the entire German Olympic team, a post he held for eight years. He had an abundance of "*Rückgrat*"—backbone.

At the end of 1986 Schmitt left Tauber for Bayer Leverkusen, at that time the third largest sports club in Germany, with ten thousand members. Because it was far more than a fencing club, with major nationally ranked teams in soccer, basketball, and boxing, Beck's influence there was minimal. In September 1986 Schmitt hoped his results would be good enough to qualify him for the Masters' competition, open to the top eight épéeists in the world. The venue was Tauber. All the sports media were to be there, and he crept in at eighth and final place. The event was by direct elimination, and in his first bout against the number one seed and current world No. 1, Alex Pusch, he won with something to spare. Next came the Italian champion, Angelo Mazzoni, whom he also beat. In the final match he was up against Eric Srecki of France, future Olympic gold medalist and twice world champion. Again, he triumphed. "I had won the Masters—in Tauber! It was the worst possible result for Beck. But it was only then that I saw that my fencing well wasn't enough—I really had to defend myself against this guy." But how could Schmitt, not even a national team member, take on one of the most powerful figures in German sport? In the end, Beck would take the fight to him.

In the next Olympic year, 1988, competition for the German épée team was intense. At a top international event held north of Milan, a non-Tauber German fencer was scrambling to qualify out of a stiff pool when Schmitt's old rival Mazzoni came up to tell him that one of the Tauber coaches (who had been Schmitt's main teacher there) had approached him with an offer of money if he lost his fight against a Pole named Mariusz Stralka, a recent addition to the Tauber stable. This would have had the effect of eliminating the German fencer, possibly ending his hopes of qualifying for Seoul. "They've asked me," said Mazzoni, "but I'm not going to do it."*

Schmitt reported this to the German Federation, but no one was interested. Eventually Mazzoni took the story to a sports journalist and listed a whole series of bribes that Tauber officials had made to foreign fencers. Eastern European fencers were being offered as much as 1,000 DM to throw a fight—a huge sum for them. The story first appeared in the leading Swiss paper *Neue Zürcher Zeitung*. Schmitt, approached for comment, was quoted as saying, "I can't believe that Emil Beck doesn't know what is going on."

Beck immediately sued for defamation—in an attempt, Schmitt believes, to gag him over the weeks leading up to Seoul. The president of the Italian federation, Renzo Nostini, informed Mazzoni that should he travel to Germany to testify on Schmitt's behalf he would find himself removed from the national team. At first Schmitt was determined to fight, but he was persuaded to put the matter off till the Games were over. "After we had all agreed on this, some journalists wrote 'Success for Beck,' but that was absolute rubbish. After the Games, Beck dropped the case completely."

On the fencing strip, Schmitt's progress continued, and he duly qualified for the German team. That July, a training camp was organized in Portugal, a chance to relax before the Games. Schmitt told the German Federation he couldn't make it, as it clashed with his university exams, but that he would continue to train on his own, which he did, taking his coach and younger brother off to Majorca. At this point, one of the leading German officials, an ally of Beck, wrote to the federation, asking for Schmitt to be excluded from the Olympic team. The national sports press reported that without Schmitt Germany would jeopardize its chance of winning gold. The federation met and voted 7–1—in Schmitt's favor.

At Seoul, the entire German team had one of its worst Olympics, win-

---

* It is said that in the same competition, another leading Tauber fencer, now ranked at six in Germany, deliberately lost a fight so that his fellow German, Achim Bellman—a Leverkusen fencer, ranked one place above him—would not get through. A second Italian international, Stefano Bellone, has told me that he too was approached by Tauber personnel and asked to throw fights for cash. It was part of the overall Beck philosophy: he needed to build up his fencers' self-esteem, and if he could, unknown to them, buy them some initial victories, the impetus should make them go on and win.

ning only two golds. One was in swimming. The other was in men's épée, where Arnd Schmitt, only twenty-three and in his first Olympic final, was unstoppable. At the moment of his victory, TV cameras showed Beck with both hands over his face.

"I can understand it all, in a way," says Schmitt. "Tauber is the biggest fencing center in the world. To keep it running, you have to be successful. He couldn't have someone like me outside the Tauber circle." He looked over my shoulder for a moment, then added, "There is a German saying, '*Der Zweck heiligt die Mittel.*'—To achieve what you want you may do anything you want—but it's meant ironically—no one agrees with that. Except Beck."

The Tauber coach may have felt chastened but he remained irrepressible—and was apparently out for revenge. The following year, at the international épée event in London, Schmitt made the final. Through the same official who had pressed to have Schmitt expelled, Beck asked for a certain referee to officiate Schmitt's fight. The Englishman in charge, Keith Smith, was surprised but agreed. Come the bout, the chosen director gave decision after decision against Schmitt, but the German still won. And went on winning: he took the world cup for the first time in 1987, then the world title in 1999, marking him, with Alex Pusch, one of the two most successful épéeists in German history.

Schmitt had agreed before our meeting in Bonn to talk for up to an hour. In the end we spoke for well over three. As the conversation went on, he continued to finger the brown file that lay between us. At last he picked it up and withdrew several sheets of paper. "These will show you that in Tauber it was an open secret that bouts, referees, and high officials were being bought." I glanced at the pages—testimony after testimony of fencers and officials about illicit financial transactions. Some of those who had given information about Beck's dealings were just names; others were fencers I knew well and had come across in competition for years. I looked across at Schmitt. "I was sent it anonymously," he said.

Yet all this was going on at the same time that Tauber fencers continued to win medals at all levels, good work in the local community flourished, and handicapped and young people alike found in "TBB" a second home. Beck's empire seemed too firmly established to be more than slightly embarrassed by Schmitt's testimony. Beck was now in his mid-sixties but still ambitious. Then in 1999 a new story broke.

Beck had become determined that when he retired his younger son, Rene, a fencing coach, would take over from him. However, Rene Beck is far from being a master of international standing and had little support at the club. Anyway, people mused, surely the succession would pass to Matthias Behr. Behr's father had died in a car accident in 1959, and he was almost Beck's adopted son. Not emotional like his mentor, Behr had a quiet way of doing things that has drawn people to him. His first marriage foundered under the weight of his commitment to fencing, but he had been married again, to a Tauber club mate and fellow Olympic gold medalist, Zita Funkenhauser, and only a week before the Olympics were due to start Zita had given birth to twins. There were complications, and Behr said he must stay behind. Beck said he would have to attend, but Behr stood firm. From that point on the relationship unraveled. As Schmitt put it, "Matthias realized that for years he had loyally cheated on Beck's orders, and that he was wrong."

At the end of the 1990s results started to fall off, and other nations overtook Germany on the medals list; by 1996 the country that had been ranked third in the world had slipped to seventh place. Sponsorship fell away, and even loyal Mercedes-Benz questioned whether the huge wage bill could be justified. At the beginning of July Beck publicly attacked Behr and his other loyal lieutenant, Alex Pusch, in front of forty of their colleagues as "lazybones" with "the wrong attitude." The same week the *Frankfurter Allgemeine Zeitung* reported that a group of senior fencers had asked Beck to resign. The reasons given were his offensive behavior and his authoritarian style of leadership. A younger successor was needed. The article sided with Behr, who said he had endured three years of persecution for his supposed "lack of commitment." Pusch declared, "I want my dignity and reputation back."

From July 7 through to the end of the month, hardly a day passed without some major German newspaper story based on the troubles at Tauber. On the fifteenth the *Süddeutsche Zeitung* reported that all parties had agreed to "bury the hatchet" and that a newfound team spirit prevailed; a week later one of the club's world champions stormed out, saying that Pusch and Behr had been made scapegoats for Tauber's current lack of success. Three days later the *Stuttgarter Zeitung* reported new accusations of financial fraud against Beck, who had moved into a flat intended for fencers.

Beck's handling of government subsidies was paraded mercilessly. Retired international fencers were due to receive some 300 DM each in public money every month as payment for acting as sparring partners for younger fencers. This money, it was claimed, Beck had retained and spent on his own priorities. He was referred to as "Emil Everywhere," one of the most powerful men in the sports industry, holding more than ten posts in various associations and unions. Behr was reported not to want Beck's job—his marriage was more important. And so it went on, the pride of Germany unraveling for all to see.

Eventually Beck was fined just 25,000 DM, and his responsibilities were split up among a group of subordinates. A year later, when I interviewed him at the Tauber center, he had retired from his various posts and seemed to be functioning as a kind of professor emeritus. People treated him carefully, with an exaggerated respect, humoring him but still slightly afraid of the short, corpulent figure who had so recently wielded so much power: a dethroned Napoleon, wandering around his Elba. How was he spending his time? Improving his golf handicap, he said: at 28, it was too high. And there were his homing pigeons, a flock he had tended lovingly for years (a hobby he shares with another noted sportsman—Mike Tyson). I asked him whether, if he had his life over again, he would do anything differently—anything at all. No, he said, he wouldn't change a thing.

Shortly after my visit Beck was accused of syphoning off some 275,000 DM *a year* from various grants and subsidies he had been given to administer. At that time no one claimed he was using the money for personal gain; it was just that he had seemed to regard this money as his own, to distribute and spend as he saw fit. "It's a tragedy—it's the right word, yes?" said Behr, finally installed as the club's manager. "But we can't help him now." No charges were ever filed against Tauber's creator, whose death in 2006 attracted glowing obituaries.

Beck was obviously an exceptional motivator, and his slant on teaching initiated a revolution. Maybe the lack of success in his final years—no gold at Sydney, just a couple of silvers and three bronzes—was an indictment of his championing hard work over technique; maybe the fencing world had simply become more competitive. But how had one man been able to corrupt a whole generation? German fencing glosses over Beck's legacy, because to criticize his methods would be to call into question all those medals, those concrete achievements. "Germany isn't a country that builds its self-image through its sporting successes," Arnd Schmitt told me, but I wonder. People see in Beck the most successful master in the history of swordplay, and certainly the center he created in his hometown surpasses all other sports centers throughout the world, a stupendous achievement. What would I have done, had I been brought up in that system? Or if my twenty-five-year-old daughter Mary, who is now in the British épée team, but struggles to beat top Continental opposition, had been offered the chance of such world-class coaching from an early age? I thought of King Midas, even of the Struldbruggs in *Gulliver's Travels*, but most of Faustus, bartering his soul for immortality:

> Cut is the branch that might have grown full straight,
> And burned is Apollo's laurel bough,
> That sometime grew within this learned man.

WHAT WILL BE EMIL BECK'S LEGACY? WILL FENCING IN GERMANY and beyond be able to put its house in order? That Arnd Schmitt should emerge as an athlete of sufficient integrity to take on the Tauber system and sufficient character to triumph, and with such great skill that he could also become a world and Olympic champion is heartening, and it did force officials throughout Europe to rethink their priorities. "When someone as talented and driven as Emil Beck emerges, it's hard not to give them near-total power," commented one leading German official who is also high on the FIE. "But we've learned that the cost can be too high." Even so, Beck's disgrace did not immediately alter the way fencers acted. During the Barcelona Olympics of 1992, four Russian épéeists and the world saber champion, Viktor Kirienko, held a press conference to announce that they would not fight for their country in the team events unless their government honored its promise to pay them $1,500 each for the gold medals they had won at the 1991 world championships. In the end they *did* fence—but only after Boris Yeltsin himself had assured them that the money would be paid. The Russians were not unusual: the Italian team at those Games won $40,000 per gold medal; Germans can expect 30,000 DM for winning an Olympic gold medal. Most national teams are the same: the Hungarian fencers who did not go to Los Angeles in 1984 because of the boycott received thousands of forints in compensation. Nor is any of this new. The cheating virus has been present for at least forty years, during which period the sport has changed not only its ethos but also its technical character, and the two are interdependent. The electric box was introduced at the Berlin Games in 1936. Fencers, and coaches like Beck, quickly realized that the new system made formerly accepted techniques redundant—there was no need to *look* elegant when registering a hit was the only thing that counted. Everything in the sport focused on that machine: the tail wagged the dog. The laws of right of way and what constituted an attack, the basic vision of fencing introduced by the French in the eighteenth century, were flouted as fencing got faster and faster, and even the traditional differences among foil, épée, and saber began to erode. A top Soviet official, a General Popov, was quoted in the French magazine *Escrime,* coining the aphorism, "The symbolism of the action has been replaced by the reality of the touch."

In an attempt to make the sport suitable for television, the FIE has introduced see-through masks, colored clothing, and an elaborate qualifying formula for major championships. One is reminded of H. L. Mencken's admonition "To every grave problem there is an answer that is simple, easy, and wrong." But other changes are on the right tack. There is a move afoot to reduce the "blockage" time at foil and saber, to make it harder for fencers' lights to go off together; to increase the contact time of the foil tip upon its target, to eliminate flick hits; to reduce the distance between the two *en garde* lines by a meter, making it harder to get a "run-up" to attacks; and, as has already and sadly happened with saber, to eliminate the flèche. No one wants to throw away the electric box, but such innovations could dilute its predominance. Ironically, these changes, if implemented, would help return fencing to classical modes—not because it would make for a more beautiful sport but because preelectric fencing was governed by what the human eye could take in. If people fence classically, it is easier for audiences to understand, and that could promote the sponsorship and TV coverage that fencing so desperately needs.

In the late 1980s the FIE moved its main headquarters from Paris to Lausanne, seat of the International Olympic Committee. If this was an attempt to gain more say in the corridors of sporting power, it backfired. Juan Antonio Samaranch, the IOC's dictatorial head, largely ignored the newly elected head of world fencing, the seventy-one-year-old businessman, René Roch, and made it clear that he wanted the Olympic fencing program streamlined—or the sport might be dropped from the Games altogether.*

---

* Samaranch finally retired at the beginning of 2001. His successor was the Belgian Jacques Rogge, a former Olympic yachtsman. Fencing was lucky. For years the frontrunner for the post had been a Canadian lawyer, Dick Pound, who had made no secret of his wish to drop the sport on the grounds that it did not pay its way, people didn't want to watch it, and sponsorship was minimal. But Pound had another reason: in 1988 the Canadian Fencing Association got itself into a muddle when a member of its saber squad said that the marking system should have qualified him for the Seoul

Recently I lunched with an old friend, Ioan Pop, a Romanian who reached the Olympic saber finals in 1976 and is now technical director for the FIE. "If we are out of the Olympics, we are finished," Ioan told me. "Every sport tries to get better and better for TV. We can't perform a miracle—just one day to the next, little by little, try to make things better. Maybe get like tennis." At least, he noted, fencing is no longer dominated by the five traditional leading powers. At Sydney the men's foil event had been won, for the first time, by a South Korean; the saber by a Romanian, another first; China had taken two team medals. So the old order is changing, and this may have helped fencing's cause when René Roch met Jacques Rogge in early February 2002.

Rogge grew up in Ghent, which has a strong tradition of swordplay. He assured Roch that the sport would stay in the Olympics at least till 2008, with two hundred contestants and women fencing saber for the first time. Roch for his part promised to reform foil, particularly definitions of the attack. "Foil is like ice skating at the moment," he explained to me a few days after his meeting with Rogge. "We need something objective."[3] So fencing kept its place at the Olympic table, a vital victory.

Within two months, the whole settlement had unraveled. A plan to replace the traditional team events was vehemently opposed, particularly by the more powerful fencing nations. When in May it was announced that, to keep within the ten-event limit, team events at men's saber and women's foil would be discarded, there was uproar. Top international competitions in Madrid, Paris, Padua, and Warsaw were disrupted, striking finalists reading out prepared texts to the TV cameras to denounce the sport's leadership.

The IOC looked on appalled, disgusted at fencing's ability to pierce itself in the foot. Couldn't the world's swordsmen agree on anything among themselves? At the same time, Roch's attempts to take the sport back to its classical roots were blocked at congress after congress. The summer of 2002 found Olympic swordsmen in rancorous confusion.

Yet was any of this really new? It all seemed one more convulsion in a history of revolutions. Amid the uproar blademakers were reporting record sales, as more and more people took to the fencing strip.

I had my own slightly odd taste of this when in the autumn of 2002

---

team and challenged the association in court. Pound was retained by the association but lost, at great cost—and was left wondering what kind of sport it was that could get itself into such a mess.

my old saber coach Bob Anderson recruited me to join the cast of that year's James Bond adventure, *Die Another Day*. My job was to be a "specialist extra" for the fencing scene, set inside one of London's gentlemen's clubs on Pall Mall. Throughout filming, there had been one constant topic: Would Madonna turn up? She was said to have put off her one scene time and time again, adding thousands to the budget, and gossip on the set was that her fee would be a million dollars for just a single day's shooting. She was forty-four, a mother of young children: How would she look? She was to play the part of Verity, the club's fencing coach, and originally she was to have been one of Bond's ex-girlfriends, but she objected to being his castoff and rewrote both her lines and his, remodeling herself as a lesbian, beyond Bond's reach.

On the day she was due to make her long-awaited appearance, the rest of us turned up, as usual, at seven in the morning, ready for action. At eight, I was backstage looking at the previous day's rushes, when I became aware of an eerie silence on set: Madonna had arrived. She wandered nonchalantly across the fencing room in a black Versace outfit that included a figure-hugging corset that she would later ask Bond to do up for her. Her black leotard was so tight it looked like cling-film. Her arms, muscular as a gymnast's, were bare, and as she sauntered across stage she licked at a red lollipop.

A few minutes passed, then entered Pierce Brosnan, and the two stars eyed each other like boxers weighing up who has the heavier punch. Eventually the director called for action, and Brosnan reentered the salle to ask if he could have a lesson. Madonna, though physically adept, had trouble with the moves, and the scene required several takes. As the two stars waited for the camera to be reset, they chatted together, and Madonna turned the conversation to fencing. "Have you had a go at this?" she asked. "It's great." One more convert.

By Way of the Sword

> *The exercising of weapons putteth away aches, griefs, and diseases, it increaseth strength and sharpeneth the wits, it giveth a perfect judgment, it expelleth melancholy, choleric, and evil conceits, it keepeth a man in breath, perfect health, and long life.*
>
> —GEORGE SILVER, *Paradoxes of Defence*, 1599

> *Doesn't everyone wish he could fence? . . . It is violence refined into beauty; it has associations with love, honor and suicidal pride. We think of great fencers—unlike great footballers or great junk-bond salesmen—as superior beings; air and fire, rather than earth and water. We think of Cyrano, Zorro and the Three Musketeers.*
>
> —JAMES TRAUB, *GQ*, 1994

THE TWO TEENAGERS STOOD STARING AT EACH OTHER, NEITHER moving. Both had been told to strike quickly and without warning; both were justly afraid of the other. It was the tensest moment those watching could remember. The date was 1965, the place Rotterdam; the occasion, the fight-off for the world youth épée title.

The final four had fenced a round robin, but the Austrian and the Russian had trailed in third and fourth places, with a tie for first between the Frenchman, Jacques Brodin, and the Swede, Hans Jacobsson. The two fought off, but when time was called at six minutes they were level. In those days fencers did not continue until a deciding hit—"sudden death," as it is appositely known. Instead they had had to fight a second barrage, and when time was called Jacobsson and Brodin were tied again, at 3–all. Over the final and the two fight-offs they had been equal on aggregate hits. The organizers conferred, then told the combatants to battle it out once more; if this match remained undecided, they would share the championship.

So they squared off, Hans Jacobsson—slim, blond, a classical épéeist who would be part of his country's all-conquering team in the 1970s—and Jacques Brodin, already a senior world finalist, short, broad-shouldered, skin darkened by southern sun, adept at snaking out attacks to his opponent's toe or wrist. In his fight in the round robin he had hit the Swede three times this way, all the more remarkable in that he held his épée by the pommel, shunning the protection of his guard but giving him crucial extra inches. He was the reigning champion and had first won the title four years before. The two were finely matched; now it was a question of character. Whose nerve would break?

Neither took the initiative, and the entire audience was on the edge of their seats wondering who would make the first move, asking themselves what *they* would do under such circumstances. Would one last all-out attack be worth it, at the very last moment of full time? Were both under orders to do nothing, or was it mutual fear? What did each want more—the chance to be cochampion or to risk everything to be supreme? *"He either fears his fate too much / Or his deserts are small / That puts it not unto the touch / To win or lose it all."*[1]

The seconds ticked away—four minutes, five . . . still neither man ventured forward. At last the buzzer sounded for the full six minutes. For the only time in fencing history, a title was split following three rounds of barrages.*

---

* Titles per se had been shared twice before. In 1935 *four* fencers divided the men's foil championship. More intriguingly, we have met Ellen Müller-Preis as the Olympic champion of 1932 and the bronze medalist of 1936. Here is the official British report on the Monte Carlo world championships of 1950:

> Ladies Individual—The final of eight was fought on a very hot afternoon. In the last bout Renée Garilhe, the French champion, beat the title-holder Ellen Müller-Preis of Austria so that both ended in a tie with two defeats each. During this last fight of the regular final Mrs Preis fell and aggravated an injury to her knee which had caused her to retire from the team matches. The fence-off was a most painful affair as Mrs Preis hobbled on to the strip and came on guard with many gestures of physical distress. Miss Garilhe obviously felt herself unable to go for her and in fact the director [referee] asked her not to bustle Mrs Preis. Two half-hearted attacks from Miss Garilhe were stopped and a third parried. With the score 3-1 for Mrs Preis the latter broke down and seemed unable to get on guard. The French captain Levy then asked his lady to leave the strip. The jury of appeal decided that the fence-off could not be regarded as properly fought and declared the two ladies equal winners. This seemed the only possible solution but the Austrians have protested.

It is possible that some arrangement had been reached between the French and Swedish teams, but I like to think not; rather, that this was a defining moment in competitive swordplay. Often have I wondered what I might have done in similar circumstances, never having faced such a challenging moment; but in the 1970 Commonwealth Games, my first appearance on the English team, I did fight a match that felt dramatic enough at the time. I was competing for the bronze medal against an experienced Scot, appropriately named Gordon Wiles; the score had reached 4–4. As soon as the referee said "Play!" each of us would attack, time and again, unwilling to trust the last hit to defense. Finally Wiles went back into a parry, which I evaded to take my first international medal.

Many years later, when in 1998 I moved to America, I came across an old wool mat, about three and a half by two feet, that my father had knitted to commemorate that victory. It portrays two figures in white lunging at each other against a black background. Two blocks of squares record the score: four hits against five. At the top my father had carefully put in "Commonweath [sic] Games 1970" in white and sky blue. Wiles, blackhaired in real life, has brown hair; mine is pink.

I remember thinking of my father's attitude to sport and how completely honorable he had been—even to the point of foolhardiness: it would never have occurred to him to cheat or to behave ungenerously to an opponent. And then my thoughts drifted to a more poignant moment, ten years before. My mother was dying in an East Sussex hospital. I had traveled down from London to sit with my father at her bedside. It was nearly midnight when the doctors told us there was nothing to be gained by sitting with her further, and despite my father's protests we were ushered out and made our way back to my parents' house. My parents had twin beds; to keep my father company, I slept in my mother's that night. At about three in the morning the telephone rang and my father answered it.

There was nothing we could do immediately, so we lay silently where we were. I think my father believed that I had managed to drop off again. After a while I heard a knocking, endlessly repeated every few seconds. At first I was mystified, then I realized: my father was hitting his chin with

---

Despite the protest, the decision stood, and both women were named champion. But why did the Austrians protest? In 1950?²

In 1932, when Müller-Preis won Olympic gold, she was faced with another fight-off—against the British foilist Judy Guinness, who lost 3–5 after *twice* acknowledging hits the judges had missed. This must count as the most self-denying act of sportsmanship that fencing has witnessed.

his fist, to stop himself crying out: even though I was over forty, I was his child, and he was determined to shield me.

What does this have to do with fencing? First, it is a reminder that defense lies at the heart of the sport. My father believed, from feelings of love and duty, that he should act in a certain way. I do not want to put him on a pedestal (he would quickly have stepped off it), but often while writing this book I have reflected how he would have reacted to various aspects of the history of swordplay. I think he would have been bewildered—that people should ever remotely have regarded cheating as an option or even seen sport as an end in itself.

His grandaughter, Mary, started to fence épée when she was twelve. In January 2002, when she was fifteen, I took her to compete in the Northern Irish Open. We stayed the night with friends of mine, the Haldanes. Fiona, a longtime international, has often won the women's épée title. As ill luck would have it, Mary's first fight the next day was with Fiona, and she was quickly down 2–0. I was fencing on another piste and when I got to her saw that Mary had won the bout 5–3. I congratulated her, and she replied ruefully that she felt she had cheated. "Cheated?" I know I looked aghast. "Yes," said Mary, perfectly serious. "I used speed." This was an interesting insight. She hadn't behaved wrongly in any ethical sense, but she had been taught to use her brains and technique; employing the natural speed of a teenager was somehow a wrong way to win.

WHY DOES ANYONE FENCE IN THE FIRST PLACE? I STILL COMPETE and enjoy it as much as ever. And although nowadays I am at best no more than an occasional irritant to a top fencer, in the last twenty-five years a veterans' circuit has been built up, for those age forty and over, and since 1998 there has been a world championship, as well as a thriving European championship, the most recent of which drew more than thirteen hundred entrants to Hénin-Beaumont, near Lille, in 2011. The standards vary wildly: some competitors are at no more than county level, but by the last eight most of those involved are ex-internationals, still burning to win.

In May 1997 I traveled to San Remo for the European championships along with Kathy, my girlfriend, now my wife. She has never fenced but to my surprise enjoys watching—"You can tell so clearly what people are like from the way they perform." Besides, San Remo has its own pleasures: an Edwardian-era spa not far east of Nice, it boasts a huge casino, built in 1905, and fine public gardens. The competition was held in one of the town's grand houses, the Villa Ormand, and we found ourselves lunging and parrying among fountains, exotic Mediterranean plants, and an entire Japanese garden in miniature. In more than one sense, the veterans look after themselves.

There were two opening rounds. Early on I lost a fight to Péter Bakonyi, a member of Hungary's gold-medal-winning team in the 1966 world championships. Then came direct elimination. I fought my way through to the last eight, where I faced a compact Ukrainian who did not pose too much of a problem. In the semifinal I drew Bakonyi again. He still had a marvelous hand, but his legs were another matter, and this time I squeaked home 10–8.

In the final my opponent was a German, Wolfgang Marzodko, an ebullient competitor who had been Germany's number one in the mid-1970s and was good enough to have reached the last twelve at the Budapest Open, the strongest saber event on the calendar. He had put on weight since then but was still a difficult proposition—as well as being the defending champion. A sizable crowd gathered, and I was aware how much the British contingent was willing me on when one of our women rushed up to wish me good luck and whisper a word of advice. Again the winner of the bout would be the first to land ten hits, and I took an early lead. Then, to my frustration, the match started slipping away. I found myself continually caught by Marzodko's left-handed prime parries, which, perfectly timed, seemed to sweep up any attack, from whatever direction. Soon I was down 7–9, one hit away from defeat. Out of the corner of my eye I could see Kathy pacing up and down the line of spectators, muttering to herself as I went further behind. What was she saying? But I had to think about the match and how I was going to take the next three hits . . .

On the referee's "Allez," I decided that I would try defending, and as Marzodko launched himself at me I managed to choose the right line, successfully making my parry before landing a riposte: 8–9. There was no time for deliberation, as once again he drove down the piste, gathering himself for a more careful attack. I threw out my blade and landed on his wrist. Lucky; but that made it 9–all. On the final hit I was sure he would go back to what had worked so well for him, waiting for me to attack so as to catch me again in that blasted prime parry. I shortened my step forward and made a simple lunge. It caught him a split second earlier than he'd expected, and although he got his blade to mine I was through, brushing his jacket at midchest. That meant 10–9, and the European championship. A cup for veterans, maybe, but I was happy.

Ten minutes later, as I bent down from the winners' rostrum to accept the trophy from an august Eduardo Mangiarotti, Wolfgang glanced up to ask, "What was it that girl said to you just before we fenced?" I smiled. "She told me to forget that you were a friend of mine and that I had to concentrate on winning." "That is funny," he replied. "I was thinking the same thing." Then the national anthem was played and it was all over and time for me to search out Kathy. I had a question of my own.

"What was it you were muttering during the bout?" She didn't reply at first, then blushed. "I was telling myself, 'If he loves me he'll win, if he loves me he'll win.'" I didn't say anything then, just took her in my arms—and reflected that fencing is, after all, a romantic sport.

Afterword

O TTO VON BISMARCK ONCE FOUGHT A DUEL WITH SAUSAGES—or so several readers of this book have informed me. Shouldn't I have included this detail? Sadly, the story is, if not entirely apocryphal, too far from the truth. In 1863 a cholera epidemic swept through much of Europe. Slaughterhouses in lower and central Germany were blamed, but the various governments seemed unconcerned. Bismarck's comment on the matter, "The less people know about how sausages and laws are made, the better they will sleep at night," led to his being repeatedly hectored by an eminent pathologist and politician named Rudolf Virchow. Enraged by Virchow's criticisms, Bismarck ordered his seconds to arrange a duel.

Virchow consented, with one stipulation. As the challenged party, he had choice of weapons, and he selected two gigantic pork sausages, one safe to eat, the other laced with trichinae, which could inflict a slow and lingering death. Virchow passed back the message "Let His Excellency decide which he wishes to eat, and I shall eat the other." Bismarck called off his challenge at once, reasoning that a man might die with some sort of honor on a dueling field but never by poisoning from a sausage. His assistants replied, "His Highness has destroyed the sausages and asks that you be his guest at dinner this evening. After due consideration he feels he may have been slightly in error." So, after all, there was no duel, nor is there firm evidence that the challenge was ever given.[1]

Sausages may hold their special place in the history of dueling, but in the five years since *By the Sword* was first published I have come across several more challenges with swords worthy of mention. Georges Clemenceau, so formidable a swordsman himself, in 1888 volunteered to second his political ally Charles Floquet, then France's elderly prime minister. His opponent was Floquet's leading political adversary, General Georges-Ernest-Jean-Marie Boulanger, who at one time seemed likely to lead a coup d'état against the republic. Boulanger had insulted Floquet in the Chamber of Deputies, charging that he had "lied impudently" during a debate. Having choice of weapons, Boulanger selected swords—this against a man of sixty, some ten years his senior. The two rivals, stripped to the waist, met on the exercise ground of a private garden in Neuilly. In the first exchange, Floquet was slightly cut on his left leg, while Boulanger had his right forefinger punctured. At the second pass, the elder man had his left hand opened, but Boulanger was far more seriously wounded. Floquet's rapier had pierced Boulanger's throat a good two inches, passing through the jugular and the carotid artery and nearly severing the phrenic nerve, and the seconds immediately called off the fight. After two days, Boulanger was out of danger, but he had been mortally shamed. Three years later, discredited and exiled, he shot himself through the head on his mistress's grave.[2]

The duel between Floquet and Boulanger took place toward the end of the period in French history when dueling was often more absurd than dangerous. In 1830, the writer Charles Augustin Saint-Beuve (1804–69) fought one of the owners of Le Globe in heavy rain; Saint-Beuve held an umbrella throughout the duel, claiming that he did not mind dying but he would not get wet. In 1870, the great Édouard Manet, angered by the brief review his friend, the critic Louis Duranty, had made of two of his paintings, fought sword to sword in the forest of Saint-Germain (Émile Zola being Manet's second) in a duel that lasted three days, before Duranty was wounded above the right nipple. The adversaries remained friends thereafter.

Near-duels—such as the Bismarck sausage exchange—are often ridiculous but nonetheless interesting. In 1954, Ernest Hemingway was called out in Cuba, but declined. Jack London was challenged at foil and duly beaten by his young opponent, Charmian Kittredge, whom he proceeded to marry. As recently as October 1997 reports appeared that a duel had been arranged between a mayor in southern Italy and certain Mafia capi. I investigated and found that, indeed, one Giovanni Maria Calabretta, of Vaccarizzo Albanese, mayor of some 512 families in the province of Cosenza, "tired of continuous acts of vandalism and of daily anonymous threats," had put up posters all over town challenging local leaders of the Honored Society, but this was left to languish.

When Vladimir Nabokov was twelve years old, he was told that his father, Vladimir Dmitrievich, a member of the Duma, had been drawn into a duel that might prove deadly. "The most powerful of the Rightist newspapers employed a shady journalist to concoct a scurrilous piece containing insinuations that my father could not let pass," Nabokov recounts in his memoir, *Speak, Memory*.[3] "Since the well-known rascality of the actual author of the article made him 'nonduelable,' (*neduelesposobnyy*, as the Russian code had it), my father called out the somewhat less disreputable editor of the paper."

Young Vladimir had himself been taking fencing lessons for almost a year, "from a wonderful rubbery Frenchman," M. Loustalot, who came almost daily to spar with his father. Nabokov "would dash, with my fur coat on, through the green drawing room . . . toward the library, from which came a medley of stamping and scraping sounds. There, I would find my father, a big, robust man, looking still bigger in his white training suit, thrusting and parrying, while his agile instructor added brisk exclamations (*'Battez!' 'Rompez!'*) to the click-clink of the foils." Now he had to consider his father using those same movements in a fight for his life. "A Russian duel was a much more serious affair than the conventional Parisian variety." It took the editor several days to decide whether or not to accept the challenge, during which Nabokov *fils* filled his mind with foreboding:

> What would his adversary choose, I kept asking myself—the blade or the bullet? Carefully, I took the beloved, the familiar, the richly alive image of my father at fencing and tried to transfer that image, minus the mask and the padding, to the dueling ground, in some barn or riding school. I visualized him and his adversary, both bare-chested, black-trousered, in furious battle, their energetic movements marked by that strange awkwardness which even the most elegant swordsmen cannot avoid in a real encounter.

To his relief, he returned home one day to find that the challenge had met with a belated apology. "I saw my mother's serene everyday face, but I could not look at my father." Tragedy was not to be stayed, however: one night in 1922, at a public lecture in Berlin, Nabokov's father threw himself in front of the lecturer, an old friend, and took two bullets from a couple of Russian Fascists. He knocked down one assassin, but the other discharged a third and fatal shot.

This kind of memory I find extremely moving. Equally interesting are the journals of Paul Gauguin. When I first researched *By the Sword* I discovered that Gauguin had fenced, but I imagined it a schoolboy activity, never a serious hobby. I could not have been more wrong. "No more paint-ing, no more literature; the time has come to talk of arms," he writes, cov-ering fencing in four different towns for five pages. "One must always begin the study of arms with foils," he goes on.

> That is the best foundation. But one has to apply this knowledge quite differently in a duel, where the question is not one of cor-rectly touching certain specified spots; here everything counts. One must consider that on the field dangerous strokes are also danger-ous for oneself. . . . In fencing there are no dogmas, any more than there are secret thrusts.

He does not record whether he ever had to fight a duel himself.

Gauguin was one of the many pupils of Adolphe Grisier (along with a Russian czar and Alexandre Dumas), and once he felt proficient he of-fered to teach his friend Vincent van Gogh. Van Gogh became sufficiently exasperated with his fellow painter's belligerence that he wrote to his brother complaining sarcastically, "Fortunately Gauguin and I and other painters are not yet armed with machine guns and other very destructive instruments of war. I for one am quite decided to go on being armed with nothing but my brush and pen. But with a good deal of clatter, Gauguin has nonetheless demanded in his last letter 'his masks and fencing gloves' hidden in the little closet in my little yellow house. I shall hasten to send him his toys by parcel post."[4]

Nevertheless, it was during his stay with van Gogh in Arles that Gau-guin witnessed one of the most famous cuts in history. One morning, hav-ing stayed overnight at a small hotel, he made his way to van Gogh's house to find a great crowd gathered: his friend "had cut off his ear close to the head." Gauguin continues:

> When he was in a condition to go out, with his head enveloped in a Basque beret which he had pulled far down, he went straight to a certain house where for want of a fellow-countrywoman one can pick up an acquaintance, and gave the manager his ear, carefully washed and placed in an envelope. "Here is a souvenir of me," he said.

Stories of the famous and their adventures steel in hand are difficult to resist. Not only, for instance, was Marx a keen fencer (as I have recorded), but so too was his collaborator Engels. Jean Sibelius completed an orchestral piece, *Fäktmusik* ("Fencing Music"), and August Strindberg a short story in which a practice foil sets off a life-changing brawl. Originally I had recorded that Conan Doyle never fenced; but in his memoirs he mentions crossing swords with "a medical man from Southsea," who insisted that Doyle wear a heavy plastron. "A necessary precaution, for the doctor's foil broke and the sharp point created went deeply into the padding: I learned a lesson that day."[5]

This brings me to other errors in *By the Sword*. Several readers wrote about wrong dates (luckily, still in single figures) or mistakes of emphasis. Some of these are matters of judgment. A reviewer on Amazon chided me for relegating the infamous "Coup de Jarnac" of 1547, after which French kings "forced dueling to be an illegal act," to no more than a sidebar on secret thrusts. The duel, "Henning O." from Stockholm wrote, "had implications on fencing and how it was being regarded. Rarely in history we can point at an individual event and say: Here is a turning point, here history actually changed direction." It is true that the king, Henri II, was so disgusted by what he witnessed that he turned against any form of judicial settlement by arms; but since within a year of his ruling, duels in his kingdom were as rife as ever, I find it difficult to see his proclamation as radical. (Across the Channel, a century on, Oliver Cromwell issued a similar proclamation against dueling, and—according to Jonathan Swift, who was in a position to know—encouraged his court to tease and josh one another, hoping that factitious insults would prevent real ones. He was no more successful than Henri.) A more telling point is that the duel of honor, as taken up throughout most of Western Europe, derived primarily from the Italian Renaissance idea of the gentleman; I might have given this more emphasis.

Another Internet reviewer, "Suspira" from Pittsburgh, Pa., turned to swordplay in films, and wrote in defense of Tyrone Power, saying that Flynn was never an accomplished swordsman, whereas Power was "an EXPERT swordsman who NEVER—read this—NEVER used a double." She was not the only reader to have defended Power, but her contention is simply not true: Power's fencing in *The Mark of Zorro* was all done by Albert Craven, the son of Fred Craven, the film's fight arranger, and while Flynn was no fencing aficionado, he was such a fine sportsman that I doubt if the pudgy, ill-balanced Power could have bested him—but then again, everyone has their view on imaginary contests.

An interesting piece of history concerns stirrups. This may seem arcane, but the introduction of stirrups, one of the greatest inventions in the history of warfare, which I had dated from 378 A.D., provided horsemen with greater purchase to strike a foe, helping swords gain ascendancy over other weapons. Reviewers argued that stirrups were not employed before Charles Martel, Duke of the Franks (688–741 A.D.), and were not in general use before the late eighth or even ninth century. My argument was that the Romans did not know of the stirrup, and so gave up a vital advantage to the Visigoths in the Battle of Adrianople (present-day Edirne, in European Turkey) in 378. A letter published in the rarified pages of the *Australian Army Journal*[6] convincingly argues that the stirrup was known at least by 175 A.D., when used by eight thousand Sarmatian heavy cavalry, part of the Roman auxiliary forces. Thereafter, Roman commanders appear to have made a deliberate choice not to use the stirrup, finding instead the Celtic horned saddle perfectly adequate for mounted operations. Further, the employment of physically larger Gallo-Roman and Germanic troops at Adrianople led to the issue of longer and heavier swords throughout the army. The Romans lost at Adrianople through poor generalship. This leaves open the question of why the sword quickly triumphed over so many other weapons, which my book has been able to address only in part.

More glaring was my underestimation of the degree of skill possessed by medieval swordsmen. As has been pointed out since publication, medieval fighting relied heavily on parry as well as thrust. For example, Manuscript I.33, the oldest fencing treatise in existence, displays parries with the blade on about 35 of its 64 illustrations. Overall, it contains all the core principles behind modern fencing: timing, distance, line, blade sensitivity, parries, beats, binds, and on through the repertoire (and also includes the earliest mention of a lady fencer, one Walpurgis, who appears in four of the illustrations). I concede that these systems were both sophisticated and complex, my error being that I relied less on original sources than on the writings of such nineteenth-century commentators as Egleton Castle and M. J. O'Rourke, who generally disparaged the skills of medieval swordsmen, describing swords throughout this period as heavy and unwieldy. This prejudice lasted at least until the 1950s (though it still rings through in the writings of Charles de Beaumont, for one), but modern scholarship argues that by far the majority of swords weighed no more than three pounds.[7] I also trusted the view of the great expert on European arms R. Ewart Oakeshott, who held that fighters of that time preferred not to use their blades for defense but to move out of the way. Maybe they did; but the knowledge of how to parry was there.

Oakeshott, who died in October 2002, is only one of several key experts on arms and swordfighting to have passed away in the last six years. Others include the great Hungarian épeé coach Bela Rerrich, Emil Beck, Christian d'Oriola, Ellen Müller-Preis, and Jerzy Pawlowski (as well as his CIA nemesis, Philip Agee). In 2004, Müller-Preis, frail but full of vigor at ninety-two, put in an unexpected appearance at the World Veteran Championships in Krems, just outside Vienna. Even before her record-breaking career was over, she had forged another as a professor at the University for Music and Performing Arts in Vienna, introducing a technique for breathing and movement that allowed the voice to float freely.

After admonishing me for incorrect breathing ("It will shorten your life, young man!"), she turned to discussing Helene Mayer. "She never beat me, you know," she said proudly, in her excellent English (a forgivable exaggeration: see page 343). "In the years following Amsterdam, she got quite a bit heavier, and I would wait for her attack, when there would be a moment when her body subsided into her lunge, then I'd riposte under her sword arm. It was her one weakness, and I always exploited it."

During the last half-decade, several interesting books on fencing have been published, from histories of dueling, such as Barbara Holland's survey *Gentlemen's Blood* (2003) to facsimile editions of many of the earliest treatises. My favorite is probably James Landale's *The Last Duel* (2005), which tells the story behind the last recorded fatal duel on Scottish soil. It mentions, among other unusual facts, that the queen still retains an official champion, whom she can call out to defend her if she is challenged: the current incumbent, Lieutenant Colonel John Dymoke, came into the office in 1946, is now over eighty, and has yet to appear on Her Majesty's behalf. Landale also unearths an apposite epigraph from Evelyn Waugh's 1955 novel *Officers and Gentlemen*, second in his Sword of Honor trilogy:

"Guy, what would you say if you were challenged to a duel?"
"Laugh."
"Yes, of course."
"What made you think of that now?"
"I was thinking about honor. It is a thing that changes, doesn't it?
I mean, a hundred and fifty years ago we would have had to fight
if challenged. Now we'd laugh. There must have been a time
hundreds of years or so ago when it was rather an awkward question."

Just as the meaning of honor changes, so does the nature of the honorable sport of fencing itself. Since 2002, at international level it has become ever more professional (my daughter, who in 2005 won the British épée title, then put off her studies to be a doctor for two years to become a fulltime athlete, which she viewed as the only way to win an Olympic place at the 2012 Games). Each year, the rules change to accommodate the demands of TV and sponsors; while at the Games in Athens, the men's saber final had neither wires nor boxes, but special lights fixed inside the masks, lighting up when a fencer scored. From 2009 on, foilists have had to contend with the mask bib being part of the target, which has changed technique all over again.

There are new heroes, new nations in contention. Stanislav Pozdniakov of Russia (born 1973) has won two Olympic individual golds and five individual world titles and shares four team titles: the best record ever. The Italian Valentina Vezzali (born 1974) has won three Olympic individual foil golds, a silver, and five world championship titles, two silvers and two bronzes—as well as five team golds. In 2006 she published her autobiography, *A Volto Scoperto* (*With Uncovered Face*), making her possibly the only living fencer to have published her memoirs while still actively competing. Both champions achieved their extraordinary success amid the fiercest competition ever.

If France, Italy, Russia, and Hungary remain world leaders (only this year did I learn that the Hungarian for boxing translates literally to "fencing with fists," a real sign of national priorities), they have been joined by countries such as Korea and China. African and South American nations now host major events. Over the last six or seven years, the United States has threatened to join the elite: fourth in both men's saber and men's foil at Athens, it gained its first-ever Olympic gold in 2004, when a last-minute replacement, Mariel Zagunis (the daughter of Olympic rowing parents), won the women's saber. Over the last eight years the United States has easily the best record of any nation at that event, with at least five different women winning major titles.

A final story. An oddity of swordplay is that it appeals to the widest range of people. One of the least likely fencers must surely be the great German philosopher Friederich Nietzsche (1844–1900), a man plagued all his short life with health problems. Yet in the early 1860s we find him at university, drinking, rejoicing in the nickname "Gluck"—and swordfighting. According to his friend Paul Deussen, "Nietzsche practiced as well as he could, and he also managed to get a challenge to a duel." Apparently the future author of the Superman (*übermensch*) philosophy went out drinking one night and asked an Armenian fellow student if he would "hang one" on him—scar him in a formal duel. Nietzsche was even at that age "somewhat corpulent . . . and moreover very myopic," but was not a whit abashed by what he had let himself in for. Come the chosen day, Deussen records:

> The blades were tied and the sharp rapiers flashed around their bare heads. After barely three minutes the opponent applied a cut diagonally across the bridge of Nietzsche's nose right where too hard a pinch leaves a red mark. The blood was dripping to the ground, and the experts determined it to be sufficient atonement for all past injury. I loaded my well-bandaged friend into a carriage and took him home to bed, cooled the wound diligently, denied him visitors and alcohol, and in two or three days our hero had recuperated except for a tiny diagonal scar across his bridge of the nose, which he kept all his life and which did not look bad on him.[8]

The experience must have given Nietzsche comfort, because he later wrote (in *Human, All Too Human*) that dueling was "a great blessing." In all its modern forms, our masks securely in place, it surely is.

Richard Cohen, New York, January, 2012

Notes

PROLOGUE

1. Egerton Castle, *Schools and Masters of Fence from the Middle Ages to the Eighteenth Century, with a Sketch of the Development of the Art of Fencing with the Rapier and the Small Sword* (London: Arms and Armour, 1969). Despite Castle's immense influence, his shortcomings have been recently pointed out, partly by William Gaugler in *History of Fencing* (Bangor, Maine: Laureate Press, 1998), and with formidable insight by Sydney Anglo in *The Martial Arts of Renaissance Europe* (New Haven: Yale University Press, 2000).
2. Edward Rice, *Captain Sir Richard Francis Burton* (New York: Scribner's, 1990), p. 19.
3. Rabbi J. L. Zlotnik, *Swearing by a Sword* (Johannesburg, 1948), p. xxxviii.
4. Bill Bryson, *The Times*, September 26, 2000.
5. Sir John Keegan, *A History of Warfare* (London: Hutchinson, 1993), p. 10.

CHAPTER 1: HOW IT ALL BEGAN

1. R. Ewart Oakeshott, *The Archaeology of Weapons* (New York: Barnes & Noble, 1994), p. 25.
2. See Julius Palffy-Alpar, *Sword and Masque* (Philadelphia: F. A. Davis, 1967), p. 2, for both this assertion and the quotation, not sourced, from the *Mahabharata*.
3. Quoted in J. K. Anderson, *Military Theory and Practice in the Age of Xenophon* (Berkeley: University of California Press, 1970), p. 85.
4. Plato, *Laws*, VIII, 834 (New York: Basic Books, 1980).
5. Thomas Wiedemann, *Emperors and Gladiators* (1992), p. 96. See also Ralph Jackson, ed., *Gladiators and Caesars* (London: British Museum Press, 1992), pp. 46–7.
6. Lucius Annaeus Seneca, Twenty-second Epistle, "Ad Lucilium" (Cambridge, Mass.: Harvard University Press).
7. Vegetius, quoted in George Watson, *The Roman Soldier* (Ithaca, N.Y.: Cornell University Press, 1969), p. 57. See also Renatus Flavus Vegetius, *De re militari*, vol. 1, pp. 11, 12, 14, 17, and Niccolò Machiavelli, *L'Arte della guerra*, vol. 2 (Rome: Salerno, 2001), p. 372.
8. Cornelius Tacitus, *Agricola*, 36.
9. Dionysius of Halicarnassus, vol. 14, pp. 9–10. See also *The Roman Antiquities of Dionysius of Halicarnassus*, tr. Edward Spelman, Loeb Library, 1937–40, pp. 269–77.
10. Oakeshott, *The Archaeology of Weapons*, p. 51.
11. Ibid., p. 83.

12. Garabed Artin Davoud-Oghlou, *Histoire de la législation des anciens Germains* (Berlin: G. Reimer, 1845).

13. R. Ewart Oakeshott, *A Knight in His Armour* (London: Lutterworth, 1961), p. 13.

14. Richard C. McCoy, *The Rites of Knighthood: The Literature and Politics of Elizabethan Chivalry* (Berkeley: University of California Press, 1989).

15. Chrétien de Troyes, quoted in Richard Barber and Juliet Barker, *Tournaments, Jousts, Chivalry and Pageants in the Middle Ages* (Woodbridge, Suffolk [England]: Boydell Press, 1989), p. 126.

16. Oakeshott, op. cit., p. 190.

17. Norman Housley, *Crusading and Warfare in Medieval and Renaissance Europe* (Aldershot [England], 2001), p. 258.

18. Theodore Cook, Preface to Richard Burton, *The Sentiment of the Sword* (London: Horace Cox, 1911).

19. R. Ewart Oakeshott, *European Weapons and Armour: From the Renaissance to the Industrial Revolution* (Guildford: Lutterworth, 1980), p. 30.

20. Stephen Hand, in an e-mailed letter to the author dated 4 December 2002.

CHAPTER 2: ENTER THE MASTER

1. Castle, *Schools and Masters of Fence*, chap. 2.

2. Elizabeth L. Eisenstein, *The Printing Revolution in Modern Europe* (Cambridge, England: Cambridge University Press, 1983), p. 92.

3. Sydney Anglo, *The Martial Arts of Renaissance Europe* (New Haven: Yale University Press, 2000), p. 322, fn. 63.

4. In England in 1597, the warrior class numbered about 30,000, of whom 60 would have been lords, 500 knights, and some 5,800 squires and gentlemen. Together with their families, they constituted about 0.6 percent of the population. In no European country did the warrior class much exceed 1 percent.

5. R. Ewart Oakeshott, *The Sword in the Age of Chivalry* (Guildford: Lutterworth, 1964), p. 25. On Luther, see Karl von Raumer, *Geschichte der Pädagogik* (Gütersloh: C. Bertelsmann, 1843–54), vol. 1, pp. 142–3.

6. Anthony Holden, *Big Deal: One Year as a Professional Poker Player* (New York: Bantam, 1995), p. 302.

7. F. C. Grove, Introduction to W. H. Pollock, *Fencing* (London: Longman, 1897), p. 6.

8. Ramon Martinez, "Spanish Fencing in the Sixteenth Century," *The Sword*, April 1998, pp. 25 ff.

9. Roger Ascham, *Toxophilus* (London: A. Murray, 1868).

10. Holinshed, quoted in Aylward, *The English Master at Arms*, p. 17.

11. Ascham, *Toxophilus*.

12. George Silver, *Paradoxes of Defence, Wherein Is Proved the True Ground of Fight to Be in the Short Ancient Weapons, Etc.* (London: E. Blount, 1599), reissued in *The Works of George Silver*, ed. Cyril G. R. Mathey (London: G. Bell, 1898).

13. Craig Turner and Tony Soper, *Methods and Practice of Elizabethan Swordplay* (Carbondale: Southern Illinois University Press, 1990), pp. xiv ff.

14. Grove, op. cit., Introduction, p. 4.

15. Castle, *Schools and Masters of Fence*, p. 16. See also Turner and Soper, *Methods and Practice*, p. 7, and G. W. Thornbury, *Shakespeare's England* (London: Longman, 1856), p. 182.

16. Anglo, *The Martial Arts of Renaissance Europe*, p. 11.
17. F. Scott Fitzgerald, "Tarquin of Cheapside," *Tales of the Jazz Age* (New York: Scribner's, 1922).

CHAPTER 3: A WILD KIND OF JUSTICE

1. *Encyclopaedia Britannica*, eleventh ed., 1910, vol. 11, p. 638, "Duel."
2. Major Ben Chambers Truman, *The Field of Honor, Being a Complete and Comprehensive History of Dueling in All Countries; Including the Judicial Duel of Europe, the Private Duel of the Civilized World, and Specific Descriptions of All the Noted Hostile Meetings in Europe and America* (New York: Fords, Howard, and Hulbert, 1884).
3. Cornelius Tacitus, *Germania* (Oxford: Clarendon Press, 1999), ch. 5.
4. See Charles Mackay, *Extraordinary Popular Delusions and the Madness of Crowds* (New York: Harmony Books, 1980), p. 649 ff.
5. See Keith Thomas, *Religion and the Decline of Magic* (New York: Scribner's, 1971), p. 29.
6. *Encyclopaedia Britannica*, ninth ed., p. 87.
7. See *Biographia Britannica*, vol. 4, *The Lives of the Most Eminent Persons* (London: Rivington, 1789), pp. 445–7. The entry admits that Crichton's reputation rests largely on the writings of Urquhart, "a fanciful seventeenth-century writer," who in 1652, during a period of captivity, penned *Discovery of a Most Exquisite Jewel*, which includes his cameo on Crichton.
8. See John Fleck, "A Jewel of a Duel," *The Sword*, July 1992, pp. 14 and 19.
9. Chamberlain, in *Handbook of American Indians*, vol. 2, p. 77, quoted in *Encyclopedia of Religion and Ethics*, "Duel," p. 117.
10. See Turner and Soper, *Methods and Practices of Elizabethan Swordplay*, p. 61.
11. Samuel Pepys, *Diary and Correspondence*, vol. 2 (London: H. Colburn, 1849), p. 165.
12. Andrew Steinmetz, *The Romance of Duelling* (London: Chapman and Hall, 1868), pp. 36–7.
13. William Douglas, *Duelling Days in the Army* (London: Ward and Downey, 1887), p. 204.
14. Captain John Godfrey, *Treatise Upon the Science of Defence* (London, 1747), pp. 40–1.
15. *The Spectator*, no. 99.
16. See John Robert Moore, *Daniel Defoe: Citizen of the Modern World* (Chicago: University of Chicago Press, 1970), pp. 24–5.
17. See Lewis Gibbs, *Sheridan: His Life and His Theatre* (New York: Morrow, 1948), pp. 35–8. See also Linda Carlyle McCollum, "No, By God I Won't!" The Richard Sheridan/Thomas Mathews Duels, printed on the Internet by the Society of American Fight Directors.
18. Steinmetz, *The Romance of Duelling*, p. 43.
19. Ibid., p. 678.
20. Nicholas Boyle, *Goethe: The Poet and the Age*, vol. 1 (Oxford: Oxford University Press, 1991).
21. See letter of October 16, 1777.
22. John Milton, *Defensio Secunda*, vol. 8, pp. 60–62, quoted in William Riley Barker, *Milton: A Biography* (Oxford: Clarendon, 1996), p. 252.
23. William Hickling Prescott, *The History of the Conquest of Mexico*, 3 vols. (New York: Harper, 1843).

24. Mary Purcell, *The First Jesuit* (Westminster, Md.: Newman, 1957), pp. 22–3; see also Henry Dwight Sedgwick, *Ignatius Loyola: An Attempt at an Impartial Biography* (New York: Macmillan, 1923).

25. These and other quotations are taken from George Walter Thornbury, *Haunted London* (London: Hurst and Blackett, 1865), p. 52 ff.

26. See Sir Ian Gilmour, *Riot, Risings and Revolution: Governance and Violence in Eighteenth-Century England* (London: Hutchinson, 1992), p. 266.

27. See Roy Goodall, "Duelling Stories: No. 16. A Lordly Affair," *The Sword/Fencing* (joint issue), Autumn 1977, pp. 24–5.

28. William Makepeace Thackeray, *The History of Henry Esmond* (New York: Garland, 1989), p. 325.

CHAPTER 4: FRANCE IN THE AGE OF THE MUSKETEERS

1. Nancy Mitford, *Voltaire in Love* (London: Hamish Hamilton, 1957), pp. 35–6. See also James Parton, *Life of Voltaire* (Boston: Houghton Mifflin, 1881), p. 189.

2. David Bodanis, $E = mc^2$ (New York: Walker, 2000), pp. 58–67.

3. François Billacois, *The Duel: Its Rise and Fall in Modern France*, ed. and tr. by Trista Selous (New Haven: Yale University Press, 1990), pp. 65–6.

4. See Anthony Levi, *Cardinal Richelieu* (London: Constable, 2000), pp. 104–6.

5. Michel Eyquem de Montaigne, *The Complete Essays*, vol. 2, essay 17, (London: Penguin, 1987), p. 730. In *The Consolations of Philosophy* (London: Hamish Hamilton, 2000). Alain de Bolton says simply, "He had never been good at sports" (p. 153).

6. See René Descartes, *Correspondences*, ed. C. Adam and G. Milhaud, vol. 1 (Paris: F. Alcan, 1936), pp. 129–31; for details about *The Art of Fencing*, see Anglo, *The Martial Arts of Renaissance Europe*, p. 140.

7. Charles Louis de Secondat, Baron de Montesquieu, *L'Esprit des lois* (Paris: Garnier, 1868).

8. Quoted by Oakeshott, *The Archaeology of Weapons*, p. 236.

9. Will and Ariel Durant, *The Age of Louis XIV* (New York: Simon and Schuster, 1963), p. 2. In May this year, a major new work on fencing in France from the sixteenth to the eighteenth century appeared—*Le Sentiment du Fer*, by Pascal Brioist, Herve Drévillon, and Pierre Serna (Orleans: Champ Vallon, 2002).

10. Richard Francis Burton, Huntington Library, Pasadena, California, Box 1, 107.

11. F. C. Grove, op. cit., Introduction, p. 18.

12. See J. D. Aylward, "Bygones," *The Sword*, Winter 1957, pp. 93 ff.

13. Geoffrey F. Hall, and Joan Sanders, *D'Artagnan, The Ultimate Musketeer* (New York: Houghton Mifflin, 1964); see also Jean Lucas-Dubreton, *The Fourth Musketeer* (New York: Coward-McCann, 1928).

14. Cameron Rogers, *Gallant Ladies* (New York: Harcourt, 1928), pp. 177–206. The other quotations about La Maupin are from the same chapter.

15. G. Letaintorier-Fradin, *La Maupin, sa vie, ses duels, ses aventures* (Paris: Flammarion, 1904). In the accounts of two other historians of the period, Andrew Steinmetz and Arsène Vigéant, La Maupin is said to have killed all three men outright.

16. Grove, op. cit., Introduction, p. 20.

17. Rafael Sabatini, *Master-at-Arms* (Boston: Houghton Mifflin, 1940), p. 11.

18. M. S. Coryn, *The Chevalier d'Eon, 1728–1810* (London: Butterworth, 1932), p. 23.

19. See Robert Baldick, Introduction to Frédéric Gaillardet, *Mémoires du Chevalier d'Eon* (London: Blond, 1970), pp. xv–xvi.

20. Octave Homberg, *D'Eon de Beaumont, His Life and Times* (London: Secker, 1911), pp. 20–1.

21. Horace Bleakley, *Casanova in England, Being the Account of the Visit to London in 1763–4 of Giacomo Casanova, Chevalier de Seingalt* (London: John Lane, 1923), p. 141.

22. Homberg, *D'Eon de Beaumont*, pp. 272–3.

23. Gaillardet, *Mémoires du Chevalier d'Eon*, p. 311.

24. Coryn, *The Chevalier d'Eon*, p. 218.

25. Carl Thimm, *A Complete Bibliography of Fencing & Duelling, as practised by all European nations from the Middle Ages to the present day* (London and New York: John Lane, 1896), p. 249.

26. Steinmetz, *The Romance of Duelling*, p. 280.

27. Arsène Vigéant, *Un Maître d'armes sous la Restauration* (Paris: Motleroz, 1883).

28. Taken from an original screenplay/novel outline by Daniel Marciano. See also Gabriel Letainturier-Fradin, *Les Joeurs d'épée en France* (Paris: Flammarion, 1907), p. 328.

29. Henry Angelo, *Reminiscences of Henry Angelo, with Memoirs of His Late Father and Friends* (London: Colburn and Bentley, 1830).

30. Steinmetz, *The Romance of Duelling*, p. 281.

31. See Alain Guédé, *Monsieur de Saint-Georges, le Nègre des lumières* (Arles: Actes Sud, 1999).

32. Simon Schama, *Citizens* (New York: Knopf, 1989), p. 5.

33. See Richard Cobb, *Reactions to the French Revolution* (Oxford: Oxford University Press, 1972), p. 280, and *Death in Paris* (Oxford: Oxford University Press, 1978), p. 5.

34. J. M. Thompson, *Napoleon Bonaparte, His Rise and Fall* (London: Basil Blackwell, 1963). See also Vincent Cronin, *Napoleon Bonaparte* (New York: Morrow, 1972), p. 42.

35. Truman, *The Field of Honor*, p. 460.

36. See Arsène Vigéant, *Jean-Louis* (Paris: Motteroz, 1883), tr. Michel Sebastiani, Princeton, N.J., 1999, private ms.

CHAPTER 5: THE GREAT SWORDMAKERS

1. Raoul Sudre, *The Fencing News*, vol. 1, no. 10, June 1980.

2. See G. B. Depping, *Wayland Smith: A Dissertation on a Tradition of the Middle Ages from the French of G. D. Deeping and Francisque Michel* (London: W. Pickering, 1847).

3. Alexandre Dumas, *My Memoirs, 1826–36*, vol. 5 (London: Methuen, 1907–9).

4. Alfred, Lord Tennyson, "The Passing of Arthur" (London: Macmillan, 1884).

5. André de Liancour, *Le Maistre d'armes, ou, l'exercice de l'épée seule*, 1686, cited in J. D. Aylward, *The Sword*, Winter 1957.

6. Anthony Harding, *Swords and Hilt Weapons* (London: Weidenfeld & Nicolson, 1989), p. 12.

7. Burton papers, Huntington Library, Box 14, 10; *Sheffield Daily Telegraph*, April 10, 1895, quoting article in *The Magazine of Art*.

8. "Medieval Metal Masters," *Discovery*, January 2000; see also James Trefil, "Supersteel of the Ancients," *Science Digest*, February 1983.

9. Anjana Ahuja, "Blade of Damascus," *The Times*, December 14, 2000.

10. *The Sword Book in Honchō Gunkikō and the Book of Same*, tr. Henri L. Joly and Inada Hogitaro (New York: C. E. Tuttle, 1963), p. 92, fn.

11. James E. Gordon, *The New Science of Strong Materials: or, Why You Don't Fall Through the Floor* (London: Penguin, 1968).

12. Jacob Bronowski, *The Ascent of Man* (Boston: Little, Brown, 1973).

13. Theophilus Presbyter, *Scheme of Various Arts*, 1847. Quoted in Gordon, *The New Science of Strong Materials*, p. 239.

14. Steinmetz, *The Romance of Duelling*.

15. Félix del Valle y Díaz, *La Espada en Toledo* (Toledo: Gráficas Minaya, 1997).

16. Albert Weyersberg, *The Solingen Sword Manufacture down through the Ages* (Solingen, 2001).

17. Frederick J. Stephens, *Daggers, Swords and Bayonets of the Third Reich* (Wellingborough [England]: Patrick Stephens, 1989), p. 13.

18. J. R. R. Tolkien, *The Lord of the Rings* (Boston: Houghton Mifflin, 1991), pp. 686–7.

19. Major James P. Atwood, *The Daggers and Edged Weapons of Hitler's Germany* (Savannah, Ga.: Militaria Publications, 1965).

20. Jacob Bronowski reminds us in *The Ascent of Man* (op. cit.), that the "making of a sword, like all ancient metallurgy, is surrounded with ritual, and that is for a clear reason. When you have no written language, when you have nothing that can be called a written formula, then you must have a precise ceremonial that fixes the sequence of operations so that they can be exact and memorable."

21. Sir John Keegan, *A History of Warfare* (London: Hutchinson, 1993), p. 45

22. Bruce Chatwin, "The Estate of Maximilian Tod" (London: Cape, 1990).

23. Richard Storry, *A History of Modern Japan* (Harmondsworth, Middlesex: Penguin, 1960), p. 42; in his study *Armed Martial Arts of Japan* (New Haven: Yale University Press, 1998), G. C. Hurst gives the figure as "often resulting in more than 30,000 layers of steel" (p. 33).

24. Bronowski, *The Ascent of Man*.

25. Inazo Nitobe, *Bushido: The Soul of Japan* (New York: Putnam, 1907).

CHAPTER 6: THE PERFECT THRUST

1. Burton, *The Sentiment of the Sword*, pp. 100, 122.

2. *Encyclopaedia Britannica*, eleventh ed., 1911, "Fencing."

3. Arsène Vigéant, *Almanac of Fencing* (Paris: Motteroz, 1889).

4. Egerton Castle and Agnes Castle, "The Great Todescan's Secret Thrust," in *Flower o' the Orange* (London: Macmillan, 1908), pp. 226–7.

5. See Umberto Eco, "A Treatise on the Science of Arms," in *The Island of the Day Before*, ed. (New York: Harcourt Brace Jovanovich, 1995.

6. See Joseph J. Snyder, "Bruce Lee's Adaptation of European Fencing Techniques," *American Fencing*, March–April 1983.

7. Rafael Sabatini, *Scaramouche* (New York: Grosset and Dunlap, 1923), pp. 224–35.

8. Arturo Pérez-Reverte, *The Fencing Master* (New York: Harcourt Brace, 1999).

9. "The Development of Fencing," *St James's Budget*, April 2, 1881.

10. Julio M. Castello, "Revolution or Evolution—Or What?" *American Fencing*, March–May 1988, p. 8.

11. Arturo Pérez-Reverte, *The Flanders Panel* (New York: Harcourt Brace, 1990).

12. Arturo Pérez-Reverte, *The Nautical Chart* (New York: Harcourt Brace, 2001), p. 295.

13. James Henry Carlisle, *Two Great Teachers: Johnson's Memoir of Roger Ascham; and selections from Stanley's Life and Correspondence of Thomas Arnold, of Rugby* (Syracuse, N. Y.: Bardeen, 1890), p. 1. See also Kenneth Jay Wilson, *Incomplete Fictions* (Washington, D.C.: Catholic University of America Press, 1985).

14. Plato, *Phaedrus*, 277B, quoted in Lawrence V. Ryan, *Roger Ascham* (Stanford, Calif.: Stanford University Press, 1963).

CHAPTER 7: WHERE THE SWORD IS THE SOUL

1. See Kurt Singer, *Mirror, Sword and Jewel: A Study of Japanese Characteristics* (New York: George Braziller, 1973), p. 25.

2. *Cambridge History of Japan*, vol. 4, *Early Modern Japan* (New York: Cambridge University Press, 1988–99), p. 483.

3. The Buddhist scholar Yamaga Soko (1622–85), quoted in Conrad D. Tottman, *Japan Before Perry: A Short History* (Berkeley: University of California Press, 1981), p. 155.

4. Frank Brinkley, *Samurai: The Invincible Warriors* (Burbank, Calif.: Ohara Publications, 1975), p. 32.

5. Charles Boxer, *The Christian Century in Japan* (Oxford: Oxford University Press, 1951), p. 235.

6. Brinkley, *Samurai*, pp. 37–8.

7. H. Paul Varley, *The Samurai* (London: Weidenfeld & Nicolson, 1970), p. 24.

8. Robert Baldick, *The Duel: A History of Duelling* (New York: Potter, 1965), p. 154.

9. "Dueling in Japan," *The Times*, September 27, 1890; quoted in Thimm, *A Complete Bibliography of Fencing and Duelling*, p. 459.

10. The earliest accounts of Musashi's contests appear in *Niten Ki* (*Two Heavens Chronicle*), a record compiled by his pupils a generation after his death. This narrative is drawn mainly from two sources: Dave Lowry, *Bokken: Art of the Japanese Sword* (Burbank, Calif.: Ohara, 1986), pp. 19–21, and the translator's introduction to Miyamoto Musashi, *Book of Five Rings*, pp. 16–20.

11. Eiji Yoshikawa, *Musashi* (New York: Harper and Row/Kodansha International, 1971), pp. 944, 967.

12. Ibid., p. 970.

13. See Daisetz T. Suzuki, *Zen and Japanese Culture* (Princeton, N.J.: Princeton University Press, 1970), pp. 61–2.

14. Musashi, *The Book of Five Rings*, p. 44.

15. G. Cameron Hurst III, *Armed Martial Arts of Japan: Swordsmanship and Archery* (New Haven: Yale University Press, 1998), p. 207.

16. Suzuki, *Zen and Japanese Culture*, p. 94.

17. Kōyō gunkan, *Gorinsho, Hagakure Shū. Sagara Tōru, hen.* (Tokyo: Chikuma Shobō, 1969).

18. Ibid.

19. Suzuki, *Zen and Japanese Culture*, p. 72.

20. See Henry Scott Stokes, *The Life and Death of Yukio Mishima* (London: Peter Owen, 1975); also the film by Paul Schrader, *Mishima: A Life in Four Chapters*, music by Philip Glass; Francis Ford Coppola and George Lucas, executive producers.

21. Varley, *The Samurai*, pp. 32–6. See also A. B. Mitford (later Lord Redesdale), *Tales of Old Japan* (London: Macmillan, 1883), pp. 355–60, where he describes a *hara-kiri* execution he witnessed in Kobe in 1868.

22. Yukio Mishima, *Runaway Horses* (New York: Knopf, 1973), p. 95.

23. Truman, *The Field of Honor*, p. 129.

24. Quoted in Henry Scott-Stokes, *The Life and Death of Yukio Mishima* (New York: Farrar, Straus, Giroux, 1974), p. 14.

25. Quoted in Ivan Morris, *The Nobility of Failure, Tragic Heroes in the History of Japan* (New York: Holt, 1975), p. 314.

26. Kurt Singer, *Mirror, Sword and Jewel: A Study of Japanese Characteristics*, p. 41.

27. Noel Perrin, *Giving Up the Gun* (Boston: Godine, 1979).

28. Hurst, *Armed Martial Arts of Japan*, pp. 220–1.

29. Perrin, *Giving Up the Gun*, p. 42.

30. Keegan, *A History of Warfare*, p. 42.

31. See Jared Diamond, *Guns, Gems and Steel: The Fates of Human Societies* (New York: Norton, 1997), pp. 257–8.

32. *Homba*, tr. Michael Gallagher (New York, 1973), pp. 75–6.

33. Perrin, *Giving Up the Gun*, pp. 42, 72–3.

34. Hurst, *Armed Martial Arts of Japan*, p. 157.

CHAPTER 8: POINTS OF HONOR

1. Quoted in Baldick, *The Duel*, pp. 183–4.

2. Blaise Pascal, *Lettres écrites à un provincial* (Paris, 1967), letter 7, pp. 96–108; see also Billacois, *The Duel*, pp. 138–9.

3. Jean-Jacques Rousseau, *Confessions* (London: Penguin, 1953), Book V. I have slightly altered this translation, to make sense of the fencing terminology.

4. Leigh Hunt, *Table-Talk* (London: Smith, Elder, 1851), p. 87.

5. Anne Brontë, *The Tenant of Wildfell Hall* (New York: Harper Bros., 1848), pp. 276–8.

6. See also Maisie Ward, *Robert Browning and His World: The Private Face 1812–61* (New York: Holt, 1967), p. 126.

7. Arthur Schopenhauer, *The Pessimist's Handbook* (Lincoln: University of Nebraska Press, 1964), pp. 79–106.

8. Immanuel Kant, *Philosophy of Law* (Edinburgh: T. and T. Clark, 1887), pp. 202–3.

9. Jeremy Bentham, *An Introduction to the Principles of Morals and Legislation* (London: W. Pickering, 1823).

10. *Pall Mall Gazette*, September 4, 1874. See also Joseph Hamilton, *The Only Approved Guide through All the Stages of a Quarrel* (London: Hatchard, 1829), p. 5.

11. Joanne B. Freeman, *Affairs of Honor* (New Haven: Yale University Press, 2001), p. 178.

12. Steinmetz, *The Romance of Duelling*, p. 65.

13. Ibid., pp. 121 ff.

14. Robert Louis Stevenson, *St. Ives, Being the Adventures of a French Prisoner in England* (New York: Scribner's, 1905), pp. 18–23.

15. F. Paulsen, *A System of Ethics* (New York: Scribner's, 1879), p. 569.

16. Cecil Woodham-Smith, *The Reason Why* (London: Constable, 1952), p. 76.

17. Joseph Conrad, *A Set of Six* (New York: Doubleday, 1925), p. 259.

18. Horace Bleackley, *Casanova in England*, pp. 227–8.

19. Dorothy L. Sayers, *Gaudy Night* (New York: Harper's, 1936), p. 399.

20. Woodham-Smith, *The Reason Why*, p. 77.

21. Ibid., p. 83.

22. Antony Simpson, "Dandelions on the Field of Honour: Dueling, the Middle Classes, and the Law in Nineteenth-Century England," *Criminal Justice History* 9 (1988), pp. 138–9.

23. *Pall Mall Gazette*, October 6, 1890.

24. Gelli, *Il Duello*, quoted in F. R. Bryson, *The Sixteenth-Century Italian Duel* (London, 1938), pp. 209–13.

25. Rebecca West, *1900* (London: Weidenfeld & Nicolson, 1982), p. 66. This would probably have been with pistols. As Kevin McAteer writes (op. cit.), "While the Italians, French and Austro-Hungarians were roused by the zip and pace of tensile swordplay, increasingly in the first half of the nineteenth century Germans were drawn to the more flaccid demands of marksmanship" (p. 45).

26. Edwin Emerson, *German Swordplay* (Philadelphia: Graf and Breuninger, 1936), p. 59.

27. See Baldick, *The Duel*, p. 147.

28. Adolph Kohut, *Das Buch berühmter Duelle* (*The Book of Famous Duels*) (Berlin: Deutscher Verlag, 1888), p. 171.

29. George D. Painter, *Marcel Proust: A Biography*, vol. 1 (London: Chatto & Windus, 1961), pp. 210–11.

30. Mark Twain, *A Tramp Abroad*, first published 1880 (London: Penguin, 1997), pp. 38, 46.

31. Joseph Conrad, *A Set of Six*, p. 247. See also Olivia Coolidge, *The Three Lives of Joseph Conrad* (New York: Houghton Mifflin, 1972), pp. 61 ff., and Georges Jean-Aubrey, *The Sea-Dreamer: A Definitive Biography of Joseph Conrad* (New York: Doubleday, 1957), pp. 72–5.

32. Gregor Dallas, *At the Heart of a Tiger* (London: Macmillan, 1993), pp. 211–2.

33. Lucien Prévost-Paradol, *La France nouvelle* (Paris, 1868), pp. 352–3. See also Robert Walter-Reichert, *Prévost-Paradol, His Life and Work* (New York: New York University Press, 1952).

34. Ernest LeGouvé, *Un Tournoi au XIX siècle* (Paris: Hetzel, 1873), pp. 166–78.

35. Anatole France, "La Vie à Paris," *Le Temps*, July 18, 1886.

36. Robert A. Nye, "Fencing, the Duel and Republican Manhood in the Third Republic," *Journal of Contemporary History*, 1990, 25 (2–3), p. 370; also quoted in Georges Bibesco and Féry d'Esclands, *Conseils sur les duels* (Paris: A. Lemerre, 1900), pp. 131–2.

37. Nye, ibid., p. 366.

38. See Anatole de la Forge, preface to *Le Jeu de l'épée, leçons de Jules Jacob*, ed. Emile André and P. Ollendorf, 1887, p. xxxvi.

39. Gabriel Letainturier-Fradin, *Le Duel* (Paris: Flammarion, 1892), pp. 3–4.

40. G. K. Chesterton, "The Duel of Dr. Hirsch," *The Father Brown Crime Stories* (New York: Avenel, 1990), p. 400, and "The Chief Mourner of Marne," *Authors' Bounty*, collected by Cecil Hewetson (London: National Literary Society for Hospitals, 1936), p. 82.

41. Wythe Williams, *The Tiger of France: Conversations with Clemenceau* (New York: Ovell, Sloan and Pearce, 1949), pp. 262 ff.

42. Irina Reyfman, *Ritualized Violence, Russian Style: The Duel in Russian Culture and Literature* (Stanford, Calif.: Stanford University Press, 1999), p. 75.

43. Ibid., p. 63.

44. Ibid., p. 44.

45. Montesquieu, *L'Esprit des lois*.

46. Edwin Emerson, "Pushkin's Duels," *Washington Journal*, 1942; see also *Sidelights of History* (Washington, D.C.: *The Washington Journal*, 1943), p. 428.

47. See Michel Alaux, *Modern Fencing* (New York: Scribner's, 1975).

48. S. L. Abramovich, *Pushkin v 1836 godu*, second rev. ed. (Leningrad, 1989), p. 279.

49. Leo Tolstoy, *War and Peace* (New York: Simon and Schuster, 1942), p. 339.

50. Anton Chekhov, *The Duel and Other Stories* (New York: Macmillan, 1926), p. 133.

51. Fyodor Dostoevsky, *Zapisnaia tetrad 1875–76*, p. 109.

52. Ibid., p. 182.

53. See Ute Frevert, "Honour and Middle-Class Culture: The History of the Duel in England and Germany," in *Bourgeois Society in Nineteenth-Century Europe*, ed. Jurgen Kocka and Allan Mitchell (Oxford, Providence: Berg, 1993), p. 223.

54. Burton, *The Sentiment of the Sword*, p. 114.

CHAPTER 9: A PURSUIT FOR GENTLEMEN

1. Francis Wheen, *Karl Marx* (London: Fourth Estate, 1999), p. 16.

2. Wilhelm Liebknecht, *Karl Marx: Biographical Memoirs*, first published 1896, English translation published 1901 (London: Journeyman Press, 1975).

3. Karl Marx, *Early Writings*, ed. T. B. Bottomore (London: Watts, 1963), p. 171.

4. Fenton Bressler, *Napoleon III: A Life* (New York: Carroll and Graf, 2000), p. 182.

5. Leslie A. Marchand, *Byron: A Biography* (New York: Knopf, 1957), p. 110.

6. Grove, op. cit., pp. 24–5.

7. Charles Louis de Beaumont, *A History of the London Fencing Club*, privately printed (London: Billings and Son, 1956).

8. A. de Saint-Albin, *Les Salles d'armes de Paris* (Paris: Glady Frères, 1875).

9. Burton, *The Sentiment of the Sword*, p. 107.

10. Anglo, *The Martial Arts of Renaissance Europe*, p. 34; Castle, *Schools and Masters of Fence*, p. 7.

11. See Albert La Marche, *Traite de l'épée* (Paris: 1884); Jules Jacob, *Le Jeu de l'épée* (Paris: P. Ollendorff, 1887); Ambroise Baudry, *L'Escrime pratique au*

XIX siècle (Paris: 1893); Anthime Spinnewyn, *L'Escrime a l'épée* (Paris: J. Rothschild, 1898).

12. Leslie J. Workman, in *The New Arthurian Encyclopedia*, ed. Norris J. Lacy (New York: Garland, 1991), p. 31.

13. See J. Bouchier, "Duels in the Waverley Novels," *N&Q*, ninth series, vol. 1 (January 15, 1898, p. 42, and February 26, 1898, p. 170).

14. S. Weir Mitchell, *The Adventures of François, Foundling, Thief, Juggler and Fencing Master During the French Revolution* (New York: Century, 1898), p. 129.

15. Alexandre Dumas, *Mes Memoires* (Paris: Gallimard, 1954–8), vol. 3, pp. 72–3.

16. See S. Guy Endore, *King of Paris* (New York: Simon and Schuster, 1956), p. 281.

17. Guy de Maupassant, *Bel-Ami* (London: Penguin Books, 1961), pp. 182–5.

18. See William S. Baring-Gould, *The Annotated Sherlock Holmes* (New York: Clarkson Potter, 1967): "There is no canonical report of Holmes with sword in hand, and it seems safe to assume that he seldom or never touched a foil or épée after his early acquaintanceship with Watson" (p. 157).

19. Léon Bertrand, *Cut and Thrust* (London: Athletic Publications, 1927), p. 6.

20. John J. MacAloon, *This Great Symbol* (Chicago: University of Chicago Press, 1981), p. 51.

21. Eugen Weber, "Pierre de Coubertin," *Journal of Contemporary History* (special edition), *Organized Sport in France*, 1970, p. 3.

22. Baron Pierre de Coubertin and Louis Pascaud, *Traite d'escrime equestre* (Auxerre: 1906). See also Truman, *The Field of Honor*, pp. 130–1.

23. See Richard Mandell, *The First Modern Olympics* (Berkeley: University of California Press, 1976), pp. 68–9. See also David C. Young, *The Modern Olympics—A Struggle for Survival* (Baltimore: John Hopkins University Press, 1996).

24. Baron Pierre de Coubertin, *Mémoires olympiques*, rev. ed. (Lausanne: International Olympic Committee, 1979).

25. Theodore Cooke, *The Cruise of the Branwen*, privately printed, 1908. See also Richard Cohen, "The Forgotten Olympics," *The Spectator*, September 1988.

26. Marguerite Joseph-Maginot, *The Biography of André Maginot: He Might Have Saved France* (New York: Doubleday, 1941).

27. See William Manchester, *The Last Lion: Winston Spencer Churchill, Visions of Glory, 1874–1932* (Boston: Little, Brown, 1983), p. 256.

28. Arthur Conan Doyle, "How the Brigadier Slew the Brothers of Ajaccio," *The Complete Brigadier Gérard* (Edinburgh: Canongate, 1995).

29. "Wizard in Oz" (editorial), *The Times*, October 2, 2000.

30. See "Fencing and Military Training," *American Fencing*, February 1954.

31. George S. Patton, *The Patton Papers*, vol. 1, ed. Martin Blumenson (Boston: Houghton Mifflin, 1972), p. 230.

32. Ibid.

CHAPTER 10: SWASHBUCKLING

1. David Shipman, *The Story of Cinema* (New York: St. Martin's Press, 1982), p. 17.

2. See *The New York Times*, April 22, 1913.

3. Rudy Behlmer, "Swordplay on the Screen," *Films in Review*, July 1965, pp. 362–75.

4. Mark Twain, *The Adventures of Tom Sawyer* (Oxford: Oxford University Press, 1996), pp. 83–4.

5. William Hobbs, *Fight Direction for Stage and Screen* (London: Heinemann, 1995), p. 18. Hobbs adds that Irving was so shortsighted that once, when playing a scene with an actress portraying a blind girl, he dropped his glasses on stage, and the "blind" girl had to retrieve them.

6. See Jeffrey Richards, *Swordsmen of the Screen: From Douglas Fairbanks to Michael York* (London: Routledge & Kegan Paul, 1977), p. 13. This is by far the best book on the subject.

7. Ibid., p. 44.

8. Basil Rathbone, *In and Out of Character* (New York: Doubleday, 1956), p. 152.

9. Richards, *Swordsmen of the Screen*, p. 40.

10. Marion Davies, *The Times We Had* (New York: Ballantine, 1977), p. 34 ff.

11. *Variety*, September 2, 1921.

12. See Les Hammer, "Ralph Faulkner: The Last Swashbuckler," *American Fencing*, March–May 1987, p. 5. Hammer is currently writing a biography of Faulkner, to be published by Scarecrow Press. See also Tony Thomas, Rudy Behlmer, and Clifford McCarty, *The Films of Errol Flynn* (New York: Citadel, 1969).

13. Sheridan Morley and Ruth Lean, *Gene Kelly: A Celebration* (London: Pavilion, 1996), p. 82.

14. Rafael Sabatini, *Scaramouche*, pp. 35, 339.

15. Aldo Nadi, *The Living Sword, A Fencer's Autobiography* (Sunrise, Fla.: Laureate Press, 1995), p. 367.

16. See Thomas H. Cragg, "The Amazing Scaramouche," *The Sword*, July 1993, pp. 33–5.

17. William Goldman, *The Princess Bride* (New York: Ballantine, 1973), the "good parts" version, "based on the original novel by S. Morgenstern."

18. See William Hobbs, *Fight Direction for Stage and Screen*, p. 11.

19. Alfred Hutton has several good stories about Rob Roy's swordsmanship in *The Sword and the Centuries* (Pennsylvania: Stackpole Books, 2003), cf. pp. 310–18.

CHAPTER 11: ON MOUNT RUSHMORE

1. Gutzon Borglum, letter to Eleanor Roosevelt, May 13, 1936; see Simon Schama, *Landscape and Memory* (New York: Knopf, 1995), p. 395.

2. Edwin Emerson, "George Washington's Lighter Vein," *The Washington Journal*, February 22, 1942.

3. Dumas Malone, *Jefferson and His Time*, vol. 1, *Jefferson the Virginian* (Boston: Little, Brown, 1948), p. 47.

4. C. Brian Kelly, "Mary Todd Lincoln, Troubled First Lady," in *Best Little Ironies, Oddities and Mysteries of the Civil War*, ed. C. Brian Kelly (Nashville, Tenn.: Cumberland House, 2000), p. 368.

5. See Douglas L. Wilson, "Lincoln's Affair of Honor," *The Atlantic Monthly*, February 1998, pp. 64–71.

6. See Francis Fisher Browne, *The Every-day Life of Abraham Lincoln* (Lincoln: University of Nebraska Press, 1995); Mariah Vance, *Lincoln's Unknown Pri-*

vate Life: An Oral History by his Black Housekeeper, Mariah Vance, 1850–1860 (Mamaroneck, N.Y.: Hastings House, 1995); Douglas L. Wilson, *Lincoln Before Washington: A New Perspective* (Urbana: University of Illinois Press, 1997); Jean H. Baker, *Mary Todd Lincoln* (New York: Norton, 1999).

7. William H. Baumer and the West Point staff, *Sports as Taught and Played at West Point* (Harrisburg, Penn.: Military Service Publishing, 1939), p. 109.

8. See U. S. Grant III, *Ulysses S. Grant, Warrior and Statesman* (New York: Morrow, 1969), p. 34.

9. Douglas Southall Freeman, *Lee* (New York: Scribner's, 1936), vol. 4, p. 1350.

10. Ibid., pp. 142–3, fn.

11. Theodore Roosevelt, *Autobiography* (condensed ed.) (New York: Scribner's, 1958), p. 17.

12. See Donald George Wilhelm, *Theodore Roosevelt as an Undergraduate* (Boston: J. W. Luce, 1910), p. 57.

13. F. G. Blakeslee, "Fencing, the Sport of President Roosevelt," *Pearson's Magazine*, November 1904, p. 12.

14. Edmund Morris, *Theodore Rex* (New York: Random House, 2002), pp. 185, 200.

15. Margaret Truman, *Harry S Truman* (New York: Morrow, 1973).

16. Mary Ethel Noland, Oral history interview for the Harry S Truman Library, June 1966, p. 71.

17. *The Academy*, October 30, 1875, p. 454; in the papers of R. F. Burton, Huntington Library, Box 15, 1.

18. Quoted in Baldick, *The Duel*, p. 115.

19. Lyle Saxon, *Fabulous New Orleans* (New York: Appleton-Century, 1939), p. 192.

20. Ibid., p. 189.

21. William Oliver Stevens, *Pistols at Ten Paces: The Story of the Code of Honor in America* (Boston: Houghton Mifflin, 1940), p. 130.

22. David T. Courtwright, *Violent Land: Single Men and Social Disorder from the Frontier to the Inner City* (Cambridge, Mass.: Harvard University Press, 1996).

23. Lyman Beecher, "The Remedy for Duelling," sermon delivered at the Presbytery of Long Island at Aquebogue, April 16, 1806, in the Huntington Library.

24. Mark Twain, *Life on the Mississippi* (London: Penguin, 1984), p. 273, fn.

25. Chambers, *The Field of Honor*, p. 77.

26. *Philadelphia Times*, January 1884, as related in ibid., p. 113.

27. Williamson, *Bowie Knives*, pp. 40–53; see also Raymond W. Thorp, *Bowie Knife* (Albuquerque: University of New Mexico Press, 1948).

28. Kentucky Constitutional Convention Debates, 1849, 82.

29. *Cockrum v. State*, 24 Tex. 394, 396 (1859); see Clayton E. Cramer, *Concealed Weapon Laws of the Early Republic: Dueling, Southern Violence and Moral Reform* (Westport, Conn.: Praeger, 1999), p. 88.

30. Stevens, *Pistols at Ten Paces*, pp. 39–40.

31. Mackay, *Extraordinary Popular Delusions and the Madness of Crowds*, p. 692.

32. Nathaniel Hawthorne, *The American Magazine of Useful and Entertaining Knowledge*, August 1836.

33. See James R. Mellow, *Nathaniel Hawthorne in His Times* (Boston: Houghton Mifflin, 1980), pp. 104–7.

34. B. C. Chambers, *The Field of Honor*, p. 144.
35. Bernice Larson Webb, *The Basketball Man: James Naismith* (Lawrence: University of Kansas Press, 1973), pp. 125–6.
36. Alex Solomon, "Did You Know?" *American Fencing*, August 1954.
37. This exchange, and the earlier details of the story, were told me by a senior U.S. fencer who overheard the conversation.
38. Peter Westbrook and Tej Hazarika, *Harnessing Anger: The Way of an American Fencer* (New York: Seven Stories Press, 1997), p. 32.
39. Joyce Wadler, "A Saber Rattler Teaching Sportsmanship," *The New York Times*, September 6, 2000.
40. Brian Cazeneuve, "Duel Purpose," *Sports Illustrated*, November 22, 1999, p. 94.

CHAPTER 12: SPILLED BLOOD

1. *The Sword*, July 1995, p. 5.
2. Lucius Apuleius, *The Golden Ass*, chap. 2 (New York: The Modern Library, 1928). For Ludovicus Vives, see www.swordswallower.org/swordswallowing.html.
3. Unknown magazine; in Box 1, Richard Francis Burton papers for *The Book of the Sword*, vols. 2 and 3, Huntington Library.
4. See *The Sword*, January 1985, p. 18, and Emile Mérignac, *Histoire de l'escrime*, vol. 2, *From Middle Ages to Modern Times* (Paris, 1883).
5. G. K. Chesterton, *The Innocence of Father Brown* (New York: Avenel, 1990), p. 222.
6. Bernard Cornwall, *Sharpe's Waterloo* (London: Harper Collins, 1990).
7. Christoph Amburger, *Hammerterz Forum* (Multi Media Books, 1996), p. 103.
8. Josef Schmied-Kowarzik and Hans Kufahl, *Das Duellbuch* (Leipzig, 1896), p. 158.
9. Dr. Richard Wiseman, *Of Wounds, of Gun-shot Wounds, of Fractures and Luxations*, 1676, p. 341. He goes on to tell the story of a surgeon who, failing to remove the shaft of an arrow, in despair asked the patient "in what posture of the body he received the Wound. Understanding it was done on Horseback, he placed him in a riding posture, and immediately drew out the Weapon."
10. Nadi, *The Living Sword*.
11. Burton, *The Sentiment of the Sword*, p. 105.
12. A. R. Crawfurd, *The Medical Hazards of Fencing*, pp. 360–70.
13. Charles Nicholl, *The Reckoning: The Murder of Christopher Marlowe* (London: Picador, 1993), p. 18.
14. Richard Francis Burton, Box 1, Huntington Library, op. cit.
15. *American Fencing*, Summer 1962.
16. Letter in *American Fencing*, Winter 1962.
17. Westbrook and Hazarika, *Harnessing Anger: The Way of an American Fencer*, pp. 97–8.

CHAPTER 13: SCARS OF GLORY

1. Twain, *A Tramp Abroad*, pp. 27, 31.
2. William Howitt, *Student Life in Germany* (London: Routledge, 1849).
3. Robert Southcombe, "Fencing and Fascism," *The Sword*, Summer 1977.

4. Twain, *A Tramp Abroad*.
5. J. M. Hart, *German Universities: A Narrative of Personal Experience, Together with Recent Statistical Information, Practical Suggestions, and a Comparison of the German, English and American Systems of Higher Education* (New York: Putnam, 1874), pp. 73–4.
6. Ibid., p. 79.
7. Jerome K. Jerome, *Three Men on the Bummel* (London: Penguin, 1999).
8. See Peter Gay, "Mensur—The Cherished Scar" in *The Cultivation of Hatred* (New York: Norton, 1989). Gay argues that the German student duel is the perfect example of the clash between two basic drives in man, that toward physical aggression and that to control such urges.
9. R. B. Haldane, *An Autobiography* (London: Hodder, 1929), p. 14.
10. Isabel Lady Burton, *The Life of Captain Sir Richard Francis Burton* (New York: Appleton, 1893).
11. John Lothrop Motley, *Morton's Hope, or The Memoirs of a Provincial* (New York: Harper, 1839), two vols.
12. Nicholas Mosley, *Hopeful Monsters* (London: Secker, 1990), pp. 103–4.
13. R. G. S. Weber, *The German Student Corps in the Third Reich* (London: Macmillan, 1986), p. 28.
14. Jerome K. Jerome, *My Life and Times* (London: Hodder & Stoughton, 1926), p. 207.
15. Desmond Stewart, *Theodor Herzl* (New York: Doubleday, 1974), p. 84. In 1904, a Jewish student was four times as likely to be involved in a duel as his Gentile counterpart.
16. Ibid.
17. Marianne Weber, *Max Weber: A Biography* (New York: Wiley, 1975), p. 69.
18. *Pall Mall Gazette*, March 12, 1890.
19. See John Van der Kiste, *Kaiser Wilhelm II: Germany's Last Emperor* (Stroud: Sutton, 1999), p. 20.
20. *St James's Gazette*, May 9, 1891.
21. Weber, *The German Student Corps in the Third Reich*, p. 162. The Corps in particular were organized democratically, according to accepted constitutions—hardly a good philosophical match for the hierarchic *Fuhrerprinzip* of the Nazis.

    Horst Wessel, the Nazi martyr, was a member of two Corps before organizing Hitler's Stormtroopers in the communist workers' districts of Berlin; in 1930, aged twenty-two, he was killed, supposedly by communists, and a poem he had written became the official anthem of the Nazi Party. While photos of his elaborate funeral and subsequent memorial services show a "grief-stricken" Hitler surrounded by Corps students decked out in full regalia, the Nazis themselves took great pains to point out that Wessel's stature in their pantheon was "not because of, but despite the fact that he was a Corps student."
22. Sylvia Sprigge, "The German Scene," *Encounter*, November 1954.
23. Christoph Amberger, *The Secret History of the Sword* (Baltimore: Hammerterz Forum, 1996), pp. 52–3.

CHAPTER 14: THE FASCIST SPORT

1. Peter Padfield, *Himmler: Reichsführer SS* (London: Macmillan, 1990), p. 56.

2. Paul Preston, *Franco* (New York: HarperCollins, 1993), p. 10.
3. R. J. B. Bosworth, *Mussolini* (New York: Arnold/OUP, 2002), p. 106.
4. Richard Collier, *Duce!: The Life of Benito Mussolini* (London: Collins, 1971), p. 57. See also Denis Mack Smith, *Mussolini* (London: Weidenfeld & Nicolson, 1981).
5. C. Dall'y Ungaro, *Mussolini e lo Sport* (Mantua, 1928), p. 8. See also R. J. B. Bosworth, *Mussolini* (New York), pp. 109 and 211.
6. Benito Mussolini, *My Autobiography* (New York: Scribner's, 1928).
7. Aldo Santini, *Nedo Nadi* (Livorno: Belforte Editions, 1989).
8. Robert Skidelsky, *Oswald Mosley* (London: Weidenfeld & Nicolson, 1975).
9. Sir Oswald Mosley, *My Life* (London: Nelson, 1968), p. 292.
10. Ibid., p. 368.
11. André Brissand, *The Nazi Secret Service* (London: Bodley Head, 1972).
12. Charles Wighton, *Heydrich* (London: Odhams, 1962).
13. G. S. Graber, *The Life and Times of Reinhard Heydrich* (London: Hale, 1981).
14. Wighton, *Heydrich*, p. 30.
15. Padfield, *Himmler*, p. 379.
16. From a short story by Wojciech Zabłocki, who had been told the tale directly from Koza-Kozarski.

CHAPTER 15: THE WOMAN WHO SALUTED HITLER

1. From a newspaper clipping in Helene Mayer's personal scrapbooks, now in the possession of her sister-in-law, Erica Mayer.
2. Ellen Preis, *Olympiasieg* (Vienna: Payer, 1936), p. 72.
3. "Maxine Mitchell, Grand Lady of Fencing," *American Fencing*, December 1989–February 1990, p. 7.
4. Richard Mandell, *The Nazi Olympics* (New York: Macmillan, 1971), p. 76.
5. Milly Mogulof, *Foiled! Hitler's Jewish Olympian—The Helene Mayer Story* (Oakland, Calif.: R. D. R. Books, 2002). This study was my main source for the chapter, but on the Nuremberg laws see also David Edmonds and John Eidinow, *Wittgenstein's Poker* (New York: Ecco Press, 2001), p. 114 and 107.
6. In the French daily newspaper *Pariser Tageblatt*, date unknown.
7. Interview with Gretel Bergmann, Queens, New York, 2001. Then eighty-four, she would have gone on for longer than the two hours she did but had to leave for her weekly ten-pin bowling session.
8. Interview with Paul Jenkins, Los Angeles, September 2000. His source was Hans Halberstadt, a native of Offenbach who represented Germany at the 1928 Olympics, where he first befriended Mayer. He was harassed by the Nazis and briefly imprisoned in Buchenwald before moving to San Francisco, where he founded his own club and where throughout her time in America he was Mayer's coach.
9. Adrienne Blue, *Faster, Higher, Further: Women's Triumphs and Disasters at the Olympics* (London: Virago, 1988).
10. Mandell, *The Nazi Olympics*, p. 182.
11. Susan D. Bachrach, *The Nazi Olympics: Berlin 1936* (Boston: Little, Brown, 2000).
12. Interview with Erica Mayer, Frankfurt, October 2000.

CHAPTER 16: THE CHAMPIONS

1. Vittorio Lambertini, *Trattato di scherma* (Bologna, 1870); quoted in William Gaugler, *Fencing Terminology* (Sunrise, Fla.: Laureate Press, 1997), p. 19.

2. Quoted in William M. Gaugler, *The History of Fencing* (Sunrise, Fla.: Laureate Press, 1998), p. 281.

3. Quoted in Lauriano Gonzales, *Greco uomini e maestri d'armi* (Rome, 1992).

4. Luigi Barbasetti, *La scherma di spada* (Milan, 1902).

5. Aldo Santini, *Nedo Nadi;* see also Roma Nadi, *Biography of Nedo Nadi.*

6. Aldo Nadi, *The Living Sword* (Sunrise, Fla.: Laureate Press, 1995); his other work, *On Fencing,* first published in 1943, has only recently been reprinted (Laureate Press, 1995), its original copper plates having been diverted to arms manufacture during the Second World War.

7. Leo Nunes, *American Fencing,* December 1953.

8. Aldo Nadi, "On Professionals," *American Fencing,* September 1952.

9. Nadi, *The Living Sword,* p. 268. Aldo Nadi's work was written by him in sometimes awkward English. I have applied some slight editing, to make it easier for the reader. However, the page references are to the Laureate Press edition.

10. Eduardo Mangiarotti, letter to the author, May 17, 2001. See also Eduardo Mangiarotti and Aldo Cerchiari, *La vera scherma* (Milan: Longanesi, 1966).

11. Christian D'Oriola, letter to the author, June 11, 2000.

12. Gillian Donaldson, née Sheen, in conversation with R. C. Winton, "50 Years Ago," *The Sword,* 1998, p. 24.

13. C. L. de Beaumont, in *American Fencing,* December 1955.

14. Julius Alpar, "A Fencing Master's Impressions of the 1958 World Championships," *American Fencing,* February 1959.

15. "An Interview with Christian d'Oriola," *The Sword,* Spring 1975, pp. 14–16.

16. Nadi, *The Living Sword,* pp. 381 ff.

17. This is Cavaliere Morelli Tia, *Lame, incrociate scherma e duello* (*Crossed Swords, Fencing and the Duel*) (Bari: Edizione Albo d'Oro degli Schermitori, 1904).

18. *Escrime,* September 2001, p. 40.

19. Barbara Tuchman, *Practicing History* (New York: Knopf, 1981), p. 27.

CHAPTER 17: EXODUS

1. Christopher Felix, *The Spy and His Masters* (London: Secker, 1963), p. 174.

2. Giuseppe Radaelli, *Istruzione per la scherma di spada e di sciabola,* 1876. See also Salvatore Pecoraro and Carlo Pessina, *La scherma di sciabola* (Rome, 1910).

3. Amberger, *The Secret History of the Sword,* p. 11.

4. See Marcello Garagnani, *L'Escrime Française,* February 1957, no. 111.

5. Lajos Csiszar, "Hungarian Sabre Fencing—Its Notable Success," *American Fencing,* February 1950.

6. See John Lukacs, *Budapest 1900: A Historical Portrait of a City and Its Culture* (London: Weidenfeld & Nicolson, 1988), p. 184.

7. László Szepesi, "Saber in Sunshine," privately circulated memoir.

8. Noel Barber, *Seven Days of Freedom: The Hungarian Uprising 1956* (New York: Macmillan, 1973), p. 216; see also "The Exodus from Hungary," *United Nations Review,* 1957.

9. Julius Palffy-Alpar, *Sword and Masque* (London: Davis, 1967).

10. Dr. Béla Bay with Anna L. Reti, *Paston es paston kivul* (Budapest: Sports-propaganda, 1979).

11. Rudolf Kárpáti, *Karddal a vilag korul* . . . (Budapest: Sport Budapest, 1965).

12. N. Norman Shneidman, *The Soviet Road to Olympus* (London: Routledge and Kegan Paul, 1979), and Sandor David, *Arany evitzedek* (Budapest).

13. Francis Zold, "Today's International Fencing Scene," *American Fencing*, December 1960.

CHAPTER 18: THE BURDEN OF GOLD

1. Wojciech Zabłocki, letter to the author, January 2000.

2. C. L. de Beaumont, "Commentary on 1957 World Championships," *American Fencing*, December 1957, p. 6. See also "Memoire 3," *L'Equipe*, October 28, 2001.

3. Zbigniew Czajkowski, letter to the author, March 11, 2001.

4. Jerzy Pawłowski, *Trud olimpijskiego złota* (*The Burden of Olympic Gold*) (Warsaw, 1972).

5. "The Broken Sabre," *Time* (European ed.), August 25, 1975. See also *Sportowiec* (*The Sportsman*), August 1975.

6. Marius Valsamis, conversation with author, November 1999.

7. Witold Woyda, conversation with author, May 2001.

8. In his memoir, *Szermierka na Szable* (Warsaw, 1952), Kevey places the bout in 1949, with a nineteen-year-old Zabłocki as protagonist, beating not Horvath but Gerevich 5–3. Both Pawłowski and Zabłocki, however, agree on the version of the story quoted here. As Kevey's account comes first, it probably was an early run of the same tactic—one which Pawłowski later typically embroidered.

9. Phillip Agee, *Inside the Company: CIA Diary* (London: Penguin, 1975).

10. Phillip Agee, *On the Run* (Secaucus, N.J.: Lyle Stuart, 1987), pp. 138–9, 174–5. See also Wendell L. Minnick, *Spies and Provocateurs* (Jefferson, N.C.: McFarland, 1992), p. 174.

11. *Time*, August 25, 1975.

12. *Neue Züricher Zeitung*, sometime in 1975; see Richard Cohen, "The Polish Connection," *The Sword*, "The Broken Sabre." Spring 1977, p. 18.

13. Jerzy Kosinski, *Blind Date* (New York: Houghton Mifflin, 1977), pp. 151 ff.

14. *Der Spiegel*, 1975.

15. "*Der Spion, der in der Kalte blieb-*," interview with Roman Zajkowski, *Sport am Montag*, October 28, 1991.

16. Ibid.

17. Walter Köestner, in conversation with the author, March 2001.

18. Iwona Jurczenko, "Szczery szpieg," *Pravo i zycia* (*Truth and Life*), May 2, 1992, p. 20; see also *Ciag Dalszy*, 18 April 1976, *Proces Szpiega* by Maria Osiadacz.

19. Jerzy Pawłowski, *Najdluzszy pojedynek* (*My Longest Duel*) (Warsaw: Druk I Oprawa, 1994).

20. Letter from Wolfgang P. Lange, to *Der Spiegel*, January 2, 1990.

21. Simon Barnes, *The Times* (writing about the Russian gymnast Svetlana Khorkina), September 2000.

CHAPTER 19: HONOR BETRAYED

1. Steven Ungerleider, *Faust's Gold: Inside the East German Doping Machine* (New York: St. Martin's, 2001).
2. Burton, *The Sentiment of the Sword*, p. 69.
3. *Encyclopaedia Britannica,* eleventh ed., 1911, "Epée."
4. Malcolm Fare, Luke Fildes, and Edmund Gray, *The Epée Club: 100 Years,* p. 59.
5. See Simon Barnes, *The Times,* April 2, 1997.
6. Brigadier General R. J. Kentish, "Disqualify Us at Your Peril," *The Independent,* August 6, 1992. See also Curtis Ettinger, *American Fencing,* April 1958, p. 12.
7. Walter Köestner, conversation with the author, March 2001.
8. Sandor David, *Arany evtizedek* (Budapest, 1986).
9. See Peter Jacobs, "The Scandal of the Combines," *The Sword,* Summer 1971, pp. 9–12.
10. "Contretemps," "The Sheriff of Dodge City," *The Sword,* Spring 1977, pp. 14–15.
11. Guido Malacarne, Letter to the Editor, *The Sword,* Spring 1977, pp. 3–4.
12. In an interview for the BBC in a program on Olympic Games cheating, broadcast on Christmas Day 2000, narrator Kevin Mosley, series producer Ian Bent.
13. *The Times,* November 10, 1994. The editorial arose from accusations that the ex–Liverpool goalkeeper, Bruce Grobbelaar, had taken bribes to let the ball into his net. "For a sportsman to play to lose is the ultimate professional foul."

CHAPTER 20: THE DEMON BARBER

1. Emil Beck, *Tauberbischofsheimer Fechtlektionem* (Bartels & Wernitz, 1978).
2. Richard Moll, *Die Fecht-Legende von Tauberbischofsheim* (Laub, 1987).
3. René Roche, in conversation with the author, February 15, 2002.

EPILOGUE: BY WAY OF THE SWORD

1. James Graham, Marquis of Montrose, *My Dear and Only Love* (c. 1640) in *The Collected Poems of James Graham, First Marquis of Montrose,* ed. Robin Graham Bell (New York: David Lewis, 1970).
2. C. L. de Beaumont, "1950 World Championships," *American Fencing,* October 1950, p. 8.

AFTERWORD

1. Cf. Richard F. Mould, *Mould's Medical Anecdotes: Omnibus Edition* (Bristol, U.K.: Institute of Physics Publishing, 1996), pp. 185, 324, 371.
2. Cf. an eyewitness account in *Illustrated London News* for July 13, 1888.
3. Vladimir Nabokov, *Speak, Memory* (New York: Putnam, 1966), pp. 181, 188–193.
4. *Letters of Vincent van Gogh* (New York: New York Graphic Society, 1958), vol. 3, p. 122; cf. also *The Intimate Journals of Paul Gauguin* (New York: Dover, 1997), p. 107 ff.

5. Arthur Conan Doyle, *Memories and Adventures* (Boston: Little, Brown, 1924), p. 287.

6. Lieutenant Commander Glenn Kerr, *Australian Army Journal*, vol. 2, no. 1, 2003, pp. 287–8.

7. For an excellent counterargument, cf. Clements, John, "What Did Historical Swords Weigh?" and "The Weighty Issue of Two-Handed Greatswords," website of *Arma*, the Association for Renaissance Martial Arts.

8. Sander L. Gilman, ed., *Conversations with Nietzsche: A Life in the Words of His Contemporaries* (New York: Oxford University Press, 1987), pp. 22–3.

Acknowledgments

During my years working as a book editor, the "acknowledgment pages" were most often a last-minute chore, along with checking the dedication and bibliography, the contents page and the index, the "bumph" that make up the editorial packaging of any book. It is only now, realizing the quantity and quality of help that I have obtained in writing this, my own first book, that I am fully aware of the extraordinary help authors are given. This manuscript certainly would not have existed without the generosity and wisdom, often over several months, of a vast range of people, and whatever I add in the next few lines cannot do justice to what I have received from them.

On a general plane, I want to thank Göram Abramsson, the late Ella Adler, Christoph Amberger, Bob Anderson, Stuart Applebaum, Clare Viscountess Asquith, Albert Axelrod, Péter Bakonyi, Emil Beck, Matthias Behr, Stefan Bellone, Daniel Bermond, Jacek Bierkowski, Stefanie Bierwerth, Oliver Biggadike, Robert Blum, Enis Boar, Robert Bookman, Carl Borack, Margaret Brown, Logan Browning, Kevin Brownlow, Wilma Caraley, Betsy Carter, Leonard Chase, Ben Cheever, Eric Chinski, Anders Cohen, Janet, Lady Cooksey, Chris Coppens, Andrew Cornford, Dr. Raymond Crawfurd, Manette Cuenin, Gregor Dallas, John and Nina Darnton, Sandor David, Raffaella de Angelis, Gianfranco della Barba, Ferenc Denes, Mark Derez, Vassil Etropolski, Nick Evangelista, Jochen Farber, Fritz Fitting, Thomas Fleming, Jim Fox, Lady Antonia Fraser, Peter Frohlich, René Geuna, Sir Martin Gilbert, Eva and Janos Glakowski, William Goldman, Wolfgang Gorke, Valerie Grove, Mark Gumley, Dr. Clare Halsted, Stephen Hand, John Harlow, Barna Heder, Cornelia Hanisch, Jorge Herralde, William Hobbs, Courtney Hodell, Gary Hoenig, Anthony Holden, Bill Hoskyns, Edgar House, Peter Jacobs, Allan Jay, Dom Philip Jebb, Paul Jenkins, Charles Kaiser, Susan Kamil, Dr. Jeno Kamuti, Dr. Czesław Karkowski, Jack Keane, Alexander Kerekes, Joe Klein, Walter Köestner, Aladar Kogler, the late Oscar Kolombatovitch, Janek Koniusz, Rick Kot, Jean-François Lamour, Wolfgang

Langer, Karl Lennartz, Elisabeth Lensing, Ingrid Losert, Roland Losert, Mary S. Lovell, Boris Lukomski, Linda McCollum, Guido Malacarne, Claudio M. Mancini, Eduardo Mangiarotti, Monica Martin, Alice Mayhew, the late Micky Meszena, Edmund Morris, Alexander Mosley, David Nasaw, László Nedeczky, Christian d'Oriola, Chaba Palaguy, Ryszard Parulski, Barry Paul, Graham Paul, Steve Paul, Petia Tersieva Pavlova, Jerzy and Iwonka Pawłowski, Nicolo Perno, Alan Petty, Tibor Pezsa, Laszlo Pongo, Ioan Pop, Michael Proudfoot, Dietrich and Guido Quanz, Mark Rakita, Gunnar Redmalm, Kari Reinhart, Béla Rerrich, Réne Roch, Zina Rohan, Martha Roselli, Ron Rosenbaum, Professor John Sanders, Lutz Schirmacher, Arnd Schmitt, Dr. Ulrich Schulke, Carl Schwende, Andy Shaw, Christo Smirnenski, Robert Spaething, Libby Spurrier, Linden Stafford, Thomas Staley, Susan Tifft, Mario Trimble, Margaret Truman, Wolf-Peter Unshelm, Peter Urban, Patrick Vajda, Paul-Claude Wackermann, Derek Ware, Peter Westbrook, Francis Wheen, Catherine Whitaker, Maciej Wierzynski, Robert Winton, David Wise, Ziemek Woldiekowski, Witek Woyda, Ralph Zimmerman, and Dr. Francis Zold. I have also enjoyed the camaraderie and complicity of the fencers at the New York Athletic Club.

Among the libraries and other institutions that have assisted me, the New York Public Library has been my constant workplace. "Swords" itself has 241 entries, "Fencing" 261, and "Duel" 523. There are eleven books to consult on dueling legislation alone. The University Library at Louvain has an even larger specialist holding, thanks to the late Archie Corble. I have also consulted the Stadt Bibliothek, Cologne; the Toledo Museum; the Huntington Library, Pasadena; the Churchill Archive, Cambridge; the Harry S Truman Library, Independence, Missouri; the U.S. Military Academy, West Point; the Harry S. Ransom Center, Austin; the Bibliothèque Nationale, Paris; the Film Library of the Museum of Modern Art, New York (with particular thanks to Charles Silver); the London Library; and the Victoria and Albert Museum, where Anthony North was especially helpful.

I am grateful to HarperCollins and to Toby Eady Associates for permission to quote from Bernard Cornwell, *Sharpe's Waterloo;* to Laureate Press, for permission to quote from Aldo Nadi, *The Living Sword;* to Seven Stones Press, for permission to quote from Peter Westbrook and Tej Hazarika, *Harnessing Anger;* and to Grove Press, for permission to quote from Jerzy Kosinski, *Blind Date.*

During the course of research I traveled to twelve countries, and relied on friends to translate texts for me. On Italy's history Franco Luxardo in

Padua and Paolo Roselli in New York were of immeasurable help. Wolfgang Marzodko in Germany and Wojciech Zabłocki and Zbigniew Czajkowski in Poland were valuable critics as well as general facilitators, as were Daniel Marciano and Gerrard Six in France and László Jacob on Hungarian history. Nicolas Halsted helped my schoolboy French over several hurdles, while Richard Gradkowski and Jeffrey R. Tishman kept a firm eye on my historical lapses. Joel Glucksman gave important advice on matters literary and cinematic and Marius Valsamis on medical and other issues too numerous to mention. The chapter on Helene Mayer could not have been written without the help of Milly Mogulof. Sonny Mehta first urged me to write a history of swordplay. "Take risks," he said. Malcolm Fare read the manuscript when it was over eight hundred pages long, yet still persevered and has helped me at every stage of its writing. Presiding over all, in matters great and small, has been Timothy Dickinson, whose vast knowledge and wonderful enthusiasm have improved this book in every way: I cannot thank him enough.

I have been fortunate in my publishers, both in New York and in London. Ann Godoff first commissioned the book and has kept a watching brief on its progress throughout. Joy de Menil has, all too literally, put her back into ensuring that I learned what it was like to be properly edited; and Barbara Bachman has been a marvelous designer. Robin Rolewicz, Joy's assistant, patiently dealt with the peculiar neuroses of an ex-publisher/author. At Macmillan in London, Jeremy Trevathan's calm confidence bolstered me during my moments of doubt, and one by one, it seems, his staff would sidle into his office to confess that they, too, had once fenced: an ideal fifth column. The Robbins Office—David, John, Sandy, Summer, Bob, and Edward—have become past masters of riposte and counterriposte, while their boss, Kathy Robbins, has managed to combine the roles of agent, author's spouse, faith healer, psychiatrist, entertainment officer, financial overseer, soothsayer, and best friend in a way that I know is unique. I have been, and am, very lucky.

Notwithstanding all the assistance listed above, there are sure to be lacunae, mistakes, and other shortcomings in this book. As any past fencer will quickly recognize, such errors are solely the responsibility and fault of . . . the referee.

Richard Cohen, New York, May 2002

Index

Page numbers in *italics* refer to illustrations.

RICHARD COHEN is the former publishing director of Hutchinson and of Hodder & Stoughton and the founder of Richard Cohen Books. Five times U.K. national saber champion, he was selected for the British Olympic team in 1972, 1976, 1980, and 1984. He won the Veteran Saber World Championship in 2004 and 2005 and is the current European Veterans champion. He has written for *The New York Times,* ESPN, and *Departures,* as well as for most leading London newspapers. *Chasing the Sun,* a cultural and scientific history of the Sun, will be published in 2009. He lives in New York City with his wife, Kathy.